Web Authoring
Desk Reference

Aaron Weiss

Rebecca Tapley

Robert C. Benedict, Jr.

Kim Daniels

Steven Mulder

Jeff Kawski

Hayden
Books

President
Richard Swadley

Associate Publisher
John Pierce

Publishing Manager
Laurie Petrycki

Managing Editor
Lisa Wilson

Director of Marketing
Kelli Spencer

Product Marketing Manager
Kim Margolius

Acquisitions Editor
Patty Guyer

Development Editors
Jim Chalex
Steven Mulder

Copy Editors
Terrie Deemer
Meshell Dinn

Production Editors
Jim Chalex
Katie Kunzler

Technical Editors
George Pytlik
Brad Siefert

Publishing Coordinator
Karen Flowers

Cover Designer
Aren Howell

Book Designer
Sandra Schroeder

Manufacturing Coordinator
Brook Farling

Production Team Supervisor
Laurie Casey

Production Team
Lori Cliburn, Linda Knose,
Malinda Kuhn, Rowena
Rappaport, Scott Tullis,
Christy Wagner

Indexer
Chris Barrick

Web Authoring Desk Reference

©1997 Hayden Books

Library of Congress Catalog Number: 96-79744
ISBN: 1-56830-352-1

Copyright © 1997 Hayden Books

Printed in the United States of America 1 2 3 4 5 6 7 8 9 0

Warning and Disclaimer

Trademark Acknowledgments

All terms mentioned in this book that are known to be trademarks or services marks have been appropriately capitalized. Hayden Books cannot attest to the accuracy of this information. Use of a term in this book should not be regarded as affecting the validity of any trademark or service mark.

About the Authors

Aaron Weiss is a longtime Internet enthusiast and aspiring agoraphobe. Aaron has hammered and co-hammered out several books on Internet topics, such as the recent *The Complete Idiot's Guide to JavaScript, Second Edition* (Que). In addition, he has convinced a variety of editors at *Internet World* magazine to publish dozens of his articles over the years, including a monthly series on JavaScript techniques.

Rebecca Tapley is a full-time author, project developer, and web page designer. Her publishing credits include *The Official Gamelan Java Directory* (Ziff-Davis Press), *The HTML 3 Personal Trainer* (IDG Books), and *How to Use Netscape Communicator* (Ziff-Davis). She also developed the flagship title of Hayden Books' successful *Magic* series, *Photoshop Type Magic*. She is a member of WebGrrls International and Women In Technology International.

Her primary extracurricular interest at the moment (other than sleep) is looking for an old house to renovate in the greater Boston area, but she also writes game storylines and does t'ai chi chuan. Her web site can be found at `http://web.wn.net/~usr/rtapley/web/home.html`.

Robert C. Benedict, Jr. is a writer and engineer working in the Silicon Valley. His writing credits include *Using Harvard Graphics for Windows, Using Norton Utilities for Macintosh,* and *Quick and Dirty Harvard Graphics Presentations* for Que Corp. His software development work includes both software engineering and project management. For Intuit Inc., Mr. Benedict was Quicken Project Manager for Central Europe and the Pocket Quicken Project Manager in the United States. He was also an engineer on Pocket Quicken. Prior to Intuit, Mr. Benedict was a founding engineer at Arbor Software Corp. working on the Essbase server and an engineer on Harvard Graphics at Software Publishing Corp.

Kim Daniels is Director of Software Development for Acadia Software in Boxborough, MA. She specializes in client/server database application development using Delphi, as well as various Internet database development tools. Daniels is a contributing author for *JavaScript Unleashed* (two editions). She received a BS in Management Information Systems from Rensselaer Polytechnic Institute in Troy, New York. She welcomes your comments at `kdaniels@acadians.com`.

When not scouring used bookstores in search of gorgeous, musty-smelling old media, **Steven Mulder** delights in cavorting in the electronic fields of new media. In his non-spare time, Mulder manages the online bookstore and toils over the design of ZDNet University in Cambridge, MA, where computer classes are served web-style. He is also author of *Web Designer's Guide to Style Sheets*.

`http://ziff.shore.net/~courses/mulder/`

Dedication

This book is for Steve.

—Rebecca Tapley

Acknowledgments

Aaron Weiss:

Primary and colorful kudos to my weary-eyed editor, Jim Chalex, who has spent far too many metabolic resources in the service of this tome. Take pride: you've earned the unique boast, *"I read the whole thing!"*

Rebecca Tapley:

Many thanks to Jim Chalex and Terrie Deemer for all their trials, tribulations, and very hard work; thanks also to Patty Guyer, Robyn Holtzman, and the rest of the Hayden people; thanks to the Production and Design teams for their many contributions; and, as always, special thanks to Chris VanBuren, Cathy Elliott, and everyone else at Waterside Productions who make it easier for me to do what I do.

Robert C. Benedict, Jr.:

I would like to thank Hayden Books for allowing me an opportunity to write for them on this book. In particular, many thanks to Patty Guyer, who signed me to do the project. Thanks also to Jim Chalex for taking over the project and seeing it to completion. Special thanks to Steve Mulder for his insight into the market and help in interpreting information and changes in company directions. Thanks and congratulations to the other authors, Jeff Kawski, Rebecca Tapley, Aaron Weiss, Kim Daniels, and Steve Mulder for their great work on the project. Thanks to Terrie Deemer, Brad Seifert, and all the others who worked on completing the book. And lastly, many thanks to friends and family who continue to support me in my writing and work. Thanks!

Hayden Books

The staff of Hayden Books is committed to bringing you the best computer books. What our readers think of Hayden is important to our ability to serve our customers. If you have any comments, no matter how great or how small, we'd appreciate your taking the time to send us a note.

You can reach Hayden Books at the following:

Hayden Books
201 West 103rd Street
Indianapolis, IN 46290
317-581-3833

Email addresses:

America Online:	Hayden Bks
Internet:	hayden@hayden.com

Visit the Hayden Books web site at http://www.hayden.com

Contents at a Glance

Table of Contents

JavaScript Style Sheets Basics 85

A 101

B

145

Table of Contents by Language

HTML

HTML (WebTV)

JavaScript/JScript/VBScript

JavaScript

VBScript

Cascading Style Sheets

JavaScript Style Sheets

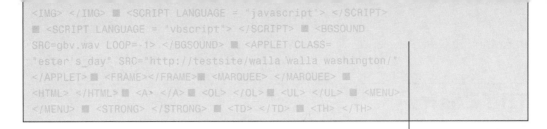

Introduction—Using the *Web Authoring Desk Reference*

Where Do I Start?

Now that you've got the *Web Authoring Desk Reference* (WADR) in your hands and you're ready to put it to use, there are some important things to be aware of before you dive in. This section will give you the information you'll need about this book in order to get the most out of it.

The Concept

The driving idea behind the WADR is to have all the Tags, Attributes, Objects, Event Handlers, Functions, Methods, and Properties at your fingertips, in an easy-to-use A–Z format. So, keeping this in mind, one must realize that all of the web designing languages espoused herein are compiled in the *same A–Z section*. In other words, you will find all the JavaScript mixed in with the VBScript, mixed in with the HTML, and so on—all in alphabetical order. The best way to think of it is like a dictionary containing the most important languages in the world—but instead of English, Spanish, and Japanese, this book has web designing languages.

To facilitate your search, we have provided you with two different methods to find the entry you're looking for. First, there is a table of contents by *language*, which will give the alphabetical listings by the type of language a particular entry is a part of. Second, we've got a good old index, much like ones you've undoubtedly used before.

In addition to the entries in this book, which will give you the basic facts and some helpful tips, we have also compiled a Basics section for each of the languages used in order to get you up and running, or to clean off some rusty neurons you haven't used in a while.

The Basics

The following languages all have their own section devoted to getting a more inexperienced user up to speed with a particular technology:

- HTML
- WebTV
- Cascading Style Sheets
- JavaScript (with Microsoft's JSCRIPT)
- VBScript
- Dynamic HTML
- JavaScript Accessible Style Sheets

These Basics sections will acquaint you with a language, and hopefully give you enough information to use the entries in this book you might otherwise not bother with. Of course, in the end, you'll want to use a combination of all these languages in order to cater to your web audience and create the most interesting, interactive web sites you can.

But, in most cases, you will not get a complete understanding of a language just from reading one of the Basics sections. We suggest seeking out other books on the various languages if you want to learn more than we provide here.

In any case, the Basics sections should deepen your understanding of all the languages used in this book, and hopefully get you started on the road to better, more dynamic web pages.

The Entries

Once you've read the basic sections, the only thing left to do is to refer to the A–Z reference for the tag or property or object (et al.) that you're looking for. Because each of these languages have their own idiosyncrasies, it's important to know a little bit about each one so you can understand these differences. But without much difficulty, you should be able to navigate each entry with ease. Let's check out an example from the book:

<CAPTION>

Category: HTML

Browser Support		Navigator 3	Navigator 4	Explorer 3	Explorer 4
	Macintosh	☐	▆	☐	☐
	Windows	☐	▆	☐	☐

May Contain `<A>`, `<APPLET>`, `<B>`, `<BASEFONT>`, `<BIG>`, `<BR>`, `<CITE>`, `<CODE>`, `<DFN>`, `<EM>`, `<FONT>`, `<I>`, `<IMG>`, `<INPUT>`, `<KBD>`, `<TT>`,

```
<STRIKE>, <SMALL>, <SUB>, <SUP>, <STRONG>, <SAMP>, <MAP>,
<SELECT>, <TEXTAREA>,   <U>, <VAR>
```

May Be Used In `<TABLE>`

Syntax `<CAPTION>…</CAPTION>`

The `<CAPTION>` tag is used to specify a table caption...

Now let's walk through each element of this entry:

- **`<CAPTION>`** is the entry name. In this case, it's the `<CAPTION>` tag. This will, of course, vary depending on what language an entry is a part of. For instance, if you were looking at a JavaScript entry, the title of each entry would be an Object. More on this later...

- **Category** tells you pretty much what you'd expect it to...that this tag is a part of HTML. Of course, if the language were different, this entry would reflect that by having Cascading Style Sheets instead of HTML, for instance.

- **Browser Support** gives you a run-down on which browsers and platforms give full, partial, or no support to a particular entry. A filled box means full support, a half-full (half-empty?) box means partial support, an empty box means no support. If a box shows partial support, the partiality will be elucidated in the definition.

- **May Contain/May Be Used In** is a special category designed for HTML entries. See the "HTML Basics" section for more information.

- **Syntax:** `<CAPTION>…</CAPTION>` is the syntax used for this entry. For more information about how to use each tag properly, or any other language element, refer to the Basics section.

- **Body Text** gives you the specifics. What does an entry do? What can it be used for? When might I want to use it in conjunction with other entries? Read this to find out the nitty-gritty details. Remember—the smaller headers within the body text in HTML entries (this applies for WebTV, too) are *attributes* that can be used in conjunction with whatever tag you happen to be reading.

And that pretty much does it for the headers of the entries. Remember—the syntaxes will be different depending on what language you're in—so take care as you include these elements into your web pages.

JavaScript, JScript, and VBScript Quirks

Because JavaScript is an inherently different language than, say, HTML, there are variations in the way each entry is handled. The most important aspect of JavaScript, JScript, and VBScript (henceforth referred to collectively as *scripting languages*) to keep in mind is that they have several elements that make up their basic structure. Unlike HTML, which has only tags and attributes, Scripting languages have several more elements:

- Objects
- Properties
- Event Handlers
- Methods
- Functions

With these five elements, one can put together a script to embed in an HTML document. Check out the "JavaScript Basics" or "VBScript Basics" chapter for more info.

In the WADR, we decided to make the Object take on the bulk of the responsibility by making it the entry header. Then, depending on the Object, we have also included the properties, event handlers, and methods that *can be used with that specific object.* Therefore, within a particular object, there will be any number of properties, event handlers, and methods that you might want to use in conjunction with the object you are in. This is exactly like the HTML entries and their attributes (which are subsumed within the tag), except instead of tags and attributes, it is objects and properties (etc.) that are subsumed.

Also, as you're reading a JavaScript, VBScript, Cascading Style Sheets, or JavaScript Style Sheets entry, keep an eye out for the "Type" bullet (directly below the "Category" bullet). This will alert you to the fact that a particular element is either a function, property, or an operator, because there are some irregular entries in each of these languages.

General Quirks

Here are some of the interesting elements you'll find as you read this book:

NOTE Notes are meant to give you extemporaneous information that, if you only want the bare-bone essentials, can be skipped. But we urge you to read all the notes, because they will contain useful information, "on the side," for your betterment.

DESIGN NOTE Design Notes are for the people who want to know about how different elements will look on their web pages. All sorts of advice about color, page-layout, and all other things "artistic" will be found here.

 Internet Explorer notes will contain information about, you guessed it, Internet Explorer.

N Similarily, Netscape notes will contain information about Netscape's browsers.

WARNING   Watch out for the Warnings, because they will steer you clear of possible pitfalls.

TIP   Tips will give you valuable information about maximizing your time and "did you knows" about the entries.

Conclusion

So, now that you're ready to crack the spine and dive in, make sure to keep these "nuances" in mind. If you ever have a question about an entry, chances are you will find the answer in our Basics sections, or in a more complete tutorial-based book. Remember, this book is meant to give you the hard facts and a *little* inspiration (we'll leave most of the creative genius behind your web pages up to you).

```
<IMG> </IMG> ■ <SCRIPT LANGUAGE = "javascript"> </SCRIPT>
■ <SCRIPT LANGUAGE = "vbscript"> </SCRIPT> ■ <BGSOUND
SRC=gbv.wav LOOP=-1> </BGSOUND> ■ <APPLET CLASS=
"ester's_day" SRC="http://testsite/walla walla ......ngton/"
</APPLET> ■ <FRAME></FRAME>■ <MARQUEE> </MARQUE.
</HTML>■ <A> </A>■ <OL> </OL>■ <UL> </UL>■
■ <STRONG> </STRONG> ■ <TD> </TD> ■ <TH> </TH>
```

Basics

HTML

If you've turned to this section of the book, you probably feel (or know) you need a no-nonsense, plain English introduction to HTML. In this section of the book, that's exactly what you get.

This Basics section covers what HTML is and is not; the different kinds of software you can use to create web pages; some simple guidelines for naming and arranging individual pages within your web site; fundamental HTML page structure; and how to read and use the HTML entries in this book.

What HTML is and is Not

HTML, which stands for HyperText Markup Language, is a kind of document structure shorthand based on a much larger language called SGML (Standard Generalized Markup Language). Whereas SGML (which you don't really need to know much about) is lengthy, complicated, and technical, HTML is just the facts—the facts you use to describe the content of a web page. This is an important point to remember: writing HTML is not like writing a letter in a word processing program. You are instead writing a sequence of instructions that a browser—a software package that interprets SGML—translates into the final product: a web page.

The Evolution of HTML

HTML was originally created to give all kinds of professionals on the World Wide Web a standard, uniform way of presenting information. The WWW started out as a small government and academic network used to exchange technical, scientific, and computer information— mostly words and numbers—so early versions of HTML and web browsers were relatively simple. This is why many HTML tags, or individual instructions, have been created for formal writing, such as superscript and subscript, definitions, and outline headers. In the early days, the kinds of information traveling along the superhighway (so to speak) were chemical formulae, doctoral theses and articles, and other exclusively "highbrow" kinds of content. No official celebrity web sites, no online magazines, not even a search engine to be found. (Hard to imagine, isn't it?)

When the rest of the world caught on to "the web," as it is now familiarly called, web page authors demanded a more flexible writing system that could handle images, sounds, movies, and all the other page elements now being regarded as necessary or even ordinary. New browsers such as Netscape Navigator suddenly appeared featuring many new tags and attributes that worked well when viewed with Navigator, but not with any other browser software. This is still, largely, the reason why the same web page looks different when viewed in two browsers, or doesn't work in the second browser at all. With the release of each new browser, and then each new version of each browser, new tags were introduced that provided more design options but didn't work with the competition's software. Web page authors who wanted everyone on the web, using all different browsers, to see their pages the same way found themselves in a bind.

Today, this same problem has become, paradoxically, much simpler and more complicated. With the founding of the World Wide Web Consortium (the W3C), a nonpartisan "standard" for HTML usage has been established and is generally followed. Yet the progress of web technology continues to test the limits of the imagination and SGML with the arrival of style sheets, Java applets, virtual reality, and the like. There is still no truly, absolutely reliable web page except for the very simple sort found later in this section, and no one is content to read just plain text anymore.

To compound the problem, platform issues have become increasingly important. Even though most people surfing the web use a PC, most people who design web sites use a Macintosh. And even with every tag, attribute, and value working correctly, the same web page looks different on a PC than it looks on a Mac.

This, in a nutshell, is why this book was written—to give HTML users access to the most definitive list possible of all tags, all attributes, and all values with descriptions of what works when and when it doesn't.

Basic HTML Structure

The following parts of this Basics section will introduce you to some generalities and some specifics about using HTML, along with some helpful advice you may want to follow while making web pages.

The Two Golden Rules

Many people look at HTML for the first time and become instantly intimidated. Why all the brackets? And the equal signs? There are a couple readable sentences there, but the rest of it looks like Swahili. So these people decide writing HTML is difficult, complicated, and only for computer programmers. And they give up before they even give HTML a chance.

The first basic idea behind HTML is simple: all web pages have certain elements in common. There's text, links to other web pages, images, lists, and so forth. HTML, then, identifies each element to the browser based on a system of *tags*, pairs of short universal instructions. The opening tag—a word or abbreviation in brackets, like <LIST>—tells the browser, "Everything after this tag is a list." Then the closing tag—which is almost identical to the opening tag except for a backslash, like </LIST>—tells the browser, "This is the end of everything in the list."

The second basic idea behind HTML is equally simple: unless you're told otherwise, always think in pairs. It takes a page of HTML instructions to produce a web page; 95 percent of the time, if you write down an opening tag, you'll need a closing one. If you include an *attribute*, a secondary instruction you write inside a tag, you'll need to assign it a *value*—a number, the address of another web page, a file name, or another piece of information to tell an attribute what to do. If you become accustomed to this basic philosophy early on, you may find learning HTML to be much easier.

The World's Simplest Web Page

With these two basic ideas in mind, then, let's review the structure of a basic, no-frills web page. (Indents and line numbers have been added to these HTML examples for reference only—do not add similar indents or add line numbers to actual HTML pages once you start creating them.)

```
1          <HTML>
2              <HEAD>
3                  <TITLE>The title goes here.</TITLE>
4              </HEAD>
5                      <BODY>
6                      The contents of the web page go here.
7                      </BODY>
8          </HTML>
```

That's all there is to it. Let's go line by line.

The <HTML> tag on line 1 is the first tag you write at the top of every web page. It tells the browser that everything between it and the closing </HTML> tag (on line 8) is HTML.

The <HEAD> tag on line 2 contains information about the entire HTML document, including the <TITLE> that appears on line 3 before the closing </HEAD> tag on line 4. All the text written within <TITLE> tag appears on the top edge of the browser window, but it also serves as a description of the page's contents for some search engines and as a bookmark description in Netscape Navigator and Internet Explorer.

The <BODY> tag on line 5 contains instructions for all the text, images, and other visible information—everything between it and the closing </BODY> tag on line 7 (minus tags, attributes, and values) will appear on your web page. And that's all there is to the simple fundamentals.

Attributes and Values

Previously in this section, attributes and values were mentioned as examples of the Second Golden Rule (think in pairs). An *attribute*, again, is an extra bit of instruction included within a tag while a value is its finishing touch. To illustrate what an attribute and a value can do, one of each will be added to the simple HTML written above. This time, though, the HTML will be written without indents and line numbers, flush left, as you'd write it for real:

```
<HTML>
<HEAD>
<TITLE>The title goes here.</TITLE>
</HEAD>
<BODY ALIGN=right>
The contents of the web page go here.
</BODY>
</HTML>
```

ALIGN is a <BODY> tag attribute that customizes alignment, and right is one of several established values it recognizes. Because the ALIGN attribute and right value are enclosed within the <BODY> tag—the end bracket comes immediately after the last letter in right—this tells the browser, "Everything contained inside the <BODY> tag is aligned right." Without the ALIGN attribute or the right value, everything specified by the <BODY> tag would be aligned left.

Writing HTML: Browsers and Writing Programs

In order to build a web page, you need two things: a writing program for writing the HTML and a browser to view your results. Because there are only two browser software packages mentioned in the HTML entries in this book—Netscape Navigator (version 3 and the browser in Netscape Communicator) and Internet Explorer (versions 3 and 4)—this choice is fairly simple.

However, you don't need to go out and purchase or download any additional software to write HTML. Both Macs and PCs come with programs you can use already installed (SimpleText and Notepad, respectively). Otherwise, you can use any word processing program like Microsoft Word or WordPerfect, as long as you save your HTML in a text-only format. There are also HTML editing programs such as BBEdit for Mac and for the PC that you may eventually find useful if you really get into authoring web pages—but none of the products mentioned in these last two categories are necessities.

How to Use the HTML Entries in this Book

When you look up an HTML tag in this reference book, you'll find it listed alphabetically by its first letter. You will also find that almost every tag entry is laid out the same way, so here's an explanation for what's included.

Contents at a Glance

The first section of an HTML tag entry looks something like this:

<TABLE>

Category: HTML

Browser Support		Navigator 3	Navigator 4	Explorer 3	Explorer 4
	Macintosh	■	■	■	■
	Windows	■	■	■	■

May Contain z

May Be Used In <BLOCKQUOTE>, <BODY>, <CENTER>, <DD>, <DIV>, <FORM>, <LI>, <TD>, <TH>

Attributes ALIGN, BACKGROUND, BGCOLOR, BORDER, BORDERCOLOR, BORDERCOLORDARK, BORDERCOLORLIGHT, CELLPADDING, CELLSPACING, CLASS, CLEAR, FRAME, HEIGHT, ID, NOWRAP, RULES, VALIGN, WIDTH

Syntax <TABLE>...</TABLE>

The May Contain list specifically runs down other HTML tags that work when enclosed within the tag in question. In this example, only two tags can be used within the <TABLE> tag, and as noted, <CAPTION> can only be used once. The May Be Used In list, on the other hand, runs down other HTML tags that can safely enclose the tag in question. This list is usually much longer, and no HTML tag can (or should) be given in both places.

The rest of the specifics about an entry head like this one are discussed in the Introduction of this book.

It is also worth noting that both Netscape Communicator and Internet Explorer 4 were only available in beta while most of this book was being written, so it is quite possible that there are tags, attributes, or attribute values that may or may not work in the final versions. You will have to experiment a little to make some things work, and you will have to do a little of your own testing.

Attributes, Values, and Examples

The rest of an HTML tag entry features a list of a tag's attributes listed alphabetically, followed in the text with an explanation of its performance, its limitations, and sometimes suggested alternatives if there are platform or other issues involved. Each attribute section will display example HTML detailing its correct usage and related visual examples—usually one per browser or platform. It may seem at times as though there are too many examples (some tag attributes, for example, have as many as ten possible values). The purpose of so many figures is intended to show you any differences between HTML as it is displayed from browser to browser and platform to platform, because most people using this book will not have the luxury of an actual Mac and a PC sitting side by side. Remember, most professional web page designers use a Mac, but most people using the web are on a PC—so writing HTML must in some way account for this mixed audience.

Some Final Tips and Suggestions

Now that you've learned some simple ideas and instructions to keep in mind, and you know how to use the HTML entries in this book, here's a final list of tips to send you on your way:

- Type any example HTML exactly as it appears on the page. Put spaces where they're supposed to be, and leave them out where they're not. This sounds like paranoia but it's not—even the most seemingly inconsequential extra space can wreak havoc.

- Talk to your Internet Service Provider before adding certain intermediate- to advanced-level features to your web page (forms and their related gateway programs, JavaScripts, and VBScripts). If your ISP doesn't support the feature you want to use, then you've saved yourself the work beforehand.

- Visit some of your favorite web pages and download the source code—this is the HTML the author of that web page wrote when he or she created it. You can learn a lot about HTML usage and syntax by studying other people's work.

- Expect the unexpected. Your HTML *will* look lovely on one browser and look horrible on another. You *will* write something that won't work and you may not immediately know why. But, you *will* also get the hang of it and end up with something cool. This is all part of the learning process, so patience is required.

```
<IMG> </IMG> ■ <SCRIPT LANGUAGE = "javascript"> </SCRIPT>
■ <SCRIPT LANGUAGE = "vbscript"> </SCRIPT> ■ <BGSOUND
SRC=gbv.wav LOOP=-1> </BGSOUND> ■ <APPLET CLASS=
"ester's_day" SRC="http://testsite/walla walla  ngton/"
</APPLET> ■ <FRAME></FRAME>■ <MARQUEE> </MARQUE
</HTML> ■ <A> </A> ■ <OL> </OL> ■ <UL> </UL> ■ <
■ <STRONG> </STRONG> ■ <TD> </TD> ■ <TH> </TH>
```

Basics

WebTV

WebTV is exactly what its name implies, the World Wide Web viewed on a television. Using your TV screen as the monitor, a computer-like device that connects you to the Internet, and the WebTV remote control used as a mouse or input device, you view web pages and explore links the same way you use a browser on your computer. In fact, the WebTV hardware has a built-in browser called the WebTV Internet Terminal, which supports most of the functionality of the Netscape Navigator and Microsoft's Internet Explorer.

Combining the Internet with your TV has some interesting advantages over using a computer. Many advertisers and television shows include web URLs in their ads. In fact, most new movies released have information about the film, the stars, and even a preview of interesting pre-release clips available on the web. If you see a preview of a movie that looks interesting, with the WebTV product, you could switch over quickly to the Internet and investigate further without having to move to your desk or start up your computer. In some cities, you can even go a step further by looking up the theaters where the film is playing and buying tickets all over the Internet.

The WebTV system is unique in its approach to bring the Internet to people, but it also presents some interesting challenges for web designers. Could you imagine having to continually click the remote to see each page of a show? How long would a viewer stay on a certain channel if they could hear the voices but had to wait a few seconds for the images to download? The point is, WebTV changes the interface and viewer interaction enough where you might want to consider certain aspects of the system when creating your pages.

The following sections explore this topic a bit further in an effort to help you design your site to work well with WebTV. The first section, "What is WebTV?," goes into more depth covering the different aspects of the system including the methods of input by the user. The next section, "Designing for WebTV," builds on this to provide suggestions and tips for creating content that is appealing on the WebTV interface.

What is WebTV?

Perhaps two more accurate questions would be: what makes up the WebTV system and how does a viewer interact with the Internet using the system? As stated earlier, the WebTV system consists of a specialized computer device that connects to your television much like a VCR. This device also connects to your phone line, like a computer modem, which in turn connects to the Internet. Data and images come in on the phone line and go out on the TV cable to display on your screen. Once the page is displayed, you see a yellow highlight that indicates the active link or hot spot on the page. To surf to the next page, you use the arrow keys on the remote control to move the highlight to the link you want and simply press the Go button on the remote. It's that simple!

Browsers must support a lot more functionality than highlighting links and viewing pages. Most support the ability to go back to a previous page or manually enter a URL in addition to activating a link. The WebTV browser supports all these features and more. But while computer browsers present this functionality with toolbars, menus, and other computer user interface elements, WebTV focuses mostly on the display of the page. At the bottom of the screen, you should see the title bar, which includes the name of the page, scroll arrows, and indicators when more content is available by scrolling. What you don't see is the browser application that has displayed the page.

In WebTV, the functionality of the browser is available either on the WebTV remote control or on the Options panel that is displayed when the viewer presses the Options button on the remote. To jump to a page, for example, you use the Go button on the remote control. To save the current page on a list of favorite places similar to bookmarks, you display the Options panel and click the Save button.

TIP   In WebTV, put all links right on the page. Do not rely on quickly available toolbars and other functionality for users to Navigate your site. You may want to consider using frames and providing a table of contents page that is always visible.

The final piece of the system relates to data input such as entering text on a form. To enter text, viewers need a keyboard and with WebTV, they have a choice of two. Most WebTV systems offer an optional hardware keyboard that simplifies input similar to a computer. The other keyboard is referred to as an onscreen keyboard. You display this keyboard by pressing a button on the remote control. When the viewer enters a text input field, they must invoke the onscreen keyboard if they do not have a hardware version. On the other hand, you can also automatically display the keyboard with special WebTV HTML features, speeding up viewer interaction with your site. The point is, using good design skills, and staying aware of the aspects of the WebTV system, you can create interactive sites that are fun and informative whether displayed on a PC browser or in WebTV. For WebTV, the next section provides some helpful guidelines and tips for achieving this goal.

Designing for WebTV

In the previous discussion, you learned that browsing the web on a computer or TV is basically the same. Viewers see your pages, explore URLs, and enter data into forms. This means that your site, whether designed for WebTV or a computer, will work just fine on either system. The information and tips in this section focus on optimizing for WebTV and preventing you from doing something that may not work well.

A good example of this is the use of a keyboard since some WebTV viewers will not have hardware keyboards. With the `showkeyboard` attribute, which is not supported in other browsers and therefore ignored, you display this keyboard automatically when a viewer enters a text input field.

Screen Limitations of WebTV

The first and most important issue to consider when designing for WebTV is the display of pages on a TV screen. The TV display is fixed in size and width as opposed to computer screens, which vary in size and color depth. The WebTV screen is limited to 544 pixels wide by 378 pixels high (actually, the true size is 560 by 380, but borders and the title bar utilize some of that space). Furthermore, the latest release of WebTV 1.1 does not support horizontal scrolling, although this issue may be addressed in future releases. Pages that are too wide are scaled to fit on the screen. Graphics may become less clear and scaling the images may increase the time it takes to load the page. For WebTV, make sure all your pages fit horizontally on the screen to insure the images are clear and appealing.

The height is also an issue even though vertical scrolling is supported. Most computer displays these days use a resolution of 800 pixels wide by 600 pixels high. This height is almost double the WebTV screen. A page that fits completely on a computer may in fact take up two WebTV screens. This cannot be completely avoided if your site will be viewed on both systems. However, if you insure your page fits neatly in 600 pixels, and the most significant content is in the first 400 or so pixels, the page should be functional and work just fine in WebTV.

User Interaction with WebTV

Watching TV is simple. You point the remote at the screen, press a button, and you're channel surfing. With WebTV, you have a remote too. You even point it at the screen and push buttons to change channels, or with the web, to view pages. To change a web page, however, you must first move a yellow highlight to a hypertext link or portion of an image map before pressing the Go button to explore the link. This difference is important to keep in mind. Make sure your pages have relevant links and are not overloaded with links to any related topic. If possible, keep links close together and avoid separating links by several pages of content. WebTV will not automatically scroll if the viewer highlights a link that is not currently visible.

TIP   If you have long pages on your site that take up more than two screen fulls in WebTV, you may want to provide links at the beginning of the page that jump to sections later in the page. This will enable the user to quickly find the information they need without having to scroll.

The point is, one of the goals of designing your site for both a computer and WebTV is to try to limit the number of additional steps a viewer must perform to complete an action. For example, using the `selected` attribute, you can designate a default link for the WebTV highlight. If this is the most likely link the viewer will take, then the viewer need only hit the Go button and will avoid having to press the arrow key repeatedly to move the highlight to the link before hitting Go.

With the onscreen keyboard, extra steps are simply unavoidable. Five fingers on a full size keyboard are much faster than selecting each key step by step on the screen. However, since many sites have no input requirements, there is no real need for a keyboard. WebTV provides some HTML extensions to help bridge the gap for designers. The following list provides some suggestions for working with, or around, the onscreen keyboard:

- Limit text input to only necessary fields.
- Use selection lists and buttons for input whenever possible.
- Use special attributes and tags, such as `showkeyboard` and `number`, to help viewers complete the actual input.

Performance Considerations

As the number of computer users and web sites increases, performance related to the time it takes to load and display a web page is a major issue. Of course, faster modems and more capable display cards still have a long way to go before they match the time it takes to display a new show when you change the channel on the television. The extra benefit of text intermixed with graphics, of interactive information as opposed to pre-programmed shows, and the ability to explore various links may ease the pain somewhat. Still, the designers of WebTV recognize that the performance of analog shows is an additional scale their success will be measured against.

Consequently, WebTV has optimized the system in certain places to reduce the time between when a user selects a URL and when they see the result of that action. Displaying text is today quite fast. But, when you add graphics to your site, which is important for creating interesting and helpful pages, the time it takes to see a page increases somewhat—especially on slower systems. One of the ways WebTV alleviates this is to pre-allocate space for graphics.

If you always specify the height and width of an image, even if that image does not require these parameters, WebTV can load faster because the size needed to store and display the image is known in advance. WebTV also supports a `transparency` attribute for graphics and text that determines how full or complete the image is drawn on the screen. The value ranges from 0 to 100 with an image of transparency 100 fully visible and a transparency of 0 fully opaque. WebTV has optimized for a 50 transparency, which still makes images completely visible yet allows WebTV to finish rendering the image in a faster time.

Summary of Important WebTV Design Tips

The WebTV system follows the same principals of any other Internet browser. Sites that work on your computer will also work in WebTV. If you follow some of the suggestions and guidelines presented in this chapter, your viewers should be able to utilize your site whether they see it on their computer or television. Given some of the subtle differences, however, the following list of suggestions should insure your success regardless of how your data is viewed:

- Be aware of the 544 pixel width limit
- Use height and width attributes for images to increase performance
- Use normal JPEG images and set transparency to 50
- Try to limit content to fewer screenfulls utilizing extra pages
- Use links on long pages to jump quickly to content and avoid scrolling

<IMG> </IMG> ■ <SCRIPT LANGUAGE = "javascript"> </SCRIPT>
■ <SCRIPT LANGUAGE = "vbscript"> </SCRIPT> ■ <BGSOUND
SRC=gbv.wav LOOP=-1> </BGSOUND> ■ <APPLET CLASS=
"ester's_day" SRC="http://testsite/walla walla ...ngton/"
</APPLET> ■ <FRAME></FRAME>■ <MARQUEE> </MARQUE...
</HTML> ■ <A> </A>■ <OL> </OL>■ <UL> </UL>...
■ <STRONG> </STRONG> ■ <TD> </TD> ■ <TH> </TH>

Basics

Dynamic HTML

Evolution is a natural part of most emerging technologies like the Internet. Each year, developers and companies listen to their users and look at the existing state of their technologies and try to determine what the next step is. Although the web offers so much today, some issues and problems exist that are leading developers to advance their Internet solutions. Anyone who has waited more than a few seconds for a slower server to process a single mouse click, or has spent more time scrolling up and down pages than actually reading the page content, is familiar with the downfalls of the web. Despite the interactive claims, the web is not as interactive as it could be, especially with access times that delay the reaction to simple user events like a mouse click.

The good news, however, is that new browsers and functionality are coming along to advance us a step farther and address some of these issues. Dynamic HTML is just such an evolving area focused on making the web more interactive. The powerful scripting of Dynamic HTML allows for handling interaction entirely on the end user's computer without sending and receiving information over the Internet. The reaction to the input is much faster, and the load on the network infrastructure is significantly reduced.

Part of making a web page more interactive involves creating dynamic content. This is content that is presented different ways to the viewer depending even though the actual substance hasn't changed. For example, a page displays a table of sales figures throughout the year. The viewer may want to see the table arranged by product or by region. He might click on a cell to see special notes such as the formula used to calculate the cell contents. With dynamic content, the user performs an action and the presentation of data is changed, yet no interaction with the Internet was required!

Looking at examples will help you understand a little more about the focus of Dynamic HTML. Layers, as supported by the upcoming Netscape Navigator 4.0 release, is one example of Dynamic HTML focused on more interactive web pages. With layers, you combine objects in a grouping and then set the position of the groups including stacking one on top of another. Layers are an excellent example of dynamic content.

In Figure 1, you see what looks like a standard web page on travel destinations. On the top, you see a <select> control where the city San Francisco is selected. When the user selects a different city, the content of the page changes without waiting for an update from the server or even jumping to another anchor on the page! The response to the user selection is fast and immediate (if this image were a live site, you could really say the layers at work).

Figure 1

A dynamic page using layers.

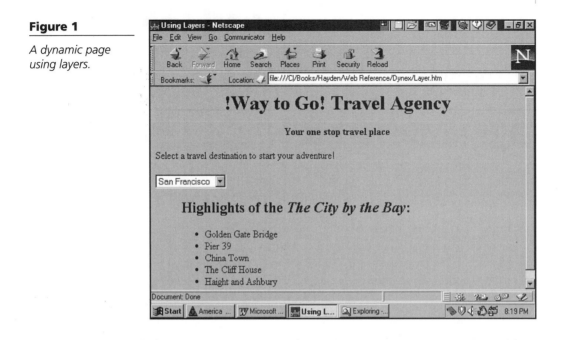

| NOTE | At the time this information was written, both Netscape Navigator 4.0 and Microsoft Internet Explorer 4.0 were at the preview release stage. All of the information and examples in this section are based on these releases. Things may change, however, before both products are released, which may affect this layering example and the other information provided here. This is just something to keep in mind while reading this section (and this book). |

Companies like Microsoft and Netscape, and the World Wide Web Consortium (an organization dedicated to recommending standards and defining the aspects of the web at http://www.w3.org), are working together to define Dynamic HTML and develop the technologies that will make it happen. The next section, "Understanding Dynamic HTML," expands on the introduction presented here including a discussion of what Microsoft and Netscape are defining as their solution for this area. The section "Using Dynamic HTML" discusses some of these technologies, including layers, to give you a better understanding of what you will be able to do to create more dynamic and interactive web sites.

Understanding Dynamic HTML

Dynamic HTML is a major focus of the next round of browsers, especially from Netscape and Microsoft. Many Internet companies agree on the major areas of the web that need improvement. However, what technology or solution best achieves this end is still under discussion. Later in this section, you will see what each of these companies are using to solve the Dynamic HTML issue. Most notably, there are some differences (and, of course, some similarities). The entire push for this technology, however, can really be summed up in two ways:

- More interactive web pages
- Less network traffic

More interactive pages is simple to explain. Rather than just provide a static page that the viewer reads, developers want more interaction like you find in desktop software today. For example, instead of simply reading a static HTML table, readers want to sort the table in different ways to digest the data. The point is to handle the user events, such as mouse clicks and keyboard entry, entirely on the end user system. Response is immediate and network traffic is reduced.

To help understand this, look at the next example that combines scripting user events with an interactive page. The example shows a page of figures displayed in a table. The figures happen to be sales numbers of a company, but imagine it could also contain stock quotes or a companies financial that have been posted on the Net for the benefit of potential investors. In such a table, the user could click on any cell and learn a little more about the data presented there such as how the data was collected.

Figure 2 shows the table along with the additional notes about why sales in the North for Q4 were so low. Users can click on any table cell and receive additional helpful information. Best of all, the entire interaction happens on the end user's computer without sending and receiving data across the Internet. All it takes is some special scripting added to the specific table cell.

Figure 2

Clicking a cell in this table displays information about the cell next to the table.

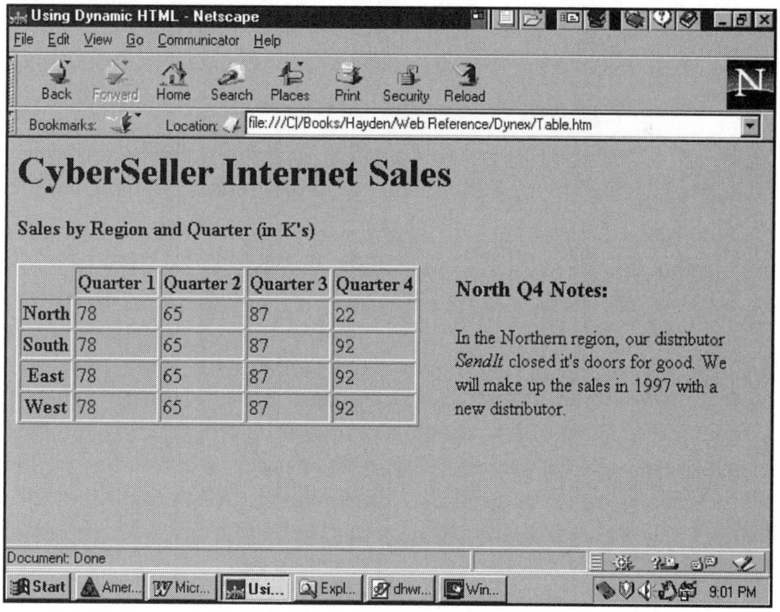

The code for the cell will look something like the following. All you have to add is the script routine for showNorthQ4Notes using a special window or layer to display the notes. It's that simple:

```
<td onclick="showNorthQ4Notes(); return false;" >
```

With the diversity of the web, many companies are working to define this new technology and they do not always agree. The following two sections explain what Microsoft and Netscape are doing to help you create dynamic web sites.

Microsoft's Dynamic HTML

Microsoft's definition of Dynamic HTML seems focused on two major components. The first is the Document Object Model. In a nutshell, this means making sure every item on a web page is an object that can be scripted. They have also added some advanced scripting capabilities which enable you fine control over user input and your page's responses to the user. Here are the major components of the Microsoft solution:

- Cascading Style Sheets
- Document object model and extensive scripting
- Absolute positioning via Cascading Style Sheets
- Multimedia controls with the Internet Client Side SDK
- Dynamic tables including data binding with the Internet Client Side SDK

For information on Cascading Style Sheets, see the "Cascading Style Sheet Basics" chapter in this book. The information in that section also covers absolute positioning and many other features. The document object model is covered more in depth later in this section. The Internet Client SDK (Software Development Kit) offers multimedia and other new functionality to web developers and also provides a way to develop your own add on technology. The SDK is best explored directly on the Microsoft site listed in the following note.

> To learn more about Internet Explorer, check out Microsoft's web site at http://www.microsoft.com/ie/.

Netscape's Dynamic HTML

The Netscape Dynamic HTML solution depends less on scripting of all objects and includes more functionality to support interactive pages. Many of the technologies can be used right away without making calls to external objects or creating scripts. The advantage of this is today's web designers can add interactive elements to their pages by just adding new HTML tags (and simple scripts). The downside is the extensive scripting in the Microsoft solution is more flexible in the long run. Flexibility is almost always related to complexity, which is something to keep in mind. Here are the major items in the Netscape solution:

- Cascading Style Sheets
- Layers
- Absolute positioning via Cascading Style Sheets and Layers

- Canvas mode
- Dynamic fonts

For information on Cascading Style Sheets, see the "Cascading Style Sheet Basics" chapter in this book. Layers are covered later in this chapter, and you can also see the tags `<layer>` and `<ilayer>` in this book. Canvas mode is a special adjunct to the `window.open` script command for opening the browser in a special mode similar to a kiosk. See the `window.open` command for more information. Finally, dynamic fonts are described a bit later.

N | To learn more about the Netscape Navigator, check out Netscape's site at `http://www.netscape.com/comprod/products/communicator/`.

TIP | In the two previous lists for Microsoft's and Netscape's Dynamic HTML definition, you see some items that are common to both browsers. If you want to create pages that work well for both, focus on using equally supported technologies such as Cascading Style Sheets. Also, try to pick a scripting language, such as JavaScript, which is likewise well supported.

Using Dynamic HTML

If you have read this chapter on Dynamic HTML up to now, you should understand two major points. First, you should understand the objectives of Dynamic HTML. Second, you should have a feeling for the emerging nature of this technology. You can see that in the differences in the different company solutions and the availability of information. These next sections should make the overall picture more clear with some specific explanations about some of these technologies.

Cascading Style Sheets

Cascading Style Sheets provide additional functionality to make a web page more interactive on the end user system. The idea behind CSS is to provide a mechanism to more precisely control the appearance and layout of a web page. You define characteristics such as the font to use for all headings or the way text should wrap around images. You then link this styling information to one or more of your web pages and create a final page that really goes beyond what is currently available today.

For Dynamic HTML, this means creating a more finished web page that the user interacts with on his computer without necessarily going up to the web. For example, you can position elements on the page the same way a software developer must do when creating a dialog box or product user interface. For a more complete explanation of CSS, see the "Cascading Style Sheet Basics" chapter in this book.

Dynamic Object Model

The dynamic object model involves the complete scripting of objects. In the HTML world, the objects are the items on the page. The scripting utilizes all the existing scripting languages including JavaScript, Jscript, and VBScript, which are all covered in this book. A major goal of Dynamic HTML and the next generation web technology is to enable designers to create truly dynamic and creative web pages. Scripting objects provides the ultimate in flexibility. Basically, you can take any item on your page and manipulate it using scripts. You can change the object properties or perform other actions in response to an external event such as user input or time.

The first part of the dynamic object model is to make everything on a web page an object. You do this with the id attribute of each tag. Every tag in your page can have a unique name or id (in fact, each id must be unique). Once named, you can reference the object directly with the name as with the following example:

```
<h1 id=PageTitle onmouseover="HiLite">
My Page</h1>
<script language=JavaScript
function HiLite () {
 PageTitle.style.fontStyle = "bold";
}
</script>
```

The <h1> header, and the text within, are all part of the object titled *PageTitle*. When the user moves the mouse over this object, the event onmouseover is invoked and the routine *HiLite* is called. The script sets the text to bold, hence the name *HiLite*.

onclick is another example of a user event that enables you to respond when a user clicks on the object. Any time the user selects or clicks an item, you can respond anyway you want using a script. This makes your pages completely dynamic.

If that weren't enough, some of the things you do with objects are not only limited to the existing scripting languages and HTML objects. Using the <object> tag and the Microsoft Client SDK, you can create code to support new objects including calls that manipulate the object. In the SDK, you get multimedia and data binding support that you can call directly from a script or HTML tag. You can also create a special control, called an ActiveX control, and then make calls to it on your page. For example, you could develop a control that accesses a news information service and use the <object> tag to automatically update your web page. ActiveX and Dynamic HTML make a powerful combination. To truly understand this, you should download the Client SDK from the Microsoft site and start programming.

NOTE   To learn more about web objects, visit the World Wide Web consortium site at http://www.w3.org. You will see many of the actual specifications for objects and object embedding. Most of the documents presented at this site have been written by employees of Microsoft and Netscape. The information provides an insight into what the future might hold for the web.

Layers

Layers are an integral part of Netscape's Dynamic HTML solution. With layers, you can dynamically change page content or create simple animation like flipping the pages of an old-time cartoon book. On your web page, you create layers by grouping page elements between the <layer> and </layer> tags (see the write-up for this tag, as well as for the <ilayer> tag and layer object in this book for more information). You then place the layer grouping anywhere you want on your page. The ability to group and precisely locate HTML elements is already a major step toward creating fantastic web pages. But with layers, additional properties enable you to hide and show an entire layer, and to stack them in a specific order one on top of the other. Creating such a stack, and then hiding each layer one by one using a script is a good way to create animation.

As for dynamic content, the following example shows what you can do. The !Way to Go! travel agency has a web site. On their site, a viewer can select different travel destinations to see what the hot attractions are and make travel arrangements. The current HTML solution requires that each time the viewer changes the city, information must be sent to the server causing a new page to be sent to the viewer. As with the following example, however, each destination could also be defined as a layer, and all destinations could be downloaded at one time. When the user selects a new place, the page is changed automatically without interaction on the server. Figure 3 shows the page. From the user's point of view, the page looks no different despite the fact that several layers of HTML elements have been defined on the page.

Figure 3

Select a different city and new information appears on the page without sending anything to the server!

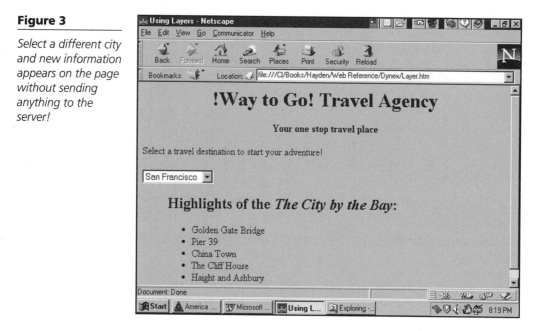

The code for this page is listed below (keep in mind, for illustration purposes, the rest of the data for the travel agency has been left off, otherwise the code would be quite long). Three layers are defined between the <layer> and </layer> tags, one for the three major US cities San Francisco, New York, and Los Angeles. The San Francisco or "SF" layer is visible while the other two have been hidden. The positions of the layers, as defined with the left and top attributes, are all exactly the same. That way, when the user selects information about a different city, the data on the page about the new city will appear in exactly the same place. The content will change right before the viewer's eyes! When the user selects a city in the <select> control, triggering an onchange event (this event occurs when the user changes the selection in the form), the script routine showCity is executed. This routine hides all the other layers and then makes the appropriate one visible:

```
<html>
<head>
<title>Using Layers</title>
</head>
<body>
<center>
<h1>!Way to Go! Travel Agency</h1>
<h4>Your one stop travel place</h4>
</center>
<p>Select a travel destination to start your adventure! </p>
<form name=myform>
<select name=cities
  onchange="showcity(this.selectedindex); return false;">
<option selected>San Francisco
<option>New York
<option>Los Angeles
</select>
</form>
<layer name="sf" left=50 top=180>
<h2>Highlights of the <i>The City by the Bay</i>:</h2>
<ul>
<li> Golden Gate Bridge
<li> Pier 39
<li> China Town
<li> The Cliff House
<li> Haight and Ashbury
</ul>
</layer>
<layer name="ny" left=50 top=180 visibility="hide">
<h2>Highlights of the <i>The Big Apple</i>:</h2>
<ul>
<li> Broadway
```

```
<li> Times Square
<li> The Empire State Building
<li> The Statue of Liberty
<li> Central Park
</ul>
</layer>
<layer name="la" left=50 top=180 visibility="hide">
<h2>Highlights of the <i>The City of Angels</i>:</h2>
<ul>
<li> Hollywood
<li> Disneyland
<li> Venice Beach
<li> The Santa Monica Pier
<li> Universal Studios
</ul>
</layer>
<script>
function showcity(iindex) {
 document.layers["sf"].visibility = "hide";
 document.layers["ny"].visibility = "hide";
 document.layers["la"].visibility = "hide";
 document.layers[iindex].visibility = "show";
}
</script>
</body>
</html>
```

Dynamic Fonts

Dynamic fonts is a misleading name. You might think that this feature describes fonts that change—well, dynamically—like growing bigger on the page or morphing into something else. In fact, the change that occurs is on the end user's system. As a web designer, you have fonts on your system that you use when doing creative work. With CSS, you can link in a variety of fonts on your web page and really enhance the appearance. But what happens when those fonts are not on the viewer's computer? CSS has an algorithm to find a suitable replacement. The best solution would be to transfer the fonts with the page so that it looks exactly the same on their computer as it does on yours. And that's what the dynamic fonts feature does.

Using a plug-in supplied by Netscape and a modification to the <link> or <style> tags, you can link your own fonts, or commercially available fonts, with your web page and the browser will insure that the page is displayed with the correct font. When the viewer clicks a link or explores your site, the fonts are downloaded with the page and read in by the browser when the page is displayed. Your page looks the same on the end user's system as it did when you designed it! The following code is an example of what the HTML side of this equation should like (see the write-ups for the two tags previously mentioned for more information):

```
<LINK REL=fontdef SRC="http://www.mysite.com/fonts.pfr>
```

> **NOTE** At the time of this writing, Netscape was the only company supporting this feature and only examples of the functionality were available. The technology is promising though, and a visit to the Netscape site should provide more complete information along with the required software to pack your fonts with your web pages. See `www.netscape.com` for more information.

> **NOTE** Check out the fonts and technology at the Bitstream site at `http://www.bitstream.com/world/`.

```
<IMG> </IMG> ■ <SCRIPT LANGUAGE = "javascript"> </SCRIPT>
■ <SCRIPT LANGUAGE = "vbscript"> </SCRIPT> ■ <BGSOUND
SRC=gbv.wav LOOP=-1> </BGSOUND> ■ <APPLET CLASS=
"ester's_day" SRC="http://testsite/walla walla      ngton/"
</APPLET> ■ <FRAME></FRAME>■ <MARQUEE> </MARQUE
</HTML> ■ <A> </A>■ <OL> </OL>■ <UL> </UL>
■ <STRONG> </STRONG> ■ <TD> </TD> ■ <TH> </TH
```

Basics

Cascading Style Sheets

The World Wide Web has achieved something that many developers and designers have tried to do since first battle between Macintosh and Windows machines—that is, create an environment where a developer could produce a single end-user product that would work, for the most part, on all the major platforms. If you are familiar with HTML, you know this was achieved by developing a set of standards or tags that could easily be interpreted by computers that had an HTML compatible browser. For example, <h1> is a level 1 header, a descriptor for how to display text in a certain font, style, and size. Tags similar to this were used instead of specific font names or technologies for font display that may not be universally available. <h1> is not a platform-specific entity and its display is handled, or interpreted, by the browser.

The first instances of HTML focused on a universally accessible environment. However, developers and designers require more when making products despite the desired result of cross platform success. You need more than just heading levels 1 to 7. You need fonts and graphics and control over layout and many of the things you are familiar with in a word processor or desktop publishing application. The issue is then simple. How do you provide the same or similar capability that is currently available on today's computers and still make it compatible with the diversity of the web? The answer is Cascading Style Sheets.

Cascading Style Sheets (CSS) provide a way to control the layout, font characteristics, and other aspects of the display of your pages, and it achieves this in a way that supports the platforms (Macintosh, Windows, Unix, and so on) of the web. You can create a style sheet that defines the fonts to use with the different headers and add styling, like bold or italics, to emphasize the text. You can define margins for your page elements, wrap text around those elements, and even add a border to make things really pop off of your page. You can also put all your style rules and definitions in a separate file and link that file to all the pages on your web site. You create a universal look and feel for all your web pages. Best of all, you can change that look in a single location that affects the entire site. No more editing every single page to just change a heading style or background color! Figures 1 and 2 show an example of what you can do with style sheets with a web page displayed without and with style.

Figure 1

A non-styled web page.

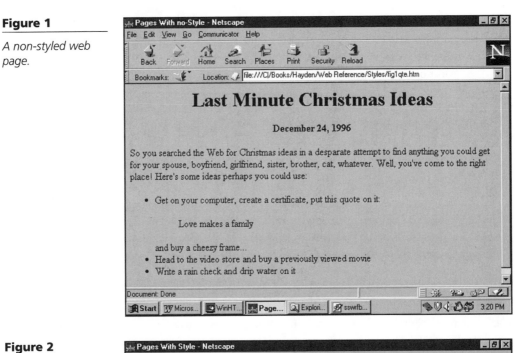

Figure 2

The same page using a Cascading Style Sheet.

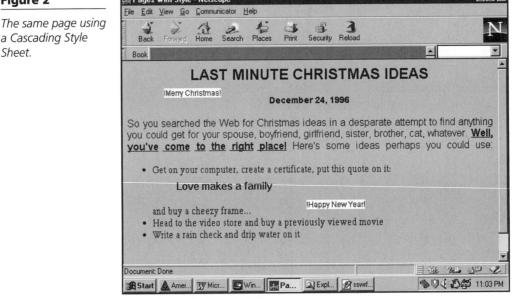

In the following sections, you will see how to define the styles or rules of a Style Sheet and how to link them into your web pages. You also learn more about how rules are (or should be) interpreted by your browser and some of the specialties of setting up a Style Sheet. The latter part of this section will cover the major features of CSS including fonts, page layout, and positioning elements anywhere on the page you want.

One final note about CSS. CSS is an emerging standard and technology in a world that two large corporations, Microsoft and Netscape, and others are competing to define. As much as the diversity of the web is an asset, it can also be a liability—especially with emerging technologies like CSS. Most of the information presented in these sections is compatible with the major players. However, not all browsers support CSS in the same way nor do they support all the functionality in the recommendation of the World Wide Web Consortium (the organization that helps to define standards like HTML on the web at `http://www.w3.org`). Keep that in mind when you use CSS and read this book. All write-ups include a Browser Support section which explains what browsers support the given feature. There is also a variety of notes and tips specific to the different browsers to help you deal with incompatibilities and missing functionality. The point is, pay attention to this information and it will help you design styles and pages that truly work across the entire web!

Elements of Style Sheets

Cascading Style Sheets work by adding or replacing the attributes of existing HTML tags. You define rules and then link those rules to your pages by entering them directly in an HTML document or providing a link to a separate file. It's that simple. Style sheets have those three components: the affected HTML element, the rule or new styling attributes, and the link to the HTML page. With that type of simplicity, you might think that perhaps this feature is limited to, say, only changing the font of a header or making a block quote red. In fact, that couldn't be farther from the truth. Here are just a few of the possibilities of what you can achieve with CSS:

- Have text appear in the font of your choice.
- Specify the size of text in points, pixels, and many other units.
- Set specific top, bottom, left, and right margins on text or images.
- Add any color or background color to elements.
- Float text or images and wrap text around them.
- Precisely position images or text down to the exact pixel.

The simplicity is in the use of CSS, but the power is in the flexibility and control you have when you use styles. The following example pulls all this together in a simple way that produces a significant effect. In the example, your web site reviews recently published fiction and you use block quotes to display material from the books. You really need all your quotes to stand out from the page and what better way to do this than to make them red! To do it, you can define a Style Sheet rule like the following:

```
blockquote { color : red }
```

The complete syntax of this statement and CSS rules is discussed in the section "Defining a Style" later in this chapter. But you can see above, you provide the HTML tag (`blockquote`) and some descriptions about how to display or handle that tag (`color : red`). Next, you link that style to your web page in one of the many ways discussed in the section "Linking in Style Sheets." An example of how to link in styles is the following code. This code brings in all the styles from the local file *mystyle.css:*

```
<head>
<link rel=stylesheet type="text/css" href="mystyle.css">
</head>
```

Lastly, and most importantly, you open up your browser and see how your pages look with the new or modified styles. See Figure 3 for an example of emphasizing a block quote. (For the purpose of this figure, the actual attribute used was underlined because the image is not a color image. See text-decoration for more information on this effect.)

Figure 3

Block quotes are especially empha-sized with underlin-ing or other effects.

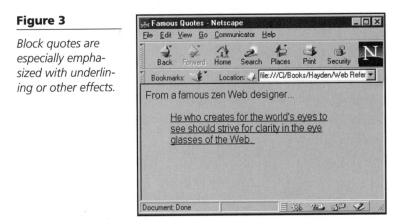

> **TIP** Make sure you really review your pages in the major browsers when working with Cascading Style Sheets. Because this technology is new, some of the functionality is implemented differently by different browsers, and in some cases it's not supported at all. This is generally a good idea anyway before bringing new material online.

The next section gets into more specifics about defining a CSS rule.

Defining a Style

A CSS rule contains two major components. The first component is the *selector,* which is an HTML tag. The selector tells the browser what elements the rule should be applied to. In the example from earlier in this chapter, which is repeated below, blockquote is the selector:

```
blockquote { color : red }
```

A single rule can have one or many selectors and each one limits the number of possible HTML elements that are affected by the rule.

The second part is the *declaration,* which tells the browser how to execute the rule. The declaration also has two parts, the *property* and the *value,* which are surrounded by brackets and individually separated by a colon. The property tells the browser what part of the tag to affect and the value tells it how to make the change. In the example, the rule sets the color, which is a property of blockquote, to the value red.

Currently, CSS supports about 50 properties and each one of those has a specific set of values that can be used. The properties and values are covered in depth throughout this book. Similar to selectors, you can have one or more declarations (and even values in some cases) with a single rule. The example below is a bit more complex (though still fairly easy to understand):

```
p i : { color : blue; font-weight : bold }
```

This example uses multiple selectors to determine what part of the page to affect. The combination of the <p> and <i> tags informs the browser to only look at italicized text within <p> and </p> tags. You might do this to draw your viewer's attention specifically to text within the paragraph (for example, look at the previous paragraph where the terms of a rule are defined). The rule tells the browser to make this text bold and display it in the color blue for added effect. The section "Cascading and Interpreting Styles" expands on the complexities of rules including guidelines for how to use multiple rules that might affect the same text. Here's an example of why you might want to do that:

```
blockquote : { color : blue }
blockquote i : { color : red; font-weight : bold }
```

These rules combine the two concepts of the previous examples. That is, you want quotes to stand out on your page. And within a quote, you want to emphasize specific text such as a reference to other material. The rules are interpreted as follows:

- Make all block quotes blue.
- Emphasize italicized text within the quote by making it red and bold.

In this next example, you learn how CSS can really define the look of your web pages. You see a single selector, <h1>, with many declarations. Multiple declarations are separated by a semicolon. All of these declarations modify the appearance of fonts or text for all h1 headers affected by this rule:

```
h1              { font-family: helvetica;
                font-weight: bold;
                font-size: 24pt }
```

The rule uses the font Helvetica for h1 headers, and additionally, displays the headers bold at a point size of 24. It completely changes the look of the header including the font used for the text!

As stated before, you can also group multiple selectors in the same rule. If you separate them by a space, the selectors act together to limit the type of elements affected by the rule. If the selectors are separated by commas, as with the example below, than each selector is treated individually as if it was a separate rule:

```
h1, h2, blockquote { font-family: helvetica;
                     font-size: 24pt }
```

Elements designated as <h1>, <h2>, and <blockquote> will be displayed with the Helvetica font at 24 point. This rule does not mean that the element must have all three tags in affect. Any one of them will do.

The syntax for CSS rules are simple as you have seen throughout this section. Without being an expert, it is easy to read a rule and understand how it will affect the elements. In fact, this syntax can be summarized in just a few statements:

- Each rule has a selector and declaration.
- Each declaration has a property and a value.
- Each declaration is surrounded by brackets.
- Each property and value is separated by a colon.
- Selectors separated by spaces are combined to narrow the selection.
- Selectors separated by commas share the same rule.
- Multiple declarations are separated by semicolons.

There are a few exceptions to the above statements. Some properties take multiple values at the same time while others can take a variable number of values. All of these cases are documented for the specific properties throughout the book. But, in general, this list should help you create most of your rules and Style Sheets.

Linking in Style Sheets

Once you define your rules, the next step is to link that information to your HTML pages. There are several ways you can do this depending on what you need to do.

For example, if you are working on just a single web page, you can enter the style rules right in the HTML text. If you are working with a large web site, and you want all pages on the site to have a consistent look, you would want to put all your styles in a single file and then link that file to every page in your site. The methods used for linking in or adding styles include the following:

- Link to an external style sheet from your HTML document
- Embed a style sheet within your HTML document
- Add styles inline in your HTML document
- Import one style sheet into another style sheet

In the first case, linking an external sheet, you enter all your styles in a separate text file and store it with your HTML pages. Each HTML page must then contain a link statement that refers to the file. When the browser loads the page, it will see the link statement and incorporate the styles from the file. In fact, you can link in one or many pages in most cases helping you better organize your styles (a file for font styles, a file for layout styles, and so on). With an external file or files, you only need to change styles in a single location and all your web pages are updated. As a result, your web site will have a consistent and familiar look that will aid viewers when they navigate the site.

External files are just text files, like an HTML page, that contain style information as opposed to HTML tags and data. The information in the file is interpreted similar to HTML. Empty spaces and multiple lines are ignored. For example, a file named *style1.css* could contain the following lines:

```
body   { background: white;
         font-family: helvetica }
h1     { font-weight: bold;
         font-size: 24pt;
         color: blue }
h2     { font-weight: bold;
         font-size: 18pt;
         color: green }
p, li { font-size: 14pt }
```

_____ **TIP**   To help you organize your files, you should save your Style Sheet files with a *.css* extension as with *style1.css*.

After creating the file, you must add the link to your web page using the `<link>` tag in the `<head>` section of your page. This tag tells the browser to load the specified Style Sheet file and use its contents as instructions for displaying the page. Note that you can link to a Style Sheet file using a relative path (such as `href="../styles/style1.css"`) or a complete URL (`href="http://www.mulder.com/style1.css"`). Some browsers support more than one link as well.

In the example below, you see the `type="text/css"` attribute that appears in the `<link>` tag. This specifies the MIME type, which tells the browser what type of information is found in the file (for more information on mime types, see Appendix E). Browsers that do not support the `"text/css"` type can ignore style sheets altogether. The following example links in the file *style1.css* (see Figure 4 for the result):

```
<html>
<head>
 <title>Style Sheets Are Here!</title>
 <link REL=stylesheet href="style1.css" type="text/css">
</head>
<body>
 <div align=center>
 <h1>Welcome to the Wonderful World<br>of <i>Style Sheets!</i></h1>
```

```
<div align=left>
Making rules is easy, and linking is easy:
<ol>
 <li>Create the rules.
 <li>Save them in a separate text document.
 <li>Link to the style sheet document from your HTML document.
 <li>And give many pages style all at once!
 </ol>
 <h2>How to Create the Rules</h2>
 First, buy this book…
</body>
</html>
```

Figure 4

A web page with linked style sheet controlling the appearance of text.

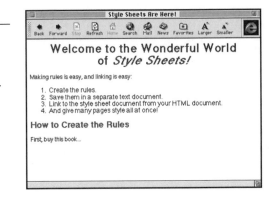

It's important that you use `type="text/css"` with your `<link>` tag, because otherwise Navigator might give you an error.

Netscape Navigator 4 does not support links to multiple style sheets. If you link to more than one .css file from your HTML file, Navigator will use only the *first* one.

Explorer 3 on the Mac supports multiple linked style sheets, but the Windows 95 version does not. In the latter browser, only the *last* .css document linked to will be used. In Explorer 4, this problem is fixed; multiple linked style sheets are supported.

You do not have to put your styles in a separate file to have them change the appearance of your page (if you are working with a lot of pages, you really should). You can embed the styles in the `<head>` tag in the same way they appear in a separate file. To do this, you put them within a `<style>` and `</style>` tags and include the `type="text/css"` in the first tag to inform the browser how to handle the rules. By putting the styles in the `<head>`, the rules still affect the entire web page just as if they were imported from a separate file. The following example demonstrates this:

```
<html>
 <style type="text/css">
 <!--
  body  { background: white;
          font-family: helvetica }
  h1    { font-weight: bold;
          font-size: 24pt;
          color: blue }
  h2    { font-weight: bold;
          font-size: 18pt;
          color: green }
  p, li { font-size: 14pt }
 -->
 </style>
<head>
```

> **TIP** **Hide style sheet tags from older browsers!** Some browsers that don't support style sheets will treat your style rules as text and display the rules themselves. These browsers will ignore the `<style>` tags, but not the rules themselves. If you enclose the rules in a comment, between the `<!--` and `-->` tags, as with the example above, you should be fine in both cases. Newer browsers will interpret the rules while older ones will treat them as comments and therefore ignore them.

In addition to putting all your styles in the `<head>`, you can also put a style inline to limit the elements affected by the style. For example, you may want a specific header to utilize some of the special font attributes that are available with CSS, but you do not necessarily want every header to have those attributes. You achieve this result with an inline style applied directly to the header tag. You use the same `<style>` tag as before with embedded styles, but you put it within the declaration of the tag you wish to change. That modified tag acts as an implied selector so you only need supply the declarations (from before, that is the property and value). The following example shows an inline style:

```
<h1 style="color: gray; margin-left: 0.7in">
```

> **N** Navigator 4 doesn't support inline styles at all.

You can also use inline styles to change the appearance of an entire section of an HTML page. One way to do this is with the `<div>` tag as in the example below:

```
<div style="color: blue; margin-left: 0.7in; font-family: helvetica">
<h1>Add styles inline for local effects</h1>
```

```
<code>Or don't if you don't want to.</code>
<p>It's up to you.</p>
</div>
```

The final method for including styles is to import the styles from one file into another file. You create each file following the instructions from before. You then add an *import* statement in the first file that will import or bring in the styles from the second file. You must supply a URL to do this as with the example below:

```
body   { background: white;
         font-family: helvetica }
p, li { font-size: 14pt }
@import url(style4.css)
```

Of course, you still need to link to first file into your web page. The biggest advantage of this method is purely organization of your files.

Internet Explorer 3 or 4 does not support importing external style sheets at all.

Netscape Navigator 4 doesn't either.

Cascading and Interpreting Styles

Most of the examples and discussion up to now have focused on single rules affecting single HTML tags. In a few cases, you saw how rules can be combined. In reality, the capabilities of CSS really expands when you combine multiple styles and rules in a single sheet. Combining styles is referred to as *cascading styles* (hence the name Cascading Style Sheets). For example, you could apply general font characteristics to your <body> tag to change the overall appearance of the text. You could then specify some special attributes on top of that for quoted text or reference material. All this is done in the following example (see Figure 5 for the results):

```
<html>
<head>
<title>Famous Quotes</title>
</head>
<style type="text/css">
<!--
body { font-family : ariel }
blockquote { font-weight : bold }
blockquote i { text-decoration : underline }
-->
</style>
<body>
```

```
<p>From a famous zen web designer…</p>
<blockquote>
He who creates for the world's eyes to
see should strive for clarity in the
<i>eye glasses</i> of the web.
</blockquote>
</body>
</html>
```

Figure 5

An example of combining styles.

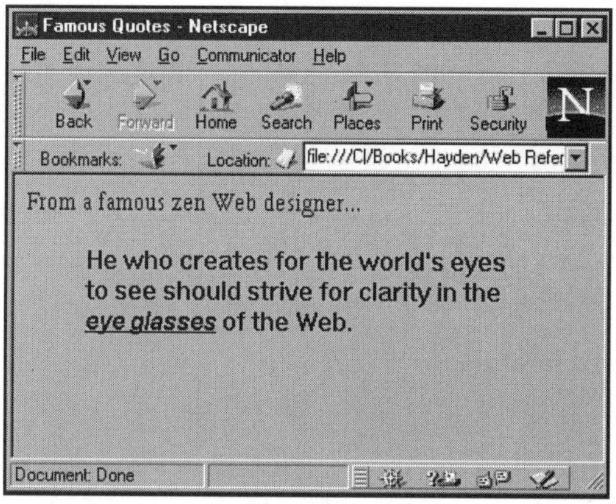

Combining styles is very powerful, but it can also lead to conflicts. For example, what happens if one style makes italics red while another makes italics in paragraphs blue? Or what happens when you link in a style sheet that sets the font family to helvetica but the HTML page itself has an embedded style which sets the family to ariel? Understanding how the browser makes each decision, about which styles to apply, is key to understanding and using CSS.

In making these decisions, browsers follow a *cascading order of rules,* which is a list of instructions that tells the browser exactly what rules should be used. The rules are based on the different ways styles can be added to a page as discussed in the section "Linking in Style Sheets" earlier in this chapter. The ideal browser (Explorer comes closer than Navigator for this) gives higher priority to link methods that occur higher in the following list:

1. Inline
2. Embedded
3. Linked
4. Imported
5. Reader (not supported by Explorer or Navigator at this time)
6. Browser default (internal to browser)

In an ideal world, inline styles will always be more important embedded styles, which will take precedence over linked styles, and so on.

Netscape Navigator 4.0 treats linked styles as more important than embedded styles.

Explorer for Mac rates things correctly, but the Windows 95 versions (3.0 and 4.0) act like Navigator and give more importance to linked styles than to embedded styles.

TIP   **The bottom line:** For now, there's one best strategy if you want to be safe in both browsers. *Use all embedded styles or all linked styles, but don't mix and match.*

The next set of rules gives another example of how multiple styles are interpreted. For example, if you have two inline styles that change the color of italicized text, the browser must decide which color to use. The following lists the steps the browser must take to resolve the conflict:

1. Sort the declarations by importance.
2. Sort by specificity of selector. More specific selectors override more general ones.
3. Sort by order specified in the code. Later entries are sorted higher than earlier ones.

The best way to understand this is to work through an example. Assuming all styles below where linked in the same way (and thus have the same importance), the blockquote text is ultimately displayed in red, italic text is green, but blockquote italicized text is blue:

```
blockquote { color : red }
i { color : green }
blockquote i { color : blue }
```

For this example, step 1 is not an issue because all styles are assumed to have been linked in the same way. Step 2 causes the last rule, which is the most specific, to win out over the other two. Step 3 is not used.

One last point, a conflict can also arise when style rules run into HTML tags that also try to influence style. For example, you might have a `<font size=2>` tag in your web page and import the style `{ font-size : 24pt }`. Essentially, HTML style tags are treated as lower priority than style sheet rules and so the 24pt rule would be used.

Inheritance

Inheritance relates to the issue of applying styles, or determining when to apply styles, as with the previous section. Specifically, this term refers to a situation where an earlier style affects a more general HTML tag and yet a more specific set of tags is in effect. The best way to understand inheritance is through an example. Suppose you set up the following style sheet in your HTML document:

```
h1 { color: green }
```

All the text within a level-one heading will appear in green. But then suppose you want to put a phrase in italics via HTML:

```
<h1>
Style sheets are here, so web designers better <i>get with it!</i>
</H1>
```

<i> hasn't been defined by a style sheet rule. However, the italicized text occurs within <h1></h1>, so it *inherits* the declarations of <h1>. Inherited styles are very powerful, enabling you to change the appearance of more global tags and still have those changes carry through the entire document.

Inheritance starts at the top-level elements in HTML, which means the <html> is first followed by the <body> tag. After those tags come the heading tags (<h1>, <h2>, and so on) and other block-level tags (tags that create their own line breaks, such as <blockquote> and <table>), followed by the "flow" tags such as <b> and <i>.

There are some style properties that are not inherited from parent to child. For example, it makes sense that the background property does not inherit, because once you've set the overall background once, there's no need to do so over and over!

Classes and IDs

This section covers style sheet syntax, which provides you greater flexibility when defining and using rules. Classes enable you to create sub-sets of attributes to act as specific selectors or to be applied to specific HTML tags. For example, you may have three different ways you want to display a quote depending on where the text is displayed in your page. You create the three classes in your style sheet and then reference a specific class in your HTML page. The following example illustrates three classes for the <p> tag:

```
P.cour   { color: blue;
           font-family: courier }
P.chi    { color: red;
           font-family: chicago }
P.arial  { color: gray;
           font-family: arial }
```

You can name the classes anything you want. From then on, when you want to use the various styles on the page, you simply activate them within the HTML like the example below. The class attribute tells the browser which variant of <p> to use. Here's the HTML text (see Figure 6 for the result):

```
<p class=cour>This line is styled in Courier, in a blue color.</p>
<p class=chi>This line is styled in Chicago, in a red color.</p>
<p class=arial>This line is styled in Arial, in a gray color.</p>
<p>And this line ain't styled at all.</p>
```

Figure 6

Three classes of <p> mean three different appearances of body text.

Netscape Navigator doesn't like it when you use numbers as class names (it ignores those classes entirely).

You can also define a class a bit more generally and have it affect multiple tags. You define the class name and declarations, and then apply the new class to other rules or tags as with the example below:

```
.bluetext  { color : blue }
blockquote.bluetext { font-weight : bold }
```

The *bluetext* class acts as an additional selector for the second rule. Hence, only text within the <blockquote> that is displayed in the color blue will be bold. The assumption here is if the text is already blue, you want the text to stand out from the page so make it bold as well. The general classes can also be applied as styles using the `class` property of a tag:

```
<P class=bluetext>This line is blue.</P>
```

A few final notes about classes:

- You can use the classes in any order or amount within the web page after you've defined them.

- Each selector can have only one class. So you can't have a class called `h1.arial.bluetext`, for example.

- You can't use the `class` attribute twice for the same tag.

- The normal inheritance rules (see the section earlier in this chapter) will apply to classes. They inherit styles from their "parent" tags.

Similar to classes, an `id` can be used to define a style or rule. The `id` involved is the same attribute introduced in HTML 3.0 and follows the same guidelines including that the `id` must be a unique value for the length of a document. For example, you could set up this rule:

```
#r174p { color: maroon }
```

Then, you could refer to it later in your web page (with the `ID` attribute) to make any bit of text maroon:

```
<H3 ID=r174p>Behold maroon text!</H3>
<P>And one more maroon word right <B ID=r174p>here</B>.</P>
```

Just like classes, styles defined with ids can be applied as styles or used as selectors.

Modifying Links

A common effect used on web pages is to change the color of text links from the defaults (using the html <body> attributes link, alink, and vlink). The creators of style sheets wisely expanded upon this feature allowing you to globally change link color, font, and other characteristics over many web documents.

Essentially, style sheets have three predefined classes (the official name is "pseudo-classes") for the <a> tag:

- ■ a:link—for unvisited links (before clicking)
- ■ a:visited—for visited links (after clicking)
- ■ a:active—for active links (during clicking)

You can use these classes to set any font or text formatting options you like, including color, font-size, font-weight, and text-decoration (see details on all of these elsewhere in this book). Best of all, you don't have to use a class attribute because the browser will track which links are unvisited, active, or visited. Here's an example of changing the link attributes:

```
A:link     { background: gray;
             font-size: 16pt }
A:visited  { background: blue;
             font-size: 14pt }
A:active   { background: white;
             font-size: 16pt;
             font-weight: bold }
```

Explorer 3 doesn't support the A:active class. However, anything that you set for the A:link class will be inherited by both A:active and A:visited. So if you set links to red and don't specify a color for visited links, then both active links and visited links will also be red. Explorer 4 does support a:active.

Explorer 3 for Macintosh supports A:visited, but the Windows 95 version doesn't seem to at all, but instead simply inherits the characteristics of A:link.

Netscape Navigator 4 doesn't support link effects.

> **TIP** One effect that may make web designers happy is removing the underline from links. By setting `text-decoration` to `none` in a link class, you can finally get rid of that pesky, ugly line:
>
> A:link { text-decoration: none }

And once again, like `classes` and `ids`, link classes can also be used as contextual selectors, which means you can set the border color of linked images like so:

```
A:link IMG { border: blue }
```

Working with Style Sheets

If you've read this chapter on Cascading Style Sheets Basics, you hopefully know everything you need to know to add style to your web pages. And if you are a web designer, your mind is already applying what you read to your existing sites or sites you plan to do in the near future. CSS is like that, the more you learn and see, the more properties you read about, the more you realize you can achieve. With that in mind, the next sections take some of the bigger web issues addressed by CSS and present the solutions to those issues. You see plenty of examples of how to combine properties and use styles to make your web site really hum.

Positioning and Layout

CSS provides a level of control when positioning and formatting pages that is simply not possible in current HTML. For starters, CSS allows you to place an element anywhere you want on the page regardless of what is currently displayed (granted, you want to be careful not to clobber the underlying element or create a mess). You can position items relative to each other to make sure one graphic always rests to the lower right of another or that text flows around an image. The point is, you no longer have to rely on "where elements fall on the page" or where the browser places elements.

To understand the positioning capabilities of CSS, it is helpful to first learn more about the way objects are formatted or treated in relation to the "box" around them. In style sheets, every single block-level element (tags such as <p> and <h1>, which automatically define their own block or paragraph) has what is called a *box*. With the box, you control margins, borders, floating images, and perform other elegant layout capabilities. The box is the sum of the following parts (see Figure 7):

- The *element* itself (text, image, animation, or whatever)
- The *padding* around the element
- The *border* around the padding
- The *margin* around the border

Figure 7

The basic formatting model within style sheets.

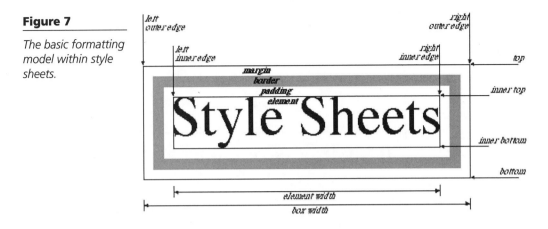

You set the size of the padding, border, and margin around each element with properties like padding, border, and margin. With those same properties, you can also adjust the color and style of the border. The size of the element's box is the sum of all of these parts, as Figure 7 shows. You also see other terminology introduced:

- *top* is the top of the box including any padding, border, and margin.
- *inner top* is the top of the actual element, without any padding, border, or margin.
- *inner bottom* is the bottom of the actual element.
- *bottom* is the bottom of the entire box.
- *left outer edge* is the left edge of the entire box, including padding, border, and margin.
- *left inner edge* is the left edge of the actual element, without padding, border, or margin.
- *right inner edge* is the right edge of the actual element.
- *right outer edge* is the right edge of the entire box.

Width refers to the width of the element: the distance between the left inner edge and the right inner edge. *Height* is the height of the element: from inner top to inner bottom. Here's an example of how these boxes interact:

```
<HTML>
<HEAD>
 <TITLE>Defining the Box</TITLE>
</HEAD>
<BODY>
 <DIV>
 <P>This line is one paragraph.</P>
 <UL>
 <LI>This is line one.
 <LI>This is line two.
 </UL>
```

```
   </DIV>
   </BODY>
   </HTML>
```

In the formatting model, each of these block elements gets its own box, with padding, border, and margin (see Figure 8).

Figure 8

Boxes within boxes: the formatting model in action.

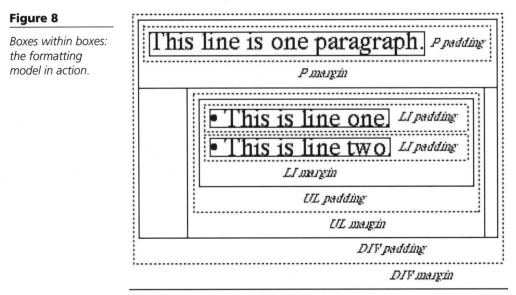

The distance between two elements is controlled by the size of their margins. If you have multiple margins that are adjoined (so there's nothing between them, including content, padding, and border), then those margins are collapsed and the larger of the margin sizes is used. In the previous example, between the first line and the first bulleted text, the <p> margin, <ul> margin, and <li> margin would be collapsed as long as no borders or padding existed between any of them (refer to Figure 10). Margins can also be negative. In this situation, for two adjoining margins, the negative margin should be subtracted from the positive margin.

Now that you understand boxes, you are ready to learn about the position property, which is the key to page layout in CSS. When combined with the top and left properties, you define where any element (text or replaced element) appears onscreen. Using these properties, you can set *absolute* positions on the page or *relative* positions, which are related to other elements.

Absolute Positioning

When you absolutely position an element, you give it a specific rectangular area that will contain the contents of the element. This new rectangle is controlled independently of any other element on the page with the top and left properties as with the following example:

```
<html>
<style type="text/css">
<!--
 body { background: white }
 div  { position: absolute;
        left: 40px;
        top: 70px }
 P    { position: absolute;
        left: 200px;
        top: 100px }
-->
</style>
<head>
<title>Absolute Positioning</title>
</head>
<body>
Here is some body text that appears after body but before
any other HTML tags. Standard stuff.
<div>Now I've started a division, and the text you see
here is within div. It gets positioned independently,
based on the coordinate system defined by body.
<p>And here is P text within the div. It's positioned
independently based on div's coordinate system.</p>
</div>
</body>
</html>
```

The result is shown in Figure 9. The `<div>` text is positioned absolutely and the browser creates a new coordinate system based on its parent element, `<body>`. The `<div>` text (the "box" around `<div>`, actually) begins at a point that is 40 pixels from the left edge of `<body>`'s normal display area, and 70 pixels down from the top. Similarly, when the browser sees that `<p>` is a child of `<div>`, it creates yet another coordinate system for `<p>` that is based on the starting point of `<div>` text (the upper-left corner of the box that surrounds the `<div>` element). So, from that point, it goes across 200 pixels and down 100 pixels, and then begins to display `<p>` text.

Figure 9

Absolute positioning means you can control layout according to coordinate systems.

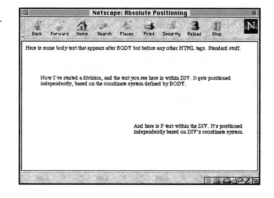

Absolute positioning can also be used on replaced elements such as images as with the following example:

```
<html>
 <style type="text/css">
 <!--
  body { background: black;
         color: white }
  .a   { position: absolute;
         left: 300px;
         top: 0px }
  P    { position: absolute;
         left: -40px;
         top: 80px }
 -->
 </style>
<head>
 <title>Absolute Positioning</title>
</head>
<body>
 <h2>Muir Woods: Your Path to Peace</h2>
 <span class=a><img src="woods.jpg">
 <p>Stepping into Muir Woods is like stepping into the
 quietest part of your soul. The wind in the trees slows
 the racing mind...</p>
 </span>
</body>
</html>
```

Figure 10 shows the result. The image is positioned 300 pixels from the left edge of <body> (which is also the edge of the browser window). Because the top value is set to 0 pixels, it's brought right up to the top edge of the window (definitely something difficult to do in standard HTML!). Then, the line of <p> text is positioned based on the coordinate system the image creates: 80 pixels down from the top of the image, and –40 pixels to the right (that is, 40 pixels to the left) of the image's left edge.

Figure 10

Absolute positioning with images and negative values can create interesting results.

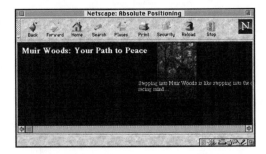

Relative Positioning

As the name implies, relative positioning means placing one element relative to or in relation to another. The new position of the element is relative to its parent. This type of positioning is more or less the way elements are placed in current HTML. In the following example, the <i> text is within the header tags <h4>. The italicized text is therefore the child of the header, and the header text is the parent. When the child text is positioned, it will be placed relative to the header text and not to the borders of the page.

```
<html>
 <style type="text/css">
 <!--
  body { background: white }
  i    { position: relative;
         left: 10px;
         top: 50px }
 -->
 </style>
<head>
 <title>Relative Positioning</title>
</head>
<body>
 <h4>Here's some normal body text.
 <i>When you position an element with relative, it's placed relative to its
parent element, more or less like we're used to in HTML. But even though the
element does retain its natural formatting on the page, it can receive some of
the special abilities that absolute offers.
  </i></h4>
</body>
</html>
```

The browser is told to position the italicized text relative to the header text. Specifically, the instructions are to begin displaying the italicized text 10 pixels across and 50 pixels down from *where it would otherwise be displayed* by default (see Figure 11). There is a coordinate system at work here, but the coordinates begin *not* at the beginning of an element, but at the "end." So, after the period after "text," the browser goes down 50 pixels and across 10 before displaying the other text.

Figure 11

Relative positioning moves the element from the position it would otherwise occupy.

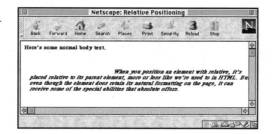

For more information on positioning, see the full description of the position, left, and top properties in this book. You may also want to hit line-height, text-align, vertical-align, height, and width. Lastly, for setting box properties, make sure you check out margin, padding, and border.

One last topic, CSS can also handle three-dimensional layout. You can place objects on top of each other in a certain order creating some interesting effects. The z-index property is the key to this as discussed in this book. Related to this, though not part of CSS, are layers, which enable you to group items together as well as set the position. See <layer> and <ilayer> for more information.

Working with Fonts

In the current browser world, many browsers come with only two predefined fonts: normal and monospaced. There's not a lot you can do with only two fonts at your disposal. After all, it seems ridiculous to have 30 or so fonts on a machine and only two on your web page. CSS is the first definitive step in changing all that. Style sheets enable web authors to finally specify particular fonts by name, and at the same time define things such as point size, italics style, small caps, and different weights of bold. These properties have long since become standard issue in the world of desktop fonts.

Netscape started to address this with the <font> tag. You can control font face, size, and so on. But that control is neither flexible enough nor open enough. <font size>, for example, enables you to specify text size from a value of 1 through 7. But with style sheets, you can specify absolutely *any* size you want—either smaller or larger than is possible through traditional HTML. Also, you can adjust size using a variety of units (such as points, pixels, and ems) that weren't possible to use before. Netscape might have introduced some font control through HTML tags, but style sheets give you more complete control than ever before possible.

To get a feel for what you can now do with fonts, here's a list of the font and text tags available with CSS:

- font-family—sets the font like arial, helvetica, and so on
- font-size—sets the size using pts, units, and so on
- font-style—supports italic and oblique
- font-weight—supports different degrees of bold
- font-variant—special caps effects like small caps
- text-transform—special case effects like lowercased text
- text-decoration—special line effects like underlining

To see what you can do, take a look at this example:

```
<html>
<head>
<title>Famous Quotes</title>
</head>
```

```
<style type="text/css">
<!--
body { font-family : helvetica }
p { font-size : 14pt }
p b {font-size : 20pt }
blockquote { font-family : ariel;
                  font-size : 16pt }
blockquote i { text-transform : uppercase }
blockquote b { text-decoration : underline }
blockquote b i { font-size : 20pt }
-->
</style>
<body>
<p>From a famous <b>zen web </b> designer...</p>
<blockquote>
He who creates for the <b>world's</b> eyes to
see should <b><i>strive for clarity</b></i> in the
<i>eye glasses</i> of the web.
</blockquote>
</body>
</html>
```

The result is displayed in Figure 12. First, the HTML text sets an overall font for the <body> of the document to helvetica. The next set of styles applies to paragraphs. The point size is 14 for <p> unless the text is specially emphasized with the <b> tag, in which case the size is made larger for extra emphasis. For quotes, the <blockquote> tag uses the ariel font. Italicized text with the <i> tag is displayed all in capitals and text with the <b> tag is underlined. Lastly, for <blockquote> text combined with <i> and <b>, the text is made especially large to really pop off the page.

Realize, of course, that this example is overloaded with font effects to make a point. You should avoid doing too much with text attributes, otherwise some of your emphasis and formatting may get lost.

Figure 12

*An example of
working with fonts.*

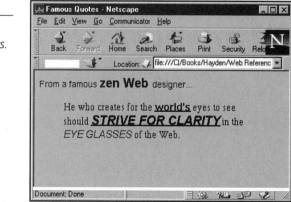

> **NOTE** For a refresher on the elements of fonts and typography, the artistry of using type, and the technology of applying them across platforms, check out Sean Cavanaugh's *Digital Type Design Guide* (Hayden Books).

One final note, if you've worked for any length of time in desktop publishing or design, you know that the world of fonts is a messy world. For one thing, there's more than one type of font format, though PostScript Type 1 fonts and TrueType fonts now dominate. But what's even more problematic is that the actual names of fonts (and their associated variants, such as Bold, Oblique, Heavy, and so on) are not at all consistent, especially as you cross platforms between Mac and Windows. The CSS addresses this issue by trying as best as possible to match font names with the fonts on the end user system. For more information on this, see the description of the font-family tag in this book.

Consistency

A consistent look and feel is very important to many software developers and producers on the web. Could you imagine starting a software package where every dialog box looks different? How about a web site where pages follow different color schemes, some have a table of contents while others scatter links and buttons throughout the page?

The point is, a consistent web site brings a familiar environment to the viewer in which they spend more time looking at the actual content and less time trying to find the content among the graphics or figuring out how to navigate to other pages. CSS helps a great deal with this issue especially if you put all your styles in a single file and link that file to all your web pages. All pages have the same properties for fonts, colors, the background, and so on, and the viewer always knows where he is and what to do.

There is one huge benefit related to consistency especially if you are a web master maintaining a rather large web site. You have many megabytes of corporate data and news releases or content that you have carefully formatted into a great, consistent-looking site. Each page has a table of contents on the side and a texture bitmap in the background and a consistent heading on the top of every page that includes the corporate logo. One day, your company PR firm checks the site and casually informs you the colors you have chosen don't match the company logo correctly. You kiss your weekend goodbye as you think of changing each and every page. Now, if you use CSS and put all your styles in one sheet linked to all your web pages, you could make this change while you are still on the phone!

When creating your consistent look, a good way to approach this is start at the top and work down. For example, look at the entire page and set properties that affect the overall look first. You can set a background color to something subtle such as "#FF7777," which is a light salmon like color. Then, you keep this color in mind when you set the colors of your text and other attributes. Best of all, CSS properties are designed to allow you to take this approach. Here's a list of suggestions you could do:

- Define the background with `background` properties
- Use the same font with the `font-family` style
- Set block level characteristics such as `color`, `text-align`, and `text-indent`
- Set text characteristics on flow elements like headings with `font-size`, `font-weight`, and other properties

VBScript

Just as JavaScript offers a tempting path toward web page nirvana, VBScript is a capable peer. "VB," as in "Visual Basic," is Microsoft's popular full-blown programming language, commonly used to develop software applications. VBScript is a simplified spawn of Visual Basic, stripped down of some complexities, and biased toward use in web pages. By and large, JavaScript and VBScript are competing web programming languages—both offer many of the same capabilities (in fact, they share the same set of objects). However, VBScript is a somewhat more fully evolved language than is JavaScript. For the vast majority of readers, however, the differences between the two languages will boil down to syntax and support.

Of course, this chapter is not intended to be a thorough course in programming, or even VBScript itself. Rather, we'll look at how VBScript code is constructed, and how to incorporate it into your web pages. In doing so, you'll be able to make sense of the A–Z reference in this book.

The VBScript Bio

VBScript is a programming language, sometimes called a "scripting language," which enables you to add logic and control to your web pages. If you're already familiar with any programming language, adding VBScript to your belt notches shouldn't be terribly difficult. As its full name (Visual Basic) implies, VBScript draws its syntax and style largely from the popular old beginner's language BASIC. If you learned to program any time during the freewheeling 1980s, you've probably spent some quality time with BASIC already. If not, think of BASIC as the esperanto of programming langauges—lacking in elegance, perhaps, but simple to read and write.

Like JavaScript, VBScript is a "client-side" programming language—it's *fast*. That means no more waiting for data to be sent to the server for a reaction. VBScript resides within the web page and runs entirely on the user's computer, allowing it to produce near-instantaneous results.

Thin Support

For VBScript-enabled web pages to function properly, the user's particular web browser must support VBScript. As of this writing, the only browser to support VBScript is Microsoft Internet Explorer. Therefore, you'll only even want to consider using VBScript (rather than JavaScript) if your pages are aimed primarily, or exclusively, at Internet Explorer users. Although this restriction is probably a major blow to widespread VBScript across the heterogeneous Internet, many organizations maintain intranets that rely entirely on one browser. Thus, in an Internet Explorer-based intranet environment, programming with VBScript is well worth consideration.

> **NOTE** If you are using or programming for Internet Explorer 3, you should install Microsoft's VBScript 2 Update. This upgrades the original VBScript support to include some functions that are included in the A–Z reference.
>
> You can find the VBScript 2 Update at: `http://www.microsoft.com/vbscript/`

Stick to the `<script>` Tag

As a client-side language, VBScript code resides within the HTML for the web page itself. With one notable exception (event handlers, to be explained later), VBScript code must always appear between HTML `<script>`…`</script>` tags. This tag tells the script-aware browser that the content within should be processed as script code, and not as information to appear directly on the web page. Web browsers that don't support any scripting language won't recognize the `<script>` tag, so we'll have to add a little trick to prevent them from misinterpreting the code.

Taking a simple example, the following is a short section of VBScript code, as it should appear within an HTML document:

```
<script language="VBScript">
<!-- hide this code from non-VBScript browsers
 document.bgColor="steel blue"
 document.fgColor="black"
-->
</script>
```

In the previous `<script>` tag, we specify the attribute `language` as "VBScript". Obviously, this tells the browser that the program code is written in VBScript, rather than, say, JavaScript. To avoid ambiguity, you should always specify the `language` attribute.

As mentioned earlier, not all browsers support scripting. Because they don't "know" the `<script>` tag, they'll simply ignore it. But what of the code in between? Typically, script-ignorant browsers will attempt to display the program code as web page content—resulting in an onscreen mess. The solution is to enclose the script inside an HTML comment tag, so that non-scripting browsers ignore it. As seen earlier, you start the comment tag with `<!--`, placed immediately after the opening `<script>` tag, and end the comment with `-->`, placed immediately before the closing `</script>` tag.

We can roughly divide an HTML document into two main sections: the `<head>` section and the `<body>` section (see the "HTML Basics" chapter for more about these tags). When VBScript code (within appropriate `<script>` tags) is placed within the `<body>` section of a document, it is executed in the order in which it appears.

Typically, you place VBScript procedures (`sub` and `function` procedures, explained later) within the `<head>` section of a document. A VBScript procedure is a subroutine—a bit of code that you will "call" from elsewhere in the VBScript program. VBScript within the `<head>` section is not executed immediately; rather, it is "remembered" by the page, and used later when called upon.

```
<html>
<head><title>Example HTML Document with VBScript Code</title>
<script language="VBScript">
 …procedure definitions…
</script>
</head>
<body>
 …HTML of page content…
<script language="VBScript">
 …any VBScript to execute after page has loaded…
</script>
</html>
```

The exception to these script placement discussions are event-handlers, which, as we see later in this chapter, are VBScript code or procedure calls that can be integrated into existing HTML tags or defined using a variation on the `<script>` tag.

Making a Statement

VBScript "commands" are known as statements, and like English-language statements, can be constructed of any valid grammatical components. For an instance, consider a basic VBScript assignment statement:

```
total = 100
```

This statement assigns the value 100 to the variable `total`. Generally, you place one statement per line, although you may optionally use a colon delimiter to place multiple statements on one line:

```
total = 100:price = 20
```

Spacing, such as around the equal signs, or line indentations are a matter of personal preference and have no impact on execution.

Like an English paragraph, a VBScript program is made up of a series of statements. A statement itself is made up of one or more expressions. For instance, the example `total=100` is an assignment statement, because it consists of one expression—an assignment.

The expression, in turn, is made up of yet smaller components; in the example seen, a variable, an operator (the equals signs), and a numeric literal. Let's consider, in turn, each of the components that can go into creating an expression and, thus, a statement.

Values

In VBScript, all types of values are known by one name: a *variant*. The variant can contain any "type" of data, such as a number, a string, or a calendar date. Technically, these "types" of data are known as *subtypes*. Because VBScript is relatively intelligent (so they say), it implicitly understands how to properly handle any subtype without requiring a prior declaration.

Subtypes exist because different sorts of values need to be handled differently. For instance, adding time to a calendar date is not the same as adding characters to a string, or subtracting an integer from another integer. VBScript will assume your values belong to a particular subtype based on how they are expressed. Table 1 summarizes the VBScript subtypes and what values they may contain.

Table 1 VBScript Variant Subtypes

Subtype	Value(s)
Empty	Variant has not been initialized. Contains a value of 0 if used in a numeric expression or a value of "" if used in a string expression.
Null	Nothing—not 0 or an empty string, simply no value.
Boolean	Either **true** or **false**.
Byte	An integer from 0 to 255.
Integer	An integer from –32,768 to 32,767.
Date (Time)	A date between January 1, 100 and December 31, 9999.
String	A string of any characters. May be up to 2 billion characters long (RAM-willing!)

In most cases, you won't need to directly know what subtype your values fall within. However, there are certain cases when you'll want to convert a value from one subtype to another, for which there are several VBScript conversion functions listed in the A–Z reference.

Any time you explicitly state one of the previous values in VBScript code, it is known as a *literal*. In the example assignment statement (`total=100`), 100 is a literal. The alternative way of expressing a value is a *variable*.

A variable is a word or label that acts as a placeholder, or referent, to a value. Although the label remains the same, the value itself may vary. So, for instance, we could conjure up a variable named `total`, and assign it the numeric value 100. At a later time, the value of `total` might change, for instance, as the result of a calculation whose result is assigned to `total`.

You can make up virtually any variable name, keeping the following few rules in mind:

■ The variable name cannot conflict with a built-in VBScript keyword.

- The variable name must begin with an alphabetic letter, although it may contain numerals or underscores (_) beyond the first character.
- The variable name cannot contain any whitespace or punctuation characters.
- The variable name cannot exceed 255 characters in length.

VBScript is not case-sensitive, which means it does not distinguish between uppercase and lowercase versions of a letter. Thus, the variable name `Total` is equivalent to `total` or `TOTAL`.

Valid Variable Names	Invalid Variable Names
cost	1cost
loop2	loop 2
for_	_for
Names_3_1	names!3.1

Lastly, you can create a variable that contains a set of values, rather than only one value. Such a variable is known as an *array*. The array contains a set of *elements*, each referenced by an *index*. Each element is a variable in its own right, and can contain a value.

Array syntax:

```
arrayname(index)
```

Imagine an array named `users`, which contains three elements. You could then access or modify the values of:

```
users(0)
users(1)
users(2)
```

As you can see, array indexing begins with number 0. The element in the array is treated just like any other variable; that is:

```
users(0)="fred"
```

> **NOTE** Although both VBScript and JavaScript support arrays in a similar fashion, notice that in VBScript you enclose the element index within parentheses: `arrayname(index)`.

Operators

Expressions are also built using *operators*. An operator, although difficult to define, is easier to illustrate. Pressed for a definition, though, we can think of a VBScript operator like a friendly telephone operator—a medium between two parties. In the case of a VBScript operator, those two parties may be two variables, or a variable and a literal, or two expressions (the only exception to this being unary negation, which requires only one variable or literal on which to operate).

VBScript operators can be divided into several classes, depending on the purpose of the operator. For instance, let's begin by looking at the arithmetic operators.

Table 2 Arithmetic Operators

Arithmetic Operator	Purpose	Example Expression
+	Addition	`total+10`
−	Subtraction	`10-3`
*	Multiplication	`units*price`
/	Division	`retail/2`
\	Integer Division	`10/3 (yields 3)`
÷	Modulus (remainder of a division)	`10÷3 (yields 1)`
^	Exponentiation	

VBScript possesses one unary operator, the unary negation. Simply a minus sign, the unary negation only takes one value; for example:

`-total`

The unary negation operator simply calculates the negative of the value supplied.

Although not strictly an arithmetic operator, the string concatenation operator (&) is classified as one. String concatenation is the process of combining two string values, as follows:

`"every good boy"&" deserves a fridge"`

This yields a single string value "every good boy deserves a fridge".

Another popular class of operators are known as *comparison operators*. These are used to—you guessed it—compare one expression, variable, or value against another. Typically, you use comparison operators within conditional statements (such as an *if...then...else*, as we'll see later), which direct the flow of program execution depending on the results of the comparison.

Table 3 Comparison Operators

Comparison Operator	Purpose	Example Expression
=	Test for equality	`year=1972`
<>	Test for inequality	`year<>1997`
>	Greater than	`age>17`
<	Less than	`height<65`

Comparison Operator	Purpose	Example Expression
>=	Greater than or equal to	`age>=21`
<=	Less than or equal to	`terms<=2`

Remember, this chapter is not a comprehensive look at all VBScript components. There are additional classes of operators, but the salty point here is that you use variables, literals, and operators to build expressions. Expressions, in turn, are combined into statements, and statements become VBScript programs.

Program Flow—Conditionals and Loops

By default, statements in VBScript are executed sequentially; that is, in the order in which they appear. This is known as *program flow.* There are many instances where you want to institute an alternative program flow—two main examples are conditionals (execute certain lines of code under certain conditions) and loops (execute certain lines of code repeatedly for a specified number of cycles or until a certain condition is met).

Controlling program flow is an integral part of any programming language, and VBScript proffers its share of techniques. Each program flow statement has its own syntax to remember, as illustrated in the following brief synopses.

if...then...else

Logically, this statement works as it reads in English—*if* a certain condition exists *then* execute the following code, or *else* execute the following. The *else* clause is optional, as you may not require an "otherwise" condition.

Syntax:

```
if condition then
 VBScript code to execute when condition is true
else
 VBScript code to execute when condition is false
end if
```

In the previous example, *condition* is usually an operator expression, such as in `if profit>=1000`. You can place as many lines of code as necessary after the `then` and after the `else`. Unlike JavaScript, VBScript does not use curly braces to enclose clauses; rather, it relies on the keyword `else` and/or `end if` to signal the end of a clause.

while

The *while* statement creates a loop situation, wherein the specified VBScript code is executed repeatedly as long as a specified condition remains true.

Syntax:

```
while condition
  VBScript code to execute repeatedly as long as condition remains true
wend
```

Again, condition is usually an operator expression, such as while seconds<60.

do...loop

The *do...loop* statement is a more elaborate and flexible version of the *while* loop. Using a *do...loop*, you can execute a block of VBScript code repeatedly either *while* a condition is true or *until* a condition turns true.

Syntax 1:

```
do while condition
  VBScript code to execute repeatedly as long as condition remains true
loop
```

Syntax 2:

```
do until condition
  VBScript code to execute repeatedly until condition is true
loop
```

VBScript also provides, as a free bonus, the *exit do* statement. Placing this statement somewhere within the execution block of the *do...loop* (such as an *if...then*) will abort the loop without waiting for the condition to be satisfied. Typically, you use the exit *do* statement as clause of an *if...then* to check for and avoid the possibility of being caught in an endless loop.

for...next

The loopy *for...next* statement provides you a compact way to control the loop's cycle. By specifying the counting variable, the starting and ending values, and an optional step increment, the loop iterates in time with the counter. In short, the *for...next* statement is used to cycle a loop a specified number of times.

Syntax:

```
for countvariable=startvalue to endvalue step stepvalue
  VBScript code to execute repeatedly until counter has finished
next
```

If you specify a *stepvalue* that is negative, the loop will attempt to count "down" from your *startvalue* to your *endvalue*. Of course, if the former is smaller than the latter, the loop will never execute because you cannot count down from a smaller number to a greater one. Optionally, you can omit the *step* keyword and value altogether and an increment of +1 will be assumed. Let's look at a couple examples to clear up any possible confusion.

Example 1:

```
for j=1 to 100
 VBScript code to execute
next
```

This loop will iterate 100 times, each time incrementing the value of j by 1.

Example 2:

```
for j=1 to 100 step 2
 VBScript code to execute
next
```

Like the *do…loop* statement, the *for…next* statement includes a free *exit for* statement. Placing it within the execution code of the loop will abort the loop immediately.

Following Procedures

Think of the prepackaged cold cuts at the supermarket, in the refrigerated section near the frankfurters and bacon. You could, for instance, construct an efficient (if somewhat bland) lunch using two slices of bread and a package of those cold cuts. In fact, a VBScript procedure is very similar—a pre-created bit of code that you call upon when needed in a larger project. Procedures are created to perform a specific task—whenever your VBScript program requires that task to be performed, it "calls" the appropriate procedure.

In truth, VBScript offers two types of procedures: subroutines and functions. Both serve much the same purpose, with a small but significant difference—to be explained momentarily.

Subroutines Defined

If the lunchmeat example seems a bit oblique, consider a simple VBScript subroutine, whose job is to rest the form fields on the page to a pre-determined set of defaults. When your program needs to reset the form fields, such as when the user clicks a "Reset" button, you can invoke the "resetfields" subroutine.

As briefly explained earlier, you typically include VBScript procedures within the <head> tags of the HTML document. This way, they are all loaded into memory by the time the page executes your JavaScript code. Imagine, then, that we're placing our code within the <head> tags, and let's define a subroutine—known in VBScript as a *sub*.

To define a sub procedure, you must give it a name (with the same restrictions as choosing a variable name), and specify any *parameters* the sub will accept. A parameter is a value that is passed to the procedure when it is called.

Syntax:

```
sub subName (parameter1,parameter2,etc)
 VBScript code to execute when this procedure is called
end sub
```

The parameter names specified are used as variables within the procedure body. Whatever values are passed to this sub, when it is called, will be assigned to the specified variable names in the parameter list. Thus, if the values 10 and 15 are passed to the example sub, then within the sub procedure, the variable parameter1 will begin with a value of 10 and parameter2 will begin with a value of 15. Some procedures may not require any parameters, in which case you simply place nothing between the parentheses; that is, subName ().

Sub procedures have one limitation, however: they can't return a value. Enter the *function*, which is a procedure much like the sub except that it can also return a value.

Function-ing

Imagine this simple hypothetical procedure: you want to send the procedure two variables, A and B, and the procedure should return a value of true if A is greater than B, or a false otherwise. Sounds like a VBScript function.

In nearly all respects, the function procedure looks just like the sub procedure, save for returning a value:

Syntax:

```
function funcName (parameter1,parameter2,etc)
 VBScript code to execute when this procedure is called
 funcName=returnvalue
end function
```

Recall the function that compares A and B—let's call this function *compare_ab()*. Remembering to place it within the <head> tags of the HTML document, this function might look something like:

```
<html><head><title>Page Title</title>
<script language="VBScript">
function compare_ab (val_a,val_b)
 if val_a > val_b then
  compare_ab=true
 else
  compare_ab=false
end function
</script>
</head><body>
...rest of HTML document...
</body></html>
```

Were we to add any more sub or function procedures to this page, they would be inserted before the closing </script> tag.

Due to the way in which you invoke ("call") subs and functions, it's best to use function procedures when a value must be returned, and a sub procedure otherwise.

Placing the Call

When a VBScript procedure is invoked, we say that it has been *called*. The manner in which you call a procedure depends on whether it is sub or function.

Sub syntax:

```
subName parameter1,parameter2
```

or

```
call subName(parameter1,parameter2)
```

Notice that if you choose to use the "call" keyword then you must enclose the parameters within parentheses. Otherwise, there is no difference between the two syntaxes.

Examples:

```
resetform
call resetform()
showhand victor,loser
call showhand(victor,loser)
```

Because functions *return* a value, they can only be called from within an expression where the returned value is appropriate. For instance, consider the assignment statement:

```
total=calcTotal(sales,price)
```

We must imagine that the function *calcTotal()* returns a value, which is then assigned to the variable `total`. Or, we might call our *compare_ab()* function as the condition in an *if...then* statement:

```
if compare_ab(val_a,val_b)=true then
 code for true clause
else
 code for false clause
end if
```

Object-ified

One of the most important and useful concepts in both VBScript and JavaScript is the object. In fact, many of the VBScript entries in the A–Z reference section of this book revolve around the object. Objects provide scriptable access to interpret and/or modify many characteristics of the web page. Both VBScript and JavaScript share the same set of web-related objects, and share nearly the exact same syntax in their use. But let's begin at the bottom, and look at just what an object is.

Think of an object as a category, or a class. Within this category reside a series of related items. For instance, picture your tax return filing cabinet (you *do* have a tax return folio, don't *you?*!). Within this possibly mythical filing cabinet reside related folders—receipts, income statements, canceled checks, and so forth. In this metaphor, then, the filing cabinet is the object. In more literal terms, the document loaded within the browser window is also an object. Within the object are a bunch of related "things." Now, "things" is a terribly vague word, so what sorts of "things" can reside within the object? Two things: properties and methods.

Properties

A property represents some relevant characteristic of the object. Remember that the currently loaded document is an object—in fact, it is officially called the `document` object. This object possesses a variety of properties, related to characteristics such as the background color of the page, the foreground color, the color of unvisited hyperlinks, all the images on the page, and so on.

Each of these properties has a predefined name, and we refer to an object's property using the syntax:

```
object.property
```

So, if you look up the `document` object in the A–Z reference section of this book, you'll see that it contains a property named `bgColor`. Sensibly, this property refers to the background color of the document. A property is similar to a VBScript variable, in that you can access the value it contains, or assign it a new value. The latter is often, but not always true—some properties are *read-only*, and you cannot modify the values they contain.

As it happens, the `document` object's `bgColor` property can be read or modified. So, you could, for instance, use an *if…then…else* statement to determine if the current background color is black:

```
if document.bgColor=0 then
 action to take if black
else
 action to take if not black
```

Alternatively, you could assign a new value to the `bgColor` property:

```
document.bgColor="blue"
```

In this example, the background color of the document would instantly become blue. Not all assignments to a property will result in an immediate effect—such details are noted in the object reference entries for each property.

Methods

Whereas a property is essentially a variable tied to an object, a method is a procedure (a sub or a function) tied to an object. Just as the `document object` contains a set of properties, it also contains a set of methods. Each method is a procedure that performs some action relevant to the object. Some of these procedures return a value although some don't. These methods, although they are procedures, are built-in to VBScript, not defined within the page itself. Again, as with properties, methods are outlined in detail for each object within the A–Z reference section of this book. Unlike the different syntaxes between calling subs and functions, you can use the following syntax to call any method:

```
object.method(parameters)
```

Consider the `write()` method of the `document` object. When called this method will output HTML content to the document within the browser window.

```
document.write("<H1>Learning VBScript is Thrilling!</H1>")
```

Calling the *write()* method of the *document* object.

It's true—using an object's properties and methods is relatively straightforward. The power of objects lies in their ability to provide script access to a wide variety of characteristics of the web page.

The Great Event

We close out the "VBScript Basics" chapter with a look at events and event-handling. Although you now have a basic understanding of how to put together VBScript code, and how to access and manipulate web pages through objects, you may wonder what "triggers" any of this code to execute in the first place. An excellent query! Events, my friend, events.

A VBScript *event* occurs whenever an event-triggering action takes place. Vague, I know, but events are easier illustrated than explained (he says sheepishly). For instance, when a user clicks the mouse button on a hyperlink or form field button, an event known as the `Click` event is triggered. As with objects, VBScript and JavaScript share much the same set of events, for compatibility sake. The following table summarizes some common events, mutual to VBScript and JavaScript, and what triggers them to occur.

Table 3   Common Events

Event Name	Triggered By
Click	Mouse click on a hyperlink or form field button.
MouseOver	Mouse pointer moved over a hyperlink or image map area.
MouseOut	Mouse pointer moved away from a hyperlink or image map area.
Focus	Bringing focus to a page element through the mouse or tab key.
Blur	Removing focus from a page element by clicking or tabbing elsewhere.
Submit	Submitting a form through the "Submit" button.
Reset	Resetting a form through the "Reset" button.

As usual, this is not a comprehensive list of all events, but it includes the most commonly used.

Finger on the Trigger

When an event occurs, you can trigger some VBScript code to execute. Pairing VBScript code with a particular event is known as an *event-handler*. In talking about an event-handler, you use the terminology onEvent; for instance, we could speak of the onClick event-handler. VBScript offers two equal but syntactically different ways of constructing an event-handler. The "short" way is best when the event-handler contains very little code, such as a procedure call. The "long" way is more suited to an event-handler that requires several lines of VBScript code.

The "Short Way" Event-Handler

Short event-handlers are added as an attribute to the HTML tag for which the event applies.

Syntax:

```
<tag attribute1 attribute2 onEvent="VBScript code to trigger"
➥language="VBScript">
```

Consider, for example, the HTML <input> tag, which you can use to create a form field button. A basic button might be defined as follows:

```
<input type="button" value="Click me!">
```

However, you can easily add a short onClick event-handler to this button:

```
<input type="button" value="Click me!" onClick="call clickfunc()"
➥language="VBScript">
```

In the previous example, if a Click event occurs at this button, the VBScript sub procedure *clickfunc()* is called. Commonly, short event-handlers are used to call a sub procedure, which handles the work. You'll typically code procedures to handle various events on the page, and call those procedures from event-handlers, such as illustrated previously.

The "Long Way" Event-Handler

Alternatively, your event-handler could contain explicit VBScript code, rather than a procedure call. It'd be a tight squeeze to fit several lines of VBScript within the onEvent attribute, so VBScript provides an alternative syntax. You can add a new <script> tag after the HTML tag that defines the VBScript code for the event.

Syntax:

```
<tag attribute1 attribute2>
<script for="elementName" event="onEvent" language="VBScript">
 …VBScript statements to execute for this event…
</script>
```

Consider the following example, which changes a variety of page characteristics when the button named "but1" is clicked:

```
<input name="but1" type="button" value="Click me!">
<script for="but1" event="onClick" language="VBScript">
 document.bgColor="black"
 another VBScript statement
 another VBScript statement
 …etc…
</script>
```

In using this event-handler syntax, you must be sure to specify the name attribute for the HTML element, because it must be referred to in the for attribute of the <script> tag. Although both the short and long versions of VBScript event-handlers work equally well, the "long way" offers better readability in cases where your event-handler requires several VBScript statements. Having said that, using the "short way" enables you to more easily re-write your code in JavaScript syntax, if necessary, because JavaScript only support the "short way" event-handler syntax.

Additional Reading

As promised, this VBScript Basics chapter has been exactly that—basic. If you have any background experience with BASIC or Visual Basic, you can easily pick up VBScript by reading the Microsoft VBScript reference documents (http://www.microsoft.com/vbscript). If you need more of a leg-up than some online tutorials, there are a few VBScript books hiding on the shelves at the local Café, err, Big Book SuperStore.

VBScript Unleashed, Second Edition, published by Sams.net

Teach Yourself VBScript in 21 Days, published by Sams.net

```
<IMG> </IMG> ■ <SCRIPT LANGUAGE = "javascript"> </SCRIPT>
■ <SCRIPT LANGUAGE = "vbscript"> </SCRIPT> ■ <BGSOUND
SRC=gbv.wav LOOP=-1> </BGSOUND> ■ <APPLET CLASS=
"ester's_day" SRC="http://testsite/walla walla     agton/"
</APPLET> ■ <FRAME></FRAME>■ <MARQUEE> </MARQUE
</HTML>■ <A> </A> ■ <OL> </OL>■ <UL> </UL>■
■ <STRONG> </STRONG> ■ <TD> </TD> ■ <TH> </TH>
```

Basics

JavaScript

Add some JavaScript code to your web pages and they'll really sing and dance. This book is full—literally—of JavaScript objects and functions, but to press them for all they're worth, you may want a good overview of JavaScript the language. Space and scope considerations prevent this chapter from becoming a full-blown JavaScript instructional, but we'll look at what JavaScript is and how you make use of it in your web pages.

Helping JavaScript Help You

JavaScript is a programming language, sometimes called a "scripting language," which enables you to add logic and control to your web pages. If you're already familiar with any programming language, picking up the details of JavaScript shouldn't be terribly difficult. Ancestrally, JavaScript draws from traditional programming languages such as Pascal and traditional scripting languages such as PERL. It's also important to note that JavaScript shares relatively little in common with Java (which draws from C and C++), other than that they're both programming languages (and that a marketing department chose to link them together by name, and name only).

Using JavaScript, you can design your web pages to act and react, by modifying content onscreen or interpreting actions from the user. For example, you can change an image on the page when a user selects a certain option in a form. Or, you can also code non-interactive JavaScript routines, such as animating a "ticker tape" style scrolling message.

Because JavaScript is a "client-side" programming language, it's effects are *fast*. That means no more waiting for data to be sent to the server for a reaction. JavaScript resides within the web page, and runs entirely on the user's computer, allowing it to produce near-instantaneous results.

Support, Support, and JScript?

For JavaScript-enabled web pages to function properly, the user's particular web browser must support JavaScript. As of this writing, only two web browsers support JavaScript—Netscape Navigator and Microsoft Internet Explorer. Furthermore, various versions of each browser may support different versions of JavaScript. It can become confusing. Again, as of this writing, there are three versions of JavaScript—1.0, 1.1, and 1.2. Each successive version adds some new functionality to the previous version. Keep this in mind when using the JavaScript reference in this book, because some browsers may not have certain support features of JavaScript, depending on the versions involved.

In some instances, you may also see reference to "JScript." In brief, JScript is the name Microsoft has given to their JavaScript support in Microsoft Internet Explorer. JScript is essentially the same as JavaScript, although there are minor quirky differences here and there, as noted in the JavaScript reference entries. The following chart summarizes the browsers and which versions of JavaScript they support.

Version	Supported By
JavaScript 1.0	Netscape Navigator 2.0, Microsoft Internet Explorer 3.0 (JScript)
JavaScript 1.1	Netscape Navigator 3.0, Microsoft Internet Explorer 4.0 (JScript)
JavaScript 1.2	Netscape Navigator 4.0

NOTE   If you are using or programming for Internet Explorer 3, you should install Microsoft's JScript 2 Update. This upgrades the original JScript support to be somewhat more compatible with JavaScript 1.0, as well as adding a small amount of JavaScript 1.1 compatibility.

You can find the JScript 2 Update at: `http://www.microsoft.com/jscript/`

Stick to the `<script>` Tag

As a client-side language, JavaScript code resides within the HTML for the web page itself. With one notable exception (event handlers, to be explained later), JavaScript code must always appear between HTML `<script>`…`</script>` tags. This tag tells the JavaScript-aware browser that the content within should be processed as JavaScript code, and not as information to appear directly on the web page. Web browsers that don't support JavaScript won't recognize the `<script>` tag, so we have to add a little trick to prevent them from misinterpreting the JavaScript code.

Taking a simple example, the following is a short section of JavaScript code, as it should appear within an HTML document:

```
<script language="JavaScript">
<!-- hide this code from non-JavaScript browsers
 document.bgColor="steel blue"
 document.fgColor="black"
-->
</script>
```

In the example `<script>` tag shown, we specify the attribute `language` as "JavaScript." As you'll see if you read the "VBScript Basics" chapter, JavaScript isn't the only language that uses the `<script>` tag, hence it is best to specify the `language` attribute.

As mentioned earlier, not all browsers support JavaScript. Because they don't "know" the `<script>` tag, they'll simply ignore it. But what about the code in between? Typically, JavaScript-ignorant browsers will attempt to display the JavaScript code as web page content—resulting in an onscreen mess. The solution is to enclose the JavaScript code inside an HTML comment tag, so that non-JavaScript browsers ignore it. As seen earlier, you start the comment tag with `<!--`, placed immediately after the opening `<script>` tag, and end the comment with `-->`, placed immediately before the closing `</script>` tag.

We can roughly divide an HTML document into two main sections: the `<head>` section and the `<body>` section (please refer to the "HTML Basics" chapter if you need your memory refreshed). When JavaScript code (within appropriate `<script>` tags) is placed within the `<body>` section of a document, it is executed in the order in which it appears.

Typically, you place JavaScript functions within the `<head>` section of a document. A function is like a subroutine—a bit of code that you will "call" from another line of JavaScript elsewhere (we'll look at functions more closely later). JavaScript within the `<head>` section is not executed immediately; rather, it is "remembered" by the page, and used when other lines of JavaScript call on it.

```
<html>
<head><title>Example HTML Document with JavaScript Code</title>
<script language="JavaScript">
 …function definitions…
</script>
</head>
<body>
 …HTML of page content…
<script language="JavaScript">
 …any JavaScript to execute after page has loaded…
</script>
</html>
```

The exception to the these script placement guidelines are event-handlers, which, as we'll see later in this chapter, are JavaScript code or function calls that are integrated into existing HTML tags.

Making a Statement

JavaScript "commands" are known as statements, and like English-language statements, can be constructed of any valid grammatical components. For an example, consider a basic JavaScript assignment statement:

```
total = 100;
```

This statement assigns the value 100 to the variable `total`. Some programmers choose to place a semicolon at the end of each JavaScript statement, as seen in this brief example, although it is not necessary unless you want to place multiple statements on a single line of text (a holdover from ancestral languages). Like an English paragraph, a JavaScript program is made up of a series of statements. A statement itself is made up of one or more expressions. For instance, the previous example is an assignment statement, because it consists of one expression—an assignment.

The expression, in turn, is made up of yet smaller components; in the previous example, a variable, an operator (the equals signs), and a numeric literal. Let's consider in turn, each component that goes into creating an expression and, thus, a statement.

Values

There are four types of values in JavaScript: numeric, string, boolean, and null. Each value is a different way of representing some "type" of content. Unlike some stricter programming languages, JavaScript enables you to use any of these values without having to make prior declarations.

- **Numeric values** are any number! Some examples include: 2, 150, 320.113, –54020113, and 2E–4.
- **String values** consist of any string of characters enclosed within single or double quotation marks. Note that JavaScript *is* case-sensitive, meaning that an uppercase letter is considered to be a different character from its lowercase counterpart. Some examples include: "harry", "Mark", "free42", and 'willy__*!()'.
- **Boolean values** are either true or false. They are represented by the keywords **true** or **false**.
- **Null values** have no value. This is *not* zero or an empty string value, as both of those *are* values. Null means *nada*, no value at all. It is represented by the keyword **null**.

When you directly refer to one of the previous values in JavaScript code, it is known as a *literal*. In the example assignment statement, the 100 is the numeric literal. The alternative value to a literal is a *variable*.

A variable is a word or label that acts as a placeholder, or reference, to a value. Although the label remains the same, the value itself may vary. So, for instance, we could conjure up a variable named `total`, and assign it the numeric value 100. At a later time, the value of `total` might change, for instance, as the result of a calculation whose result is assigned to `total`.

You can make up virtually any variable name, keeping the following few rules in mind:

- The variable name cannot conflict with a built-in JavaScript keyword.
- The variable name must begin with a letter or underscore (_), although it may contain numerals beyond the first character.
- The variable name cannot contain any white space or punctuation characters.

Valid Variable Names	Invalid Variable Names
cost	1cost
loop2	loop 2
_for	for
names_3_1	names!3–1

Lastly, you can create a variable that contains a set of values, rather than only one value. Such a variable is known as an *array*. The array contains a set of *elements*, each referenced by an *index*. Each element is a variable in its own right, and can contain a value.

Array syntax:

```
arrayname[index]
```

Imagine an array named `users`, which contains three elements. You could then access or modify the values of:

```
users[0]
users[1]
users[2]
```

As you can see, array indexing begins with number 0. The element in the array is treated just like any other variable; that is:

```
users[0]="fred"
```

> **NOTE**   Although both JavaScript and VBScript support arrays in a similar fashion, notice that in JavaScript you enclose the element index within brackets: `arrayname[index]`.

Operators

Expressions are also built using *operators*. An operator, although difficult to define, is easier to illustrate. Pressed for a definition, though, we can think of a JavaScript operator like a friendly telephone operator—a medium between two parties. In the case of a JavaScript operator, those two parties may be two variables, or a variable and a literal, or two expressions. There are, though, as you'll see, a couple of operators that "operate" with only one party.

JavaScript operators can be divided into several classes, depending on the purpose of the operator. For instance, let's begin by looking at the arithmetic operators in Table 1.

Table 1   Arithmetic Operators

Arithmetic Operator	Purpose	Example Expression
+	Addition	`total+10`
−	Subtraction	`10-3`
*	Multiplication	`units*price`
/	Division	`retail/2`
%	Modulus	`10%3` (remainder of a division)

There are some additional operators that can also roughly be classified as arithmetic, although they only require one expression on which to operate. Consequently, Table 2 lists those that are known as *unary* operators (whereas the previous operators are called *binary*).

Table 2   Unary Operators

Unary Operator	Purpose	Example Expression
++	Increment by 1	`total++`
—	Decrement by 1	`total--`
−	Negation	`-total`

Another popular class of operators known as *comparison operators* are listed in Table 3. These are used to—you guessed it—compare one expression, variable, or value against another. Typically, you use comparison operators within conditional statements (such as an *if...else*, as we'll see later), which direct the flow of program execution depending upon the results of the comparison.

Table 3   Comparison Operators

Comparison Operator	Purpose	Example Expression
==	Test for equality	`year==1972`
!=	Test for inequality	`year!=1997`
>	Greater than	`age>17`
<	Less than	`height<65`
>=	Greater than or equal to	`age>=21`
<=	Less than or equal to	`terms<=2`

Remember, this section is not a comprehensive look at all JavaScript components. There are several classes of operators, although the salient point here is that you use variables, literals, and operators to build expressions. Expressions, in turn, are combined into statements, and statements become JavaScript programs.

Program Flow—Conditionals and Loops

By default, statements in a JavaScript program are executed sequentially; that is, in the order in which they appear. This is known as *program flow*. There are many instances where you want to institute an alternative program flow—two main examples are conditionals (execute certain lines of code under certain conditions) and loops (execute certain lines of code repeatedly for a specified number of cycles or until a certain condition is met).

Controlling program flow is an integral part of any programming language, and JavaScript is no different. Each program flow statement has its own syntax to remember, as illustrated in the following brief synopses.

if...else

Also known as *if...then...else*, this statement works as it reads in English—if a certain condition exists execute the following code, otherwise (else) execute the following. The *else* clause is optional, as you may not require an "otherwise" condition.

Syntax:

```
if (condition)
 { JavaScript code to execute when condition is true }
else
 { JavaScript code to execute when condition is false }
```

In this example, *condition* is usually an operator expression, such as if (profit>=1000).

while

The *while* statement creates a loop situation, wherein the specified JavaScript code is executed repeatedly as long as a specified condition remains true.

Syntax:

```
while (condition)
 { JavaScript code to execute repeatedly as long as condition remains true }
```

Again, *condition* is usually an operator expression, such as while (seconds<60).

for

The *for* statement also creates a loop, but provides you with a compact way to control the loop's cycle. The *for* statement takes three parameters, which indicate the starting value of the loop control variable, the condition under which to continue the loop, and an expression that updates the loop control variable. Complicated sounding? Not so bad, actually.

Syntax:

```
for (loopvar=initialvalue; condition; update expression)
 { JavaScript code to execute repeatedly as long as condition remains true }
```

A common, basic example of the *for* statement looks like the following:

```
for (j=0; j<100; j++)
 { …statements… }
```

In the previous example, we use the variable j to control the loop, and assign it an initial value of 0. The loop repeats as long as the condition, j<100, remains true. After each iteration of the loop, j is updated with the unary increment j++, which adds 1 to j. Thus, the statements within this *for* loop will be executed 100 times, as j counts up from 0 to 99.

Keep in mind that in all cases, the *statements* that are placed between curly braces may be any number of JavaScript code lines, not only one. Of course, the previous program flow statements are not the only available in JavaScript, but this is meant to be a tasty overview, not a formal course.

The Call of the Function

Think of the prepackaged cold cuts at the supermarket, in the refrigerated section near the frankfurters and bacon. You could, for instance, construct an efficient (if somewhat bland) lunch using two slices of bread and a package of those cold cuts. In fact, a JavaScript function is similar—a pre-created bit of code that you call upon when needed in a larger project. Functions are created to perform a specific task—whenever your JavaScript program requires that task to be performed, it "calls" the appropriate function.

If the lunchmeat example seems a bit oblique, consider a simple JavaScript function, whose job is to compare two numeric variables A and B, and return a value of true if A is greater than B, or false otherwise. In other parts of your JavaScript code, whenever you need to compare A and B, you simply call this function.

As briefly explained earlier, you typically include your JavaScript functions within the <head> tags of the HTML document. This way, they are all loaded into memory by the time the page executes your JavaScript code. How do you code a function, though? With a function definition!

Functions Defined

To define a function, you must give it a name (with the same restrictions as choosing a variable name), and specify any *parameters* the function will accept. A parameter is a value that is passed to the function when it is called.

Syntax:

```
function functionName (parameter1,parameter2,etc)
 { JavaScript code to execute when this function is called }
```

For instance, recall the "compare A and B" function described earlier. This function would require two parameters passed to it—A and B! So, the function definition for the compare function might look like:

```
function compare_ab (val_a,val_b)\
{ JavaScript code }
```

The parameter names specified are used as variables within the function body. Whatever values are passed to this function, when it is called, will be assigned to the specified variable names in the parameter list. Thus, if the values 10 and 15 are passed to the function *compare_ab()*, then within the function, the variable val_a will begin with a value of 10 and val_b will begin with a value of 15. Some functions may not require any parameters, in which case you simply place nothing between the parentheses; for example functionName ().

Let's now imagine the entire *compare_ab()* function written out. Recall that it is placed within the <head> tag of the HTML document.

```
<html><head><title>Page Title</title>
<script language="JavaScript">
function compare_ab (val_a,val_b)
  { if (val_a > val_b) { result=true }
    else { result=false }
return result
  }
</script>
</head><body>
...rest of HTML document...
</body></html>
```

Were we to add any more functions to this page, they would be inserted before the closing </script> tag.

Placing the Call

When a JavaScript function is invoked, we say that it has been *called*. You can call a function as a stand-alone statement or as an expression within a statement.

Stand-alone syntax:

```
functionName(parameters)
```

Examples:

```
compare_ab(total,sales)
showhand(victor)
fadeColors()
```

Some functions *return* a value, which enables them to be used within an expression. For instance, consider the assignment statement:

```
total=compare_ab(total,sales)
```

We know, from the example shown in the "Functions Defined" section, that the function *compare_ab()* returns a value of true or false. Using the function call illustrated, this value is then assigned to the variable `total`. Functions are frequently called from within an event handler, which we'll see near the end of this chapter.

Object-ified

One of the most important and useful concepts in JavaScript is the object. In fact, most of the JavaScript entries in the entire reference section of this book revolve around the JavaScript object. Objects provide JavaScript access to interpret or modify many characteristics of the web page. But let's start at the beginning, and look at just what an object is.

Think of an object as a category, or a class. Within this category reside a series of related items. For instance, picture your tax return filing cabinet (you *do* have a tax return folio, don't *you*?!). Within this possibly mythical filing cabinet reside related folders—receipts, income statements, canceled checks, and so forth. In this metaphor, then, the filing cabinet is the object. In more literal terms, the document loaded within the browser window is also an object. Within the object are a bunch of related "things." Now, "things" is a terribly vague word, so what sorts of "things" can reside within the object? Two things: properties and methods.

Properties

A property represents some relevant characteristic of the object. Remember that the currently loaded document is an object—in fact, it is officially called the `document` object. This object possess a variety of properties, related to characteristics such as the background color of the page, the foreground color, the color of unvisited hyperlinks, all the images on the page, and so on.

Each property has a predefined name, and we refer to an object's property using the syntax:

```
object.property
```

So, if you look up the `document` object in the A–Z reference section of this book, you'll see that it contains a property named `bgColor`. Sensibly, this property refers to the background color of the document. A property is similar to a JavaScript variable, in that you can access the value it contains, or assign it a new value. The latter is often, but not always true—some properties are *read-only*, and you cannot modify the values they contain.

As it happens, the `document` object's `bgColor` property can be read or modified. So, you could, for instance, use an `if...else` statement to determine if the current background color is black:

```
if (document.bgColor==0) { action to take if black }
 else { action to take if not black }
```

Alternatively, you could assign a new value to the `bgColor` property:

```
document.bgColor="blue"
```

In the previous example, the background color of the document would instantly become blue. Not all assignments to a property will result in an immediate effect—such details are noted in the object reference entries for each property.

Methods

Whereas a property is essentially a variable tied to an object, a method is a function tied to an object. Just as the `document` object contains a set of properties, it also contains a set of methods. Each method is a function that performs some action relevant to the object. These methods, although they are functions, are built-in to JavaScript, not defined within the page itself. Again, as with properties, methods are outlined in detail for each object within the A–Z reference section of this book. You call a method just like a function (because it *is* a function):

```
object.method(parameters)
```

Consider the `write()` method of the `document` object. When called this method will output HTML content to the document within the browser window.

```
document.write("<H1>Learning JavaScript is Thrilling!</H1>")
```

It's true—using an object's properties and methods is relatively straightforward. The power of objects lies in their capability to provide script access to a wide variety of characteristics of the web page.

The Main Event

We close out the "JavaScript Basics" chapter with a look at events and event-handling. Although you now have a basic understanding of how to put together JavaScript code, and how to access and manipulate web pages through objects, you may wonder what "triggers" any of this JavaScript code to execute in the first place. Or, you may wonder why roadkill so often lies on the side of the road, out of harm's way—how did they get killed, then? In truth, we're only planning to address the former curio.

A JavaScript *event* occurs whenever an event-triggering action takes place. Vague, it's true, but events are easier illustrated than explained (like making a peanut butter and banana sandwich). For instance, when a user clicks the mouse button on a hyperlink or form field button, an event known as the `Click` event is triggered. The following chart summarizes some common JavaScript events, and what triggers them to occur.

Event name	Triggered by
Click	Mouse click on a hyperlink or form field button.
MouseOver	Mouse pointer moved over a hyperlink or imagemap area.
MouseOut	Mouse pointer moved away from a hyperlink or image map area.
Focus	Bringing focus to a page element through the mouse or Tab key.

Event name	Triggered by
Blur	Removing focus from a page element clicking or by tabbing elsewhere.
Submit	Submitting a form through the "Submit" button.
Reset	Resetting a form through the "Reset" button.

As usual, the preceding table is not a comprehensive list of all JavaScript events, but it should communicate the concept.

Finger on the Trigger

When an event occurs, you can trigger some JavaScript code to execute. Pairing JavaScript code with a particular event is known as an *event-handler*. In talking about an event-handler, you use the terminology onEvent; for instance, we could speak of the onClick event-handler. Typically, event-handlers are added as an attribute to the HTML tag for which the event applies.

Syntax:

```
<tag attribute1 attribute2 onEvent="JavaScript code to trigger">
```

Consider, for example, the HTML <input> tag, which you can use to create a form field button. A basic button might be defined as follows:

```
<input type="button" value="Click me!">
```

However, you can easily add an onClick event-handler to this button:

```
<input type="button" value="Click me!" onClick="clickfunc()">
```

In the previous example, if a Click event occurs at this button, the JavaScript function *clickfunc()* is called. Commonly, event-handlers are specified to call a particular function—this is a main reason why JavaScript functions are so important. You'll typically code functions to handle various events on the page, and call those functions from event-handlers such as that illustrated previously.

Alternatively, your event-handler could contain explicit JavaScript code, rather than a function call. Consider the following variation, which changes the background color of the page when the button is clicked:

```
<input type="button" value="Click me!" onClick="document.bgColor='red'">
```

Notice that the event-handler must always be enclosed within quotation marks. As seen earlier, if your JavaScript code requires quotation marks itself, you must use single-quotation marks within the JavaScript code (if you used double-quotation marks to enclose the entire event-handler). You can also use single-quotation marks to enclose the event-handler, and double-quotation marks within the JavaScript code—it doesn't matter, as long as you are consistent.

Additional Reading

As promised, this "JavaScript Basics" chapter has been exactly that—basic. If you're programming experience has grown rusty or you have no such history, you can browse plenty of free JavaScript documentation, with examples and reference, at Netscape's web site:

`http://home.netscape.com/eng/mozilla/3.0/handbook/javascript/index.html`

In addition, there are numerous more detailed books that can lead you through the ins and outs of JavaScript. If the sight of the bookshelf at Borders is too daunting, consider some of these titles:

- *JavaScript Interactive Course*, by Alman Danesh, published by Waite Group Press
- *Teach Yourself JavaScript 1.1 in a Week*, also by Alman Danesh, published by Sams.net
- *The Complete Idiot's Guide to JavaScript, Second Edition*, by Aaron Weiss, published by Que

```
</A> ■ <UL> </UL> ■ <UL> </UL> ■ <MENU> </MENU> ■ <STRONG> </STRONG>
■ <TD> </TD> ■ <TH> </TH> ■ <TABLE> </TABLE>  ■ <IMG> </IMG> ■
<SCRIPT LANGUAGE = "javascript"> </SCRIPT>
■ <SCRIPT LANGUAGE = "vbscript"> </SCRIPT> ■ <BGSOUND SRC=gbv.wav
LOOP=-1> </BGSOUND> ■ <APPLET CLASS= "ester's      SRC="http://
testsite/walla walla washington/" </APPLET> ■
QUEE> </MARQUEE> ■    <HTML> </HTML> ■ <A> </A>
UL> ■ <MENU> </MENU> ■ <STRONG> </STRONG> ■
```

Basics

JavaScript Style Sheets

The concept of style sheets for use with HTML has given developers a more powerful way to express style, enhance presentation, and define more consistent looks in HTML documents. A style sheet consists of one or more style definitions for HTML properties (fonts sizes, font styles, text alignment, font and background colors, margins, padding, line height, and so on) that can be linked to an HTML document to give consistent styles throughout the document.

JavaScript Style Sheets, which are introduced in and currently only available for use with Netscape Navigator 4, go one step beyond the functionality of Cascading Style Sheets by enabling style sheets to be accessed through JavaScript code and functions; thus allowing developers the access to change styles at run time and document load time based on user input, HTML changes, or browser sizes.

In the following sections, you learn how to use JavaScript Style Sheets to enhance your document, how to best define and work with styles, and the limitations of JavaScript Style Sheets.

The current definition and standards for JavaScript Style Sheets can be found at http://developer.netscape.com/library/documentation/communicator/stylesheets/jss25.htm#1016694. Because JavaScript Style Sheets is Netscape only, there are no standards as of yet from the World Wide Web Consortium, although they are being reviewed at this time and there may be more on JavaScript Style Sheets in the future.

Basic JavaScript Style Sheet Concepts

JavaScript Style Sheets are implemented within your HTML document, using similar methods to linking generic JavaScript statements to the document. JavaScript Style Sheets definitions may be completely contained within the HTML document or they may be defined in external files and linked from within the HTML document. The external storage and retrieval of style sheets is similar to the external storage of JavaScript code.

The benefit to keeping style sheets defined externally from your HTML document is that you are able to use the JavaScript Style Sheets for multiple documents and thus maintain a consistent style throughout a group of HTML documents or even entire web sites.

Styles Defined

Styles are properties that can be "assigned" to HTML elements to change the look or behavior of the elements. You will learn the various ways to assign the properties later in this chapter. One generic example of a JavaScript Style Sheets property is the `color` property.

```
tags.h1.color="green";
```

The preceding code sample is an example of how to make all `<h1>` elements green. This type of assignment applies to all `<h1>` elements, but can be overridden using other methods of JavaScript Style Sheets definition. In the preceding code sample, the four pieces of the code are broken down as follows:

- `tags` is one of the methods of defining JSSS styles that will be discussed in detail later in this chapter. The `tags` definition describes the element immediately following it in the dot notation.
- `h1` is the HTML element that is being assigned a style. This may be any valid HTML element.
- `color` is the style that is being defined for the element. This may be any valid JSSS style.
- `green` is the value of the style color.

Setting Up Styles within a Document

To define styles within the HTML document Styles, the new html element of `<style>` is used. The `type` attribute of the `<style>` element is where the Style is defined to be accessible through JavaScript. By using the element definition `<style type="text/javascript">`, you are telling the browser that the style sheet being defined is a JavaScript Style Sheet.

Figure 1 is an example of a document that is using JavaScript Style Sheets. The following code listing, which is used for Figure 1, shows a simple JavaScript Style Sheet definition that will make all `<h1>` headers italicized and 12 point font height.

```
<html>
<head>
<style type="text/javascript">
```

```
tags.h1.fontStyle="italic";
tags.h1.fontSize="12";
</style>
</head>
<body>
<h1> This header does not look like a normal header</h1>
<h1> All headers will change and show the new style</h1>
<h2> All h1 headers that is. This is an h2 header.</h2>
</body>
</html>
```

Figure 1

*HTML document
with JavaScript Style
Sheets.*

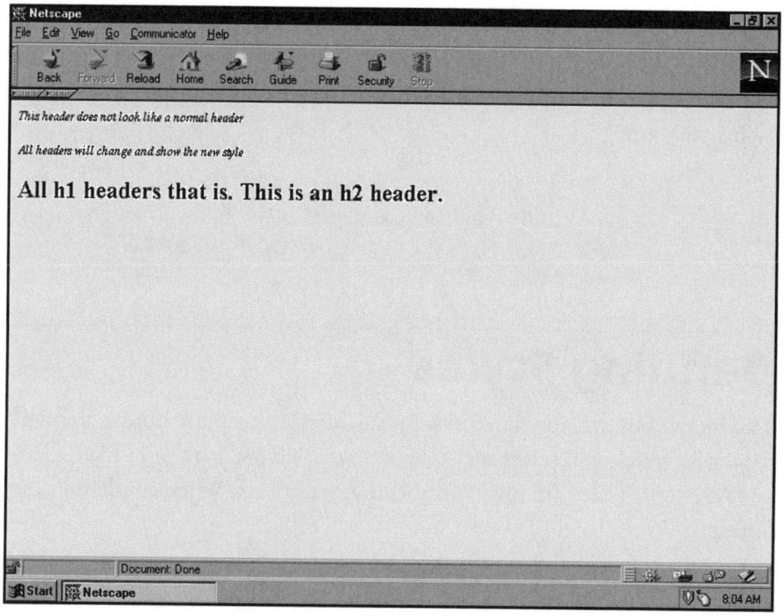

Linking External Style Sheets

External JavaScript Style Sheets are built similar to the JavaScript Style Sheets defined within the document. The style sheet is stored as a URL containing the Style definitions, with all HTML elements excluded. For example, the <style></style> should be left out of the definition because the type of style will be defined when the external style sheet is linked to the document. External style sheets are associated with the document by using either the <link> element to link in a style sheet, or by specifying a source for the <style> element.

<link> element

The <link> element has three properties used to fully define it. They are rel, type, and href. For style sheets, the rel=stylesheet, the type="text/javascript", and the href is the complete URL to the style sheet.

```
<head>
<link rel=stylesheet type="text/javascript"
href="http://www.acadians.com/generic/styles/compstyle.html">
</head>
```

`<style>` element

To link style sheets directly into the `<style>` element, use the `<style>` element with the `href` attribute reference. This format is also useful if multiple JavaScript Style Sheets need to be linked to one HTML document.

```
<style type="text/javascript"
href="http://www.acadians.com/generic/styles/compstyle.html">
</STYLE>
```

Multiple style sheets can be implemented by defining multiple `<style></style>` pairs, one for each style sheet.

> **NOTE** When using multiple style sheets, styles in the latter style sheet will override any styles that conflict with those defined in the former.

Defining Styles

The method by which you access, or call, a style sheet attribute is defined as the selector. It is the means by which you select the style that you will use for the HTML element (that is, `<h1>`, `<body>`, `<p>`). There are four selectors defined for use when implementing JavaScript Style Sheets:

- `tags`
- `classes`
- `id`
- `style` attribute of HTML element

Any styles defined with the `tags` method need not be called explicitly; they are called by default.

> **NOTE** The innermost style defined for an element has precedence over any parent styles that have been defined.

Later in this chapter is a list of style properties that are currently available with JavaScript Style Sheets. Each style is defined in more detail in the alphabetical listing in this book.

tags

The tags attribute can be thought of as a reference to HTML elements (or tags). The full syntax of this definition is document.tags, but because the tags object always applies to the current document, the document object is unnecessary. Thus, the following statements are identical:

```
document.tags.h1.fontSize = "12";
```

```
tags.h1.fontSize = "12";
```

Following the tags object in the definition is the element to which it applies (<h1> in the previous sample), or the all element can be used to apply to all tags.

```
tags.all.fontSize = "12";
```

Immediately following the HTML element is the style for the element, which is being defined, and the value for those styles.

classes

Using the classes attribute of the <style> element, style classes can be defined for use with specific HTML elements or all elements. The element will take on all properties of the classes (that are applicable) to which it belongs.

```
<style type="text/javascript">
classes.classone.all.textDecoration = "underline";
classes.classtwo.h1.textDecoration = "overline";
classes.classtwo.h1.color = "blue";
</style>
```

In the previous style definition, all elements belonging to the class *classone* will be displayed with underlined text, and <h1> elements belonging to the class *classtwo* will be displayed in blue and have an overline. The style *classtwo* could be applied to other elements but they will not inherit the style because they are not elements belonging to the original class definition. Only <h1> elements can belong to the class *classtwo* and take on its properties.

The following listing uses both classes and tags style definitions and the results can be seen in Figure 2. Note the paragraph that does not reflect any of the styles. Because no specific style is given and there is no style defined for <p> tags, this paragraph will be rendered in the default properties for the <p> element.

```
<html>
<head>
<style type="text/JavaScript">
classes.larger.all.fontSize = "20";
tags.h1.textDecoration = "underline";
classes.nextclass.p.fontWeight = "bold";
</style>
</head>
```

```
<body>
<h1>This header is underlined because of the tags style</h1>
<p class="nextclass">This will be a bold paragraph</p>
<p class="larger">This paragraph has a font Size of 20</p>
<blockquote class="larger">This blockquote also has a font Size of
 18</blockquote>
<p>This will NOT be a bold, 20 point paragraph because it
doesn't use either class definition and also has not tags
style defined for it.</p>
</body>
</html>
```

Figure 2

Using multiple style definitions.

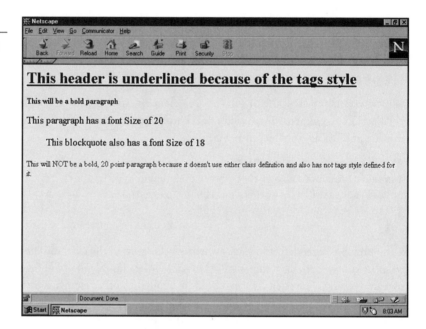

id

Using `ids` in Style definitions is similar to using classes in style definitions. The following sample defines an `id` called acadiaid that has a line height of 10. Any element can be defined with the acadiaid and will take on the defined style. Note that in Figure 3, any element that has acadiaid as a style has a line height of 10.

```
<html>
<head>
<style type="text/javascript">
ids.acadiaid.lineheight = .75;
```

```
</style>
<body>
<h1 id="acadiaid">This header has a line height change</h1>
<p id="acadiaid">This paragraph has a line height change</p>
<p>This paragraph does not have a line height change</p>
<p id="acadiaid">This paragraph has a line height change</p>
<div>This text does not have a line height change</div>
</body>
</html>
```

Figure 3

Using the id definition method.

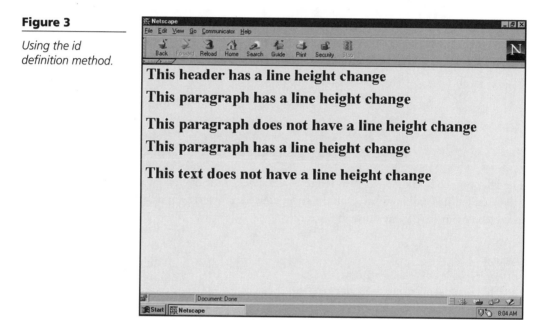

Any element defined using the `acadiaid` will have the style defined for the `id`. Although the preceding example is a valid definition, the `id` method is normally used only to override previously defined styles for an element. They are not as generic as the `tags` and `classes` definitions and are not flexible. Figure 4 shows the display of more common use of `id`.

Figure 4

Overriding a style.

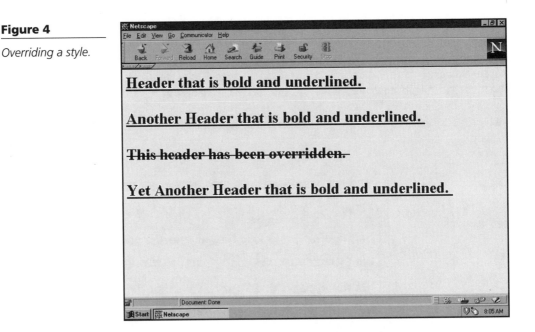

The following code sample was used to create the styles in the document in Figure 4. All `<h1>` will be underlined and bold based on the styles created. However, for a particular `<h1>` we want it to be bold but have a line through instead.

```
<html>
<head>
<style type="text/javascript">
tags.h1.textdecoration = "underline";
tags.h1.fontWeight = "bold";
ids.acadiaid.textdecoration = "line-through";
</style>
<body>
<h1> Header that is bold and underlined.</h1>
<h1> Another Header that is bold and underlined.</h1>
<h1 id="acadiaid"> This header has been overridden.</h1>
 <h1> Yet Another Header that is bold and underlined.</h1>
</body>
</html>
```

`style` element selector

The least used selector involves defining a style for a particular instance of an element. This allows specific style definitions for each element. Styles are infrequently defined in this manner, because of the difficulty in editing the style in the future. This method is used for similar reasons with `ids` but is less flexible because the style is hidden in the body of the document and is more difficult to change.

```
<p style="lineHeight='24'">
```

This will make this particular <p> a height of 24.

> N   This method of style definition does not work in Netscape Navigator 4, prerelease 5.

Using Combinations of Style Definitions

Using JavaScript Style Sheets, style selectors can be mixed and used in conjunction with each other to achieve the desired effect. The following code listing shows that a mix of style definitions of the same and different types can achieve the effects in Figure 5. Multiple attributes of the same selector (two `classes` attributes used in conjunction) and attributes of different selector types (one `classes` and one `id` attribute) can be combined in one HTML element to achieve combined style effects.

```
<html>
<head>
<style type="text/javascript">
tags.h1.textDecoration="underline";
tags.h1.fontSize="12";
classes.headerclass.fontStyle="italic";
ids.testid.fontSize="20";
classes.newheader.h1.verticalAlign = "sub";
</style>
</head>
<body>
<h2> This header will be underlined and 12 point font</h2>
<h1 class="headerclass" ID="testid"> This header will be italic and point size
➥20</h1>
<h1 class="newheader" class="headerclass"> This header will be italic and
➥superscript.</h1>
<h2> This will be default text </h2>
</body>
</html>
```

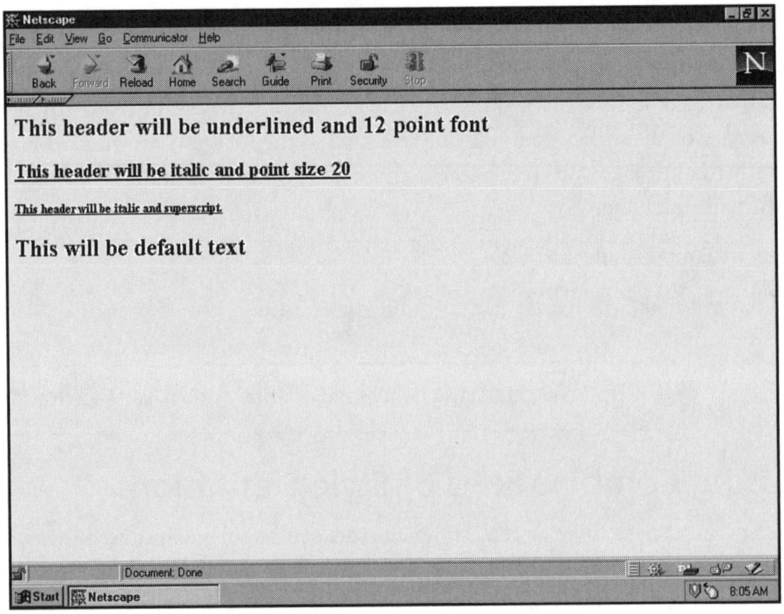

Figure 5

Mixing style definitions to create the desired effect.

Contextual Selectors

The JavaScript method `contextual()` can be used with style definitions to broaden the criteria for which styles are defined. When defining style sheets, you may, for example, only want `<blockquote>` elements that are contained within `<p>` elements to be italicized and all other `<blockquote>` elements (those not within `<p>` elements) to retain their original default styles. `Contextual()` selector means that the styles will be applied only if the context of the elements defined by `contextual()` are met. The values within the `contextual()` statement may be any combination of HTML elements and previously defined `classes`, `ids`, or `tags`.

All `<blockquote>` elements contained within `<p>` will be italic:

`tags.contextual(tags.p, tags.blockquote).fontWeight = "italic";`

All `<div>` elements that have any ancestor with *haydenclass* used as a style will be bold:

`tags.contextual(classes.hayden.all, tags.div).fontWeight = "bold";`

All `<p>` elements that have an ancestor of *acadiaid* will have a line height of 10:

`tags.contextual(ids.acadiaid, tags.p).lineHeight = "10";`

JavaScript Style Sheets Properties

The following properties can be used in JavaScript Style Sheets:

Font Properties

- ■ `fontSize`—point size of font
- ■ `fontStyle`—italics, small caps, other font styles

Text Properties

- **lineHeight**—distance between text lines
- **verticalAlign**—alignment of other text in relation to this text
- **textDecoration**—underline, overline, line-through
- **textTransform**—capitalization of text
- **textAlign**—alignment of the text within the element itself

Block Level Formatting Properties

- **margins()**—left, right, top, bottom margins for the element
- **paddings()**—space inserted between border of the element and the actual element content
- **borderWidths()**—set the border around the element
- **borderStyle**—type of border around the element
- **width**—width of the element
- **height**—height of the element
- **align**—alignment of the content of the element in relation to the document
- **clear**—defines whether the element can have other elements floating on either side of it

Color Properties

- **color**—text color of the element
- **backgroundImage**—the image to display in the background of the element
- **backgroundColor**—the color for the background of the element, not the text

Classification Properties

- **display**—defines the type of element: inline, blocklevel, list item
- **listStyleType**—defines the type of list style for list items
- **whitespace**—defines how whitespace is treated in the element

---

WARNING When defining units of width in JavaScript Style Sheets, watch the sum of the horizontal properties. The total of all horizontal properties cannot exceed the defined width of the document. If the width is exceeded, then JavaScript Style Sheets will automatically calculate values, which rank lowest in horizontal property priority. The following list is the ranking priority for calculating horizontal widths in JavaScript.

1. Left border

2. Right Border

continues

3. Left Padding

4. Right Padding

5. Width

6. Left Margin

7. Right Margin

8. Auto

Using Styles with JavaScript Functions

Because JavaScript is a scripting language, JavaScript Style Sheet definitions can be incorporated into the scripts and be accessible from function calls. The function in the following code sample will be called to change the style of <p> elements based on the user's input to a checkbox field. In the listing, the function change_style() is used when the user selects the checkbox. Until the user supplies the input, the styles remain unapplied.

```
<html>
<head>
<script language = "JavaScript">
</script>
<style type="text/JavaScript">

function change_style(){
tags.p.fontSize="20";
}
tags.p.apply  = change_style();
</style>
</head>
<body>
<form>
<input
       type = CheckBox
       name = "CBOne"
       value = "BStyle1"
OnClick = "change_style()">
CheckBox
<p>
<p> This is a 20 point line when the box is checked, otherwise it
is 14 point.</p>
</form>
</body>
</html>
```

The result of this example before checking the box is shown in Figure 6, and the result after checking the box is shown in Figure 7.

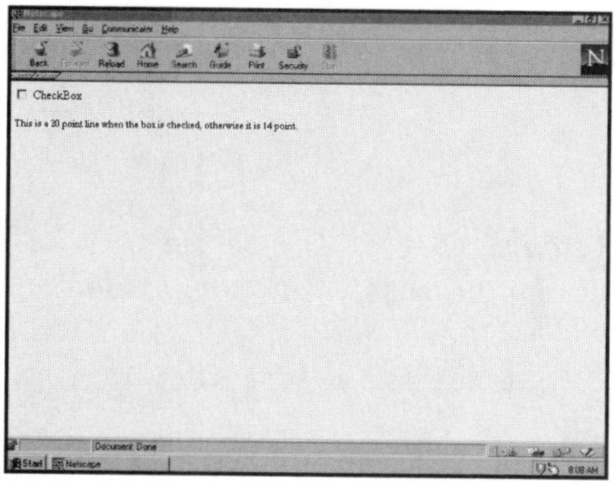

Figure 6

Before checking the box.

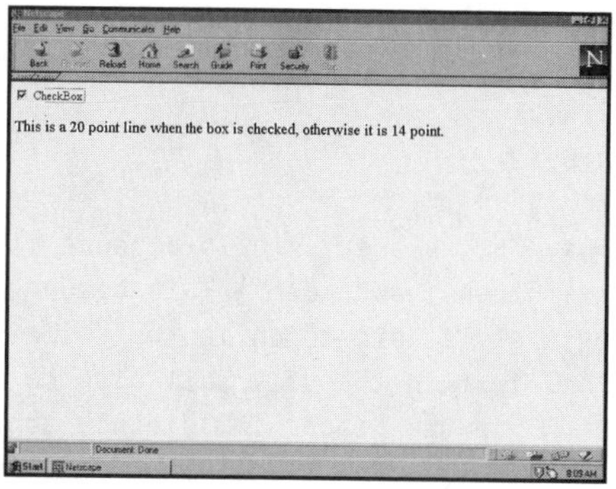

Figure 7

After box has been checked.

This example demonstrates the flexibility now available to developers by combining JavaScript and style sheets. The core of JavaScript Style Sheets revolves around the capability to use JavaScript function calls and assigned values in style sheets. Developers now have the capability to base styles on user input and to programmatically select and change styles based on the document and browser. JavaScript Style Sheets means that styles do not have to be static following page generation but can be updated as the document requires.

Inheritance

The concept of inheritance does apply to JavaScript Style Sheets. You must remember that certain styles can be inherited from parents to children and children must be given overriding styles if you want the styles to be applicable to the parents only. For the definitions used here, parent and children refer to HTML elements that are grouped or contained within other elements. The <body> element can have many children within it, including <h1> or <div>, whereas the <p> element will have fewer children (<em> is an example). For the majority of styles, the child inherits the styles of a parent if and only if the child has the same properties.

> **NOTE** For the most part, styles that are not inherited will be obvious. If the child does not have the property of the parent then the child cannot inherit the style.

A style that is defined for a child (or redefined for a child) will always take precedence and override the parent style. To override globally set styles, a child style can be defined in the style sheet definition using tags, classes, or ids.

```
<html>
<head>
<style type="text/javascript">
tags.body.fontWeight ="bold";
classes.headerclass.h1.fontWeight ="900";
</style>
</head>
<body>
<h1> This header is bold because it is inherited from the parent</h1>
<h1 class="newheader"> This header is bolder because it is overridden
by a style definition in the child</h1>
This text in the body will also be bold, but not the bolder that is
Shown in the header immediately above.
</body>
</html>
```

Note in Figure 8 that the font weight defined in the body of the preceding code sample is inherited by the first <h1> (child), and also by the text within the body; but that the second <h1> is overridden by a class-defined style for that child.

Figure 8

Style inheritance.

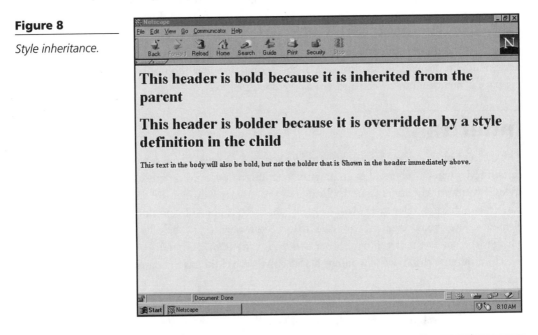

Order of Precedence for Tags, Classes, and Ids

The order of precedence for styles should be determined during document development so that the developer can accurately predict which styles will be applied when, and in what instances styles will and will not be overridden. Neglecting to carefully predict the order of precedence may cause unwanted styles when each possible option has not been fully tested. If styles are based on function calls, then you should carefully look at the final styles when each function is called, and in which order. If you count on the functions always being called in order, and then for some reason they are not; this could make for a rather strange, unanticipated combination of styles.

To find the value or precedence of a style of an element (and property), it is necessary to apply the following predefined set of rules:

1. Locate all references to the element by any selector.

2. Sort the references by explicit weight.

3. Sort by origin of style sheet: default values are overridden by user's style sheets, which are overridden by author style sheets.

4. Sort by specificity, give one point for each of the following three options, then sum the points to get specificity:

   ■ number of `id` attributes

   ■ number of `class` attributes

   ■ number of `tag` names referenced

5. Sort by order specified. For two rules with identical weights, the latter rule will take precedence.

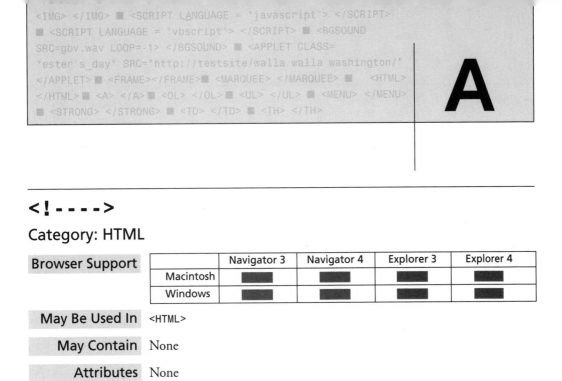

<!---->

Category: HTML

Browser Support

	Navigator 3	Navigator 4	Explorer 3	Explorer 4
Macintosh	■	■	■	■
Windows	■	■	■	■

May Be Used In <HTML>

May Contain None

Attributes None

Syntax <!--…-->

This funny-looking element, <!-- -->, is an older, more formal way of indicating a *comment*—a block of text in the HTML page included for basic information and backward-compatibility between earlier and later browser versions. Text specified within this element will not appear on a web page unless it contains <HTML>-specified code.

Hence, the following example:

```
<!--This line of text, traditionally referred to as an author's comment, will not
appear on the web page.-->
```

An updated way of creating comments is as follows:

```
<COMMENT>This page was created using HTML 3.2 specifications.</COMMENT>
```

<COMMENT>-specified text won't appear in your web page, either, but it better conforms to the overall appearance of more recent HTML. However, to provide for the many web users still surfing with Navigator 2.0 and other early browsers, you can utilize both methods of including comments, depending upon your preferences, although neither is required to make an HTML document work properly.

<A>

Category: HTML

Browser Support		Navigator 3	Navigator 4	Explorer 3	Explorer 4
	Macintosh	▇	▇	▇	▇
	Windows	▇	▇	▇	▇

May Contain   <APPLET>, <B>, <BASEFONT>, <BIG>, <BR>, <CITE>, <CODE>, <DFN>, <EM>, <FONT>, <I>, <IMG>, <INPUT>, <KBD>, <MAP>, <SAMP>, <SELECT>, <SMALL>, <STRIKE>, <STRONG>, <SUB>, <SUP>, <TEXTAREA>, <TT>, <U>, <VAR>

May Be Used In   <ADDRESS>, <APPLET>, <B>, <BIG>, <BLOCKQUOTE>, <CAPTION>, <CENTER>, <CITE>, <CODE>, <DD>, <DT>, <FONT>, <H1>, <H2>, <H3>, <H4>, <H5>, <H6>, <I>, <KBD>, <LI>, <P>, <SAMP>, <SMALL>, <STRIKE>, <STRONG>, <SUB>, <SUP>, <TD>, <TH>, <TT>, <U>

Attributes   <CLASS>, <HREF>, <ID>, <METHODS>, <NAME>, <REL>, <REV>, <TARGET>, <TITLE>, <URN>

Syntax   <A>...</A>

The <A> tag is the backbone of every web page—it is used to make navigational anchors within a single web page for easier movement up and down, and/or for making links to other parts of the web.

Either the NAME or the HREF attribute, which can both specify a reference point, must be used. The closing, or </A> tag, is also required.

CLASS

The CLASS attribute is used to specify the name of a style sheets as it applies to a specific selection on a web page. See the "Cascading Style Sheets Basics" chapter and any individual, related style sheets entries elsewhere in the book for more information.

HREF

The HREF attribute is the most common and flexible of all <A> tag attributes. You use it to:

- specify a document name if you are linking to another page within the same web site
- specify the file name of an image, sound, movie, or a compressed archive to which you are linking
- specify an address if you are linking to another part of the Internet, such as (but not only) another web site
- specify your email address if you're creating a feedback link

A

It can accomplish even more when it's used in combination with other <A> tag attributes. These additional features of the HREF attribute will be shown in the sections dealing with the other necessary attributes—this section addresses only what you can do with HREF alone.

Whether you are using the HREF attribute to link to another page in your web site, an image, a sound or movie, a compressed archive, or any other kind of file, the HTML you would write is the same. In the following example, the words "my biography page" are linked to the document biopage.html like this:

```
See <A HREF="biopage.html">my biography page</A> for more information about my
life.
```

To create a similar link to another kind of file, substitute that file name with biopage.html as shown above. Figure 1 shows what this basic link-making HTML will look like in Netscape Navigator 3 for Macintosh.

Figure 1

Linking to another page in the same web site using the <A> tag and HREF attribute.

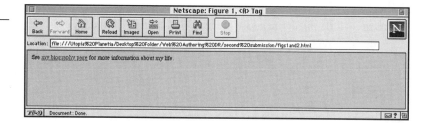

Notice that the space between the words "See" and "my" and "page" and "for" is placed outside the <A> tag. If you were to include these spaces within the <A> tag, you'd be including them in the linked text as shown in Figure 2, which looks funny.

Figure 2

Placing spaces between linked and unlinked words within the <A> tag— they should be placed outside the <A> tag so the text looks correct on the web page.

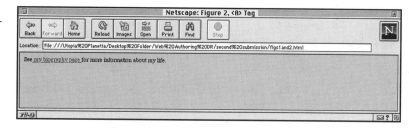

NOTE It is also in keeping with current online procedure to include any punctuation (periods, commas, and so on) within a link if the link comes at the end of a sentence.

If you want to create a link between the web page you're working on and a web page within a different folder in your web site, a few extra characters are needed. Using the previous example, the document `biopage.html` is located in a different folder. In this case, write:

```
See <A HREF="../biopage.html">my biography page</A> for more information about my
life.
```

The dots and backslash tell the browser to back up one extra level or folder within your web site—if you forget to include these extra characters, users who click this link will get an error message saying `biopage.html` is missing or not available.

You can also use the HREF attribute to link a user to another site elsewhere on the web by specifying the site's URL.

```
For more information on Martin Luther King, Jr., visit <A HREF="http://
www.provider.com/~johndoe/mlkbio.html">John Doe's MLK page</A> for an excellent
look at this activist's life.
```

You must include the entire address of the URL, http:// and all, or visitors to your page who try to use this link will get an error message.

You can also use the HREF attribute to direct visitors to other areas of the Internet, such as:

```
<A HREF="ftp://...>
```

Connects users anonymously to a public ftp site.

```
<A HREF="gopher://...>
```

Connects users to a gopher server.

```
<A HREF="news://...>
```

Connects users to a usenet newsgroup, although each individual local news server is not guaranteed to carry access to every newsgroup.

```
<A HREF="newsrc://...>
```

Connects users to a particular newsrc file that lists the newsgroups carried by the local news server.

```
<A HREF="telnet://...>
```

Connects users to an active Telnet session.

```
<A HREF="wais://...>
```

Connects users to a Wide Area Index Server (WAIS).

Another popular use of the HREF attribute is the creation of an email or feedback link. This is an easy way to enable visitors to your web site get in touch with you, so if `johndoe@provider.com` is your email address, you'd write the following HTML:

```
Please <A HREF="mailto:johndoe@provider.com">email me</A> with your comments,
complaints, and threats.
```

The `mailto` command tells your browser software to bring up a blank email message, as shown in Figures 3 and 4.

Figure 3

Using the HREF attribute to create an email link...

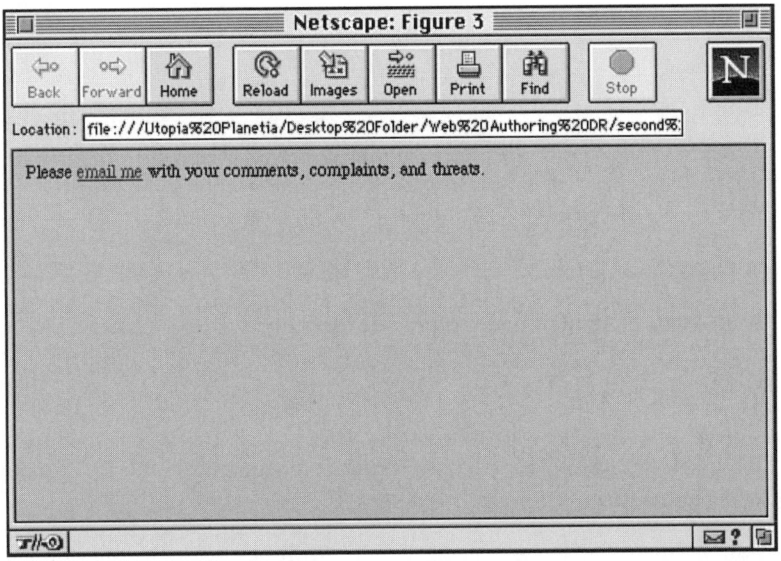

Figure 4

...and the appropriate response.

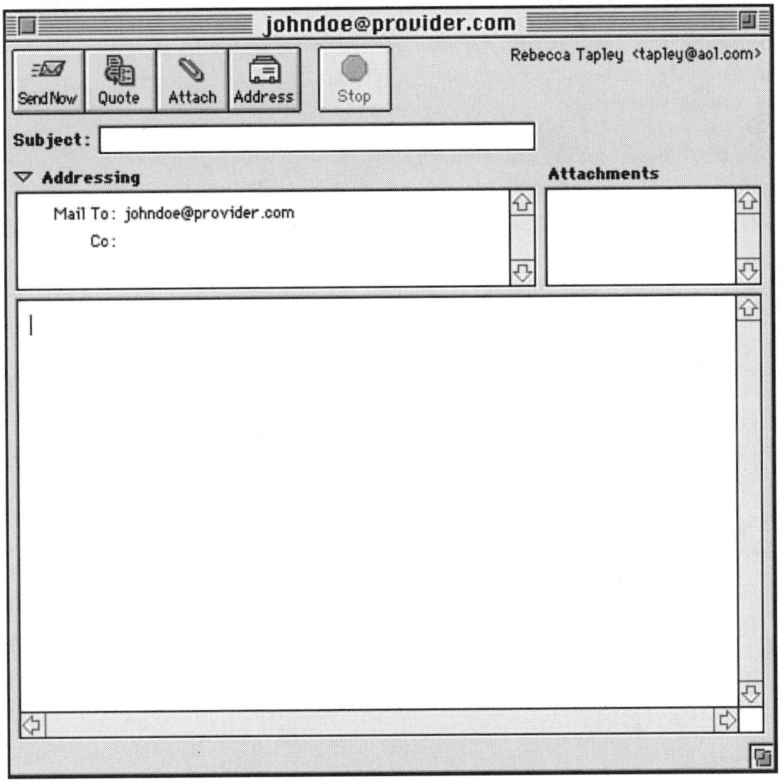

The HREF attribute also plays a part in creating internal links or anchors within a web page when used in combination with the NAME attribute. See the later section on NAME for more information on how to create these kinds of links.

ID

The ID attribute is used to distinguish individual selections in a web page as pertaining to the use of style sheets. See the "Cascading Style Sheets Basics" chapter and any individual, related style sheets entries elsewhere in the book for more information.

METHODS

The METHODS attribute is used to provide extra information about what a user can do with a link.

NAME

The NAME attribute is used with the HREF attribute to specify internal links within a web page. This enables users to easily navigate a lengthy document or a series of images without manually scrolling down the page.

In this example, there is a virtual gallery of paintings by the painter John William Waterhouse. Links to the actual images using the HREF attribute are created like this:

```
<A HREF="#section1">Hylas and the Nymphs</A><BR>
<A HREF="#section2">The Lady of Shalott</A><BR>
<A HREF="#section3">The Sorceress</A><BR>
```

The pound sign and the section names will instruct the browser to automatically jump down to each individual painting further down the page when the user clicks the link. To complete these internal links, use the NAME attribute along with the section name you established above and the name of each painting as shown:

```
<A NAME="section1"><P><HR></A><IMG SRC="hylas.jpg"> Hylas and the Nymphs
<A NAME="section2"><P><HR></A><IMG SRC="shalott.jpg"> The Lady of Shalott
<A NAME="section3"><P><HR></A><IMG SRC="sorceress.jpg"> The Sorceress
```

Figures 5 and 6 show what these internal links look like when displayed in Internet Explorer 3 for the Macintosh.

Unlike other attributes, NAME is case-sensitive; which means, in the example listed above, "section1" as written after the HREF attribute must also be listed as "section1" with no capital letters after the NAME attribute, or the link will not work.

A

Figure 5

Using the NAME and HREF attributes to create internal links—when a user clicks the name of a painting...

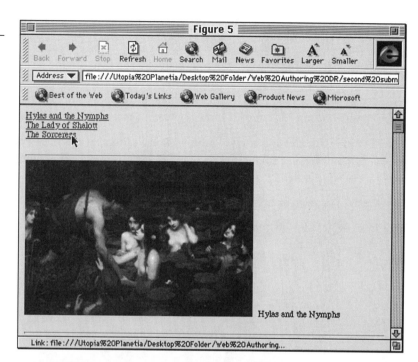

Figure 6

...the browser jumps to the image further down the page.

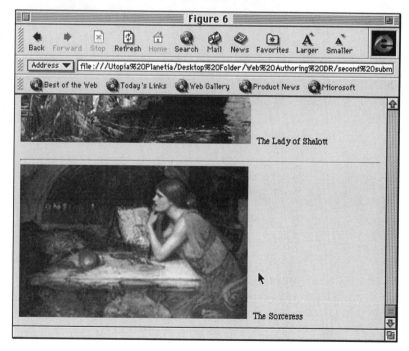

When creating internal links, use tags that create blank space on a web page. In this example, the <P> and <HR> tags are placed inside the <A> tag to add a blank line and a hard rule for better readability. They instruct the browser to bring users to a place on the page where users can see a little blank space all the way around the paintings. If you were to place the <P> and <HR> tags outside the <A> tag, or eliminate them altogether, the browser would align the top edge of the painting with the top edge of your browser window, making it seem cut off.

A final touch when creating internal links is to add a link that returns users to the top of the page at natural breaking points. Figures 7 and 8 demonstrate the function of this link created with the HREF attribute:

```
<P><A HREF="museum.html">Return to the top</A>
```

This link enables users to quickly return to the list of paintings at the top of the page.

Figure 7

Clicking this internal link...

Figure 8

...returns the user to the top of the page.

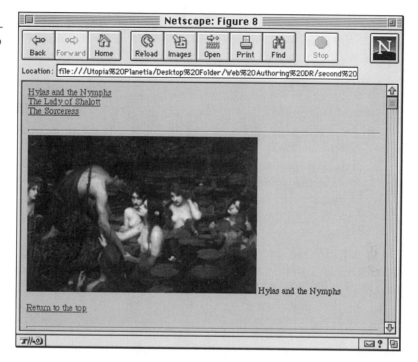

REL

The REL attribute describes the relationship of one internal link to another; it is only used with the HREF attribute. The default value is SAME—the same page you are visiting—if none of the following values are specified using REL instead:

NEXT

The link specified by the HREF attribute is the next one in a sequence of linked pages.

PARENT

The current web page in which the link is specified by the HREF attribute is the parent of the destination page.

PREVIOUS

The link specified by the HREF attribute is the previous one in a sequence of linked pages.

The REL attribute is not widely used. Even though it has been supported by the last few versions of HTML (since version 2.0), there really is no standard list of values for it. Its presence or absence does not affect your web page if you are using the <A> tag and HREF and NAME attributes to create a series of internal links.

REV

The REV attribute is related to REL as it describes a reverse relationship to whatever value you assign. This just means that if you establish a REL attribute value of NEXT, the REV value would be PREVIOUS to complete the link. However, REV is also not widely used (it also does not affect the outcome of a page containing internal links) so there is also no list of standard values for this <A> tag attribute.

TARGET

The TARGET attribute is used in conjunction with the HREF attribute to open the link you create in a completely new browser window. Only users of Navigator and Internet Explorer can successfully use this feature into their web pages—Mosaic and other such browsers do not recognize TARGET or any TARGET-specified instructions.

For example, if shrine.jpg is the name of the image you want linked and newframe is the name of the new browser page you want TARGET to specify, you would write:

```
Here's another painting by John William Waterhouse: <A HREF="shrine.jpg"
TARGET="newwindow">The Shrine.</A>
```

When the user clicks the link, a brand new browser window will spontaneously open, containing the specified image.

Figures 9 and 10 show this HTML in action.

Figure 9

Using the HREF and TARGET attributes to open a link in a new browser window— click the link…

A

Figure 10

*...and the image
opens in a different
browser window.*

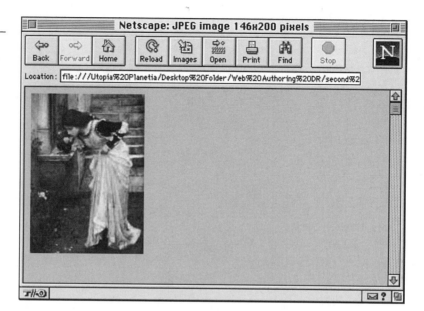

> **NOTE** You can use JavaScript to establish a specific height and width for the type of **TARGET**-created page mentioned here. See the "JavaScript Basics" chapter of this reference for more information.

The TARGET attribute can also be used with a handful of pre-established values. Here is a list of those values:

BLANK

The linked page or URL opens into a new, unnamed, blank browser window.

PARENT

The linked page or URL opens in the parent window of the web page where the link is located.

SELF

The linked page or URL opens in the same window where the link is located.

TOP

The linked page or URL opens in the full body of the open window.

Figure 11

*Using the TARGET
attribute and the
BLANK, PARENT, SELF,
and TOP values—the
results are all
identical and
resemble Figure 10.*

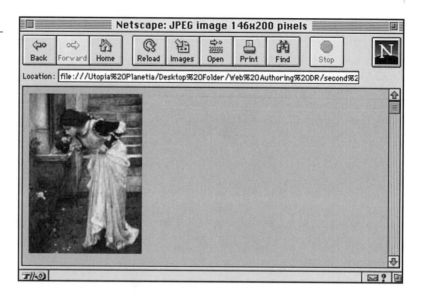

TITLE

The TITLE attribute of the <A> tag serves a strictly informational purpose and is not necessary to your web page like the <TITLE> tag. It is used in conjunction with the HREF attribute to display the title of a linked page, location, or image, usually in the title bar of the browser window.

If you wanted, for example, to specify the title "The Shrine" as the last painting referred to in this section, and you wanted this painting to be displayed in its own window, the HTML on your primary page would look like this:

```
Here's another painting by John William Waterhouse: <A HREF="shrine.jpg"
TARGET="newwindow"TITLE="The
Shrine">The Shrine.</A>
```

Interestingly enough, the TITLE tag does not affect the actual title of the new window spawned by clicking its related link. The "title" as it appears in Netscape Navigator 3.0's title bar is shown in Figure 12—the image file type and its dimensional measurements in pixels. Internet Explorer 3.0, however, displays the title of the image file in its location bar, as shown in Figure 13.

A

Figure 12

The title of the new window as displayed in Navigator 3.0 for the Macintosh.

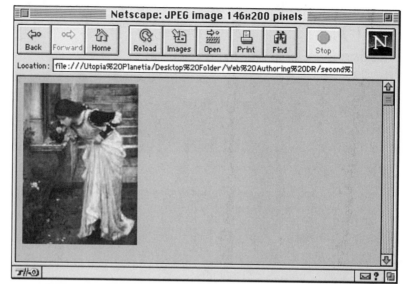

Figure 13

The title of the new window as displayed in Internet Explorer 3.0 for the Macintosh—also unrelated to the TITLE attribute and also boring.

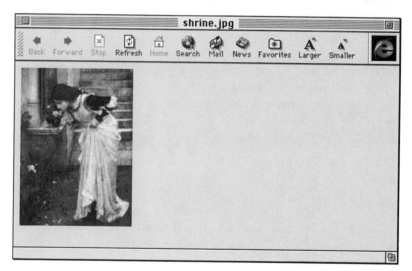

URN

The URN attribute specifies a uniform resource name for a target document—the exact use and parameters for this attribute have not yet been decided, so using it is not recommended at this writing.

Abs ( )

Category: VBScript

| Type | Function |

Browser Support		Navigator 3	Navigator 4	Explorer 3	Explorer 4
	Macintosh				■
	Windows			■	■

Syntax Abs(*number*)

The Abs() function returns the absolute value of a numeric expression—*number*. The absolute value of a number is the unsigned, positive value of the number.

For example, calling

Abs(-42)

will return the value 42.

Similarly, calling

Abs(42)

also returns the value 42. Absolute values are typically used when you want to know the magnitude of a variable, without caring about its sign. For instance, when comparing two people's ages, 83 and 24: you may care only that the difference is 59 years.

Abs(83-24)

or

Abs(24-83)

both yield 59.

If *expression* is a null value, the function will return null. If *expression* is an uninitialized variable, the value 0 is returned. A non-numeric *expression* will cause an error.

<ADDRESS>

Category: HTML

Browser Support		Navigator 3	Navigator 4	Explorer 3	Explorer 4
	Macintosh	■	■	■	■
	Windows	■	■	■	■

May Contain	<A>, <APPLET>, <B>, <BASEFONT>, <BIG>, <BR>, <CITE>, <CODE>, <DFN>, <EM>, <FONT>, <I>, <IMG>, <INPUT>, <KBD>, <MAP>, <P>, <SAMP>, <SELECT>, <SMALL>, <STRIKE>, <STRONG>, <SUB>, <SUP>, <TEXTAREA>, <TT>, <U>, <VAR>
May Be Used In	<BLOCKQUOTE>, <BODY>, <CENTER>, <DD>, <DIV>, <FORM>, <LI>, <TD>, <TH>
Syntax	<ADDRESS>...</ADDRESS>

The <ADDRESS> tag is an older tag traditionally used to indicate author information, such as the name, mailing address, author credits, and so on, at the bottom of an HTML document. <ADDRESS> renders all the text it specifies in italics and may also indent it, so a closing, or </ADDRESS> tag, is required.

Hence, the following example:

```
<ADDRESS>
This HTML document was written by Gizmo Ferreolus, 123 Main Street, Anytown, ST,
01234, USA.
</ADDRESS>
```

If you want this address to display formally with line breaks, use the <BR> tag as shown here:

```
<ADDRESS>
This HTML document was written by<BR>
Gizmo Ferreolus<BR>
123 Main Street<BR>
Anytown, ST 01234<BR>
USA<BR>
</ADDRESS>
```

Figures 1, 2, 3, and 4 illustrate the difference between using the <ADDRESS> tag in Netscape Navigator 3 and Internet Explorer 3 on both Macintosh and Windows. Figures 5 and 6 show the same <ADDRESS>-specified text with <BR> line breaks added. See the entry on the <BR> tag elsewhere in the book for more information on creating horizontal space and line breaks.

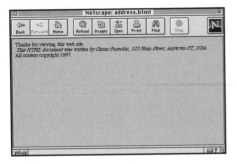

Figure 1

<ADDRESS>-specified text without line breaks in Netscape-Navigator 3 for Macintosh.

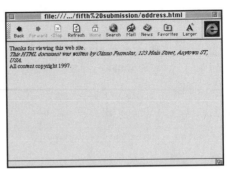

Figure 2

<ADDRESS>-specified text without line breaks in Internet Explorer 3 for Macintosh.

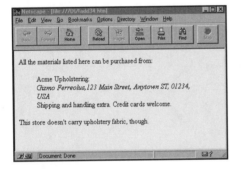

Figure 3

<ADDRESS>-specified text without line breaks in Netscape Navigator 3 for Windows.

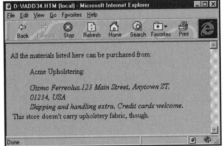

Figure 4

<ADDRESS>-specified text without line breaks in Internet Explorer 3 for Windows.

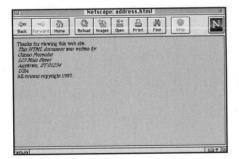

Figure 5

<ADDRESS>-specified text with line breaks in Netscape Navigator 3 for Macintosh (just for comparison).

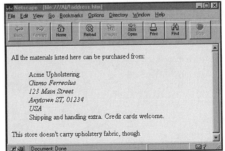

Figure 6

<ADDRESS>-specified text with line breaks in Internet Explorer 3 for Windows (just for comparison).

align

Category: JavaScript Style Sheets

Type	Property			

Browser Support

	Navigator 3	Navigator 4	Explorer 3	Explorer 4
Macintosh		■		
Windows		■		

Applies To   All elements

Inherited   No

Syntax   align = "*value*"

align is the property that enables you to control the placement of an element on the HTML page. This property is normally used for image elements and aligning them with the surrounding text, but there is no reason that this property cannot be used for any element. For example, it is possible to use the align property with the <p> element and attempt to align it with other surrounding text, but the the results may not always be as expected. There are only three possible values for the align property:

- "left" positions the element to the left side of the page (after accounting for any margin properties) and other surrounding elements, such as text will float to the right side.
- "right" positions the element to the right side of the page (again, after accounting for any margin properties) and other surrounding elements, such as text, will float to the left side.
- "none" is the default property value for the align property. The value of "none" will cause the element to be displayed exactly where it falls within the text.

The use of the align property with the <img> is shown in the following code segment.

```
<style TYPE="text/javascript">
tags.img.align = "right"
</style>
```

In this example, the important elements are as follows:

- tags is one of the methods of defining JSSS styles. The tags definition describes the element immediately following it in the dot notation will be one of the accepted HTML elements.
- img is the HTML element that is being assigned a style. This may be any valid HTML element.
- align is the style that is being defined for the element. This may be any valid JSSS style.
- "right" is the value of the style align.

> **NOTE** The align property has the same functionality as the CSS (Cascading Style Sheet) `float` property. `float` is a reserved word in JSSS (JavaScript Style Sheets) and cannot be used as a property name.

Using the `align` element gives you control over how elements are generally placed in the document. A good example of this is the image element. For consistency, you may want all of your images to align on the right margin and have all left descriptions to the left of the image. The following example shows how this can be accomplished:

```
<html>
<style TYPE="text/javascript">
tags.img.align = "right"
</style>
<body>
<img SRC=scisess.gif>
<p>Display text to the left side of the first image and
after putting in enough text to fit to the left of the
first image, the second image will display in the same
manner.
<img SRC=sciex.gif>
<p>Display more text to the left side of the second image
</body>
</html>
```

Each image in the document will be displayed the right side of the page with text floating to the left side.

Anchor

Category: JavaScript, JScript, and VBScript

Type	Object

Browser Support		Navigator 3	Navigator 4	Explorer 3	Explorer 4
	Macintosh	■	■	☐	■
	Windows	■	■	■	■

Subset Of	Document object

Syntax	document.anchors[*idx*]

An anchor is a hyperlink that has been given a name. Hyperlinks can point to anchors in a document by using a hash mark (#) in the URL, as follows:

A

`http://www.site.com/page.html#anchorName`

Within a script, the `Anchor` object is an array of all anchors in the document. The array will contain all the named `<a>` tags (those which contain a specified `name` attribute) in the order that they appear in the document.

The anchor object is read-only, and it has no properties. In other words, it serves no real purpose. Typically, one might use the `length` property of the related `anchors` array to determine the total number of anchors in a document—however, that is a subject of the `document` object (see `Document` object).

> **NOTE**   If the hyperlink containing the anchor also specifies a destination (that is, the `<a>` tag has an `href` attribute), the hyperlink will also be contained as a `link` object in the `links` array.

Applet
Category: JavaScript 1.1

Type	Object

Browser Support		Navigator 3	Navigator 4	Explorer 3	Explorer 4
	Macintosh	■	■	☐	☐
	Windows	■	■	☐	☐

Subset Of	Document object

Syntax	`document.appletName.property` OR
	`document.applets[index].property`

Java applets are included in a web page using the HTML `<applet>` tag. The `Applet` object enables the script to interact—to a limited extent—with the Java applet included in the `<applet>` tag. For this interaction to function, you must specify the `mayscript` attribute in the `<applet>` tag, which explicitly permits the Java applet to "talk" with JavaScript.

> **NOTE** Java, although not directly related to JavaScript, is a complex programming language that enables authors to create self-contained programs ("applets") that can be included on a web page. Java applets can range from small visual enhancements such as dancing text, to complex applications such as an interactive subway map. Because Java applets are platform-independent, they can be run by any user on any machine as long as his browser supports Java. For more information on Java, check out its home site at `http://www.javasoft.com`.

 Internet Explorer 3 does not support the `applet` object. Nor does Internet Explorer 4, as of this writing.

Each `applet` object is an element in the `applets[]` array, which itself is a property of the document object (see document object). You can access reference an `applet` object either via the `applets[]` array or by name, if a name attribute was specified in the `<applet>` tag.

An `applet` object doesn't possess any intrinsic properties or methods; rather, it can access any public properties or methods of the Java applet itself. A "public" property or method is one that has been specifically defined as accessible in the Java applet source code.

Interacting with Java applets in this way using JavaScript is known as LiveConnect. Although Java is far too complex and out of scope for this discussion, detailed information on LiveConnect can be found at Netscape's web site: `http://home.netscape.com/eng/mozilla/3.0/handbook/javascript/livecon.htm`

Imagine, for instance, that your HTML document includes a Java applet named `myApplet`. This applet has been created with the public methods `start()` and `stop()`, which cause the action of the applet to start and stop, respectively. Assuming that you specified the `mayscript` attribute in the `<applet>` tag, you could use a script statement such as:

`document.myApplet.start()`

to start the applet's behavior, or

`document.myApplet.stop()`

to stop the applet's behavior. This can be tied into an `onClick` event-handler, for instance, on a form field button:

```
<input type="button" name="go" value="Click to start applet"
➥onClick="document.myApplet.start()">
```

```
<input type="button" name="stop" value="Click to stop applet"
➥onClick="document.myApplet.stop()">
```

A

Of course, if `myApplet` is the first applet in the HTML document, it could also be referenced as `document.applets[0]`.

Because every Java applet is different, and often created by different authors, the set of available public properties and methods for the `applet` object is always different.

If you write your own Java applets, it's simple to consciously create public properties and methods meant to be accessed from JavaScript. However, when you use Java applets from other authors, they may or may not be coded to easily interact with JavaScript. You may need to read the source code of the Java applet to learn which public properties and methods it supports. Needless to say, this would require some knowledge of Java!

<AREA>

Category: HTML

Browser Support

	Navigator 3	Navigator 4	Explorer 3	Explorer 4
Macintosh	■	■	■	■
Windows	■	■	■	■

May Contain   None

May Be Used In   <MAP>

Attributes   ALT, CLASS, COORDS, HREF, ID, NOHREF, NOTAB, SHAPE, TABINDEX

Syntax   <AREA>...</AREA>

The <AREA> tag is used to specify individual active areas on a client-side imagemap within the <MAP> tag. See the <MAP> tag entry for a complete description and explanation of what an imagemap is and how it works.

The <AREA> tag and its attributes must be placed within the <MAP> tag, but a closing, or </AREA> tag, is not needed.

ALT

If a visitor is using a text-only browser, the ALT attribute displays a string of text instead of the imagemap. In the following example, `imagemap` is the name of the imagemap:

```
<MAP NAME=imagemap><AREA ALT="Support Bill Gates and Get Internet Explorer! Or,
snub Bill Gates and get Netscape Navigator!"></MAP>
```

> **NOTE**   If there is a problem with the imagemap, an image-enabled browser such as Netscape Navigator and/or Internet Explorer will display the <ALT>-specified string of text.

> **DESIGN NOTE**   If you're using an imagemap on your web page, it is always a good idea to include a corresponding group of text links somewhere nearby. This is not only for the benefit of visitors using text-only browsers (who will have no other means to navigate your web site), but it's also for visitors using image-enabled browsers, too. Internet Explorer, for example, will wait to load your imagemap like all the other images on your page until after all the text has appeared—a text link menu enables impatient visitors get on with it, without having to wait.
>
> Also, many web surfers who have image-enabled browsers will turn the graphics off altogether so they can move about with more speed. Writing some intriguing or curiosity-inspiring <ALT> text may get these visitors to turn graphics on so they can see what your site has to offer.

CLASS

The CLASS attribute is used to specify the name of a style sheet as it applies to a specific selection on a web page. See the "Cascading Style Sheets Basics" chapter and any individual, related style sheets entries elsewhere in the book for more information.

COORDS

The COORDS attribute specifies the coordinates that define each individual section or "hot spot" within an imagemap. It is directly related to the shape type value specified by the SHAPE attribute—a rectangular hot spot requires four coordinates (the four corners); a circular hot spot requires three (two center measurements and the radius); and a polygonal hot spot requires three or more pairs of coordinates depending on what you want.

This part of the <AREA> entry is otherwise known as High School Geometry Revisited (or It Came From Planet Geometry, for those of us who are math-impaired). Browsers read COORD-specified measurements as (x, y) points on a grid, as most clearly demonstrated in the first of the following examples. This sample HTML specifies a rectangular hot spot with imagemap as the name of the graphic that appears on the web page:

```
<MAP NAME=imagemap><AREA SHAPE="RECT" COORDS="0, 0, 99, 99"></MAP>
```

The coordinates are specified in image pixels, with (0, 0) representing the top-left corner and (99, 99) representing the bottom-right corner.

This next example demonstrates how to specify a circular imagemap hot spot, again, with imagemap as the name of the imagemap:

```
<MAP NAME=imagemap><AREA SHAPE="CIRC" COORDS="10, 10, 5"></MAP>
```

This circle has a radius of 5 pixels with the center point (X) located at 10 pixels and the center point (Y) also located at 10 pixels.

A polygonal hot spot is specified using pairs of coordinates that are connected in the order you list them, with the last pair being connected to the first. This example HTML specifies a triangular hot spot with `imagemap` representing the name of the imagemap:

```
<MAP NAME=imagemap><AREA SHAPE="POLY" COORDS="10, 50, 15, 20, 20, 50"></MAP>
```

The edge locations of this triangle, therefore, are located at (10, 50), (15, 20), and (20, 50).

Assembling an entire imagemap is accomplished by listing several `COORDS`-specified hot spots. The following example is a 200×80 pixel button bar, with `imagemap` again representing the image:

```
<MAP NAME="imagemap">
<AREA SHAPE="RECT" COORDS="10, 10, 40, 70">
<AREA SHAPE="RECT" COORDS="60, 10, 90, 70">
<AREA SHAPE="RECT" COORDS="110, 10, 140, 70">
<AREA SHAPE="RECT" COORDS="160, 10, 190, 70">
</MAP>
```

If you're up on your geometry, you may recognize some overlap between some of the hot spots specified in the last example—it's important to remember that if there's overlap between two hot spots, the first one listed will take precedence and will be slightly larger than the second. This will not affect the appearance of your imagemap. As you've seen, the HTML used to specify hot spots does not display on a web page—but if the overlap is significant, the clickable area of the second hot spot may be reduced enough to make it difficult to locate and use.

Also, you can set the `COORDS` attribute to DEFAULT no matter what `SHAPE` you specify, in which case you do not need to establish specific coordinates. Be sure to test this setting thoroughly, however, as the DEFAULT-specified clickable area may be too large or too small for the design of your imagemap.

HREF

The `HREF` attribute specifies the URL of the web page or site linked to a particular hot spot on your imagemap. In the following example, `resume.html` is the web page to which this hot spot is linked:

```
<MAP NAME="imagemap"><AREA SHAPE="RECT" COORDS="10, 10, 40, 70"
HREF="resume.html"></MAP>
```

DESIGN NOTE If you need to add blank or padding space to properly position certain hot spots, you can use the `NOHREF` attribute to specify an area on an imagemap as plain, unlinked space. See the `NOHREF` section of this entry for more detailed information.

ID

The ID attribute is used to distinguish individual selections in a web page as pertaining to the use of style sheets. See the "Cascading Style Sheets Basics" chapter and any individual, related style sheets entries elsewhere in the book for more information.

NOHREF

The NOHREF attribute specifies an exact region on your imagemap as plain, unlinked page space. It becomes useful if the design of your imagemap requires you to pad or place unlinked space between hot spots so that the HTML will exactly correspond to the design of your image.

In the following example, the third hot spot in this button bar is deliberately left unlinked to properly position the rest:

```
<MAP NAME="imagemap">
<AREA SHAPE="RECT" COORDS="10, 10, 40, 70" HREF="links.html">
<AREA SHAPE="RECT" COORDS="60, 10, 90, 70" HREF="index.html">
<AREA SHAPE="RECT" COORDS="110, 10, 140, 70" NOHREF>
<AREA SHAPE="RECT" COORDS="160, 10, 190, 70" HREF="gallery.html">
</MAP>
```

Alternating linked and unlinked space in your imagemap does not affect the appearance of your web page, but it does affect the position and amount of clickable space assigned to each hot spot. Test your imagemap thoroughly to make sure there is proper overlapping and/or an adequate amount of page space assigned to each active hot spot.

NOTAB

The NOTAB attribute enables you to pass over a hot spot if you have used the TABINDEX attribute to create a tabbing sequence. (Visitors browsing with Internet Explorer can use the Tab key to move from one hot spot to another on an imagemap if you create a tabbing sequence with TABINDEX and numbers—see the section on TABINDEX later on in this entry.)

Neither NOTAB nor TABINDEX works in Netscape Navigator.

In the following example, NOTAB has been assigned to the unlinked or plain hot spot on this imagemap while TABINDEX is used to create a numerical sequence of all the active hot spots:

```
<MAP NAME="imagemap">
<AREA SHAPE="RECT" COORDS="10, 10, 40, 70" HREF="links.html" TABINDEX=1>
<AREA SHAPE="RECT" COORDS="60, 10, 90, 70" HREF="index.html" TABINDEX=2>
<AREA SHAPE="RECT" COORDS="110, 10, 140, 70" NOHREF NOTAB>
<AREA SHAPE="RECT" COORDS="160, 10, 190, 70" HREF="gallery.html" TABINDEX=3>
</MAP>
```

A visitor using the Tab key to navigate through this imagemap will simply jump from the second hot spot to the fourth, passing over the third hot spot altogether.

SHAPE

The SHAPE attribute specifies the general SHAPE type of a hot spot within an imagemap. It is directly related to the COORDS attribute that specifies the exact location of points, planes, sides, and other geometric SHAPE measurements—you'll want to refer to the COORDS section of this entry to get the whole story on how to specify a hot spot shape.

The SHAPE attribute has six values, but it can only define three general geometric forms:

RECT or RECTANGLE

Specifies the general shape of the hot spot will be rectangular.

CIRC or CIRCLE

Specifies the general shape of the hot spot will be circular.

POLY or POLYGON

Specifies the general shape of the hot spot will be a polygon, or any closed plane figure with straight-plane sides (the POLYGON example in the COORDS section is a triangle).

In the following example, imagemap describes the type of file, and the numerical values specify the exact coordinates of the hot spot's sides:

```
<MAP NAME=imagemap><AREA SHAPE="RECT" COORDS="0, 0, 99, 99"></MAP>
```

> **DESIGN NOTE**
> The SHAPE-specified parameters of a hot spot do not affect the appearance of your imagemap, but they do affect the amount of clickable space a hot spot will have on the page. Your imagemap will be much easier for visitors to use if you make each hot spot as large as possible—don't assign a circular SHAPE to a square-drawn button, for example, because this means you lose valuable page area.

TABINDEX

The TABINDEX attribute specifies a hot spot's position in the tabbing order. Visitors browsing with Internet Explorer can use the Tab key to move from one hot spot to another on an imagemap if you create a tabbing sequence with TABINDEX and numbers. However, TABINDEX is not supported by Netscape Navigator.

In the following example, TABINDEX has been used to specify a tabbing sequence of 1 through 3:

```
<MAP NAME="imagemap">
<AREA SHAPE="RECT" COORDS="10, 10, 40, 70" HREF="links.html" TABINDEX=1>
<AREA SHAPE="RECT" COORDS="60, 10, 90, 70" HREF="index.html" TABINDEX=2>
<AREA SHAPE="RECT" COORDS="110, 10, 140, 70" NOHREF NOTAB>
<AREA SHAPE="RECT" COORDS="160, 10, 190, 70" HREF="gallery.html" TABINDEX=3>
</MAP>
```

Notice that the third hot spot on this imagemap, which is unlinked or plain as specified by the NOHREF attribute, has also been left out of the tabbing sequence via the NOTAB attribute. The NOTAB attribute enables visitors to pass over this third hot spot in the tabbing sequence because it serves no practical purpose. (See the NOTAB section earlier in this entry for more information— NOTAB, like TABINDEX, is not supported in Netscape Navigator.)

TITLE

The TITLE attribute is an Internet Explorer–only feature that enables you to specify text that appears in a small, pop-up balloon when Windows' balloon Help feature is turned on.

In the following example, each hot spot in the imagemap is given a brief description specified by the TITLE attribute:

```
<MAP NAME="imagemap">
<AREA SHAPE="RECT" COORDS="10, 10, 40, 70" HREF="links.html" TABINDEX=1
TITLE="Hot links I like">
<AREA SHAPE="RECT" COORDS="60, 10, 90, 70" HREF="gallery.html" TABINDEX=2
TITLE="I like Monet, too">
</MAP>
```

Area

Category: JavaScript 1.1

		Navigator 3	Navigator 4	Explorer 3	Explorer 4
Type	Object				
Browser Support					
	Macintosh	■	■	☐	■
	Windows	■	■	☐	■
Subset Of	Document object				
Properties	hash, hostname, host, href, pathname, port, protocol, search, target				
Events	onmouseover, onmouseout				
Syntax	document.links[*idx*].*property*				

An image map is a graphic image that contains regions of hyperlinks; that is, clicking within an area of the image activates a hyperlink to a URL. Client-side image maps require no communications with the server to determine to which URL a portion of the image should link. Image maps are created in HTML using the <map> tag, and their associated hyperlinks are created using the <area> tag within the <map> tag.

Internet Explorer 3 does not support the `area` object. Image map areas created using the HTML <area> tag are not included as hyperlinks within the `links []` array.

`Area` objects *are* `link` objects. They reside in the `links[]` array of the document object. There is an area object for each <area> tag in the document. Because `area` objects and `link` objects are exactly the same, they are indexed according to their order in the HTML. Consider the following HTML excerpt:

```
<a href="http://www.site.com">Great Web Site</a>
<img src="mapimage.gif" width=40 height=20 usemap="#imagemapname">
<map name="imagemapname">
<area name="firstregion" coords="0,0,50,25"  href="http://www.othersite.com">
</map>
<a href="http://www.thirdsite.com">My favorite site of all</a>
```

In the preceding example, there are three hyperlinks, two of which are created using the <a> tag and one of which is created with the <area> tag. Because they are all indexed into the `document` object's `links[]` array in order, the object

`document.links[0]` would contain the `link` object for "Great Web Site".

`document.links[1]` would contain the area object for the <area> tag named *firstregion*.

`document.links[2]` would contain the `link` object for "My favorite site of all".

The `Area` object has the same set of properties and all but one of the methods as the `link` object.

hash **property**

The `hash` property reflects the anchor portion of a URL. This includes the hash mark (#) and everything after it. For instance, consider a hyperlink which points to a URL with an anchor named `july`.

```
<area name="firstregion" coords="0,0,50,25"  href="http://www.site.com/
whatsnew.html#july>
```

Assuming that the preceding is the first hyperlink in the HTML document, then the script statement

```
anchtext = document.links[0].hash
```

would assign the value "#july" to the variable `anchtext`.

You can also assign a new anchor name to the `hash` property, thereby redirecting the `area` object. In other words, recalling the preceding example, the script statement

```
document.links[0].hash="august"
```

would modify the hyperlink to point to

```
http://www.site.com/whatsnew.html#august
```

Modifying the `hash` property is a convenient way to dynamically redirect a hyperlink depending on a certain condition.

For instance, you might have a "What's New" page that contains anchors for each month. When the page loads, your script could determine the current date using the `date` object and modify the `hash` property for the link leading to the "What's New" page. Therefore, when the user clicks the "What's New" hyperlink, she'll always be taken to the most current anchor in the page.

`hostname` **property**

The `hostname` property reflects the host name or IP address contained in a URL. For instance, consider a hyperlink that points to a URL with the host name `www.site.com`.

```
<area name="firstregion" coords="0,0,50,25"  href="http://www.site.com/
whatsnew.html>
```

Assuming that the above is the first hyperlink in the HTML document, then the script statement

```
hosttext = document.links[0].hostname
```

would assign the value "`www.site.com`" to the variable `hosttext`.

You can also assign a new host name to the `hostname` property, thereby redirecting the `area` object. In other words, recalling the example above, the script statement

```
document.links[0].hostname="www.anothersite.com"
```

would modify the hyperlink to point to

```
http://www.anothersite.com/whatsnew.html#august
```

Modifying the `hostname` property is not commonly done; however, in such cases, you'll want to modify the entire URL, via the `area` object's `href` property.

`host` **property**

`host` property is almost exactly the same as the `hostname` property. The only difference is that the `host` property will reflect the server port number if specified in the URL, whereas the `hostname` property will not. Consider the hyperlink

```
<area name="firstregion" coords="0,0,50,25"  href="http://www.site.com:6000/
whatsnew.html>
```

In this URL, server port 6000 is specified. Most URLs do not contain a server port, which cause them to default to 80—the web server standard port. Assuming that the above is the first hyperlink in the HTML, then

```
hosttext = document.links[0].host
```

would assign the value "www.site.com:6000" to hosttext, whereas

```
hosttext = document.links[0].hostname
```

would have assigned the value "www.site.com" to hosttext. This is the only difference between the two properties.

> Within Internet Explorer 3 or 4, the host property always contains a port number, even if one was not specified in the URL. Thus, if the location object contained the URL "http://www.site.com", the host property would contain "www.site.com:80". Recall that 80 is the default port when unspecified. Also note that this is the opposite behavior of Netscape, which does not include the port if unspecified in the URL.

href property

href property reflects the entire URL specified in the hyperlink <area> tag. Recall the hyperlink

```
<area name="firstregion" coords="0,0,50,25"  href="http://www.site.com/
whatsnew.html#july>
```

Assuming that this is the first hyperlink in the HTML document, the script statement

```
url = document.links[0].href
```

would assign the value "http://www.site.com/whatsnew.html#july" to the variable url.

Modifying the href property is the most common way to redirect the destination of a hyperlink. For instance, imagine a page that contains a series of form fields, and an imagemap containing an area with an icon representing "next page."

However, just *which* page is the next page depends on options the user has selected in the various form fields. Therefore, you could write a script function that would test the state of the form fields and, depending upon the results, assign a new URL to the area object.

```
document.links[0].href="newURL"
```

When would this function be executed? Well, there is no onClick event handler for the area object as there is for the link object. Thus, a function that modifies the href property would have to be triggered by some other event, such as an onMouseOver event on the area object, or an onClick event for one of the form fields.

> **TIP** It's important to understand that assigning a new URL to an area object's href property does *not* immediately load that page. Rather, it merely redirects where the hyperlink *will* lead when and if the user clicks it.

pathname **property**

pathname property reflects the file path portion of a URL. This begins with the first backslash following the host name or port number up until the end of the URL or the presence of a hash mark or question mark.

For instance, consider a hyperlink that points to the following URL:

```
<area name="firstregion" coords="0,0,50,25"  href="http://www.site.com/
whatsnew.html#july">
```

Assuming that the above is the first hyperlink in the HTML document, then the script statement

```
pathtext = document.links[0].pathname
```

would assign the value "/whatsnew.html" to the variable pathtext.

You can also assign a new file path to the pathname property, thereby redirecting the area object. In other words, recalling the example above, the script statement

```
document.links[0].pathname="/oldwhatnews.html"
```

would modify the hyperlink to point to

```
http://www.site.com/oldwhatsnew.html#july
```

Notice that the anchor name "july" was not lost from the URL. Assigning a new file path to the pathname property only modifies that portion of the URL—the rest of it remains unchanged.

However, the pathname property is rarely modified. Generally speaking, when you want to redirect an area object you should assign the new URL in its entirety to the href property.

port **property**

port property reflects the port number, if specified, for the URL contained in the area object. Given the hyperlink

```
<area name="firstregion" coords="0,0,50,25"  href="http://www.site.com:4096/
whatsnew.html>
```

the script statement

```
urlport = document.links[0].port
```

would assign the value 4096 to the variable urlport.

Few URLs specify a port number, however, because most web servers use the default port number 80. If no port number is specified in the URL, the port property will be empty (it will *not* contain the value 80).

Unlike Netscape, when within Internet Explorer 3 and 4 and no port number is specified in the location object, the port property *will* contain the value 80 (the default port for web servers).

Although unlikely, you could also assign a new port number to the `port` property, and the URL to which that `area` object points will change accordingly.

```
document.links[0].port=6000
```

`protocol` **property**

`protocol` property reflects the document delivery protocol for the URL contained in the `area` object, up to and including the colon. Given the hyperlink

```
<area name="firstregion" coords="0,0,50,25"  href="http://www.site.com/
whatsnew.html>
```

the script statement

```
urlprotcol = document.links[0].protocol
```

would assign the value "`http:`" to the variable `urlprotocol`. Of course, "`http:`" is the protocol prefix which describes all web pages, so it is the most common protocol to turn up in the `protocol` property. Other, far less common possibilities include

Value	Protocol Description
`file:`	document is retrieved either from the local computer or remotely via FTP
`ftp:`	document is retrieved via FTP
`gopher:`	document is retrieved via the old Gopher protocol
`mailto:`	hyperlink launches new email message to specified address
`javascript:`	hyperlink leads to JavaScript statements

Although rarely modified, you could assign a protocol to the `protocol` property, and the URL to which that `area` object points will change accordingly.

```
document.links[0].protocol="ftp:"
```

`search` **property**

`search` property reflects the query string, if specified, for the URL contained in the `area` object, including the preceding question mark. Query strings are data submitted via the "get" method to a web page. Given the hyperlink

```
<area name="firstregion" coords="0,0,50,25"  href="http://www.site.com/
whatsnew.html?m=2&d=10>
```

the script statement

```
urlquery = document.links[0].search
```

would assign the value "?m=2&d=10" to the variable urlport. The query string is a series of variable and value pairs, which are passed along to a CGI program on the server side for processing. Form data, which is submitted via the "get" method, is sent using a query string URL.

You could supply a hyperlink with a new query string by assigning it to the search property.

```
document.links[0].search = "?m=5&d=14"
```

target property

target property reflects the name of the window or frame in which to display the clicked hyperlink, as specified by the target attribute of the <area> tag. By default, a hyperlink with no set target attribute will open into the same window, overwriting the contents of the current page.

However, some pages contain multiple frames, or some scripts open new windows onscreen. You can redirect a hyperlink to open into a particular frame or window.

```
document.links[idx].target="frameOrWindowName"
```

Frame names are created within the <frame> tag subordinate to the <frameset> tag. Window names are created using the open() method of the window object (see the Window object).

There is also a set of built-in targets, which you can assign to the target property to achieve the following results:

Target	Result
"_top"	opens hyperlink into full size of current window
"_parent"	opens hyperlink into parent window of current window
"_self"	opens hyperlink into same window which hyperlink was clicked
"_blank"	opens hyperlink into a new, blank, unnamed window

onMouseOver event handler

Located within the <area> tag, the onMouseOver event handler will activate when the user moves the mouse onto the image region containing the hyperlink, *before* it is clicked. Often, this event handler is used to display a description of the hyperlink in the browser's status bar (at the bottom of the browser window border).

For instance:

```
<area name="firstregion" coords="0,0,50,25" href="http://www.site.com/
whatsnew.html onMouseOver="window.status='The Latest and Greatest Sites';return
true">
```

When the mouse passes over this image region, the browser's status message will display the specified description, as seen in Figure 1.

Figure 1

Customizing the browser status message using the area object's onMouseOver *event handler.*

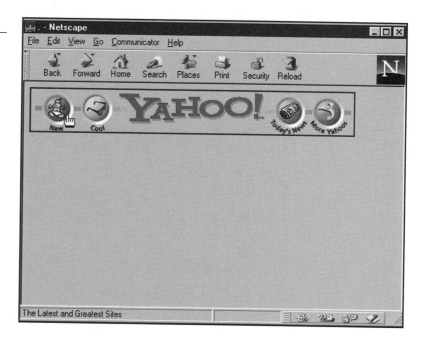

Notice that the onMouseOver event handler returns a value of true—this is necessary for the event handler to function properly.

onMouseOut event handler

Located within the <area> tag, the onMouseOut event handler will activate when the user moves the mouse out of the image region containing the hyperlink. Typically, the onMouseOut event handler will contain statements to disable any functions invoked by the onMouseOver event handler.

In the onMouseOver example earlier, the window status message was modified by the event handler. However, this message remains on the window until the mouse moves over another hyperlink. Clearly, you'd want to remove the status message immediately after the mouse vacated the hyperlinked image region. Simply add an onMouseOut event handler to the <area> tag to assign an empty string to the window object's status property. The result can be seen in Figure 2.

```
<area name="firstregion" coords="0,0,50,25"  href="http://www.site.com/
whatsnew.html  onMouseOver="window.status='The Latest and Greatest News';return
true"  onMouseOut="window.status='';return true">
```

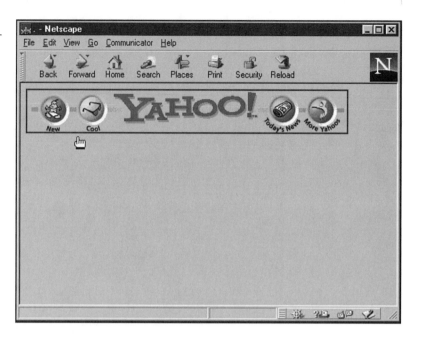

Figure 2

Using the onMouseOut event handler, the status message disappears when the mouse moves out of the hyperlinked image region.

Array

Category: JavaScript, JScript

Type	Object	

Browser Support

	Navigator 3	Navigator 4	Explorer 3	Explorer 4
Macintosh	■	■	☐	■
Windows	■	■	■	■

Subset Of	Nothing
Properties	length
Methods	join(), reverse(), sort()
Syntax	To create an array: *arrayName* = new Array([*size*]) OR
	arrayName = new Array([*element list*])
	To use an array: arrayName[*index*] OR
	arrayName.propertyName OR
	arrayName.methodName(parameters)

As anyone familiar with programming languages may know, an array is a *container*—a "supervariable" that can contain several or more values. Another way to think of an array is as an ordered collection of data. An array contains *elements*, where each element is a variable and may contain any valid value (string, numeric, and so on). The array may contain any number of elements, from none to thousands. The elements are referenced via their *index*, or position in the array. Typically, arrays are used to contain a related set of data. An array named colors, for instance, may contain four elements, each of which holds a string representing a color. You can reference each of the elements in `colors[]` as:

```
colors[0]
colors[1]
colors[2]
colors[3]
```

Each of the preceding elements can be accessed or modified like any other variable, such as

```
colors[0]="red"
```

or

```
document.bgColor=colors[1]
```

You create a JavaScript or JScript array using the *new* statement. There are three slightly different variations on creating an array with the new statement, depending upon your needs or preference:

1. `colors = new Array(5)`

   An array named `colors` contains five elements. Initially, each element contains a value of null.

2. `colors = new Array("red","green",30)`

   This array, named `colors`, initially contains three elements: the first (index 0) containing the value "red," the second containing "green," and the third containing 30. This construction is not much different from step 1, except that the array elements initially contain the values specified rather than nulls.

3. `colors = new Array()`

   The most general form of array creation, this array creates an array named `colors`, with no specified length or element values. As you'll see in a moment, elements can be added to the array at any later time. Use this construction when your script doesn't know how many elements are needed, or what values they should contain at creation time.

In all cases above, you *must* properly capitalize Array. You can change the size of an array at any time—simply assign a value to an array element with an index number higher than any previous index number. For instance, consider the array:

```
colors = new Array("red","green",30)
```

This array contains three elements, index numbers 0, 1, and 2. To add a fourth item to this array at index 3:

```
colors[3]=someValue
```

You don't even have to add the new element immediately after the previous highest index. Considering the preceding array again, the assignment:

```
colors[6]=someValue
```

would expand the `colors` array to contain seven elements. While `colors[6]` would contain *someValue*, `colors[4]` and `colors[5]` would contain null values until you assign values to them.

TIP Keep in mind, too, that an array element can contain *any* type of value, including another array! For instance:

`colors[7]=new Array(3)`

Following the above statement, `colors[7]` is now an array itself, initially containing four null elements. To refer to an individual element in this array, simply follow the same *arrayName[idx]* syntax: `colors[7][1]` would refer to the second element in the array `colors[7]` (which itself is the eighth element of the array `colors`—whew!).

Arrays are especially convenient when you need your script to cycle through a set of values. For instance, when outputting a series of strings to a page, those strings could be assigned to elements of an array. Imagine that your array is named `outstr`. You can then use a `for` loop to cycle through the array elements, outputting each to the page:

```
for (j=0; j<10; j++)
{ document.write(outstr[j]) }
```

The above loop will output, in sequence, the contents of `outstr[0]`, `outstr[1]`, `outstr[2]`, and so forth, up to and including `outstr[9]`.

In most cases, when dealing with an array, you actually work with individual elements of the array, as exemplified above. However, an array is also an object, and as such, contains a property and several methods that concern the whole array. These are described in the following section.

`length` property

The `length` property is the number of elements in the array, sometimes described as the "size" of the array. This is a read/write property; you can assign a new value to `length` to decrease or increase the size of the array. If you decrease the array smaller than the index of any elements, those elements are deleted from the array.

Imagine the array:

`computer = new array(5)`

Initially, `computer.length` would yield the value 5. You could resize `computer` to contain 10 elements using the statement

`computer.length=10`

Any new elements created as a result initially contain a value of null.

join() method

The join() method combines the values of all elements in the array and returns one string, with a comma separating each value. You may optionally specify an alternate separator string as a parameter to the join() method. For instance, imagine that you start with the following array:

```
count = new Array("one", "two", "three")
```

You call the join() method in the context of an assignment:

```
str = count.join()
```

The preceding command would assign the string "one,two,three" to the variable str.

If you make the statement:

```
str = count.join(" and a ")
```

then the join() method would return the string "one and a two and a three."

Lastly, if you'd prefer not to include any delimiting character:

```
str = count.join("")
```

would return the string "onetwothree."

reverse() method

The flip-flop method—reverse()—simply inverts the order of the elements in the array. The first element becomes the last, the last the first, and so on. For instance, imagine that you begin with:

```
month=new Array("jan","feb","mar","apr","may","jun")
```

In the above array, month[0] contains "jan", month[1] contains "feb", and so on until month[5] which contains "jun".

After executing the statement:

```
month.reverse()
```

now, month[0] contains "jun", month[1] contains "may", month[2] contains "apr", and so on until month[5] which now contains "jan".

The reverse() method does not change the size of the array or the element values themselves—it merely reverses their index order.

sort() method

As its name implies, the sort() method re-orders the elements in the array in accordance with a sort order. You may use either the built-in (default) dictionary-style sort order (alphabetical), or create your own sorting function (passed as a parameter to the method).

Imagine that you begin with the following array:

```
labels = new Array("toyota",5,"intel","idek",20)
```

If you don't specify the name of a *compareFunction*, the sort() method will re-order these elements such that they conform to dictionary alphabetic sort-order. As a consequence, the statement:

```
labels.sort()
```

would yield the new index order:

```
labels[0] contains "20"
labels[1] contains "5"
labels[2] contains "idek"
labels[3] contains "intel"
labels[4] contains "toyota"
```

Notice that "20" is sorted above "5"—this is because alphabetic sorting converts all numeric values to strings, and compares them alphabetically rather than numerically. Therefore, because "2" (the first "letter" of "20") comes before "5," it is sorted earlier.

Alternatively, you could write your own function for sorting the array elements. Specify this function name as a parameter to the sort() method:

```
arrayName.sort(compareFunction)
```

Your custom function should take two parameters, a and b. This function should:

- Return a value less than zero if a should be sorted before b.
- Return zero, if a and b are equivalent and remain in their current places.
- Return a value greater than zero if a should be sorted after b.

For instance, suppose you want to create a function that performs a numerical sort, rather than alphabetical.

```
function compareNumbers(a, b)
{ return a - b }
```

Imagine the following array:

```
numbers = new array( 20, 5, 75, 111)
```

numbers.sort() would index the elements in the order: 111, 20, 5, 75.

numbers.sort(compareNumbers) would index the elements in the order: 5, 20, 75, 111.

___TIP___ When coding your own *compareFunction*, remember that the *sign* of the returned value is what's important, not its magnitude. You can utilize any logic you want when comparing a and b, but be careful to return any positive number, zero, or any negative number, depending upon how you want a and b to be sorted with respect to each other.

Array()

Category: VBScript

Type	Function

Browser Support

	Navigator 3	Navigator 4	Explorer 3	Explorer 4
Macintosh	☐	☐	☐	■
Windows	☐	☐	■	■

Syntax `Array(arglist)`

The `array()` function is used to quickly create an array. An array is a set of elements, each of which may contain any type of value. The `arglist` parameter is a comma-delimited list of values, each of which will be assigned to succeeding elements. For example:

```
dim colors
colors = array("red", "green", 25)
```

The array `colors` now contains three elements: the first element contains the value "red", the second contains "green", and the third contains the value 25. You refer to array elements using the array name followed by parenthesis containing the element's index number. The first element in the array is at index number 0. In other words:

```
colors(0)  contains "red"
colors(1)  contains "green"
colors(2)  contains 25
```

You can view or modify the contents of an array element just as any other variable.

```
colors(1)="yellow"
document.write("Your favorite color is "&colors(1))
```

If no `arglist` is specified, an array of zero length is created, in which case you need to resize the array if it is to contain any elements. To resize an array, either one that began with zero length, or one that contained some number of elements (such as the colors array example), use the construction redim preserve `arrayName(newSize)`. For instance, the colors array created previously contains three elements. To resize the array to 10 elements, while preserving the contents of the first three, you would write:

```
redim preserve colors(9)
```

Remember that indexing begins at number 0, so the previous statement resizes the array to contain 10 elements. If you omit the `preserve` keyword, the array will be resized, but its current contents will be lost.

Asc()

Category: VBScript

		Navigator 3	Navigator 4	Explorer 3	Explorer 4
Type	Function				
Browser Support	Macintosh	☐	☐	☐	■
	Windows	☐	☐	■	■
Syntax	Asc(string)				

The `asc()` function returns the ANSI character code of the first character in *string*. An error is generated if an empty *string* value is passed to the function. Although VBScript is not case-sensitive, ANSI codes are different for lower- and uppercase characters.

asc("a") returns 97

asc("A") returns 65

The numbers returned previously are specified by the ANSI character code set standard, which assigns a value to each possible character.

If you need to access byte data within a *string*, use the alternative construction `ascB(string)`, which returns the first byte contained within *string*, when *string* contains byte data.

On systems which use the 32-bit Unicode character set, use the construction `ascW(string)` to return the Unicode character code for the first character of *string*.

ANSI codes, such as those returned by `asc()`, are also commonly used in the `chr()` function, for outputting non-typable characters (see the `Chr()` function).

For detailed information on character codes and the ANSI and Unicode character sets, visit `http://www.bbsinc.com/iso8859.html`.

Atn()

Category: VBScript

		Navigator 3	Navigator 4	Explorer 3	Explorer 4
Type	Function				
Browser Support	Macintosh	☐	☐	☐	■
	Windows	☐	☐	■	■
Syntax	Atn(number)				

The `atn()` function calculates and returns the arctangent of *number*. The expression *number* represents the ratio between two sides of a right triangle, and the value returned represents the size of the angle in radians. Returned values may range from –pi/2 to pi/2.

A

> **NOTE** VBScript does not provide any `asin()` or `acos()` functions. The `atn()` function can be used in the following formulas to produce these functions.
>
> Inverse sine:
>
> `atn(x / sqr(-1 * x * x + 1))`
>
> Inverse cosine:
>
> `atn(-1 * x / sqr(-1 * x * x + 1)) + 2 * atn(1)`

<audioscope>

Category: HTML

Browser Support	WebTV Internet Terminal
Applies To	Sound files
Attributes	`align, border, gain, height, leftcolor, leftoffset, maxlevel, rightcolor, rightoffset, width`
Syntax	`<audioscope>…</audioscope>`

The `<audioscope>` tag displays the amplitude of the currently playing sound file as an animated graphical image. While the sound plays, the viewer can see a graphical image that matches the sounds they hear. Because WebTV supports stereo sound, viewers are able to see separate graphs for the left and right channels.

`<audioscope height=200 width=200 gain=5>`

> **NOTE** Be aware of your screen dimensions when using the `<audioscope>` tag. The WebTV screenwidth is limited to 544 pixels. Viewers are not accustomed to scrolling to see the rest of their show on a TV and will not be accustomed to scrolling web pages. To limit the size of your image, use the `height` and `width` attributes.

align

The `align` attribute aligns the adjacent text with the image of the sound file. This helps associate the text, which may explain the image or describe the sound, with the image of the sound wave. For the `<audioscope>` tag, WebTV HTML extensions support additional keywords to place the text including `top`, `middle`, `bottom`, `left`, `right`, `absmiddle`, `baseline`, and `absbottom`. The default value is `baseline`.

`<audioscope align=middle>`

border

The border attribute sets the border displayed around the <audioscope> image in pixels. The default value is 1. You can use a thick border to draw attention to the image by increasing the overall size of the graphic on the page.

```
<audioscope border=3>
```

gain

The gain attribute determines the magnitude of the amplitudes displayed in the graph. The value for gain acts as a multiplier increasing the size and making the individual amplitudes more distinct on a larger scale. The default value is 1. This attribute does not effect the actual sound coming out of your speakers. The gain is separate fromthe height attribute, discussed later in this chapter. In this situation, the gain affects the image within the graph, while the height affects the overall size of the entire image.

```
<audioscope gain=5>
```

height

The height attribute sets the height of the overall image of the sound in pixels. You use the height attribute to insure the complete image is visible within the bounds of the WebTV screen. This is separate from the gain attribute, which determines the height or size of the wave within the image.

```
<audioscope height=100 width=200>
```

leftcolor

The leftcolor attribute determines the color of the graph of the left channel of a stereo sound. Both the left and right channels can have separate colors helping your viewers visually distinguish them onscreen. The default color is #8ece10. Colors can be specified using names or RGB values. Refer to Appendix B for alisting of color names and RGB values.

```
<audioscope leftcolor="green" leftoffset=2>
```

> **TIP** Use both the leftcolor and leftoffset attributes together to visually distinguish the left and right channels of the stereo sound when you use the <audioscope> tag.

leftoffset

The leftoffset attribute sets the vertical position of the left channel of a stereo sound within the <audioscope> image. It determines the bottom or starting point for each amplitude displayed for the channel. You enter an integer that works as added or subtracted from the original starting point. A positive value raises the amplitudes higher in the image. A negative value lowers them. You can use the `leftoffset` attribute, in conjunction with the `leftcolor` attribute, to visually distinguish the left and right channels of your sound by displaying one channel higher than the other and in a different color.

```
<audioscope leftcolor="green" leftoffset=2>
```

maxlevel

The `maxlevel` attribute sets the maximum value for amplitude of the sound that can bedisplayed in the graph. If the amplitude is higher than the value, including with or without the `gain` attribute, the image is clipped to fit within the level. You use the `maxlevel` tag to insure the sound wave image fits nicely within the bounds of the image.

```
<audioscope maxlevel=10>
```

rightcolor

The `rightcolor` attribute determines the color of the graph of the right channel of a stereo sound. Both the left and right channels can have separate colors, helping your viewers visually distinguish them on screen. The default color is #ce8e10, which is orange. Colors can be specified using names of RGB values. Refer to Appendix B for a listing of color names and RGB values.

```
<audioscope rightcolor="blue" rightoffset=-2>
```

TIP   Use both the `rightcolor` and `rightoffset` attributes together to visually distinguish the left and right channels of the stereo sound when you use the `<audioscope>` tag.

rightoffset

The `rightoffset` attribute sets the vertical position of the right channel of a stereo sound within the `<audioscope>` image. It determines the bottom or starting point for each amplitude displayed for the sound. You enter an integer that works as added or subtracted from the original starting point. A positive value raises the amplitudes higher in the image, while a negative value lowers the starting point. You can use the `rightoffset` attribute, in conjunction with the `rightcolor` attribute to visually distinguish the left and right channels of your sound by displaying one channel higher than the other and in a different color.

```
<audioscope rightcolor="blue" rightoffset=-2>
```

width

The `width` attribute sets the width in pixels of the sound image. You use the `width` attribute to insure the complete image is visible within the bounds of the WebTV screen.

```
<audioscope height=100 width=100>
```

</STRONG> ■ <TD> </TD> ■ <TH> </TH> ■ <TABLE> </TABLE> ■ C
<IMG> </IMG> ■ <SCRIPT LANGUAGE = "javascript"> </SCRIPT>
■ <SCRIPT LANGUAGE = "vbscript"> </SCRIPT> ■ <BGSOUND
SRC=gbv.wav LOOP=-1> </BGSOUND> ■ <APPLET CLASS=
"ester's_day" SRC="http://testsite/walla walla washington/"
</APPLET> ■ <FRAME></FRAME>■ <MARQUEE> </MARQUEE> ■   <HTML>
</HTML> ■ <A> </A> ■ <OL> </OL> ■ <UL> </UL> ■ <MENU> </MENU>
■ <STRONG> </STRONG> ■ <TD> </TD> ■ <TH> </TH>

B

<B>

Category: HTML

Browser Support

	Navigator 3	Navigator 4	Explorer 3	Explorer 4
Macintosh	■	■	■	■
Windows	■	■	■	■

May Contain <APPLET>, <B>, <BASEFONT>, <BIG>, <BR>, <CITE>, <CODE>, <DFN>, <EM>, <FONT>, <I>, <IMG>, <INPUT>, <KBD>, <MAP>, <SAMP>, <SELECT>, <SMALL>, <STRIKE>, <STRONG>, <SUB>, <SUP>, <TEXTAREA>, <TT>, <U>, <VAR>

May Be Used In <ADDRESS>, <APPLET>, <B>, <BIG>, <BLOCKQUOTE>, <CAPTION>, <CENTER>, <CITE>, <CODE>, <DD>, <DT>, <FONT>, <H1>, <H2>, <H3>, <H4>, <H5>, <H6>, <I>, <KBD>, <LI>, <P>, <SAMP>, <SMALL>, <STRIKE>, <STRONG>, <SUB>, <SUP>, <TD>, <TH>, <TT>, <U>

Attributes None

Syntax <B>...</B>

The <B> tag is used to render text in bold. Everything written between the opening and closing, or </B>, tags will be displayed on a web page in bold as shown in the following example:

```
<B>This text is bolded using the B tag.</B>
```

Figure 1 illustrates what this HTML would look like in Netscape Navigator 3 for the Macintosh.

Figure 1

Text displayed in boldface using the <B> tag.

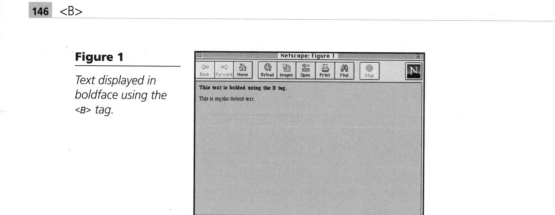

NOTE   Remember that there is a point size variance between the way text displays on the Macintosh versus text display on a PC—the default font sizes on a PC are larger, and this largeness will increase even further if you add bold. (Neither PCs themselves nor PC browsers compensate for this effect at this writing.)

---

background

Category: Cascading Style Sheets

Browser Support

	Navigator 3	Navigator 4	Explorer 3	Explorer 4
Macintosh	☐	☐	▬	☐
Windows	☐	▬	▬	▬

Syntax   `background: background-color value background-image url color background-repeat value background-attachment value background-position value`

Applies To   Depends (see descriptions of other background properties)

The background property enables you to combine all other background-related properties in a single statement. With background, you can specify a background image, color, repeat, attachment, and/or position all at once. You need not provide all properties, just the ones you want to use. For explanations of each property, see the individual descriptions in this book.

```
body { background: url(stripes.gif) center bottom }
```

```
body { background: url(background.gif) white repeat-x 50% 100% }
```

See the entries for `background-attachment`, `background-color`, `background-image`, `background-position`, and `background-repeat` for specific information on what settings to use for the `background` style. Also, you should make sure to check these individual styles for values that work (and don't work) with the `background` style as well.

B

Here's an example of combining several properties with background:

```
body { background: url(../graphics/face.gif) white repeat-y fixed 85% 18% }
```

In this example, the rule tells the browser to display the background image (face.gif) in the following way (see Figure 1 for the result):

- Use white as the backup solid background color.
- Place the initial image 85% across and 18% down the browser window.
- Tile the image vertically (down) but not horizontally.
- Fix the background so that it doesn't scroll with the page's contents.

Figure 1

The page loads with the background images placed precisely...

background-attachment

Category: Cascading Style Sheets

Browser Support		Navigator 3	Navigator 4	Explorer 3	Explorer 4
	Macintosh	☐	☐	■	☐
	Windows	☐	☐	■	■

Applies To All elements

Syntax background-attachment: *value*

The background-attachment property enables you to define whether a background image should be fixed in relation to the browser window, or whether it should "scroll" with the text of the web page. You can specify two values for this property:

- scroll means the background image will scroll along with the page's contents.
- fixed is a new option for web designers. The background image will not scroll, but remain fixed in place.

The default value is scroll. This value is what happens normally without using this property as well. Figure 1 shows a page when the background-attachment property is set to fixed.

```
body { background-image: url(stripes.gif);
       background-attachment: fixed }

body { background-image: url(background.gif) };
       background-attachment: scroll }
```

Figure 1

Using a fixed background-attachment that stays in place no matter where you scroll...

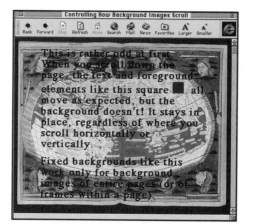

NOTE

It's important to note that background-attachment works only on *page* background images—that is, backgrounds that are styled to the <body> tag. Backgrounds styled to other elements cannot be declared fixed.

 Reminder: With Explorer 3, you have to use the background property to get these values to work; background-attachment won't work.

---

background-color

Category: Cascading Style Sheets

Browser Support

	Navigator 3	Navigator 4	Explorer 3	Explorer 4
Macintosh	☐	☐	☐	☐
Windows	☐	▬	☐	▬

Applies To   All elements

Syntax   background-color: *value*

The background-color property enables you to specify the background color of any given text element or group. Without style sheets, you could previously only set the background of an entire page or work with tables. The value can be a color value specified with a reserved color name such as green or a hexadecimal value such as #ff0000. See Appendix B for more information on working with colors and HTML.

```
h1 { background-color: blue }
```

```
h1 { background-color: #ff0000 }
```

You can also use the keyword `transparent` for `background-color`, which simply means there is no background. The current background shows through behind the text. This is especially important when you consider inheritance as discussed in the "Cascading Style Sheets Basics" chapter. In the following three lines of code, the `<i>` tag will inherit the white color of the `<body>` tag unless there is a preceding header `<h1>`, in which case the text will have a light blue color that matches the other items under the `<h1>`. Transparent is the default background color for items on your page.

```
body { background-color: white }
h1   { background-color: lightblue }
i    { background-color: transparent }
```

Explorer 3 does support background colors, but *only* if you use the "shorthand" version of the property: `background` (see the section on this style for details). Instead of using `background-color` as the property, you have to use `background`, or it won't work. Why? Because Internet Explorer 3 came out while the Cascading Style Sheets spec was still evolving, and at the time there was just one broad `background` property proposed. Explorer 4 works fine with either `background-color` or `background`.

Navigator 4 doesn't support the `transparent` setting of the `bacground-color` style.

Here's an example of using many different background colors on the same page:

```
<html>
 <style type="text/css">
 <!--
  body       { background-color: white }
  h1         { background-color: orange }
  blockquote { background-color: blue }
  b          { background-color: lime }
  i          { background-color: yellow }
 -->
 </style>
<head>
 <title>Specifying Background Colors</title>
</head>
<body>
 <h1>Hi, I'm a level-one heading with
 <b>a few words of bold</b> and
 <i>a few words of italics</i>.</h1>
```

```
<p>New paragraph here. Let's insert just a little
<b>bold</b> and <i>italics</i>.</p>
<blockquote>A blockquote here. Let's insert just a little
<b>bold</b> and <i>italics</i>.</blockquote>
</body>
</html>
```

The result is rather odd-looking (see Figure 1). If anything, this indicates you should be careful when using too many background colors on one page.

Figure 1

Watching the background colors fight it out.

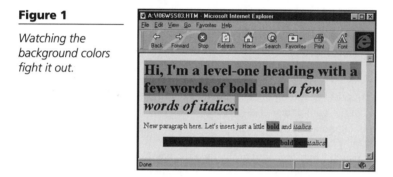

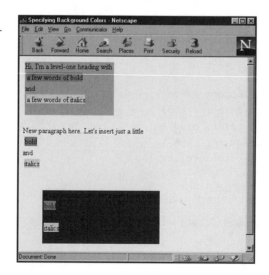

Navigator sometimes has trouble when you change styles in the middle of a paragraph. Figure 2 shows how Navigator breaks to a new line every time the background color changes. The text is also not styled as you'd expect: the `<h1>` text isn't larger and bold, the `<i>` text isn't italicized, and so on.

Figure 2

Navigator displays the same page—but adds line breaks!

B

As you can see in the figures, in Explorer 3 and Navigator 4 background color doesn't mean the whole paragraph is enveloped in a single colored rectangle that goes all the way to the browser window. The color appears only where it's actually behind text; the result is a "ragged right" of rows of background color.

> Explorer 4, however, handles this differently: the background color extends to the edge of the element's possible display area, forming a large rectangle for each block-level element (see Figure 3).

Figure 3

Explorer 4 extends background color as it should.

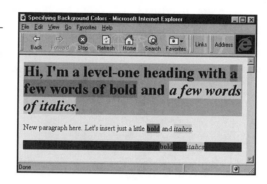

backgroundColor
Category: JavaScript Style Sheets

Type	Property				
Browser Support		Navigator 3	Navigator 4	Explorer 3	Explorer 4
	Macintosh		■		
	Windows		■		
Applies To	All elements				
Inherited	No				
Syntax	backgroundColor = "*value*"				

backgroundColor is the JSSS (JavaScript Style Sheets) property that gives color to the background of an HTML element. backGroundColor may be used with any HTML element; although there are some HTML elements where the results may not be seen well (that is, with <img> the image itself would hide the background color that has been applied). This property will add distinction to your document, but excessive use will make the document overbearing and probably turn people off. This is not the color of the text in an element, for instance <h1>, but instead the color behind the text. There is only one value that can be used for backgroundColor, and this is:

■ `"color"` is the only acceptable value for this JSSS property, although `"color"` can be expressed in two distinct manners. Either the explicit color reference, `backgroundColor = "red"`, or the RGB value in the range from 0–255, `backgroundColor = 250`. Both of these types of values are acceptable. (See Appendix B for more information on color values.)

An example of overuse of the `backgroundColor` property would be making your corporate style to have all `<h1>` and `<h2>` elements have a `backgroundColor` style of red or bright yellow. Certain colors are harsh on the eyes and trying to read through pages on a site where the `backgroundColor` of the headers was something bright would tend to deter a user form returing to the site.

Remember that `backgroundColor` is not inherited so you cannot assume that all child elements will have the same background color, and this could make for some rather interesting documents.

A useful example of the `backgroundColor` property is defined in the following code example, and displayed in Figure 1.

```
<html>
<head>
<style type="text/javascript">
function pushbutton() {
classes.pushedclass.p.backgroundColor = "gray"
}
</style>
</head>
<body>
<p class="pushedclass"> This is a paragraph in document.
<form>
<input
        type = button
        name = "ChangeBackground"
        value = "Change Background"
        OnClick = "pushbutton()">
</form>
<p class="pushedclass"> This is the second paragraph in the document
<div> this division would not change because backgroundColor
is not inherited.
</body>
</html>
```

This code shows the syntax for referencing JSSS styles in JavaScript functions. Because these JSSS styles are JavaScript-based, they can be used in code as well as just predefined styles. The single line of JSSS code `classes.pushedclass.p.backgroundColor = "gray"` is contained within a JavaScript function that is called when the button on the form is pushed. This line of code defines a JSSS class called "pushedclass" for use with the `<p>` element. The style for all `<P>` elements that reference this style will be to have a background color of gray.

When the button on the form is pushed, all paragraphs that are defined with the class `"pushedclass"` will change their background color to gray.

Figure 1

A document with grayed text after button push.

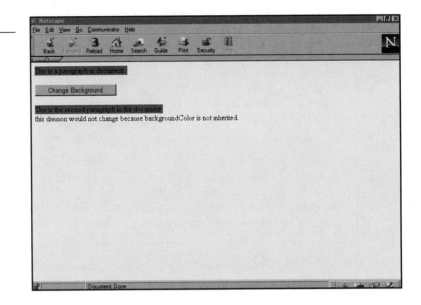

The previous code example is a subtle use of the property where a paragraph is given a gray background depending on the user's answer to a push button question. The use of `backgroundColor` will in effect "gray out" some unimportant text, and make it less noticeable, but not completely eliminate the text from the document.

background-image

Category: Cascading Style Sheets

Browser Support

	Navigator 3	Navigator 4	Explorer 3	Explorer 4
Macintosh			■	
Windows		■	■	■

Applies To   All elements

Syntax   background-image: *url color*

The `background-image` works identical to the `background-color` in that you can affect the background of any item on your page. Of course, you're using image files as backgrounds instead of solid colors. You specify an image file with a URL. You can even specify a backup color that "sits" behind the image. The color is displayed if the file at the URL is not located or cannot be displayed. You can also specify none for this property, which is useful if you don't want to include a background image behind a child element that would otherwise inherit a background image.

```
h1 { background-image: url(stripes.gif) }
```

Explorer 3 supports background images, but *only* if you use `background` (not `background-image`). All the values that follow in this section (and the next several) can still be specified through `background` (see the last section).

 Using image URLs works fine with Explorer 3 unless you're using a *linked* style sheet (see "Cascading Style Sheets Basics" for more information). Then it doesn't display the image at all. Make sure to use embedded or inline styles for background images.

N Navigator 4 can recognize background images when applied to <body>, but it *doesn't* recognize background images when applied to anything else. Also, when applying background images to the <body> tag, you have to use `background`, not `background-image`—for the same reason you have to do so with Internet Explorer 3.

Background images enable effects never before possible, or at least ones that are much more bandwidth-friendly. You can overlay text onto images to liven up headlines, and use text over images as callouts pointing to specific areas, for example on a map (see Figure 1).

Figure 1

Use background images, and suddenly all sorts of creative effects are possible.

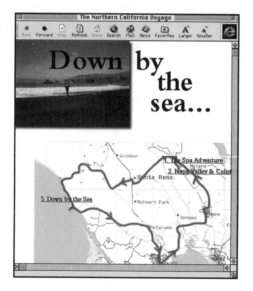

By the way, you can indeed use background images in combination with solid color backgrounds.

backgroundImage

Category: JavaScript Style Sheets

Type	Property				

Browser Support		Navigator 3	Navigator 4	Explorer 3	Explorer 4
	Macintosh	☐	■	☐	☐
	Windows	☐	■	☐	☐

Applies To All elements

Inherited No

Syntax `backgroundImage = "url"`

`backgroundImage` is best used to define an image that will be used as the background to the HTML element. This property would be used in place of a background color or pattern. `backgroundImage` can be used as a style for a single block of text (`<p>`), a group of elements in a document (all text related elements, `<p>`, `<h1>`, `<h2>`) or the entire document. `backgroundImage` will display an image behind the text of the element. Because this property is applicable for all HTML elements, caution should be used when applying the property because different results may occur, depending on the type of HTML element. The `backgroundImage` property has one possible value:

■ `"url"` is the only value that can be used. It can either be specified as the full URL path to the image file, or it can be a relative path to the current style sheet or document. Use caution when using relative URL's in style sheets because the "relative" location may change based upon the document in which the style is being used. The full path would be: `"http://www.acadians.com/kim/images/styles/image1.jpg"`, while the relative could just be `"/images/styles/image1.jpg"`.

Use `backgroundImage` with caution in style sheets. Be sure not to define styles for your documents that are overpowering and might turn users away from your pages.

For instance, the following JavaScript Style Sheet, when used in your document or linked to your document from external style sheets, overpowers the entire document and makes it too difficult to read.

```
<html>
<head>
<style type="text/javascript">
tags.body.backgroundImage = "bpaper.jpg"
</style>
</head>
<body>
The body of the document is very difficult to read with
this image behind it.
```

```
<p> This is another paragraph of text that is very hard to
read.
</body>
</html>
```

The tags line of code in the preceding example is the JSSS definition for this example. The breakdown of this line of code is as follows:

- tags denotes that this style is applicable to an HTML element. This notation tells JSSS that the property immediately following in the dot notation will be a valid HTML element.

- <body> is the HTML element to which the style will be applied. The preceding example is defining a style for the entire <body> of the HTML document. This can be any valid HTML element.

- backgroundImage is the style that will applied to the <body> element. This example is defining the background image that will display behind the entire body of the HTML document. Any valid JSSS style property can be used here.

- "bpaper.jpg" is the value of the style that will be applied. In this case, backgroundImage for this <body> can be found in the .jpg file. Each style has its own set of defined values.

The use of the backgroundImage can really enhance your documents, but watch the use of them or your documents will end up looking like Figure 1.

Figure 1

backgroundImage
that isn't readable.

background-position

Category: Cascading Style Sheets

B

Browser Support		Navigator 3	Navigator 4	Explorer 3	Explorer 4
	Macintosh	☐	☐	▬▬	☐
	Windows	☐	☐	▬▬	▬▬

Applies To Block level and replaced elements

Syntax background-position: *value*

The background-position property enables you to set the position of an image added with background-image. You specify a position length, a percentage, or a keyword such as center and the image is adjusted behind the element. In the following example, you see the two properties combined to add and position a background on a web page. If tiling of the image is in effect, the tiling begins at the new position of the background.

```
body { background-image: url(stripes.gif);
       background-position: center bottom }

body { background-image: url(background.gif) };
       background-position: 50% 100% }
```

> With Explorer 3, you have to use the background property and not background-image to get these values to work. Also, in Explorer 3, background-position works *only* on background images styled to the <body> tag. You can't control the position of an image background behind a <p> element, for example—just the entire page.

Percentage values for background-position always appear as a pair. The first value always refers to the horizontal positioning; the second declares the vertical positioning. Values can range from 0% to 100%. Using this rule and values of 0%, the browser places the upper-left corner of the background image exactly at the upper-left corner of the "box" that surrounds the actual content of element. This is the default placement. In this next example, the position is defined at 50% of the horizontal and vertical:

```
BODY { background-image: url(background.gif);
       background-position: 50% 50% }
```

For this rule, the browser takes the point halfway (50%) over in the background image (the horizontal center, that is) and places it halfway across the <body> element (the browser window). In other words, it centers the background image horizontally. Also, it places the vertical middle of the background image halfway down the browser window, thus centering the image vertically. Now that the initial tile is placed, the browser tiles the background image across (to the right) and down the way it normally does (see Figure 1).

Figure 1

*The initial back-
ground image is
aligned in the exact
center of the
window, then tiled.*

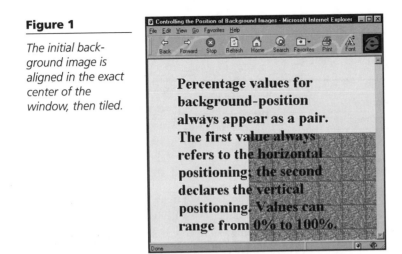

If the values are identical, such as 35% 35%, you can simply state the value once, and the browser will assume you mean 35% for both horizontal and vertical placement. A final note about percentage values: resizing the browser window will cause the background image to move, because the percentages depend on the size of the window.

Positioning background images by length value works much the same way as percentages. The first number declares a horizontal distance from the top left, and the second number a vertical distance from the top left. You can use any of the length units discussed in Appendix D. You may specify one or two values as well.

 Explorer 3 does not accept length values for `background-position`.

Your final option for `background-position` is to use a keyword. Here are all the keywords and their corresponding percentage values:

- `top` (0%)
- `bottom` (100%)
- `left` (0%)
- `right` (100%)
- `center` (50%) (may be used for horizontal and vertical)

As always, the first value specifies horizontal placement, and the second vertical placement.

```
body { background-image: url(face.gif);
       background-repeat: repeat-y;
       background-position: top center }
```

B

In this example, the center of the top of the background image is placed at the center of the top of the window (see Figure 2). In other words, top is the same as specifying 0%, and center is the same as 50%. A value of center top would mean exactly the same thing; order is irrelevant. (Note that for this example, horizontal tiling is turned off with background-repeat set to repeat-y.)

Figure 2

The result of top center positioning.

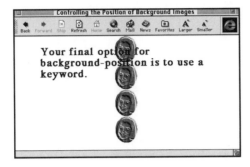

 Explorer 3 also supports a value of middle—middle specifies only vertical positioning, although center can specify both vertical and horizontal positioning.

If only one position is specified, then the browser will usually assume the other should be center.

Well, Explorer 3 handles this a bit differently:

- Specify only left, and Explorer adds top
- Specify only right, and Explorer adds bottom
- Specify only top, and Explorer adds left
- Specify only bottom, and Explorer adds left
- Specify only center, and Explorer adds center
- Specify only middle, and Explorer adds left

A final note about background images and positions: If an image doesn't scroll but is fixed on the browser window (via fixed), then any position values are relative to the entire window, not just to the element.

background-repeat

Category: Cascading Style Sheets

Browser Support		Navigator 3	Navigator 4	Explorer 3	Explorer 4
	Macintosh	☐	☐	■	■
	Windows	☐	☐	■	▬

Applies To All elements

Syntax `background-repeat: value`

With `background-repeat`, you can finally control exactly how background images tile or don't tile across an area. For textured backgrounds, you may still want to repeat the image. For more graphic images, however, such as landscapes or scenes, removing the tiling enables you to display only one copy of the image regardless of the size of your page or the size of browser window. To use this property, there has to be a background image defined through `background-image` or `background`. The four values for the repeat are:

- `no-repeat` means the background image won't repeat at all, but instead display just once.
- `repeat` causes the background image to repeat (tile) as it normally does (horizontally and vertically) to fill the entire space.
- `repeat-x` makes the background image tile only horizontally.
- `repeat-y` forces the background image to tile only vertically.

The default value is `repeat`. If `background-repeat` is not used or specified the effect of `repeat` will occur (the images will repeat to fill the entire space).

```
h1 { background-image: url(stripes.gif);
     background-repeat: repeat-x }
```

```
h1 { background-image: url(background.gif) };
     background-repeat: no-repeat }
```

 Reminder: With Explorer 3, you have to use the `background` property to get these repeat values to work; `background-repeat` won't work.

<BASE>

Category: HTML

Browser Support		Navigator 3	Navigator 4	Explorer 3	Explorer 4
	Macintosh	■	■	■	■
	Windows	■	■	■	■

May Contain	None
May Be Used In	<HEAD>
Attributes	HREF, TARGET
Syntax	<BASE>...</BASE>

The <BASE> tag is used to verify the exact location of a web page by listing a URL. It should always appear within the <HEAD> tag, as follows, or it will not work:

```
<HEAD>
<BASE HREF="www.provider.com/page1.html">
</HEAD>
```

Notice, though, that a closing tag, or </BASE>, is not always required.

The <BASE> tag is not often necessary because web browsers will usually know the location of a web page. However, if someone uses a mirrored site to find your web page (not a common occurrence) you should include the <BASE> tag in the HTML of your page to resolve relative URLs.

<BASE> can also be particularly useful for pages that might be moved around—especially for pages that might briefly appear as indexes and then become archived in another folder. The base URL for things such as links and graphics then remains the same as it was for the original index document.

For example, in an HTML document that contains

```
<BASE HREF="http://www.provider.com">
```

the relative URL

```
<IMG SRC="johndoe/page1/image1.gif">
```

corresponds with this image's full URL, which is

```
http://www.provider.com/johndoe/page1/image1.gif
```

You'd need to use the <BASE> tag to specify the entire URL; otherwise, someone linking to your site from a mirrored site would not be able to download the image.

> **NOTE**   The <BASE> URL may be overridden by an HTTP header if it's included. See HTTP for more information.

HREF

The HREF attribute is used to specify the web page's URL, just as it's used as part of the LINK and ANCHOR tags, or any other tag that requires a specific location.

TARGET

The TARGET attribute specifies precisely where all the links on the web page should load up. The _window value loads up all links or images on the page into a specific window, as indicated by an alphanumeric sequence or one of the following:

_blank	Loads the link or image into an unnamed, new blank window
_parent	Loads the link or image into the immediate parent window
_self	Loads the link or image into the same window
_top	Loads the link or image into the entire, full body of the window

<BASEFONT>

Category: HTML

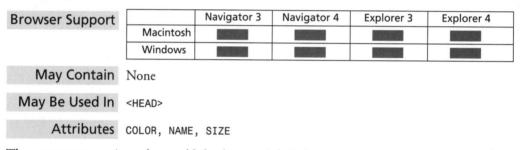

Browser Support		Navigator 3	Navigator 4	Explorer 3	Explorer 4
	Macintosh	▪	▪	▪	▪
	Windows	▪	▪	▪	▪

May Contain None

May Be Used In <HEAD>

Attributes COLOR, NAME, SIZE

The <BASEFONT> tag is used to establish a base or default font name, color, and point size for a specific block of text. A closing, or </BASEFONT>, tag is not required, but this tag must be placed within the <HEAD> tag, usually situated at the top of the HTML document.

<BASEFONT> has three attributes: COLOR, used to customize the font color; FACE, used to customize the font type; and SIZE, used to customize the font size. Each of these attributes may be used independently, so that if, for example, a COLOR attribute is specified but not FACE and/or SIZE, the font type and font size will remain at their default settings.

COLOR

The COLOR attribute specifies the color of the base font using either color names or hexadecimal values, enabling you to display page text in some other color than its default, black.

The following examples, then:

<HEAD><BASEFONT COLOR=green></HEAD>

or

<HEAD><BASEFONT COLOR="#008000"></HEAD>

will produce the same color—in this case, a bright kelly or grass green.

B

DESIGN NOTE   If you ever have the opportunity to view the same web page on a Macintosh and a PC sitting side by side, take it—even if this book contained color figures, it still couldn't depict the subtle differences between different monitors because of color calibration. In other words, you can look at the same web page on two different machines, of similar or different platforms, and the colors won't look exactly the same. You can't compensate for this hardware dilemma in HTML, but it is something you should consider when designing a web page.

There are 16 colors you can specify by name and many more to choose from if you specify them by hexadecimal value. Color information and codes are discussed thoroughly in Appendix B, so see it for more details.

FACE

The FACE attribute enables you to specify one or more particular fonts if you don't like the Macintosh or PC default settings.

Hence, the following example

```
<HEAD><BASEFONT FACE="Courier, Chantilly, Chicago"><HEAD>
```

will establish Courier as the font for all text on the web page. If a visitor's computer doesn't have Courier installed, the browser will look for Chantilly, and then Chicago if necessary. If none of the fonts specified by the FACE attribute are present, then the browser will revert to the default font as if the FACE attribute wasn't even present.

DESIGN NOTE   If you change the base font, choose common fonts that most visitors to your web page will have on their computers.

Why do typefaces look different on a Macintosh versus a PC if the HTML is exactly the same?

First, the most common typefaces look slightly different on a Macintosh versus a PC and vice versa—close, but not quite the same. Second, there's the issue of size—12-point type on a Macintosh does not resemble 12-point type on a PC. Why do fonts appear larger on a Windows monitor than on a Macintosh monitor? It's yet another frustrating hardware discrepancy, like the color difference dilemma, that you cannot solve with regular HTML.

DESIGN NOTE   Style sheets will give you more choices and more control over fonts. See the "Cascading Style Sheets Basics" chapter and have a look at Appendix C on fonts.

SIZE

The Internet Explorer–specific SIZE attribute specifies the relative size of the base font. The SIZE-specified value isn't measured in points as in desktop publishing or word processing programs, but by the numbers 1 through 7, with 7 being the largest and 3 being the default. To increase or decrease this default size, you would use the <FONT> tag in the body of the HTML document with its SIZE attribute and a value of –7 to 7, depending upon how you want to vary your text size.

In the following example, the base font size has been specified to 2, increasing the font size by two increments above the default of 3, while the <FONT> tag and related SIZE attribute are also used to increase and decrease the relative size:

```
<HEAD><BASEFONT SIZE=2></HEAD>
<BODY>
<P>The size of this text is only affected by the BASEFONT tag.<BR>
<P><FONT="1">The size of this text has been enlarged by the FONT tag.<BR>
<P><FONT="-2">The size of this text has been decreased by the FONT tag.<BR>
</BODY>
```

You can conversely decrease the base font in degrees by using negative numbers, –1 through –7, if you prefer. It's important to note, however, that all relative font settings elsewhere in your HTML document will be established based on the SIZE-specified number. So if you choose either a very small or very large SIZE value now and a very small or very large <FONT> setting later on, you may find you've created problems.

You also need to take the differences between browsers and the differences between platforms into account—as mentioned, SIZE is, at this writing, not supported by Navigator. Navigator, therefore, will ignore all your careful SIZE settings and display all text at an approximate default of 3.

At the same time, keep in mind that all these <BASEFONT> and subsequent <FONT> settings are relative numbers that only enable you to control the relationship between settings in your page. A visitor to your web site could have a very different default font size established on their computer from the default size established on yours. So you should always use the <BASEFONT> and <FONT> tag relationship with moderation and realistic expectations.

See the <FONT> tag entry elsewhere in the book for more information.

DESIGN NOTE The irony of all this numerical monkey business is, even with all these settings, you *still* don't have much choice when it comes to the appearance of text on your web page—and when it comes to Navigator (the most popular web browser software in the world), you have none at all! This is where the beauty, ease, and usefulness of style sheets comes in—see the "Cascading Style Sheets Basics" chapter for more information on how to take better control of your fonts.

<BGSOUND>

Category: HTML

Browser Support		Navigator 3	Navigator 4	Explorer 3	Explorer 4
	Macintosh	☐	☐	■	■
	Windows	☐	☐	■	■

May Contain   None

May Be Used In   `<BODY>`

Attributes   `SRC, LOOP, DELAY`

Syntax   `<BGSOUND>...</BGSOUND>`

The `<BGSOUND>` tag is an Internet Explorer–specific sound tag that enables you to create a soundtrack for your web site that plays in the background while users browse each individual page. The `SRC`, `LOOP`, and `DELAY` attributes work together to specify the sound or music file you want to play, how many times you want the file to play, and, if you want the file to play more than once, how long of a pause or delay should pass before the sound file starts again.

The `BGSOUND` tag and its attributes belong at the beginning of every web page's HTML document, inside the `<BODY>` tag with other `<BODY>`-related attributes (it is considered a background element). A closing, or `</BGSOUND>`, tag is not necessary.

It should be noted, though, that visitors to your web page will have no warning that a `BGSOUND`-specified soundtrack will play unless you add a warning message to your page. Visitors will also be unable to control the soundtrack, which they may find irritating, especially if the volume on their computer is turned up and they don't realize it until your soundtrack kicks in.

`<BGSOUND>` has other limitations—the sound file will only play while Internet Explorer is actually running as the foreground application, and even then, only when the window containing the tag is the frontmost window in Internet Explorer 3. Also, Explorer will also restart the soundtrack from the beginning each time the browser window is brought to the foreground.

You should also think about the file format of the sounds you want to use on your web page, as format issues can bring on as many headaches as the syntax of your HTML.

NOTE   There's no Navigator-only equivalent for the `<BGSOUND>` tag, but you can use the `<EMBED>` tag to give visitors a sound file they can play, stop, and loop at will. It is possible to use both the `<BGSOUND>` and the `<EMBED>` tags in one HTML document if you want to cover all your bases (so to speak)—you'll learn how to do this later on in this entry and in the `<EMBED>` tag entry.

SRC

The SRC attribute specifies the sound file you want to use as your soundtrack. In the following example, sound.wav is the name of the sound file:

```
<BGSOUND SRC="sound.wav">
```

SRC is the one <BGSOUND> attribute you will always need to use if you want to add background sound to your web page. The other attributes are all optional.

LOOP

The LOOP attribute tells the browser how many times to play the sound file. The LOOP value can be either a number or INFINITE. Strangely, using either the number 1 or the INFINITE value produces the same result: a nonstop, continuous soundtrack. The minimum number of loops you can specify, therefore, is 2.

In the following example, the number 5 stands for five loops:

```
<BGSOUND SRC="sound.wav" LOOP=5>
```

Leaving the LOOP attribute out completely is the only way to make your soundtrack sound file play only once.

DELAY

The DELAY attribute specifies the length of a pause between loops of your soundtrack in seconds.

In the following example, the DELAY value has been specified as 3 to establish a three-second delay between each loop:

```
<BGSOUND SRC="sound.wav" LOOP=5 DELAY=3>
```

If you don't use the DELAY attribute, your soundtrack sound file will play endlessly with no pauses between loops, which might also annoy a visitor to your web page.

<BIG>

Category: HTML

Browser Support		Navigator 3	Navigator 4	Explorer 3	Explorer 4
	Macintosh	■	■	■	■
	Windows	■	■	■	■

May Contain <APPLET>, <B>, <BASEFONT>, <BIG>, <BR>, <CITE>, <CODE>, <DFN>, <EM>, <FONT>, <I>, <IMG>, <INPUT>, <KBD>, <MAP>, <SAMP>, <SELECT>, <SMALL>, <STRIKE>, <STRONG>, <SUB>, <SUP>, <TEXTAREA>, <TT>, <U>, <VAR>

May Be Used In <ADDRESS>, <APPLET>, <B>, <BIG>, <BLOCKQUOTE>, <CAPTION>, <CENTER>, <CITE>, <CODE>, <DD>, <DT>, <FONT>, <H1>, <H2>,

```
<H3>, <H4>, <H5>, <H6>, <I>, <KBD>, <LI>, <P>, <SAMP>,
<SMALL>, <STRIKE>, <STRONG>, <SUB>, <SUP>, <TD>, <TH>,
<TT>, <U>
```

Syntax `<BIG>...</BIG>`

The `<BIG>` tag is used to increase the point size of plain text by one size to 14. Everything written between the opening and closing, or `</BIG>`, tags will be displayed on a web page one point size larger than the default size of 12.

The `<BIG>` tag is used to increase the point size of a specified block of text by one screen font size increment. In other words, text as displayed on a web page is sized in 8-, 10-, 12-, 14-, 18-, and 24-point increments, so that if the rest of the text on a web page is 12-point, any text specified as `<BIG>` will be 14-point instead.

In the following example, regularly sized and appearing text is outside the `<BIG>` tags:

```
This is normal size text. <BIG> But this text has been made larger using the BIG
tag.</BIG>
```

Figure 1 shows a comparison of regular, default-sized text and `<BIG>`-specified text.

Figure 1

The top line of text is regular size, while the second is tagged as `<BIG>`.

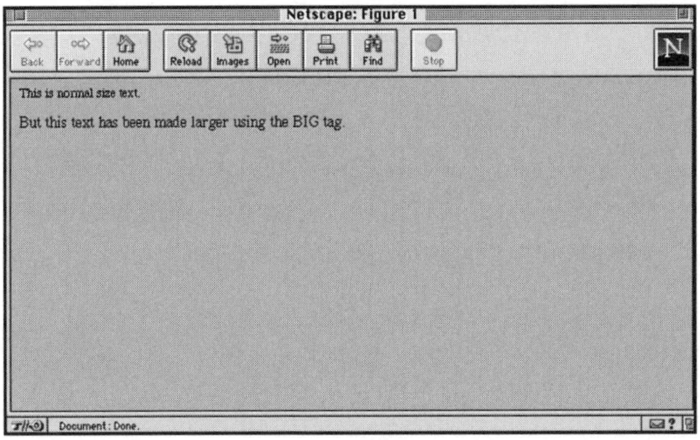

`<blackface>`

Category: HTML

Browser Support WebTV Internet Terminal

Applies To Text

Syntax `<blackface>...</blackface>`

You use the `<blackface>` tag to display text with a double boldface attribute. This emphasizes the text over other items on your page including text displayed in normal boldface.

```
<blackface> Up To The Minute World News </blackface>
```

<BLINK>

Category: HTML

Browser Support

	Navigator 3	Navigator 4	Explorer 3	Explorer 4
Macintosh	■	■	☐	☐
Windows	■	■	☐	☐

May Contain <B>, <BIG>, <CITE>, <CODE>, <DFN>, <EM>, <I>, <KBD><SAMP>, <SMALL>, <STRIKE>, <STRONG>, <SUB>, <SUP>, <TT>, <U>

May Be Used In <ADDRESS>, <APPLET>, <B>, <BIG>, <BLOCKQUOTE>, <CAPTION>, <CENTER>, <CITE>, <CODE>, <DD>, <DT>, <FONT>, <H1>, <H2>, <H3>, <H4>, <H5>, <H6>, <I>, <KBD>, <LI>, <P>, <SAMP>, <SMALL>, <STRIKE>, <STRONG>, <SUB>, <SUP>, <TD>, <TH>, <TT>, <U>

Syntax <BLINK>…</BLINK>

The <BLINK> tag is a Navigator-only text effect tag that causes all the text between the beginning and closing, or </BLINK> tags, to blink. Using <BLINK> by itself does not otherwise affect text appearance, but you can use other tags to customize the size, color, font, and so on of the blinking text.

There is no Internet Explorer–equivalent tag at this writing—IE displays <BLINK>-specified text as regular, static words.

In the following example, "ON SALE NOW" is the text that will blink:

```
<P>The soundtrack is available on CD.<BR>
<BLINK>ON SALE NOW!</BLINK>
```

<BLOCKQUOTE>

Category: HTML

Browser Support		Navigator 3	Navigator 4	Explorer 3	Explorer 4
	Macintosh	■	■	■	■
	Windows	■	■	■	■

May Contain `<A>, <ADDRESS>, <APPLET>, <B>, <BASEFONT>, <BIG>, <BLOCKQUOTE>, <BR>, <CENTER>, <CITE>, <CODE>, <DFN>, <DIR>, <DIV>, <DL>, <EM>, <FONT>, <FORM>, <H1>, <H2>, <H3>, <H4>, <H5>, <H6>, <HR>, <I>, <IMG>, <INPUT>, <KBD>, <MAP>, <MENU>, <OL>, <P>, <PRE>, <SAMP>, <SELECT>, <SMALL>, <STRIKE>, <STRONG>, <SUB>, <SUP>, <TABLE>, <TEXTAREA>, <TT>, <U>, <UL>, <VAR>`

May Be Used In `<BODY>, <CENTER>, <DD>, <DIV>, <FORM>, <LI>, <TH>, <TD>`

Syntax `<BLOCKQUOTE>…</BLOCKQUOTE>`

The `<BLOCKQUOTE>` tag is traditionally used to set off quotations by indenting both the right and left margins. Some earlier browsers will also italicize the specified text, and in every case, no additional HTML is needed to create paragraph breaks or blank lines above or below. The closing, or `</BLOCKQUOTE>`, tag is required.

In the following example, the text that precedes and follows the `<BLOCKQUOTE>`-specified paragraph would conform to normal, plain text defaults:

```
<P>Lao Tzu said:
<BLOCKQUOTE>If there is right in the soul, there will be beauty in the person,
➥</BLOCKQUOTE>
and continued to add that such striving would ultimately bring about world
➥peace.<BR>
```

Figures 1, 2, 3, and 4 display this `<BLOCKQUOTE>` text in Navigator and Internet Explorer for both the Mac and the PC. Note the differences, especially, between the way Navigator and Explorer do and don't include blank padding space.

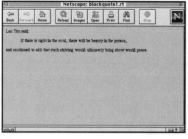

Figure 1

<BLOCKQUOTE> text as displayed in Navigator 3 for the Macintosh.

Figure 2

<BLOCKQUOTE> text as displayed in Internet Explorer 3 for the Macintosh.

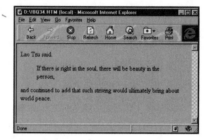

Figure 3

<BLOCKQUOTE> text as displayed in Navigator 3 for Windows.

Figure 4

<BLOCKQUOTE> text as displayed in Internet Explorer 3 for Windows.

> **DESIGN NOTE** <BLOCKQUOTE> should only be used to offset small portions of text, not to create generous margins around large blocks of text. Not only are there better, newer tags for this purpose, but there are better, newer methods of designing page layout (using tables and/or style sheets). Also, some browsers display <BLOCKQUOTE>-ed text in italics, which can be very difficult to read.

<BODY>

Category: HTML

Browser Support

	Navigator 3	Navigator 4	Explorer 3	Explorer 4
Macintosh	■	■	■	■
Windows	■	■	■	■

May Contain <A>, <ADDRESS>, <APPLET>, <B>, <BASEFONT>, <BIG>, <BLOCKQUOTE>, <BR>, <CENTER>, <CODE>, <CITE>, <DFN>, <DIR>, <DIV>, <DL>, <EM>, <FONT>, <FORM>, <H1>, <H2>, <H3>, <H4>, <H5>, <H6>, <HR>, <I>, <IMG>, <INPUT>, <KBD>, <MAP>, <MENU>, <OL>, <P>, <PRE>, <SAMP>, <SELECT>, <STRIKE>, <STRONG>, <SMALL>, <SUB>, <SUP>, <TABLE>, <TEXTAREA>, <TT>, <U>, <UL>, <VAR>

May Be Used In	<HTML>
Attributes	ALINK, BACKGROUND, BGCOLOR, BGPROPERTIES, CLASS, ID, LEFTMARGIN, LINK, TEXT, TOPMARGIN, VLINK
Syntax	<BODY>…</BODY>

The <BODY> tag is used to contain and define the actual contents of your HTML document. There are about a dozen <BODY> tag attributes that can affect all aspects of your web page's appearance—color, text, background, margins, and links—so refer to their individual headings for all the details.

You would place the opening <BODY> tag at the top of your HTML page along with all its various attributes so that everything listed after them—text, images, and links—would be properly displayed according to your <BODY> attribute choices. Accordingly, the closing <BODY> tag should be the next to last item in your entire HTML document. For example, if you place

```
<BODY BGCOLOR="yellow" LINK="purple" BACKGROUND="bckgrnd.gif">
```

at the top of your HTML document before writing the text and inserting the images and links, you would insert </BODY> as the very last item after your last line of text or your last image or link.

> **NOTE** If you're going to use many <BODY> attributes—more than you can comfortably pick out with one glance at your HTML document—it may be better to list them alphabetically rather than logically. (The order in which attributes are listed doesn't affect the way your browser interprets them, as long as they don't provide conflicting instructions.) In other words, if you're not using many other attributes, you might group LINK, ALINK, and VLINK together because these three are all related. But if you're using eight or ten attributes, for example, listing them in alphabetical order will pay off if you have to make changes.

ALINK

The ALINK attribute lets you customize the color of active links on your web page. This is the color that appears when a visitor rolls the cursor over a link and holds down the mouse key on it. You can use either color names or hexadecimal values to name the particular color you want—keeping in mind, however, that the Mac and Windows browser default color is cherry red.

If, for example, you want to specify the ALINK color on your page as teal, you could use the color name

```
<BODY ALINK="teal">
```

or the hexadecimal value

```
<BODY ALINK="#008080">
```

and the result would be the same color.

Remember, there are 16 color names that will always produce similar results regardless of computer platform because they originated as the standard Windows VGA palette. But, hexadecimal values will give you more flexibility and choice, even though they're obviously harder to remember. For the complete list of color names and more details on hexadecimal values and colors, see Appendix B.

> **NOTE**   David Siegel's *Creating Killer Web Sites* (Hayden Books) contains excellent information on colors and color palettes. Or, check out Lynda Weinman's *Coloring Web Graphics* (New Riders Publishing), and her online hexadecimal color charts at `http://www.lynda.com/colors/hexv.html/`.

BACKGROUND

The BACKGROUND attribute enables you to use an image as a background pattern or texture. It is *tiled*, or repeated, sort of like wallpaper, behind the text and graphics on your web page. Regardless of how long or wide your web page displays, browsers will automatically resize and rescale a BACKGROUND-specified image to cover the entire open window.

If `pattern.gif`, for example, is the texture you want to use as a background, you'd write:

```
<BODY BACKGROUND="pattern.gif">
```

> **DESIGN NOTE**   There are two design issues to keep in mind when using a BACKGROUND-specified image. First, never, *ever* use an image that makes it hard for people to see the text and images on your page—nobody will care how cool it looks if they can't read your page contents.
>
> Second, you must bow to the lowest common denominator where color monitors are concerned. Although most monitors display images in millions of colors, some people deliberately set their monitors to 256 or even 16 colors for faster navigation (as they disable images in their browser preferences, for the same reason). So your beautifully detailed, 24-bit image will be wasted—and it will take forever to load up.

BGCOLOR

The BGCOLOR attribute is used to specify a solid background color for an entire web page, either as a color name or as a hexadecimal value.

For example, if you chose maroon as your solid background color, the HTML would be

```
<BODY BGCOLOR="maroon">
```

or

```
<BODY BGCOLOR="#800000"
```

and you'd get a similar color.

As of this writing, there's no way to assign different background colors to different, specific areas of one web page using a background <BODY> attribute. You do have more discretion over area-specific color if you're using frames or tables. See the <TABLE> and <FRAME> sections for more information if this is what you want to do.

Again, for a complete list of colors you can assign by name and for more detailed information on hexadecimal color values, see Appendix B.

> **NOTE** Never use a background color that will interfere with the color of your text—this is easier to do than you may think, too. PC monitors display all colors several shades darker than Mac monitors do, so as a rule you should avoid all dark background colors unless you also specify your text color as something light (white, yellow, and so on). See the TEXT attribute section later in this entry for more information on customizing text color.

> **DESIGN NOTE** You should also consider whether or not your web page will be printed out—such as an online newsletter, index, meeting minutes, or something similar. A PC will print out a web page with a white background, but a Macintosh prints it as is, which is sure to drain all the ink from anybody's printer if the page background color is dark.

BGPROPERTIES

The BGPROPERTIES attribute is a way of "watermarking" or assigning a fixed background image to your web page that does not scroll or tile.

If you were to assign watermrk.gif as your background using BGPROPERTIES, the HTML would look like this:

```
<BODY BACKGROUND="watermrk.gif" BGPROPERTIES=FIXED>
```

BGPROPERTIES only works in Internet Explorer 3, so it's advantageous to also specify a tiling pattern using the BACKGROUND attribute or a solid background color using BGCOLOR:

```
<BODY BACKGROUND="watermrk.gif" BGPROPERTIES=FIXED BGCOLOR="yellow">
```

This modified HTML will give Netscape and other non-IE browsers something to interpret. Otherwise, Netscape will tile the watermark pattern as if it were a BACKGROUND-specified image, which may not be in keeping with your page design.

CLASS

The CLASS attribute is used to specify the name of a style sheets as it applies to a specific selection on a web page. See the "Cascading Style Sheets Basics" chapter and any individual, related style sheets entries elsewhere in the book for more information.

ID

The ID attribute is used to distinguish individual selections in a web page as pertaining to the use of style sheets. See the "Cascading Style Sheets Basics" chapter and any individual, related style sheets entries elsewhere in the book for more information.

LEFTMARGIN

The LEFTMARGIN attribute is an Internet Explorer–only feature that sets the left margin for the entire web page, overriding the default left margin setting. You can specify this new margin in pixels or inches, but if it's set to zero, the left margin will sit on the exact left edge of the page, right along the left side of the browser window.

If you wanted to set the left margin to approximately three inches, the HTML using a general pixel equivalent would be:

```
<BODY LEFTMARGIN="pixel">
```

> **NOTE** Roughly, one inch of space on a web page is equivalent to 72 pixels. This inches-to-pixels estimate works with any attribute that establishes space, such as LEFTMARGIN.

LINK

The LINK attribute enables you to customize the color of *unvisited* links, or links a visitor has yet to click, on your web page. You can use either color names or hexadecimal values to name the particular color you want—keeping in mind, however, that the Mac and Windows browser default color is royal blue.

> **DESIGN NOTE** Always remember that it is easy for the web surfer to customize their own link colors—both Netscape and Microsoft build this capability into their browsers' preferences files. So you cannot truly ever assume you know a web page's "default" colors.

Setting the LINK attribute to lime using a color name would look like:

```
<BODY LINK="lime">
```

and using the hexadecimal equivalent of lime would look like:

```
<BODY LINK="#00FF00">
```

For the complete list of color names and more details on hexadecimal values and colors, see Appendix B.

> **NOTE**   David Siegel's *Creating Killer Web Sites* (Hayden Books) contains excellent informa-
> tion on colors and color palettes. Or, check out Lynda Weinman's *Coloring Web
> Graphics* (New Riders Publishing), and her online hexadecimal color charts at
> `http://www.lynda.com/colors/hexv.html/`.

TEXT

The TEXT attribute changes the default color (black) of the plain, unlinked text on your web
page. Just as with the ALINK, LINK, and VLINK attributes, and the background color attribute
BGCOLOR, you use color names or hexadecimal values to choose a customized TEXT color.

TEXT is limited to the same restrictions as the other color-determining <BODY> attributes: you
cannot use TEXT to vary your basic text color from section to section, unless you're using frames
or tables. If this is what you want to do, see the FRAMES and TABLES entries elsewhere in this
book.

> **NOTE**   The same color considerations apply to using the TEXT attribute properly as they do
> to using the BACKGROUND attribute—you must choose readable colors that will not
> disappear or blur against the page background. Also, remember the PC color shift:
> PCs display all colors as darker than Macintosh displays colors, so maroon, brown,
> and/or forest green text can all look black on a PC and fine on a Macintosh.

To specify your basic body text color as purple using a color name, write:

```
<BODY TEXT="purple">
```

or to use the equivalent hexadecimal value, write:

```
<BODY TEXT="#800080">
```

For a complete list of color names, and more about hexadecimal color values, see Appendix B.

TOPMARGIN

The TOPMARGIN attribute, which can only be read by Internet Explorer 3, enables you to establish
a top margin in pixels. Similarly to the LEFTMARGIN attribute, if you set a TOPMARGIN specification
of zero, your page contents will appear at the very top of the page along the edge of the browser
window.

Set the TOPMARGIN attribute at 288 pixels, or four inches, for example, by writing:

```
<BODY TOPMARGIN="288">
```

VLINK

The VLINK attribute enables you to customize the color of visited links on your web page. You
can use either color names or hexadecimal values to name the particular color you want.

Setting the VLINK attribute to silver using a color name would look like:

```
<BODY VLINK="silver">
```

and using the hexadecimal equivalent of silver would look like:

```
<BODY VLINK="#C0C0C0">
```

For the complete list of color names and more details on hexadecimal values and colors, see Appendix B.

> **NOTE** David Siegel's *Creating Killer Web Sites* (Hayden Books) contains excellent information on colors and color palettes. Or, check out Lynda Weinman's *Coloring Web Graphics* (New Riders Publishing), and her online hexadecimal color charts at `http://www.lynda.com/colors/hexv.html/`.

border

Category: Cascading Style Sheets

Browser Support

	Navigator 3	Navigator 4	Explorer 3	Explorer 4
Macintosh	☐	☐	☐	☐
Windows	☐	☐	☐	☐

Applies To All elements

Syntax `border: color style width`

border is a shorthand property for defining the entire border around an element of object. The border is a box displayed around an element such as text or graphics. You specify up to three values for the border including a style, color, and width. The values you give are used around the entire object similar to using the border-top, border-bottom, border-left, and border-right properties. See the descriptions for border-style, border-color, and border-width for information on the values you can use for each setting.

```
h1 { border-bottom: thin solid blue }
```

```
<h1 style="border-bottom: dotted 8mm">
```

> If you want to display a border in Netscape Navigator 4 for Windows, you must use one of the following styles: bottom-border-width, top-border-width, left-border-width, right-border-width, or border-width. See the entries for these styles elsewhere in this book. Using border-style alone will not display a border.

Internet Explorer does not support borders of any kind.

border-bottom

Category: Cascading Style Sheets

Browser Support		Navigator 3	Navigator 4	Explorer 3	Explorer 4
	Macintosh	☐	☐	☐	☐
	Windows	☐	☐	☐	☐

Applies To All elements

Syntax `border-bottom: color style width`

border-bottom is a shorthand property for defining all aspects of just the *bottom* border in exactly the same way as `border-top`. You define up to three values for the border including a style, color, and width. If you include fewer than three, then the other aspects take on their default values. Because all the keywords involved are unique, the order of the values isn't important. See the descriptions for `border-style`, `border-color`, and `border-width` for information on the values you can use for each setting.

```
h1 { border-bottom: thin solid blue }
```

```
<h1 style="border-bottom: dotted 8mm">
```

If you want to display a bottom border in Netscape Navigator 4 for Windows, see the `bottom-border-width` style discussed in this book.

border-bottom-width

Category: Cascading Style Sheets

Browser Support		Navigator 3	Navigator 4	Explorer 3	Explorer 4
	Macintosh	☐	☐	☐	☐
	Windows	☐	■	☐	☐

Applies To All elements

Syntax `border-bottom-width: value`

The `border-bottom-width` property displays a border on the bottom of an element and dictates the width of the border. You may specify a length in units, or use one of the keywords thin, medium, or thick to set the width. The border appears as a line underneath the element. The default value is medium. Figure 1 shows using a bottom border to emphasize text.

```
h1 { border-bottom-width: thick }
```

```
h1 { border-bottom-width: 8mm }
```

Figure 1

Using a bottom border to emphasize text.

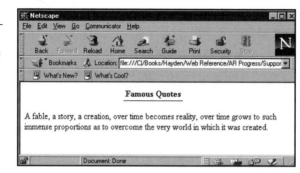

Bottom borders only display if you use the `border-bottom-width` style in Netscape Navigator 4 for Windows. The `border-bottom` style does not work in any version. Other styles, such as `border-style` and `border-color`, must be used in conjunction with `border-bottom-width`.

borderBottomWidth

Category: JavaScript Style Sheets

Type	Property

Browser Support

	Navigator 3	Navigator 4	Explorer 3	Explorer 4
Macintosh		▰		
Windows		▰		

Applies To	All elements

Inherited	No

Syntax	`borderBottomWidth = "value"`

`borderBottomWidth` is used to the set the width of the bottom border of an HTML element. This property can be used alone or in conjunction with any or all of the other `borderWidth` properties: `borderLeftWidth`, `borderTopWidth`, `borderRightWidth`. The `borderWidth` properties can take only one value:

■ The value of "`number`" defines the width of the border on the bottom of the element. "`number`" can be defined using any of the valid units of measurement available for HTML: points, em units, or pixels. For more information on units of measurement, see Appendix D.

Any of the following values for `borderBottomWidth` is valid to specify the width:

```
tags.p.borderBottomWidth = "3px"

tags.p.borderBottomWidth = "3em"

tags.p.borderBottomWidth = "3pt"
```

Defining a border width for only a single side of a border will can look strange in your document; but may prove useful depending on the style that you are attempting to achieve in your document.

An example of a border defined for only a single side of an HTML element is shown in the following code:

```
<html>
<head>
<style type="text/javascript">
classes.pclass.p.borderBottomWidth = "5px"
</style>
</head>
<body>
<p class="pclass"> This paragraph will have a border around it
marking it off from other paragraphs in the document.
<p> This paragraph below, does not have the same border.
</body>
</html>
```

Important to note in this code is the line `classes.pclass.p.borderBottomWidth = "5px"` which defines the border that we are referencing.

- `classes` denotes that this style is defined for a specific class only. This notation tells JSSS that the property immediately following in the dot notation will be a class name.

- `pclass` is the name of the class. This class name can be any alphanumeric combination, and will be referenced each time the class is used.

- `<p>` is the HTML element that the class will be valid for use with. This can be any valid HTML element.

- `borderBottomWidth` is the style that will applied to the `<p>` elements that use the style. Any valid JSSS style property can be used here.

- `"5px"` is the value of the style that will be applied. Each style property has its own set of define valid values.

The result of the preceding code is shown in Figure 1.

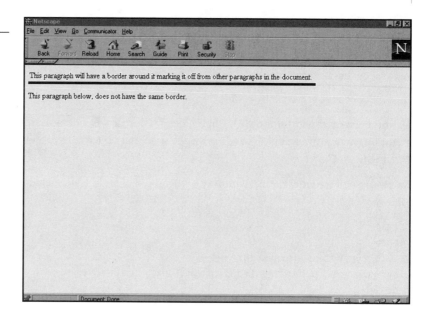

Figure 1

Bottom border is wider than on the other three sides.

Notice that below the paragraph there is a thick border line that does not exist on the other three sides of the paragraph.

border-color

Category: Cascading Style Sheets

Browser Support

	Navigator 3	Navigator 4	Explorer 3	Explorer 4
Macintosh	☐	☐	☐	☐
Windows	☐	■	☐	☐

Applies To All elements

Syntax *border-color: top_value left_value bottom_value right_value*

You use the border-color to define the color given to any or all of the four borders around an element. You can use any color name or value that is discussed in Appendix B. You can list one color to be used for the entire border, or up to four colors, which will be interpreted in this order: top, right, bottom, left. If no border-color is listed, then the border will take on the color of the element it surrounds.

```
h1 { border-color: #ff0000 }
```

```
h1 { border-color: olive green blue }
```

B

> If you want to display a border in Netscape Navigator 4 for Windows 95, you must use one of the following styles: `bottom-border-width`, `top-border-width`, `left-border-width`, `right-border-width` or `border-width`. See the entries for these styles elsewhere in this book. Using `border-color` alone will not display a border.

borderColor

Category: JavaScript Style Sheets

| | Type | Property |

Type Property

Browser Support

	Navigator 3	Navigator 4	Explorer 3	Explorer 4
Macintosh	☐	■	☐	☐
Windows	☐	■	☐	☐

Applies To All elements

Inherited No

Syntax `borderColor = "value"`

Once a `borderStyle` has been defined for an element, that border can be given color. `borderColor` cannot be defined without `borderStyle`, because as you see in `borderStyle`, element borders do not exist until they are defined with `borderStyle`. The `borderStyle` and `borderColor` are officially applicable for use with all HTML elements. A border can be defined around text elements and image elements. It can be seen through testing that better results are achieved with some HTML elements over others; but the style can applied to all elements if so desired. `borderColor` can take one of two values:

- ■ `"none"` is the value of `borderColor` that causes the border to have no color. This value is most useful for turning off a color that set with a previous `borderColor` style.

- ■ The other value is the `"colorvalue"` for the color. The color value can be assigned with two methods. The first is to used the named color, `"pink"`. The second is to use the 6–digit hexadecimal color, `"#FF0000"`, also a pink. (See Appendix B for more detail on color values.)

Based on the possible value choices, the following two styles would produce similar colors around the borders of the elements.

```
tags.p.color = "pink"

tags.p.color = "#FF0000"
```

As with any colors used in HTML, `borderColor` should also be used with caution in style sheets. The border for any particular element type may not always be the same, depending on the user input. Be careful not to define border colors that conflict with previously defined colors in other parts of the document.

The following code is an example of changing the border color of an element based on user input. Using the `tags` style property, the `borderColor` is defined as green.

```
<html>
<head>
<script LANGUAGE="JavaScript">
<!--
//-->
</script>
<style TYPE="text/javascript">
function ColorBorder() {
tags.body.borderStyle = "single";
tags.body.borderColor = "green";
}
</style>
Since this text is in the header of the document, it will not have a border
around it.
</head>
<body>
<p>This is the text in the body of my document. It will have a border around it
after I click the button
<form>
<input
          type = button
          name = "ChangeColor"
          value = "Change Color"
          OnClick = "ColorBorder()">
</form>
</body>
</html>
```

Using colored borders can make your documents more bold and let you be more creative in the styles that you define for your documents.

WARNING   The `borderColor` property does not display correctly in Netscape Navigator 4.0, because the required `borderStyle` property is not functioning.

border-left

Category: Cascading Style Sheets

Browser Support		Navigator 3	Navigator 4	Explorer 3	Explorer 4
	Macintosh	☐	☐	☐	☐
	Windows	☐	☐	☐	☐

Applies To All elements

Syntax `border-left: color style width`

`border-left` is a shorthand property for defining all aspects of the *left* border in exactly the same way as `border-top`. You define up to three values for the border including a style, color, and width. If you include fewer than three, then the other aspects take on their default values. Because all the keywords involved are unique, the order of the values isn't important. See the descriptions for `border-style`, `border-color`, and `border-width` for information on the values you can use for each setting.

```
h1 { border-left: thin solid blue }
```

```
<h1 style="border-left: dotted 8mm">
```

N— If you want to display a left border in Netscape Navigator 4 for Windows, see the `left-border-width` style discussed in this book.

border-left-width

Category: Cascading Style Sheets

Browser Support		Navigator 3	Navigator 4	Explorer 3	Explorer 4
	Macintosh	☐	☐	☐	☐
	Windows	☐	■	☐	☐

Applies To All elements

Syntax `border-left-width: value`

The `border-left-width` property dictates the width of the left border. You may specify a length in units, or use one of the keywords `thin`, `medium`, or `thick` to set the width. The border appears as a box around the element. The default value is `medium`.

```
h1 { border-left-width: thick }
```

```
h1 { border-left-width: 8mm }
```

Figure 1

Using a left border for special effects.

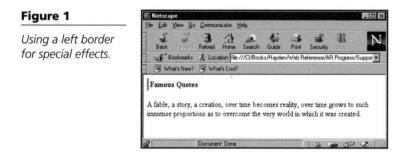

Left borders only display if you use the `border-left-width` style in Netscape Navigator 4 for Windows. The `border-left` style does not work in any version. Other styles, such as `border-style` and `border-color`, must be used in conjunction with `border-left-width`.

borderLeftWidth

Category: JavaScript Style Sheets

Type	Property

Browser Support		Navigator 3	Navigator 4	Explorer 3	Explorer 4
	Macintosh	☐	■	☐	☐
	Windows	☐	■	☐	☐

Applies To	All elements

Inherited	No

Syntax	`borderLeftWidth = "value"`

`borderLeftWidth` is used to the set the width of the left border of an HTML element. `borderLeftWidth`, as with any other `borderWidth` property, can be applied as a property to all HTML elements, although the results may vary depending on the element. For example, an `<img>` can take a `borderLeftWidth` but depending on the actual image, the border may not be visible. This property can be used alone or in conjunction with any or all of the other `borderWidth` properties: `borderBottomWidth`, `borderTopWidth`, `borderRightWidth`. `borderLeftWidth` also can only take one value:

B

■ The value of `"number"` defines the width of the border on the left side of the element. `"number"` can be defined using any of the valid units of measurement available for HTML: points, em units, or pixels. For more information on units of measurement, see Appendix D.

Any of the following values for `borderLeftWidth` is valid to specify the width:

```
tags.p.borderLeftWidth = "10px"
```

```
tags.p.borderLeftWidth = "1em"
```

```
tags.p.borderLeftWidth = "1pt"
```

Defining a border width for only some of the borders will look strange but could useful depending on the style that you are attempting to define in your document.

The following code segment and resulted document, shown in Figure 1, show the use of multiple lines of JSSS styles to define more than one style for a class:

```
<html>
<head>
<style type="text/javascript">
classes.pclass.p.borderBottomWidth = "5px"
classes.pclass.p.borderLeftWidth = "10px"
</style>
</head>
<body>
<p class="pclass"> This paragraph will have a border around it
marking it off from other paragraphs in the document.
<p> This paragraph below, does not have the same border.
</body>
</html>
```

Figure 1

The bottom and left sides have border.

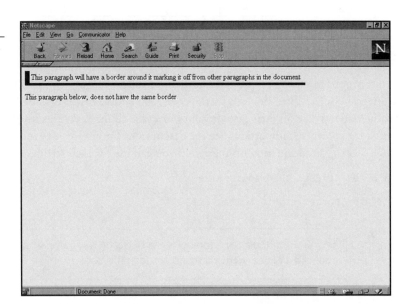

Using the two lines of style code

```
classes.pclass.p.borderBottomWidth = "5px"
classes.pclass.p.borderLeftWidth = "10px"
```

borders have been defined for the bottom and left sides of all paragraphs that are defined with `pclass`. Notice that there a many similarities between the two definitions. The lines can be broken down as follows:

- `classes` is the property that tells JSSS that the code immediately following will define a style class.

- `pclass` is the name of the class. This class name can be any alphanumeric combination, and will be referenced each time the class is used.

- `<p>` is the HTML element that the class will be valid for use with. (This can be any valid HTML element.) In our example, all `<p>` can take the pclass in their definition, but they do not have to take the class.

- `borderBottomWidth` and `borderLeftWidth` are the styles that will applied to the `<p>` elements that use the style. Any valid JSSS style property can be used here.

- `"5px"` and `"10px"` are the values of the style that will be applied. Our example uses the px (pixel) unit of measurement.

border-right

Category: Cascading Style Sheets

Browser Support		Navigator 3	Navigator 4	Explorer 3	Explorer 4
	Macintosh				
	Windows				

Applies To All elements

Syntax `border-right: color style width`

`border-right` is a shorthand property for defining all aspects of just the *right* border. You can include from one to three values for style, color, and width. If you include fewer than three, then the other aspects take on their default values. Because all the keywords involved are unique, the order of the values isn't important. See the descriptions for `border-style`, `border-color`, and `border-width` for information on the values you can use for each setting.

```
h1 { border-right: thin solid blue }
```

```
<h1 style="border-right: dotted 8mm">
```

N If you want to display a top border in Netscape Navigator 4 for Windows, see the `bottom-border-width` style discussed in this book.

border-right-width

Category: Cascading Style Sheets

B

Browser Support		Navigator 3	Navigator 4	Explorer 3	Explorer 4
	Macintosh				
	Windows		■		

Applies To All elements

Syntax border-right-width: *value*

The border-right-width property dictates the width of the right border. You may specify a length in units, or use one of the keywords thin, medium, or thick to set the width. The border appears as a box around the element, or in this case, the right border is displayed only on the right side. The default value is medium.

```
h1 { border-right-width: thick }
```

```
h1 { border-right-width: 8mm }
```

Figure 1

Using both a right and bottom border to emphasize text.

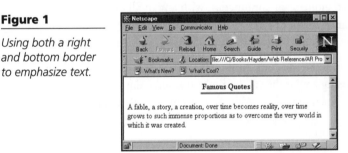

N

Right borders only display if you use the border-right-width style in Netscape Navigator 4 for Windows. The border-right style does not work in any version. Other styles, such as border-style and border-color, must be used in conjunction with border-right-width.

borderRightWidth

Category: JavaScript Style Sheets

| | Type | Property |

| **Type** | Property |

Browser Support			Navigator 3	Navigator 4	Explorer 3	Explorer 4
	Macintosh		☐	▇	☐	☐
	Windows		☐	▇	☐	☐

| **Applies To** | All elements |

| **Inherited** | No |

| **Syntax** | `borderRightWidth = "value"` |

`borderRightWidth` is used to set the width of a border on the right side of an HTML element. `borderRightWidth`, as with any other `borderWidth` property, can be applied as a property to all HTML elements, although the results may vary depending on the element. For example, an `<img>` can take a `borderRightWidth` but depending on the actual image, the border may not be visible. This property can be used alone or in conjunction with any or all of the other `borderWidth` properties: `borderBottomWidth`, `borderTopWidth`, `borderLeftWidth`. `borderRightWidth` has only one value that can be assigned to it:

■ The value of `"number"` defines the width of the border on the right side of the element. `"number"` can be defined using any of the valid units of measurement available for HTML: points, em units, or pixels. For more information on units of measurement, see Appendix D.

Any of the following values for `borderRightWidth` is valid to specify the width:

```
tags.p.borderRightWidth = "10px"
tags.p.borderRightWidth = "1em"
tags.p.borderRightWidth = "1pt"
```

Defining a border width for only some of the borders will look strange but could useful depending on the style that you are attempting to define in your document.

The following code, which defines borders for three of the four sides of a paragrpah, will produce Figure 1:

```
<html>
<head>
<style type="text/javascript">
classes.pclass.p.borderBottomWidth = "5px"
classes.pclass.p.borderLeftWidth = "10px"
classes.pclass.p.borderRightWidth = "10px"
</style>
</head>
<body>
```

B

```
<p class="pclass"> This paragraph will have a border around it
marking it off from other paragraphs in the document.
<p> This paragraph below, does not have the same border.
</body>
</html>
```

Figure 1

*The bottom, left,
and right sides have
borders.*

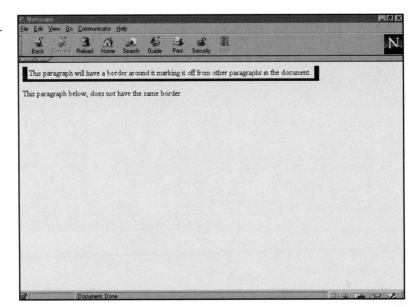

In the previous code listing, the important lines of code to note are the three contained within the `<style>` tags. These lines can be broken down as follows:

- `classes` denotes that this style is defined for a specific class only. This notation tells JSSS that the property immediately following in the dot notation will be a class name.
- `pclass` is the name of the class. This class name can be any alphanumeric combination, and will be referenced each time the class is used.
- `<p>` is the HTML element that the class will be valid for use with. This can be any valid HTML element.
- `borderBottomWidth`, `borderLeftWidth`, and `borderRightWidth` are the styles that will applied to the `<p>` elements that use the clases. Any valid JSSS style property can be used here.
- `"5px"` and `"10px"` are the values of the styles that will be applied. Each style property has its own set of define valid values.

border-style

Category: Cascading Style Sheets

Browser Support		Navigator 3	Navigator 4	Explorer 3	Explorer 4
	Macintosh				
	Windows		■		

Applies To All elements

Syntax `border-style: top_value left_value bottom_value right_value`

You use the `border-style` to define a style given to the four borders around an element. The border is a box displayed around the element. You may also set the style to one of the following values:

- `none`—no border is displayed at all, even if there is a `border-width` value
- `dotted`—a dotted line
- `dashed`—a dashed line
- `solid`—a solid line (this is the default value)
- `double`—two lines; the sum of the two lines and the space between them equals the value on `border-width`
- `groove`—a 3D groove in colors based on the value of `border-color`
- `ridge`—a 3D ridge in colors based on the value of `border-color`
- `inset`—a 3D inset in colors based on the value of `border-color`
- `outset`—a 3D outset in colors based on the value of `border-color`

The last four values are best used in conjunction with `border-color`. Values for the colors are discussed in Appendix B. Figure 1 shows examples of some of the styles listed here.

```
h1 { border-style: solid }
```

If you want to display a border in Netscape Navigator 4 for Windows, you must use one of the following styles: `bottom-border-width`, `top-border-width`, `left-border-width`, `right-border-width`, or `border-width`. See the entries for these styles elsewhere in this book. Using `border-style` alone will not display a border.

Netscape Navigator 4 for Windows does not support `dashed` and `dotted` borders.

Figure 1

Examples of the borders you can use to emphasize text and elements.

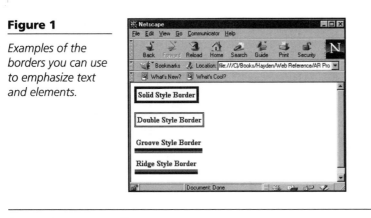

borderStyle

Category: JavaScript Style Sheets

Type	Property

Browser Support

	Navigator 3	Navigator 4	Explorer 3	Explorer 4
Macintosh		▬		
Windows		▬		

Applies To All elements

Inherited No

Syntax borderStyle = "*value*"

Setting the borderStyle style gives the power to define borders around any valid HTML element. Most elements do not normally have a border, so borderStyle not only sets the style of the border, but also in essence defines the existence of a border for the element. The are three possible borderStyles:

- ■ "none" is the default style and can be used to disable the border style if a previous style had been applied.
- ■ "solid" will cause a solid line border to be displayed around the element.
- ■ The "3-D" value defines a border style that has a three-dimensional appearance.

A useful implementation of borderStyle in JavaScript Style Sheets is during data entry sessions when output is displayed based on user input. A good example is an HTML form within an HTML document that has input fields, check boxes, or radio buttons for the user to click. Based on the user's input to the buttons, HTML text elements (like <p> or <body>) or output fields (which are initially empty) will receive data and a border can be displayed around them to enhance their look on the page and make them more apparent to the user. This works well when certain text is more important to one set of users than another. The user type can be determined based on a radio button click and then text important to the user can be highlighted for the user using a borderStyle.

The following code listing is an example of this scenario:

```
<HTML>
<HEAD>
<SCRIPT LANGUAGE="JavaScript">
<!--
//-->
</SCRIPT>
<STYLE TYPE="text/javascript">
tags.html.backgroundColor = "white";
if (tags.html.backgroundColor == "white" {
tags.body.borderStyle = "solid";
}
else {
tags.body.borderStyle = "3-D";
}
</STYLE>
Since this text is in the header of the document, it will not have a border
around it.
</HEAD>
<BODY>
<P>This is the text in the body of my document. It will have a border around it
if the background is white.
</FORM>
</BODY>
</HTML>
```

This code example shows two mutually exclusive checkboxes, that, when checked, will change the type of borderStyle used for the document.

WARNING The borderStyle property does not function correctly in Netscape Navigator 4.01. No borders are displayed around elements.

borderStyle is a valid property for every HTML element; however, some HTML elements because of their usage do not support borders, in these cases an error will not occur, the border will just not be displayed. The <em></em> element for example would not change if it had a borderStyle style applied to it.

border-top

Category: Cascading STYLE Sheets

Browser Support		Navigator 3	Navigator 4	Explorer 3	Explorer 4
	Macintosh	☐	☐	☐	☐
	Windows	☐	☐	☐	☐

Applies To All elements

Syntax `border-top: color style width`

border-top is a shorthand property for defining all aspects of just the *top* border. You can include from one to three values for style, color, and width. If you include fewer than three, then the other aspects take on their default values. Because all the keywords involved are unique, the order of the values isn't important. See the descriptions for border-style, border-color, and border-width for information on the values you can use for each setting.

`h1 { border-top: thin solid blue }`

`<h1 style="border-top: dotted 8mm">`

border-top-width

Category: Cascading Style Sheets

Browser Support		Navigator 3	Navigator 4	Explorer 3	Explorer 4
	Macintosh	☐	☐	☐	☐
	Windows	☐	■	☐	☐

Applies To All elements

Syntax `border-top-width: value`

The border-top-width property dictates the width of the top border. The border is a line displayed on top of the element. You may specify a length in units or use one of the keywords thin, medium, or thick to set the width. The border appears as a box around the element. The default value is medium.

`h1 { border-top-width: thick }`

`h1 { border-top-width: 8mm }`

Figure 1

Using a top and left border to emphasize text.

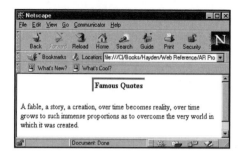

 Top borders only display if you use the `border-top-width` style in Netscape Navigator 4 for Windows. The `border-top` style does not work in any version. Other styles, such as `border-style` and `border-color`, must be used in conjunction with `border-top-width`.

borderTopWidth

Category: JavaScript Style Sheets

Type	Property

Browser Support

	Navigator 3	Navigator 4	Explorer 3	Explorer 4
Macintosh	☐	■	☐	☐
Windows	☐	■	☐	☐

Applies To All elements

Inherited No

Syntax `borderTopWidth = "value"`

`borderTopWidth` is used to set the width of the top border of any valid HTML element. `borderTopWidth`, as with any other `borderWidth` property, can be applied as a property to all HTML elements, although the results may vary depending on the element. For example, an `<img>` can take a `borderTopWidth` but depending on the actual image, the border may not be visible. This property can be used alone or in conjunction with any or all of the other `borderWidth` properties: `borderBottomWidth`, `borderLeftWidth`, `borderRightWidth`. `borderTopWidth`, like the other `borderWidth` properties, can only take on value.

- The value of "number" defines the width of the border on the top of the element. "number" can be defined using any of the valid units of measurement available for HTML: points, em units, or pixels. For more information on units of measurement, see Appendix D.

Any of the following values for borderTopWidth is valid to specify the width:

```
tags.p.borderTopWidth = "5px"
tags.p.borderTopWidth = "5em"
tags.p.borderTopWidth = "5pt"
```

Defining a border width for only some of the borders will look strange but could be useful depending on the style that you are attempting to define in your document.

In the following code listing, a top and bottom border are defined for the paragraphs. The result is seen in Figure 1.

```
<html>
<head>
<style type="text/javascript">
classes.pclass.p.borderBottomWidth = "10px"
classes.pclass.p.borderTopWidth = "10px"
</style>
</head>
<body>
<p class="pclass"> This paragraph will have a border around it
marking it off from other paragraphs in the document.
<p> This paragraph below, does not have the same border.
</body>
</html>
```

Figure 1

A bottom and top border are defined for the paragraph.

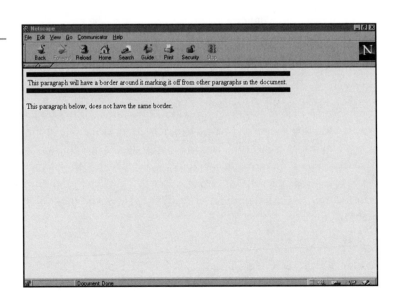

In the previous code lisitng, the important lines of code to note are the two contained within the `<style>` tags. You can see that multiple styles have been defined for the same class name. By defining styles this way, you can create full style definitions using a single class name. These lines can be broken down as follows:

- `classes` denotes that this style is defined for a specific class only. This notation tells JSSS that the property immediately following in the dot notation will be a class name.

- `pclass` is the name of the class. This class name can be any alphanumeric combination, and will be referenced each time the class is used.

- `<p>` is the HTML element that the class will be valid for use with. This can be any valid HTML element.

- `borderBottomWidth` and `borderTopWidth` are the styles that will applied to the `<p>` elements that use the clases. Any valid JSSS style property can be used here.

- `"10px"` is the value of the style that will be applied. Each style property has it's own set of define valid values.

Notice that the bottom and top borders have borders defined while the left and right sides remain normal. This type of border definition can be useful when the text above and below should be set off significantly from other text but it is not as important to separate any text or elements that may be on the left or right sides of the element.

`border-width`

Category: Cascading Style Sheets

Browser Support		Navigator 3	Navigator 4	Explorer 3	Explorer 4
	Macintosh	☐	☐	☐	☐
	Windows	☐	■	☐	☐

Applies To All elements

Syntax
```
border-top-width: top_value left_value bottom_value
right_value
```

The `border-width` enables you to set the widths of all four borders (top, left, bottom, and right) with a single property. You may specify a length in units or use one of the keywords `thin`, `medium`, or `thick` to set the width. The border appears as a box around the element. The default value is `medium`. This is a shorthand way to combine `border-top-width`, `border-right-width`, `border-bottom-width`, `border-left-width`. Refer to the descriptions of those properties for more information. You can also list fewer than four values, and they will be interpreted similarly to the `margin` property.

```
h1 { border-width: thick }
```

```
h1 { border-width: 8mm 16mm }
```

Figure 1

Using a border to emphasize text.

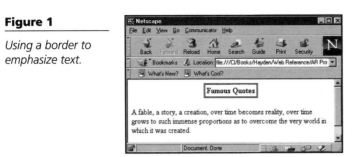

B

borderWidths()

Category: JavaScript Style Sheets

Type   Property

Browser Support

	Navigator 3	Navigator 4	Explorer 3	Explorer 4
Macintosh		■		
Windows		■		

Applies To   All elements

Inherited   No

Syntax   `borderWidths(value1,value2,value3,value4)`

`borderWidth()` is used to the set the width of all four `borderWidth` elements at the same time. This property is extremely useful when setting all four borders, because four separate `borderWidth` statements do not have to be used. Like the four other `borderWidth` properties, `borderLeftWidth`, `borderRightWidth`, `borderTopWidth`, and `borderBottomWidth`, the `borderWidths()` property also can only take one value.

■ The value of `"number"` defines the width of the border for the element. `"Number"` can be defined using any of the valid units of measurement available for HTML: points, em units, or pixels. For more information on units of measurement, see Appendix D.

Any of the following values for `borderWidths()` is valid to specify the width:

```
tags.p.borderWidths("10px", "10px", "10px", "10px")
tags.p.borderWidths("1em", "1em", "1em", "1em")
tags.p.borderWidths("1pt", "1pt", "1pt", "1pt")
```

`borderWidths()` are defined in the following order:

`tags.p.borderWidths(top,right,bottom,left)`

All four values should be specified but they do not have to be with the same value type. For instance, the following many produce some strange results but is a valid definition:

`tags.p.borderWidths("3em","5px","5ex","3px")`

The following code listing and the resultant document in Figure 1 uses the four separate border width properties to define the border widths for the class. Although correct, this definition is rather cumbersome.

```
<html>
<head>
<style type="text/javascript">
classes.pclass.p.borderBottomWidth = "5px"
classes.pclass.p.borderLeftWidth = "10px"
classes.pclass.p.borderTopWidth = "5px"
classes.pclass.p.borderRightWidth = "10px"
</style>
</head>
<body>
<p class="pclass"> This paragraph will have a border around it
marking it off from other paragraphs in the document.
<p> This paragraph below, does not have the same border.
</body>
</html>
```

The following code listing is a much cleaner and more consise `borderWidths()` definition. Although it will produce the same results, displayed in Figure 2, as the first code listing, it a better way to define borders for all four sides of an HTML element.

```
<html>
<head>
<style type="text/javascript">
classes.pclass.p.borderWidths("5px","10px","5px","10px")
</style>
</head>
<body>
<p class="pclass"> This paragraph will have a border around it
marking it off from other paragraphs in the document.
<p> This paragraph below, does not have the same border.
</body>
</html>
```

In the previous code listing, the borderWidths() line of code can be broken down as follows:

- classes is the property that tells JSSS that the code immediately following will define a style class.
- pclass is the name of the class. This class name can be any alphanumeric combination, and will be referenced each time the class is used.
- <p> is the HTML element that the class will be valid for use with. (This can be any valid HTML element.) In our example, all <p> can take the pclass in their definition, but they do not have to take the class.
- borderWidth() is the style that will applied to the <p> elements that use the style. Any valid JSSS style property can be used here.
- "5px" and "10px" are the values of the style that will be applied. Our example uses the px (pixel) unit of measurement.

Notice that in Figure 2, the borderWidths() proprerty produced indentical results to the four separate defintions of border widths shown in Figure 1.

Figure 1

Using four separate style definitions.

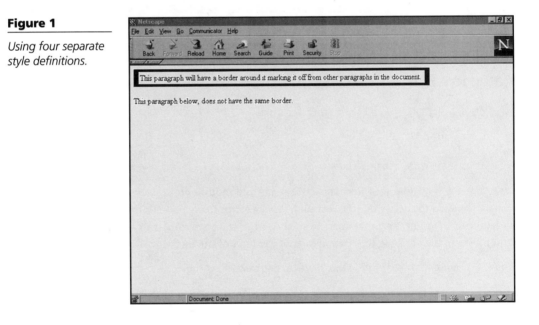

Figure 2

Using a single borderWidths() defintion.

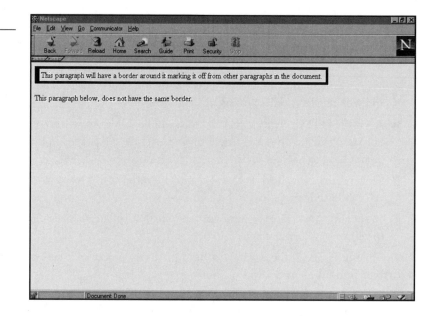

<BQ>

Category: HTML

Browser Support	WebTV Internet Terminal
Applies To	Text
Syntax	<bq>...</bq>

The <bq> tag is an alias for the <blockquite> tag and modifies text in exactly the same way. The <bq> tag is used to specify quoted text such as an excerpt from a book or play. The text is indented to the right, setting it apart from the rest of the page similar to a quote within a book. You must use the <br> tag to separate each of the lines of the quote.

```
<bq> All good things must also have a beginning. </bq>
```


Category: HTML

Browser Support

	Navigator 3	Navigator 4	Explorer 3	Explorer 4
Macintosh	▬	▬	▬	▬
Windows	▬	▬	▬	▬

May Be Used In   <A>, <ADDRESS>, <APPLET>, <B>, <BIG>, <BLOCKQUOTE>, <CAPTION>, <CENTER>, <CITE>, <CODE>, <DD>, <DFN>, <DIV>, <DT>, <EM>,

<FONT>, <FORM>, <H1>, <H2>, <H3>, <H4>, <H5>, <H6>, <I>,
<KBD>, <LI>, <P>, <PRE>, <SAMP>, <SMALL>, <STRIKE>, <STRONG>,
<SUB>, <SUP>, <TD>, <TH>, <TT>, <U>, <VAR>

B

Attributes Clear

Syntax
...</BR>

The <BR> tag is used to insert a line break or blank line between sections of content on a web page. The closing, or </BR>, tag is not required.

 is recognized by all the Navigator and Explorer versions listed in the Browser Support grid, but Internet Explorer does not recognize more than one <BR> listed successively. If you want to insert more than one blank line of space on your web page without browser considerations, use the <P> or <PRE> tags instead. See the <P> and/or <PRE> entries elsewhere in this book for more information.

CLEAR

The CLEAR attribute can be used to regulate the flow of text beside or below an image. There are four values you can assign to it:

Value	Result
all	The next portion of text in the web page will appear at the next full left and right margins beneath the image.
left	The next portion of text in the web page will appear beneath the image at the next full left margin.
none	The next portion of text in the web page will appear immediately beneath the image—this is the default CLEAR attribute setting.
right	The next portion of text in the web page will appear beneath the image at the next full right margin.

CLEAR-specified settings will only work in tandem with an image that has been ALIGN-ed left or right. Without these alignment specifications written in (even though left is the <IMG> ALIGN attribute default setting), the image will not "float" and the text will not wrap.

In the following example, shalott.jpg is the name of the inserted image and its alignment is specified as left:

```
<IMG SRC="shalott.jpg" ALIGN=left><BR CLEAR=right>This painting by John William
Waterhouse depicts Elaine, the Lady of Shalott from the legend of King Arthur.
```

Figures 1 through 8 illustrate all four CLEAR values using this example image and HTML in Navigator and Internet Explorer for the Mac.

Figure 1

Positioning an image and surrounding text using CLEAR all in Navigator 3 for the Mac.

Figure 2

Positioning an image and surrounding text using CLEAR left in Navigator 3 for the Mac.

Figure 3

Positioning an image and surrounding text using CLEAR none in Navigator 3 for the Mac.

Figure 4

Positioning an image and surrounding text using CLEAR right in Navigator 3 for the Mac.

Figure 5

Positioning an image and surrounding text using CLEAR all in Internet Explorer 3 for the Mac.

Figure 6

Positioning an image and surrounding text using CLEAR left in Internet Explorer 3 for the Mac.

B

Figure 7

Positioning an image and surrounding text using CLEAR none in Internet Explorer 3 for Windows.

Figure 8

Positioning an image and surrounding text using CLEAR right in Internet Explorer 3 for Windows.

Figures 9 through 16 illustrate all four CLEAR values using this same example image and HTML in Navigator and Internet Explorer for Windows.

Figure 9

Positioning an image and surrounding text using CLEAR all in Navigator 3 for Windows.

Figure 10

Positioning an image and surrounding text using CLEAR left in Navigator 3 for Windows.

Figure 11

Positioning an image and surrounding text using CLEAR none in Navigator 3 for Windows.

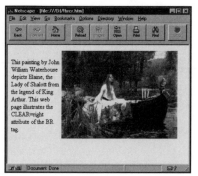

Figure 12

Positioning an image and surrounding text using CLEAR right in Navigator 3 for Windows.

Figure 13

Positioning an image and surrounding text using CLEAR all in Internet Explorer 3 for Windows.

Figure 14

Positioning an image and surrounding text using CLEAR left in Internet Explorer 3 for Windows.

 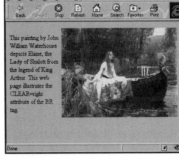

B

Figure 15

Positioning an image and surrounding text using CLEAR none in Internet Explorer 3 for Windows.

Figure 16

Positioning an image and surrounding text using CLEAR right in Internet Explorer 3 for Windows.

As is obvious in these examples, the authoritative description of what a tag or attribute will do can be very different from how things actually turn out. Remember that each browser—on each platform—interprets space differently, particularly when text and images are next to each other.

Button

Category: JavaScript, JScript, VBScript

| | Type | Object |

Type Object

Browser Support

	Navigator 3	Navigator 4	Explorer 3	Explorer 4
Macintosh	■	■	☐	■
Windows	■	■	■	■

Subset Of Form object

Properties `form, name, type, value`

Methods `blur(), focus(), click()`

Event Handlers `onBlur, onFocus, onClick, onMouseDown, onMouseUp`

Syntax `document.formName.buttonName.property` OR
`document.forms[index].elements[index].property` OR
`document.formName.buttonName.method(parameters)` OR

The button object provides script access to several characteristics of an HTML button form field element, created using the <input> tag as follows.

```
<input
    type="buttonType"
    name="buttonName"
    value="buttonText"
    [onBlur="eventHandler"]
    [onClick="eventHandler"]
    [onFocus="eventHandler"]>
```

There are, in addition to the standard generic all-purpose button, two special types of buttons: the submit and reset buttons. Typically, these buttons are used for communicating data to CGI programs on the server. Each of these buttons are a separate input type and have their own JavaScript objects, separate from the button object being discussed here (see Reset object and Submit object).

form **property**

form property is the read-only reference to the form object that contains the button object. This is a useful way to refer to another object in the same form. For instance, imagine a scenario where you want to reference a text object, named *text1*, which resides within the same form as the button object, button1. This can be used to code in shorthand, or eliminate the need to explicitly reference the full path to every element within a single form, as in the code excerpts:

JavaScript
```
path=document.forms[0].button1
value1=path.value
value2=path.form.text1.value
```

VBScript
```
set path=document.forms(0).button1
value1=path.value
value2=path.form.text1.value
```

name **property**

The name property is the read-only name of the button object, specified by the name attribute in the <input> tag.

```
objname = document.formname.buttonname.name
objval = document.formname.objname.value
```

type **property**

The type property is the input type specified by the type attribute in the <input> tag. Of course, this always contains the value "button" when referencing a button object.

```
objtype = document.formname.buttonname.type
```

Internet Explorer 3 does not support the `type` property.

value property

`Value` property is the read-only text displayed on the button, specified by the `value` attribute in the `<input>` tag. You *cannot* modify the text on the face of the button using the value property— it *is* read-only. In the case of a button which has no `value` attribute specified in HTML, its value property will contain an empty string.

```
caption = document.formname.buttonname.value
```

blur() method

The `blur()` method simulates the user losing focus from the button. Therefore, if the user currently has focus on the button, somehow triggering the following code would remove the focus:

```
document.formname.buttonname.blur()
```

focus() method

Click me!   The `focus()` method simulates the user gaining focus on the button. When the button element has focus, a thin dotted line appears around its perimeter.

You could use this method to direct a user's attention and input to a particular button.

```
document.formname.buttonname.focus()
```

WARNING   Be careful if and when you use the `focus()` method on a button that also contains an `onFocus()` event handler. In some scenarios within Netscape, this may result in an infinite loop wherein the `onFocus` event handler is repeated seemingly indefinitely. If your page is not operating as intended, this may be a cause to investigate.

click() method

The `click()` method simulates the user pressing the left (or only) mouse button atop the button element.

```
document.formname.buttonname.click()
```

NOTE   Whether or not simulating such an event triggers the `onClick` event handler depends on the browser being used. Within both Internet Explorer 3.0 and Navigator 3.0, the `click()` method of the button object *does not* trigger an `onClick` event handler to be called. Within Internet Explorer 4.0 and Navigator 4.0, this `click()` method *does* trigger an `onClick` event handler for this button element.

onBlur event handler

Located within the <input> tag, the onBlur event handler will activate when the user loses focus (that is, clicks or tabs elsewhere in the browser) from the button.

```
<input type="button" name=buttonname value="captiontext" onBlur="eventHandler">
```

onFocus event handler

Located within the <input> tag, the onFocus event handler activates when the user brings focus to the button element. When the user is using a mouse, the only way to bring focus to the button is to click on it—therefore, the onClick event handler is more commonly used. However, the user can also bring focus to the button using the Tab key, which consecutively brings focus to each element on the page. In this case, the onFocus event handler could be triggered without also triggering an onClick event.

```
<input type="button" name=buttonname value="captiontext" onFocus="eventHandler">
```

 Tab keying onto a button in Internet Explorer 3.0 does not trigger an onFocus event, even though the button does gain focus visually.

onClick event handler

Located within the <input> tag, the onClick event handler activates when the user clicks on and releases from the button. Commonly applied to a variety of circumstances, the onClick event often triggers a script function that acts on the form data. For instance, imagine a form that contains fields requesting the user's current loan balance and annual interest rate. This form could also contain a button that, when clicked, triggers an onClick event that calculates and displays the user's monthly payment.

The HTML creating the form would look something like the following:

JavaScript

```
<form name=interest>
<input type="text" name=balance width=10>Please enter your current balance<br>
<input type="text" name=apr width=3>Please enter your APR %<br>
<input type="button" name=button1 value="Click to calculate monthly payment"
onClick="calcpay(this.form.balance.value,this.form.apr.value)">
</form>
```

VBScript

```
<form name=interest>
<input type="text" name=balance width=10>Please enter your current balance<br>
<input type="text" name=apr width=3>Please enter your APR %<br>
<input type="button" name=button1 value="Click to calculate monthly payment"
onClick="calcpay  document.interest.balance.value,document.interest.apr.value">
</form>
```

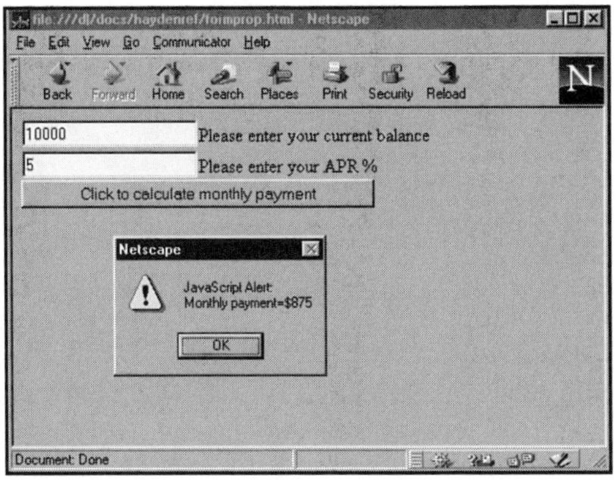

Figure 1

A simple form with a button element. When this button is clicked, an onClick event is triggered— in this case, calling a custom JavaScript function named calcpay( ).

B

onMouseDown event handler

Located within the <a> tag, this will activate when the user presses the mouse button on the button, but before the mouse button is released. This event handler can be used to determine if a user is "holding" the mouse button down over the button, as opposed to clicking (pressing and releasing).

For instance:

```
<input type="button" name=buttonname value="captiontext"
onMouseDown="eventHandler">
```

NOTE The onMouseDown event handler is only supported beginning with the version 4 releases of Netscape Navigator and Internet Explorer.

onMouseUp event handler

Located within the <a> tag, this activates when the user releases the mouse button on the button, after pressing it. In releasing the mouse button, the user has completed a click—however, the onMouseUp event occurs just prior to the onClick event. If your onMouseUp event handler returns true, the onClick event will be triggered and/or the form will be submitted; if this event handler returns false, no onClick event will occur.

For instance:

```
<input type="button" name=buttonname value="captiontext"
onMouseUp="eventHandler">
```

NOTE The onMouseUp event handler is only supported beginning with the version 4 releases of Netscape Navigator and Internet Explorer.

```
</STRONG>   </TD> </TD>    <TH>  </TH>    <TABLE> </TABLE>
<IMG> </IMG>   <SCRIPT LANGUAGE = "javascript"> </SCRIPT>
  <SCRIPT LANGUAGE = "vbscript"> </SCRIPT>   <BGSOUND
SRC=gbv.wav LOOP=-1> </BGSOUND>   <APPLET CLASS=
"ester's_day" SRC="http://testsite/walla walla washington/"
</APPLET>   <FRAME></FRAME>  <MARQUEE> </MARQUEE>     <HTML>
</HTML>   <A> </A>  <OL> </OL>   <UL> </UL>   <MENU> </
MENU>   <STRONG> </STRONG>   <TD> </TD>   <TH> </TH>
```

C

<CAPTION>

Category: HTML

Browser Support		Navigator 3	Navigator 4	Explorer 3	Explorer 4
	Macintosh	■	■	■	■
	Windows	■	■	■	■

May Contain <A>, <APPLET>, <B>, <BASEFONT>, <BIG>, <BR>, <CITE>, <CODE>, <DFN>, <EM>, <FONT>, <I>, <IMG>, <INPUT>, <KBD>, <MAP>, <SAMP>, <SELECT>, <SMALL>, <STRIKE>, <STRONG>, <SUB>, <SUP>, <TEXTAREA>, <TT>, <U>, <VAR>

May Be Used In <TABLE>

Syntax <CAPTION>…</CAPTION>

The <CAPTION> tag is used to specify a table caption. The caption belongs within the <TABLE> tag, like all other <TABLE> elements, but not within a row or cell. By default, a caption will appear horizontally centered within the borders and rules of its table, and a closing, or </CAPTION> tag, is required.

It is always a good idea to use the <TABLE> tag's BORDER and CELLPADDING attributes, if only just during the first few rough drafts of a table. BORDER by itself draws in all the internal and external lines so you can see where the boundaries of the table have been placed, and CELLPADDING gives cell text some room so you can see the effects of row, column, and cell vertical and horizontal alignment specifications. See the <TABLE> tag entry elsewhere in the book for more information.

The following example displays the proper placement of the <CAPTION> tag text:

```
<TABLE BORDER CELLPADDING=10>
<TR>
<CAPTION>The caption text, if there is any, goes here.</CAPTION>
<TD>Cell No. 1</TD><TD>Cell No. 2</TD>
</TR>
<TR>
<TD>Cell No. 3</TD><TD>Cell No. 4</TD>
</TR>
</TABLE>
```

<CAPTION> text will be automatically broken and wrapped within its cell, so no attributes or extra tags are needed to make it fit.

ALIGN

The ALIGN attribute specifies different alignments in the two different browsers covered in this book.

In Navigator, the ALIGN attribute can be used to center-, left-, or right-align a caption above a table or to center-align a caption below a table. In Internet Explorer, the ALIGN attribute center-, left-, or right-aligns a caption above a table only. Web page authors must utilize the Internet Explorer–specific VALIGN attribute to position a caption below a table. See the VALIGN section of this entry for more information.

Altogether, the ALIGN attribute has five values:

Value	Result
bottom	The caption text will appear centered below the table. Internet Explorer does not support this value.
center	The caption text will appear centered above the table. This is Explorer's ALIGN attribute default.
left	The caption text will appear left-aligned above the table. Navigator does not support this value.
right	The caption text will appear right-aligned above the table. Navigator does not support this value.
top	The caption text will appear centered above the table—this is also Navigator's ALIGN attribute default.

In the following example, center has been specified as the ALIGN setting:

```
<TABLE BORDER CELLPADDING=10>
<CAPTION ALIGN=center>This is the table caption.</CAPTION>
<TR>
<TD>Cell No. 1</TD><TD>Cell No. 2</TD>
</TR>
<TR>
<TD>Cell No. 3</TD><TD>Cell No. 4</TD>
</TR>
</TABLE>
```

Figures 1 through 6 display all the ALIGN options available in Navigator 3 and Internet Explorer 3 for the Mac and for Windows.

C

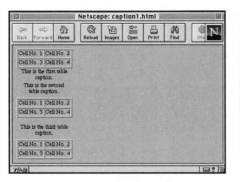

Figure 1

ALIGN options in Navigator 3 for the Mac—bottom, center, and/or top.

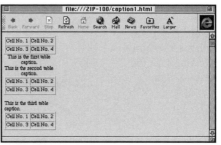

Figure 2

Three of six ALIGN options in Internet Explorer 3 for the Mac—bottom, center, and left.

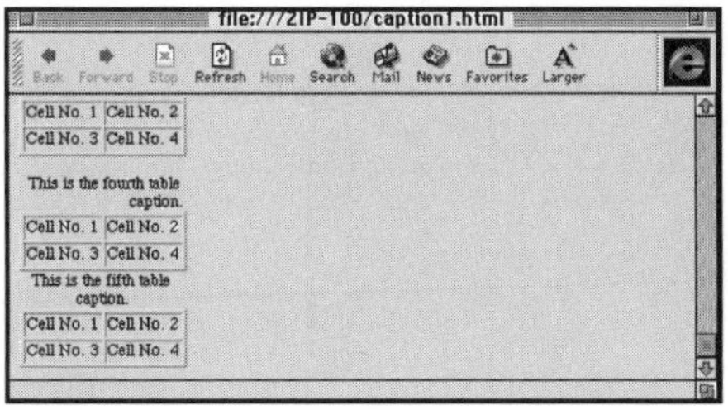

Figure 3

The rest of the six ALIGN options in Internet Explorer 3 for the Mac—bottom, center, and left.

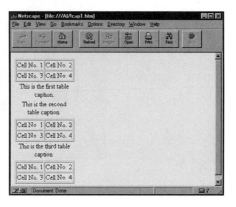

Figure 4

ALIGN options in Navigator 3 for Windows—bottom, center, and/or top.

Figure 5

Three of six ALIGN options in Internet Explorer 3 for the Mac—bottom, center, and left.

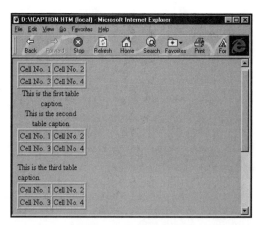

Figure 6

The rest of the six ALIGN options in Internet Explorer 3 for the Mac— bottom, center, and left.

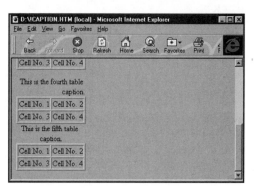

VALIGN

The VALIGN attribute is an Internet Explorer–only attribute that specifies a table caption placed either above or below the table body. At this writing, Internet Explorer for the Mac does not support VALIGN, so it is actually an Explorer-for-Windows-only attribute.

VALIGN has two values:

Value	Result
bottom	The table caption will appear centered below the table body.
top	The table caption will appear centered above the table body. This is the VALIGN attribute default.

In the following example, bottom has been specified as the VALIGN value:

```
<TABLE BORDER CELLPADDING=10>
<CAPTION VALIGN=bottom>This is the table caption.</CAPTION>
<TR>
<TD>Cell No. 1</TD><TD>Cell No. 2</TD>
```

```
</TR>
<TR>
<TD>Cell No. 3</TD><TD>Cell No. 4</TD>
</TR>
</TABLE>
```

The ALIGN attribute has also been specified with a value of bottom so that the table caption will appear in the same place in Navigator as it will in Explorer. See the ALIGN attribute section within this entry for more information.

Figure 7 displays captions specified by VALIGN as both top and bottom, in Internet Explorer 3 for Windows.

Figure 7

VALIGN top and bottom in Internet Explorer 3 for Windows.

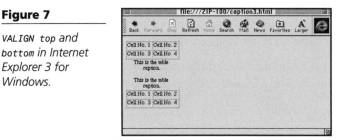

CBool()

Category: VBScript

| Type | Function |

Browser Support

	Navigator 3	Navigator 4	Explorer 3	Explorer 4
Macintosh				■
Windows			■	■

Syntax CBool(expression)

The CBool() function converts the result of expression into a Boolean value of true or false. If expression evaluates to 0 then false is returned; if expression evaluates to a non-zero number then true is returned.

CBool(5-5)   returns false

CBool(42-5)   returns true

If expression cannot evaluate to a number, then a run-time "type mismatch" error will occur. The exceptions to this rule are the strings "true" and "false", which if the result of expression, are returned respectively by CBool().

CBool("hiya") returns type mismatch error

CByte()

Category: VBScript

Type	Function

Browser Support

	Navigator 3	Navigator 4	Explorer 3	Explorer 4
Macintosh	☐	☐	☐	■
Windows	☐	☐	■	■

Syntax CByte(expression)

The CByte() function converts the expression to an 8-bit byte value. The expression must evaluate to a numeric value between 0 and 255. If the numeric value is outside this range, an overflow error will occur. Floating-point numeric values are rounded to the nearest integer and expressions other than numeric values passed to the function will cause an error.

On the surface, this function seems to return the same number that it was passed. Although true, you'd use this function when performing byte arithmetic (calculations using byte values).

```
CByte(100-20)          returns          80

CByte(256)             returns          overflow error
```

DESIGN NOTE The CByte() function is rather esoteric, and rarely used, because VBScript is not very strict about data types. In general, you'll only need to look up this function if you are specifically looking for its action, which is seldom if ever.

CCur()

Category: VBScript

Type	Function

Browser Support

	Navigator 3	Navigator 4	Explorer 3	Explorer 4
Macintosh	☐	☐	☐	■
Windows	☐	☐	■	■

Syntax CCur(expression)

The CCur() function converts expression to a currency value. The only requirement is that expression evaluate to any numerical value; any other expressions passed to the function will cause an error. You would use this function when performing calculations with dollar amounts.

```
CCur(100.23)    returns          100.23

CCur("bob")     returns          Type mismatch error
```

Because thousands of different thousands and decimal separators are used in currency representation throughout the world, use the CCur() function to convert monetary values into an "internationally aware," a currency data type subtype.

| DESIGN NOTE | The CCur() function is rather esoteric, and rarely used, because VBScript is not very strict about data types. In general, you'll only need to look up this function if you are specifically looking for its action, which is seldom if ever. |

CDate()

Category: VBScript

| Type | Function |

Browser Support

	Navigator 3	Navigator 4	Explorer 3	Explorer 4
Macintosh	☐	☐	☐	▉
Windows	☐	☐	▉	▉

| Syntax | CDate(date) |

The CDate() function converts the date parameter to a date subtype. The expression must be a string with a date or time that conforms to one of the following formats:

Format	Example
hh:mm	19:26
hh:mm:ss	19:26:47
hh:mm [AM/PM]	7:26 PM
hh:mm:ss [AM/PM]	7:26:47 PM
mm-dd-yy	3-11-97
mm-dd-yyyy	3-11-1997
mm/dd/yy	3/11/97
mm/dd/yyyy	3/11/1997
month dd, yyyy	March 11, 1997

A valid date must also be in the range of January 1, 1000 and December 31, 9999—any other expressions passed to the function will cause an error. Alternatively, you can also specify date as a negative integer, which will be interpreted as that many days prior to December 30, 1899.

CDate("may 20 1988")	returns	5/20/88
CDate("13:20:00")	returns	1:20:00 PM
CDate(-10)	returns	12/20/1899

CDbl( )

Category: VBScript

Type Function

Browser Support

	Navigator 3	Navigator 4	Explorer 3	Explorer 4
Macintosh	☐	☐	☐	■
Windows	☐	☐	■	■

Syntax CDbl(expression)

The CDbl() function converts expression to a double-precision floating-point value. Any numerical value can be passed to this function; any non-numeric expressions will cause an error.

Double-precision floating point values may reside within the range $-1.79769313486232E308$ to $-4.94065645841247E-324$ for negative values and $4.94065645841247E-324$ to $1.79769313486232E308$ for positive values.

DESIGN NOTE The CDbl() function is rather esoteric, and rarely used, because VBScript is not very strict about data types. In general, you'll only need to look up this function if you are specifically looking for its action, which is seldom if ever.

<CENTER>

Category: HTML

Browser Support

	Navigator 3	Navigator 4	Explorer 3	Explorer 4
Macintosh	■	■	■	■
Windows	■	■	■	■

May Contain <A>, <ADDRESS>, <APPLET>, <B>, <BASEFONT>, <BIG>, <BLOCKQUOTE>, <BR>, <CENTER>, <CITE>, <CODE>, <DFN>, <DIR>, <DIV>, <DL>, <EM>, <FONT, <FORM>, <H1>, <H2>, <H3>, <H4>, <H5>, <H6>, <HR>, <I>, <IMG>, <INPUT>, <KBD>, <MAP>, <MENU>, <OL>, <P>, <PRE>, <SAMP>, <SELECT>, <SMALL>, <STRIKE>, <STRONG>, <SUB>, <SUP>, <TABLE>, <TEXTAREA>, <TT>, <U>, <UL>, <VAR>

May Be Used In <BLOCKQUOTE>, <BODY>, <CENTER>, <DD>, <DIV>, <FORM>, <LI>, <TD>, <TH>

Syntax <CENTER>...</CENTER>

The <CENTER> tag is used to center text and images on a web page. The closing, or </CENTER>, tag is required and it also serves to reset alignment.

Hence, the following example:

```
This text is aligned normally.<BR>
<CENTER><IMG SRC="image1.gif"></CENTER>
This text is also aligned normally.
<CENTER>This text, like the image above, is centered.</CENTER>
```

Figures 1, 2, 3, and 4 display this example HTML in Netscape Navigator and Internet Explorer, for the Mac and for Windows.

Figure 1

Positioning an image and text using the <CENTER> tag in Netscape Navigator 3 for the Mac.

Figure 2

Positioning an image and text using the <CENTER> tag in Internet Explorer 3 for the Mac.

Figure 3

Positioning an image and text using the <CENTER> tag in Navigator 3 for Windows.

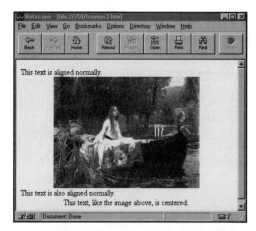

Figure 4

Positioning an image and text using the <CENTER> tag in Internet Explorer 3 for Windows.

> **DESIGN NOTE**
>
> The performance of the <CENTER> tag, like the <BASEFONT> and <B> tags, is affected by the difference between the way a web page is displayed by a Macintosh versus display on a PC. Remember that it's not just the size of the individual letters that's larger on a PC—it's also the size of individual spaces. So a <CENTER>-defined object or block of text will take up more room on a web page than on a Macintosh. You should allow for this variance in your web page design.

Checkbox

Category: JavaScript, JScript, VBScript

Type	Object

Browser Support		Navigator 3	Navigator 4	Explorer 3	Explorer 4
	Macintosh	■	■	☐	■
	Windows	■	■	■	■

Subset Of	Form object
Properties	checked, defaultchecked, form, name, type, value
Methods	blur(), focus(), click()
Events	onBlur, onFocus, onClick
Syntax	document.formName.checkboxName[index].property OR
	document.forms[index].elements[index].property OR
	document.formName.checkboxName[index].method(parameters) OR
	document.forms[index].elements[index].method(parameters)

The checkbox object is an on/off form field element. Checking the checkbox will result in an "on" (true) setting, while an unchecked checkbox will result in an "off" (false) setting. Checkboxes are commonly used for single questions that only have two possible answers. For instance, the question "Are you a smoker?" can only be answered yes or no. For questions that can be answered from a group of choices, see the Radio object and Select object.

A checkbox object is created using the <input> tag. The default value of the checkbox will be unchecked unless the checked attribute is supplied.

```
<input
    type="checkbox"
    name="checkboxName"
    value="valueToSubmit"
    [checked]
    [onBlur="eventHandler"]
    [onClick="eventHandler"]
    [onFocus="eventHandler"]>
    CheckBoxText
```

Figure 1

A checkbox form field.

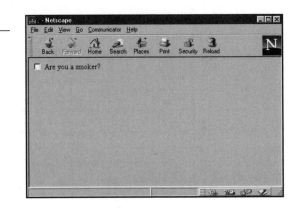

checked **property**

`checked` property is a Boolean value indicating the status of the checkbox. The value will be true for a checked checkbox and false for an unchecked checkbox.

```
checkval = document.formname.checkboxname.checked
```

Alternatively, by setting this property to true or false with script code, the appearance of the checkbox will change accordingly.

```
document.formname.checkboxname.checked=true
```

Figure 2

A selected checkbox form field.

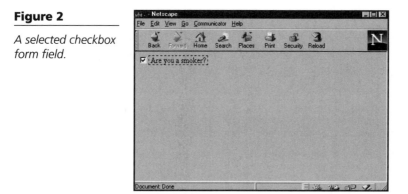

defaultChecked **property**

`defaultChecked` property is a Boolean value of true or false that denotes the default value of the checkbox; it is indicated by whether the `checked` attribute was supplied or not in the `<input>` tag.

```
defval = document.formname.checkboxname.defaultChecked
```

You can modify whether the checkbox will be checked by default, if the form is reset, by assigning a value to the `defaultChecked` property.

```
document.formname.checkboxname.defaultChecked=true
```

form **property**

`form` property is the read-only reference to the form object that contains the checkbox object. This is a useful way to refer to another object in the same form. For instance, imagine a scenario where you want to reference a text object, named *text1*, which resides within the same form as the currently interesting checkbox object, *check1*. This can be used to code in shorthand, or eliminate the need to explicitly reference the full path to every element within a single form, as in the code excerpts:

JavaScript

```
path=document.forms[0].check1
```

```
value1=path.value
value2=path.form.text1.value
```

VBScript

```
set path=document.forms(0).check1
value1=path.value
value2=path.form.text1.value
```

name property

name property is the read-only name of the group within which the checkbox object resides, specified by the name attribute in the <input> tag.

```
objname = document.formname.checkbox.name
objval = document.formname.objname.value
```

type property

Type property is the input type specified by the type attribute in the <input> tag. Of course, this always contains the value "checkbox" when referencing a checkbox element.

```
objtype = document.formname.checkboxname.type
```

Internet Explorer 3 does not support the type property.

value property

value property is the read-only text specified by the value attribute in the <input> tag. This is not the text that is displayed by the checkbox. Rather, it is the value that is sent to the server when this checkbox is checked on as the form data is submitted.

```
checkval = document.formname.checkboxname.value
```

If the value attribute was not specified in the HTML, this property defaults to the string "on."

Within Internet Explorer 3, if the value attribute was not specified in the HTML, this property contains an empty value.

blur() method

The blur() method simulates the user losing focus from the checkbox. Therefore, if the user currently has focus on the checkbox, triggering the following code would remove the focus:

```
document.formname.checkboxname.blur()
```

Internet Explorer 3.0 does not support the blur() method for the checkbox object.

`focus()` method

The `focus()` method simulates the user gaining focus on the checkbox. You could use this method to "force" a user to pay attention to a particular checkbox.

```
document.formname.checkboxname.focus()
```

WARNING Be careful if and when you use the `focus()` method on a checkbox that also contains an `onFocus()` event handler. In some scenarios within Netscape, this may result in an infinite loop wherein the `onFocus()` event handler is repeated seemingly indefinitely. If your page is not operating as intended, this may be a cause to investigate.

 Internet Explorer 3.0 does not support the `focus()` method for the checkbox object.

`click()` method

The `click()` method simulates the user clicking on the checkbox. Essentially, this has the same effect as assigning a true value to the checkbox object's `checked` property: the clicked checkbox will become checked onscreen, and its `checked` property will contain the value `true`.

```
document.formname.checkboxname.click()
```

Within Navigator and Internet Explorer 4, the `click()` method also triggers any `onClick` event handler defined for the particular radio button.

Within Internet Explorer 3, the `click()` method does not trigger an `onClick` event handler, although it does set the clicked object's value property to true and redraws the onscreen checkbox.

`onBlur` event handler

Located within the `<input>` tag, the `onBlur` event handler will be triggered when the user loses focus (that is, clicks or tabs elsewhere in the browser) from the checkbox element.

```
<input type="checkbox" name=checkboxname onBlur="eventHandler">
```

 Internet Explorer 3.0 does not support the `onBlur` event handler for the checkbox object.

onFocus event handler

Located within the <input> tag, the onFocus event handler will activate when the user brings focus to the checkbox element. When the user is using a mouse, the only way to bring focus to the checkbox is to click on it—therefore, the onClick event handler is more commonly used. However, the user can also bring focus to the checkbox using the Tab key, which consecutively brings focus to each element on the page. In this case, the onFocus event handler could be triggered without also triggering an onClick event handler.

```
<input type="checkbox" name=checkboxname onFocus="eventHandler">
```

> Internet Explorer 3.0 does not support the onFocus event handler for the checkbox object.

onClick event handler

Located within the <input> tag, the onClick event handler will activate when the user clicks on and releases from the checkbox. Typically, the onClick event handler is used when you want to trigger an action immediately conditional upon the state of a particular checkbox. For instance, imagine that you have a checkbox that, if checked, makes the page background black and foreground white, for easier contrast on some monitors. You would use an onClick event handler to trigger a change in the page's background and foreground color.

```
<input type="checkbox" name="color"Ø
onClick="document.bgcolor='black';document.fgcolor='white'">Check this to set
your color preference to white on black
```

Chr()

Category: VBScript

	Type	Function

Browser Support		Navigator 3	Navigator 4	Explorer 3	Explorer 4
	Macintosh				■
	Windows			■	■

	Syntax	Chr(number)

The chr() function returns the ANSI character specified by the ANSI code *number*. The character code *number* must be a numeric expression ranging from 0 to 255—any other value will cause an error.

chr(65) returns   A

chr(34) returns   "

chr(39) returns   '

The numbers passed to chr() are specified by the ANSI character code set standard, which assigns a value to each possible character.

The chr() function is especially useful when you need to output single or double quotation marks:

```
document.write("Look at my "&chr(34)&"quote marks"&chr(34)&"!")
```

The preceding statement would produce the output:

```
Look at my "quote marks"!
```

If you need to return a byte from a string containing byte data, use the alternative construction:

```
chrB(byteString)
```

On systems that use the 32-bit Unicode character set, use the construction chrW(*number*) to return the Unicode character for the character code *number*.

For detailed information on character codes and the ANSI and Unicode character sets, visit `http://www.bbsinc.com/iso8859.html`.

CInt()

Category: VBScript

	Type	Function

Browser Support

	Navigator 3	Navigator 4	Explorer 3	Explorer 4
Macintosh	☐	☐	☐	■
Windows	☐	☐	■	■

Syntax CInt(expression)

The CInt() function will convert the numeric *expression* to an integer value, rounding to the nearest integer if necessary. Fractional values of exactly .5 are rounded to the nearest even integer. Note that integer values may range from –32,768 to 32,767. Any other expressions passed to the function will cause an error.

cint(43)	returns	43
cint(43.5)	returns	44
cint(42.5)	returns	42

<CITE>

Category: HTML

Browser Support		Navigator 3	Navigator 4	Explorer 3	Explorer 4
	Macintosh	■	■	☐	■
	Windows	■	■	■	■

May Contain `<APPLET>`, `<B>`, `<BASEFONT>`, `<BIG>`, `<BR>`, `<CITE>`, `<CODE>`, `<DFN>`, `<EM>`, `<FONT>`, `<I>`, `<IMG>`, `<INPUT>`, `<KBD>`, `<MAP>`, `<SAMP>`, `<SELECT>`, `<SMALL>`, `<STRIKE>`, `<STRONG>`, `<SUB>`, `<SUP>`, `<TEXTAREA>`, `<TT>`, `<U>`, `<VAR>`

May Be Used In `<ADDRESS>`, `<APPLET>`, `<B>`, `<BIG>`, `<BLOCKQUOTE>`, `<CAPTION>`, `<CENTER>`, `<CITE>`, `<CODE>`, `<DD>`, `<DT>`, `<FONT>`, `<H1>`, `<H2>`, `<H3>`, `<H4>`, `<H5>`, `<H6>`, `<I>`, `<KBD>`, `<LI>`, `<P>`, `<SAMP>`, `<SMALL>`, `<STRIKE>`, `<STRONG>`, `<SUB>`, `<SUP>`, `<TD>`, `<TH>`, `<TT>`, `<U>`

Syntax `<CITE>…</CITE>`

`<CITE>` is an older tag used to specify a citation—a reference to a book, paper, or other published source material in a formal academic or scientific publication. Everything written between the beginning and closing, or `</CITE>` tags, will be italicized as shown in the example:

`<CITE>This text is specified as a citation using the CITE tag.</CITE>`

Figure 1 displays this HTML in Navigator 3 for the Mac.

Figure 1

Text written as a citation by using the `<CITE>` tag compared to plain default text.

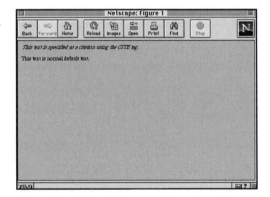

There's no functional difference between text that has been italicized using the `<I>` tag versus the `<CITE>` tag, as shown in Figure 2, so use either tag to italicize text as you prefer. Also see the `<I>` tag entry elsewhere in the book for more information.

Figure 2

The <CITE> tag versus the <I> tag— no difference.

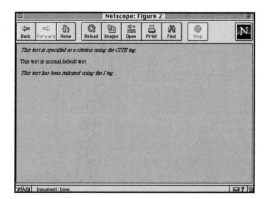

`classes`

Category: JavaScript Style Sheets

Type	Selector	

Browser Support

	Navigator 3	Navigator 4	Explorer 3	Explorer 4
Macintosh		▓▓▓▓		
Windows		▓▓▓▓		

Applies To	All elements
Inherited	Yes
Syntax	`classes.classname.element.proprety = "value"`

The `classes` property is a JavaScript object property that is one of three properties (the others are `tags` and `ids`) that can be used to define styles in JavaScript Style Sheets.

The `classes` property is defined using dot notation and takes a class name as its first modifier. You may use any valid alphanumeric combination as a class name. The second modifier of the `classes` property is any valid HTML element. For example, `classes.bodyclass.body.` or `class.h1class.h1.` are both valid "tags.element" combinations. The usage of "all" is also a valid modifier, and `classes.class1.all.` will define a class style that can be used for all elements.

The property modifier of this object can be any valid JavaScript Style Sheets property, which are listed in this book's alphabetical listing with the category: JavaScript Style Sheets, and type: property.

The `classes` property must always be used with the `<style></style>` elements; thus defining it as a property used only for JavaScript Style Sheets.

By defining your styles using the `classes` property, you will need to reference the style definition in the document, thus giving you the capability to control the usage of the style to only specific instances of the element.

In the following example, `<h2>` headers are underlined only if they have the class definition. The class is defined within the `<style></style>` tags, and then explicitly referenced with the `<h2>` element.

```
<html>
<head>
<style type="text/javascript">
classes.h2class.h2.textDecoration ="underline";
</style>
</head>
<body>
<h1> This header will not be underlined.
<h2> Note that the style has only been applied to the h2 header
<h2 class="h2class"> This header will be underlined.
</body>
</html>
```

The single line of code between the `<style></style>` elements is the important line when defining `classess`. There are five elements to note in the example:

- `classes` is the property that tells JSSS that the code immediately following will define a style class.
- `h2class` is the name of the class. This class name can be any alphanumeric combination, and will be referenced each time the class is used.
- `<h2>` is the HTML element that the class will be valid for use with. This can be any valid HTML element.
- `textDecoration` is the style that will applied to the `<h2>` elements that use the style. Any valid JSSS style property can be used here.
- `"underline"` is the value of the property that will be applied. Each style property has its own set of defined values.

The results of this code are shown in Figure 1.

Figure 1

Underlined <h2>
elements.

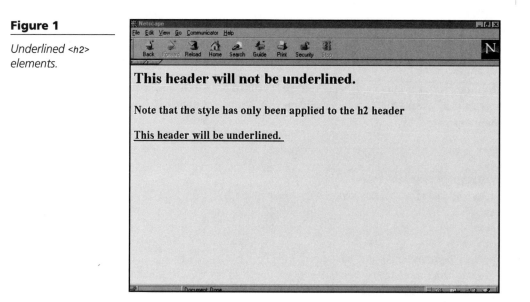

It is also worthy to note that some styles can be inherited to child elements, so when using the high-level `classes` property, remember that this style may not be for just <h2>, but also for all child elements.

clear

Category: Cascading Style Sheets

Browser Support

	Navigator 3	Navigator 4	Explorer 3	Explorer 4
Macintosh	☐	■	☐	☐
Windows	☐	■	☐	☐

Applies To   All elements

Syntax   `clear: value`

The `clear` property enables you to specify if an element will allow the floating of other elements around the given element. If you use the `float` property to wrap text and images around an element, you use `clear` to negate the effects of `float`. This property is the equivalent of using `<br clear=x>` in current HTML.

`clear` can be used with text as well as with replaced elements such as images. See `float` for more information about wrapping text and images. The possible values for `clear` include `left` and `right` for the left and right side of an element respectively. You may also specify `both`, which combines these two, and `none`, which turns off the effects of `clear`.

```
h1 { clear: right }
```

```
<h1 style="clear: both">
```

clear

Category: JavaScript Style Sheets

	Type	Property

Browser Support

	Navigator 3	Navigator 4	Explorer 3	Explorer 4
Macintosh	☐	▆	☐	☐
Windows	☐	▆	☐	☐

	Applies To	All elements
	Inherited	No
	Syntax	clear = "*value*"

The clear JavaScript Style Sheet style enables you to define the usage of "floating" elements in your document. An example floating HTML element is <img> element. The <img> when used near text elements, <p> or <h1>, will appear to float around the text. Normally certain HTML objects are allowed to be floating objects, but using the clear style you can define the usage, or rather lack of usage, of floating objects for particular elements, or for the entire document. There are four valid values for the clear property:

- "none" specifies that no clear styles are in place and the default floating will be allowed around this particular element.

- "left" specifies that floating elements will not be allowed to the left of this element. They will be "cleared" from the left side, and this element will be displayed below the floating elements.

- "right" specifies that floating elements will not be allowed to the right of this element. They will be "cleared" from the right side, and this element will be displayed below the floating elements.

- "both" specify that floating elements will not be allowed to either side of this element. They will be "cleared" from the left and right sides, and this element will be displayed below the floating elements.

The clear style is probably only relevant in the circumstance where you want to pin objects in a specific area of the document. Normally the flow of an HTML page is designed to have images and graphics flow or float in the text on the page.

The following example uses clear for the <h2> elements, thus disallowing the element to have the <img> float to its left or right. <h1> elements will still have the <img> floating around it but not the <h2>.

```
<html>
<head>
<style type="text/javascript">
tags.h2.clear = "both";
```

```
</style>
</head>
<body>
<img src="school.gif">
<h1> This header can have elements floating to its left and
right because it is not an h2 header.
<img src="school.gif">
<h2> This header will never have any elements floating to its left or rigt.
<img src="school.gif">
<p> The h2 header will always display below the floating elements
associated with it in the document.
</body>
</html>
```

In the previous example, because the clear style is only defined for <h2> headers, all other headers can have floating elements. But the <h2> headers will always display below any floating elements.

In this example, the important elements are as follows:

- tags is one of the methods of defining JSSS styles. The tags definition describes the element immediately following it if the dot notation will be one of the accepted HTML elements.

- h2 is the html element that is being assigned a style. This may be any valid HTML element.

- clear is the style that is being defined for the element. This may be any valid JSSS style.

- "both" is the value of the style clear.

clip

Category: Cascading Style Sheets

Browser Support		Navigator 3	Navigator 4	Explorer 3	Explorer 4
	Macintosh	☐	☐	☐	☐
	Windows	☐	☐	☐	☐

Applies To All elements with position of absolute

Syntax clip: rect (top, left, bottom, right)

The clip property enables you to control the clipping of elements (text or replaced elements). You define an area and any part of the element or image within the area is displayed while any part outside the area is not. Items that fall on the boundary of the element are displayed right up to the boundary making them appear cut or "clipped."

For the shape of the clipping region, you use a `rect`. The values correspond to the top, left, bottom, and right sides of the rectangle and are relative to the origin of the element. You can also use `auto` for any coordinate, which means the image is not clipped along that boundary.

```
h1 { clip: rect(10px 20px 30px 40px) }
```

```
h1 { clip: rect(25% auto 5% auto) }
```

C

> **NOTE** No browser supports `clip` at the present time.

CLng()
Category: VBScript

| Type | Function |

Browser Support		Navigator 3	Navigator 4	Explorer 3	Explorer 4
	Macintosh	☐	☐	☐	■
	Windows	☐	☐	■	■

| Syntax | `CLng(expression)` |

The `CLng()` function converts the *expression* to a long subtype value. Any numerical value can be passed to this function; any non-numeric expressions will cause an error.

Long subtype values may reside within the range –2,147,483,648 to 2,147,483,647.

> **NOTE** The `CLng()` function is rather esoteric, and rarely used, because VBScript is not very strict about data types. In general, you'll only need to look up this function if you are specifically looking for its action, which is seldom if ever.

<CODE>
Category: HTML

Browser Support		Navigator 3	Navigator 4	Explorer 3	Explorer 4
	Macintosh	■	■	☐	■
	Windows	■	■	■	■

| Applies To | Text |

| Syntax | `<CODE>...</CODE>` |

<CODE> is an older tag used to specify a section of programming code. Everything written between the beginning and closing, or </CODE> tags, will be displayed in a monotype font as shown in the example:

```
<CODE>This text is specified as programming code using the CODE tag.</CODE>
```

> **NOTE** The <CODE> tag works with Macintosh and Windows 95 machines for Netscape Navigator 3 and Internet Explorer 4; there is no Macintosh support in Internet Explorer 3. The only browser to support all platforms is Netscape Navigator 4.

Figure 1 displays this HTML in Navigator 3 for the Macintosh.

Figure 1

Text written as programming code by using the <CODE> tag compared to plain default text.

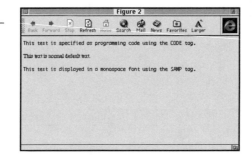

There's no functional difference between text displayed in a monospace font using the <CODE> tag versus using the <SAMP> tag, as shown in Figure 2. Use either of these tags for monospaced plain text as you prefer.

Figure 2

The <CODE> tag versus the <SAMP> tag—no difference.

There is a difference between the default monospace fonts in Navigator versus Internet Explorer; Figure 3 displays the same HTML as shown in Figure 2, but in Internet Explorer 3 for Windows.

Figure 3

The <CODE> tag versus the <SAMP> tag—there is a difference between Navigator and Internet Explorer 3.

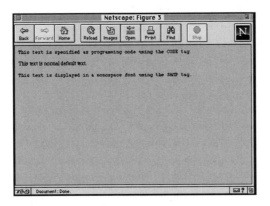

C

<COL>

Category: HTML

Browser Support

	Navigator 3	Navigator 4	Explorer 3	Explorer 4
Macintosh			■	■
Windows			■	■

Attributes ALIGN, SPAN

Syntax <COL>...</COL>

The <COL> tag is an Internet Explorer–only element used to specify text alignment for table columns. It is used in tandem with the <COLGROUP> tag to specify settings for individual columns within a column group. A closing, or </COL> tag, is not required.

See the <COLGROUP> tag entry elsewhere in the book for more information on how it and the <COL> tag work together.

ALIGN

The ALIGN attribute specifies vertical alignment of text within the cells of a single column in a column group. It has three values:

center

The text is centered within the cells in the column. This is the ALIGN attribute default.

left

The text is left-aligned within the cells in the column.

right

The text is right-aligned within the cells in the column.

In the following example, the <COLGROUP> tag and its HALIGN and SPAN attributes have been used to specify a horizontal alignment for all three columns. The <COL> tag and the ALIGN attribute have been used to specify center, left, and right vertical alignments:

```
<TABLE>
<COLGROUP HALIGN=center SPAN=3>
<COL ALIGN=center>
<COL ALIGN=left>
<COL ALIGN=right>
<TR>
<TD>Cell No. 1</TD><TD>Cell No. 2</TD><TD>Cell No. 3</TD>
</TR>
<TR>
<TD>Cell No. 4</TD><TD>Cell No. 5</TD><TD>Cell No. 6</TD>
</TR>
<TR>
<TD>Cell No. 7</TD><TD>Cell No.8</TD><TD>Cell No. 9</TD>
</TR>
</TABLE>
```

The text in each individual column has the same horizontal alignment but different vertical alignments—from left to right, center, left, and right, respectively.

DESIGN NOTE There are no equivalent or similar alignment tags in Navigator. It is however, worthwhile to remember that Navigator is still the most popular web browser (at this writing), so any table features you specify with Explorer-only tags like <COL> and <COLGROUP> will not be seen by the majority of visitors to your page.

SPAN

The SPAN attribute specifies how many columns in a column group will be affected by the ALIGN attribute (or any other <COLGROUP> settings, should more attributes and values be created for it in the future).

In the following example, there are four individual columns in the column group specified by the <COLGROUP> tag.

```
<TABLE>
<COLGROUP>
<COL ALIGN=left SPAN=2>
<COL ALIGN=right SPAN=2>
<TR>
<TD>Cell No. 1</TD><TD>Cell No. 2</TD><TD>Cell No. 3</TD><TD>Cell No. 4</TD>
</TR>
<TR>
<TD>Cell No. 5</TD><TD>Cell No. 6</TD><TD>Cell No. 7</TD><TD>Cell No. 8</TD>
</TR>
```

C

```
<TR>
<TD>Cell No. 9</TD><TD>Cell No. 10</TD><TD>Cell No. 11</TD><TD>Cell No. 12</TD>
</TR>
</TABLE>
```

Only two \<COL\> tags are used to specify vertical alignment because each of them uses the SPAN attribute. Therefore, the first two columns are affected by the ALIGN value of left, and the last two columns are affected by the ALIGN value of right.

Figures 1 and 2 illustrate this example HTML in Internet Explorer 3 for the Macintosh and for Windows.

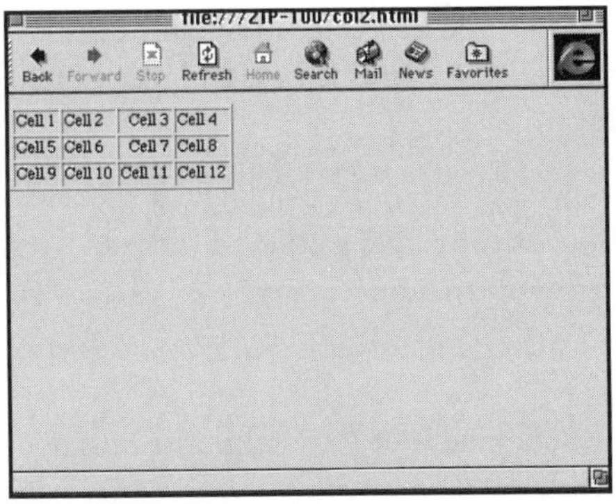

Figure 1

Using SPAN in Internet Explorer 3 for the Macintosh.

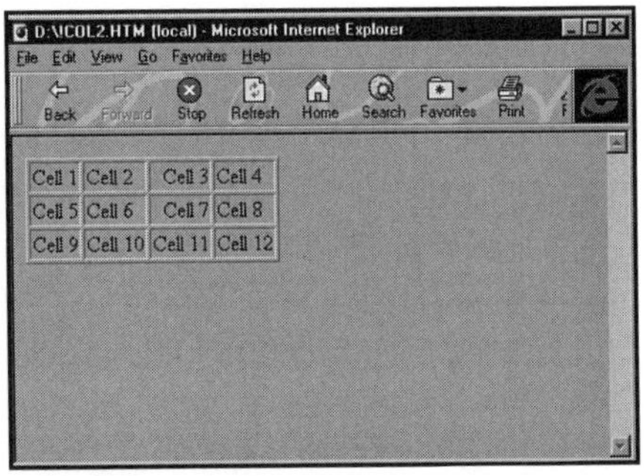

Figure 2

Using SPAN in Internet Explorer 3 for Windows.

\<COLGROUP\>

Category: HTML

Browser Support		Navigator 3	Navigator 4	Explorer 3	Explorer 4
	Macintosh	☐	☐	■	■
	Windows	☐	☐	■	■

Attributes HALIGN, SPAN, VALIGN, WIDTH

Syntax \<COLGROUP\>...\</COLGROUP\>

The \<COLGROUP\> tag is an Internet Explorer–only element used to establish spacing and alignment properties of individual or groups of columns in a table. There is no equivalent tag in Navigator, and the closing, or \</COLGROUP\> tag, is not required.

A *column* in an HTML table refers to a vertical stack of table cells; a horizontal line of table cells that sit side by side is called a *row*. In the following example, therefore, \<COLGROUP\> is used to differentiate between two different columns in the same table:

```
<TABLE>
<COLGROUP ALIGN=LEFT>
<COLGROUP ALIGN=RIGHT>
<TR>
<TBODY>
<TD>Cell No. 1</TD><TD>Cell No. 2</TD><TD>Cell No. 3</TD>
</TR>
<TR>
<TD>Cell No. 4</TD><TD>Cell No. 5</TD><TD>Cell No. 6</TD>
</TR>
</TABLE>
```

The first <COLGROUP> tag contains specifications for the first column of table cells, the second contains specifications for the second column, and so on (if this were a bigger table).

Note that you don't need to use attributes with the <COLGROUP> tag at all—sometimes you'll want to specify different features for a few columns within a column group and a <COLGROUP> attribute setting may make this difficult. See the SPAN attribute section of the <COL> tag entry for an example situation of when <COLGROUP> attributes are unnecessary.

HALIGN

The HALIGN attribute establishes the horizontal alignment of text within the cells of a column (or columns, if two or more have been grouped with the SPAN attribute). It has three values:

center

The text is centered horizontally within each cell in the column.

left

The text is left-aligned horizontally within each cell in the column.

right

The text is right-aligned horizontally within each cell in the column.

In the following example, each column has been specified with a different HALIGN value:

```
<TABLE>
<COLGROUP HALIGN=CENTER>
<COLGROUP HALIGN=LEFT>
<COLGROUP HALIGN=RIGHT>
<TBODY>
<TR>
<TD>Center</TD><TD>Center</TD><TD>Center</TD>
</TR>
<TR>
<TD>Left</TD><TD>Left</TD><TD>Left</TD>
</TR>
<TR>
```

```
<TD>Right</TD><TD>Right</TD><TD>Right</TD>
</TR>
</TABLE>
```

> **NOTE** To establish vertical alignment of text within column cells, see the following
> VALIGN section.

SPAN

The SPAN attribute specifies the number of columns in one group so you can change the alignment and spacing within several columns with one line of HTML.

In the following example, SPAN has been used to group the second and third rows together (hence, its value of 2):

```
<TABLE>
<COLGROUP HALIGN=CENTER>
<COLGROUP HALIGN=LEFT SPAN=2>
<TBODY>
<TR>
<TD>Cell 1</TD><TD>Cell 2</TD><TD>Cell 3</TD>
</TR>
<TR>
<TD>Cell 4</TD><TD> Cell 5</TD><TD> Cell 6</TD>
</TR>
<TR>
<TD> Cell 7</TD><TD> Cell 8</TD><TD> Cell 9</TD>
</TR>
</TABLE>
```

> **NOTE** If you have specified two or more columns to be grouped together with the
> <COLSPAN> tag but you want to specify different attributes within each column,
> use the <COL> tag. See the <COL> tag entry elsewhere in the book for more
> information on how to accomplish this task.

VALIGN

The VALIGN attribute establishes the vertical alignment of text within all the cells in a column (or columns if two or more have been grouped with the SPAN attribute).

VALIGN has three values:

bottom

The text is vertically aligned to the bottom of each cell in the column.

```
middle
```

The text is vertically centered within each cell in the column. This is the VALIGN attribute default.

```
top
```

The text is vertically aligned to the top of each cell in the column.

In the following example, each of the three columns is specified with a different VALIGN value:

```
<TABLE>
<COLGROUP VALIGN=bottom>
<COLGROUP VALIGN=middle>
<COLGROUP VALIGN=top>
<TBODY>
<TR>
<TD>Bottom</TD><TD>Bottom</TD><TD> Bottom</TD>
</TR>
<TR>
<TD>Middle</TD><TD>Middle</TD><TD> Middle</TD>
</TR>
<TR>
<TD>Top</TD><TD>Top</TD><TD>Top</TD>
</TR>
</TABLE>
```

> **NOTE** To establish horizontal alignment of text within column cells, see the HALIGN section earlier in this entry.

WIDTH

The WIDTH attribute is an optional feature that specifies the vertical width of each column in a column group in pixels, (if the group is specified with a VALIGN value).

The following example demonstrates proper use of the WIDTH attribute:

```
<TABLE>
<COLGROUP VALIGN=BOTTOM>
<COLGROUP VALIGN=TOP SPAN=2 WIDTH=25>
<TBODY>
<TR>
<TD>Cell 1</TD><TD>Cell 2</TD><TD>Cell 3</TD>
```

```
</TR>
<TR>
<TD>Cell 4</TD><TD> Cell 5</TD><TD> Cell 6</TD>
</TR>
<TR>
<TD> Cell 7</TD><TD> Cell 8</TD><TD> Cell 9</TD>
</TR>
</TABLE>
```

While WIDTH does not directly affect the appearance of a table (you don't need it even if you have specified a VALIGN value), it does sometimes help browsers to render tables more quickly. See the previous VALIGN section within this entry for more information on positioning cell column text vertically.

color

Category: Cascading Style Sheets

Browser Support		Navigator 3	Navigator 4	Explorer 3	Explorer 4
	Macintosh			■	
	Windows		■	■	■

Applies To All elements

Syntax color: *value*

The color property defines the color of an element using either a color name or hexadecimal value. Colors and their values are discussed more completely in Appendix B. If you're accustomed to dealing with color values in HTML (via the <font color> tag, for example), then color values in style sheets will seem very familiar.

```
h1 { color: aqua }
```

```
<h1 style="color: #ff0000">
```

> **NOTE** A great site to experiment with color values is HYPE's Color Specifier, located at http://www.users.interport.net/~giant/COLOR/1ColorSpecifier.html (see Figure 1). As well as showing the colors, this helpful page gives the correct color names, hexadecimal equivalents, and even RGB values for each. It's important to note that these hundreds of colors are mostly *not* in the browser-safe family and may not look great across platforms.

HYPE's Color Specifier shows all the color names you can use.

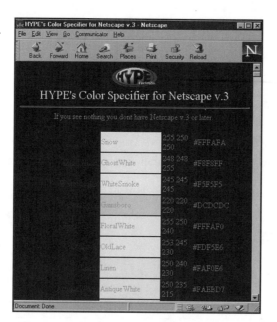

NOTE   For more detailed information on the important issues of browser color palettes and web color optimization, see David Siegel's *Creating Killer Web Sites* (Hayden Books) or Lynda Weinman's *Coloring Web Graphics* (New Riders Publishing)—both are unparalleled books. For starters, visit their respective web sites at `http://www.killersites.com` and `http://www.lynda.com`.

---

color

Category: JavaScript Style Sheets

| Type | Property |

Browser Support

	Navigator 3	Navigator 4	Explorer 3	Explorer 4
Macintosh	☐	■	☐	☐
Windows	☐	■	☐	☐

| Applies To | All elements |

| Inherited | Yes |

| Syntax | `color = "value"` |

The `color` property is the complementary property to `backgroundColor`. Although `backgroundColor` gives color to the area behind the text in the HTML element, `color` defines the color for the text of the HTML element itself. There is only one acceptable value for `color`:

■ `"color"` is the value that defines the color style, and JavaScript Style Sheets accepts the `"color"` value in two different formats. Exact color: `tags.h1.color = "green"` or rgb color: `tags.h1.color = rgb(0,255,0)`. See Appendix B for more details on colors.

`color` is a useful style when for standards purposes, every element of a particular type will always be displayed in a certain color. Or it could be used to change the color of elements in JavaScript function calls.

The following code sample is the simple definition of using `color` to define the text color for an element. Note that in Figure 1, only the paragraphs that have the class definition of `"colorclass"` are displayed in green. Those without the JavaScript Style Sheets colorclass style are the normal black text.

```
<html>
<head>
<style type="text/javascript">
classes.colorclass.p.color = "green";
</style>
</head>
<body>
<p> This paragraph will not be green because it does not have the
class definition
<p class="colorclass"> This paragraph be green because it uses the class
<h2 class="colorclass"> This header will not be green.
<p> the header will not be green because even though it uses the
class of "colorclass," this class has been defined for paragraphs
only
</body>
</html>
```

Figure 1

Changing paragraph color.

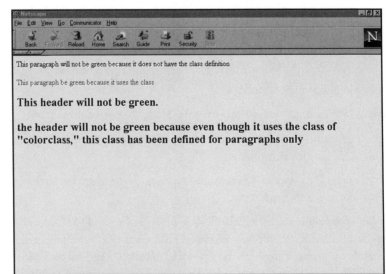

In the previous code lisitng, the important line of JSSS code is `classes.colorclass.p.color = "green";`. This line can be broken down as follows:

- `classes` denotes that this style is defined for a specific class only. This notation tells JSSS that the property immediately following in the dot notation will be a class name.

- `colorclass` is the name of the class. This class name can be any alphanumeric combination, and will be referenced each time the class is used.

- `<p>` is the HTML element that the class will be valid for use with. This can be any valid HTML element.

- `color` is the style that will applied to the `<p>` elements that use the clases. Any valid JSSS style property can be used here.

- `"green"` is the value of the style that will be applied. Each style property has its own set of define valid values.

Note that the colorclass has been defined as only a style for `<p>` elements, so when it is used as a class definition for an `<h2>` element the class is actually ignored.

<COMMENT>

Category: HTML

Browser Support		Navigator 3	Navigator 4	Explorer 3	Explorer 4
	Macintosh	■	■	■	■
	Windows	■	■	■	■

May Be Used In   `<HTML>`

Syntax   `<COMMENT>…</COMMENT>`

`<COMMENT>` is used to indicate a *comment*—a block of text in the HTML page included for basic information and backward-compatibility between earlier and later browser versions. `<COMMENT>`-specified text will not appear on a web page unless it contains HTML-specified code. The closing, or `</COMMENT>` tag, is required.

Hence, the following example:

```
<COMMENT>This page was created using HTML 3.2 specifications.</COMMENT>
```

This specification for writing comments replaces an earlier, more programming-like way of adding such text, for example:

```
<!--This line of text, traditionally referred to as an author's comment, will not
appear on the web page.-->
```

You can utilize either format of including comments in your HTML depending upon your preferences, but neither is necessary to make an HTML document work properly. However, you may want to include comments using both the `<!-->` and `<COMMENT>` tags for backward browser compatibility, because Navigator 2.0 and other, earlier browsers do not recognize the newer `<!-->` tag.

Cos()

Category: VBScript

	Type	Function

Browser Support		Navigator 3	Navigator 4	Explorer 3	Explorer 4
	Macintosh				■
	Windows			■	■

	Syntax	Cos(number)

The cos() function calculates and returns the cosine of *number*, which is an angle expressed in radians. The cosine of *number* represents the ratio between two sides of a right triangle: the length of the side adjacent to the angle divided by the length of the hypotenuse. The ratio returned can range from –1 to 1.

> **NOTE** VBScript does not provide an acos() function. Use the following formula to calculate the inverse cosine:
>
> atn(-1 * x / sqr(-1 * x * x + 1)) + 2 * atn(1)

CSng()

Category: VBScript

	Type	Function

Browser Support		Navigator 3	Navigator 4	Explorer 3	Explorer 4
	Macintosh				■
	Windows			■	■

	Syntax	CSng(expression)

The CSng() function converts the *expression* to a single-precision floating-point value. Any numerical value can be passed to this function; any non-numeric expressions will cause an error.

Single-precision floating point values may reside within the range –3.402823E38 to –1.401298E–45 for negative values and 1.401298E–45 to 3.402823E38 for positive values.

> **DESIGN NOTE** The CSng() function is rather esoteric, and rarely used, because VBScript is not very strict about data types. In general, you'll only need to look up this function if you are specifically looking for its action, which is seldom if ever.

CStr()

Category: VBScript

Type	Function				

Browser Support

	Navigator 3	Navigator 4	Explorer 3	Explorer 4
Macintosh	☐	☐	☐	■
Windows	☐	☐	■	■

Syntax CStr(expression)

The CStr() function converts the *expression* to a string value. Any value may be passed to this function, except for null, which will cause an error.

The following table lists the types of expressions and the strings returned by CStr():

Expression Type	Returned by CStr()
Boolean	A string containing "true" or "false" cstr(5>3) returns "true"
Date	A string containing the date in short-date format cstr(datevalue("jan 11 97")) returns "1/11/97"
Empty	A null string ("") cstr(string(0,"a")) returns ""
Numeric	A string containing the number cstr(100/5) returns "20"
String value	String value cstr("hello") returns "hello"

```
<IMG> </IMG> ■ <SCRIPT LANGUAGE = "javascript"> </SCRIPT>
■ <SCRIPT LANGUAGE = "vbscript"> </SCRIPT> ■ <BGSOUND
SRC=gby.wav LOOP=-1> </BGSOUND> ■ <APPLET CLASS=
"ester's_day" SRC="http://testsite/walla walla washington/"
</APPLET> ■ <FRAME></FRAME>■ <MARQUEE> </MARQUEE> ■
<HTML> </HTML> ■ <A> </A>■ <OL> </OL>■ <UL> </UL> ■ <MENU>
</MENU> ■ <STRONG> </STRONG> ■ <TD> </TD> ■ <TH> </TH>
```

D

Date

Category: JavaScript, JScript

| Type | Object |

Browser Support

	Navigator 3	Navigator 4	Explorer 3	Explorer 4
Macintosh	■	■	☐	■
Windows	■	■	■	■

Methods getDate() AND setDate(), getDay(), getHours() AND setHours(), getMonth() AND setMonth(), getMinutes() AND setMinutes(), getSeconds() AND setSeconds(), getTime() AND setTime(), getYear() AND setYear(), getTimezoneOffset(), toGMTString(), toLocaleString(), parse(), UTC()

Syntax dateName = new Date(parameters) OR dateName.method()

The Date object, although sometimes confusing, enables you to manipulate dates and times for scripting purposes. There is a wide variety of uses for this object, from setting expiration dates on cookies (see document object) to calculating a shipping date three days ahead of today.

To use the Date object, you must first instantiate it using the *new* construction:

dateName = new Date()

In the above example, *dateName* is a variable that you want to represent the Date object. When referencing the object's methods, you'll do so via this variable—such as dateName.method().

Because no parameters were specified in the new Date() construction above, the current date and time will be assigned to *dateName*. Note that "current" refers to the user's machine, not the server on which the web page resides. Therefore, if the user is in the Pacific Time Zone, new Date() will reflect Pacific time.

Alternatively, you can instantiate a Date object containing any date and time you wish. Any of the following examples are valid:

dateName = new Date("*month day, year hours:minutes:seconds*")
birthday = new Date("May 23, 1972 18:07:00")

Above, you can use any unique portion of the month name; for instance, "Jun" works just as well as "June."

```
dateName = new Date(year, month, day)
birthday = new Date(1972, 4, 23)
```

Notice above that the *month* is given as 4, although we are specifying May. Month numbering begins with 0 (January), and so May, the fifth month, is month number 4.

```
dateName = new Date(year, month, day, hours, minutes, seconds)
birthday = new Date(1972, 4, 23, 18, 07, 00)
```

In any of the above, if you omit a parameter, such as *seconds*, it is set to 0.

WARNING When setting the Date object, you *can* specify only the last two digits of the year, as in 72. The year 1972 will be assumed—don't succumb to the millenium bug! The safe bet is to specify all years in full four digits.

However you choose to set the Date object, JavaScript internally records the date as the number of milliseconds elapsed from January 1, 1970 0:00:00. Thus, you cannot set a date prior to January 1, 1970.

 In Internet Explorer 3, you cannot set a date beyond 2037—an apocalyptic vision on Microsoft's part or a bug?

After you've assigned and set a Date object to a variable *dateName*, you can use the following methods to parse the date, set the date, or convert the format of the date. The methods available in get/set pairs are listed in pairs below.

getDate() and setDate() methods

The getDate() method returns a value representing the date of the month of dateName, from 1 to 31. Similarly, you can set the date of the month for a Date object by passing *number* to setDate(), where *number* is a value between 1 and 31 inclusive.

```
datenum=dateName.getDate()
dateName.setDate(number)
```

If you exceed the end of the month—that is, pass a *number* greater than the last date in that month (such as 31 for April, which only has 30 days), the Date object will automatically be corrected to represent the correct date. Thus, if your Date object is set to April 1997, and you execute setDate(31), the Date object will be set to May 01, 1997. Any changes to the Date object *will* cascade—advancing the date may advance the month which may advance the year.

getDay() method

The getDay() method returns the day of the week as an integer, where 0 represents Sunday, 1 represents Monday, and so on, until 6 (Saturday).

```
daynum=dateName.getDay()
```

If, for instance, you set

```
datename=new Date("September 8, 1997")
```

Then `datename.getDay()` would yield 1, which represents Monday. There is no analogous `setDay()` method.

getHours() and setHours() methods

The `getHours()` method returns a value representing the hour of time in `dateName`, from 0 (Midnight) to 23 (11 pm). Similarly, you can set the hour for a `date` object by passing *number* to `setHours()`, where *number* is a value between 0 and 23 inclusive.

```
hour=dateName.getHours()
dateName.setHours(number)
```

If you exceed the 23 hour mark—that is, pass a *number* greater than 23 as the hour, the `Date` object will be set to hour *number*–24 and the day and date will advance accordingly. Thus, if your `Date` object is set to April 29, 1997 15:00:00, and you execute `setHours(24)`, the `Date` object will be set to April 30, 1997 00:00:00. Any changes to the `Date` object *will* cascade—advancing the hour may advance the day which may advance the month which may advance the year.

getMonth() and setMonth() methods

The `getMonth()` method returns a value representing the month of the year in `dateName`, from 0 (January) to 11 (December). Similarly, you can set the month for a `Date` object by passing *number* to `setMonth()`, where *number* is a value between 0 and 11 inclusive.

```
month=dateName.getMonth()
dateName.setMonth(number)
```

If you exceed the month 11 mark—that is, pass a *number* greater than 11 as the month, the `Date` object will be set to month *number*–12 and the year will advance accordingly. Thus, if your `Date` object is set to October 10, 1997 (month 9) and you execute `setMonth(13)`, the `Date` object will be set to February 10, 1998 (month 1).

getMinutes() and setMinutes() methods

The `getMinutes()` method returns a value representing the minutes past the hour in `dateName`, from 0 to 59. Similarly, you can set the minutes for a `Date` object by passing *number* to `setMinutes()`, where *number* is a value between 0 and 59 inclusive.

```
minute=dateName.getMinutes()
dateName.setMinutes(number)
```

If you exceed the 59 minute mark—that is, pass a *number* greater than 59 as the minute, the `Date` object will be set to *number*–60 minutes and the hour will advance accordingly. Thus, if your `Date` object is set to 10:30:50, and you execute `setMinutes(60)`, the `Date` object will be set to 11:00:50. Any changes to the `Date` object *will* cascade—advancing the minutes may advance the date which may advance the month which may advance the year.

getSeconds() and setSeconds() methods

The getSeconds() method returns a value representing the seconds past the minute in dateName, from 0 to 59. Similarly, you can set the seconds for a Date object by passing *number* to setSeconds(), where *number* is a value between 0 and 59 inclusive.

```
second=dateName.getSeconds()
dateName.setSeconds(number)
```

If you exceed the 59 second mark—that is, pass a *number* greater than 59 as the second, the Date object will be set to *number*–60 seconds and the minute will advance accordingly. Thus, if your Date object is set to 08:30:10, and you execute setSeconds(70), the Date object will be set to 08:31:10. Any changes to the Date object *will* cascade—advancing the seconds may advance the minutes which may advance the date which may advance the month which may advance the year!

getTime() and setTime() methods

The getTime() and setTime() methods enable you to work with JavaScript's internal millisecond representation of the Date object. The getTime() method returns the number of milliseconds elapsed from January 1, 1970 0:00:00 for dateName. Similarly, you can quickly set a Date object by passing *milliseconds* to the setTime() method.

```
ms=dateName.getTime()
dateName.setTime(milliseconds)
```

Of course, you're not likely to know offhand how many milliseconds have elapsed since 1970, which is why you typically set the Date object using the month and date syntax seen earlier. However, you may find the getTime() and setTime() methods useful for assigning the value of one Date object to another:

```
date1=new Date("January 3, 1998")
date2=new Date()
 …some other script statements…
 date2.setTime(date1.getTime())
```

Additionally, you may sometimes find it quicker to advance a date by adding milliseconds rather than accessing the correct method for date, hours, minutes, and so on. Considering that there are 1,000 milliseconds in a second, you could quickly advance a Date object by, say, 4 hours:

```
dateName.setTime(dateName.getTime()+1000*60*60*4)
```

getYear() and setYear() methods

The getYear() and setYear() methods can be used to read or modify the year stored in the Date object. However, the value returned and *number* passed vary depending upon the browser.

```
yr=dateName.getYear()
dateName.setYear(number)
```

Within Netscape Navigator

The getYear() method returns a two-digit value if the year is less than 2000, otherwise a full four-digit value is returned. Thus, if you had

```
set dateName=new Date("October 10, 1947")
```

then

```
dateName.getYear()
```

would return the value 47. Had you set the year to 2047, this method would return the value 2047.

For all years, you can pass a full four-digit value as *number* to setYear, such as

```
dateName.setYear(1972)
```

or

```
dateName.setYear(2010)
```

If you pass only a two-digit *number*, the preceding "19" is assumed. Therefore,

```
dateName.setYear(72)
```

would set the year to 1972.

Within Internet Explorer 3

The getYear() method returns the value of *year*–1900; that is, the number of years elapsed since 1900. If the Date object's year is 1988, then this method would return the value 88. For the year 2010, this method returns the value 110.

Similarly, to use setYear(), you must pass a *number* which represents *year*–1900. Thus, to set the Date object to the year 1998, use

```
dateName.setYear(98)
```

To set the date to 2022, use

```
dateName.setYear(122)
```

 At the time of this writing, it is unknown how Internet Explorer 4 handles the getYear() and setYear() methods.

getTimezoneOffset() method

The getTimezoneOffset() method returns the difference in minutes between the user's local time and GMT. You can use this method to locate the time zone of the user's machine. Keep in mind that many regions change their clocks for Daylight Savings Time, and so their offset may not remain constant all year.

```
tz=dateName.getTimezoneOffset()
```

Because this method returns the offset in minutes, you may find it more sensible to calculate the offset in hours:

```
tzhours=dateName.getTimezoneOffset()/60
```

For instance, if a user is located in the Eastern Time Zone, his offset would be –5 hours from GMT when not during Daylight Savings, and –4 hours from GMT during Daylight Savings.

toGMTString() method

The toGMTString() method returns the date and time in Internet GMT format, which corrects for time zone differences.

```
gmt=dateName.toGMTString()
```

For instance, if you set

```
exp=new Date("April 15, 1997 12:00:00")
```

on a user's machine located in the Eastern Time Zone, then the statement

```
document.write(exp.toGMTString())
```

would output the date in GMT format similar to:

```
Tue, 15 Apr 1997 15:00:00 GMT
```

Commonly, the toGMTString() method is used when setting cookies, because their expiration dates require the GMT format (see document object).

toLocaleString() method

The toLocaleString() method returns the date and time in the format configured on the user's particular computer. For instance, local conventions for displaying the date and time may vary from one country to another—usually, the user's operating system has been configured to display date and time according to local tradition.

```
local=dateName.toLocaleString()
```

For instance, if you set

```
exp=new Date("February 23, 1996 16:00:00")
```

on a user's machine located in the United States which has been configured to display dates in *mm/dd/yy* format, then the statement

```
document.write(exp.toLocaleString())
```

would output the date as:

```
02/23/97 16:00:00
```

Generally, you would use the toLocaleString() method when displaying a date to the user, so that it is shown in a format he is familiar with. For instance, in many countries other than the U.S., people are used to seeing the day listed before the month, as in *dd/mm/yy*.

parse() method

The parse() method is considered *static*, meaning that it is not tied to a particular instantiation of the object; it is always used in the construction Date.parse(), unlike the methods described above.

This method accepts a date string and returns the number of milliseconds elapsed since January 1, 1970 00:00:00. It is equivalent to setting a Date object and then returning the value of the getTime() method.

You can pass the date string in a variety of formats, as illustrated below:

`Date.parse("Dec 25, 1997")`	Assumes time 00:00:00 in local time zone
`Date.parse("Thu, 25 Dec 1997 13:30:00")`	Assumes local time zone
`Date.parse("Thu, 25 Dec 1997 13:30:00 GMT")`	Greenwich Mean Time
`Date.parse("Thu, 25 Dec 1997 13:30:00 GMT-0500")`	Eastern Time Zone (non-Daylight Savings)

Because this method returns a value representing milliseconds, you would generally pass this value into the setTime() method for a Date object. Commonly, this is done when you want to set the time for a Date object that has already been created. Imagine that your script has already instantiated the Date object dateName. To set the time for dateName at any time in your script, use a statement such as the following:

`dateName.setTime(Date.parse("May 23, 1998"))`

UTC() method

The UTC() method is much like the parse() method, except that it accepts date and time as comma delimited values. It returns the number of milliseconds elapsed for the specified date and time since January 1, 1970 0:00:00. As a static method, UTC() is only used in the construction Date.UTC(), never with an actual Date object. The UTC() method accepts integers in the following format.

`Date.UTC(year,month,date[,hours][,minutes][,seconds])`

The hours, minutes, and seconds parameters are optional. The integer formats are the same as those used in the "get" and "set" methods:

year	Greater than 1900
month	Between 0 (January) and 11 (December)
date	Between 1 and 31
hours	Between 0 and 23
minutes	Between 0 and 59
seconds	Between 0 and 59

Because this method returns a value representing milliseconds, you would generally pass this value into the setTime() method for a Date object. Commonly, this is done when you want to set the time for a Date object that has already been created. Imagine that your script has already instantiated the Date object dateName. To set the time for dateName at any time in your script, use a statement such as the following:

```
dateName.setTime(Date.UTC(1997,4,23,18,6,0))
```

Date
Category: VBScript

| Type | Function |

Browser Support

	Navigator 3	Navigator 4	Explorer 3	Explorer 4
Macintosh	☐	☐	☐	■
Windows	☐	☐	■	■

Syntax `Date`

The Date function simply returns the current date from the user's machine. The date is returned in the format "mm/dd/yy" or "mm/dd/yyyy" (if the year is not in the 1900s).

You don't need to use a set of parentheses when calling the date function.

```
date        returns 4/18/97
```

```
today = date
```

The above example assigns the current date to the variable today. Notice that the date function does *not* return the time, only the month, day, and year.

DateAdd()
Category: VBScript

| Type | Function |

Browser Support

	Navigator 3	Navigator 4	Explorer 3	Explorer 4
Macintosh	☐	☐	☐	■
Windows	☐	☐	■	■

Syntax `DateAdd(interval, number, date)`

The DateAdd() function returns a new date by adding or subtracting an amount of time to a specified starting *date*. The *date* parameter may be a date *dd-mmm-yy* or time *hh:mm:ss* or both. You use the *interval* and *number* parameters to specify the amount of time to add or subtract.

The *interval* parameter is one of the below string values, which represents the unit of time to add:

"yyyy"	year
"q"	quarter
"m"	month
"y"	day of year
"d"	day
"w"	weekday
"ww"	week of year
"h"	hour
"m"	minute
"s"	second

The *number* parameter specifies how many intervals to add to *date* (if *number* is negative then that many intervals are subtracted from *date*).

The date returned by the function will be calculated into a valid date, automatically taking into account leap years and other calendar variations.

dateAdd("yyyy", 2, "25-Jan-97")	returns	1/25/99
dateAdd("m", 1, "25-Jan-97 13:10:00")	returns	2/25/97 1:10:00 PM
dateAdd("d", 1, "27-Feb-96")	returns	2/28/96
dateAdd("h", -7, "05:00:30")	returns	10:00:30 PM

DateDiff()

Category: VBScript

Type Function

Browser Support

	Navigator 3	Navigator 4	Explorer 3	Explorer 4
Macintosh	☐	☐	☐	■
Windows	☐	☐	■	■

Syntax DateDiff(interval, date1, date2 [, firstDayOfWeek][, firstWeekOfYear])

The DateDiff() function determines the amount of time, in *intervals*, between *date1* and *date2*. Optionally, you can specify the preferred *firstDayOfWeek* and/or *firstWeekOfYear*.

You can measure the time difference in any valid *interval* unit, where *interval* is a string value containing one of the below:

`"yyyy"`	year
`"q"`	quarter
`"m"`	month
`"y"`	day of year
`"d"`	day
`"w"`	weekday
`"ww"`	week of year
`"h"`	hour
`"m"`	minute
`"s"`	second

The `DateDiff()` function is best illustrated by example:

`datediff("yyyy","May 23 1972","May 23 1997")`	returns	25
`datediff("ww","May 23 1997","June 2 1997")`	returns	2
`datediff("d","January 1 1990","March 1 1990")`	returns	59
`dateDiff("d","April 21", "April 23 1998")`	returns	367
`dateDiff("d","April 23", "April 21")`	returns	−2

As seen in the final example above, if you specify *date1* as later than *date2*, a negative value is returned.

In the last two examples above, the current year (1997) is assumed for *date1* (and for *date2* in the last example) because it was not specified.

The *firstDayOfWeek* parameter specifies, for the purposes of calculation, which day is the first day of the week. If you omit this parameter, Sunday is assumed by default. Additionally, the *firstWeekOfYear* parameter is used to specify the first week of the year. If omitted, the week that contains January 1st will be assumed to be the first week of the year. See the two tables below for valid values for the *firstDayOfWeek* and *firstWeekOfYear* parameters.

firstDayOfWeek may be any of the following constants or values:

`vbUseSystem`	0	Uses National Language Support setting
`vbSunday`	1	Sunday (*default*)
`vbMonday`	2	Monday

vbTuesday	3	Tuesday
vbWednesday	4	Wednesday
vbThursday	5	Thursday
vbFriday	6	Friday
vbSaturday	7	Saturday

For example, to specify Monday as the first day of the week in a `DateDiff()` calculation, you can use either:

```
datediff("d","September 1 1992","October 10 1994",vbMonday)
```

or

```
datediff("d","September 1 1992","October 10 1994",2)
```

firstDayOfYear may be any of the following constants or values:

vbUseSystem	0	Uses National Language Support setting
vbFirstJan1	1	Start with the week in which January 1 occurs (*default*)
vbFirstFourDays	2	Start with the week that has at least four days in the new year
vbFirstFullWeek	3	Start with the first full week of the new year

For example, to specify Sunday as the first day of the week and to count the first full week of the year as the first week in a year, you can use either:

```
datediff("d","September 1 1992","October 10 1994",vbSunday,vbFirstFullWeek)
```

or

```
datediff("d","September 1 1992","October 10 1994",1,3)
```

DatePart()
Category: VBScript

Type	Function

Browser Support

	Navigator 3	Navigator 4	Explorer 3	Explorer 4
Macintosh				■
Windows			■	■

Syntax `DatePart(interval, date, [, firstDayOfWeek ][, FirstWeekOfYear])`

The `DatePart()` function extracts and returns a specified time *interval* from a *date*. Optionally, you can specify a preferred *firstDayOfWeek* and/or *firstWeekOfYear*, which may affect the calculation of certain intervals by changing the offset, as seen in later examples.

You can extract from *date* any valid *interval* unit, where *interval* is a string value containing one of the below:

`"yyyy"`	year
`"q"`	quarter
`"m"`	month
`"y"`	day of year
`"d"`	day
`"w"`	weekday
`"ww"`	week of year
`"h"`	hour
`"m"`	minute
`"s"`	second

The `DatePart()` function is best illustrated by example:

`datepart("yyyy","May 23 1972")`	returns 1972
`datepart("ww","June 1 1997")`	returns 23
`datepart("h","March 3 1995 14:05:00")`	returns 14

If you do not specify the year, the current year is assumed.

The *firstDayOfWeek* parameter specifies, for the purposes of calculation, which day is the first day of the week. If you omit this parameter, Sunday is assumed by default. Setting this parameter affects calculations that return the w (weekday) or ww (week of year) interval.

Additionally, the *firstWeekOfYear* parameter is used to specify the first week of the year. If omitted, the week that contains January 1st will be assumed to be the first week of the year. This impacts calculations which return the ww (week of year) interval.

See the two tables below for valid values for the *firstDayOfWeek* and *firstWeekOfYear* parameters.

firstDayOfWeek may be any of the following constants or values:

`vbUseSystem`	0	Uses National Language Support setting
`vbSunday`	1	Sunday (*default*)
`vbMonday`	2	Monday

vbTuesday	3	Tuesday
vbWednesday	4	Wednesday
vbThursday	5	Thursday
vbFriday	6	Friday
vbSaturday	7	Saturday

For example, to specify Monday as the first day of the week in a `DatePart()` calculation, you can use either:

```
datepart("w","September 1 1992",vbMonday)
```

or

```
datepart("w","September 1 1992",2)
```

firstDayOfYear may be any of the following constants or values:

vbUseSystem	0	Uses National Language Support setting
vbFirstJan1	1	Start with the week in which January 1 occurs (*default*)
vbFirstFourDays	2	Start with the week that has at least four days in the new year
vbFirstFullWeek	3	Start with the first full week of the new year

For example, to specify Sunday as the first day of the week and to count the first full week of the year as the first week in a year, you can use either:

```
datepart("ww","September 1",vbSunday,vbFirstFullWeek)
```

or

```
datepart("ww","September 1",1,3)
```

DateSerial()

Category: VBScript

Type	Function

Browser Support		Navigator 3	Navigator 4	Explorer 3	Explorer 4
	Macintosh	☐	☐	☐	■
	Windows	☐	☐	■	■

Syntax	`DateSerial(Year, Month, Day)`

The DateSerial() function returns the date value specified by the numeric *year*, *month*, and *day* parameters. While *month* and *day* may be any integer, the *year* must be between 0 and 9999—year values between 0 and 99 will be interpreted as the years 1900 to 1999. To specify a date outside the 1900–1999 range, use a complete four digit value.

The exact format of the date value returned depends on the localization of the user's system. In these examples, the system is localized to U.S. standard *mm/dd/yyyy* format.

dateserial(72,5,23)   returns 5/23/72

dateserial(2010,10,15) returns 10/15/2010

Values for *month* range from 1 (January) to 12 (December), while *day* may range from 1 to 31. However, month and day values that fall outside their respective range will add or subtract time accordingly.

dateserial(90,15,1)   returns 3/1/91

In the example above, the value 15 for *month* evaluates to month 3 (15–12), while the year is advanced by one.

You can use the DateSerial() function to quickly add or subtract time to or from a date. For instance, the below example adds 5 days to and subtracts 11 years from the date June 1, 1999:

dateserial(99-11,1+5,6)   returns 6/6/88

There are only two circumstances under which the DateSerial() function will return an error: If any parameter falls outside the range −32,768 to 32,767 or if the entire date falls outside the valid date range of January 1, 100 to December 31, 9999.

dateserial(32768,30,5) returns overflow error

dateserial(10000,1,1) returns invalid procedure call error

DateValue()
Category: VBScript

| | Type | Function |

Browser Support

	Navigator 3	Navigator 4	Explorer 3	Explorer 4
Macintosh				■
Windows			■	■

| | Syntax | DateValue(date) |

The DateValue() function simply takes a string expression which represents a *date*, and returns a date subtype localized to the user's system settings. For example:

datevalue("Feb 1 1981")	returns 2/1/81
datevalue("8,9,67")	returns 8/9/67
datevalue("April 21")	returns 4/21/97

D

In the last example above, the current year (1997) is assumed because it was not specified in *date*.

The *date* parameter may also contain time information, but the time will not be returned. However, if the specified time is invalid, an error *will* be generated.

datevalue("June 1 1988 12:00:00")	returns 6/1/88
datevalue("June 1 1988 40:75:00")	returns type mismatch error

Day()
Category: VBScript

Type	Function

Browser Support		Navigator 3	Navigator 4	Explorer 3	Explorer 4
	Macintosh	☐	☐	☐	■
	Windows	☐	☐	■	■

Syntax Day(date)

The Day() function returns a value, from 1 to 31, which represents the day of the month for *date*. If the *date* contains an invalid day of the month, an error will occur.

day("October 10 1947")	returns 10
day("Feb 29 1996")	returns 29
day("2,29,97")	returns type mismatch error

If you pass a null *date* to Day() then the value null is returned.

<DFN>

Category: HTML

Browser Support

	Navigator 3	Navigator 4	Explorer 3	Explorer 4
Macintosh	☐	☐	■	■
Windows	☐	☐	■	■

May Contain

<A>, <APPLET>, <B>, <BASEFONT>, <BIG>, <BR>, <CITE>, <CODE>, <DFN>, <EM>, <FONT>, <I>, <IMG>, <INPUT>, <KBD>, <MAP>, <SAMP>, <SELECT>, <SMALL>, <STRIKE>, <STRONG>, <SUB>, <SUP>, <TEXTAREA>, <TT>, <U>, <VAR>

May Be Used In

<A>, <ADDRESS>, <APPLET>, <B>, <BIG>, <BLOCKQUOTE>, <CAPTION>, <CENTER>, <CITE>, <CODE>, <DD>, <DFN>, <DIV>, <DT>, <EM>, <FONT>, <FORM>, <H1>, <H2>, <H3>, <H4>, <H5>, <H6>, <I>, <KBD>, <LI>, <P>, <PRE>, <SAMP>, <SMALL>, <STRIKE>, <STRONG>, <SUB>, <SUP>, <TD>, <TH>, <TT>, <U>, <VAR>

Syntax   <DFN>...</DFN>

The <DFN>, or definition tag, is used to accentuate a term the first time it is mentioned in a web page. This is a formal, older tag traditionally used in scientific or academic papers; it usually renders all text specified by it in italics. The closing, or </DFN> tag, is required.

Hence, the following example:

```
<P>British science-fiction hero Dr. Who traveled in a time machine called the
<DFN>Tardis</DFN>.<BR>
```

Figures 1 and 2 display this example HTML in Internet Explorer 3 for the Mac and for Windows.

Figure 1

Highlighting a definition using the <DFN> tag in Internet Explorer 3 for the Mac.

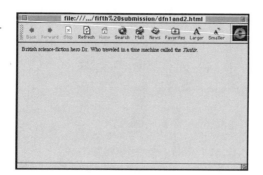

Figure 2

Highlighting a definition using the <DFN> tag in Internet Explorer 3 for Windows.

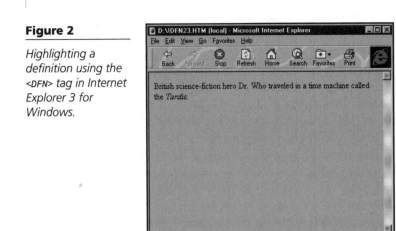

D

Navigator does not support the <DFN> tag, and some earlier versions of Internet Explorer and once-standard browsers like Mosaic may not display <DFN>-specified text as described here.

If you want to italicize text in your web page with complete, crossplatform certainty, use the <I> tag instead. See the <I> tag entry elsewhere in this book for more information.

<DIR>

Category: HTML

Browser Support		Navigator 3	Navigator 4	Explorer 3	Explorer 4
	Macintosh	▬	▬	▬	▬
	Windows	▬	▬	▬	▬

May Contain   <LI>

May Be Used In   <BLOCKQUOTE>, <BODY>, <CENTER>, <DD>, <DIV>, <FORM>, <LI>, <TD>, <TH>

Attributes   COMPACT

Syntax   <DIR>...</DIR>

The <DIR> tag is a rarely used list tag that specifies a list of individual, unordered (or nonalphabetized) items on a web page, similar to the results specified by the <UL> tag. Each item in a <DIR>-specified list should be no longer than 20 characters, as browsers typically arrange <DIR> lists in 24-character wide columns. A closing, or </DIR> tag, is also required.

Also, an <LI> tag must be placed before each list item or the browser won't recognize them—you can add a <BR> tag to create <LI>-like line breaks, but you won't get the proper spacing or the bullets. In other words, there's not much point.

The following is an example list containing the kinds of items well-suited to a <DIR> type of list:

```
<P>Requirements:<BR>
<DIR><LI>4 hours of English
<LI>4 hours of History or Humanities
<LI>4 hours of Science
<LI>4 hours of Art
<LI>2 hours of Physical Education
</DIR>
```

Figures 1, 2, 3, and 4 illustrate this example HTML in Navigator 3 and Internet Explorer 3 for the Macintosh and for Windows.

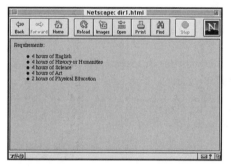

Figure 1

A <DIR> list in Navigator 3 for the Macintosh.

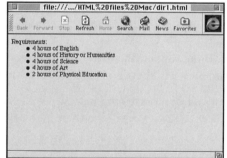

Figure 2

A <DIR> list in Internet Explorer 3 for the Macintosh.

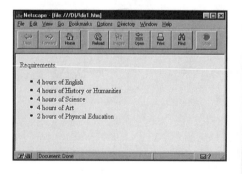

Figure 3

A <DIR> list in Navigator 3 for Windows.

Figure 4

A <DIR> list in Internet Explorer 3 for Windows.

See the <UL> tag entry elsewhere in the book for more information.

> **NOTE**   Using a block element, a list element, or a table with the <LI> tag as an item in a <DIR> or a <MENU> list is "not permitted"—that's tech-talk for it won't work. In other words, you cannot bold something with the <B> tag, or specify a phrase with <H3>, and/or write a table into a <DIR>- or a <MENU>-specified list.

COMPACT

The COMPACT attribute is used to tell the browser that items in the list are short, so the list can be tightened accordingly. When this attribute is used within a <DL> list in Navigator 3, for example, the browser will display two items on one line.

In <DIR> lists, however, neither Navigator nor Internet Explorer 3 will display COMPACT-specified lists any differently than regular <DIR> lists, even when the list items are only one character long. So use of this attribute in these two browsers, on either the Macintosh or the Windows platforms, seems to serve no purpose.

`display`

Category: Cascading Style Sheets

Browser Support		Navigator 3	Navigator 4	Explorer 3	Explorer 4
	Macintosh		■		
	Windows		■		

Applies To All elements

Syntax `display: value`

The `display` property changes the way objects are treated by your browser. You can modify Hypertext links so that they are always treated as items in a list, for example. As another example, you can make a non-block element, such as bold text, into a block element such as a paragrpah. You decide if or how an element is treated and displayed including as a block-level element, an inline element, or an item in a list. You also can define if the item is displayed at all. Using `display`, you can take all the advantages of working with one type of element, and utilize those advantages when working with a completely different element.

Traditionally, all HTML tags come with built-in assumptions about what they are. Tags like <p> and <h1> are block-level, because they automatically create their own new line breaks and thus their own "box." Other HTML tags are automatically treated as inline elements such as <i> and <code>. They define styles within a line instead of starting a new line. Then there are list-item HTML tags, such as <li>. With the `display` property, you can override these default assumptions making <p> an inline element or <i> a block-level element. You do this by specifying the `display` property with one of the keywords `block`, `inline`, `list-item`, and `none`, which affect the given element according to the keyword used. An item with `none` is not displayed.

```
h1 { display: list-item }

<h1 style="display: block">
```

If you give an element a `display` value of `block`, the browser will treat it like it does any other block-level element: the element will get its own box, and be appropriately positioned relative to other boxes on the page—via padding, border, and margin. In this simple example below, `<b>` is treated as a block-level element, though it normally would not. When displaying bold text, then the browser should give the text its own line, just as it would for an `<h1>` or other such block-level element (see Figure 1).

```
<html>
 <style type="text/css">
 <!--
   body { background: white;
          font-size: 20px }
   B    { display: block }
 -->
 </style>
<head>
 <title>Specifying Display Classification</title>
</head>
<body>
 <p>Welcome to the <b>display property</b>, which enables you to
 set how an element is treated by a browser.</p>
</body>
</html>
```

Figure 1

<b> is now a block-level element.

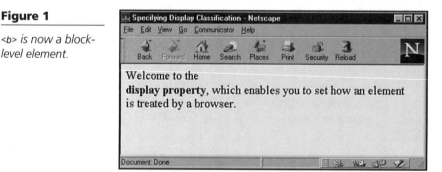

Navigator 4 inserts a line break *before* the new `block` element, but as you can see, it doesn't do so *after* the element as it also should.

Similarly, you can also force elements to become inline or list-item elements:

```html
<html>
 <style type="text/css">
 <!--
  body { background: white;
         font-size: 20px }
  h1    { display: inline }
  .a    { display: list-item }
 -->
 </style>
<head>
 <title>Specifying Display Classification</title>
</head>
<body>
 <p>Welcome to the <h1>display property</h1>, which enables you to
 set how an element is treated by a browser.</p>
 <span class=a><img src="face.gif"></span>
 <span class=a><img src="face.gif"></span>
 <span class=a><img src="face.gif"></span>
</body>
</html>
```

Without styles, this page would consist of three blocks of text, then three inline graphics in the next line. But since <h1> is declared as an inline element, there should be only one paragraph of text. And since the graphics are list items, they should each be on their own lines and with preceding bullet symbols (see Figure 2).

Figure 2

Navigator displays the newly defined items as it should, though the preceding bullets are missing.

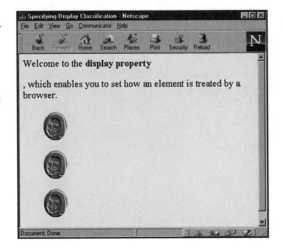

`display`

Category: JavaScript Style Sheets

		Navigator 3	Navigator 4	Explorer 3	Explorer 4
Type	Property				
Browser Support	Macintosh	☐	■	☐	☐
	Windows	☐	■	☐	☐
Applies To	All elements				
Inherited	No				
Syntax	display = "*value*"				

display is one of three classification properties, along with listStyleType and whiteSpace, in JavaScript Style Sheets. These properties are not used to explicitly set visual styles of the element, but instead to associate it with a HTML style that is already found in generic HTML. Each of the following four values, except for "none", is found as a default classification in HTML.

- ■ "block" defines the element to be a block level element, like <p> in HTML. Block-level elements will start on a new line.

- ■ "inline" classifies an element as being in line with other elements surrounding it, like the <em> element is used in HTML.

- ■ "list-item" defines the element to be a list item, and thus part of a list. The example in HTML is <li>.

- ■ "none" does not turn off previous classifications, but instead gives the element no display properties; thus the element is not shown.

Using the display property you can define styles that override the default behavior of an element and have those styles be used consistently throughout the document. The following code sample and Figure 1, show that a style defined for <em> elements can change the <em> elements from being in line elements to block level elements.

```
<HTML>
<HEAD>
<style type="text/javascript">
tags.em.display = "block";
</style>
</HEAD>
<BODY>
<p> This is my document and the <em> stuff in the middle
here should be </em> on the same line as the paragraph.
<p> But instead it is split out like block-level elements.
</BODY>
</HTML>
```

Figure 1

<em> is now block-level.

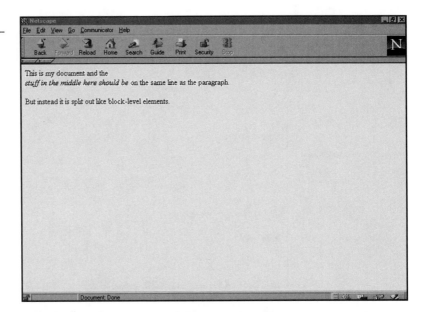

Another use of the display style is for turning off the display of certain elements based other document properties. In the following example, if the background color of the document is white then <em> text does not display.

```
<HTML>
<HEAD>
<SCRIPT LANGUAGE="JavaScript">
<!--
//-->
</SCRIPT>
<style type="text/javascript">
tags.body.backgroundColor = "white"
if (tags.body.backgroundColor == "white") {
tags.em.display = "none";
}
</style>
</HEAD>
<BODY>
<p> If the background is white then this is the only
text to display. <em> And this text will show if the background
is any other color </em>
</BODY>
</HTML>
```

This is used when information is not valuable to certain types of users and would clutter important information. Figures 2 and 3 show the results based on the changing of the background color.

Figure 2

*With a background
color of white.*

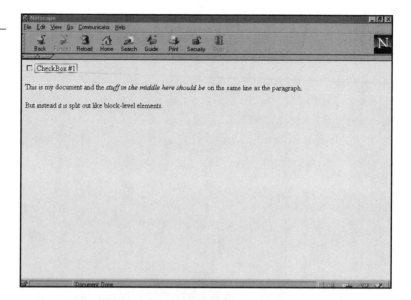

Figure 3

*With a background
color of gray.*

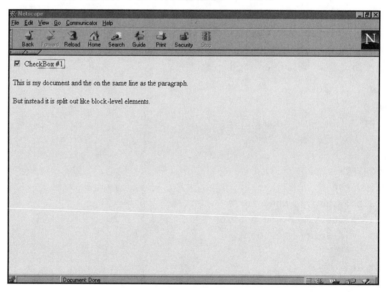

The previous code listing is simple HTML form definition using JavaScript. The important line
of JSSS is contained within the JavaScript function

```
function turnoffem () {
tags.em.display = "none";
}
```

The JSSS can be broken down as follows:

- **tags** is one of the methods of defining JSSS styles. The **tags** definition describes the element immediately following it in the dot notation will be one of the accepted HTML elements.

- **em** is the html element that is being assigned a style. This may be any valid html element.

- **display** is the style that is being defined for the element. This may be any valid JSSS style.

- **"none"** is the value of the style **display**. This value means that the HTML element defined with this style will not be displayed.

D

<DIV>

Category: HTML

Browser Support		Navigator 3	Navigator 4	Explorer 3	Explorer 4
	Macintosh	■	■	■	■
	Windows	■	■	■	■

May Contain <A>, <ADDRESS>, <APPLET>, <B>, <BASEFONT>, <BIG>, <BLOCKQUOTE>, <BODY>, <BR>, <CENTER>, <CITE>, <CODE>, <DFN>, <DIR>, <DIV>, <DL>, <EM>, <FONT>, <FORM>, <H1>, <H2>, <H3>, <H4>, <H5>, <H6>, <HR>, <I>, <IMG>, <INPUT>, <KBD>, <MAP>, <MENU>, <OL>, <P>, <PRE>, <SAMP>, <SELECT>, <SMALL>, <STRIKE>, <STRONG>, <SUB>, <SUP>, <TABLE>, <TEXTAREA>, <TT>, <U>, <UL>, <VAR>

May Be Used In <BLOCKQUOTE>, <CENTER>,<DD>, <FORM>, <LI>, <TD>, <TH>

Attributes ALIGN, CLASS, ID, LANG, NOWRAP

Syntax <DIV>...</DIV>

The <DIV> or division tag is used to create differently aligned or styled sections within a web page. Traditionally the <DIV> tag was used to create individual chapters, abstracts, or appendixes, but its usefulness has greatly increased with the introduction of style sheets. A closing, or </DIV>, tag is required.

ALIGN

The ALIGN attribute is used to specify the default horizontal alignment. It has four values:

center Text within the <DIV> tag is centered.

justify Text within the <DIV> tag is justified to both the right and left margins.

left Text within the <DIV> tag is aligned to the left edge of the browser window. This is the default ALIGN value.

right Text within the <DIV> tag is aligned to the right edge of the browser window.

Figures 1 through 8 display this example HTML in Netscape Navigator 3 and Internet Explorer 3 for Mac.

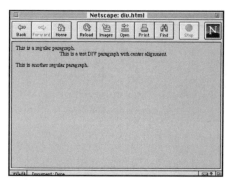

Figure 1

Aligning text within a <DIV> tag using the center value in Netscape Navigator 3 for Mac.

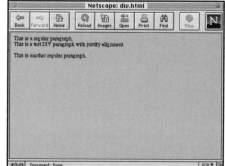

Figure 2

Aligning text within a <DIV> tag using the justify value in Netscape Navigator 3 for Mac.

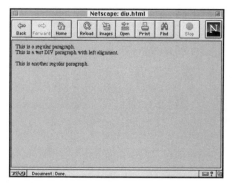

Figure 3

Aligning text within a <DIV> tag using the left value in Netscape Navigator 3 for Mac.

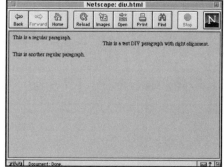

Figure 4

Aligning text within a <DIV> tag using the right value in Netscape Navigator 3 for Mac.

One note about using <DIV> ALIGN center: originally, Netscape browsers did not support the <DIV> tag at all, so the <CENTER> tag was added. Both tags are retained as part of the HTML 3.2 standard because <CENTER> is widely used, but older versions of Navigator and text-only browsers may not recognize <DIV> ALIGN center at all.

D

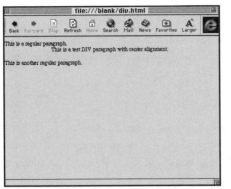

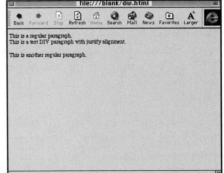

Figure 5

Aligning text within a <DIV> tag using the center value in Netscape Navigator 3 for Windows.

Figure 6

Aligning text within a <DIV> tag using the justify value in Netscape Navigator 3 for Windows.

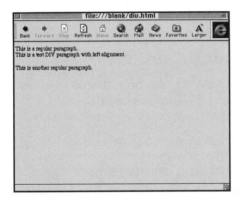

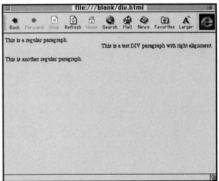

Figure 7

Aligning text within a <DIV> tag using the left value in Netscape Navigator 3 for Windows.

Figure 8

Aligning text within a <DIV> ta g using the right value in Netscape Navigator 3 for Windows.

Also, because <DIV> behaves like a block element, it will override any existing <P> tag specifications. That is, if you stick a <DIV>-specified section of text in the middle of a <P>-specified paragraph, any <P>-specified alignment or style properties will not hold to the text or images that follow the <DIV> section. So if you include a <DIV>-specified section within a <P> paragraph, you must add a line break <BR> to "reset" or reinstate <P> tag specifications.

CLASS

The CLASS attribute is used to specify the name of a style sheets as it applies to a specific selection on a web page. See the "Cascading Style Sheets Basics" chapter and any individual, related Style Sheets entries elsewhere in the book for more information.

ID

The ID attribute is used to distinguish individual selections in a web page as pertaining to the use of style sheets. See the "Cascading Style Sheets Basics" chapter and any individual, related style sheets entries elsewhere in the book for more information.

LANG

The LANG attribute is an Internet Explorer–specific feature used to indicate an ISO- or International Standards Organization-designated abbreviation. If you are using the <DIV> tag to assign style sheet specifications to a section of text, you would use the LANG attribute to specify a particular character set or alphabet.

NOWRAP

The NOWRAP attribute prevents lines of text from being automatically wrapped by the browser reading the web page. It is not supported by Netscape Navigator 3, Internet Explorer 3 for Mac, or Netscape Navigator 3 for Windows.

For example, in this HTML a short poem is offset from two other sections of text using the <DIV> tag and the NOWRAP attribute:

```
<P>This text is normal plain text that follows default attributes.

<DIV NOWRAP>This text will not break no matter how long, lengthy, or wordy this
paragraph gets, nor how narrow the browser window gets.</DIV><BR>
This text is also normal plain text following default attributes.</P>
```

Figure 9 displays this example HTML in Internet Explorer 3 for Windows.

Figure 9

Using the NOBR attribute in Internet Explorer 3 for Windows.

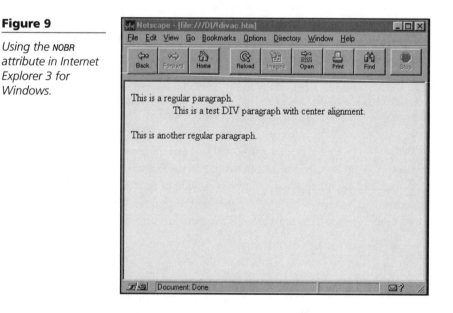

<DL>

Category: HTML

		Navigator 3	Navigator 4	Explorer 3	Explorer 4
Browser Support	Macintosh	■	■	■	■
	Windows	■	■	■	■

D

May Contain <DD>, <DT>

May Be Used In <BLOCKQUOTE>, <BODY>, <CENTER>, <DD>, <DIV>, <FORM>, <LI>, <TD>, <TH>

Attributes CLASS, COMPACT, ID

Syntax <DL>...</DL>

The <DL> tag creates a list of items with related definitions. Each item in a <DL> list is enclosed within the <DT> tag with the corresponding definition enclosed within the <DD> tag immediately afterwards. A closing, or </DL> tag, is required.

The following example is a simple <DL> list:

```
<DL>
<DT>Breakfast
<DD>Bagel and coffee eaten in the car.
<DT>Lunch
<DD>Burger and fries eaten at the desk.
<DT>Dinner
<DD>Pizza eaten in front of the TV.
</DL>
```

Typically, the <DT>-specified terms would appear flush against the left margin with each related <DD>-specified definition just below, indented on its own line.

Figures 1, 2, 3, and 4 illustrate this simple <DL> list in Netscape Navigator 3 and Internet Explorer 3 for the Mac and for Windows.

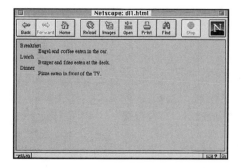

Figure 1

A simple <DL> list in Navigator 3 for the Mac.

Figure 2

A simple <DL> list in Internet Explorer 3 for the Mac.

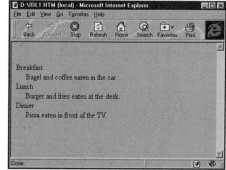

Figure 3

A simple <DL> list in Navigator 3 for Windows.

Figure 4

A simple <DL> list in Internet Explorer 3 for Windows.

> **NOTE** The <DD> and <DT> tags are only used here to describe how a <DL> list is constructed. See the separate <DD> and <DT> entries elsewhere in the book for more information on how these tags work.

Remember also that a <DL> list may only contain text items specified with either the <DD> or the <DT> tags—no plain untagged text, no tables, no forms, no images, nothing.

CLASS

The CLASS attribute is used to specify the name of a style sheets as it applies to a specific selection on a web page. See the "Cascading Style Sheets Basics" chapter and any individual, related style sheets entries elsewhere in the book for more information.

COMPACT

The COMPACT attribute tells the browser that items in the <DL> list are short, so the list can be tightened accordingly. Some browsers, for example, will list more than one item on one line.

In the following example, none of the list elements exceed 10 characters, roughly half the width of a regular or default list column width:

```
<DL COMPACT>
<DT>Cat
<DD>meow
<DT>Dog
<DD>woof
<DT>Cow
<DD>moo
</DIR>
```

Figures 5 and 6 illustrate this example HTML in Navigator 3 for the Mac and for Windows. Internet Explorer 3 does not support this <DL> tag attribute.

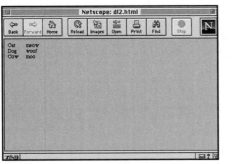

Figure 5

A <DL> list in Navigator 3 for the Mac.

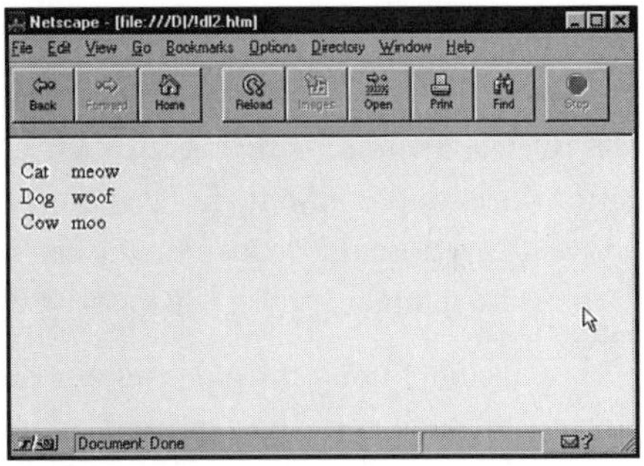

Figure 6

A <DL> list in Navigator 3 for Windows.

ID

The ID attribute is used to distinguish individual selections in a web page as pertaining to the use of style sheets. See the "Cascading Style Sheets Basics" chapter and any individual, related style sheets entries elsewhere in the book for more information.

Document

Category: JavaScript, JScript, and VBScript

Type	Object

Browser Support		Navigator 3	Navigator 4	Explorer 3	Explorer 4
	Macintosh	■	■	☐	■
	Windows	■	■	■	■

Subset Of	Window object

Properties	alinkcolor, anchors(length), applets(length), bgcolor, cookie, domain, embeds(length), fgcolor, forms(length), images(length), lastmodified, linkcolor, links(length), referrer, title, URL, vlinkcolor

Methods	clear(), close(), getSelection(), open(), write(), writeln()

Syntax	document.*property* OR document.*method*

The document object is a large object encompassing all the elements that you see in the content section of the browser window, as illustrated in Figure 1. Many of the document object's properties reference subordinate objects, such as link, anchor, form, applet, image, and area (the latter three supported only in JavaScript 1.1 and higher). Keep in mind that the contents of a *window* comprise the document object—because a frame is a window, a page containing multiple frames also contains multiple document objects, as shown in Figure 2.

Other document object properties can directly alter characteristics of the currently loaded document, such as the background color (bgColor) and foreground color (fgColor). You can even make behind-the-scenes changes, such as creating cookies that can be used to "tag" individual users to your site (via the cookie property).

Figure 1

All characteristics of this page (colors, hyperlinks, form fields, and so on) are contained within the document object.

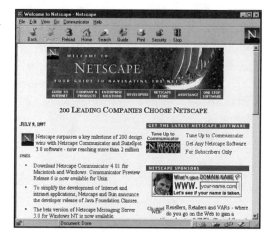

Figure 2

Each frame is a window, therefore each frame contains an independent document object.

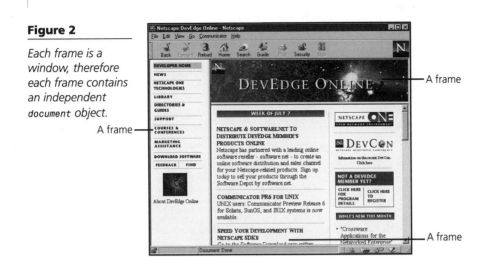

A frame

A frame

A frame

D

Using the document object's `open()`, `write()`, and `writeln()` methods, you can also create entirely new web pages on-the-fly by outputting HTML content to a newly opened browser window.

alinkColor property

The `alinkColor` property is the color of active links in the document. "Active links" refers to the brief moment after a hyperlink has been clicked, before the link is followed (while the mouse button is still depressed). Typically, the link changes color after being clicked as a way to provide feedback to the user, proving that an action has occurred.

Modifying this property changes the color for all active links in the document—you cannot modify only some of them.

```
document.alinkColor="#00a855"
```

TIP   All color values are specified as a hexadecimal triplet. The triplet indicates the RGB color values in the form of "#RRGGBB," where each color is a hexadecimal value between 00 and FF. Alternatively, you may instead specify a predefined color name; for instance:

```
document.alinkColor="green"
```

You can refer to Appendix B for predefined color names and their associated hexadecimal triplet values.

When you modify the `alinkColor` property on a page within Navigator or Internet Explorer 4, the page will immediately reflect the change. That is, the next time the user clicks a hyperlink, it will take on the newly specified color.

Internet Explorer 3 does not feature active links—that is, no color changes take place when the user clicks a hyperlink. Although the `alinkColor` property is supported for compatibility reasons, modifications to it have no effect on the page.

anchors[] property

The anchors property is an array of all the anchor objects in the document. An anchor is a hyperlink that has been given a name via the name attribute of the <a> tag. Each element in the `anchors[]` array is references ann anchor object. Anchor objects are indexed in the array in the order in which they appear in the HTML source. (See the anchor object.)

To reference a particular anchor object:

```
document.anchors[index].property
```

length property

The `anchors[]` property also possesses a `length` property of its own. This property reflects the total number of anchors on the page. As such, it also reflects the number of anchor object elements in the `anchors[]` array.

```
total=document.anchors.length
```

applets[] property

The applets property is an array of all the Java applet objects in the document. An applet is included in the document via the <applet> tag. Each element in the `applets[]` array is an applet object. Applet objects are indexed in the array in the order in which they appear in the HTML source. (See applet object.)

To reference a particular applet object:

```
document.applets[index].property
```

or

```
document.applets[index].method()
```

length property

The `applets[]` property also possesses a `length` property of its own. This property reflects the total number of Java applets on the page. As such, it also reflects the number of applet object elements in the `applets[]` array.

```
total=document.applets.length
```

Internet Explorer 3 does not support the `applets[]` property. At the time of this writing, it is unknown how Internet Explorer 4 may support this property.

bgColor property

The `bgColor` property is the background color of the document, originally determined by the `bgcolor` attribute of the `<body>` tag. Modifying this property results in an immediate onscreen effect, as the background color of the document changes to the newly specified color.

```
document.bgColor="#FAFAFA"
```

TIP All color values are specified as a hexadecimal triplet. The triplet indicates the RGB color values in the form of "#RRGGBB," where each color is a hexadecimal value between 00 and FF. Alternatively, you may instead specify a predefined color name, for instance:

```
document.bgColor="steelblue"
```

You can refer to Appendix B for predefined color names and their associated hexadecimal triplet values.

DESIGN NOTE When changing the background color of the document, don't forget about the foreground color! Modifying only the background color might result in unreadable text if the current foreground color doesn't contrast well with the new background color. (See the `fgColor` property.)

cookie property

A cookie is a string value that is stored on the user's machine, either in RAM or on the hard drive. For security reasons, cookies are the only way to save or retrieve information on the user's machine.

Generally, a bit of information about the user is stored in the cookie, and it is then retrieved when the user re-visits your page on another occasion. This enables your page to "remember" certain characteristics of the individual user, such as his email address, or site preferences that he has previously chosen. The cookie does *not* enable you to read any data from the user's machine other than the cookie itself.

Two typical uses of cookies:

1. Single-session cookies. Stored in the user's RAM, this cookie only lasts for as long as the user's browser is currently running. Commonly, single-session cookies are used in "shopping cart" scenarios, where a user selects items of interest across several pages within a Web site. This enables the "cashier" page to "remember" all the items the user has picked up along the way while browsing that particular site.

2. Long-term cookies. Stored on the user's hard drive, this cookie lasts for as long as you define it to, anywhere from minutes to years. Often, long-term cookies are used to remember characteristics of a user. For instance, you might use a cookie to simply note the date of the current visit to your page. The next time that user visits, you'll be able to recall the date he last visited, and perhaps update him on any important information since then. Other long-term cookies are used to keep track of a set of preferences. Suppose a visitor to your site is using your search engine, and he configures your search engine to yield 100 hits at a time sorted by date. You could store these preferences with a long-term cookie, and when the user next visits your page, you can automatically configure the search engine options to match his preferences.

WARNING There are many restrictions placed upon cookies for the sake of security. Consider:

- The cookie cannot contain more than 4K of data.

- The cookie is never *executed*, its contents can merely be read by a web page script.

- The cookie can only directly be read by web pages, within the same domain, specified by the cookie's creator.

- Cookies *cannot* be used to "see" any other data on the user's computer, nor can they determine the user's email address or identity, unless the user has voluntarily submitted such information.

Having said that, when a user does submit his identity, he may not realize that it will be used in a cookie unless your page provides such a notice. Although the technology does not require that you obtain consent to use submitted information in a cookie, many feel that ethical considerations should take precedence.

To set a cookie, use the following script statement.

```
document.cookie = "cookieName=cookieValue
    [;expires=GMTdate]
    [;domain=domainName]
    [;path=pathName]
    [;secure]"
```

At the very least, every cookie has a name and string value. This is the *only* data that can be retrieved by the cookie. The string value contains the data you want to "save." You may express this data in any way you want, since you must code the script that retrieves and makes sense of it. There are a few restrictions, though: the cookie value cannot contain any whitespaces, semicolons, or commas.

The `expires` parameter specifies a date in GMT format when the cookie will expire. After the cookie has expired, it cannot be retrieved by the web page, just as if it were never created.

In JavaScript, for example, you can use the `toGMTString()` method of the `date` object to create an expiration date (see `date` object).

In VBScript, the various date related functions can be used to create a valid date. I would have loved to include VBscript tip on how to convert a date to GMT, however after much research I've failed to come up with a way. VBScript doesn't seem to know about time zones, which is necessary to represent a date in GMT (must subtract or add time zone number of hours and minutes from local date).

D

Omitting the `expires` parameter will cause the cookie to be deleted as soon as the browser is exited, thereby creating a single-session cookie. Setting the `expires` parameter to a date prior to the current date immediately expires the cookie. This is how you can force a cookie to be deleted before its original expiration date—re-create the cookie, but with an `expires` date earlier than the present.

The `domain` parameter indicates which network domain is allowed to access the cookie. By default, cookie access is restricted the host name of the server from which the cookie was set. You may set this to a narrower domain to restrict cookie access to specific pages on that server.

For example, if Macmillan Computer Publishing wanted only the pages on `goodbooks.mcp.com` to have access to a cookie, they would set `domain=goodbooks.mcp.com`. You can further restrict cookie access to particular pages using the `path` parameter below.

The `path` parameter, in a way similar to the `domain` parameter, indicates which pathname in the domain may access the cookie. Setting `path` to "/" would allow access to all paths in the domain. Setting `path` to "/home/user2" would restrict cookie access to pages which reside within the specified `domain` *and* reside within the file path "/home/user2" on the server. The `path` parameter defaults, if omitted, to the full path of the page that created it.

If the `secure` parameter is specified, only pages communicating over a secure (HTTPS) channel will be allowed to access the cookie. If omitted, the cookie can be accessed over any connection, secure or insecure.

Imagine that we want to set a cookie, which is named `email`, and the value `beagle@woof.com`. The cookie expires on January 1, 1999. It can only be accessed from within the domain `bookseller.virtualworld.com`, and from within the path `/bookseller/orderform`, but *it* does not require a secure connection.

```
document.cookie="email=beagle@woof.com; expires=Fri, 01 Jan 1999 00:00:00 GMT;
domain=bookseller.virtualworld.com; path=/bookseller/orderform"
```

Retrieving the `cookie` property will yield all the cookie name and value pairs that meet the domain, path, and secure requirements. The pairs will all be contained in a single string, separated by a semicolon and a space. Thus, the statement

```
cookies=document.cookie
```

would assign a string such as the following to the variable `cookies`, assuming a page that has created three cookies with identical domain, path, and secure requirements:

```
userID=16; passwd=slobber; email=beagle@woof.com
```

To extract the cookie data from the returned string, such as above, you need to write your own script. Typically, you would use string methods, such as JavaScript's `indexOf()`, `charAt()`, `substring()`, and `lastIndexOf()` (all methods of the `string` object) or VBScript's `inStr()`, `right()`, `left()`, and `mid()` functions to parse for the desired cookie name and value.

> **NOTE** In continuing to pursue their own interests, and making life difficult for us in the process, Navigator supports the creation of 20 cookies per domain, while Internet Explorer 3 only supports 1 cookie per domain. Therefore, if you intend to cater to Internet Explorer visitors, try to pack as much data into a single cookie as possible (up to the maximum of around 4K).

> **TIP** Because the cookie format can be rather difficult to understand, a JavaScript guru named Bill Dortch of hIdaho Design has released some generic cookie functions to the public domain. You can either use or learn from these script functions to manage cookies in your own pages. The cookie functions are available at `http://www.hidaho.com/cookies/cookie.txt`.

domain property

Initially, the `domain` property reflects the domain name of the server from which the web page was delivered. However, this property serves a great purpose in protecting certain security interests.

It would be a security risk to allow a script in a web page to access properties of any other page that is currently open. This is the reason Netscape has introduced *data tainting*, which prevents or allows certain properties from being accessed by other scripts.

However, in some cases there is good cause for a web page from one server to share data with a page for another server—specifically, within sites that use multiple servers. A classic example is the Yahoo catalog, which maintains its table of contents on the server `www.yahoo.com` and its search engine on `search.yahoo.com`.

By setting the `domain` property, you can allow your script to access other pages which share the same `domain` property. Thus, if the page from `www.yahoo.com` and the page from `search.yahoo.com` both set their respective `domain` property to `yahoo.com`, they can share each other's properties.

```
document.domain=yahoo.com
```

Of course, there are limitations on how you can set the `domain` property. Before you modify this property, it is automatically set to the domain name of the server from which the page was loaded. You can only modify the `domain` property to a suffix of this domain name. In other words, if your page originated from `fuzzy.wuzzy.com`, you can only set the `domain` property to a domain ending in `wuzzy.com`.

Lastly, you can only modify the domain property one time in your page's script—it then becomes read-only for the duration of that script.

 Internet Explorer 3 does not support the domain property.

embeds[] property

The embeds property is an array of all the embedded objects in the document. An embedded object is included in a document using the <embed> tag. Typically, an embedded object is a file of a particular data type that requires a plug-in to be launched.

For instance, if you embed a QuickTime movie in the web page, the browser will try to launch the QuickTime plug-in to view it (if that plug-in has been installed by the user—see plug-in object).

Only embedded objects that are Java-enabled can be accessed via the embeds[] property. If an embedded object is Java-enabled, you can access its fields and methods using the construction

```
document.embeds[index].field
```
or
```
document.embeds[index].method()
```

However, these fields and methods vary from object to object, so you must consult the documentation provided by the manufacturer of the object for further reference.

length property

The embeds[] property also possesses a length property of its own. This property reflects the total number of embedded objects on the page.

```
total=document.embeds.length
```

 Internet Explorer 3 does not support the embeds[] property.

fgColor property

The fgColor property is the foreground color of the document, originally determined by the fgcolor attribute of the <body> tag. This property determines the default color of text content, which does not have a particular color specified by the color attribute of the <font> tag. Modifying this property results in an immediate onscreen effect, as the foreground color of the document changes to the newly specified color.

```
document.fgColor="#000000"
```

> **TIP** All color values are specified as a hexadecimal triplet. The triplet indicates the RGB color values in the form of "#RRGGBB," where each color is a hexadecimal value between 00 and FF. Alternatively, you may instead specify a pre-defined color name; for instance
>
> ```
> document.fgColor="black"
> ```
>
> You can refer to Appendix B for pre-defined color names and their associated hexadecimal triplet values.

> **DESIGN NOTE** When changing the foreground color of the document, don't forget about the background color! Modifying only the foreground color might result in unreadable text if the current background color doesn't contrast well with the new foreground color. (See the `bgColor` property.)

forms[ ] property

The `forms` property is an array of all the `form` objects in the document. A form is included in the document via the `<form>` tag. Each element in the `forms[ ]` array is a `form` object. Form objects themselves contain numerous subproperties which are, themselves, objects representing each possible form field (such as the `checkbox` object, `text` object, and so on). Form objects are indexed in the array in the order in which they appear in the HTML source. (See `form` object.)

To reference a `form` object:

`document.forms[index].property`

or

`document.forms[index].method()`

length property

The `forms[ ]` property also possesses a `length` property of its own. This property reflects the total number of forms on the page. As such, it also reflects the number of `form` object elements in the `forms[ ]` array.

`total=document.forms.length`

images[ ] property

The `images` property is an array of all the `image` objects in the document. An image is included in the document via the `<img>` tag. Each element in the `images[ ]` array is an `image` object. Image objects are indexed in the array in the order in which they appear in the HTML source. (See `image` object.)

To reference an image object:

`document.images[index].property`

length **property**

The `images[]` property also possesses a `length` property of its own. This property reflects the total number of images on the page. As such, it also reflects the number of image object elements in the `images[]` array.

`total=document.images.length`

 Internet Explorer 3 does not support the `images[]` property.

lastModified **property**

The `lastModified` property is the local date and time in which the document was last modified. This value is not a `date` object, but a string in the format specific to the file system of the machine that maintains the page. Not all servers report a modification date, in which case this property may contain the value 0 or January 1, 1970.

Typically, this property is used to add a footnote at the bottom of a Web page reflecting its last date of update:

JavaScript

`document.writeln("<h5>Page last modified: "+document.lastModified+"</h5>")`

VBScript

`document.writeln("<h5>Page last modified: "&document.lastModified&%"</h5>")`

linkColor **property**

The `linkColor` property is the color of unselected, unvisited links in the document, originally determined by the `link` attribute of the `<body>` tag.

Modifying this property after the page has been loaded will have no onscreen effect—it should be modified at the time of HTML evaluation. This means that to be effective, a statement such as the one below must reside within `<script>` tags which are within the `<body>` tags of the document.

To assign a new color to all unvisited hyperlinks:

`document.linkColor="#E8A0B2"`

Within Internet Explorer 3 and 4, modifications to the `linkColor` property *do* immediately change the color of links onscreen.

> **TIP** All color values are specified as a hexadecimal triplet. The triplet indicates the RGB color values in the form of "#RRGGBB," where each color is a hexadecimal value between 00 and FF. Alternatively, you may instead specify a pre-defined color name; for instance
>
> ```
> document.linkColor="firebrick"
> ```
>
> You can refer to Appendix B for pre-defined color names and their associated hexadecimal triplet values.

links[] property

The links property is an array of all the link objects in the document, and in the case of JavaScript 1.1 and higher, area objects. A link object hyperlink is included in the document via the `<a>` tag, while area object hyperlinks are image map regions created with the `<area>` tag. Each element in the links[] array is either a link object or an area object (the latter in JavaScript 1.1 and higher only, Netscape Navigator 3+ or Internet Explorer 4 only). Link and area objects are indexed in the array in the order in which they appear in the HTML source. (See the link object and the area object.)

To reference a link or area object:

```
document.links[index].property
```

> Internet Explorer 3 does not support the **area** object; therefore, hyperlinks created using the `<area>` tag are *not* included in the links[] array. As a result, the elements in the links[] array within Netscape and Internet Explorer 4 may not be at the same indexes as those in the links[] array within Internet Explorer 3.

length property

The links[] property also possesses a length property of its own. This property reflects the total number of hyperlinks on the page. As such, it also reflects the combined number of link objects and area object elements in the links[] array.

```
total=document.links.length
```

> Internet Explorer 3 does not support the **area** object; therefore, the **length** property only reflects the number of hyperlinks of the **link** object type (those created using the `<a>` tag).

D

location **property**

The Location property is a string URL of the document containing the hypertext links that referred to this document. It has the same value as the document.URL property.

plug-ins[] **property**

This plug-ins[] property is merely a synonym for the embeds[] property of this same document object. To prevent confusion in reading your scripts, it is advised that you use the embeds[] property syntax. (See embeds[] property.)

Don't confuse this plug-ins property with the plug-ins[] property of the navigator object!

 Internet Explorer 3 does not support the plug-ins[] property.

referrer **property**

The referrer property is the URL of the document from which the user linked to the current document. It's not quite as confusing as it may sound: you click a hyperlink on page A which brings you to page B. Within page B, then, the referrer property is the URL of page A.

Using this property, you can sometimes determine from which page a user reached your own page.

```
origin=document.referrer
```

The referrer property will be empty if the user did not reach your link via a hyperlink; for instance, if he typed your URL directly into his browser, or opened a bookmark (also known as a "Favorite" in Internet Explorer).

title **property**

The title property reflects the "title" of the document, as included between the <title> tags in the HTML source. This property is read-only.

```
doctitle=document.title
```

URL **property**

The URL property is the full URL of the current document—a read-only property. It contains the same value as that in window.location.href, unless you've redirected the page by modifying location.href. (See location object, window object.)

```
currenturl=document.url
```

vlinkColor **property**

The vlinkColor property is the color of unselected, previously visited links in the document, originally determined by the vlink attribute of the <body> tag.

Modifying this property after the page has been loaded will have no onscreen effect—it should be modified at the time of HTML evaluation. This means that to be effective, a statement such as the one below must reside within `<script>` tags which are within the `<body>` tags of the document.

```
document.vlinkColor="#ff0000"
```

 Within Internet Explorer 3 and 4, modifications to the `vlinkColor` property *do* immediately change the color of visited links on the screen.

TIP All color values are specified as a hexadecimal triplet. The triplet indicates the RGB color values in the form of "#RRGGBB," where each color is a hexadecimal value between 00 and FF. Alternatively, you may instead specify a pre-defined color name; for instance

```
document.vlinkColor="red"
```

You can refer to Appendix B for pre-defined color names and their associated hexadecimal triplet values.

clear() method

If an output stream has been opened for the document (see `open()` method), the `clear()` method will close the output stream and write the contents of the stream to the browser window. Any previous content in that browser window will first be cleared. For all intents and purposes, you should use the `close()` method to perform this same function (see `close()` method).

The following code example first opens the output stream and then clears the current document window.

```
document.open()
document.clear()
```

close() method

The close() method closes an output stream which has been opened to the document. When the output stream is open, it becomes filled with data via the `write()` and/or `writeln()` methods. When you call the `close()` method, the data in the output stream is sent to its destination—usually, the browser window. Technically, that destination is determined by the MIME type specified, if any, in the `open()` method (see `open()` method).

Under most circumstances, the `open()` method will be used to open an output stream to a browser window (also known as "layout" or the MIME type `text/html`). In these cases, when you call the `close()` method, the destination document is cleared and output from any `write()` or `writeln()` statements is displayed.

D

Visually, calling the `close()` method stops the "busy" icon in the browser—the "comet shower" in Navigator and the spinning globe in Internet Explorer—if it was in a busy state.

```
document.open()
document.write("<h1>Test Results Page</h1>")
 document.write("<h2><em>Below is a table summarizing your results</em></h2>")
 document.write(results())
document.close()
```

In the code excerpt above, none of the data output to the document stream (the three `document.write()` calls) will appear in the browser window until the `document.close()` call is executed.

getSelection() method

The `getSelection()` method returns a string containing any data which the user has selected on the page. To select data on the page, the user must have held down the left (or only) mouse button while dragging across some text, highlighting it. It is this text which is returned by the `getSelection()` method.

> **NOTE**   The `getSelection()` method is new to JavaScript 1.2. At the time of this writing, only Netscape Navigator 4 supports JavaScript 1.2. Microsoft Internet Explorer 4 does not yet appear to support the `getSelection()` method.

Consider, for instance, the example page shown in Figure 3. Notice the portion of text which has been selected by the user.

Figure 3

The selected text will be returned as a string via the `getSelected()` method—new to JavaScript 1.2.

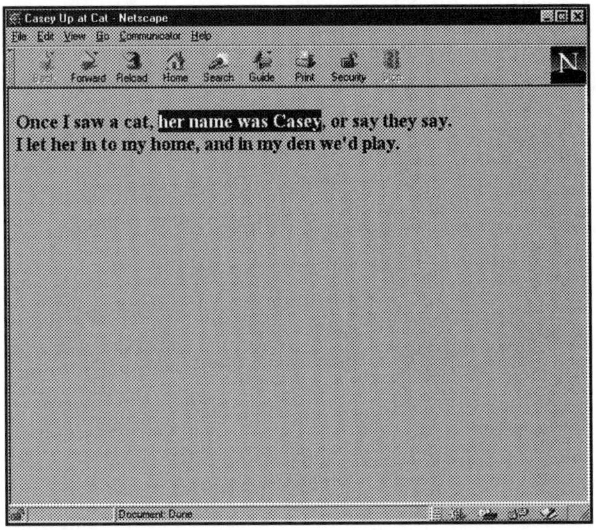

If the page in Figure 3 contained a script which contained the statement:

```
seltxt=document.getSelected()
```

The string value "her name was Casey" would be assigned to the variable `seltxt`.

open() method

The open() method opens an output stream to the document. An output stream accepts data, usually text, which will later be sent to an output destination—usually, the document window. The open() method uses the construction:

```
document.open(["mimeType"],[replace])
```

If you do not specify a MIME type (e.g. `"image/jpeg"` or "text/plain"), the default `text/html` will be used. In the majority of instances, where you want to output content to a document window, you do not need to specify a MIME type (see Appendix F).

If you specify the parameter `replace`, the new document will preserve the same history list as the originating document. This prevents the `history` object's length from being incremented when you output to a document window. (See `history` object.)

In most cases where you want to use the `write()` and `writeln()` methods to output data to a document, you *do not* need to use the `open()` or `close()` methods. These methods are primarily used if and when you intend to output non-HTML data, such as plain unformatted text, or encoded data for a plug-in.

When using the `open()` method, output data will not be sent to its destination (such as the browser window) until the `close()` or `clear()` method is called.

If you have opened additional browser windows by using the `window` object's `open()` method (see `window` object), you can `open()` the outputstream to the specified window:

```
windowName.document.open()
```

write() method

The write() method is used to output data (usually HTML) to a source (usually a browser window). Before outputting data, you must first open the outputstream by calling the `open()` method. Unless it follows the `open()` method, which specifies an alternative MIME type, the `write()` method implicitly outputs data of the MIME type `text/html`.

The write() method accepts any string, literal, variable, or expression. Thus, it can be used as simply as in

```
document.write("Hello there")
```

or to format HTML content as in

```
document.write("<h3>Results Table:</h3><br><table cols=4 width='100%'>")
```

or a more complex combination of variables and literals, as in

```
document.write("<strong>I pronounce you, "+firstname+", King of thy Castle, and
ruler until the year "+(yr+100)+"</strong>")
```

Typically, you use a series of write() calls to "build" the HTML of the page you wish to output to the document window. If you have opened additional browser windows, you can use the window object's open() method (see window object), to direct the write() method to the specified window:

windowName.document.write()

The immediate impact of using the write() method depends on when it is called. If you call the write() method while the HTML source is being evaluated—that is, somewhere within the <body> tags—it will append its output to the original HTML. For instance, consider the following tiny HTML source:

```
<html><body>
<h1>This is original content from the HTML source<h1>
<script language="JavaScript">
document.write("<hr><h2>This is new content generated by the write() method
</h2>")
</script>
</body></html>
```

The above HTML would produce a page which looks like Figure 4.

Figure 4

When you use the write() method to output HTML during loading of the page, it is appended to the original HTML source.

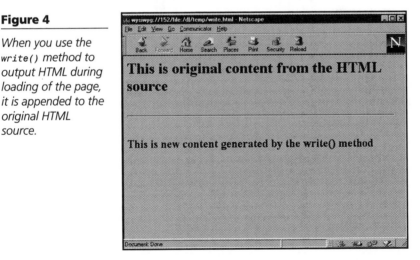

On the other hand, you could call the write() method after the page has already loaded—for instance, in an event handler. Consider the example above, but we'll move the write() method to an onClick event handler for a button.

```
<html><body>
<h1>This is original content from the HTML source<h1>
<form>
<input type="button" value="Click me"
onClick="document.open();document.write('<hr><h2>This is new content generated by
the write() method</h2>');document.close()">
</form>
</body></html>
```

When this page is first loaded, it looks like Figure 5. After clicking the button, the write() method is called, which first clears the document before outputting new HTML, as seen in Figure 6.

Figure 5

The write() method is now in an onClick event handler for the button.

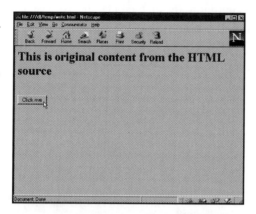

Figure 6

When the event handler is called, the write() method causes the current document to be cleared before outputting the new HTML.

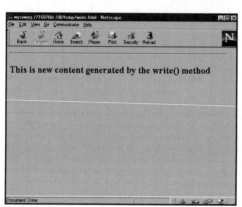

writeln() method

Nearly identical to the write() method, the writeln() method merely appends a newline character to the end of its output. Note, though, that the newline character is ignored in HTML, except within special instances such as the <pre> tag (which displays pre-formatted ASCII text). Thus, unless outputting formatted data which makes use of the newline character, the writeln() method offers no advantage over the write() method. Other than the addition of the newline character, this method operates identically to write(). (See the write() method.)

`<EM>`

Category: HTML

Browser Support

	Navigator 3	Navigator 4	Explorer 3	Explorer 4
Macintosh	▬	▬	▬	▬
Windows	▬	▬	▬	▬

Applies To None

May Contain `<APPLET>`, `<B>`, `<BASEFONT>`, `<BIG>`, `<BR>`, `<CITE>`, `<CODE>`, `<DFN>`, `<EM>`, `<FONT>`, `<I>`, `<IMG>`, `<INPUT>`, `<KBD>`, `<MAP>`, `<SAMP>`, `<SELECT>`, `<SMALL>`, `<STRIKE>`, `<STRONG>`, `<SUB>`, `<SUP>`, `<TEXTAREA>`, `<TT>`, `<U>`, `<VAR>`

May Be Used In `<ADDRESS>`, `<APPLET>`, `<B>`, `<BIG>`, `<BLOCKQUOTE>`, `<CAPTION>`, `<CENTER>`, `<CITE>`, `<CODE>`, `<DD>`, `<DT>`, `<FONT>`, `<H1>`, `<H2>`, `<H3>`, `<H4>`, `<H5>`, `<H6>`, `<I>`, `<KBD>`, `<LI>`, `<P>`, `<SAMP>`, `<SMALL>`, `<STRIKE>`, `<STRONG>`, `<SUB>`, `<SUP>`, `<TD>`, `<TH>`, `<TT>`, `<U>`

Attributes None

Syntax `<EM>...</EM>`

The `<EM>` tag is an older tag that emphasizes a section of text. Everything written between the beginning and closing, or `</EM>` tags, will be displayed in italics as shown in the example:

```
<EM>This text is italicized using the EM tag.</EM>
```

Figure 1 displays this HTML in Navigator 3 for the Mac.

Figure 1

Text emphasized with italics by using the <EM> tag compared to plain default text.

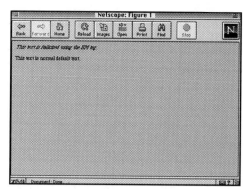

There's no functional difference between text displayed in italics using the <EM> tag versus using the <I> tag and/or the <CITE> tag, as shown in Figure 2. Use any of these tags for italicizing plain text as you prefer.

Figure 2

The <EM> tag versus the <I> tag and the <CITE> tag—there's no difference.

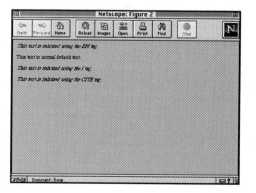

<EMBED>

Category: HTML

Browser Support		Navigator 3	Navigator 4	Explorer 3	Explorer 4
	Macintosh	■	■	■	■
	Windows	■	■	■	■

May Contain None

May Be Used In <BODY>

Attributes ALIGN, AUTOSTART, BORDER, HEIGHT, HSPACE, NAME, PALETTE, PLAYBACK, SRC, UNITS, VSPACE, WIDTH

Syntax <EMBED>...</EMBED>

The `<EMBED>` tag introduces embedded sound, video, or VRML objects into a web page. Then a browser's plug-ins automatically and appropriately handle these objects once the page loads, so that visitors to your site can see or hear this multimedia the way you intend. An end tag, or `</EMBED>`, is required.

You also have to consider file format and browser version issues for any multimedia you specify using the `<EMBED>` tag.

> **NOTE** `<EMBED>` is not the HTML purist's first choice for embedding objects—the `<OB-JECT>` tag is preferred by some site designers, but `<EMBED>` has greater compatibility with earlier versions of HTML. See the `<OBJECT>` tag entry elsewhere in the book for more information.
>
> Also, `<EMBED>` is not the tag to use for importing JavaScript or Java applets into your web page. In Netscape, Java applets are included by way of the `<APPLET>` tag, whereas Internet Explorer uses the `<OBJECT>` tag. JavaScript, on the other hand, is a completely different ball game—read the JavaScript section of this book for more information.

ALIGN

The `ALIGN` attribute is one of three placement attributes that specifies where an `<EMBED>`-generated control panel appears on your web page.

In the following example, `film.mov` specifies the name of the QuickTime movie being embedded:

```
<EMBED ALIGN=right HEIGHT=250 WIDTH=250 UNITS=pixels SRC=film.mov></EMBED>
```

Notice that the `HEIGHT`, `SRC`, `WIDTH`, and `UNITS` attributes have also been specified—this is because you cannot properly test or use the alignment attribute by itself. You must specify the name of the object for starters (`SRC`, as already noted) and also its size (`HEIGHT` and `WIDTH`) along with how you are measuring height and width (`UNITS`). Without establishing these attributes and their values, in this particular example, you won't be able to see the movie clip or the control box, because QuickTime's default box size is too small.

There are 10 `ALIGN` attribute values:

`baseline`

The control panel aligns with the bottom horizontal edge of the player window. Netscape Navigator 3 and Internet Explorer 3 for Mac do not support this value.

`bottom`

The control panel aligns with the bottom horizontal edge of the player window.

`center`

The control panel aligns with the center of the player window.

left

The control panel aligns with the left side of the browser window. This is the ALIGN attribute's default setting.

middle

The control panel aligns with the center of the player window. Netscape Navigator 3 and Internet Explorer 3 for Mac do not support this value.

textbottom

The control panel aligns with the bottom edge of the player window. Internet Explorer 3 for Mac does not support this value.

textmiddle

The control panel aligns with the middle of the player window. Netscape Navigator 3 and Internet Explorer 3 for Mac do not support this value.

texttop

The control panel will align with the top. Netscape Navigator 3 and Internet Explorer 3 for Mac do not support this value.

top

The control panel aligns with the top edge of the player window.

right

The control panel aligns with the right side of the browser window.

AUTOSTART

The AUTOSTART attribute enables you to specify whether or not a sound or video file will begin playing automatically once the page is loaded.

AUTOSTART has only one value, true, which disables Netscape Navigator's and Internet Explorer's control box and plays the sound or video file immediately. It is used in tandem with the PLAY-BACK attribute, which specifies the number of times the file will loop (a PLAYBACK value of 0 (zero) will make the file loop continuously).

In this example, film.mov is instructed to play immediately as soon as it is loaded up, and to loop three times:

```
<EMBED AUTOSTART=true PLAYBACK=3 SRC=film.mov></EMBED>
```

If a sound or video has no AUTOSTART value specified in their HTML, visitors must click the control box play button to make the example movie begin playing.

BORDER

The BORDER attribute specifies a black border around the object player window in pixel increments.

In the following HTML, the border width has been specified at 4 pixels:

```
<EMBED BORDER=4 SRC=film.mov></EMBED>
```

HEIGHT

The HEIGHT attribute works in tandem with the WIDTH and UNITS attributes to establish the size of the player window.

In the following example, film.mov represents the object embedded in the web page:

```
<EMBED HEIGHT=150 WIDTH=150 UNITS=pixels SRC=film.mov></EMBED>
```

Because the UNITS attribute is specified as "pixels," the movie player box will be 150×150 pixels in size.

It always pays to test the height and width measurements of a player box, as each sound and video clip and VRML world have different dimensions. You can never rely on the HEIGHT and WIDTH attribute defaults to be sufficient—if the dimensions are too small, both Navigator and Explorer compensate by only showing the middle of the object, which usually hides the player box controls.

HSPACE

The HSPACE attribute of the <EMBED> tag is very similar to the HSPACE attribute of the <IMG> tag—when the embedded object is ALIGN-ed left or right, the HSPACE and VSPACE attributes specify blank space buffer zones between the object and any text surrounding it.

In the following example, film.mov represented the file name of the object embedded in the web page:

```
<EMBED SRC=film.mov ALIGN=right HSPACE=15 VSPACE=20></EMBED>
```

Don't confuse the HSPACE and VSPACE with the HEIGHT and WIDTH attributes—you do not need to specify an increment with the UNITS attribute here, as this kind of blank space is only measured in pixels.

PALETTE

The PALETTE attribute specifies a foreground and a background color for the player box in hexadecimal values or color names.

In the following example, film.mov represents the file name of the embedded object:

```
<EMBED SRC=film.mov PALETTE=#ffccff/#ffffff></EMBED>
```

The first color value specified is the foreground color and the second is the background color.

> **NOTE** PALETTE does not work in Netscape Navigator nor Internet Explorer for the Macintosh.

PLAYBACK

The PLAYBACK attribute is used specifically for sound or video files as a companion attribute to AUTOSTART. The numerical value assigned to PLAYBACK determines how many times the sound or video file will loop (if you specify this value as 0 (zero) it will play continuously).

In the following example, film.mov will play four times because of the PLAYBACK setting of 4:

```
<EMBED SRC=film.mov AUTOSTART=true PLAYBACK=4></EMBED>
```

Remember you need to include the entire string "AUTOSTART=true" to get the sound or video file to play immediately. See the AUTOSTART section of this entry for more information.

> **NOTE** The PLAYBACK attribute does not work in Navigator 3 or Explorer 3 for the Mac.

SRC

The SRC attribute is used to specify the file name of the sound file, movie clip, or VRML world to be embedded in your web page.

In the following example, film.mov represents the object to be embedded:

```
<EMBED SRC=film.mov></EMBED>
```

This is the one attribute you are required specify within the <EMBED> tag. All the other <EMBED> attributes rely upon this information and will not work without it.

UNITS

The UNITS attribute specifies the type of measurement stated by the HEIGHT and WIDTH attributes. It has two values:

pixels

The HEIGHT and WIDTH measurements will be rendered in pixels. This is the UNITS attribute default.

en

The HEIGHT and WIDTH measurements are rendered in increments equivalent to half the point size of the specified page text. The point size defaults for all four browsers is 12.

The difference between pixels and ens is quite significant, especially given the difference in font display on a Macintosh versus a PC. Keep these variables in mind when decided how to use HEIGHT and WIDTH.

VSPACE

The VSPACE attribute of the <EMBED> tag is very similar to the VSPACE attribute of the <IMG> tag—when the embedded object is ALIGN-ed left or right, the HSPACE and VSPACE attributes specify blank space buffer zones between the object and any text surrounding it.

In the following example, `film.mov` represented the file name of the object embedded in the web page:

```
<EMBED SRC=film.mov ALIGN=right HSPACE=15 VSPACE=20></EMBED>
```

The difference between the HSPACE value (15) and the VSPACE value (20) better suits the rectangular shape of the EMBED-generated player box. You may have to experiment with these values if the EMBED-specified object is differently shaped.

WIDTH

The WIDTH attribute works in tandem with the HEIGHT and UNITS attributes to establish the size of the player window.

In the following example, `film.mov` represents the object embedded in the web page:

```
<EMBED HEIGHT=150 WIDTH=200 UNITS=en SRC=film.mov></EMBED>
```

Because the UNITS attribute is specified as "en," the movie player box will be 150×200 ens in size. ("En" represents an increment equal to half the height of the web page text—12 points by default unless otherwise specified by the <FONT> tag.)

It always pays to test the height and width measurements of a player box, as each sound and video clip and VRML world have different dimensions. You can never rely on the HEIGHT and WIDTH attribute defaults to be sufficient—if the dimensions are too small, both Netscape Navigator and Internet Explorer compensate by only showing the middle of the object, which usually hides the player box controls.

escape()
Category: JavaScript, JScript

	Type	Function

Browser Support

	Navigator 3	Navigator 4	Explorer 3	Explorer 4
Macintosh	■	■	☐	■
Windows	■	■	■	■

Syntax `escape(string)`

The `escape()` function returns a *string* encoded in the Latin ISO-1 character set, where spaces, punctuation, and other special characters are represented as escape codes, in the string format "%xx"; for instance:

```
escape("Hey buddy")            returns the string    "Hey%20buddy"
```

In the preceding example, the escape code %20 represents a space.

This function is commonly used when you need to pass data in a manner that disallows spaces, punctuation, and other special characters. The escaped string can be converted back into its original form in the receiving program by unescaping the string (see also the `unescape()` function).

For instance, when you set a cookie (a bit of information stored on the user's computer which your page can recall at a later visit—see the `document` object), its value is not allowed to contain any spaces or special punctuation. Therefore, it's common practice to escape the cookie value string before setting it.

```
document.cookie("cookiename="+escape(cookievalue))
```

You may also want to use the `escape()` function on strings before passing them to a server via a form submission, because some server-based scripts will not properly understand data that contains whitespace or punctuation marks.

eval()

Category: JavaScript, JScript

Type	Function; also, a method of all objects

Browser Support

	Navigator 3	Navigator 4	Explorer 3	Explorer 4
Macintosh	■	■	☐	■
Windows	■	■	■	■

Syntax `eval(string)`

The `eval()` function is used to evaluate, and possibly execute, the contents of *string*. This function enables you to "store" JavaScript statements or expressions in string form until you want them to be evaluated or executed. This function is best illustrated by an example. Imagine that you assign the string:

```
total="orders * gross"
```

Because the preceding is a string assignment, no calculation of `orders * gross` is made. Rather, the entire expression `"orders * gross"` is assigned to the variable `total`. At a later point in your script, you could use the `eval()` function in a context such as:

```
document.write("Total cost="+eval(total))
```

In the preceding statement, when JavaScript sees the expression `eval(total)`, it will execute `orders * gross`. This is a basic example. Typically, you use the `eval()` function to construct on-the-fly JavaScript expressions or statements. Imagine that your script needed to output the `status` property of a window object. However, the script doesn't know in advance which window object. So, you've also coded a function, named `getWinName()`, which returns the name of the window of interest.

```
winname=getWinName()
documenwrite("The status bar reads: "+eval(winname+".status"))
```

Notice, in the preceding example, the construction `eval(winname+".status")`. If, for instance, winname had the value "win2," then this construction would be calling `eval("win2.status")`. As you can see, the `eval()` function enables you to construct expressions on-the-fly, allowing for context-dependent coding.

You can pass any valid JavaScript expressions or statements in the *string* sent to `eval()` function, and they will be evaluated on-the-spot.

Event

Category: JavaScript 1.2

| | Type | Object |

Browser Support

	Navigator 3	Navigator 4	Explorer 3	Explorer 4
Macintosh	☐	■	☐	☐
Windows	☐	■	☐	☐

Subset Of Nothing

Properties layerX, layerY, modifiers, pageX, pageY, screenX, screenY, target, type, which

Syntax event.property

The event object is a rare bird—unlike other objects, the event object changes according to the most recent event (such as a `Click` event). To use this flighty object, you must pass it along to your event-handler. Within the event-handler, you may access the event object's properties to learn more about the current event (such as which mouse button was pressed, the location of the mouse pointer at the time, and so on). Although the event object has a set of informative properties as discussed later, each event only carries a subset of these properties. For example, the `Click` event does not provide cursor position information (among others, the `layerX`, `screenX`, and `pageX` properties are empty). Refer to the chart at the end of this entry to see which JavaScript events carry which event object properties.

As stated earlier, to use the event object you must first pass it to your event-handler. Consider the following HTML examples:

```
<input type="button" name="order" value="Click to Order"
onClick="window.alert('Triggered by the event:'+event.type)">

<a href="http://www.page.com" onlick="dolink(event)">Next Page</a>
```

In the first example, the event object and its `type` property are called right in the `onClick` event-handler. In the second example the `onClick` event-handler calls the fictional function *dolink()*, and passes along the event object as a parameter. The *dolink()* function itself may then use the event object's informative properties.

```
function dolink(evt)
{posx=evt.pageX
 poxy=evt.pageY
 …etc…
}
```

Next in this entry are the properties that the event object *may* contain. All of these properties are read-only and cannot be directly modified. Remember, though, that each event supports only some of these properties—see the Event Property charts for an overview of which events support which properties.

layerX property

In supporting events, this property contains the horizontal position of the mouse pointer (in pixels) with relation to the *layer* in which the event occurred, where zero represents the leftmost edge of the current layer. You can use the layerX property in combination with the layerY property to learn the pointer coordinates when a supporting event happened. Remember, though, that these coordinates are measured with respect to the layer—see also pageX and screenX for coordinates measured along different criteria.

In the case of the resize event, the layerX property contains the width of the object (window or frame) after it has been resized.

layerY property

In supporting events, this property contains the vertical position of the mouse pointer (in pixels) with relation to the *layer* in which the event occurred, where zero represents the topmost edge of the current layer. You can use the layerY property in combination with the layerX property to learn the pointer coordinates when a supporting event happened. Remember, though, these coordinates are measured with respect to the layer—see also pageY and screenY for coordinates measured along different criteria.

In the case of the resize event, the layerY property contains the height of the object (window or frame) after it has been resized.

modifiers property

In the case of mouse button or keypress related events, the modifiers property is used to determine which, if any, modifying keys (such as Shift, Control, or Alt) were depressed during the event. To best use the modifiers property, you should include it in a JavaScript condition as follows:

```
if (event.modifiers & Event.ALT_MASK) {…}
```

In the previous example, the *if* condition will be true if the event was accompanied by the ALT key. If the above line is included within an event-handler function, be sure to change event.modifiers to reflect whatever parameter name you chose for the incoming event object; for example, if (evt.modifiers & Event.ALT_MASK).

Following this model, you should use the following JavaScript conditions to test for the following modifying keys:

`(event.modifiers & Event.ALT_MASK)`	Alt key
`(event.modifiers & Event.SHIFT_MASK)`	Shift key
`(event.modifiers & Event.CONTROL_MASK)`	Ctrl key
`(event.modifiers & Event.META_MASK)`	Meta key (only some keyboards have a Meta key, such as the open apple key on the Mac)

pageX property

In supporting events, this property contains the horizontal position of the mouse pointer (in pixels) with relation to the *page* in which the event occurred, where zero represents the leftmost edge of the browser viewing area. You can use the `pageX` property in combination with the `pageY` property to learn the pointer coordinates when a supporting event happened. These coordinates are measured with respect to the page—see also `layerX` and `screenX` for coordinates measured along different criteria.

pageY property

In supporting events, this property contains the vertical position of the mouse pointer (in pixels) with relation to the *page* in which the event occurred, where zero represents the topmost edge of the browser viewing area. You can use the `pageY` property in combination with the `pageX` property to learn the pointer coordinates when a supporting event happened. Remember, though, that these coordinates are measured with respect to the page—see also `layerY` and `screenY` for coordinates measured along different criteria.

screenX property

In supporting events, this property contains the horizontal position of the mouse pointer (in pixels) with relation to the *screen* in which the event occurred, where zero represents the leftmost edge of the user's desktop. You can use the `screenX` property in combination with the `screenY` property to learn the pointer coordinates when a supporting event happened. These coordinates are measured with respect to the entire desktop screen—see also `layerX` and `pageX` for coordinates measured along different criteria.

screenY property

In supporting events, this property contains the vertical position of the mouse pointer (in pixels) with relation to the *screen* in which the event occurred, where zero represents the topmost edge of the user's desktop. You can use the `screenY` property in combination with the `screenX` property to learn the pointer coordinates when a supporting event happened. Remember, though, that these coordinates are measured with respect to the entire desktop screen—see also `layerY` and `pageY` for coordinates measured along different criteria.

target property

The `target` property contains a string representing the object where the event was originally sent. Every event supports this property. For instance, the `target` property for a `Click` event may look like:

```
<input type="button" name="order" value="Click to Order" onClick='order(event);'>
```

This resembles the line of HTML will called the event-handler. Of course, because it is here where the event was originally sent, and then later routed on to *order()*, as specified in the `onClick` event-handler.

type property

A string containing the name of the event that has occurred. Every event supports this property. Possible values for the `type` property are:

Abort	Blur	Click	Change
DblClick	DragDrop	Error	Focus
KeyDown	KeyPress	KeyUp	Load
MouseDown	MouseMove	MouseOut	MouseOver
MouseUp	Move	Reset	Resize
Select	Submit	Unload	

which property

With mouse button–related events (MouseUp, MouseDown), the `which` property contains a value representing which mouse button was involved in the event. Possible `which` values are:

1	left mouse button
3	right mouse button

In the case of keypress-related events (KeyPress, KeyUp, KeyDown), the `which` property contains the ASCII character code for the key that was involved in the event.

Event Property Charts

The following two tables show which event object properties are associated with which events. In the first table, you can look up events in the first column and see which event object properties they support in the second column. The second table displays the event object properties in the first column and the events that support them in the second column. Convenient and handy!

Table 1 Events and Supported event Object Properties

Event	Supported event Object Properties
Abort	target, type
Blur	target, type
Click	modifiers, target, type, which
	for a link only: layerX, layerY, pageX, pageY, screenX, screenY
Change	target, type
DblClick	layerX, layerY, modifiers, pageX, pageY, screenX, screenY, target, type, which
DragDrop	target, type
Error	target, type
Focus	target, type
KeyDown	layerX, layerY, modifiers, pageX, pageY, screenX, screenY, target, type, which
KeyPress	layerX, layerY, modifiers, pageX, pageY, screenX, screenY, target, type, which
KeyUp	layerX, layerY, modifiers, pageX, pageY, screenX, screenY, target, type, which
Load	target, type
MouseDown	layerX, layerY, modifiers, pageX, pageY, screenX, screenY, target, type, which
MouseMove	layerX, layerY, pageX, pageY, screenX, screenY, target, type
MouseOut	layerX, layerY, pageX, pageY, screenX, screenY, target, type
MouseOver	layerX, layerY, pageX, pageY, screenX, screenY, target, type
MouseUp	layerX, layerY, modifiers, pageX, pageY, screenX, screenY, target, type, which
Move	screenX, screenY, target, type
Reset	target, type
Resize	layerX, layerY, target, type
	notes: *width* is a synonym for layerX
	height is a synonym for layerY
Select	target, type
Submit	target, type
Unload	target, type

E

Table 2 **Event** **Object Properties and Supporting Events**

Event Object Property	Supporting Events
layerX	Click, DblClick, KeyDown, KeyPress, KeyUp, MouseDown, MouseMove, MouseOut, MouseOver, MouseUp, Resize
layerY	Click, DblClick, KeyDown, KeyPress, KeyUp, MouseDown, MouseMove, MouseOut, MouseOver, MouseUp, Resize
modifiers	Click, DblClick, KeyDown, KeyPress, KeyUp, MouseDown, MouseUp
pageX	Click, DblClick, KeyDown, KeyPress, KeyUp, MouseDown, MouseMove, MouseOut, MouseOver, MouseUp
pageY	Click, DblClick, KeyDown, KeyPress, KeyUp, MouseDown, MouseMove, MouseOut, MouseOver, MouseUp
screenX	Click, DblClick, KeyDown, KeyPress, KeyUp, MouseDown, MouseMove, MouseOut, MouseOver, MouseUp, Move
screenY	Click, DblClick, KeyDown, KeyPress, KeyUp, MouseDown, MouseMove, MouseOut, MouseOver, MouseUp, Move
target	Abort, Blur, Click, Change, DblClick, DragDrop, Error, Focus, KeyDown, KeyPress, KeyUp, Load, MouseDown, MouseMove, MouseOut, MouseOver, MouseUp, Move, Reset, Resize, Select, Submit, Unload
type	Abort, Blur, Click, Change, DblClick, DragDrop, Error, Focus, KeyDown, KeyPress, KeyUp, Load, MouseDown, MouseMove, MouseOut, MouseOver, MouseUp, Move, Reset, Resize, Select, Submit, Unload
which	Click, DblClick, KeyDown, KeyPress, KeyUp, MouseDown, MouseUp

Exp()

Category: VBScript

Type	Function				

Browser Support

	Navigator 3	Navigator 4	Explorer 3	Explorer 4
Macintosh	☐	☐	☐	■
Windows	☐	☐	■	■

Syntax Exp(*number*)

The Exp() function calculates and returns the value e raised to the power *number*: e^{number}. The value e is also known the base of the natural logarithm, and is approximately 2.718.

exp(2)   returns approximately 7.389

If *number* is greater than approximately 709.78, an error is generated.

E

```
<IMG> </IMG> ■ <SCRIPT LANGUAGE = "javascript"> </SCRIPT>
■ <SCRIPT LANGUAGE = "vbscript"> </SCRIPT> ■ <BGSOUND
SRC=gbv.wav LOOP=-1> </BGSOUND> ■ <APPLET CLASS=
"ester's_day" SRC="http://testsite/walla walla washington/"
</APPLET> ■ <FRAME></FRAME>■ <MARQUEE> </MARQUEE> ■
<HTML> </HTML> ■ <A> </A> ■ <OL> </OL> ■ <UL> </UL> ■ <MENU>
</MENU> ■ <STRONG> </STRONG> ■ <TD> </TD> ■ <TH> </TH>
```

F

FileUpload
Category: JavaScript 1.1

Type	Object				

Browser Support		Navigator 3	Navigator 4	Explorer 3	Explorer 4
	Macintosh	■	■	☐	■
	Windows	■	■	☐	■

Subset Of	Form object
Properties	form, name, type, value
Methods	blur(), focus()
Events	onBlur, onFocus, onChange
Syntax	document.formName.fileUploadName.property OR
	document.forms[index].elements[index].property OR
	document.formName.fileUploadName.method(parameters) OR
	document.forms[index].elements[index].method(parameters)

The FileUpload form field enables users to submit files with a form. The element displays a text field and a browse button. The user may enter a file name or pathname in the text field, or press the supplied Browse button and select a file from a file dialog box (Internet Explorer 4 does not offer a Browse button with the FileUpload element). This object is rarely used, both because most forms do not ask for files and many users may have hesitations about sending files from their machine to the web page. More commonly, you may see the FileUpload used in secure intranet environments. A FileUpload element is created using the <input> tag.

```
<input
   type="file"
   name="fileUploadName">
```

 Internet Explorer 3.0 does not support the FileUpload object.

`form` **property**

The `form` property is the read-only reference to the `form` object that contains the `FileUpload` object. This is a useful way to refer to another object in the same form. For instance, imagine a scenario where you want to reference a `text` object, named *text1*, which resides within the same form as the `FileUpload` object, *fileup1*. This can be used to code in shorthand, or eliminate the need to explicitly reference the full path to every element within a single form, as in the following code excerpts:

JavaScript

```
path=document.forms[0].fileup1
value1=path.value
value2=path.form.text1.value
```

`name` **property**

The `name` property is the read-only name of the `FileUpload` object, specified by the name attribute in the `<input>` tag.

```
objname = document.formname.fileuploadname.name
objval = document.formname.objname.value
```

`type` **property**

The `type` property is the input type specified by the `type` attribute in the `<input>` tag. Of course, this always contains the value "file" when referencing a `FileUpload` element.

```
objtype = document.formname.fileuploadname.type
```

`value` **property**

The read-only `value` property represents the file name or pathname of the file that the user has sel-ected. The user must enter this data. JavaScript cannot modify this property—therefore, it is not possible to force a particular file name and try to extract data from the client without his knowledge.

```
filename = document.formname.fileuploadname.value
```

`blur()` **method**

The `blur()` method simulates the user losing focus from the `FileUpload` field. Therefore, if the user currently has focus on the `FileUpload` field, somehow triggering the following code would remove the focus:

```
document.formname.fileuploadname.blur()
```

`focus()` **method**

The `focus()` method simulates the user gaining focus on the `FileUpload` field. You could use this method to call a user's attention to the field.

```
document.formname.fileuploadname.focus()
```

WARNING Be careful if and when you use the `focus()` method on a `FileUpload` element which also contains an `onFocus()` event handler. In some scenarios within Netscape, this may result in an infinite loop wherein the `onFocus()` event handler is repeated seemingly indefinitely. If your page is not operating as intended, this may be a cause to investigate.

onBlur event handler

Located within the `<input>` tag, the `onBlur` event handler activates when the user loses focus (that is, clicks or tabs elsewhere in the browser) from the `FileUpload` element.

```
<input type="file" name=fileuploadname onBlur="eventHandler">
```

onFocus event handler

Located within the `<input>` tag, the `onFocus` event handler activates when the user clicks or tabs onto the `FileUpload` field, unless the field already had focus. For instance, you might use this event handler to pop up a window of instructions when the user brings focus to the field.

```
<input type="file" name=fileuploadname onFocus="window.alert('Please select a file')">
```

onChange event handler

Located within the `<input>` tag, the `onChange` event handler activates when the user makes a change to the text field of the `FileUpload` element and then clicks or tabs away.

You could, for instance, create a function named `validfile()`, which determines if the user's input into the `FileUpload` field is a valid file name. Call this function using the `onChange` event handler.

JavaScript

```
<input type="file" name=fileuploadname onChange="validfile(this.value)">
```

VBScript

```
<input type="file" name=fileuploadname onChange="validfile
➥document.formname.fileuploadname.value">
```

Filter()
Category: VBScript

		Type	Function

Type Function

Browser Support		Navigator 3	Navigator 4	Explorer 3	Explorer 4
	Macintosh	☐	☐	☐	■
	Windows	☐	☐	■	■

F

`Filter(stringArray, value, include)`

The `Filter()` function is used to sift string matches from one array into another. Imagine that you have an array A, each of whose elements contain a string value. The `Filter()` function will analyze each element of array A and, for any element that contains a substring matching *value*, copy that element into a new array B. The result is an array B whose elements were pulled from array A based upon matching *value*. The *include* Boolean parameter specifies whether to filter matches or non-matches from array A to array B.

Imagine that you begin with an array `pets`:

`pets = array("dog barney","dog lucky","cat pippar","cat casey","dog scruffy")`

Now, you want to use the `Filter()` function to copy any elements in `pets` that contain the string "dog" to another array dogs.

`dogs = filter(pets,"dog",true)`

The resulting array `dogs` would contain three elements: "dog barney", "dog lucky", and "dog scruffy". Alternatively, the following would only copy the elements that *do not* contain "dog":

`other = filter(pets,"dog",false)`

In the preceding case, the array `other` would contain two elements: "cat pippar" and "cat casey".

If no matches are found, the `Filter()` function returns an empty array that contains no elements. If the *stringArray* is null or not one-dimensional, then an error will occur.

Fix()
Category: VBScript

| | Type | Function |

Browser Support

	Navigator 3	Navigator 4	Explorer 3	Explorer 4
Macintosh	☐	☐	☐	■
Windows	☐	☐	■	■

Syntax `Fix(number)`

The `Fix()` function returns the integer portion of a numeric expression *number*, chopping off any decimal places. It *does not* round or modify the integer portion of *number* in any way.

`fix(20.632)`	returns	20
`fix(42.11)`	returns	42
`fix(-15.63)`	returns	−15
`fix(-8.03)`	returns	−8

Note that Fix() is nearly identical in function to Int(), except that when given a negative *number*, Fix() returns the first integer greater than or equal to *number*, as illustrated in the last two preceding examples. If *number* is a null value, Fix() will return a null value; any other non-numeric expression will cause an error.

float

Category: Cascading Style Sheets

Browser Support

	Navigator 3	Navigator 4	Explorer 3	Explorer 4
Macintosh	☐	■	☐	☐
Windows	☐	■	☐	☐

Applies To All elements

Syntax float: *value*

You use the float property to flow text around an element such as an image or block-level text. This property behaves similarly to the align attribute on the <img> tag. You may specify left, right, or none for the float. A value of left displays the element on the left side of the browser window and the text wraps around it on the right. The reverse happens for the right value. With a float value of none, an element would appear as it normally does in the text. You can also use clear to negate the effects of float.

```
h1 { float: right }

<h1 style="float: left">
```

Here's an example of using float around an image. Figure 1 shows the result in which text flows nicely around the floating graphic.

```
<html>
 <style type="text/css">
 <!--
   body { background: white }
   .a   { float: left }
 -->
 </style>
<head>
 <title>Specifying Float</title>
</head>
<body>
 <span class=a><img src="../graphics/woods.jpg"></span>
 <h2>The float property also has a companion in HTML. You use float like you'd
use the ALIGN attribute on the IMG tag: to flow text around an element (in style
sheets, this element can be an image or block-level text).</h2>
 <span class=a><h1>This is floating H1 text!</h1></span>
```

```
    <h2>The float property also has a companion in HTML. You use float like you'd
use the ALIGN attribute on the IMG tag: to flow text around an element (in style
sheets, this element can be an image or block-level text).</h2>
</body>
</html>
```

Figure 1

*The text flows
around the image.*

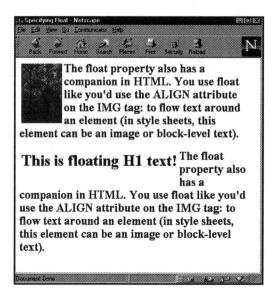

What's new (from traditional HTML) is the capability to float text around *other text*. Any block-level element, such as the <h1>, can be made to float. And if you don't want just one line of floating text, you can easily break it with
s within the block-level text (see Figure 2). An obvious use is pull-quotes from articles. This could also be used as poorman's initial caps.

Figure 2

*Add line breaks and
a little `padding`
(`margin` seems to
cause trouble) to
make floating text
blocks more useful
and attractive.*

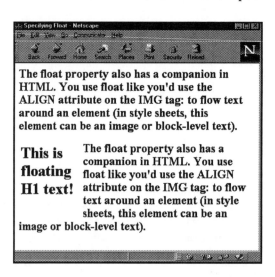

Be careful when floating things `right`. Occasionally Navigator will cut off parts of images that float right, so you end up with the right-hand side of the image missing.

font
Category: Cascading Style Sheets

Browser Support

	Navigator 3	Navigator 4	Explorer 3	Explorer 4
Macintosh	☐	■	■	☐
Windows	☐	■	■	■

Applies To   All elements

Syntax   font: *font-size line-height font-family*

The font property is a shorthand method for specifying up to three font properties simultaneously. You specify font-size, line-height, and font-family, in that order. Any value that you can normally use for these properties can also be used here. See the individual descriptions for more information. You must always specify at least size and family. Each value is separated by a space (although separating font-family names requires a comma, as usual).

```
h1 { font: 14pt/16pt arial }
```

```
h1 { font: large times }
```

<FONT>
Category: HTML

Browser Support

	Navigator 3	Navigator 4	Explorer 3	Explorer 4
Macintosh	■	■	■	■
Windows	■	■	■	■

May Contain   <A>, <APPLET>, <B>, <BASEFONT>, <BIG>, <BR>, <CITE>, <CODE>, <DFN>, <EM>, <FONT>, <I>, <IMG>, <INPUT>, <KBD>, <MAP>, <SAMP>, <SELECT>, <SMALL>, <SUB>, <SUP>, <STRIKE>, <STRONG>, <TEXTAREA>, <TT>, <U>, <VAR>

May Be Used In   <A>, <ADDRESS>, <APPLET>, <B>, <BIG>, <BLOCKQUOTE>, <CAPTION>, <CENTER>, <CITE>, <CODE>, <DD>, <DFN>, <DIV>, <DT>, <EM>, <FONT>, <FORM>, <H1>, <H2>, <H3>, <H4>, <H5>, <H6>, <I>, <KBD>, <LI>, <P>, <SAMP>, <SMALL>, <STRIKE>, <STRONG>, <SUB>, <SUP>, <TD>, <TH>, <TT>, <U>, <VAR>

Attributes   COLOR, FACE, SIZE

Syntax   <FONT>...</FONT>

The <FONT> tag changes the font, size, and color of a section of text within a web page. A closing, or </FONT> tag, is not required.

For example:

```
This is regular default text: Times 12 on a Macintosh and Times New Roman 12
on a PC.
<FONT FACE=Courier>This text is specified as Courier.
This text is still Courier…
<FONT FACE=arial, helvetica>But this text is different (Arial in Windows or
Helvetica on a Mac), because of the new FONT tag specification.
```

Figures 1, 2, 3, and 4 compare default regular text settings in Navigator 3 and Internet Explorer 3 for the Mac and for Windows.

Figure 1

Default font settings in Navigator 3 for the Mac.

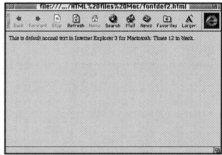

Figure 2

Default font settings in Internet Explorer 3 for the Mac.

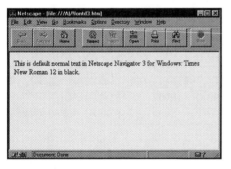

Figure 3

Default font settings in Navigator for Windows.

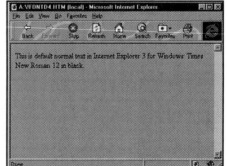

Figure 4

Default font settings in Internet Explorer 3 for Windows.

> **NOTE** The <BASEFONT> tag is only used as a reference in this entry and is not fully explained. See the <BASEFONT> entry elsewhere in the book for a more thorough explanation of its attributes and uses.

COLOR

The COLOR attribute is used to establish the color of all text in a certain section being specified by the <FONT> tag.

In the following example, the regular text that comes before and after the <FONT>-specified text is unaffected:

```
<P>Here's one line of default black text.<BR>
<FONT COLOR=blue> Here's a second line of customized, royal blue text.<BR>
<P>Here's another line of default black text.<BR>
```

"Blue" is one of 16 colors you can safely specify in English, but you are better off using hexadecimal values because they are more precise. For example, you can specify the same shade of royal blue as you did previously with a corresponding "hex" value:

```
<FONT COLOR=#0000FF> Here's a second line of customized, royal blue text.<BR>
```

See Appendix B on color for more information and extensive browser-safe color charts.

> **DESIGN NOTE** Always test font colors extensively to make sure you can read your page text, especially if you are placing white or yellow text on a background pattern. Remember, too, that PC monitors display colors significantly darker than Mac monitors do, so a dark font color against a dark background may be readable on a Mac but not on a PC.

Although the COLOR attribute is supported by recent versions of Navigator and Internet Explorer, this is not the case with earlier versions, so don't stake a lot on it. Also, both Navigator and Explorer have Preferences options that enable users to disable body colors. So if you are using COLOR to specify something that will be invisible, or nearly unreadable against a gray background (white, off-white, silver, yellow, and pastels come immediately to mind), certain visitors will be unable to read your web page.

FACE

The FACE attribute enables you to specify one or more particular font if you don't like the Mac's or the PC's default settings, or if you want to change a particular section of text to a different font than you specified using the <BASEFONT> tag.

Hence, the following example:

```
<FONT FACE=monaco, times, chantilly>This text will appear in one of the different
fonts specified here.<BR>
```

will establish Monaco as the font for all text in the specified section. If a visitor's computer doesn't have Monaco installed, the browser will look for Times and then Chantilly if necessary. If none of the fonts specified by the FACE attribute are present, then the browser will revert to the default font as if the FACE attribute wasn't even present.

Figures 5, 6, 7, and 8 compare various customized text settings in Navigator 3 and Internet Explorer 3 for the Mac and for Windows.

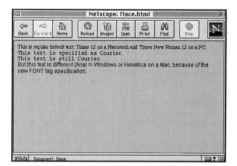

Figure 5

Customizing font settings with the <FONT> tag in Navigator 3 for the Mac.

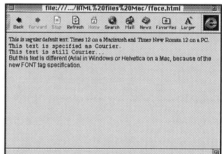

Figure 6

Customizing font settings with the <FONT> tag in Internet Explorer 3 for the Mac.

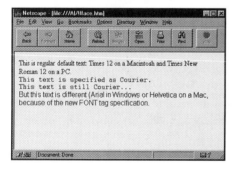

Figure 7

Customizing font settings with the <FONT> tag in Navigator for Windows.

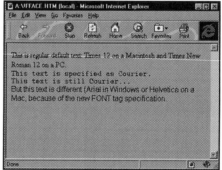

Figure 8

Customizing font settings with the <FONT> tag in Internet Explorer 3 for Windows.

DESIGN NOTE Choose common fonts that most visitors to your web page will have on their computers. Appendix C lists all the fonts that come installed on both Macs and PCs when users buy them, along with other valuable type decision information.

With respect to this Design Note, if you specify "Times" as the FACE value, this request does indeed mean "Times" on a Mac, but it means "Times New Roman" on a PC. This is because the most common typefaces (Times, Courier, Helvetica, and Arial) look slightly different on a Mac versus a PC and vice versa—close, but not quite the same.

Secondly, there's the issue of size—12-point type on a Mac does not resemble 12-point type on a PC. Why do fonts appear larger on a Windows monitor than on a Mac monitor? It's a hardware discrepancy, like the color difference dilemma that you cannot solve with regular HTML.

See the "Cascading Style Sheets Basics" chapter elsewhere in the book for ways to better control fonts, and take a look at Appendix C on platform support for fonts.

SIZE

The Internet Explorer-only SIZE attribute denotes a font size for a particular, <FONT>-specified section of a web page, similar to the way the SIZE attribute of the <BASEFONT> tag establishes a font size for all text on a web page.

However, there's one major difference that you must remember unless you want to create a mess: when you establish a <BASEFONT> SIZE setting, you are adding onto or subtracting from a universal setting of 3. But, when you establish a <FONT> SIZE setting elsewhere in the same document, *you are adding onto or subtracting from your <BASEFONT> SIZE setting*, not that universal 3.

In other words, if you greatly enlarge or reduce the overall size of text on your page with <BASEFONT> SIZE, you cannot and should not greatly increase or reduce the size of text in a specific section. You could easily end up with tiny text that's impossible to read or gigantic text you wouldn't bother with.

DESIGN NOTE It's a safer bet to use the <BIG> and <SMALL> tags to specify larger and smaller text on your web page. <BIG> translates to <FONT SIZE="+1"> and <SMALL> to <FONT SIZE="-1">, without lots of fussing and guessing. See the <BIG> and <SMALL> entries elsewhere in the book for more information.

A SIZE-specified value isn't measured in points as in desktop publishing or word processing programs, but by the numbers 1 through 7, with 7 being the largest and 3 being the default.

In the following example, the font size has been specified to +2 (the plus sign or + is necessary), increasing the font size by two increments above the default of 3:

```
<FONT SIZE=+2>
```

You can conversely decrease the base font by degrees using negative numbers, –1 through –7, if you prefer.

You also must take the differences between browsers and the differences between platforms into account—as in the case of <BASEFONT>, SIZE is, at this writing, not supported by Navigator. Navigator, therefore, will ignore all your careful SIZE settings and display all text at an approximate default of 3.

Figures 9, 10, 11, and 12 show <FONT> SIZE settings +1 through +7 on Navigator 3 and Internet Explorer 3 for the Mac and for Windows, while Figures 13, 14, 15, and 16 show the –1 through –7 settings.

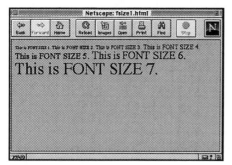

Figure 9

<FONT> SIZE settings 1 through 7 on Navigator 3 for the Mac.

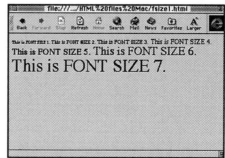

Figure 10

<FONT> SIZE settings 1 through 7 on Internet Explorer 3 for the Mac.

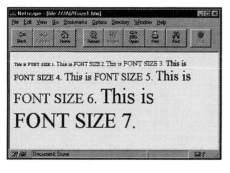

Figure 11

<FONT> SIZE settings 1 through 7 on Navigator 3 for Windows.

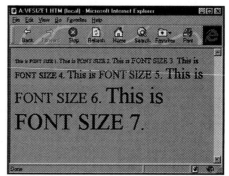

Figure 12

<FONT> SIZE settings 1 through 7 on Internet Explorer 3 for Windows.

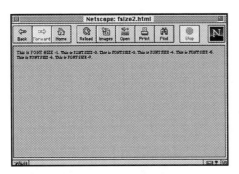

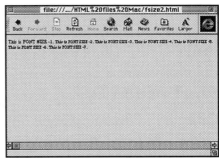

F

Figure 13

<FONT> SIZE settings –1 through –7 on Navigator 3 for the Mac.

Figure 14

<FONT> SIZE settings –1 through –7 on Internet Explorer 3 for the Mac.

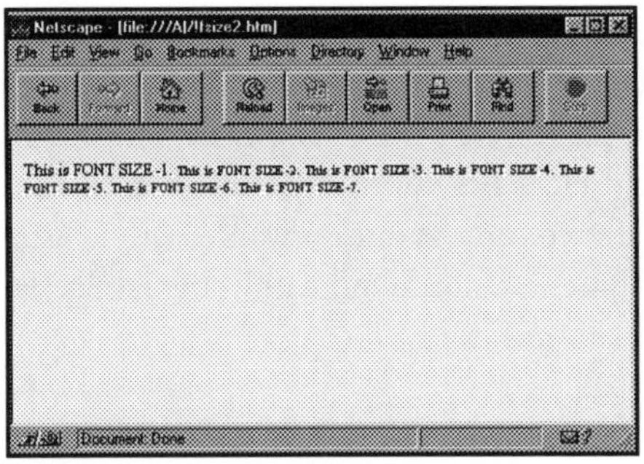

Figure 15

<FONT> SIZE settings –1 through –7 on Navigator 3 for Windows.

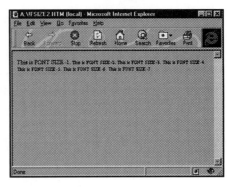

Figure 16

<FONT> SIZE settings –1 through –7 on Internet Explorer 3 for Windows.

Notice that in both Navigator and Explorer, on both platforms nonetheless, it's pretty pointless to specify anything lower than a –2 value anyway, as the text size remains constant (and pretty small) from –3 through –7.

DESIGN NOTE It's been said before but this information is worth repeating: even with all these settings, you *still* don't have much choice when it comes to the appearance of text on your web page. This is where the usefulness of style sheets comes in—see the "Cascading Style Sheets Basics" chapter of this book for more information on how to take better control of your fonts.

If you're writing a lengthy web document in traditional academic, scientific, or reporting style, you never, *ever* want to use the <FONT> tag to create headers. Indexers, both the human and the technical kind, use the six header tags (<H1>, <H2>, <H3>, <H4>, <H5>, and <H6>) to categorize and summarize web pages for proper retrieval via library online systems and popular online resources like Yahoo, Infoseek, Excite, and Alta Vista. So if your document lacks these headers, chances are good that it will not be cataloged properly.

`font-family`

Category: Cascading Style Sheets

Browser Support		Navigator 3	Navigator 4	Explorer 3	Explorer 4
	Macintosh	☐	■	■	☐
	Windows	☐	■	☐	■

Applies To All elements

Syntax `font-family: family-name family-name …`

The `font-family` property defines a prioritized list of font families used for elements on your page. When the element is displayed, the browser looks at the fonts installed on the system for the given family, and then attributes specified for the element. A *family name* is the name of a specific font family such as Palatino, Arial, and Helvetica. With any `font-family` rule, the web browser will use the first font listed as the preferred font, and use any alternatives listed if necessary if the right properties, sizes, or attributes are not found within the family. Font names containing more than one word should appear in *quotes*.

```
h1 { font-family: caslon, bookman, serif }

h1 { font-family: "gill sans", "times new roman", sans-serif }
```

Note that all the font names in the examples are lowercase. The style sheets spec recommends this spelling, and the browsers prefer it. If you're ever having problems getting a lowercase font to work, however, try a mixed-case spelling. Also, embedded style rules get double primes, and inline styles get single primes. If you forget these, the web browser ignores any spaces before or after the font name.

```
<h1 style="font-family: 'new baskerville', serif">
```

> In general, when you're establishing multiple style rules, always use `font-family` *last,* as with this example:
>
> ```
> h1 { font-size: 30pt;
>    color: red;
>    background: white;
>    margin-top: 50px;
>    font-family: chantilly, bookman, times, serif }
> ```

> The reason for this is some reports of odd problems in Internet Explorer 3. Occasionally, if `font-family` occurs anywhere but last in the list, the entire style sheet rule will fail.

> Explorer 3 and 4 for Windows 95 do not support alternative font lists. They will recognize only the first font listed, and otherwise use the default font. (The Mac version works fine.)

F

Always include a generic family as the final alternative value in the `font-family` property. That way you can ensure that even if visitors don't have any of the specific fonts you list, at least they'll see something that comes close to what you intend. A *generic family* is a more general category of font, not a particular font family. Generic font families include:

- `serif` (such as Times)
- `sans-serif` (such as Arial)
- `cursive` (such as Comic Sans, Zapf Chancery)
- `fantasy` (such as Ransom)
- `monospace` (such as Courier, Monaco)

Here are the default fonts each browser uses for the generic families:

Generic Family	NN4 (Win 95)	NN4 (Mac)	IE4 (Win 95)	IE3 (Win 95)	IE3 (Mac)
`serif`	Arial	Times	Times New Roman	Times New Roman	Times
`sans-serif`	Arial	Times	Arial	Arial	Times
`cursive`	Arial	Times	Comic Sans MS	Comic Sans MS	Times
`fantasy`	Arial	Times	Ransom	Ransom	Times
`monospace`	Arial	Times	Courier New	Courier New	Monaco

> If you have trouble with viewing a particular font in Explorer (especially on the Windows side), try adding a semicolon after font names enclosed in quotes, even if the font name is the last property in a group. For example:
>
> ```
> h1 { font-family: "comic sans ms"; }
> ```

> Explorer 3.0 for Windows 95 doesn't recognize multiple-word font names if used in *inline* styles. The following code won't work, even if you add a semicolon as in the following example:
>
> ```
> <h1 style="font-family: 'comic sans ms'">
> ```

When using specific fonts within a family, such as bold or italic, you should be careful about how you specify the `font-family` rule. For example, if you want to use the font Goudy Sans Bold, your rule might look like this:

```
h1 { font-family: "goudy sans bold", sans-serif }
```

If visitors have Goudy Sans installed on their machines but *not* Goudy Sans Bold, then the web browser will not display Goudy Sans at all, but instead will display its default sans serif font. In other words, the browser won't automatically use normal Goudy Sans and apply a bold style. The whole name you use must *exactly* match what the visitor has installed, or there won't be a match. With the following rule, the browser will use Goudy Sans, then apply bold to it via the `font-weight` property (see the section on `font-weight` for more information).

```
h1 { font-weight: bold;
     font-family: "goudy sans", sans-serif }
```

Some fonts will simply give you a hard time and not display when they should. This most likely happens because the name *we* associate with the font is not the same as the name the system and/or the browser associates with the font. In many cases, you can simply try alternative spellings for the value of `font-family`, and soon you'll find the one that works.

On the Windows side, you can pretty much trust that if a font is listed in the Font pull-down menu of Microsoft Word, then it's available in style sheets using that exact same spelling.

fontFamily
Category: JavaScript Style Sheets

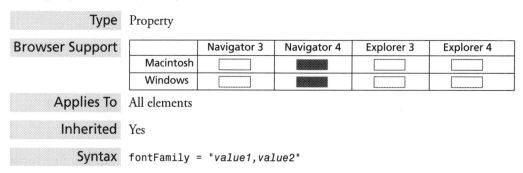

		Navigator 3	Navigator 4	Explorer 3	Explorer 4
Type	Property				
Browser Support					
	Macintosh	☐	■	☐	☐
	Windows	☐	■	☐	☐
Applies To	All elements				
Inherited	Yes				
Syntax	`fontFamily = "value1,value2"`				

The `fontFamily` property is used to define a style "set" of fonts that can be used to display the elements in a document. This style is especially useful when you want your documents to keep a

F

consistent style regardless of the browser's default fonts. `fontFamily` only has one possible value, which is the `fontFamily` set. `fontFamily` may be a single-defined font or a comma-delimited list of fonts to be tried.

By taking the time to define a generic list of fonts in the set, you can be guaranteed that your document will display in one of your desired fonts. It is best to use at least one generic font family in your list so that you get at least one font that you desire.

JavaScript Style Sheets will attempt to apply the first font in the font family set. If the first font does not exist, then it will continue down the list until an existing font is located and can be used.

For the best results, you should include at least one of the following font families:

- Monospace

- Serif

- Sans-serif

- Cursive

- Fantasy

By using one of these font families you are sure to get the font that you want on every system, but the exact font will be Windows system dependant. The exact display of the font will depend on which fonts are installed on the system, and what type of platform is being used.

The code segment following shows a definition for the fonts for `<h1>` elements. You could define the `fontSize` and `fontFamily` for `<h1>` as follows:

```
<style type="text/javascript">
with {tags.h1} do
        fontSize = "12"
        fontFamily = "Arial, Courier, Sherwood, sans-serif"
</style>
```

In the preceding sample, the JSSS code can be broken down as follows:

In this example, the important elements are as follows:

- `with {…} do` as a JavaScript function used in our example to define multiple style properties for a single HTML element `<h1>` all within a single statement.

- `tags` is one of the methods of defining JSSS styles. The `tags` definition describes the element immediately following it in the dot notation will be one of the accepted HTML elements.

- `h1` is the html element that is being assigned a style. This may be any valid HTML element.

- `fontSize` and `fontFamily` are the style properties that are being defined for the element.

- `"12"` and `"Arial,Courier,Sherwood,sans-serif"` are the values of the style properties.

The three special fonts are defined as the "first choice" fonts and the final "last choice" font is from the generic sans-serif font family. Thus, if the system has no special fonts defined, you can be sure that a sans-serif font will be used, not the user's default font.

If none of the font families defined for the style are available, then the browser will drop back down to using the default system font.

Sometimes it is necessary to define `fontFamily` styles to keep constancy in your documents as well as to be sure that the fonts are suitable to display your document as it was defined. In today's web the look of your document is as important as the text content of the document.

font-size

Category: Cascading Style Sheets

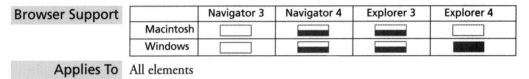

Browser Support		Navigator 3	Navigator 4	Explorer 3	Explorer 4
Macintosh		☐	■	■	☐
Windows		☐	■	■	■

Applies To All elements

Syntax `font-size: value`

The `font-size` property enables you to set the size of the font within an element. A key aspect of this property is there are a number of different ways to define the size of text, not just the traditional point size. These include:

- Points
- Relative keywords
- Absolute keywords
- Length units
- Percentage

You can specify one size relative to another or even define a size in specific units as discussed in Appendix D.

Point size refers to an imaginary box that extends from the descender line (the bottom of the "p," for example) to the ascender line (the top of the "d," for example). The actual sizes of the characters can vary quite a bit within this box. That's why two fonts that are technically the same point size don't necessarily "look" like they're the same size onscreen. Point sizes in style sheets must be specified as whole units. Something like 12.5 pt won't work; the web browser will round it down to something it understands.

For relative keywords, a value of `smaller` will adjust the size of the font down one "notch" on the scale of absolute keywords in the following list and `larger` will move it up a "notch."

```
h1 { font-size: 14pt }

h1 { font-size: larger }

h1 { font-size: 125% }
```

Navigator for the Macintosh seems to ignore point sizes completely.

F

NOTE Navigator for Windows 95 defines font sizes much smaller compared to Explorer. Definitely something to be aware of when sizing text.

Absolute keywords still specify particular font sizes, but let the browser make more of the decisions about what exact display size is best. Your choices include:

- `xx-small`
- `x-small`
- `small`
- `medium`
- `large`
- `x-large`
- `xx-large`

NOTE These seven values correspond to the seven numerical values (1–7) you can use to specify font size for Netscape Navigator via HTML tags like `<font size="3">` and `<font size="+2">`.

The following table shows what point sizes Netscape Navigator and Internet Explorer use for each of the absolute keywords for the appropriate default fonts, Times New Roman (for Windows 95) and Times (for Mac).

Absolute Keyword	NN4 (Win 95)	NN4 (Mac)	IE4 (Win 95)	IE3 (Win 95)	IE3 (Mac)
`xx-small`	12-point	12-point	8-point	6-point	9-point
`x-small`	12-point	12-point	10-point	8-point	10-point
`small`	12-point	12-point	12-point	10-point	12-point
`medium`	12-point	12-point	14-point	12-point	14-point

continues

Absolute Keyword	NN4 (Win 95)	NN4 (Mac)	IE4 (Win 95)	IE3 (Win 95)	IE3 (Mac)
large	12-point	12-point	18-point	14-point	18-point
x-large	12-point	12-point	24-point	18-point	24-point
xx-large	12-point	12-point	36-point	24-point	36-point

Check out the interesting differences between the Windows and Mac versions of Explorer (see Figures 1 and 2). The 4.0 Windows version (which should be out before this book is published) is like the 3.0 Mac version, so it looks like Microsoft is heading toward consistency.

Figure 1

Explorer 3 for Windows 95 displays keyword-sized text.

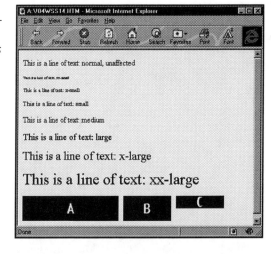

Figure 2

Explorer 3 for the Mac uses the same keyword values. Note this time that relative to identical graphics, the Mac text is bigger than the Windows text, as the previous table testifies.

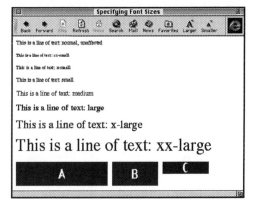

As you can see by the table, the Mac *and* Windows 95 versions of Navigator fail to recognize these absolute keyword font sizes at all.

Explorer 3 doesn't support `smaller` or `larger` at all.

Navigator in version 4 doesn't support `smaller` or `larger`.

F

Length values, less commonly used for `font-size`, include the following:

- **em**

  An em is a unit of distance equal to the point size of a font. In 14-point type, an em is 14 points wide. See Appendix A.

- **ex**

  X-height refers to the height of the lowercase letters (not including ascenders or descenders, like "h" or "p" have) of a font. See Appendix D.

When used with the `font-size` property, em and ex units refer to the font size of the *parent* element (on other properties, they refer to the size of the current element).

```
<html>
 <style TYPE="text/css">
 <!--
  p { font-size: 20pt }
  b { font-size: 1.5em }
 -->
 </style>
<head>
 <title>Specifying Font Sizes by Length Units</title>
</head>
<body>
 <p>
 Now I'm 20 points.
 <b>
 But look! Now I'm 1.5 ems of what I was before: 30 points.
 </b>
 </p>
</body>
</html>
```

In the ideal browser, text within <b> gets displayed at 30 points, which is 1.5 ems of the inherited size of 20 points. Essentially, the text is displayed at one and a half times the size of its parent.

Explorer handles **em** a bit differently. On the Mac side, it always uses the *default* font size as its base, and ignores inheritance in this instance. That is, Explorer treats 1 em <p> text as *always* 12 point, its default. 1.5 em text would always be 18 point, regardless of any other font size it inherits. So in the previous example, the text would be 18 point, not 30 point. Obviously this removes any uniqueness or value in using em for `font-size`. Explorer for the Mac treats ex exactly the same way.

On the Windows side, **em** and **ex** values are treated like they're *point* size values! 2em equals 2-point text, and so on.

Navigator doesn't support **em** or **ex**. Nor does it support percentage values for `font-size`.

Percentage values also work through inheritance. Values include any whole number.

```
<html>
 <style type="text/css">
 <!--
  P { font-size: 15pt }
  B { font-size: 300% }
  -->
 </style>
<head>
 <title>Specifying Font Sizes by Percentage</title>
</head>
<body>
 <p>
 Now I'm 15 points, and <b>now I'm 45 points!</b>
 </p>
</body>
</html>
```

The web browser takes the size of the <h1> text and makes the bold text 300% of that size. Pretty straightforward.

Explorer uses the percentage of the *default* font size, not any other size. That is, in our example, the text would be 36-point (because the default <p> size is 12-point in Explorer), not 45-point.

fontSize

Category: JavaScript Style Sheets

Type	Property				

Browser Support

	Navigator 3	Navigator 4	Explorer 3	Explorer 4
Macintosh		■		
Windows		■		

F

Applies To All elements

Inherited Yes

Syntax `fontSize = "value"`

`fontSize` is one of the most commonly used JavaScript Style Sheets properties. It is used to define the size of the font for any HTML element. There are four possible values you can assign to `fontSize`:

- ■ `"absolute-size"` refers to the six possible values that are computed from a table of font sizes to be used for font rendering. Possible values are: x-small, small, medium, large, x-large, xx-large. Normally a scaling factor of 1.5 is used between font sizes. The default absolute-size is medium and all other sizes are scaled from there.

- ■ `"relative-size"` can be defined in two ways, either textually with the two values of: larger and smaller, or numerically using +1 (for one size larger) or −1 (for one size smaller). These values are interpreted in relation to the parent font and will render this font as either one step larger or smaller than the parent. If the parent is large (or the equivalent), then larger will render as extra large.

- ■ `"fontSize"` takes a number as it's value. Where number can be defined in either point size or em units. The statements of `tags.body.fontSize = "36pt"` and `tags.body.fontSize = "3em"` are equivalent. For more information on units of measurement, see Appendix D.

- ■ `"percentage"` increases the current font size by the percentage defined. This does not function the same as relative-size, which increases in size relative to the parent but instead increases the current font size by the percentage specified.

By defining `fontSize` properties for text inside of JavaScript Style Sheets you have more control over the size of the fonts based on the current status of the document and from input that you have received from the user. A document may be generically defined with standard styles and then `fontSize` properties may be used to change styles based on user interaction with the document. It may be beneficial to increase the font size of information on your site that is more relevant to the user.

Just increasing the font size is a powerful way to make certain elements on your site more apparent while keeping them unobtrusive.

The following code uses JavaScript functions to change the `fontSize` based on the background color of the body of the document:

```
<HTML>
<HEAD>
<SCRIPT LANGUAGE="JavaScript">
<!--
//-->
</SCRIPT>
<STYLE TYPE="text/javascript">
tags.body.backgroundcolor = "gray"
if (tags.body.backgroundcolor == "white") {
tags.p.fontSize = "12pt";
classes.fontclass1.p.fontSize = "16pt";
}
if (tags.body.backgroundcolor == "gray") {
tags.p.fontSize = "12pt";
classes.fontclass2.p.fontSize = "16pt";
}

</STYLE>
Since this text is in the header of the document, it will not have a border
around it.
</HEAD>
<BODY>
<P>This is the text in the body of my document.
<p class="fontclass1"> this text is important if the background is white
<p class="fontclass2"> this text is important if the background is gray
</BODY>
</HTML>
```

Each function in the preceeding example as two similar lines of code.

```
tags.p.fontSize = "12pt";
classes.fontclass3.p.fontSize = "16pt";
```

The first line sets the font size for all `<p>` elements to 12 point and then the second line sets the font size to 16 point for a particular font class. The lines can be broken down as follows:

- `classes` and `tags` are the properties that tells JSSS that the code immediately following will define a either style class or for an HTML tag.
- `fontclass3` is the name of the class. This class name can be any alphanumeric combination, and will be referenced each time the class is used.
- `<p>` is the HTML element that the class or the `tags` definition will be valid for use with. (This can be any valid HTML element.) In our example, all `<p>` can take the fontclass3 in their definition, but they do not have to take the class.

- `fontSize` is the style that will applied to the `<p>` elements. Any valid JSSS style property can be used here.
- `"12pt"` and `"16pt"` are the values of the style that will be applied. Our example uses the pt (point) unit of measurement.

In Figure 1, the third paragraph has a larger font than the other two because it is more useful on a white background.

Figure 1

Document with a white background.

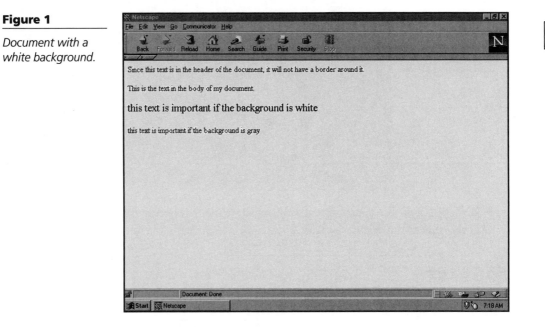

F

In Figure 2, the fourth paragraph has a larger font than the other two because it is more useful on a gray background.

Figure 2

Document with a gray background.

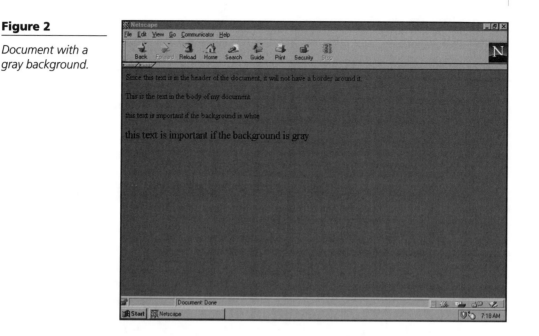

Each JavaScript Style Sheets function not only changes the font size of the paragraph in question, but will also change the default size back to 12 pt before changing the important paragraph.

`font-style`

Category: Cascading Style Sheets

Browser Support

	Navigator 3	Navigator 4	Explorer 3	Explorer 4
Macintosh		▉	▉	
Windows		▉	▉	▉

Applies To All elements

Syntax `font-style: value`

The `font-style` property enables you to add styles to the font of an element. When combined with `font-family` and `font-size`, this is a very powerful way to get extra effects for your text. You can choose between the following values for the style:

- `normal` selects a font that is classified as "normal" in the web browser's font database.
- `italic` specifies a font from the font database that is labeled "italic."
- `oblique`, not surprisingly, specifies a font that is labeled "oblique."

```
h1 { font-style: italic }
```

```
<h1 style="font-style: oblique">
```

Explorer 3 supports `italic`, but not `normal` or `oblique`.

Keep in mind that by styling a font `italic` or `oblique`, you might possibly be instructing the computer to create an artificial font by forcing the normal font into a slant. If a certain font (like Monotype Corsica) has no italic or oblique version at all, then the computer will "invent" it on the spot, and display the normal version, slanted even further than it already is. This unnatural-looking italics might not be what you want.

F

fontStyle

Category: JavaScript Style Sheets

Type	Property				
Browser Support		Navigator 3	Navigator 4	Explorer 3	Explorer 4
	Macintosh	☐	■	☐	☐
	Windows	☐	■	☐	☐
Applies To	All elements				
Inherited	Yes				
Syntax	`fontStyle = "value"`				

The `fontStyle` property is used in JavaScript Style Sheets to define the style of a font that will be used for an HTML element. Normal text font styles, italics, oblique, and small caps, are available as well as combinations of styles to give greater definition to the font styles. There are six possible values and value combinations you can assign to `fontStyle`:

- `"normal"` displays the font in the normal style. This is the default/initial value for `fontStyle`.
- `"italic"` style renders the text in the browser's default italic font style.
- `"oblique"` renders the text in the browser's default oblique font style. If the oblique style is not available, then the italic style is used.
- `"small-caps"` will render the text in small capital letters. Substitutes will be used if the browser does not support small capital letters.
- `"italic small-caps"` displays the text in italicized small capital letters.
- `"oblique small-caps"` displays the text in italicized small capital letters.

Each browser will attempt to render the `fontStyle` as defined, but if the styles cannot be accomplished as defined, the browser will make a best attempt to render it in a similar style. For example, if small-caps are not available, the browser will render the text in capital letters of a smaller font size.

Because JavaScript Style Sheets is currently only available in Netscape Navigator, you will get small-caps because Navigator supports them. If in the future other browsers support JavaScript Style Sheets but not small-caps, the browser will render the small-caps when possible.

```
tags.P.fontStyle = "italic"
```

The following example demonstrates how JavaScript can be used to manipulate the font style. If the background of the document is white, then the fontStyle for all <blockquotes> is italic, otherwise it is normal.

```
<HTML>
<HEAD>
</HEAD>
<STYLE type="text/JavaScript">
tags.body.backgroundColor = "white"
if (tags.body.backgroundColor == "white") {
tags.BLOCKQUOTE.fontStyle="italic";
}
else{
tags.BLOCKQUOTE.fontStyle="normal";
}

</STYLE>
<BODY>
<BLOCKQUOTE> This text is in italics if the background is white, otherwise it is
➥normal.
</BLOCKQUOTE>
</BODY>
</HTML>
```

Based on the background color of the document, the preceding code will display a document in two distinct formats.

In the preceeding example the important JSSS code is contained in the function

```
if (document.bgcolor = "white") {
tags.BLOCKQUOTE.fontStyle="italic";
}
else{
tags.BLOCKQUOTE.fontStyle="normal";
}
}
```

The lines can be broken down as follows:

- `tags` is the property that tells JSSS that the code immediately following will define a style for a particular HTML element.
- `<BLOCKQUOTE>` is the HTML element that the style will be valid for use with. (This can be any valid HTML element.)
- `fontStyle` is the style that will applied to the `<BLOCKQUOTE>` elements. Any valid JSSS style property can be used here.
- `"normal"` and `"italic"` are the values of the style that will be applied.

F

font-weight

Category: Cascading Style Sheets

Browser Support		Navigator 3	Navigator 4	Explorer 3	Explorer 4
	Macintosh		■	■	
	Windows		■	■	■

Applies To All elements

Syntax `font-weight: value`

The `font-weight` property enables you to adjust the boldness, or weight, of the font. The basic way to do this is through keyword or numerical values. For keywords, you can use `bold` to make a font bold, or `normal` to return the font to non-bold display. You can also use the values `lighter` and `bolder` to specify font weights that are relative to some inherited value. The numbered values range from `100` to `900` in even increments of 100 (100, 200, 300, and so on). Each of these numbers corresponds to a certain weight value. The `normal` value is the same as `400`, and `bold` is normally `700`. So `500` might be characterized as "a little bold," while `800` is "extremely bold."

```
h1 { font-weight: bold }
```

```
h1 { font-weight: 200 }
```

```
<h1 style="font-weight: lighter">
```

Explorer 3 supports `bold`, but not `normal`. Version 4 supports both. Explorer, however, has its own range of keywords that include `extra-light`, `light`, `demi-light`, `medium`, `demi-bold`, `bold`, and `extra-bold`.

Navigator for Macintosh does not support `bold` or `normal`. Numeric values are also not supported for the Mac.

If you've worked with fonts for a while, you know that they don't just come in "Normal" and "Bold" versions. There's "Regular," "Book," "Medium," "SemiBold," "DemiBold," "Heavy," "Black," and probably many more. Still, the web browser must determine how to handle each variant, and how to translate a numerical value to something appropriate in the font family. The following rules determine which arbitrary term gets associated with which numerical value:

- If the font at hand uses a numerical scale with nine values in it, then font weights can correspond easily to those values. OpenType fonts will work this way.

- If the font has a variant named "Medium," but also one named "Book," "Regular," "Roman," or "Normal," then the "Medium" variant is the one that gets a value of 500.

- Most often, the font variant named "Bold" will get the value of 700.

- If there are fewer than nine weights that come with a font family, then things get a little complicated. The browser needs to "fill in the holes" (assign the other numerical values) as follows:

  - If the value of 500 isn't assigned to any font variant, then it will get the same variant as 400.

  - If either 600, 700, 800, or 900 remains unassigned, then they are each assigned to the same variant as the next darker assigned keyword, if any, or the next lighter one otherwise. So, if there's a "Black" face that gets a value of 900, and a "Bold" face that gets 700, then 800 gets assigned to "Black," and 600 to "Bold."

  - Finally, if 100, 200, or 300 are still not assigned, then each gets assigned to the next lighter assigned keyword, (if any) or otherwise the next darker keyword. So if there's a "Medium" (500) but nothing lighter, then 100 through 300 all get assigned to "Medium" as well.

The following table explains how this works for the Chantilly font on the Mac:

Table 1 Mapping Fonts to Numeric Values with font-weight

Font Variant	Value	Value Assigned
Chantilly Light	200	100, 300
Chantilly Regular	400	500
Chantilly Bold	700	600
Chantilly Heavy	800	
Chantilly Ultra Bold	900	

If we try this out on a web page using Navigator, we can see how different weights are mapped to weights near in value. The following HTML document defines classes for each numerical value of Eras, and Figure 1 shows the result.

```html
<html>
 <style type="text/css">
 <!--
  body { background: white }
  P    { font-size: 24pt;
         font-family: eras }
  .a   { font-weight: 100 }
  .b   { font-weight: 200 }
  .c   { font-weight: 300 }
  .d   { font-weight: 400 }
  .e   { font-weight: 500 }
  .f   { font-weight: 600 }
  .g   { font-weight: 700 }
  .h   { font-weight: 800 }
  .i   { font-weight: 900 }
 -->
 </style>
<head>
 <title>Specifying Font Weights</title>
</head>
<body>
 <p class=a>Hi, I'm a line of text: value of 100</p>
 <p class=b>Hi, I'm a line of text: value of 200</p>
 <p class=c>Hi, I'm a line of text: value of 300</p>
 <p class=d>Hi, I'm a line of text: value of 400</p>
 <p class=e>Hi, I'm a line of text: value of 500</p>
 <p class=f>Hi, I'm a line of text: value of 600</p>
 <p class=g>Hi, I'm a line of text: value of 700</p>
 <p class=h>Hi, I'm a line of text: value of 800</p>
 <p class=i>Hi, I'm a line of text: value of 900</p>
</body>
</html>
```

F

Figure 1

Figure 1

Numerical weight values in action, getting their assignments based on the font variants available.

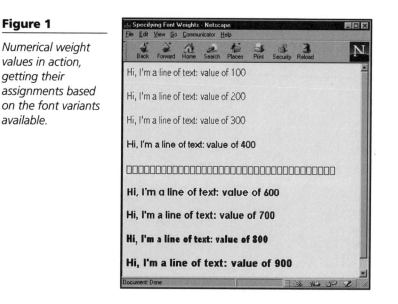

The lines with values of 100-300 are indeed Eras Light, and 400 is Medium. 500 doesn't show up at all (this seems to be a bug in the preview release that will hopefully be fixed). However, 600 and 700 are not quite different enough. Finally, although 800 and 900 are Eras Ultra, it's strange that 800 looks more condensed.

Explorer 4 only partially supports these number values. It displays the same page slightly differently: lines 100-500 are all Medium, 600-800 are Bold, and 900 is Ultra. Explorer 4 seems to display every font this way.

Internet Explorer 3 doesn't support either `bolder` or `lighter`.

Netscape Navigator also doesn't support either `bolder` or `lighter`.

fontWeight

Category: JavaScript Style Sheets

Type	Property		

Browser Support		Navigator 3	Navigator 4	Explorer 3	Explorer 4
	Macintosh	☐	■	☐	☐
	Windows	☐	■	☐	☐

F

Applies To All elements

Inherited Yes

Syntax fontWeight = "*value*"

fontWeight style properties are used to specify the weight of the font for the text of an HTML element. The weight of a font can also be called the "boldness" of the font. The five acceptable values for fontWeight are as follows:

- ■ "normal" displays the text in non-bold (or normal) font. This value works when used on text whether or not a previously specified, or inherited fontWeight has been used.

- ■ "bold" changes the text to a bold weight. In this usage, "bold" is the opposite of "normal" and is the initial value when starting the "bolding" process of a font.

- ■ "bolder" causes the font to be more bold than with the "bold" value. The value only works if the is already bold—either through inheritance, previous JavaScript Style Sheets font Weight changes, or the starting font weight was already bold.

- ■ "lighter" causes the font to be less bold than with the "bold" value. The value only works if the font is already bold—either through inheritance, previously JavaScript Style Sheets font Weight changes, or the starting font weight was already bold.

- ■ "100-900" values enable you to specify the specific font Weight and control the degree of boldness. "100" is the least bold and "900" is the most bold.

The best way to understand normal, bold, bolder, and lighter values is look at the following code sample, and Figure 1.

```
<html>
<head>
<style type="text/javascript">
classes.weight1.all.fontWeight ="normal";
classes.weight2.all.fontWeight ="bold";
classes.weight3.all.fontWeight ="bolder";
classes.weight4.all.fontWeight ="lighter";
</style>
</head>
<body class="weight2">
```

```
<p class="weight1"> normal font
<p> bold font
<p class="weight3"> bold font
<p clas="weight4"> bold font

</body>
</html>
```

Figure 1

fontWeight using textual values.

The <body> is defined with a fontWeight style, which is inherited to all <p> elements in the <body>. The normal style is used to override the original fontWeight = "bold" style, while lighter and bolder cause subtle changes in the bold style.

> **NOTE**   The difference in font weight caused by bolder and lighter are subtle and it best to test the example on your monitor.

The differences in font Weight are more noticeable using the fontWeight values of 100–900. The specific fontWeight values are used in the following code and the results are shown in Figure 2.

```
<html>
<head>
<style type="text/javascript">
classes.weight1.all.fontWeight ="100";
classes.weight2.all.fontWeight ="200";
classes.weight3.all.fontWeight ="300";
```

```
classes.weight4.all.fontWeight ="400";
classes.weight5.all.fontWeight ="500";
classes.weight6.all.fontWeight ="600";
classes.weight7.all.fontWeight ="700";
classes.weight8.all.fontWeight ="800";
classes.weight9.all.fontWeight ="900";
</style>
</head>
<body>
<p class="weight1"> gradually bolding font
<p class="weight2"> gradually bolding font
<p class="weight3"> gradually bolding font
<p class="weight4"> gradually bolding font
<p class="weight5"> gradually bolding font
<p class="weight6"> gradually bolding font
<p class="weight7"> gradually bolding font
<p class="weight8"> gradually bolding font
<p class="weight9"> gradually bolding font
</body>
</html>
```

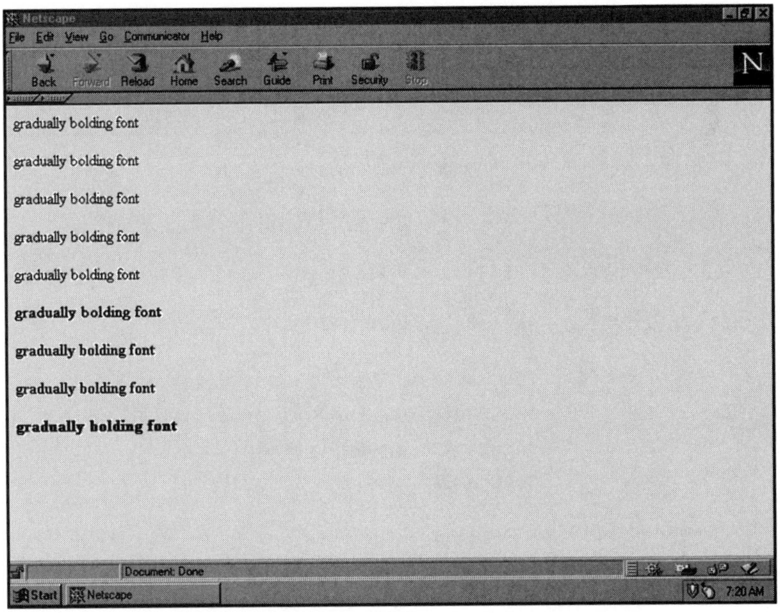

Figure 2

fontWeight using numeric values.

The change is extremely gradual for the values in the range of 100–500 and then becomes much more noticeable as the font Weight increases greatly. Each class in the previous example is defined in a simlar manner. The code can be broken down as follows:

- `classes` is the property that tells JSSS that the code immediately following will define a style class.

- `weight1` is the name of the class. This class name can be any alphanumeric combination, and will be referenced each time the class is used.

- `<p>` is the HTML element that the class will be valid for use with. (This can be any valid HTML element.) In our example, all `<p>` can take the weight1 in their definition, but they do not have to take the class.

- `fontWeight` is the styles that will applied to the `<p>` elements that use the style. Any valid JSSS style property can be used here.

- `"100"` ... `"900"` are the values of the style that will be applied.

Form
Category: JavaScript, JScript, VBScript

Type	Object			

Browser Support		Navigator 3	Navigator 4	Explorer 3	Explorer 4
	Macintosh	■	■	□	■
	Windows	■	■	■	■

Subset Of Document object

Properties `action, elements[], encoding, length, method, name, target`

Methods `reset(), submit()`

Events `onReset, onRubmit`

Syntax
```
document.formName.property OR
document.forms[index].property OR
document.formName.method() OR
document.forms[index].method()
```

The `form` object provides script access to the HTML `<form>` tag and its related characteristics. Most commonly, you'll use the `form` object to refer to one of its many subordinate properties, such as `button`, `checkbox`, `textarea`, and so on, which are objects in their own right. Using those objects, you'll read or modify the status and data input into the various form fields. You may also use the `form` object's `submit` method to send data to a server, or its `reset` method to clear form data to its default values.

You can reference a `form` object in either of two ways:

1. If the form contains a specified `name` attribute: `document.formName`
2. As part of the `forms[]` array, which is a property of the `document` object: `document.forms[idx]`

When using the `forms[]` array style of reference, keep in mind that each form on the page is indexed in the array in the order in which they are created in the HTML. Thus, the first `<form>` tag to appear in the HTML document will be referenced as `document.forms[0]`, the second will be `document.forms[1]`, and so on.

To create a form, use the `<form>` tag.

```
<form
    name="formName"
    target="windowName"
    action="serverURL"
    method=get¦post
    enctype="encodingType"
    [onReset="eventHandler"]
    [onSubmit="eventHandler"]>
</form>
```

The `form` object contains a number of objects that reflect form fields. Each of the following objects contains its own detailed entry in this book:

- `Button` object
- `Checkbox` object
- `FileUpload` object
- `Hidden` object
- `Password` object
- `Radio` object
- `Reset` object
- `Select` object
- `Submit` object
- `Text` object
- `Textarea` object

action **property**

The `action` property contains the URL specified, if any, to which the form data will be sent upon submission. Typically, the URL points to a CGI script on a server that is designed to process the form data.

Alternatively, this property can contain a *mailto:* address, to which the form data will be emailed if the user's browser is properly set up to send email.

> Internet Explorer 3 does not support modification of the `action` property; it is read-only.

You might, for instance, want to change the URL to which the form data is submitted depending on certain conditions of the form; perhaps you have one CGI program that processes the form under one circumstance, and another CGI program that operates in remaining cases.

```
document.formname.action = "submitToURL"
```

elements[] property

The `elements[]` property is an array of all the elements within the form, with the first object indicated at *elements[0]*. An "element" in this case would be any form field within the form. For instance, a form that contains one text field, one checkbox, two radio buttons, a submit button, and a reset button would be considered to have six elements (indexed 0–5 in the array).

When referencing, the `elements[]` array can be used in the place of a form field object name because it points to a form field object. For instance, if a text field named `text1` is the first element in `form1`, then you can refer to properties or methods of `text1` as either

```
document.form1.text1.property
document.form1.text1.method()
```

or

```
document.form1.elements[0].property
document.form1.elements[0].property
```

Of course, if `form1` is the first form in this document, you could replace *it* with the reference `forms[0]`, as in `document.forms[0].elements[0].property`, or any combination thereof!

encoding property

The `encoding` property is the method of encoding used for submission of the form data. It contains a string value which reflects a MIME type, such as the default encoding "application/x-www-form-urlencoded."

If not specified via the `enctype` attribute of the `<form>` tag, you should set this property to "multipart/form-data" if the form contains a FileUpload field (see the `FileUpload` object).

```
document.formname.encoding="multipart/form-data"
```

There are few other occassions where you'll need to access or modify this property from a script.

length property

The length property simply contains the number of elements (also known as form fields) within this form. Consequently, this property also reflects the number of indexes within the elements[] array.

For instance, imagine that a form contains only one form field—a checkbox:

```
idx = document.formname.lengthSC1
```

In the preceding statements, the value 1 would be assigned to idx, because this form only contains one element.

method property

The method property indicates the type of form submission. Valid values for the method property are "get" and "post." Don't confuse the word "method" here with a JavaScript method, which is a function associated with an object. A form's method specifies how the form data should be sent to the server.

The "get" method will append the form data to the URL specified in the action attribute or in the action property.

The "post" method will send the form data to the receiving URL in a data body, which the CGI program must know how to accept.

Generally, the only time you would modify this property from within a script is if you have modified the action property and the URL to send the form data to requires either the "get" or "post" method. For instance, imagine that you have redirected the form data by modifying the action property.

```
document.formname.action="newURL"
```

Because you know that the CGI program at *newURL* requires form data to be sent via "post," you'd be sure to modify the method property as well.

```
document.formname.method="post"
```

name property

The name property is the name of the form object, specified by the name attribute in the <form> tag.

Although not commonly modified via JavaScript, you could assign a new name to this form.

```
documents.forms[0].name="addressform"
```

Recall that the form's name is used when referencing it via the script, as in the syntax:

```
document.formname
```

target property

The `target` property specifies to which frame or window the server should send form processing results. You can either specify the name of the frame or window to target, or use one of the following built-in JavaScript targets:

Target	Effect
`"_top"`	Open hyperlink into full size of current window
`"_parent"`	Open hyperlink into parent window of current window
`"_self"`	Open hyperlink into same window which hyperlink was clicked
`"_blank"`	Open hyperlink into a new, blank, unnamed window

For instance, perhaps your script has created a new window named *New Window*, and you'd like server results to appear there.

```
document.formname.target="NewWindow"
```

reset() method

The `reset()` method changes all the elements in the form to their default values. This is equivalent to pressing a reset button (see the `Reset` object). Therefore, you don't necessarily need to include a reset button on your page to offer the user a way to clear the form.

```
document.formname.reset()
```

For instance, perhaps you have an image wrapped within a hyperlink. By embedding the `<img>` tag within the `<a>` tag and using an `onClick` event for the hyperlink containing the image, you could trigger the `reset()` method for the form object, thus creating a graphic image that would reset the form data when clicked.

```
<a href="" onClick="document.formname.reset()"><img src="clearform.gif"></a>
```

> **NOTE** Within Navigator and Internet Explorer 4, the `reset()` method *does* trigger any `onReset` method defined in the `<form>` tag.

 Internet Explorer 3 does not support the `reset()` method.

submit() method

The `submit()` method performs the form submission. This is equivalent to pressing a submit button. Therefore, you don't necessarily need to include a submit button on your page to offer the user a way to submit the form.

```
document.formname.submit()
```

For instance, perhaps you have an image wrapped within a hyperlink. By embedding the `<img>` tag within the `<a>` tag and using an `onClick` event for the hyperlink containing the image, you could trigger the `submit()` method for the form object, thus creating a graphic image that would submit the form data when clicked.

```
<a href="" onClick="document.formname.submit()"><img  src="submitform.gif"></a>
```

> **NOTE**   Within Navigator and Internet Explorer, the `submit()` method *does* trigger any `onSubmit` method defined in the `<form>` tag.

onReset event handler

Located within the `<form>` tag, the `onReset` event handler is executed when a `reset()` method is issued or a Reset button within the form is pressed. The event handler will execute before the form is reset. If the event handler returns a value of false, the form will *not* be reset.

For instance, imagine that you have a generic event handler function named `generic()`. When `generic()` is complete, it returns a value of true or false. The following `onReset` event handler will not proceed to resetting the form if `generic()` returns false; otherwise, the form will be reset.

```
<form name=formname method=get action="URL" onReset="return generic()">
```

Internet Explorer 3 does not support the `onReset` event handler for the `<form>` tag.

onSubmit event handler

Located within the `<form>` tag, the `onSubmit` event handler is executed when a `submit()` method is issued or a Submit button within the form is pressed. The event handler will execute before the form is submitted. If the event handler returns a value of false, the form will *not* be submitted.

For instance, imagine that you have a generic event handler function named `generic()`. When `generic()` is complete, it returns a value of true or false. The following `onSubmit` event handler will not proceed to submit the form if `generic()` returns false; otherwise, the form will be submitted.

```
<form name=formname method=get action="URL" onSubmit="return generic()">
```

Commonly, the `onSubmit` event handler is used to validate or confirm form data before it is actually sent across the network to a server. By calling data validation functions, and returning a value of false if validation fails, you can prevent the form from being submitted. This can save time and bandwidth, versus performing validation and confirmation from the server side.

<FORM>

Category: HTML

Browser Support		Navigator 3	Navigator 4	Explorer 3	Explorer 4
	Macintosh	■■■	■■■	■■■	■■■
	Windows	■■■	■■■	■■■	■■■

May Contain `<A>`, `<ADDRESS>`, `<APPLET>`, `<B>`, `<BASEFONT>`, `<BIG>`, `<BLOCKQUOTE>`, `<BR>`, `<CENTER>`, `<CITE>`, `<CODE>`, `<DFN>`, `<DIR>`, `<DIV>`, `<DL>`, `<EM>`, `<FONT>`, `<H1>`, `<H2>`, `<H3>`, `<H4>`, `<H5>`, `<H6>`, `<HR>`, `<I>`, `<IMG>`, `<INPUT>`, `<KBD>`, `<MAP>`, `<MENU>`, `<OL>`, `<P>`, `<PRE>`, `<SAMP>`, `<SELECT>`, `<SMALL>`, `<STRIKE>`, `<STRONG>`, `<SUB>`, `<SUP>`, `<TABLE>`, `<TEXTAREA>`, `<TT>`, `<U>`, `<UL>`, `<VAR>`

May Be Used In `<BLOCKQUOTE>`, `<BODY>`, `<CENTER>`, `<DD>`, `<DIV>`, `<LI>`, `<TD>`, `<TH>`

Attributes ACTION, ENCTYPE, METHOD, TARGET

Syntax `<FORM>…</FORM>`

The `<FORM>` tag is the primary tag used to create a form. The other necessary tag is `<INPUT>`, although `<SELECT>` and `<TEXTAREA>` also play a part. All three of these other tags are covered in detail in their own individual entries elsewhere in the book.

A *form* is a front-end user interface on a web page that is linked to a CGI script or other gateway program; it produces specific, pre-established results based on information a visitor types in. When a visitor types text or numbers into a form, or chooses one of a form's listed options, the form collects the information and sends it over the web to be processed by a CGI script, usually located on the web page author's server. The script determines what the visitor wants and returns the results.

The `<FORM>` tag encloses all the information needed to specify the CGI script or gateway program. A closing, or `</FORM>` tag, is required. Forms cannot be nested on a web page like tables, but you can easily list many forms on the same web page.

The front-end design of a form is relatively uncomplicated, and most HTML users have no trouble learning to use the form tags. The difference between forms and other intermediate- to advanced-level HTML (like tables and frames) however, is the necessity of the CGI script or other gateway program. These form components are written in full-fledged programming languages like C, REXX, and Perl, and that's a completely different, separate proposition from learning to write HTML.

If you want to include forms on your web page, before you write the HTML you should 1) ask your Internet Service Provider what their form limitations and requirements are, and 2) find an appropriate CGI script or gateway program. You should also look into other, more detailed HTML tutorials like *HTML 3.2 Unleashed* and *CGI Unleashed*, which cover connections to and composition of CGI scripts and gateway programs. This aspect of using forms goes beyond the scope of this book.

> **NOTE** You can also find ready-to-use CGI scripts and gateway programs on the web. Here are a few places to start your search:
>
> Matt's Script Archive
>
> `http://www.worldwidemart.com/scripts`
>
> The CGI Resource Index
>
> `http://www.cgi-resources.com`

You can still practice with and perfect using form HTML, even if you don't have the CGI script or gateway program in place. Here's the most basic <FORM> tag HTML:

```
<FORM ACTION=http://www.provider.com/cgiscript METHOD=post>
Form text contents go here.
</FORM>
```

The <FORM> tag's individual attributes are discussed in detail throughout the rest of this entry.

> **NOTE** See the <INPUT> tag entry for numerous examples of what forms look like on a web page.

ACTION

The ACTION attribute typically specifies the URL where the form data is sent to be processed by the CGI script or gateway program. It is the only required ACTION attribute and a form will not work without it.

In the following example HTML, the URL represents the location of the server where the form data will be processed:

```
<FORM ACTION="http://www.provider.com/cgi-bin/cgiscript.html" METHOD=post
Form text contents go here.
</FORM>
```

This HTML does not work by itself because it only represents half of the information needed to create a form—remember you need something on the web page for the user to interact with *and* you need a CGI script. The ACTION attribute only specifies the CGI script information, so putting the preceding HTML into a text editor and uploading it to a browser would produce a blank web page.

Some web page authors will use the ACTION attribute to create buttons which, when clicked, will take the user to another web page. Using ACTION in this manner is not highly recommended because the ACTION attribute was not created for this purpose.

If you want to give it a try, here's the "proper" HTML:

```
<FORM ACTION=links.html METHOD=get>
<INPUT TYPE=submit NAME=name VALUE="Go to the links page">
</FORM>
```

Under the best circumstances, you'll have created a typical form-like oval button with the words "Go to the links page." written on it. It won't be bordered with a link color and the cursor won't identify it as a link (the cursor arrow won't change to a pointing hand). However, you'll still have needed to make a connecting page (in this example, links.html) before creating the button, or else the process won't work at all.

ENCTYPE

The ENCTYPE (or encoding type) attribute specifies the media type of the information being processed by the <FORM> tag. Including this attribute is only necessary when the METHOD attribute's value is something other than get or post. In other words, the ENCTYPE default value ("application/x-www-form-urlencoded") is good enough most of the time.

However, if the ACTION attribute is used to specify an email value like "mailto:johndoe@provider.com" for an email form, you would specify something else:

```
<FORM ACTION="mailto:johndoe@provider.com" ENCTYPE=text/plain METHOD=post>
<INPUT TYPE=text NAME=name VALUE="Email me">
</FORM>
```

If you've really gotten into the HTML of forms and want to use this attribute to its fullest extent, check out document RFC1520 at (ftp://ftp.merit.edu/documents/rfc/rfc1520) for more information on how to propose a new METHOD value. And see the following METHOD attribute section for more information on how it is used.

METHOD

The METHOD attribute specifies how the information typed into a form should be sent to the server. It has two values:

Value	Result
get	The information will be sent in a URL and the sender will get a lengthy, customized response (as in doing a keyword search using an index). This is the METHOD attribute default.
post	The information will be sent in the body of the submission and the reader will get a short, standardized response (as in sending email or participating in a survey).

These two values will apply in almost every situation where a form is used. However, the <FORM> tag does possess the ENCTYPE attribute, which is used in the event of an exception—see the ENCTYPE attribute section for more details.

Both of the METHOD attributes listed in this section are used in every figure in the <FORM> tag entry as a whole. Please thumb through this tag entry and browse all the example HTML and related figures in the other attribute sections to get an idea of how the METHOD attribute is used.

TARGET

The TARGET attribute specifies how the response to a form request is displayed after it's received. There are four values:

Value	Result
blank	The response information is loaded into a new blank window.
parent	The response information is loaded into the parent window.
self	The response information is loaded into the same window that the form is in.
top	The response information is loaded into the full window body.

FormatCurrency( )
Category: VBScript

Type	Function				
Browser Support		Navigator 3	Navigator 4	Explorer 3	Explorer 4
	Macintosh	☐	☐	☐	■
	Windows	☐	☐	■	■

Syntax   `formatCurrency(number [,digitsAfterDecimal]`
        `[,includeLeadingDigit][,parensForNegatives][,groupDigits])`

The formatCurrency() function returns the value of *number* formatted to a currency expression in the specified format. Despite its apparent complexity, this function is rather straightforward— as illustrated in the following parameters and the examples provided:

Parameter	Result
number	The numeric value to be formatted as currency. If no other parameters are specified, the currency format is based upon the user's operating system settings. `formatCurrency(100-58)` returns $42.00
digitsAfterDecimal	An integer that specifies how many decimal places to display. `formatCurrency(100-58,3)` returns $42.000

continues

Parameter	Result
includeLeadingDigit	0: Do not add a leading zero for fractional values –1: Add a leading zero for fractional values –2: Use the system's default setting `formatCurrency(5/10,2,-1)` returns $0.50 `formatCurrency(5/10,2,0)` returns $.50
parensForNegative	0: Do not use parentheses for negative values –1: Use parentheses for negative values –2: Use the system's default setting `formatCurrency(58-100,2,0,-1)` returns ($42.00) `formatCurrency(58-100,2,0,0)` returns –$42.00
groupDigits	0: Do not group values using the system's group delimiter –1: Group values using the system's group delimiter –2: Use the system's default setting `formatCurrency(500000,2,0,-1,0)` returns $500000.00 `formatCurrency(500000,2,0,-1,-1)` returns $500,000.00

Omitting any of the preceding parameters defaults to the system's default settings (same as a value of –2 for many of the parameters). Different operating systems handle currency format defaults in different ways—in Windows 95, currency format default values are specified in the Regional Settings applet in the Control Panel, as seen in Figures 1 and 2.

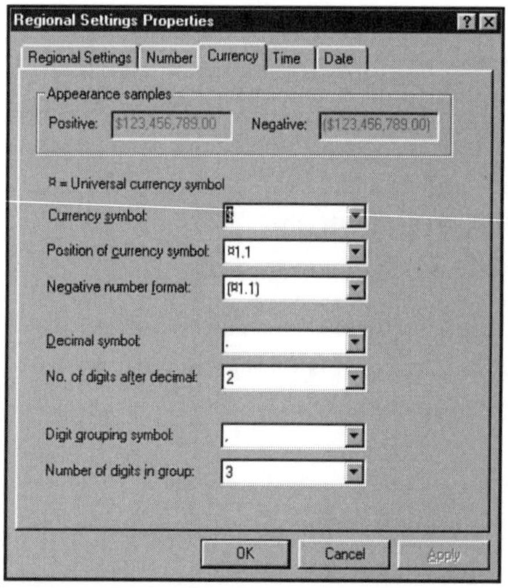

Figure 1

Setting the system default Currency format in the Windows 95 Control Panel.

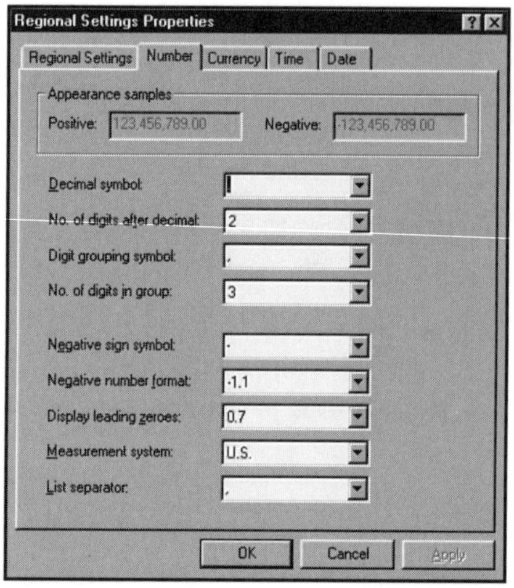

Figure 2

Setting the system default Number format in the Windows 95 Control Panel.

FormatDateTime()
Category: VBScript

Type	Function

Browser Support

	Navigator 3	Navigator 4	Explorer 3	Explorer 4
Macintosh	☐	☐	☐	■
Windows	☐	☐	■	■

Syntax   `formatDateTime(date [,NamedFormat])`

The `FormatDateTime()` function accepts the date and/or time, as expressed by *date*, and returns a date or time in the format *NamedFormat*. If *NamedFormat* is not specified, the system default date or time format is used.

The parameter *date* may contain the date and/or time in any legal format, such as:

```
formatdatetime("Jan 8 1991 05:00:00")
formatdatetime("5,23,72")
formatdatetime("1:05 PM")
```

The optional parameter *NamedFormat,* specified following *date,* may contain any of the following values:

Value	Result
0	Displays both date and/or time—date as a short date, time as a long time `formatdatetime("Sep 8 1967 13:05:00",0)` returns 9/8/67 1:05:00 PM
1	Displays only the date, in long date format as set in the operating system `formatdatetime("Sep 8 1967 13:05:00",1)` returns Friday, September 08, 1967
2	Displays only the date, in short date format as set in the operating system `formatdatetime("Sep 8 1967 13:05:00",2)` returns 9/8/67
3	Displays only the time, in long time format as set in the operating system `formatdatetime("Sep 8 1967 13:05:00",3)` returns 1:05:00 PM
4	Displays only the time, in short time format 24-hour military time `formatdatetime("Sep 8 1967 13:05:00",4)` returns 13:05

Different operating systems handle default date and time formats in different ways—in Windows 95, default date and time formats are specified in the Regional Settings applet in the Control Panel, as seen in Figures 1 and 2.

F

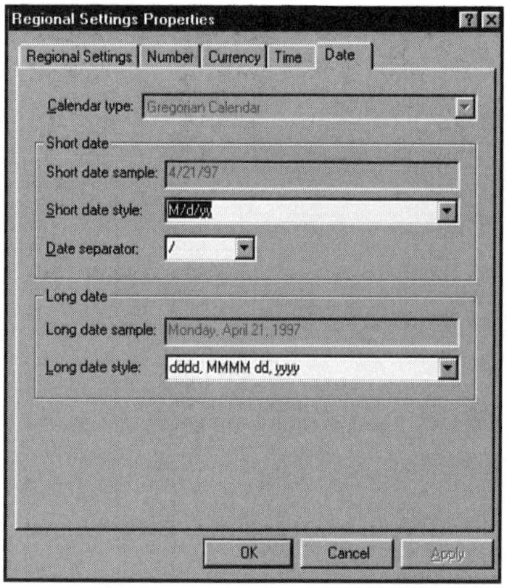

Figure 1

Setting the system date format in the Windows 95 Control Panel.

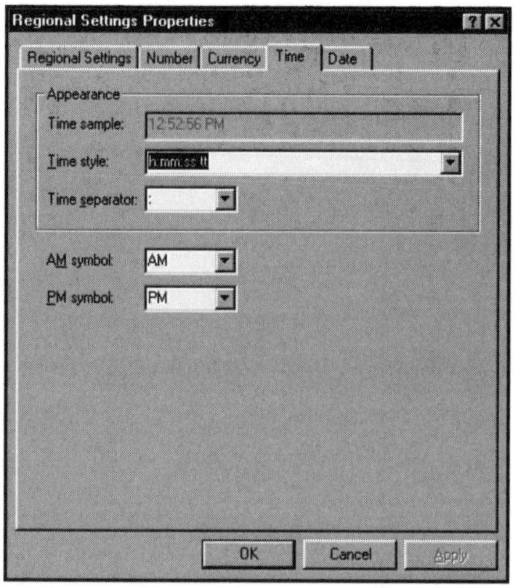

Figure 2

Setting the system time format in the Windows 95 Control Panel.

FormatNumber()
Category: VBScript

Type	Function	

Browser Support

	Navigator 3	Navigator 4	Explorer 3	Explorer 4
Macintosh	☐	☐	☐	■
Windows	☐	☐	■	■

Syntax

```
formatNumber(number [,digitsAfterDecimal]
       [,includeLeadingDigit][,parensForNegatives][,groupDigits])
```

The FormatNumber() function returns the value of *number* in the specified numeric format. Despite its apparent complexity, this function is rather straightforward—as illustrated in the following parameters and the examples provided:

Parameter	Result
number	The numeric value to be formatted. If no other parameters are specified, the number format is based upon the user's operating system settings. formatNumber(50) returns 50.00
digitsAfterDecimal	An integer that specifies how many decimal places to display formatNumber(100-50,3) returns 50.000

Parameter	Result
`includeLeadingDigit`	0: Do not add a leading zero for fractional values −1: Add a leading zero for fractional values −2: Use the system's default setting `formatNumber(2/4,4,-1)` returns 0.5000 `formatNumber(2/4,4,0)` returns .5000
`parensForNegative`	0: Do not use parentheses for negative values −1: Use parentheses for negative values −2: Use the system's default setting `formatNumber(25-100,2,-1,-1)` returns 75.00 `formatNumber(25-100,2,-1,0)` returns −75.00
`groupDigits`	0: Do not group values using the system's group delimiter −1: Group values using the system's group delimiter −2: Use the system's default setting `formatNumber(500000,2,0,-1,0)` returns 500000.00 `formatNumber(500000,2,0,-1,-1)` returns 500,000.00

Omitting any of the preceding parameters defaults to the system's default settings (same as a value of −2 for many of the parameters). Only *number* is required as a specified parameter. Different operating systems handle number format defaults in different ways—in Windows 95, number format defaults are specified in the Regional Settings applet in the Control Panel, as seen in Figure 1.

Figure 1

Setting the system default number format in the Windows 95 Control Panel.

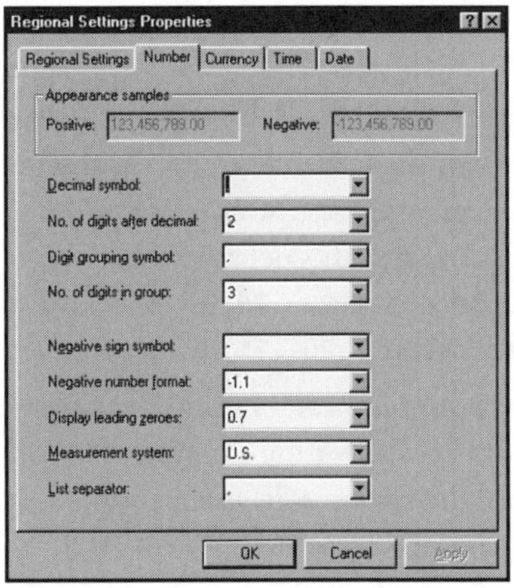

FormatPercent()
Category: VBScript

Type	Function

Browser Support

	Navigator 3	Navigator 4	Explorer 3	Explorer 4
Macintosh				■
Windows			■	■

Syntax

```
formatPercent(number [,digitsAfterDecimal]
[,includeLeadingDigit][,parensForNegatives][,groupDigits])
```

The FormatPercent() function returns the value of *number* multiplied by 100 in the specified numeric format, followed by a % sign. Despite its apparent complexity, this function is rather straightforward—as illustrated in the following parameters and the examples provided:

Parameter	Result
number	The numeric value to be formatted as a percent. If no other parameters are specified, the number format is based upon the user's operating system settings. formatPercent(.50) returns 50.00%
digitsAfterDecimal	An integer that specifies how many decimal places to display formatPercent(25/100,3) returns 25.000%
includeLeadingDigit	0: Do not add a leading zero for fractional values −1: Add a leading zero for fractional values −2: Use the system's default setting formatPercent(25/10000,4,-1) returns 0.2500% formatPercent(25/10000,4,0) returns .2500%
parensForNegative	0: Do not use parentheses for negative values −1: Use parentheses for negative values −2: Use the system's default setting formatPercent(.25-.75,2,-1,-1) returns (50.00%) formatPercent(.25-.75,2,-1,0) returns −50.00%
groupDigits	0: Do not group values using the system's group delimiter −1: Group values using the system's group delimiter −2: Use the system's default setting formatPercent(25*75,2,0,0,0) returns 187500.00% formatPercent(25*75,2,0,0,-1) returns 187,500.00%

Omitting any of the preceding parameters defaults to the system's default settings (same as a value of −2 for many of the parameters). Different operating systems handle number format defaults in different ways—in Windows 95, number format defaults are specified in the Regional Settings applet in the Control Panel, as seen in Figure 1.

Figure 1

Setting the system default number format in the Windows 95 Control Panel.

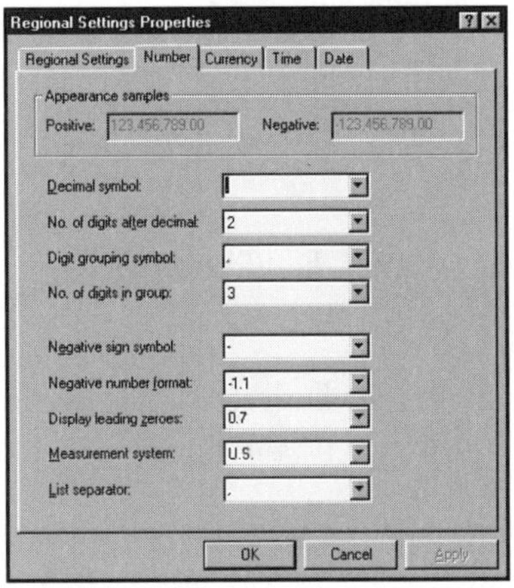

<FRAME>

Category: HTML

Browser Support		Navigator 3	Navigator 4	Explorer 3	Explorer 4
	Macintosh	▬	▬	▬	▬
	Windows	▬	▬	▬	▬

Attributes ALIGN, FRAMEBORDER, MARGINHEIGHT, MARGINWIDTH, NAME, NORESIZE, SCROLLING, SRC

Syntax <Frame>...</Frame>

The <FRAME> tag is one of two primary tags (the other is <FRAMESET>) used to create a web page using frames. It defines a single frame in a *frameset,* or arrangement of several individual frames on one web page. A closing, or </FRAME>, tag is not required.

In the following example HTML, there are three individual frames within this frameset, each individually specified by <FRAME>:

```
<FRAMESET SCROLLING=yes FRAMEBORDER=no>
<FRAME SRC=menu.html>
<FRAME SRC=links.html>
<FRAME SRC=intro.html>
</FRAMESET>
```

ALIGN

The ALIGN attribute specifies the alignment of an individual frame within a frameset and/or any surrounding text. There are five possible ALIGN values:

bottom

Any surrounding text is aligned with the bottom of the affected frame.

center

Any surrounding text is aligned with the center of the affected frame.

left

The affected frame is displayed as a floating entity flush against the left side of the browser window with any surrounding text flowed around it. This is the ALIGN attribute default.

right

The affected frame is displayed as a floating entity flush against the right side of the browser window with any surrounding text flowed around it.

top

Any surrounding text is aligned with the top of the affected frame.

FRAMEBORDER

The FRAMEBORDER attribute specifies the presence (FRAMEBORDER=1) or absence (FRAMEBORDER=0) of a 3-D border around the edge of an individual frame. The 1 value is the FRAMEBORDER default.

MARGINHEIGHT

The MARGINHEIGHT attribute specifies the amount of vertical space between the contents of a frame and its border in pixels. It is used in tandem with MARGINWIDTH, which specifies the amount of horizontal space between frame contents and the frame border, also in pixels.

MARGINWIDTH

The MARGINWIDTH attribute specifies the amount of vertical space between the contents of a frame and its border in pixels. It is used in tandem with MARGINHEIGHT, which specifies the amount of horizontal space between frame contents and the frame border, also in pixels.

NAME

The NAME attribute specifies a target name for each individual frame. Each frame should have its own unique NAME specification, though this information does not affect the way the frames display on the web page.

NORESIZE

The NORESIZE attribute prevents the browser from resizing an individual frame if the visitor changes the width or height of the open browser window.

SCROLLING

The SCROLLING attribute specifies whether or not a frame will be displayed with a click-and-draggable slider bar. The no value (SCROLLING=no) means the frame is not scrollable and the yes value (SCROLLING=yes) means it is.

Obviously, a frame need not scroll if the information it contains doesn't run off the edge or bottom of the browser window. So you should only assign the yes value to SCROLLING if it is necessary, lest you confuse visitors to your web page.

FRAME SRC

The SRC attribute specifies the file name or URL to be displayed in the frame.

Frame
Category: JavaScript, JScript, VBScript

Browser Support		Navigator 3	Navigator 4	Explorer 3	Explorer 4
	Macintosh	■	■	☐	■
	Windows	■	■	■	■

Subset Of	Window object
Properties	name, length, onblur, onfocus
Events	onblur, onfocus
Syntax	windowName.frames[index].property OR
	windowName.frameName.property

A frame *is* a window. This is the most important point. Visually, frames are independent sub-windows within a main browser window. A web page may contain frames as a way of displaying several forms of content simultaneously—for instance, the classic "table of contents" page, wherein the lefthand frame contains a series of hyperlinks and the righthand frame contains the document associated with the hyperlink. As seen in Figure 1, a page may contain any number of frames, all of which are created using the HTML <frameset> and <frame> tags. The set of frames that make up a web page is known as a "frameset."

In scripting terms, a frame object is a window object, which possesses its same properties and methods (see window object). Some of these properties and methods, however, require explanation unique to the frame object, each of which is described in the following sections.

Figure 1

A frameset containing three frames. Each frame *object is a* window *object.*

A frame object is created using the <frame> tag within a <frameset> tag.

```
<frameset
   rows="rowHeightList"
   cols="columnWidthList"
   [onBlur="eventHandler"]
   [onFocus="eventHandler"]
   [onLoad="eventHandler"]
   [onUnload="eventHandler"]>
   <frame src="URL" name="frameName">
   [ ... <frame src="URL" name="frameName">]
</frameset>
```

When referencing a frame object, you can either use its name attribute in the <frame> tag, or its index in the frames[] array. For instance, consider the frameset:

```
<frameset rows="30%,70%">
 <frame src="doc1.html" name="frame_a">
 <frame src="doc2.html" name="frame_b">
</frameset>
```

In this frameset, you can reference the frame object named "frame_a" as either

```
windowName.frame_a.property
```

or

```
windowName.frames[0].property
```

F

TIP	Because a `frame` object is also a `window` object, *windowName* could be the name of a frame, if that frame contains an HTML document which itself defines a frameset. Frames within frames are known as child-frames.

Consider a parent window with two frames: the first frame, *frame1*, contains a typical HTML document; the second frame, *frame2*, contains an HTML frameset, which defines three frames: *framea*, *frameb*, and *framec*. These three frames are child-frames of *frame2*. Thus, to reference *frameb*:

```
parent.frame2.frameb.property
```

or

```
parent.frame2.frames[1].property
```

or

```
parent.frames[1].frames[1].property
```

Frame references *can* be confusing, so pay them close attention!

name property

The `name` property reflects the name of the specified frame, as defined by the `name` attribute of the `<frame>` tag.

```
frname=parent.frames[2].name
```

The preceding example would assign the name of the third frame in the window to the variable `frname`.

length property

The `length` property is the number of child frames within the specified frame, if any. Consider a parent window with two frames: the first frame, *frame1*, contains a typical HTML document; the second frame, *frame2*, contains an HTML frameset, which defines three frames: *framea*, *frameb*, and *framec*. Thus, these three frames are child-frames of *frame2*:

```
parent.frame2.length
```

or

```
parent.frames[1].length
```

would yield the value 3. Because `frame1` does not contain any child frames, its `length` property would contain the value 0.

Figure 2

The parent window
contains two frames.
The second of these
frames contains
three child frames.
Confusing!

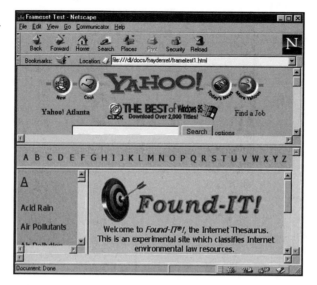

onblur property and event handler

An `onblur` event occurs when the user loses focus from the frame, either by clicking or tabbing elsewhere in the window. Unlike other HTML elements, you cannot specify a frame's event handler in its HTML tag (although there are event handlers specified in the `<frameset>` tag, these operate on the `window` object). Rather, it must be assigned to the `onblur` property of the `frame` object.

```
windowname.framename.onblur="eventHandler"
```

> **NOTE**   Notice that `onblur` is written in all lowercase, unlike many other event handlers. This is required when assigning an event handler to a `frame` object.

 Internet Explorer 3 does not support the `onblur` propery or event handler for the `frame` object.

onfocus property and event handler

An `onfocus` event occurs when the user brings focus to the frame, either by clicking on or tabbing to the frame. Unlike other HTML elements, you cannot specify a frame's event handler in its HTML tag (although there are event handlers specified in the `<frameset>` tag, these operate on the `window` object). Rather, it must be assigned to the `onfocus` property of the `frame` object.

```
windowname.framename.onfocus="eventHandler"
```

> **NOTE** | Notice that `onfocus` is written in all lowercase, unlike many other event handlers. This is required when assigning an event handler to a `frame` object.

> Internet Explorer 3 does not support the `onfocus` property or event handler for the `frame` object.

F

<FRAMESET>

Category: HTML

Browser Support		Navigator 3	Navigator 4	Explorer 3	Explorer 4
	Macintosh	■■■	■■■	■■■	■■■
	Windows	■■■	■■■	■■■	■■■

May Contain	<FRAMES, <NOFRAMES>
May Be Used In	<BODY>
Attributes	COLS, FRAMEBORDER, FRAMESPACING, ROWS, SCROLLING
Syntax	<FRAMESET>...</FRAMESET>

The <FRAMESET> tag is one of two primary tags (the other is <FRAME>) used to create a web page using frames. It encloses all the individual frames and the <NOFRAMES> alternative page, if present. A closing, or </FRAMESET>, tag is required.

In the following example HTML, there are three individual frames on this web page:

```
<FRAMESET SCROLLING=yes FRAMEBORDER=no>
<FRAME SRC=menu.html>
<FRAME SRC=links.html>
<FRAME SRC=intro.html>
</FRAMESET>
```

Without the <FRAMESET> tag, the browser reading this HTML would not recognize the <FRAME>-specified information as instructions to create frames. See the <FRAME> entry elsewhere in the book for more information on creating web pages with frames.

Experimenting with frames HTML is different from experimenting with other intermediate-level HTML (such as tables and forms) in that if you want your work in progress to display correctly, you must have your secondary pages already written—in the preceding example HTML, these pages would be menu.html, links.html, and intro.html. Also, remember these secondary pages must be kept in the same folder as your primary page, or (again) frames won't work.

COLS

The COLS attribute creates a frame within a vertical column on the web page. Its size can be specified in one of three ways: as a percentage of the overall browser window (COLS=25%), in pixels (COLS=175) or as a relative size (COLS=*).

In the following example HTML, the precision of the COLS attribute settings is evident—all three columns on this web page are specified in the three available ways:

```
<FRAMESET COLS="15%, 115, *" SCROLLING=yes FRAMEBORDER=1>
<FRAME SRC=menu.html>
<FRAME SRC=links.html>
<FRAME SRC=intro.html>
</FRAMESET>
```

FRAMEBORDER

The FRAMEBORDER attribute specifies the presence (FRAMEBORDER=1) or the absence (FRAMEBORDER=0) of a border around the frames on a web page.

FRAMESPACING

The FRAMESPACING attribute specifies an amount of space between frames in pixels (FRAMESPACING=5).

ROWS

The ROWS attribute specifies a number of rows within a frame document in one of three ways: by percentage (ROWS=20%) by pixels (ROWS=140) or by relative size (ROWS=*).

FRAMESET SCROLLING

The SCROLLING attribute specifies whether or not the user of a page with frames can or cannot scroll down within each individual frame.

If the value specified by SCROLLING is 1, a slider bar will appear on the right side of the frame that the visitor can use by clicking and dragging. If the value specified by SCROLLING is 0 (zero) or the SCROLLING attribute is not used at all, the frame will be loaded up without the slider bar. This implies there is no more information than what is displayed in the frame when the web page loads up.

<H1>

Category: HTML

Browser Support	Navigator 3	Navigator 4	Explorer 3	Explorer 4
Macintosh	■	■	■	■
Windows	■	■	■	■

May Contain   `<A>`, `<APPLET>`, `<B>`, `<BASEFONT>`, `<BIG>`, `<BR>`, `<CITE>`, `<CODE>`, `<DFN>`, `<EM>`, `<FONT>`, `<I>`, `<IMG>`, `<INPUT>`, `<KBD>`, `<MAP>`, `<SAMP>`, `<SELECT>`, `<SMALL>`, `<STRIKE>`, `<STRONG>`, `<SUB>`, `<SUP>`, `<TEXTAREA>`, `<TT>`, `<U>`, `<VAR>`

May Be Used In   `<BLOCKQUOTE>`, `<BODY>`, `<CENTER>`, `<DD>`, `<DIV>`, `<FORM>`, `<LI>`, `<TD>`, `<TH>`

Attributes   `ALIGN`

Syntax   `<H1>…</H1>`

The `<H1>` header is the level one header tag (of six header tags) typically used to indicate the title of an HTML document. Sometimes `<H1>`-specified text is repeated in the `<TITLE>` tag, although it serves different purposes—`<H1>` information is only seen within the web page while `<TITLE>`-specified text can be utilized for bookmarks, Internet Explorer window captions, and some search indexes' URL descriptions.

`<H1>` has one attribute (`ALIGN`) for establishing horizontal alignment. The closing, or `</H1>` tag, is required.

ALIGN

The `ALIGN` tag specifies the horizontal alignment of a level one header. It has three values:

`center`

The level one header is centered on the web page.

`left`

The level one header is aligned by the left margin on the web page. This is the default `ALIGN` setting, although it is technically not supported by Internet Explorer.

`right`

The level one header is aligned by the right margin on the web page. This value is not as popular as the other two—it's not supported by Internet Explorer—and may be less reliable.

Figures 1, 2, 3, and 4 display level one headers specified with all three ALIGN attribute values in Navigator 3 and Internet Explorer 3 for the Mac and for Windows.

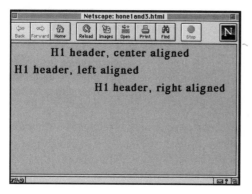

Figure 1

Level one headers center-, left-, and right-aligned, respectively, in Navigator 3 for the Mac.

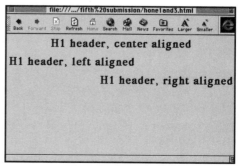

Figure 2

Level one headers center-, left-, and right-aligned, respectively, in Internet Explorer 3 for the Mac.

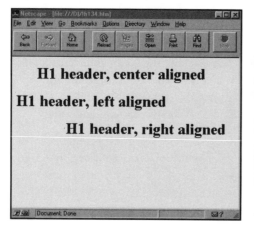

Figure 3

Level one headers center-, left-, and right-aligned, respectively, in Navigator 3 for Windows.

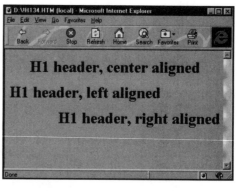

Figure 4

Level one headers center-, left-, and right-aligned, respectively, in Internet Explorer 3 for Windows.

The "typical" appearance of the six header tags as specified first in HTML 2.0 and carried through to HTML 3.2:

    <H1>   Text displayed in a very large font, bolded, and centered on the page with one or two blank lines above and below.

<H2>	Text displayed in a large font, bolded, and aligned flush left on the page with one or two blank lines above and below.
<H3>	Text displayed in a large font, italicized, and slightly indented from the left margin with one or two blank lines above and below.
<H4>	Text displayed in a normal font size, bolded, and indented farther than <H3> text with one blank line above and below.
<H5>	Text displayed in a normal font size, italicized, and indented just as far as <H4> text with one blank line above.
<H6>	Text displayed in a small font size, bolded, and indented similarly to normal text but farther than <H5> text with one blank line above.

Figures 5, 6, 7, and 8 can be used to compare all six header levels side by side in Navigator 3 and Internet Explorer 3 for the Mac and for Windows.

H

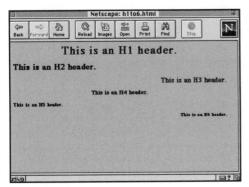

Figure 5

All six header tags in Navigator 3 for the Mac.

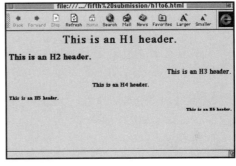

Figure 6

All six header tags in Internet Explorer 3 for the Mac.

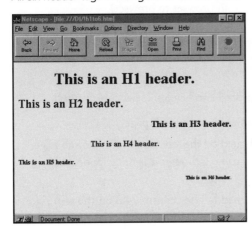

Figure 7

All six header tags in Navigator 3 for Windows.

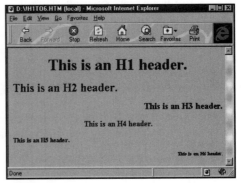

Figure 8

All six header tags in Internet Explorer 3 for Windows.

> **TIP** Some indexers (human and software both) rely on <H1> tag information to tell them the title or general subject matter of an HTML document. This information is then used to catalog and/or categorize a web page in online library systems or in popular Internet indexes like Yahoo! So, if you're looking for a way to make your page stand out for search engine robots, or human catalogers, a unique, inviting <H1> tag might be just the trick.

<H2>

Category: HTML

Browser Support

	Navigator 3	Navigator 4	Explorer 3	Explorer 4
Macintosh	▰	▰	▰	▰
Windows	▰	▰	▰	▰

May Contain <A>, <APPLET>, <B>, <BASEFONT>, <BIG>, <BR>, <CITE>, <CODE>, <DFN>, <EM>, <FONT>, <I>, <IMG>, <INPUT>, <KBD>, <MAP>, <SAMP>, <SELECT>, <SMALL>, <STRIKE>, <STRONG>, <SUB>, <SUP>, <TEXTAREA>, <TT>, <U>, <VAR>

May Be Used In <BLOCKQUOTE>, <BODY>, <CENTER>, <DD>, <DIV>, <FORM>, <LI>, <TD>, <TH>

Attributes ALIGN

Syntax <H2>...</H2>

The <H2> header is the level two header tag (of six header tags) typically used to indicate chapter titles or headings in a document. It is smaller than an <H1> header, but larger than an <H3> (although the way header tags are displayed will vary from browser to browser).

<H2> has one attribute (ALIGN) for establishing horizontal alignment. The closing, or </H2> tag, is required.

ALIGN

The ALIGN tag specifies the horizontal alignment of a level two header. It has three values:

center	The level two header is centered on the web page.
left	The level two header is aligned by the left margin on the web page. This is the default ALIGN setting, although it is not supported by Internet Explorer.
right	The level two header is aligned by the right margin on the web page. This value is not as popular as the other two—it's not supported by Internet Explorer—and may be less reliable.

Figures 1, 2, 3, and 4 display level two headers specified with all three ALIGN attribute values in Navigator 3 and Internet Explorer 3 for the Mac and for Windows.

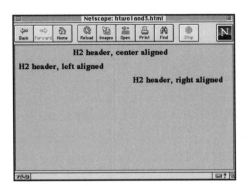

Figure 1

Level two headers center-, left-, and right-aligned, respectively, in Netscape Navigator 3 for the Mac.

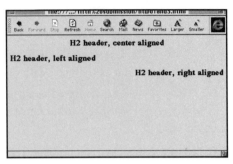

Figure 2

Level two headers center-, left-, and right-aligned, respectively, in Internet Explorer 3 for the Mac.

H

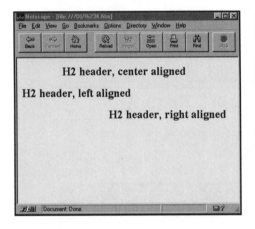

Figure 3

Level two headers center-, left-, and right-aligned, respectively, in Navigator 3 for Windows.

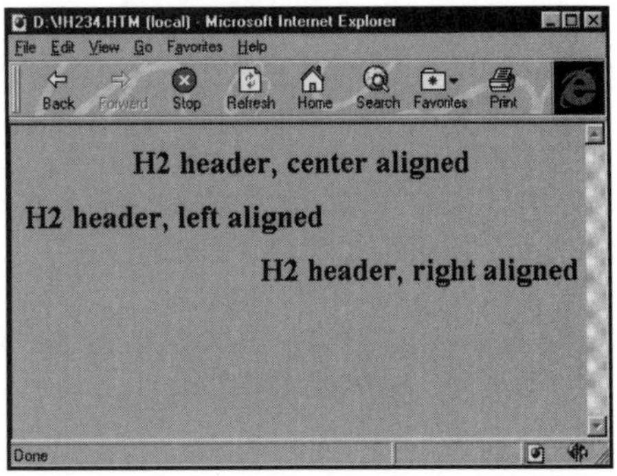

Figure 4

Level two headers center-, left-, and right-aligned, respectively, in Internet Explorer 3 for Windows.

The "typical" appearance of the six header tags as specified first in HTML 2.0 and carried through to HTML 3.2:

<H1>	Text displayed in a very large font, bolded, and centered on the page with one or two blank lines above and below.
<H2>	Text displayed in a large font, bolded, and aligned flush left on the page with one or two blank lines above and below.
<H3>	Text displayed in a large font, italicized, and slightly indented from the left margin with one or two blank lines above and below.

<H4>	Text displayed in a normal font size, bolded, and indented farther than <H3> text with one blank line above and below.
<H5>	Text displayed in a normal font size, italicized, and indented just as far as <H4> text with one blank line above.
<H6>	Text displayed in a small font size, bolded, and indented similarly to normal text but farther than <H5> text with one blank line above.

Figures 5, 6, 7, and 8 can be used to compare all six header levels side by side in Navigator 3 and Internet Explorer 3 for the Mac and for Windows.

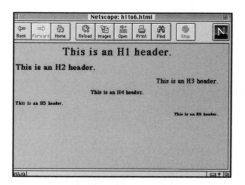

Figure 5

All six header tags in Navigator 3 for the Mac.

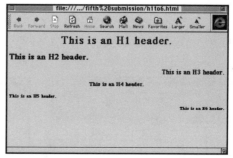

Figure 6

All six header tags in Internet Explorer 3 for the Mac.

Figure 7

All six header tags in Navigator 3 for Windows.

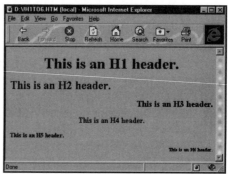

Figure 8

All six header tags in Internet Explorer 3 for Windows.

<H3>

Category: HTML

		Navigator 3	Navigator 4	Explorer 3	Explorer 4
Browser Support	Macintosh	■	■	■	■
	Windows	■	■	■	■

May Contain <A>, <APPLET>, <B>, <BASEFONT>, <BIG>, <BR>, <CITE>, <CODE>, <DFN>, <EM>, <FONT>, <I>, <IMG>, <INPUT>, <KBD>, <MAP>, <SAMP>, <SELECT>, <SMALL>, <STRIKE>, <STRONG>, <SUB>, <SUP>, <TEXTAREA>, <TT>, <U>, <VAR>

May Be Used In <BLOCKQUOTE>, <BODY>, <CENTER>, <DD>, <DIV>, <FORM>, <LI>, <TD>, <TH>

Attributes ALIGN

Syntax <H3>...</H3>

The <H3> header is the level three header tag (of six header tags) typically used to indicate chapter sections in a document. It is smaller than an <H2> header, but larger than an <H4> (although the way header tags are displayed will vary from browser to browser).

<H3> has one attribute (ALIGN) for establishing horizontal alignment. The closing, or </H3> tag, is required.

ALIGN

The ALIGN tag specifies the horizontal alignment of a level three header. It has three values:

center   The level three header is centered on the web page.

left   The level three header is aligned by the left margin on the web page. This is the default ALIGN setting, although it is not supported by Internet Explorer.

right   The level three header is aligned by the right margin on the web page. This value is not as popular as the other two—it's not supported by Internet Explorer—and may be less reliable.

H

Figures 1, 2, 3, and 4 display level three headers specified with all three ALIGN attribute values in Navigator 3 and Internet Explorer 3 for the Mac and for Windows.

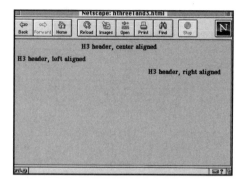

Figure 1

Level three headers center-, left-, and right-aligned, respectively, in Navigator 3 for the Mac.

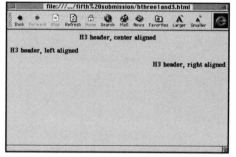

Figure 2

Level three headers center-, left-, and right-aligned, respectively, in Internet Explorer 3 for the Mac.

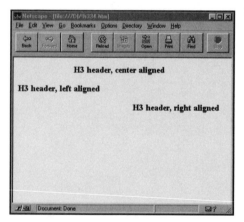

Figure 3

Level three headers center-, left-, and right-aligned, respectively, in Navigator 3 for Windows.

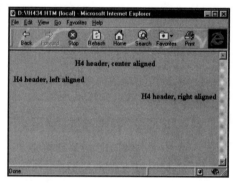

Figure 4

Level three headers center-, left-, and right-aligned, respectively, in Internet Explorer 3 for Windows.

The "typical" appearance of the six header tags as specified first in HTML 2.0 and carried through to HTML 3.2:

<H1>	Text displayed in a very large font, bolded, and centered on the page with one or two blank lines above and below.
<H2>	Text displayed in a large font, bolded, and aligned flush left on the page with one or two blank lines above and below.

<H3>	Text displayed in a large font, italicized, and slightly indented from the left margin with one or two blank lines above and below.
<H4>	Text displayed in a normal font size, bolded, and indented farther than <H3> text with one blank line above and below.
<H5>	Text displayed in a normal font size, italicized, and indented just as far as <H4> text with one blank line above.
<H6>	Text displayed in a small font size, bolded, and indented similarly to normal text but farther than <H5> text with one blank line above.

Figures 5, 6, 7, and 8 can be used to compare all six header levels side by side in Navigator 3 and Internet Explorer 3 for the Mac and for Windows.

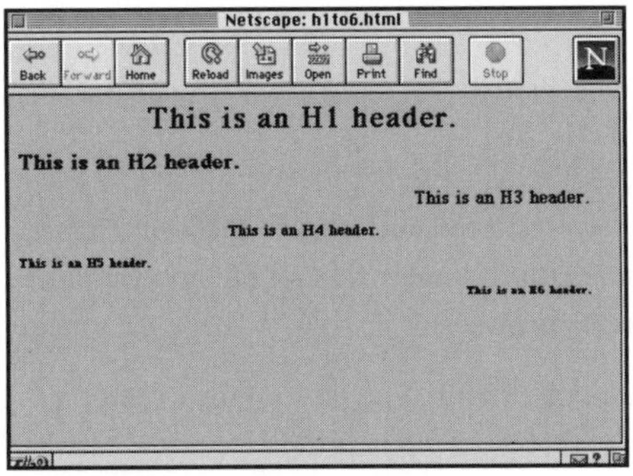

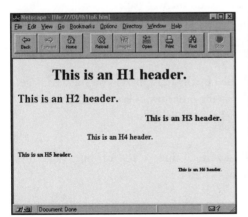

Figure 5

All six header tags in Navigator 3 for the Mac.

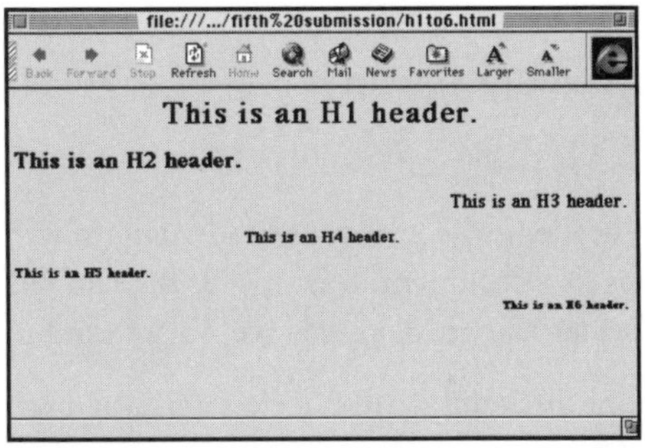

Figure 6

All six header tags in Internet Explorer 3 for the Mac.

Figure 7

All six header tags in Navigator 3 for Windows.

Figure 8

All six header tags in Internet Explorer 3 for Windows.

<H4>

Category: HTML

	Navigator 3	Navigator 4	Explorer 3	Explorer 4
Browser Support				
Macintosh	■■■■	■■■■	■■■	■■■
Windows	■■■■	■■■	■■■	■■■■

May Contain   <A>, <APPLET>, <B>, <BASEFONT>, <BIG>, <BR>, <CITE>, <CODE>, <DFN>, <EM>, <FONT>, <I>, <IMG>, <INPUT>, <KBD>, <MAP>, <SAMP>, <SELECT>, <SMALL>, <STRIKE>, <STRONG>, <SUB>, <SUP>, <TEXTAREA>, <TT>, <U>, <VAR>

May Be Used In   <BLOCKQUOTE>, <BODY>, <CENTER>, <DD>, <DIV>, <FORM>, <LI>, <TD>, <TH>

Attributes   ALIGN

Syntax   <H4>...</H4>

The <H4> header is the level four header tag (of six header tags) typically used to indicate chapter subsections in a document. It is smaller than an <H3> header, but larger than an <H5> (although the way header tags are displayed will vary from browser to browser).

<H4> has one attribute (ALIGN) for establishing horizontal alignment. The closing, or </H4> tag, is required.

ALIGN

The ALIGN tag specifies the horizontal alignment of a level four header. It has three values:

center   The level four header is centered on the web page.

left   The level four header is aligned by the left margin on the web page. This is the default ALIGN setting, although it is not supported by Internet Explorer.

right   The level four header is aligned by the right margin on the web page. This value is not as popular as the other two—it's not supported by Internet Explorer—and may be less reliable.

Figures 1, 2, 3, and 4 display level four headers specified with all three ALIGN attribute values in Navigator 3 and Internet Explorer 3 for the Mac and for Windows.

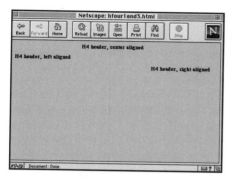

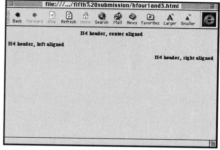

Figure 1

Level four headers center-, left-, and right-aligned, respectively, in Navigator 3 for the Mac.

Figure 2

Level four headers center-, left-, and right-aligned, respectively, in Internet Explorer 3 for the Mac.

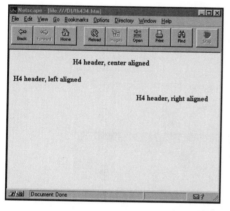

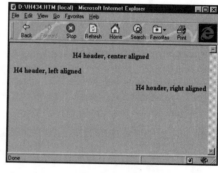

Figure 4

Level four headers center-, left-, and right-aligned, respectively, in Internet Explorer 3 for Windows.

Figure 3

Level four headers center-, left-, and right-aligned, respectively, in Navigator 3 for Windows.

The "typical" appearance of the six header tags as specified first in HTML 2.0 and carried through to HTML 3.2:

<H1>   Text displayed in a very large font, bolded, and centered on the page with one or two blank lines above and below.

<H2>   Text displayed in a large font, bolded, and aligned flush left on the page with one or two blank lines above and below.

<H3>   Text displayed in a large font, italicized, and slightly indented from the left margin with one or two blank lines above and below.

<H4>   Text displayed in a normal font size, bolded, and indented farther than <H3> text with one blank line above and below.

<H5>	Text displayed in a normal font size, italicized, and indented just as far as <H4> text with one blank line above.
<H6>	Text displayed in a small font size, bolded, and indented similarly to normal text but farther than <H5> text with one blank line above.

Figures 5, 6, 7, and 8 can be used to compare all six header levels side by side in Navigator 3 and Internet Explorer 3 for the Mac and for Windows.

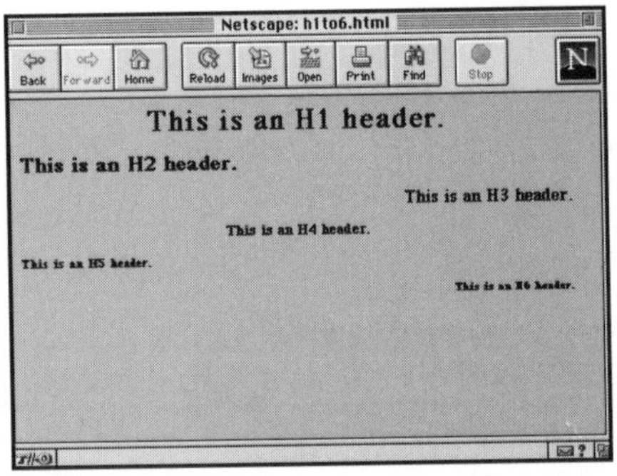

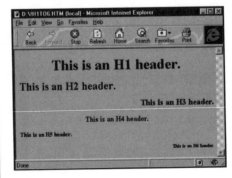

Figure 5

All six header tags in Navigator 3 for the Mac.

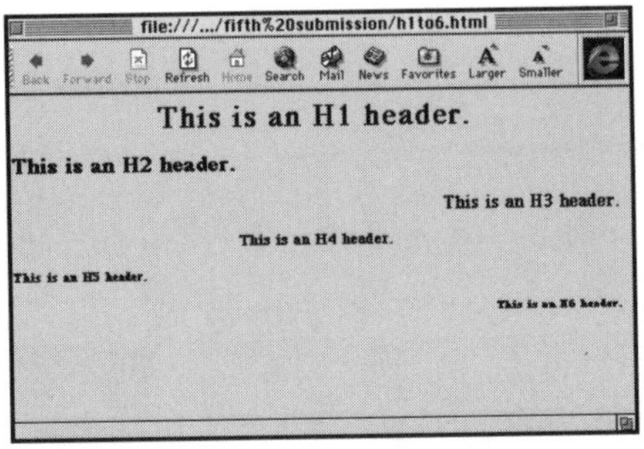

Figure 6

All six header tags in Internet Explorer 3 for the Mac.

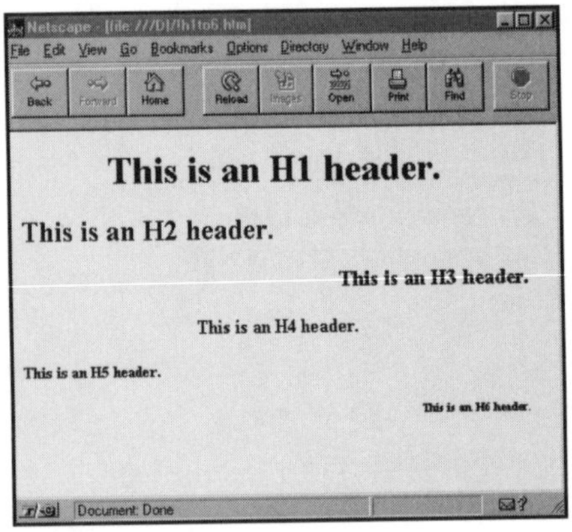

Figure 7

All six header tags in Navigator 3 for Windows.

Figure 8

All six header tags in Internet Explorer 3 for Windows.

<H5>

Category: HTML

Browser Support		Navigator 3	Navigator 4	Explorer 3	Explorer 4
	Macintosh	▇▇▇	▇▇▇	▇▇▇	▇▇▇
	Windows	▇▇▇	▇▇▇	▇▇▇	▇▇▇

May Contain <A>, <APPLET>, <B>, <BASEFONT>, <BIG>, <BR>, <CITE>, <CODE>, <DFN>, <EM>, <FONT>, <I>, <IMG>, <INPUT>, <KBD>, <MAP>, <SAMP>, <SELECT>, <SMALL>, <STRIKE>, <STRONG>, <SUB>, <SUP>, <TEXTAREA>, <TT>, <U>, <VAR>

May Be Used In <BLOCKQUOTE>, <BODY>, <CENTER>, <DD>, <DIV>, <FORM>, <LI>, <TD>, <TH>

Attributes ALIGN

Syntax <H5>...</H5>

The <H5> header is the level five header tag (of six header tags) typically, but infrequently, used to indicate subsections within <H4>-specified blocks of text. It is smaller than an <H4> header, but larger than an <H6> (although the way header tags are displayed will vary from browser to browser).

<H5> has one attribute (ALIGN) for establishing horizontal alignment. The closing, or </H5> tag, is required.

ALIGN

The ALIGN tag specifies the horizontal alignment of a level five header. It has three values:

center   The level five header is centered on the web page.

left   The level five header is aligned by the left margin on the web page. This is the default ALIGN setting, although it is not supported by Internet Explorer.

right   The level five header is aligned by the right margin on the web page. This value is not as popular as the other two—it's not supported by Internet Explorer—and may be less reliable.

Figures 1, 2, 3, and 4 display level five headers specified with all three ALIGN attribute values in Navigator 3 and Internet Explorer 3 for the Mac and for Windows.

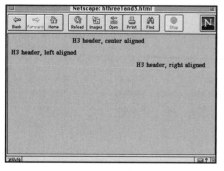

Figure 1

Level five headers center-, left-, and right-aligned, respectively, in Navigator 3 for the Mac.

Figure 2

Level five headers center-, left-, and right-aligned, respectively, in Internet Explorer 3 for the Mac.

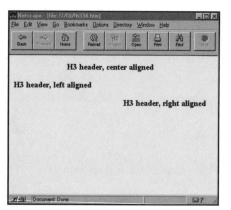

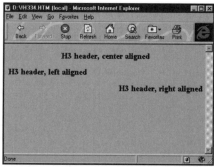

Figure 4

Level five headers center-, left-, and right-aligned, respectively, in Internet Explorer 3 for Windows.

Figure 3

Level five headers center-, left-, and right-aligned, respectively, in Navigator 3 for Windows.

The "typical" appearance of the six header tags as specified first in HTML 2.0 and carried through to HTML 3.2:

<H1> Text displayed in a very large font, bolded, and centered on the page with one or two blank lines above and below.

<H2> Text displayed in a large font, bolded, and aligned flush left on the page with one or two blank lines above and below.

<H3> Text displayed in a large font, italicized, and slightly indented from the left margin with one or two blank lines above and below.

<H4>	Text displayed in a normal font size, bolded, and indented farther than <H3> text with one blank line above and below.
<H5>	Text displayed in a normal font size, italicized, and indented just as far as <H4> text with one blank line above.
<H6>	Text displayed in a small font size, bolded, and indented similarly to normal text but farther than <H5> text with one blank line above.

Figures 5, 6, 7, and 8 can be used to compare all six header levels side by side in Navigator 3 and Internet Explorer 3 for the Mac and for Windows.

Figure 5

All six header tags in Navigator 3 for the Mac.

Figure 6

All six header tags in Internet Explorer 3 for the Mac.

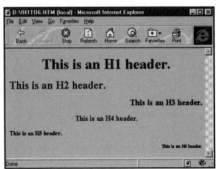

Figure 7

All six header tags in Navigator 3 for Windows.

Figure 8

All six header tags in Internet Explorer 3 for Windows.

<H6>

Category: HTML

Browser Support		Navigator 3	Navigator 4	Explorer 3	Explorer 4
	Macintosh	■	■	■	■
	Windows	■	■	■	■

May Contain   <A>, <APPLET>, <B>, <BASEFONT>, <BIG>, <BR>, <CITE>, <CODE>, <DFN>, <EM>, <FONT>, <I>, <IMG>, <INPUT>, <KBD>, <MAP>, <SAMP>, <SELECT>, <SMALL>, <STRIKE>, <STRONG>, <SUB>, <SUP>, <TEXTAREA>, <TT>, <U>, <VAR>

May Be Used In   <BLOCKQUOTE>, <BODY>, <CENTER>, <DD>, <DIV>, <FORM>, <LI>, <TD>, <TH>

Attributes   ALIGN

Syntax   <H6>...</H6>

The <H6> header is the level six header tag (of six header tags) typically, but infrequently, used to indicate subsections within <H5>-specified blocks of text. It is the smallest of all six headers, although the way header tags are displayed will vary from browser to browser.

<H5> has one attribute (ALIGN) for establishing horizontal alignment. The closing, or </H5> tag, is required.

ALIGN

The ALIGN tag specifies the horizontal alignment of a level six header. It has three values:

center   The level six header is centered on the web page.

left   The level six header is aligned by the left margin on the web page. This is the default ALIGN setting, although it is not supported by Internet Explorer.

right   The level six header is aligned by the right margin on the web page. This value is not as popular as the other two—it's not supported by Internet Explorer—and may be less reliable.

Figures 1, 2, 3, and 4 display level six headers specified with all three ALIGN attribute values in Navigator 3 and Internet Explorer 3 for the Mac and for Windows.

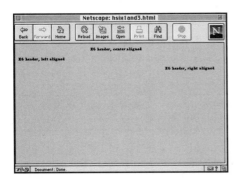

Figure 1

Level six headers center-, left-, and right-aligned, respectively, in Navigator 3 for the Mac.

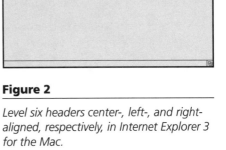

Figure 2

Level six headers center-, left-, and right-aligned, respectively, in Internet Explorer 3 for the Mac.

H

Figure 3

Level six headers center-, left-, and right-aligned, respectively, in Navigator 3 for Windows.

Figure 4

Level six headers center-, left-, and right-aligned, respectively, in Internet Explorer 3 for Windows.

The "typical" appearance of the six header tags as specified first in HTML 2.0 and carried through to HTML 3.2:

<H1>	Text displayed in a very large font, bolded, and centered on the page with one or two blank lines above and below.
<H2>	Text displayed in a large font, bolded, and aligned flush left on the page with one or two blank lines above and below.
<H3>	Text displayed in a large font, italicized, and slightly indented from the left margin with one or two blank lines above and below.
<H4>	Text displayed in a normal font size, bolded, and indented farther than <H3> text with one blank line above and below.

<H5>   Text displayed in a normal font size, italicized, and indented just as far as <H4> text with one blank line above.

<H6>   Text displayed in a small font size, bolded, and indented similarly to normal text but farther than <H5> text with one blank line above.

Figures 5, 6, 7, and 8 can be used to compare all six header levels side by side in Navigator 3 and Internet Explorer 3 for the Mac and for Windows.

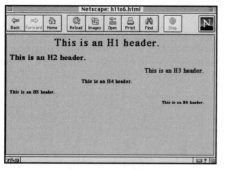

Figure 5

All six header tags in Navigator 3 for the Mac.

Figure 6

All six header tags in Internet Explorer 3 for the Mac.

Figure 7

All six header tags in Navigator 3 for Windows.

Figure 8

All six header tags in Internet Explorer 3 for Windows.

<HEAD>

Category: HTML

Browser Support		Navigator 3	Navigator 4	Explorer 3	Explorer 4
	Macintosh	■■■	■■■	■■■	■■■
	Windows	■■■	■■■	■■■	■■■

Applies To Text

May Contain <BASE>, <ISINDEX>, <LINK>, <META>, <SCRIPT>, <STYLE>, <TITLE>

May Be Used In <HTML>

Attributes None

Syntax <HEAD>...</HEAD>

The <HEAD> tag is used (in combination with many other tags) to create the HEAD section, which provides additional information about your web page. It doesn't appear or affect the actual body of your web page, and it doesn't work by itself—only with other tags.

These other, related tags that work with it are:

<BASE>   provides exact document location

<ISINDEX> enables a kind of keyword search of a web page

<META>   lists categories or subjects covered in the page, used by indexes and search engines

<LINK>   establishes basic site and page structure

<SCRIPT>   deals with inline script

<STYLE>   details style sheet information

<TITLE>   gives the title of the web page

All six of these related tags are covered in their own, separate entries elsewhere within the book, where you can find more detailed information about them.

height

Category: Cascading Style Sheets

Browser Support		Navigator 3	Navigator 4	Explorer 3	Explorer 4
	Macintosh	☐	☐	☐	☐
	Windows	☐	☐	☐	■

Applies To All elements

Syntax height: value

The height property presets height for tags or elements like the HTML height property. As with the HTML equivalent, you may specify the height in units, as discussed in Appendix D, or as a percentage. With the width and height properties, you can force text or an image to a certain dimension. You may also use the auto keyword, which allows the item to display at the height it would normally have on the page. Auto is especially useful for inherited attributes.

```
h1 { height: 200px }
```

```
h1 { height: 1.2in }
```

```
<h1 style="height: auto">
```

Explorer 4, again, applies height to only replaced elements and specifically not text. Length values work, and so do percentage values (which are relative to the height of the current browser window).

height

Category: JavaScript Style Sheets

	Type	Property

Browser Support		Navigator 3	Navigator 4	Explorer 3	Explorer 4
	Macintosh	☐	■	☐	☐
	Windows	☐	■	☐	☐

Applies To Block-level elements and replace elements

Inherited No

Syntax `height = "value"`

The height property is most useful for sizing the height of an image in the document. Although this style can be applied to all block-level elements, it is meant for changing the height of the <img> tag. Only two types of values are allowed for height:

- "length" is the numeric value for the exact height of the element.
- "auto" is the default style. "auto" is best used when the width of the element has been assigned a length and the element should be auto-sized (scaled) to the correct height.

height and width are compatible properties and you should use caution when setting both property styles. Explicitly setting both properties may produce an HTML element that is no longer displayed to scale. By specifying the height property and leaving the width as "auto" you are more likely to get a reasonably scaled element.

Using the following sample, we let the first <img> tag (defined with hclass) to "auto" scale the width after defining height, whereas in the second <img> tag (using bclass) we have set both properties:

```
<html>
<style TYPE="text/javascript">
classes.hclass.img.height = "10"
with (classes.bclass.img) {
height = "10"
width = "1000"
}
</style>
<body>
<img class="hclass" src="school.gif">
<img class="bclass" src="school.gif">
</body>
</html>
```

WARNING   The height property does not function as defined in Netscape Navigator 4.0.

The second image defined in the document would be completely out of scale and would not display well because both the height and width were defined explicitly.

The important JSSS code that was used to define the previous code sample is:

```
classes.hclass.img.height = "10"
with (classes.bclass.img) {
height = "10"
width = "1000"
```

The code can be broken down as follows:

- with {…} do as a JavaScript function used in our example to define multiple style properties for a single HTML element <img> class all within a single statement.
- classes one of the methods of defining JSSS styles. The classes definition specifies the element immediately following it in the dot notation will be a class name.
- hclass and bclass are the class names that are being defined. A class name may be any alphanumeric combination.
- img is the HTML element that is being assigned a style in both of the classes. This may be any valid HTML element.

- `height` and `width` are the style properties that are being defined for the element.
- `"10"` and `"1000"` are the values of the style properties.

This JSSS defintion uses two different methods to define JSSS class style properties. One is single complete line defintion and the other uses a `with {...} do` grouping to define multiple styles.

Hex()

Category: VBScript

| Type | Function |

Browser Support

	Navigator 3	Navigator 4	Explorer 3	Explorer 4
Macintosh	☐	☐	☐	■
Windows	☐	☐	■	■

| Syntax | `Hex(number)` |

The `Hex()` function accepts a decimal (base 10) *number* and returns its hexadecimal (base 16) equivalent value. The hexadecimal counting system contains 16 base values, represented by 0–9 and A–F. Any numerical value *number* may be passed to `Hex()`, but fractional values will be rounded to the nearest integer before conversion.

`hex(5)`	returns	5
`hex(10)`	returns	A
`hex(255)`	returns	FF
`hex(8192)`	returns	2000

Commonly, hexadecimal values are used when specifying RGB color values. You may find the `Hex()` function useful for converting decimal values between 0 and 255 into valid R, G, or B color values between 00 and FF. You can refer to the color chart (Appendix B) to see a list of common color names and their hexadecimal values.

Hidden

Category: JavaScript, JScript, VBScript

| Type | Object |

Browser Support

	Navigator 3	Navigator 4	Explorer 3	Explorer 4
Macintosh	■	■	☐	■
Windows	■	■	■	■

| Subset Of | `form object` |

Properties `form, name, type, value`

Syntax `document.formName.hiddenName.property` OR
`document.forms[index].elements[index].property` OR
`document.formName.hiddenName.method(parameters)` OR
`document.forms[index].elements[index].method(parameters)`

The `hidden` object accesses a hidden form field element that is not visible to the user. Generally, the hidden form field is used to submit values to the server that don't require user input.

For instance, perhaps you want to tell the server that form field was most recently clicked by the user (not counting the submit button!), as a type of survey of how users navigate your page. Whenever a form field is clicked, script code could then store this information in the hidden form field. After the user submits the form, the hidden information (along with the remaining data from that form) is sent to the server for processing. A hidden object is created using the `<input>` tag.

```
<input
   type="hidden"
   name="hiddenName"
   value="textValue">
```

form property

The `form` property is the read-only reference to the `form` object that contains the `hidden` object. This is a useful way to refer to another object in the same form. For instance, imagine a scenario where you want to reference a `text` object, named *text1*, which resides within the same form as the `hidden` object, *hidden1*. This can be used to code in shorthand, or eliminate the need to explicitly reference the full path to every element within a single form, as in the code excerpts:

JavaScript

```
path=document.forms[0].hidden1
value1=path.value
value2=path.form.text1.value
```

VBScript

```
set path=document.forms(0).hidden1
value1=path.value
value2=path.form.text1.value
```

name property

The `name` property is the read-only name of the `hidden` object, specified by the `name` attribute in the `<input>` tag.

```
objname = document.formname.hiddenname.name
objval = document.formname.objname.value
```

type **property**

The read-only `type` property is the input type specified by the `type` attribute in the `<input>` tag. Of course, this always contains the value "hidden" when referencing a hidden field.

```
objtype = document.formname.hiddenname.type
```

 Internet Explorer 3 does not support the `type` property.

value **property**

The `value` property is the value associated with the hidden element, specified by the `value` attribute in the `<input>` tag. You may change this value, but it will not be directly visible to the user. The value will be sent, as though it were the value in a `text` object, if the form is submitted. As stated earlier, this is a common way to pass data to the server that does not require user input.

In the following example, there is a form with two checkbox form fields and one hidden form field. When the user clicks the submit button, not only are the checkbox values returned to the server, but so is the value of the hidden element. The script code within the `onClick` event handlers for each checkbox assigns a value to the hidden element, indicating which checkbox was modified immediately prior to clicking the submit button.

```
<form name="form1"  onSubmit="window.alert(document.form1.lastcheck.value)">
 <input type="hidden" name="lastcheck">Select one or more favorite colors:<br>
<input type="checkbox" name="red"onClick="document.form1.lastcheck.value='red'">
➥Red<br>
<input type="checkbox" name="green"onClick="document.form1.lastcheck.value=
➥'green'"> Green<br>
<input type="submit" value="Submit Form">
</form>
```

The preceding sample doesn't actually pass the form data onto the server; rather, it pops up an alert window showing which checkbox was last modified (such as the `value` property of the `hidden` object).

Figure 1

By assigning a value to the hidden object, you can keep track of non-interactive form data.

history

Language: JavaScript, JScript, and VBScript

Category	Object			

Browser Support

	Navigator 3	Navigator 4	Explorer 3	Explorer 4
Macintosh	■■■■	■■■■	☐	■■■■
Windows	■■□	■■■■	■■■	■■□

Subset Of Window object

Syntax `history.property` OR
`windowName.frameName.history.property` OR
`history.method (parameter)` OR
`windowName.frameName.history.method(parameter)`

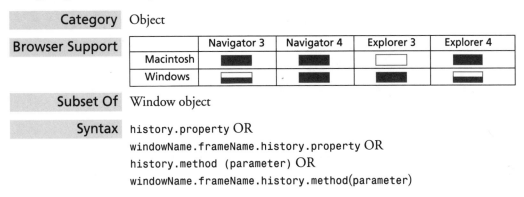

The `history` object contains the URLs previously visited by the browser. A URL list is maintained for the entire browser page, while individual URL lists are maintained by the browser for each frame in a multi-frame. All of these URLs may be accessed by the appropriate `history` object.

Unfortunately, the `history` object behaves differently between implementations of Internet Explorer and Netscape Navigator—as a result, you should read the following entries carefully depending on which browser you intend to code for.

> **NOTE**
> For Netscape Navigator 3 and Internet Explorer 4 for the PC, the `history` object works with Windows 95 only.

history[ ] array

In addition to the properties and methods described in the following paragraphs, the `history` object is also an array; each element contains a string representing the URL for that history entry. Thus, if the first element in the `history[]` array points to the main Yahoo! page, then

`history[0]`

would contain the string value `www.yahoo.com`. The elements in the `history[]` array are ordered from earliest to most recent.

current property

The `current` property is a string containing the URL of the currently loaded document, as illustrated in Figure 1. This property is only available if data tainting is enabled (see the `taint()` function).

`window3.history.current`

contains the URL for the page loaded into the window named *window3*.

```
window4.frame2.history.current
```

contains the URL for the page loaded into *frame2* of *window4*.

Figure 1

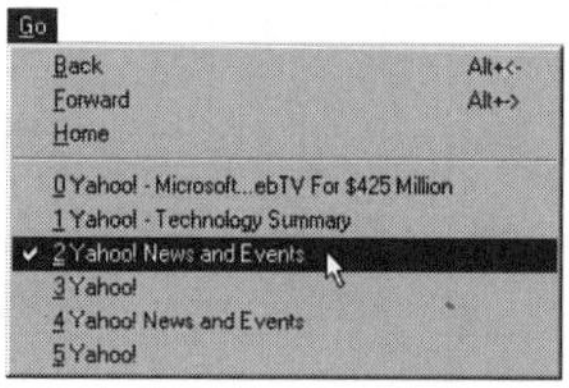

The current page in the history list, whose URL is contained in `history.current`.

Internet Explorer 3 and 4 do not support the `current` property.

length **property**

The `length` property is a integer that notes the number of URLs stored in the `history` object. In Navigator, the `length` property reflects the number of URL entries that appear under the Go menu. Within Internet Explorer, the URL entries appear under the File menu.

NOTE Within Internet Explorer 3, the `length` property **always** returns a value of zero.

next **property**

The `next` property is a read-only string containing the URL of the *next* document in the history list. By definition, the *next* document is the one more recently visited than the current document, as if the user were to click the Forward button in the browser, as seen in Figure 2. This property is only available if data tainting is enabled (see the `taint()` function).

```
window3.history.next
```

contains the URL for the page one entry more recent in *window3*.

```
window4.frame2.history.next
```

contains the URL for the page one entry more recent in *frame2* of *window4*.

Figure 2

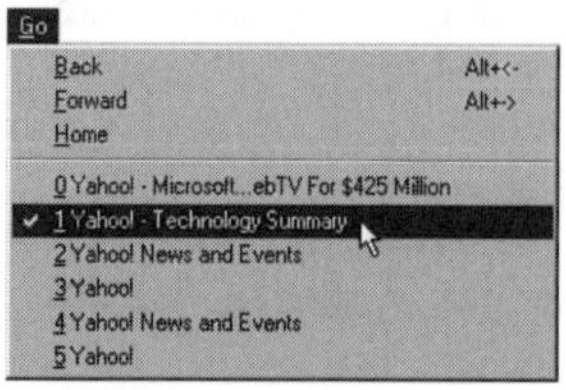

The next page in the history list, whose URL is contained in `history.next`.

Internet Explorer 3 and 4 do not support the **next** property.

previous **property**

The **previous** property is a string containing the URL of the *previous* document in the history list. By definition, the *previous* document is the one visited just before the current document, as if the user were to click the Back button in the browser, as seen in Figure 3. This property is only available if data tainting is enabled (see the **taint()** function).

```
window3.history.previous
```

contains the URL for the page one entry prior to the current document in *window3*.

```
window4.frame2.history.previous
```

Contains the URL for the page one entry prior to the current document in *frame2* of *window4*.

H

Figure 3

The previous page in the history list, whose URL is contained in history.previous.

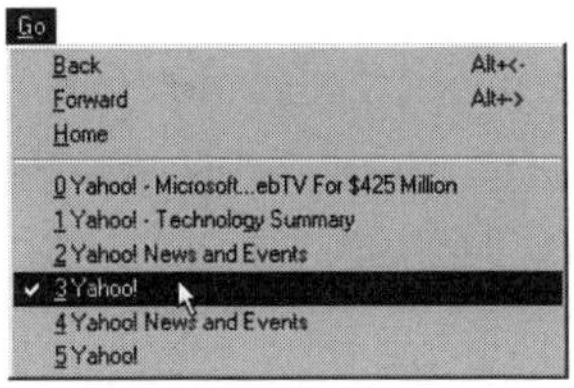

Internet Explorer 3 and 4 do not support the **previous** property.

back() **method**

The **back()** method, using the general syntax **history.back()**, sends the current window to a previous URL in the history list. However, the exact behavior of this method varies between browser versions. Specifically, Netscape Navigator and Internet Explorer 4 behave in one manner while Internet Explorer 3 behaves in a different manner. Each behavior is explained below.

Within Netscape Navigator and Internet Explorer 4

The **back()** method directs the browser window (or frame) to the URL of the previous document in the history list (if possible). For instance, the statement

```
history.back()
```

would load the page visited prior to the current page within the history list. This is as if the user had clicked the Back button one time.

The statement

```
window2.frame1.history.back()
```

appears as if the user had right-clicked within *frame1* and selected Back from the pop-up menu, loading the page previously viewed within *frame1* of *window2*.

Within Internet Explorer 3

The method `history.back(index)` directs the browser to the *indexth* URL previous to the current page in the history list. In other words, the statement

```
window.history.back(3)
```

would load the page three steps previous, from the current page, within the history list. Think of this as if the user clicked the Back button *index* times.

forward() method

The `forward()` method, using the general syntax `history.forward()`, sends the current window to the next URL in the history list. However, the exact behavior of this method varies between browser versions. Specifically, Netscape Navigator and Internet Explorer 4 behave in one manner while Internet Explorer 3 behaves in a different manner. Each behavior is explained below.

Within Netscape Navigator and Internet Explorer 4

The `forward()` method directs the browser window (or frame) to the URL of the next document in the history list (if possible). For instance, the statement

```
history.forward()
```

would load the page visited one position more recently than the current page within the history list. This is as if the user had clicked the Forward button one time.

The statement

```
window2.frame1.history.forward()
```

appears as if the user had right-clicked within *frame1* and selected Forward from the pop-up menu, loading the page viewed more recently than the current page within *frame1* of *window2*.

Within Internet Explorer 3

The method `history.forward(index)` directs the browser to the *indexth* URL next in the history list. In other words, the statement

```
window.history.forward(3)
```

would load the page three steps more recent, from the current page, within the history list. Think of this as if the user clicked the Forward button *index* times.

go(*index*) or go("*string*") method

The `go()` method, using the general syntax `history.go()`, sends the current window to a particular URL in the history list, either specified by an index from the current URL or a portion of the URL string. However, the exact behavior of this method varies between browser versions. Specifically, Netscape Navigator and Internet Explorer 4 behave in one manner while Internet Explorer 3 behaves in a different manner. Each behavior is explained in the following paragraphs.

Within Netscape Navigator and Internet Explorer 4

The methods `history.go(`*`index`*`)` or `history.go("`*`string`*`")` directs the browser window (or frame) to the *index*th URL relative to the current page. Negative *index* values move earlier in the history list while positive *index* values move forward (more recently) in the history list.

```
history.go(-3)
```

In the in the preceding example, the URL third previous from the current URL will be loaded into the browser window. This is as if the user clicked the Back button three times.

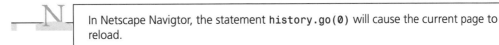

In Netscape Navigtor, the statement `history.go(0)` will cause the current page to reload.

Alternatively, you can pass a string rather than an integer to the `go()` method, as in:

```
history.go("xmas")
```

In this example, the browser will load to the most recent URL in the history list that contains the string "xmas."

Within Internet Explorer 3

The construction `history.go(`*`index`*`)` directs the browser to the *index*th URL in the history list, where the earliest item in the history list is index number 1. In other words, the statement

```
history.go(2)
```

would open the second earliest page in the history list, regardless of what page is currently loaded. Consequently, Internet Explorer 3 support for the `go()` method does not accept negative integers.

Internet Explorer 3 does not support the `go("`*`string`*`")` version of this method.

TIP   Because the `go()` method is implemented quite unusually in Internet Explorer 3, you may need to include some code in your script that tests for the user's browser version and uses the appropriate `go()` method construction.

You can do this using the `appName` and `userAgent` properties of the `navigator` object (see `navigator` object):

```
if ((navigator.appName.indexOf("Netscape")>-1) ||
(navigator.userAgent.indexOf("Mozilla/4.0")>-1))
 {statements using Netscape version of go() method}
else {statements using Explorer version of go() method}
```

In the preceding code example, the true clause will execute if the user's browser is either a version of Netscape (`navigator.appName`) or Internet Explorer 4 (`navigator.userAgent`); otherwise, the false clause is executed. This means that the Internet Explorer 3 statements will execute if the browser is anything *other than* Netscape or Internet Explorer 4.

Hour()
Category: VBScript

Type	Function

Browser Support

	Navigator 3	Navigator 4	Explorer 3	Explorer 4
Macintosh				■
Windows			■	■

Syntax	Hour(date)

The Hour() function returns the hour, between 0 and 23, within the specified *date*. The time format within *date* may be in either 24-hour time or AM/PM time.

```
hour("June 11 4:30 PM")          returns          16

hour("05:45:00")                 returns          5

hour("12:00 AM")                 returns          0

hour("22:35")                    returns          22
```

If the value *date* is null, then a null value is returned. If *date* does not contain a time, then an hour of 0 is returned; if *date* contains an invalid time, such as 25:00:00, an error will occur.

<HR>
Category: HTML

Browser Support

	Navigator 3	Navigator 4	Explorer 3	Explorer 4
Macintosh	■	■	■	■
Windows	■	■	■	■

May Contain	None

May Be Used In	<BLOCKQUOTE>, <BODY>, <CENTER>, <DD>, <DIV>, <FORM>, <LI>, <TD>, <TH>

Attributes	ALIGN, CLASS, COLOR, ID, NOSHADE, SIZE, WIDTH

Syntax	<HR>...</HR>

The <HR> tag inserts a horizontal rule. The width, color, alignment, and other characteristics of this rule can be customized with <HR>'s attributes. A closing, or </HR> tag, is not required.

Generally, <HR> is placed as shown in the following example:

```
<P>Here's a line of text.<HR>
```

No
-specified line break is needed because <HR> automatically establishes space above and below the rule it inserts.

However, there are certain situations in which the <HR> tag should be placed elsewhere—if you're creating a long document with anchor tags, for example. If this is the kind of web page you're designing, see the <A> tag entry for more details.

It is also noteworthy to mention that the length of an <HR> horizontal rule is determined by the margins where it is to be inserted, so if an image has been placed against one or both margins, the rule will draw itself according to these narrower measurements.

ALIGN

The ALIGN attribute setsthe alignment of the horizontal rule on the page. It has three values:

center	Centers the rule on the page. This is the default ALIGN setting.
left	Aligns the rule to the left of the page.
right	Aligns the rule to the right of the page.

Keep in mind that horizonal rules stretch across the entire width of the page by default (thus making these ALIGN attributes fruitless without being able to shorten the rule). To shorten a rule, use the WIDTH attribute.

CLASS

The CLASS attribute is used to specify the name of a style sheets as it applies to a specific selection on a web page. See the "Cascading Style Sheets Basics" chapter and any individual, related style sheets entries elsewhere in the book for more information.

COLOR

The COLOR attribute customizes the color of a horizontal ruler. Colors are specified either by name or by hexadecimal value, so that writing

<HR COLOR=red>

and

<HR COLOR="ff0000">

will result in the same color rule: a bright cherry red.

"Red" is one of 16 colors you can safely specify in English, but you are better off using hexadecimal values that are more precise. See Appendix B on color for more information and extensive browser-safe color charts.

NOTE Navigator 2.0 does not recognize the 16 colors you can specify in English.

H

> **DESIGN NOTE** Test rule colors extensively to make sure you can see them, especially if you are placing a white or yellow rule on a background pattern. Remember, too, that PC monitors display colors significantly darker than Mac monitors do, so a dark rule placed against a dark background may be readable on a Mac but not on a PC.

Here's the same general, but still valuable, advice about using the COLOR attribute: although it is supported by recent versions of Navigator and Internet Explorer, this is not the case with earlier versions—so don't stake a lot on it.

Also, both Navigator and Explorer have Preferences options that enable users to disable body colors. So if you are using COLOR to specify something that will be invisible, or nearly unreadable, against a gray background (white, off-white, silver, yellow, and pastels come immediately to mind), certain visitors will be unable to read your web page.

ID

The ID attribute is used to distinguish individual selections in a web page as pertaining to the use of style sheets. See the "Cascading Style Sheets Basics" chapter and any individual, related style sheets entries elsewhere in the book for more information.

NOSHADE

The NOSHADE attribute disables a horizontal rule's default shading, resulting in a plain thick line instead.

Inserting NOSHADE works like this:

```
The rule following this text is shaded.<HR>
The rule following this text is plain. <HR NOSHADE>
```

SIZE

The SIZE attribute determines the height of the horizontal rule in pixels as in the following example:

```
<HR SIZE=10>
```

WIDTH

The WIDTH attribute determines the width of the horizontal rule in one of two ways—either absolutely in pixels or relationally in a percentage.

For example:

```
<HR WIDTH=30>
```

states an absolute rule width of 30 pixels, while

```
<HR WIDTH=30%>
```

states a rule width that spans 30% of the width of the open window.

There is an advantage to specifying rule width in a percentage versus specifying it in pixels. A percentage-defined rule will expand and contract with the width of the browser window—a pixel-defined rule cannot adjust to be compatible and may look funny if a visitor has her browser window greatly reduced or enlarged.

> **DESIGN NOTE**
>
> You can always insert your own horizontal rules as `<IMG>`-defined GIFs, JPGs, or any other suitably formatted image files. Some custom horizontal rules even do tricks—rippling, blinking, fading in and out, or even burning up and exploding (as in a stick of dynamite with a long fuse that's lit as soon as the page loads up)—as they can be animations, JavaScripts, and other cutting-edge web page elements.
>
> If this is the route you want to pursue, consult the `<IMG>` tag or other appropriate entries elsewhere in this book. Don't use the `<HR>` tag and its attributes as described in this entry, or you'll add a second rule.

H

`<HTML>`

Category: HTML

Browser Support		Navigator 3	Navigator 4	Explorer 3	Explorer 4
	Macintosh	■	■	■	■
	Windows	■	■	■	■

Attributes None

Syntax `<HTML>...</HTML>`

The `<HTML>` tag is the single most important tag to remember when building a web page. It has no attributes, and therefore no values, but it must enclose all the other HTML tags, attributes, values, and web page information—with the opening tag at the beginning of the code listing and the closing, or `</HTML>`, tag at the end.

<I>

Category: HTML

Browser Support

	Navigator 3	Navigator 4	Explorer 3	Explorer 4
Macintosh	■	■	■	■
Windows	■	■	■	■

May Contain   <APPLET>, <B>, <BASEFONT>, <BIG>, <BR>, <CITE>, <CODE>, <DFN>, <EM>, <FONT>, <I>, <IMG>, <INPUT>, <KBD>, <MAP>, <SAMP>, <SELECT>, <SMALL>, <STRIKE>, <STRONG>, <SUB>, <SUP>, <TEXTAREA>, <TT>, <U>, <VAR>

May Be Used In   <ADDRESS>, <APPLET>, <B>, <BIG>, <BLOCKQUOTE>, <CAPTION>, <CENTER>, <CITE>, <CODE>, <DD>, <DT>, <FONT>, <H1>, <H2>, <H3>, <H4>, <H5>, <H6>, <I>, <KBD>, <LI>, <P>, <SAMP>, <SMALL>, <STRIKE>, <STRONG>, <SUB>, <SUP>, <TD>, <TH>, <TT>, <U>

Attributes   None

Syntax   <I>...</I>

The <I> tag renders text in italics. Everything written between the opening and closing, or </I> tags, will be displayed on a web page in italics, as shown in the example:

<I>This text is italicized using the I tag.</I>

Figure 1 displays this HTML in Navigator 3 for the Macintosh.

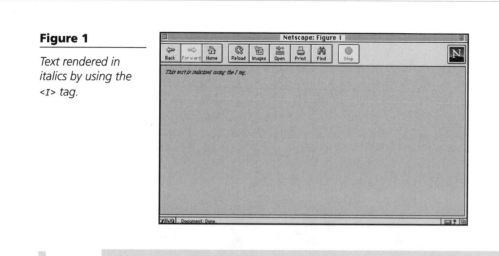

> **NOTE**   You can also create italicized text by using the **<CITE>**, **<EM>**, and/or **<VAR>** tags if you prefer. However, these tags are older and specifically refer to a technical/academic method for writing formal papers—most web pages today are more informal in nature, even a business or corporate web site.

It is worth noting that many designers and web surfers generally dislike the effect of italics, regardless of the platform or browser involved. Italicized text can appear crowded, overly slanted, and generally difficult to read, so italics should be used sparingly for overall design and netiquette considerations.

ids

Category: JavaScript Style Sheets

Type	Selector

Browser Support

	Navigator 3	Navigator 4	Explorer 3	Explorer 4
Macintosh	☐	■	☐	☐
Windows	☐	■	☐	☐

Applies To	All elements

Inherited	Yes

Syntax	`ids.idname.proprety = "value"`

The `ids` property is a JavaScript object property that is one of three properties (the others are `tags` and `classes`) that can be used to define styles in JavaScript Style Sheets. Unlike the other two properties, `ids` should be used only to define exceptions to style rules. `ids` should be used rarely and only used to override already existing exceptions.

The `ids` property is defined using dot notation and takes an id name as its first modifier. You may use any valid alphanumeric combination as an id name. The property modifier of this object can be any valid JavaScript Style Sheets property, which are listed in this book in the alphabetical listing under the category: JavaScript Style Sheets, type: property.

The `ids` property must always be used with the `<style></style>` elements; thus defining it as a property used only for JavaScript Style Sheets.

By defining your styles using the `ids` property, you will need to reference the style definition in the document; thus, giving you the capability to control the usage of the style to only specific instances of the element.

In the following simple example, `<h2>` headers have been assigned a style of underline using the `tags` property; thus all `<h2>` will be underlined. But maybe in your document, a particular `<h2>` element needs to have a line through it instead of being underlined. So an `ids` style is defined for use in overriding the underline style. The `id` is defined within the `<style></style>` tags, and then explicitly referenced with the `<h2>` element.

```
<html>
<head>
<style type="text/javascript">
tags.h2.textDecoration ="underline";
ids.hid.textDecoration ="line-through";
</style>
</head>
<body>
<h2> This header will be underlined.
<h2 ID="hid"> This header will have a line through.
<h2> This header will be underlined.
</body>
</html>
```

The results of this code are shown in Figure 1.

Figure 1

Underlined and line-through `<h2>` elements.

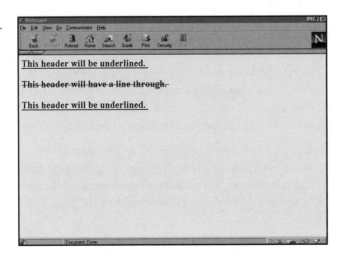

There are two lines of JSSS style code in the code used to generate Figure 1. The second part of this is the one that is important to this property.

```
ids.hid.textDecoration ="line-through";
```

This definition of a JSSS id style can be broken down as follows:

- **ids** is the property that tells JSSS that the code immediately following will define a style id that will be referenced elsewhere in the document.
- **hid** is the name of the id. This id name can be any alphanumeric combination and will be referenced each time the id is used.
- **textDecoration** is the style that will applied to the <h2> elements that use the style. Any valid JSSS style property can be used here.
- **"line-through"** is the value of the style that will be applied. Each style has its own set of defined values.

`<ilayer>`

Category: HTML

Browser Support

	Navigator 3	Navigator 4	Explorer 3	Explorer 4
Macintosh		▇		
Windows		▇		

Applies To Animation and Page Layout

May Contain None

May Be Used In None

Attributes above, background, below, bgcolor, clip, left, name, top, width, visibility, z-index

Syntax `<ilayer>…</ilayer>`

The `<ilayer>` tag defines an inline layer on your web page. A layer is a group of items such as text and images collected between the `<ilayer>` and `</ilayer>` tags. Once combined, you can manipulate the group of items simply by setting the various attributes of the `<ilayer>` tag. You can combine multiple layers to produce composite images or, by using a simple JavaScript routine, create clever animations by peeling away layers stacked upon each other.

The initial position of an inline layer is determined by the order of items on your page. You use the top and left attributes to set the relative position of the layer on the page based on the initial position. The above, below, and z-index attributes control the layering or stacking of multiple layers. The topmost layer, the one most visible on the page, is above the others and has the highest z-index or z position.

Layers can also be nested inside of each other providing you more flexibility when setting layer attributes. For example, the background color of a nested layer is inherited from the parent layer unless the nested one has set its own background color. The following example HTML document displays the animation pictured in Figure 1. The animation is the disappearing card trick. Figure 2 shows the animation on the web page.

Figure 1

These five images are stored in the files hshani1 to hshan5 in the following example.

Figure 2

The web page shows the Do Trick button and the first picture of the animation.

Here's the HTML text and JavaScript that displays the animation:

```
<html>
<head>
<title>Magic Trick</title>
</head>
<body bgcolor="white">
<b>Magic Trick</b><br>
<layer name="hand1" left=20 top=100 z-index=5>
<img src="hshani1.gif">
</layer>
<layer name="hand2" left=20 top=100 z-index=4>
<img src="hshani2.gif">
</layer>
<layer name="hand3" left=20 top=100 z-index=3>
<img src="hshani3.gif">
</layer>
<layer name="hand4" left=20 top=100 z-index=2>
<img src="hshani4.gif">
</layer>
<layer name="hand5" left=20 top=100 z-index=1>
<img src="hshani5.gif">
</layer>
```

```
<script>function doTrick() {
var i;
for (i = 0; i <= 4; i++)
document.layers[i].visibility="show";
document.layers["hand1"].visibility="hide";
document.layers["hand2"].visibility="hide";
document.layers["hand3"].visibility="hide";
document.layers["hand4"].visibility="hide";
return;}
</script>
<form>
<input type="button" value="Do Trick" OnClick="doTrick(); return false;">
</form>
</body>
</html>
```

TIP   You should always use the `name` attribute with the layers you create. This will help when using attributes such as `above` and `below`, which refer to other layers. Your JavaScripts will also be easier to create and modify if you refer to layers by name as seen in the `doTrick` function of the preceding example.

NOTE   To create a stack of layers—when displaying animation on your web page, for example—you use the `top` and `left` attributes of each subsequent layer to align it with the previously defined layer.

NOTE   Another way to think of layers is as a collection objects similar to the way graphics are grouped in a drawing or graphics application. When you work with grouped objects in drawing applications, you can make changes to the individual items within the group all at one time. Moving a group moves all the objects, keeping them in the exact same position relative to each other. The same thing occurs when you change the position of a layer with the `left` and `top` attributes. Furthermore, nesting layers is similar to combining two or more groups of objects in your drawing application.

above

The `above` attribute causes one layer to be positioned above or on top of another layer in the page. If you stack layers on top of each other by setting `top` and `left` attributes such that the layers overlap, the `above` attribute determines which of the two layers will be displayed above the other. When layers are stacked, the layer below may not be visible. To make it visible, you can remove the top layer with a JavaScript or adjust the position or size of one of the layers.

```
<ilayer name="FirstImage" above="SecondImage">
```

background

The background attribute sets the background image of a layer. The image is displayed behind all other objects in the layer. As with the background of the <body> tag, if the image is smaller than the dimensions of the layer, the image is tiled to fill the entire background.

```
<ilayer name="Car" background="images/sunset.html">
```

below

The below attribute causes one layer to be positioned below another layer in the page. If you stack layers on top of each other by setting top and left attributes such that the layers overlap, the below attribute places one layer below the other. When layers are stacked, the layer below may not be visible. To make it visible, you can remove the top layer with a JavaScript or adjust the position or size of one of the layers.

```
<ilayer name="SecondImage" below="FirstImage">
```

bgcolor

The bgcolor attribute sets the color of the background of the layer. You can specify the color with an RGB value, such as #8eve10, or with a name such as green. The color is displayed behind all items of the layer. By default, layers are transparent, meaning the underlying items on the page show through in the blank portions of the layer. See Appendix B for more information on using colors.

```
<ilayer name="Car" bgcolor="green">
```

clip

The clip attribute determines the maximum size of the layer image on the page by defining a clip rectangle. The four values of the attribute denote the left, top, right, and bottom points of the rectangle. All items on the layer that do not fit within the dimensions of the clip are cropped at the boundary. If you specify only two values with the clip attribute, these are taken as the right and bottom points respectively and the top and left values are defaulted to 0.

```
<ilayer name="Landscape" clip=300,100>
```

> **NOTE** The clip rectangle is different from the dimensions of the layer as defined with the left, top, height, and width attributes. Items such as the text or graphics that do not fit within the clip area is cropped to fit. Without the clip attribute, the text and other items are wrapped to the next line.

left

The left attribute sets the relative position of the left side of a layer in pixels based on where the layer falls on the page. The value indicates the number of pixels from the initial position to the left side of the layer. A value of 50, for example, would set the position of the left side 50 pixels over from the initial position. Negative values move the layer in the opposite direction. If a left value is not specified, the layer is placed where it falls in the among elements of the page.

```
<ilayer name="Animate1" left=50 top=50>
```

> **TIP** When creating animation with layers, it is important your graphics are aligned using the top and left attributes of each layer. Otherwise, the animation will not appear smooth—especially if the viewer perceives sudden jumps or changes in position.

name

The name attribute defines the name of the layer for the page. The name should help you uniquely identify each layer. You can then refer to the layer by name, for example, in your JavaScript code. In the example earlier in this section, each layer of the animation is numbered which helps you see which image should be displayed first, second, and so on.

top

The top attribute defines the position of the top of a layer in pixels relative to where the layer falls on the page. The value indicates the number of pixels from that position to the top of the layer. The top position of a layer nested within another layer is measured from the top of the parent layer.

```
<ilayer name="Animate1" left=50 top=50>
```

width

The width attribute determines the width in pixels of the layer image. All items that do not fit within the width of the layer are wrapped to the next line. If a width is not specified, the layer will grow as much as possible to fit all the items.

```
<ilayer name="Animate1" width=100>
```

visibility

The visibility attribute determines if a layer is visible on the page. A value of show displays the layer on the page while a value of hide does not display the layer. For nested layers, a setting of inherit sets the visibility of the layer according to the visibility of the parent or outer layer.

```
<ilayer name="Animate1" visibility=show>
```

> **TIP** Using the visibility attribute and JavaScripting, you create simple animation on your web page. Start by creating the consecutive images of your animation and positioning them on the page one on top of the other with the top and left attributes. Make sure they are in the correct order so the first image is on top and the last on bottom. Then, one by one, you set the visibility attribute to hide and your graphics will become animated.

z-index

The z-index attribute enables you to define the order of layers that are overlapped or are stacked on each other. The value is a positive or negative number, which determines the positioning in the stack. Layers with higher numbers are displayed on top of layers with lower numbers. Without the z-index attribute, layers are positioned in the order they appear in the page with the first layer displayed at the bottom of the stack and the last layer on top.

```
<ilayer name="Animate1" z-index=1>
```

Image
Category: JavaScript 1.1

		Navigator 3	Navigator 4	Explorer 3	Explorer 4
Type	Object				
Browser Support	Macintosh	■	■	☐	■
	Windows	■	■	☐	■

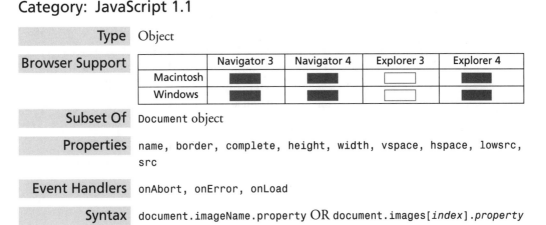

Subset Of Document object

Properties name, border, complete, height, width, vspace, hspace, lowsrc, src

Event Handlers onAbort, onError, onLoad

Syntax document.imageName.property OR document.images[index].property

Just as the name implies, the image object provides script access to a graphic image on the web page. Frequently, the image object is used to dynamically change images on the page. You can swap image files in and out of an image space on-the-fly quite easily. This technique has many uses, such as:

- Highlighted menus, where each item's image changes to a highlighted version when the mouse passes over it.

- Games, such as card-games, where you need to dynamically display a series of card faces.

- Animations, which you can control with more precision than an animated GIF, by utilizing event handlers and timed delays.

Image objects are elements in the images[] array, which itself is a property of the document object (see the document object). Each image on the page, as created using the HTML <img> tag, is indexed in source order into the images[] array.

```
<img
   [name="imageName"]
   src="imageLocation"
   [lowsrc="lowresImageLocation"]
```

```
[height="pixels"|"value"%]
[width="pixels"|"value"%]
[hspace="pixels"]
[vspace="pixels"]
[border="pixels"]
[align="left"|"right"|
    "top"|"absmiddle"|"absbottom"|
    "texttop"|"middle"|"baseline"|"bottom"]
[ismap]
[usemap="#MapName"]
[onAbort="eventHandler"]
[onError="eventHandler"]
[onLoad="eventHandler"]>
```

Additionally, you can use the new Image() constructor to create new image objects, which can be used to pre-cache images for display at a later time. Pre-caching is a technique where you load a number of images into image objects before they must appear on the page. In doing so, you can have all necessary images downloaded to the user's browser before they are displayed—as a result, when it comes time to display the image, it will appear immediately without experiencing a download delay.

For instance, imagine that your page requires five images, named sequentially "pic1.gif," "pic2.gif," and so on. To pre-cache these images, simply create and call a function such as the following:

```
function precache()
{
pics=new Array()
for (j=1;j<=5;j++}
pics[j]=new Image()
pics[j].src="pic"+j+".gif"
}
```

Now, you can dispay an image on the page using one of the images in the cache previously created. For instance, to display "pic1.gif" in the image object document.images[2]:

```
document.images[2].src=pics[1].src
```

Remember that the purpose of the preceding code is to pull the image from the cache rather than ask for it to be downloaded across the network at display-time.

NOTE Image objects created using the new Image() constructor are *not* added to the images[] array.

name property

The name property is the read-only name of the object, as specified by the name attribute of the <img> tag. It is not commonly used via script.

border property

The border property is a read-only integer that specifies the width in pixels of the border around the image. It is not commonly accessed via script, mainly because it is read-only.

```
imgborder=document.imagename.border
```

complete property

The complete property is a read-only Boolean value that is set to true when the image is completely loaded. This enables you to detect whether an image has been fully downloaded before attempting to swap it into the page, for instance. The following script excerpt uses a while loop to wait until the complete property for the image has become true.

```
while (!imagename.complete)
  { void(0) }
```

Using the preceding code prior to an image replacement ensures that the image will have been fully downloaded before it appears onscreen.

height property

The height property is a read-only integer indicating the height of the image in pixels. You cannot modify the dimensions of an image—its dimensions are created with the height and width attributes of the <image> tag.

```
imgheight=document.imagename.height
```

width property

The width property is a read-only integer indicating the width of the image in pixels. You cannot modify the dimensions of an image—its dimensions are created with the height and width attributes of the <image> tag.

```
imgwidth=document.imagename.width
```

vspace property

The vspace property is a read-only integer that specifies the amount in pixels of space inserted above and below the image. This characteristic cannot be modified via script—it is determined by the vspace attribute of the <image> tag.

```
imgvspace=document.imagename.vspace
```

hspace **property**

The hspace property is a read-only integer that specifies the amount in pixels of space inserted on the left and right of the image. Again, this characteristic cannot be modified via script—it is determined by the hspace attribute of the <image> tag.

```
imghspace=document.imagename.hspace
```

lowsrc **property**

The lowsrc property points to a low-resolution image that the browser displays if the user has a low-resolution display. In some cases, web authors specify the lowsrc attribute for the <img> tag. By modifying it, you can change which low-resolution image will be loaded.

Note, however, that changing this property *does not* result in an immediate onscreen effect. Rather, it changes which low-res image will be loaded *if* a change to the src property is made *and* the user's screen requires a low-resolution image.

```
document.imagename.lowsrc="lowres2.gif"
```

src **property**

By far, this is the most commonly used property of the image object. All the magic resides here. The src property points to the file name and/or location for the image. Modifying this property, and therefore pointing to a new image, immediately changes the onscreen image.

```
document.imagename.src="newimage2.jpg"
```

One common use of this technique is the "highlighted button menu." In concept, when the user passes his mouse pointer over a menu button image (which is also a hyperlink), the image under the pointer is replaced with an enhanced version of the same image. For instance, the new image may have bright borders, or a spotlight effect—something that brings it "alive" and alerts the user that the button is aware of his presence.

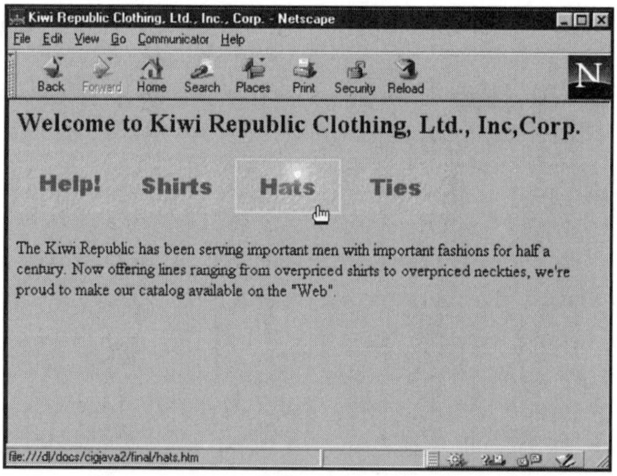

Figure 1

A highlighted button menu, courtesy of modifying the image *object's* src *property.*

Scripting the highlighted button menu is simple: attach an `onMouseOver` and `onMouseOut` event handler to the hyperlink within which the image is created in HTML:

```
<a href="help.html" onMouseOut="unselect(1);return true"
➥onMouseOver="select(1);return true"><img src="button1a.jpg" border="0"
width="100" height="50"></a>
```

When the user's mouse passes over this image, the function `select()` is called. The hypothetical `select()` function modifies the image object's `src` property to point to the highlighted version of the image.

When the user moves his mouse off the image, the hypothetical `unselect()` function is called, which modifies the `src` property again to the non-highlighted version of the image.

> **TIP** Remember that the `image` object's dimensions are *not* modifiable. Therefore, if you redirect the `src` property to a new image that has different dimensions from that defined in the `<img>` tag, the new image will be scaled to fit the original dimensions. In many cases, this scaling will result in a disfigured, if not downright ugly, appearance. Therefore, when preparing images that may replace one another on the page, be sure to keep their dimensions consistent.

onAbort event handler

Located in the `<img>` tag, the `onAbort` event handler will activate if the user aborts the downloading of an image by pressing the Stop button. You might use this event handler to trigger a function that prevents an image swap from occurring, because the image has not been fully downloaded.

```
<img src="image1.gif" width=100 height=50 onAbort="skipswitch()">
```

onError event handler

Located in the `<img>` tag, the `onError` event handler will activate if an error occurs when downloading the image. Basically, an image loading error would occur if the image file is corrupted and cannot be decoded by the browser. It's up to you what you'd like to do in such a case, rare though it is. Imagine that you've coded a function named `errhalt()`, which when called, alerts the user of the image corruption problem.

```
<img src="image1.gif" width=100 hright=50 onError="errhalt()">
```

onLoad event handler

Located in the `<img>` tag, the `onLoad` event handler will activate as soon as an image is displayed on the page. Despite its name, this event handler doesn't merely activate when an image is *loaded*. As explained earlier, images can be loaded beforehand using the `new Image()` constructor—this does *not* generate an `onLoad` event. Displaying the image on the page or, in other words, assigning a new image file to the image object's `src` property *does* generate an `onLoad` event.

Generally, this event handler is used to create animations, wherein each image, upon being displayed, triggers the onLoad handler, which replaces the image, thereby triggering the onLoad handler again! The result is a loop in which a series of images can replace each other in sequence. In the onLoad handler function, you can code any animation logic you want, such as delays in the sequence, or changes in the order of image replacement.

```
<img src="anim1.gif" name=anim width=100 width=50
onLoad="nextpic(document.anim.src)">
```

> **NOTE** If you set the image object's src property to a file that contains an animated GIF, each loop through the animation sequence will trigger an onLoad event—not each frame of the animation.

<IMG>

Category: HTML

Browser Support

	Navigator 3	Navigator 4	Explorer 3	Explorer 4
Macintosh	■	■	■	■
Windows	■	■	■	■

May Contain None

May Be Used In `<ADDRESS>`, `<APPLET>`, `<B>`, `<BIG>`, `<BODY>`, `<BLOCKQUOTE>`, `<CAPTION>`, `<CENTER>`, `<CITE>`, `<CODE>`, `<DD>`, `<DT>`, `<FONT>`, `<H1>`, `<H2>`, `<H3>`, `<H4>`, `<H5>`, `<H6>`, `<I>`, `<KBD>`, `<LI>`, `<P>`, `<SAMP>`, `<SMALL>`, `<STRIKE>`, `<STRONG>`, `<SUB>`, `<SUP>`, `<TD>`, `<TH>`, `<TT>`, `<U>`

Attributes ALIGN, ALT, BORDER, CLASS, CONTROLS, DYNSRC, HEIGHT, HSPACE, ID, ISMAP, LOOP, LOOPDELAY, LOWSRC, SRC, START, USEMAP, VRML, VSPACE, WIDTH

Syntax `<IMG>...</IMG>`

The `<IMG>` tag embeds, or integrates, all kinds of graphical content into your web page—not just images, as in the very recent past, but client-side imagemaps, video clips, and VRML (Virtual Reality Modeling Language) worlds, just to name a few examples.

All these files types require usage of the ALIGN, ALT, HEIGHT, HSPACE, SRC, VSPACE, and WIDTH attributes for proper placement on the web page. Each individual file type also requires others as listed in the following paragraphs.

A static (or unmoving) image, such as a GIF or JPG file, would benefit from the BORDER attribute if you wanted to add a frame effect, and LOWSRC if you wanted to provider users with a low-resolution alternative.

An imagemap would also require ISMAP and USEMAP to properly identify the map to the server.

A VRML world or video clip would also require CONTROLS to bring up a player control box, START to allow the user loop control, and LOOP and LOOPDELAY for repetition issues. VRML worlds specifically need DYNSRC and SRC for cross-browser, Explorer-friendly coverage, and VRML for proper identification.

See each of the individual attribute entries later on in this section for more details.

The <IMG> tag and its attributes must be placed within the <BODY> tag, but a closing, or </IMG> tag, is not needed.

> **NOTE** It is a very good idea to familiarize yourself with Navigator and Internet Explorer file format issues at this point if you haven't done so already. Otherwise, you may find you've wasted your time writing HTML to include a file that isn't supported by one browser, the other, or in some cases, both.

ALIGN

The ALIGN attribute specifies the alignment of either an embedded object or of its surrounding text. The default for both Navigator and Internet Explorer (all versions) on both the Macintosh and Windows PC platforms is TOP.

In the following example, TOP is specified as the ALIGN value and image1.gif represents the embedded image:

```
<IMG SRC="image1.gif" ALIGN=TOP>
```

The ALIGN attribute has several established values:

absbottom

Aligns the bottom edge of the object with the bottom of the current (first) line of text. It is not recognized by Internet Explorer.

absmiddle

Aligns the middle of the object with the middle of the surrounding text. It is not recognized by Internet Explorer.

baseline

Aligns the bottom edge of the object with the baseline of the current (or first) line of text. It is not recognized by Internet Explorer.

`bottom`

Aligns the bottom edge of the object with the baseline of the current (or first) line of text.

`left`

The embedded image or object "floats" on the page with its left side flush against the edge of the page and the text flows around it.

`middle`

Aligns the middle of the object with the baseline of the current (or first) line of text.

`right`

The embedded image or object "floats" on the page with its right side flush against the edge of the page and the text flows around it.

`texttop`

Permits all text that follows the embedded object to align itself with the top of the tallest character in the first line of text. It is not recognized by Internet Explorer.

`top`

Permits all text that follows the embedded object to align itself with the top edge of the object. `TOP` is the `ALIGN` attribute's default setting.

DESIGN NOTE You can force text to flow around an image by using the <BR> tag and the `CLEAR` attribute. See the <BR> tag for more information.

Figures 1 through 9 display text and image alignment using the `ALIGN` attribute and all nine values previously explained.

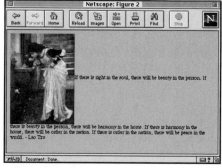

Figure 1

Text and image alignment using the `ALIGN` attribute and the `absbottom` value.

Figure 2

Text and image alignment using the `ALIGN` attribute and the `absmiddle` value.

Figure 3

Text and image alignment using the ALIGN attribute and the baseline *value.*

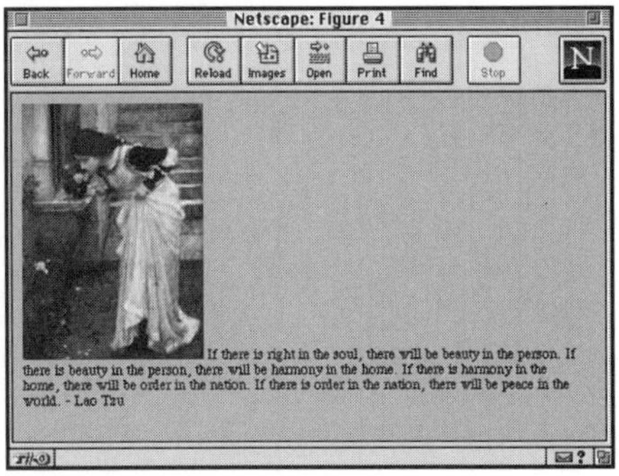

Figure 4

Text and image alignment using the ALIGN attribute and the bottom *value.*

Figure 5

Text and image alignment using the ALIGN attribute and the left *value.*

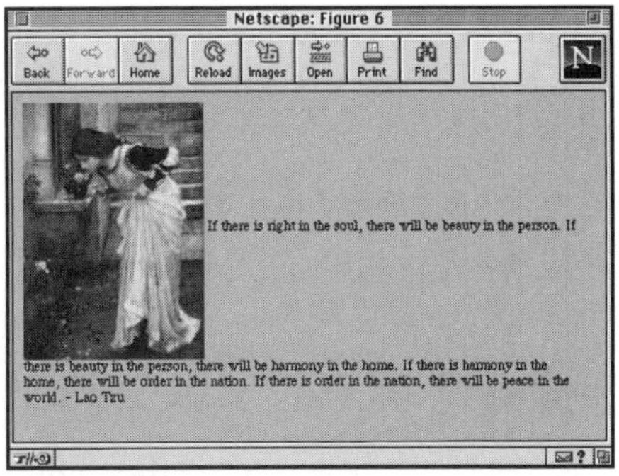

Figure 6

Text and image alignment using the ALIGN attribute and the middle *value.*

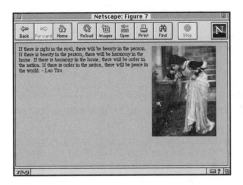

Figure 7

Text and image alignment using the ALIGN attribute and the right *value.*

Figure 8

Text and image alignment using the ALIGN attribute and the texttop *value.*

Figure 9

Text and image alignment using the ALIGN attribute and the top value, which is also the ALIGN attribute's default.

ALT

The ALT attribute specifies a string of text that will be displayed if a visitor to your web page is using a text-only browser.

It will also be displayed by an image-enabled browser if the Show Images (Navigator 3) and/or the Show Pictures (Internet Explorer) options are turned off, and by Internet Explorer while the related embedded object loads up.

In the following example, image1.gif represents the embedded object on your web page:

```
<IMG SRC="image1.gif" ALT="Either Netscape Navigator or Internet Explorer isn't
loading images, or you're using a text-only browser.">
```

BORDER

The BORDER attribute specifies the width or absence of a frame-like border, which can appear around an embedded object.

In the following example, the border thickness is set at 4 pixels and image1.gif represents the image:

```
<IMG SRC="image1.gif" BORDER=4>
```

Figure 10 displays a BORDER-specified frame of 5 pixels while Figure 11, for comparison, displays a frame of 2 pixels. The default setting for the BORDER attribute is 0, in which case there will be no border present.

The color of this border cannot be customized so it will be black, and unless you want to link this image (for which you would use the <A> tag, not <IMG>), this border's function is purely decorative.

> **DESIGN NOTE** At this writing, there's no way to customize the color of an image border using HTML. You can, however, build a colored border into your image using Photoshop, Illustrator, or another similar graphic design program—like adding a picture frame to a painting before you hang it on the wall. Then, in your HTML document, disable BORDER by specifying a value of zero to turn off the default black border previously described.

Figure 10

A BORDER-*specified frame of 5 pixels...*

Figure 11

...compared with a BORDER-*specified frame of 2 pixels.*

CLASS

The CLASS attribute is used to specify the name of a style sheets as it applies to a specific selection on a web page. See the "Cascading Style Sheets Basics" chapter and any individual, related style sheets entries elsewhere in the book for more information.

CONTROLS

The CONTROLS attribute creates a player box when you are embedding a video clip. It needs no values, so with `film.mov` representing your movie clip, here's the HTML:

```
<IMG SRC="film.mov" CONTROLS>
```

DYNSRC

The DYNSRC attribute, which stands for Dynamic Source, is an Internet Explorer–only designator for a video clip or a VRML world.

In the following example, `vrml.wrl` represents a VRML file:

```
<IMG DYNSRC=" vrml.wrl">
```

What's the advantage to using the DYNSRC over just plain SRC? You can then use the START attribute to specify when the clip or world should commence playing. Otherwise, if visitors to your page are using Internet Explorer, they'd be out of luck.

See the START and SRC attribute sections later in this entry for more information.

HEIGHT

The HEIGHT attribute is used in tandem with the WIDTH attribute to specify the size of an image in pixels. Internet Explorer uses HEIGHT- and WIDTH-specified values to draw an image's temporary placeholder while the actual file is being downloaded.

In the following example, `image1.gif` stands in for the image you'd want to embed:

```
<IMG SRC="image1.gif" HEIGHT=120 WIDTH=425>
```

There is a significant potential drawback to specifying HEIGHT and WIDTH values, however, if your specifications do not match the real dimensions of the image you're embedding. Both Navigator and Internet Explorer will use HEIGHT and WIDTH values to stretch or compress an image to fit the specifications you set, even if the results are unattractive (see Figures 12, 13, and 14).

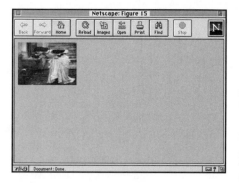

Figure 12

The result of mismatched HEIGHT-specified, WIDTH-specified, and actual image dimensions in Navigator 3 for the Macintosh.

Figure 13

The result of mismatched HEIGHT-specified, WIDTH-specified, and actual image dimensions in Navigator 3 for the Macintosh.

Figure 14

The result of perfectly matched HEIGHT-specified, WIDTH-specified, and actual image dimensions.

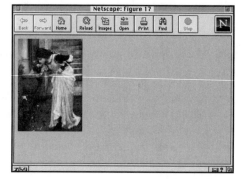

HSPACE

The HSPACE attribute is most effectively used in conjunction with the ALIGN attribute and a LEFT or RIGHT value (when an image is "floating").

It specifies a horizontal buffer zone in pixels around such an image when there is text flowing all around it—the related VSPACE attribute specifies similar vertical space.

In the following example, `image1.gif` stands for the image displayed on the web page:

`<IMG SRC="image1.gif" HSPACE=12 VSPACE=18>`

Figures 15 and 16 display a `RIGHT-ALIGN`ed image with an `HSPACE` and a `VSPACE` of 10 pixels each.

Figure 15

Nicely proportioned HSPACE and VSPACE attributes in Navigator 3 for the Macintosh.

Figure 16

Nicely proportioned HSPACE and VSPACE attributes in Internet Explorer 3 for the Macintosh.

ID

The `ID` attribute is used to distinguish individual selections in a web page as pertaining to the use of style sheets. See the "Cascading Style Sheets Basics" chapter and any individual, related style sheets entries elsewhere in the book for more information.

ISMAP

The `ISMAP` attribute used with the `SRC` attribute, properly identifies an imagemap to the browser software and the server (literally `ISMAP` means "is map"). You must use ISMAP in tandem with SRC if you are adding an imagemap to your web page. ISMAP has no values, and should be written as follows, with `imap.gif` representing the imagemap graphic:

`<<IMG> SRC="imap.gif" ISMAP>`

LOOP

The `LOOP` attribute specifies the number of times an embedded video clip will play (it is not used for audio or VRML worlds). It is used in conjunction with the `SRC`, `DYNSRC`, `LOOPDELAY`, and `START` attributes (see each of these attributes' individual sections elsewhere in this entry for more specific information).

In the following example, `film.mov` represent the name of the video clip file being played:

`<IMG SRC="film.mov" DYNSRC="film.mov" LOOP=5 LOOPDELAY=3000 START=mouseover>`

The `LOOP` setting of 5 indicates that the clip will play five times. Setting `LOOP` to –1 or INFINITE will cause the clip to play continuously.

LOOPDELAY

The LOOPDELAY attribute specifies a length of time in milliseconds, during which the video clip will pause before starting again (it is not used for audio or VRML worlds). It is used in conjunction with the SRC, DYNSRC, LOOP, and START attributes (see each of these attributes' individual sections elsewhere in this entry for more specific information).

In the following example, film.mov represents the name of the video clip file being played:

```
<IMG SRC="film.mov" DYNSRC="film.mov" LOOP=5 LOOPDELAY=3000 START=mouseover>
```

The LOOPDELAY setting of 3000 indicates that there will be a delay of three seconds between each of the five times the video clip will play (add or subtract 1000 for each second you want to shave off or add on). Eliminating the LOOPDELAY attribute altogether results in the clip playing nonstop with no delays at all.

LOWSRC

The LOWSRC attribute specifies a low-resolution version of an image as an alternate to a higher- or normal-resolution image specified with the SRC attribute.

In the following example, imagehigh.gif represents the high-resolution image and imagelow.gif represents the low-resolution image:

```
<IMG SRC="imagehigh.gif" LOWSRC="imagelow.gif">
```

This HTML comes in handy in situations where the SRC-specified image is of very good quality (in other words, a very large file because of the increased number of colors). A browser will read and load the LOWSRC image first, giving visitors something to look at while the SRC image loads in the background. Internet Explorer users will find this strategy particularly helpful, because Explorer loads text and images separately, which can make for a long wait.

SRC

The SRC attribute is used to specify the file name of the object you want to embed in your web page. It is the only required attribute you must include when using the <IMG> tag.

In the following example, image1.gif represents the name of the object being embedded:

```
<IMG SRC="image1.gif">
```

There are some related attributes you'll want to use in addition to SRC in specific circumstances. If you're embedding a video clip, you'll want to specify it twice, using both the SRC attribute and the Internet Explorer attribute DYNSRC for dynamic embedded content. The HTML for this situation would be:

```
<IMG SRC="film.mov" DYNSRC="film.mov">
```

START

START tells browsers when to begin playing the video clip depending upon which of START's two values you specify.

The START attribute works in conjunction with SRC/DYNSRC, LOOP, and LOOPDELAY (see these attributes' individual sections elsewhere in this entry for more specific information).

These values are:

`fileopen`

The video clip will begin playing as soon as the web page is fully loaded. This is the START attribute default setting so that any embedded video clip you add will automatically play unless you specify otherwise.

`mouseover`

The video clip will begin playing when and if the visitor rolls the mouse over it.

The following examples show proper use of the START attribute and the value you specify, with film.mov representing the video clip:

```
<IMG SRC="film.mov" DYNSRC="film.mov" START=fileopen LOOP=4 LOOPDELAY=3000>
```

You can specify both `fileopen` and `mouseover` together by separating them with a comma.

USEMAP

The USEMAP attribute is the link between the two elements of an imagemap: the information laid out using the <MAP> tag and the information laid out using the <IMG> tag.

In the following example, map1 is the name of the <MAP> portion and the value specified by the USEMAP attribute:

```
<IMG SRC="buttonbar.gif" BORDER=0 USEMAP="map1">
<MAP NAME="map1">
<AREA SHAPE="RECT" COORDS="10, 10, 40, 70" HREF="links.html">
<AREA SHAPE="RECT" COORDS="60, 10, 90, 70" HREF="resume.html">
<AREA SHAPE="RECT" COORDS="110, 10, 140, 70" HREF="gallery.html">
</MAP>
```

If the USEMAP and NAME values do not match exactly, the imagemap will not work because the browser will not identify these bits of HTML as two halves of one whole.

VRML

The VRML attribute serves two functions—it embeds a VRML world file into the web page and prompts the browser to provide a set of navigational controls, much as the CONTROLS attribute brings up a control panel for video clips. Like CONTROLS, VRML is an Internet Explorer–only attribute.

In the following example, `vrml.wrl` is the VRML world file being embedded:

```
<IMG SRC="stillvrml.gif" VRML="vrml.wrl" HEIGHT=250 WIDTH=300>
```

Notice that a still image, `stillvrml.gif`, has also been specified using the SRC attribute along with HEIGHT and WIDTH variables. This is a courtesy to visitors who, 1) use an older version of Internet Explorer (prior to version 2), 2) use Internet Explorer without the requisite Virtual Explorer plug-in installed, and/or 3) use Navigator. In any of these situations, the still image GIF file will be loaded instead, giving these visitors something to look at.

> **DESIGN NOTE**
>
> If you are going to include a still image alongside a VRML world in your web page, use a screen shot of your VRML world in action to pique curiosity. This will preserve the overall design of your page.

VSPACE

The VSPACE attribute is most effectively used in conjunction with the ALIGN attribute and a LEFT or RIGHT value (when an image is "floating").

It specifies a vertical buffer zone in pixels around such an image when there is text flowing all around it—the related HSPACE attribute specifies similar horizontal space.

In the following example, `image1.gif` represents the image displayed on the web page:

```
<IMG SRC="image1.gif" HSPACE=12 VSPACE=18>
```

Figures 17 and 18 display a RIGHT-ALIGNed image with an HSPACE and a VSPACE of 10 pixels each.

Figure 17

Nicely proportioned HSPACE and VSPACE attributes in Navigator 3 for the Macintosh.

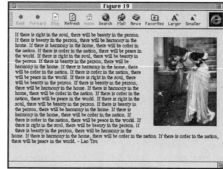

Figure 18

Nicely proportioned HSPACE and VSPACE attributes in Internet Explorer 3 for the Macintosh.

WIDTH

The WIDTH attribute is used in tandem with the HEIGHT attribute to specify the size of an image in pixels. Internet Explorer uses HEIGHT- and WIDTH-specified values to draw an image's temporary placeholder while the actual file is being downloaded.

In the following example, image1.gif represents the image you'd want to embed:

```
<IMG SRC="image1.gif" HEIGHT=120 WIDTH=425>
```

There is a potential drawback to specifying HEIGHT and WIDTH values, however, if your specifications do not match the real dimensions of the image you're embedding. Both Navigator and Internet Explorer will use HEIGHT and WIDTH values to stretch or compress an image to fit the specifications you set, even if the results are unattractive (see Figures 19, 20, and 21).

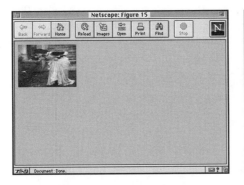

Figure 19

The result of mismatched HEIGHT-specified, WIDTH-specified, and actual image dimensions in Navigator 3 for the Macintosh.

Figure 20

The result of mismatched HEIGHT-specified, WIDTH-specified, and actual image dimensions in Navigator 3 for the Macintosh.

Figure 21

The result of perfectly matched HEIGHT-specified, WIDTH-specified, and actual image dimensions.

<INPUT>

Category: HTML

	Navigator 3	Navigator 4	Explorer 3	Explorer 4
Browser Support Macintosh	■	■	■	■
Windows	■	■	■	■

Applies To None

May Contain None

May Be Used In <A>, <ADDRESS>, <APPLET>, <B>, <BIG>, <BLOCKQUOTE>, <CAPTION>—but only within the <FORM> tag, <CENTER>, <CITE>, <CODE>, <DD>, <DFN>, <DIV>, <DT>, <EM>, <FONT>, <FORM>, <H1>, <H2>, <H3>, <H4>, <H5>, <H6>, <I>, <KBD>, <LI>, <P>, <PRE>, <SAMP>, <SMALL>, <STRIKE>, <STRONG>, <SUB>, <SUP>, <TD>, <TH>, <TT>, <U>, <VAR>

Attributes ALIGN, CHECKED, CLASS, ID, MAXLENGTH, NAME, NOTAB, SIZE, SRC, STYLE, TABINDEX, TITLE, TYPE, VALUE

Syntax <INPUT>...</INPUT>

The <INPUT> tag specifies the type of form control to be inserted in a web page—text boxes, buttons, checkboxes, and more—which the web page visitor uses to enter information. The closing, or </INPUT> tag, is not required.

For more information on creating and using forms, see the <FORM> tag entry elsewhere in the book for a place to start.

The following example represents a simple form with <INPUT> specifying the presence of a text box:

```
<FORM ACTION=http://www.provider.com/cgi-bin/survey METHOD=post>
<P>Please leave your name:
<BR><INPUT NAME=control1 TYPE=text>
</FORM>
```

Note that you can use regular text and spacing tags between the individual controls within a form, like the paragraph <P> tag, the line break <BR> tag, or the <PRE> tag, to insert a larger area of blank space in order to arrange a form's contents. See the <P> , <BR>, and <PRE> tag entries for more, broader information on how to use these tags.

Figures 1 through 4 illustrate this simple text box in Navigator 3 and Internet Explorer 3 for the Mac and for Windows.

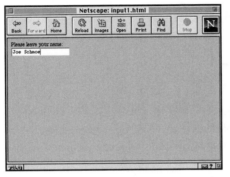

Figure 1

A text control in Navigator 3 for the Mac.

Figure 2

A text control in Internet Explorer 3 for the Mac.

Figure 3

A text control in Navigator 3 for Windows.

Figure 4

A text control in Internet Explorer 3 for Windows.

> **DESIGN NOTE**
>
> As always, you should pay attention to the subtle differences between the way Navigator and Explorer display the same HTML. In this entry, for example, forms in Navigator are displayed on the same gray background, but Explorer's form page default background color is white. There's also a different between the shape and length of text boxes, the size and appearance of text within text forms, and more.

ALIGN

The ALIGN attribute is used to wrap text around a form element on a web page, most typically with an image. It has five values:

Value	Result
bottom	Text is aligned to the bottom edge of the form.
left	Text is aligned to the left edge of the form.
middle	Text is aligned to the center of the form.
right	Text is aligned to the right edge of the form.
top	Text is aligned to the top edge of the form.

In the following example, the text is to be aligned around an image used as a feedback link:

```
<FORM ACTION=http://www.provider.com/cgi-bin/feedback METHOD=post>
<INPUT ALIGN=middle SRC=kiosk2.gif NAME=button1 TYPE=image>Click the kiosk to
send me your email
</FORM>
```

In this example, the image will appear with a link border around it, as it is linked to the CGI script named by the <FORM> tag ACTION attribute.

Figures 5 though 8 illustrate this example HTML in Navigator 3 and Internet Explorer 3 for the Mac and for Windows.

Notice in Figure 6—Internet Explorer 3 for the Mac—that Explorer doesn't draw link borders around the kiosks. Also, in Figure 8—Internet Explorer 3 for Windows—the fourth example representing the middle value remains at the default left value setting.

> **DESIGN NOTE**
>
> In the following four figures, note that there's little or no space between the text and the link border around the image. You can hide or customize the border width by using a BORDER attribute, the same way you'd use it in the <IMG> tag. See the <IMG> tag entry for more information on BORDER and other potentially useful attributes that may apply to using an image in a form.

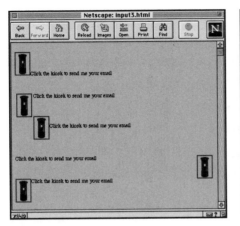

Figure 5

Using an image and the ALIGN *attribute in a form in Navigator 3 for the Mac.*

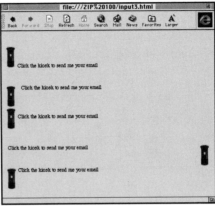

Figure 6

Using an image and the ALIGN *attribute in a form in Internet Explorer 3 for the Mac.*

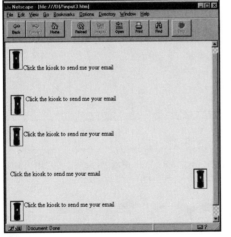

Figure 7

Using an image and the ALIGN *attribute in a form in Navigator 3 for Windows.*

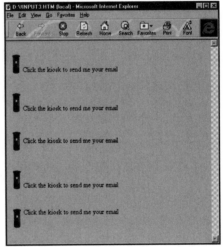

Figure 8

Using an image and the ALIGN *attribute in a form in Internet Explorer 3 for Windows.*

CHECKED

The CHECKED attribute is used to set a default "checked" or selected setting, but only when the TYPE attribute has been set to either the radio (radio button) or checkbox value. If the CHECKED attribute is not present, no default check will be present either.

In the following example, a checkbox has been specified:

```
<FORM ACTION=http://www.provider.com/cgi-bin/survey2 METHOD=post>
<P>I prefer:<BR>
<INPUT NAME=box1 TYPE=checkbox CHECKED VALUE=1>Macintosh
<INPUT NAME=box2 TYPE=checkbox VALUE=2>Windows
</FORM>
```

Figures 9 through 12 display this example HTML in Navigator 3 and Internet Explorer 3 for the Mac and for Windows.

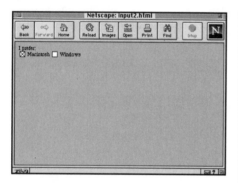

Figure 9

Using checkboxes and the CHECKED attribute in a form in Navigator 3 for the Mac.

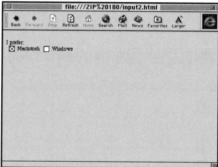

Figure 10

Using checkboxes and the CHECKED attribute in a form in Internet Explorer 3 for the Mac.

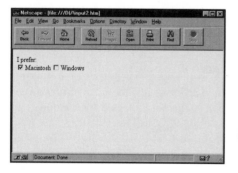

Figure 11

Using checkboxes and the CHECKED attribute in a form in Navigator 3 for Windows.

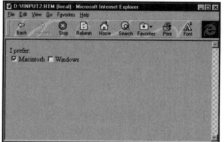

Figure 12

Using checkboxes and the CHECKED attribute in a form in Internet Explorer 3 for Windows.

CLASS

The CLASS attribute is used to specify the name of a style sheets as it applies to a specific selection on a web page. See the "Cascading Style Sheets Basics" chapter and any individual, related style sheets entries elsewhere in the book for more information.

ID

The ID attribute is used to distinguish individual selections in a web page as pertaining to the use of style sheets. See the "Cascading Style Sheets Basics" chapter and any individual, related style sheets entries elsewhere in the book for more information.

MAXLENGTH

The MAXLENGTH attribute specifies the maximum number of characters that can be typed into a text box.

In the following example HTML, the MAXLENGTH value has been established at 12 characters:

```
<FORM ACTION=http://www.provider.com/cgi-bin/password METHOD=get>
<P>Enter your password (up to 12 characters):<BR>
<INPUT NAME=textbox1 TYPE=password MAXLENGTH=12 VALUE=0>
</FORM>
```

If the user of this form types in more than 12 characters, his computer will sound an error and no more information can be put into the text box.

Notice in Figures 13 through 16, though, that the total length of the text box does not relate to the specified MAXLENGTH—you can specify the maximum length of a password to two characters and the box would remain this long.

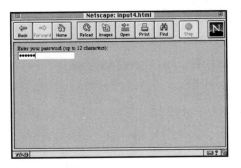

Figure 13

Using a password and the MAXLENGTH attribute in a form in Navigator 3 for the Mac.

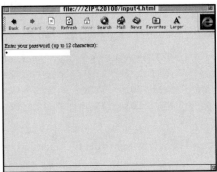

Figure 14

Using a password and the MAXLENGTH attribute in a form in Internet Explorer 3 for the Mac.

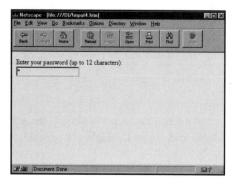

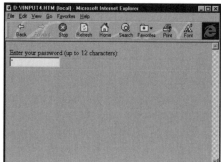

Figure 15

Using a password and the MAXLENGTH attribute in a form in Navigator 3 for Windows.

Figure 16

Using a password and the MAXLENGTH attribute in a form in the Internet Explorer 3 for Windows.

NAME

The NAME attribute specifies the description of the text control that corresponds to the gateway program that processes any information submitted via the form. Without the NAME attribute and the identifier it specifies, the gateway program will not work properly and the form user will not get a response. This is the reason why you cannot choose a form control's NAME value randomly; it must correspond to the part of the form's CGI script or other gateway program that processes the control's information.

There is one exception to the rule that each individual control has a different NAME value: if you're putting a group of radio buttons on your page for a visitor to select from, they must all be assigned the same NAME value or the selection process will not work.

In the following example, the NAME value in this series of radio buttons links all three together:

```
<FORM ACTION=http://www.provider.com/cgi-bin/colors METHOD=post>
<INPUT NAME=color TYPE=radio VALUE=0>I like blue.
<INPUT NAME=color TYPE=radio VALUE=1>I like green.
<INPUT NAME=color TYPE=radio VALUE=2>I like red.
</FORM>
```

This HTML prevents the form user from choosing more than one option, because the purpose of radio buttons is to equate one opinion per form user. See the TYPE attribute section in this entry for visual examples of how NAME is used properly.

NOTAB

The NOTAB attribute is an Internet Explorer–only attribute that permits a web author to omit one part of a form from the navigational tabbing order when used in tandem with the TABINDEX attribute.

In Explorer, visitors using a form can move from control to control using the Tab key instead of the mouse, just as they can move from hot spot to hot spot in an imagemap. In the following example HTML, the last part of this form has been left out of the tabbing sequence:

```
<FORM ACTION=http://www.provider.com/cgi-bin/comments METHOD=post>
<P>Leave your comments here:<BR>
<INPUT NAME=comments TYPE=textarea SIZE=20,10 VALUE=0 TABINDEX=1>
<INPUT NAME=submit TYPE=submit VALUE=Submit TABINDEX=2>
<INPUT NAME=reset TYPE=reset VALUE=Reset NOTAB>Clear the form
</FORM>
```

The visitor to your page who uses Explorer will have to move the mouse to the reset or "clear the form" button to click it, but he or she can simply tab down to the submit button. See the TABINDEX section of this entry for more information.

Also, the presence or absence of the NOTAB attribute does not affect the outcome or appearance of your HTML, so the only way to see it in action is to include it and test it on the screen in Explorer.

SIZE

The SIZE attribute specifies the height and width of a text control in characters when the TYPE attribute is specified as text in Internet Explorer.

The textarea value does not work properly in Navigator, so web page designers should use the <TEXTAREA> tag to create large text controls instead (see the <TEXTAREA> entry elsewhere in the book for more information).

In the following example, the text control is specified as 60 characters high and 10 characters wide:

```
<FORM ACTION=http://www.provider.com/cgi-bin/comments METHOD=post>
<P>Tell me what you think of my page:<BR>
<INPUT NAME=comments TYPE=textarea SIZE=60,10 VALUE=text>
<INPUT NAME=submit TYPE=submit VALUE=Submit>
<INPUT NAME=reset TYPE=reset VALUE=Reset>
</FORM>
```

Figure 17 illustrates this example HTML in Internet Explorer 3 for Windows.

Figure 17

Using the SIZE attribute in a form in Internet Explorer 3 for Windows.

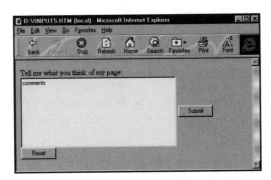

SRC

The SRC attribute specifies a file name when image is specified as the TYPE attribute value.

In the following example, tile1.gif and tile2.gif represent the two form choices:

```
<FORM ACTION=http://www.provider.com/cgi-bin/kitchen METHOD=get>
<P>Choose a tile pattern:<BR>
<INPUT SRC=tile1.gif NAME=tile1 TYPE=image VALUE=1>White tile
<INPUT SRC=tile2.gif NAME=tile2 TYPE=image VALUE=2>Cream tile
</FORM>
```

You can also use the ALIGN attribute with TYPE image to establish text flow alignment. See the ALIGN attribute section elsewhere in this entry for more information, and for examples of HTML and figures using SRC.

TABINDEX

The TABINDEX attribute is an Internet Explorer–only attribute that permits a web author to omit one part of a form from the navigational tabbing order when used in tandem with the NOTAB attribute.

In Explorer, visitors using a form can move from control to control using the Tab key instead of the mouse, just as they can move from hot spot to hot spot in an imagemap. In the following example HTML, the last part of this form has been left out of the tabbing sequence:

```
<FORM ACTION=http://www.provider.com/cgi-bin/comments METHOD=post>
<P>Leave your comments here:<BR>
<INPUT NAME=comments TYPE=textarea SIZE=20,10 VALUE=0 TABINDEX=1>
<INPUT NAME=submit TYPE=submit VALUE=Submit TABINDEX=2>
<INPUT NAME=reset TYPE=reset VALUE=Reset NOTAB>Clear the form
</FORM>
```

The visitor to your page who uses Explorer will have to move the mouse to the reset or "clear the form" button to click it, but he or she can simply tab down to the submit button. (See the NOTAB section of this entry for more information.)

Also, the presence or absence of the TABINDEX attribute does not affect the outcome or appearance of your HTML, so the only way to see it in action is to include it and test it on the screen in Explorer.

TITLE

The TITLE attribute specifies an advisory title recommended, but not needed, for use with Internet Explorer. TITLE does not affect or alter the appearance of your web page, and technically its usefulness is debatable, because most people visiting your page will (at this writing) be using Navigator.

If you want to include a title, here's the way to do it:

```
<INPUT NAME=button1 TYPE=radio TITLE=button1 VALUE=1>I use Netscape Navigator
most often.
```

This is another HTML situation where it's best to be logical, as when specfying a value for the NAME attribute—and in this example, both attributes are specified with the same description: button1. (Can't really go wrong with it either way.)

TYPE

The TYPE attribute is the most important part of the <INPUT> tag, as it specifies the kind of form control to be displayed on the web page. It also determines the necessity of using certain other attributes when different values are specified. Here are those values—there are 11 in all—along with other <INPUT> tag attributes needed to make them work properly:

button

An oval gray button will appear on the web page. A word or number can be specified to appear on the button by using the VALUE attribute, but nothing written after a space will appear on the button. In the figures shown later in this section, for example, the button reads "ClickMe" because typing "Click Me" with a space will only translate as "Click."

checkbox

A square blank clickable box appears on the web page. It can also be used with the CHECKED attribute (see its specific section elsewhere in this entry).

file

A file appears on the web page as specified by the SRC attribute (see its specific section elsewhere in this entry).

hidden

Nothing appears on the web page, but this value is necessary to process the form information properly. In this section's examples, the hidden value specifies the email address where the form results will be sent.

image

An image appears on the web page, as specified by the SRC attribute (see its specific section elsewhere in this entry).

password

A blank password box appears on the web page, but the characters typed in by the user will not appear (Navigator displays passwords as solid round bullets, while Internet Explorer displays them asterisks).

radio

A radio button, or blank round clickable area, appears on the web page. It should be used in a group or series with the same name as specified by the NAME attribute so the form user can only choose from one option presented. Using the VALUE attribute is also required (see both attributes' sections elsewhere in this entry).

reset

A button that clears and resets all controls in the form appears on the web page. The VALUE attribute can be used to specify a short reset button label, and the NAME attribute can be used to record a user's visit to the form page if it is specified (see both attributes' sections elsewhere in this entry).

submit

A button that submits the form information appears on the web page. The VALUE attribute can be used to specify a short reset button label, and the NAME attribute can be used to record a user's visit to the form page if it is specified (see both attributes' sections elsewhere in this entry).

text

A blank, single-line text box appears on the web page. The SIZE and MAXLENGTH attributes determine the box height and width, and the maximum number of characters to be typed in (see both attributes' sections elsewhere in this entry).

> **NOTE** Remember the <TEXTAREA> tag must be used along with or instead of the textarea value to create multi-line text controls in Navigator. See the <TEXTAREA> entry elsewhere in the book for more information.

The following example HTML is understandably very long—each TYPE value is presented here in tandem with the other attributes it needs:

```
<FORM ACTION=http://www.provider.com/cgi-bin/cgiscript METHOD=post>
<BR><INPUT TYPE=button NAME=control1 VALUE=ClickMe>
<BR><INPUT TYPE=checkbox NAME=control2 CHECKED>Put me on your mailing list
<BR><INPUT SRC=contents.html TYPE=file NAME=control3><BR>Type in your preference
➥or browse this site's index
<BR><INPUT TYPE=image NAME=control4 SRC=kiosk2.gif>Click the kiosk to email us.
<BR><INPUT TYPE=password NAME=control5 MAXLENGTH=6>Type in your password (6
➥character maximum)
<BR><INPUT TYPE=radio NAME=platform VALUE=0>I use Macintosh.
<BR><INPUT TYPE=radio NAME=platform VALUE=1>I use Windows.
<BR><INPUT TYPE=submit NAME=control8>
<BR><INPUT TYPE=reset NAME=control9>
<INPUT TYPE=hidden NAME="mailback" VALUE="johndoe@provider.com">
<INPUT TYPE=hidden NAME="clickme" VALUE="/~johndoe/index.html">
<BR><INPUT TYPE=text NAME=control10 MAXLENGTH=25>Leave your name or email
➥address.
</FORM>
```

Figures 18 through 21 illustrate this example HTML (nothing shows up in response to the hidden value HTML, for obvious reasons) in Navigator 3 and Internet Explorer 3 for the Mac and for Windows.

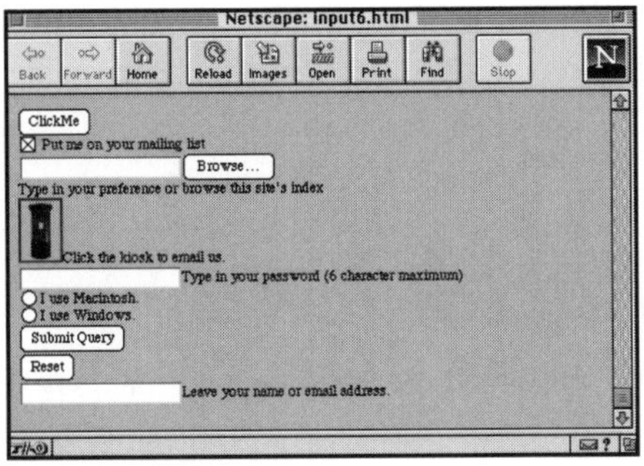

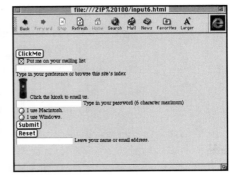

Figure 18

The TYPE attribute options in Navigator 3 for the Mac.

Figure 19

The TYPE attribute options in Internet Explorer 3 for the Mac.

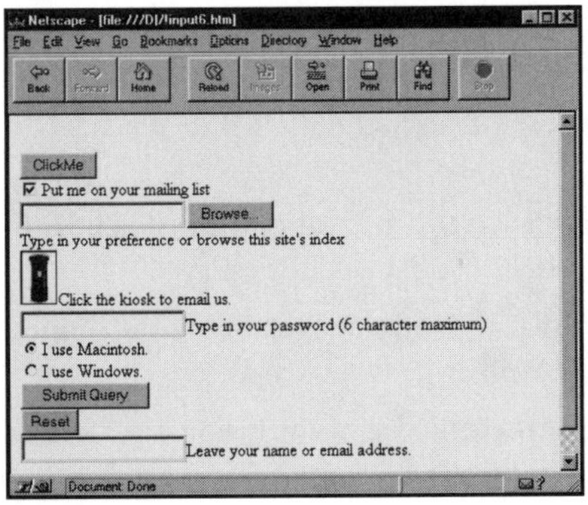

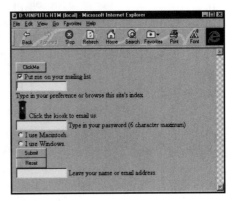

Figure 20

The TYPE attribute options in Navigator 3 for Windows.

Figure 21

The TYPE attribute options in Internet Explorer 3 for Windows.

InputBox()
Category: VBScript

Type	Function

Browser Support

	Navigator 3	Navigator 4	Explorer 3	Explorer 4
Macintosh	☐	☐	☐	▓
Windows	☐	☐	▓	▓

Syntax
```
inputBox(prompt [, title][, default][, xpos][, ypos]
[, helpfile, contextID])
```

The InputBox() function displays a dialog box, in which the user can enter data via the keyboard. The dialog box also contains an OK and a Cancel button. If the user clicks OK, any input data is returned as a string value; if Cancel is clicked, an empty string is returned.

You may configure a number of characteristics of the input box, each of which is represented by an optional parameter described in the following paragraphs.

prompt
A string expression to display in the dialog box—a directive to the user, such as "How old are you?". This string may be as long as 1024 characters. Multiple line strings are permitted—use the carriage return (chr(13)) or linefeed (chr(10)) characters or both to separate the lines. For example, `age=inputbox("How old are you?"&chr(13)&"You must be over 18 to enter this site.")`

title
A string expression to display in the title bar of the dialog box. If omitted, the application name ("Visual Basic") will be displayed.

default
A string expression to display as the default answer in the input text box. If omitted the input text box will initially be blank.

xpos
The horizontal distance of the left edge of the dialog box from the left edge of the screen—measured in twips, which are 1/20 of a point. If omitted, the dialog box is horizontally centered, which is usually the preferred placement.

ypos
The vertical distance of the upper edge of the dialog box from the top of the screen—measured in twips, which are 1/20 of a point. If omitted, the dialog box is vertically centered, which is usually the preferred placement.

helpfile
A string that names the help file to use in providing context-sensitive help. If this parameter is specified, a HELP button will be displayed in the dialog box. If *helpfile* is provided, *contextID* must also be provided. It's unlikely that you will use the *helpfile* or *contextID* parameters in the context of a web page.

contextID
The help context number for the appropriate help topic. If *contextID* is provided, helpfile must also be provided.

Typically, you'll only use the first three parameters for the InputBox() function when writing scripts for a web page. The following example prompts the user to enter his age—a default age of 18 is displayed. If the user enters a lower age, or if the user clicks the Cancel button, a message appears denying access to the site.

```
sub restrict()
age=inputbox("How old are you?"&chr(13)&"You must be over 18 to enter this
site.","Age Restriction","18")
if cint(age)<18 then
 window.alert("Sorry, site access denied."):location="http://www.yahoo.com"
 else window.alert("Welcome to House of Horrors!"):location="horrors.html"
end if
end sub
```

Instr()
Category: VBScript

| | Type | Function |

Browser Support		Navigator 3	Navigator 4	Explorer 3	Explorer 4
	Macintosh	☐	☐	☐	■
	Windows	☐	☐	■	■

| Syntax | `instr([start, ] string1, string2)` |

The Instr() function locates the position of *string2* within *string1*. You can specify a position within *string1* from which to *start* the search. The search proceeds from left to right within *string1*, beginning at the position *start*, if specified.

The function returns the starting position of *string2* within *string1*, if found—the first character in *string1* is considered to be position 1. Instr() returns a value of 0 if *string1* is empty, if *start* is greater than the length of *string1*, or if *string2* is not found within *string1*. If *string2* is empty, then the value of *start* will be returned (0 if *start* was not specified). Null is returned if either *string1* or *string2* contains null.

`instr("party time","party")`	returns	1
`instr("every good boy deserves food","boy")`	returns	12
`instr(5,"hello hello my friend","hello")`	returns	7
`instr("crackin' toast, gromit","feathers")`	returns	0
`instr(20,"jack sprat","sprat")`	returns	0

While Instr() can pinpoint the location of one string within another, it can also be used to simply identify whether one string resides within another.

For instance, consider the `appName` property of the `navigator` object (see the `navigator` object). It returns a string containing the name of the user's browser application. To determine if the user is using Internet Explorer, you'd simply test for the presence of "Explorer" within `navigator.appName`:

```
if instr(navigator.appName,"Explorer")>0 then
 statements if browser is explorer
else statements if browser is not explorer
end if
```

InstrRev( )
Category: VBScript

| Type | Function |

Browser Support

	Navigator 3	Navigator 4	Explorer 3	Explorer 4
Macintosh	☐	☐	☐	■
Windows	☐	☐	■	■

| Syntax | `instrRev(string1, string2 [,start])` |

The `InstrRev()` function locates the position of *string2* within *string1*. You can specify a position within *string1* from which to *start* the search. The search proceeds from right to left within *string1*, beginning at the position *start*, if specified. Although `InstrRev()` is quite similar to `Instr()`, note the slightly different syntax where the *start* parameter is placed.

The function returns the starting position of *string2* within *string1*, if found—the first character in *string1* is considered to be position 1. `InstrRev()` will return a value of 0 if *string1* is empty, if *start* is greater than the length of *string1*, or if *string2* is not found within *string1*. If *string2* is empty, then the value of *start* will be returned (0 if *start* was not specified). Null is returned if either *string1* or *string2* contains null.

Although `InstrRev()` searches in the opposite direction as `Instr()`, the *start* position and the returned match position are still relative to the left edge of *string1*.

`instrRev("party girl","party")`	returns	1
`instrRev("every good boy deserves food","boy")`	returns	12
`instrRev("hello hello my friend","hello",14)`	returns	7
`instrRev("crackin' toast, gromit","feathers")`	returns	0

In the preceding examples, you can see that while the `InstrRev()` search moves from right to left, the index numbers for where to begin the search and a match are still counted from left to right. Thus, "party" still occurs at position 1 within "party girl".

Generally, you would only prefer `InstrRev()` over `Instr()` when you specifically need to know the position of the rightmost occurrence of *string2* within *string1*.

Int()
Category: VBScript

		Navigator 3	Navigator 4	Explorer 3	Explorer 4
Type	Function				
Browser Support	Macintosh				■
	Windows			■	■

Syntax `Int(number)`

The `Int()` function returns the integer portion of a numeric expression *number*, chopping off any decimal places. It *does not* round the integer portion of *number* in any way, although in the case of a negative *number*, it does return the next integer less than or equal to *number*.

`int(20.632)`	returns	20
`int(42.11)`	returns	42
`int(-15.63)`	returns	−16
`int(-8.03)`	returns	−9

Note that `Int()` is nearly identical in function to `Fix()`, except in the way it handles a negative *number*, as previously explained and illustrated. If *number* is a null value, `Int()` will return a null value; any other non-numeric expression will cause an error.

IsArray()
Category: VBScript

		Navigator 3	Navigator 4	Explorer 3	Explorer 4
Type	Function				
Browser Support	Macintosh				■
	Windows			■	■

Syntax `IsArray(varname)`

The simple `IsArray()` function returns a Boolean value of true if *varname* is an array; otherwise, it returns false. Because there are no specific variable data types in VBScript, this function enables you to distinguish arrays from other variables, if necessary.

```
x=10
artest=isarray(x)
```

The `IsArray()` function will assign a value of false to `artest` because x is not an array variable. In the following examples, `IsArray()` returns a value of true to `artest` because `pets` is an array.

```
pets=array("dog","cat","snake","iguana")
artest=isarray(pets)
```

IsDate()
Category: VBScript

| | Type | Function |

		Navigator 3	Navigator 4	Explorer 3	Explorer 4
Browser Support	Macintosh	☐	☐	☐	■
	Windows	☐	☐	■	■

Syntax `IsDate(date)`

The `IsDate()` function returns a Boolean value of true if *date* conforms to a valid VBScript time or date format; otherwise, it returns false. Valid time and date variables are strings that have the following formats:

Format	Example
hh:mm	19:26
hh:mm:ss	19:26:47
hh:mm [AM/PM]	7:26 PM
hh:mm:ss [AM/PM]	7:26:47 PM
mm-dd-yy	3-11-97
mm-dd-yyyy	3-11-1997
mm/dd/yy	3/11/97
mm/dd/yyyy	3/11/1997
month dd, yyyy	March 11, 1997

Valid dates must also be within the range from January 1, 100 and December 31, 9999.

`IsDate("January 3, 1998")`	returns	true
`IsDate("frank")`	returns	false
`IsDate("12:03 PM")`	returns	true
`IsDate("50")`	returns	false

IsEmpty()
Category: VBScript

Type	Function

Browser Support		Navigator 3	Navigator 4	Explorer 3	Explorer 4
	Macintosh	☐	☐	☐	■
	Windows	☐	☐	■	■

Syntax	IsEmpty(*varname*)

The `IsEmpty()` function returns a Boolean value of true if *varname* has not been initialized, or explicitly set to empty; otherwise, it returns false. You can only pass a single variable name to `IsEmpty()`, otherwise false is returned. Typically, you initialize a variable by assigning some value to it.

Consider the variable assignments:

```
y=100
greet="hello"
```

```
isempty(y)              returns          false

isempty(greet)          returns          false

isempty(pets)           returns          true
```

The last example above returns true because the *varname* `pets` has not been initialized.

Note that a variable containing a zero-value, such as 0 for a number or "" for a string, does *not* constitute empty, and will return false from `IsEmpty()`.

```
y=0
z=" "
```

```
isempty(y)   returns    false
isempty(z)   returns    false
```

<ISINDEX>
Category: HTML

Browser Support		Navigator 3	Navigator 4	Explorer 3	Explorer 4
	Macintosh	■	■	■	■
	Windows	■	■	■	■

May Contain	None

May Be Used In	<HEAD>

Attributes	ACTION, PROMPT
Syntax	<ISINDEX>...</ISINDEX>

The <ISINDEX> tag tells a browser that your page is not only readable but also keyword-searchable. When a user conducts a search on your web page, the server then executes the results. Your server must possess a corresponding CGI search script as well, though—adding the <ISINDEX> tag by itself isn't enough.

> **NOTE** The <ISINDEX> tag was widely used before the <FORM> tag and its capabilities became available, but if you want a more complex search feature for your web page, use the <FORM> tag and related attributes instead.

ACTION

The ACTION attribute specifies the location of the search program used on your web page. So if your CGI script is called cgisearch, for example, the HTML would look like this:

```
<HEAD><ISINDEX ACTION="www.provider.com/cgisearch"></HEAD>
```

This code would direct all search queries made from your web page to the appropriate script on your server.

PROMPT

The PROMPT attribute lists a specific combination of keywords that should be used instead of the default, such as:

```
<ISINDEX ACTION="www.provider.com/cgisearch"  PROMPT="search phrase">
```

Notice that the proper format of initiating a keyword search has been given on the page as an example—this mirrors the way that "search phrase" is indicated in the HTML above: no plus signs between words, no uppercase letters needed, and so on.

---

isNaN()
Category: JavaScript, JScript

Type	Function				
Browser Support		Navigator 3	Navigator 4	Explorer 3	Explorer 4
	Macintosh	☐	☐	☐	■
	Windows	☐	☐	■	■

Syntax	isNaN(testValue)

This function is used to test whether the expression *testValue* is "Not a Number." A variable may be considered "Not a Number" if it is the result of a division by zero or some other arithmetic error. The `isNaN()` function returns true if *testValue* is "Not a Number," and false otherwise. Thus, you can use this function to test expressions that may produce an invalid result.

For instance, if your script performs calculations based on user input, you could use `isNaN()` to test whether the calculation was successful (the user may have submitted a negative value for a square root calculation).

```
if (isNaN(Math.sqrt(userinput)))
 { statements if calculation was invalid }
else { statements if calculation was valid }
```

Most commonly, though, the `isNaN()` function is used in conjunction with the `parseFloat()` and `parseInt()` functions, which are used in converting strings to numbers.

In cases where the string could not be converted into a number (because it contained a non-numeric character of some sort), those functions return "NaN," which the `isNaN()` function can test for, just as in the example above. (See the `parseFloat()` and `parseInt()` functions.)

IsNull()
Category: VBScript

| Type | Function |

Browser Support

	Navigator 3	Navigator 4	Explorer 3	Explorer 4
Macintosh	☐	☐	☐	■
Windows	☐	☐	■	■

Syntax `IsNull(expression)`

The `IsNull()` function returns a Boolean value of true if the expression evaluates to a *null* value; otherwise, it returns *false*.

A *null* value indicates that expression or variable does not contain valid data—this is different from an *empty* value, which only indicates that the variable has not been initialized. In addition, a zero-length string ("") is *not* a null value, nor is a numeric value of 0.

`isnull(instr("hello",null))`   returns   true

`isnull(instr("hello","lo"))`   returns   false

Use the `IsNull()` function to determine whether an expression evaluates to a null value.

If you pass more than one variable to `IsNull()`, it will return true *if any one of the variables contains null.*

IsNumeric( )
Category: VBScript

Type	Function

Browser Support

	Navigator 3	Navigator 4	Explorer 3	Explorer 4
Macintosh	■■■■	■■■■	☐	■■■■
Windows	■■■■	■■■■	■■■■	■■■■

Syntax IsNumeric(*expression*)

The IsNumeric() function returns a Boolean value of true if the *expression* evaluates to a number; otherwise, it returns *false*. If the *expression* contains a date value, the function will also return false. Because there are no specific variable data types in VBScript, the IsNumeric() function enables you to distinguish numbers from other variables.

```
isnumeric(200)        returns        true

isnumeric("marty")    returns        false
```

This function is most useful in preventing errors with mathematical calculations based upon user input data. You should always check variables that contain user input data before using them in a mathematical calculation. For instance, suppose that the variable age contains user input from an InputBox() function:

```
sub getage()
age=inputbox("What is your age?")
 if isnumeric(age) then statements which perform calculations with age
 else window.alert("You did not enter a valid age!"):getage()
end sub
```

In the preceding example, if the user enters data that VBScript can convert into a valid number (such as "40"), then isnumeric(age) will return true and the calculations will proceed—otherwise, the user will be scolded and asked to retry his input.

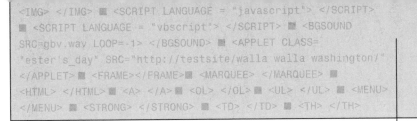

Join()

Category: VBScript

Type	Function

Browser Support

	Navigator 3	Navigator 4	Explorer 3	Explorer 4
Macintosh				■
Windows			■	■

Syntax `Join(arrayName[, delimiter])`

The `Join()` function accepts an *arrayName*, and concatenates the values of each element in the array into one long string. The *delimiter* string, if specified, is placed between each element value in the resulting string. If no *delimiter* is specified, a single space is used; if an empty string delimiter is specified (""), then no delimiter is used.

Imagine that you have created the following array:

```
pets=array("dogs","cats","lizards","ferrets","rabbits")
```

Consider, then, the following examples of the `Join()` function:

`join(pets)`	returns	"dogs cats lizards ferrets rabbits"
`join(pets,",")`	returns	"dogs,cats,lizards,ferrets,rabbits"
`join(pets," and ")`	returns	"dogs and cats and lizards and ferrets and rabbits"
`join(pets,"")`	returns	"dogscatslizardsferretsrabbits"

Note that the elements in *arrayName* need not all be string values—however, any values that are not string values will be converted into strings when concatenated to the other elements.

```
names=array("harry","bob",30,"mike")
```

`join(names,", ")`	returns	"harry, bob, 30, mike"

<IMG> </IMG> ■ <SCRIPT LANGUAGE = "javascript"> </SCRIPT>
■ <SCRIPT LANGUAGE = "vbscript"> </SCRIPT> ■ <BGSOUND
SRC=gbv.wav LOOP=-1> </BGSOUND> ■ <APPLET CLASS=
"ester's_day" SRC="http://testsite/walla walla washington/"
</APPLET> ■ <FRAME></FRAME>■ <MARQUEE> </MARQUEE> ■   <HTML>
</HTML> ■ <A> </A>■ <OL> </OL>■ <UL> </UL> ■ <MENU> </
MENU> ■ <STRONG> </STRONG> ■ <TD> </TD> ■ <TH> </TH>

K

<KBD>

Category: HTML

	Navigator 3	Navigator 4	Explorer 3	Explorer 4
Browser Support Macintosh	■	■	■	■
Windows	■	■	■	■

May Contain <APPLET>, <B>, <BASEFONT>, <BIG>, <BR>, <CITE>, <CODE>, <DFN>, <EM>, <FONT>, <I>, <IMG>, <INPUT>, <KBD>, <MAP>, <SAMP>, <SELECT>, <SMALL>, <STRIKE>, <STRONG>, <SUB>, <SUP>, <TEXTAREA>, <TT>, <U>, <VAR>

May Be Used In <ADDRESS>, <APPLET>, <B>, <BIG>, <BLOCKQUOTE>, <CAPTION>, <CENTER>, <CITE>, <CODE>, <DD>, <DT>, <FONT>, <H1>, <H2>, <H3>, <H4>, <H5>, <H6>, <I>, <KBD>, <LI>, <P>, <SAMP>, <SMALL>, <STRIKE>, <STRONG>, <SUB>, <SUP>, <TD>, <TH>, <TT>, <U>

Attributes None

Syntax <KBD>...</KBD>

The <KBD> tag is an older tag used in a tutorial or other instructional exercise to specify a bit of text to be typed in by the user. Everything written between the beginning and closing, or </KBD> tag, will be displayed in a monotype font as shown in the example:

At the login, type<KBD>GUEST</KBD> for anonymous user privileges.

Figure 1 displays this HTML in Navigator 3 for the Macintosh.

Figure 1

Text-written monospaced instructions by using the <KBD> tag compared to plain default text.

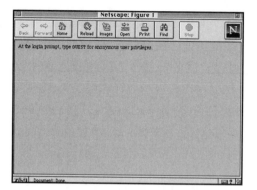

There's no functional difference between text displayed in a monospace font using the <KBD> tag versus using the <CODE> tag or the <SAMP> tag, as shown in Figure 2. Use any of these tags for monospaced plain text as you prefer—see the <CODE> and <SAMP> tag entries elsewhere for more information.

Figure 2

The <KBD> tag versus the <CODE> tag and/ or the <SAMP> tag— there's no difference.

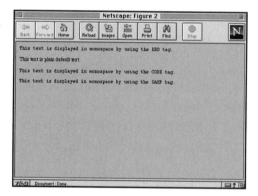

There is a difference between the way Netscape Navigator displays <KBD>-specified text versus Internet Explorer, however—Figure 3 displays the same HTML as shown in Figure 2, but the <KBD>-specified text is monospaced and bolded, too.

Figure 3

The <KBD>, <CODE>, and <SAMP> tags— Internet Explorer bolds and mono- spaces <KBD>- specified text.

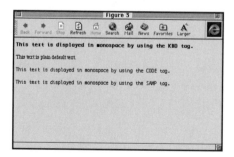

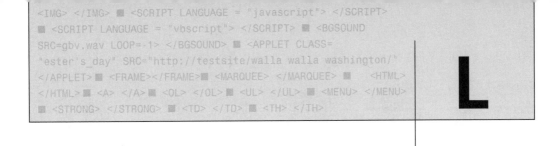

`<layer>`

Category: HTML

Browser Support		Navigator 3	Navigator 4	Explorer 3	Explorer 4
	Macintosh		▉		
	Windows		▉		

Applies To   All elements

Attributes   ABOVE, BACKGROUND, BELOW, BGCOLOR, CLIP, LEFT, NAME, TOP, WIDTH, VISIBILITY, Z-INDEX

Syntax   `<layer>…</layer>`

The `<layer>` tag defines a layer on your web page. A layer is a group of items such as text and images collected between the `<layer>` and `</layer>` tags. Once combined, you can manipulate the group of items simply by setting the various attributes of the layer. You can combine multiple layers to produce composite images or, using simple JavaScripts, create clever animations by peeling away layers stacked upon each other.

You use the top and left attributes to set the relative position of the page based on the initial position. The above, below and z-index attributes control the layering or stacking of multiple layers. The top most layer, the one most visible on the page, is above the others and has the highest z-index or z position.

Layers can also be nested inside of each other providing you more flexibility when setting layer attributes. For example, the background color of a nested layer is inherited from the parent layer unless the nested one has set its own background color. The following example HTML document displays the animation pictured in Figure 1. The animation is the disappearing card trick. Figure 2 shows the animation on the web page.

Figure 1

These five images are stored in the files hshani1 to hshan5 for the example below.

Figure 2

The web page shows the "Do Trick" button and the first picture of the animation.

```
<html><head><title>Magic Trick</title></head><body bgcolor="white">
<b>Magic Trick</b><br>
<layer name="hand1" left=20 top=100 z-index=5><img src="hshani1.gif">
</layer><layer name="hand2" left=20 top=100 z-index=4><img src="hshani2.gif"></
→layer><layer name="hand3" left=20 top=100 z-index=3><img src="hshani3.gif"></
layer><layer name="hand4" left=20 top=100 z-index=2><img src="hshani4.gif"></
layer><layer name="hand5" left=20 top=100 z-index=1><img src="hshani5.gif"></
layer><script>function doTrick() {  var i;
  for (i = 0; i <= 4; i++)    document.layers[i].visibility="show";
  document.layers["hand1"].visibility="hide";
  document.layers["hand2"].visibility="hide";
document.layers["hand3"].visibility="hide";
document.layers["hand4"].visibility="hide";  return;}</script>
<form><input type="button" value="Do Trick" OnClick="doTrick(); return false;"></
form></body></html>
```

TIP You should always use the `name` attribute with the layers you create. This will help when using attributes such as `above` and `below` which refer to other layers. Your Javascripts will also be easier to create and modify if you refer to layers by name.

NOTE To create a stack of layers, for example when displaying animation on your web page, make sure the `top` and `left` attributes of each layer are the same and the size of each image is also the same.

> **NOTE** Another way to think of layers is as a collection objects similar to the way graphics are grouped in a drawing or graphics application. When you work with grouped objects in drawing applications, you can make changes to the individual items within the group all at one time. Moving a group moves all the objects keeping them in the exact same position relative to each other. The same thing occurs when you change the position of a layer with the `left` and `top` attributes. Furthermore, nesting layers is similar to combining two or more groups of objects in your drawing application.

above

The `above` attribute causes one layer to be positioned above or on top of another layer in the page. If you stack layers on top of each other by setting top and left attributes such that the layers overlap, the `above` attribute determines which of two layers will be displayed above the other. When layers are stacked, the layer below may not be visible. To make it visible, you can remove the top layer with a JavaScript or adjust the position or size of one of the layers. See the example with the `layer` object for more information.

```
<layer name="FirstImage" above="SecondImage">
```

background

The `background` attribute sets the background image of a layer. The image, which may be any of the formats supported in HTML, is displayed behind all other objects in the layer. As with the background of the `<body>` tag, if the image is smaller than the dimensions of the layer, the image is tiled to fill the entire background.

```
<layer name="Car" background="images/sunset.html">
```

below

The `below` attribute causes one layer to be positioned below another layer in the page. If you stack layers on top of each other by setting `top` and `left` attributes such that the layers overlap, the `below` attribute places one layer below the other. When layers are stacked, the layer below may not be visible. To make it visible, you can remove the top layer with a JavaScript or adjust the position or size of one of the layers.

```
<layer name="SecondImage" below="FirstImage">
```

bgcolor

The `bgcolor` attribute sets the color of the background of the layer. You can specify the color with an RGB value, such as #8eve10, or with a name such as green. The color is displayed behind all items of the layer. By default, layers are transparent meaning the underlying items on the page show through in the blank portions of the layer. See Appendix B for more information on working with colors.

```
<layer name="Car" bgcolor="green">
```

clip

The clip attribute determines the maximum size of the layer image on the page by defining a clip rectangle. The four values of the attribute denote the left, top, right and bottom points of the rectangle. All items on the layer that do not fit within the dimensions of the clip are cropped at the boundary. If you specify only two values with the clip attribute, these are taken as the right and bottom points respectively and the top and left values are defaulted to 0.

```
<layer name="Landscape" clip=300,100>
```

> **NOTE** The clip rectangle is different from the dimensions of the layer as defined with the left, top and width attributes. Items such as the text or graphics which do not fit within the clip area is cropped to fit. Without the clip attribute, the text and other items are wrapped to the next line.

left

The left attribute sets the position of the left side of a layer in pixels. The value indicates the number of pixels from the left side of the page to the beginning of the layer. A value of 50, for example, would place the layer 50 pixels from the side of the page. If a left value is not specified, the layer is placed where it falls in the among elements of the page. If the layer is nested within another layer, the position is relative to the left side of the parent layer instead of the left side of the page.

```
<layer name="Animate1" left=50 top=50>
```

> **TIP** When creating animation with layers, it is important your graphics are aligned using the **top** and **left** attributes of each layer. Otherwise, the animation will not appear smooth especially if the viewer perceives sudden jumps or changes in position.

name

The name attribute specifies the name of the layer. In JavaScripts, the name may be used to access the layer object and the layers array of the document.

```
<layer name="Fish1">
```

top

The top attribute defines the position of the top of a layer in pixels. The value indicates the number of pixels from the top of the page. If a value is not specified, the layer is placed where it falls in the among elements of the page. The top position of a layer nested within another layer is measured from the top of the parent layer and not the page.

```
<layer name="Animate1" left=50 top=50>
```

> **TIP**
>
> When creating animation with layers, it is important your graphics are aligned using the **top** and **left** attributes of each layer. Otherwise, the animation will not appear smooth especially if the viewer perceives sudden jumps or changes in position.

width

The `width` attribute determines the width in pixels of the layer image. All items which do not fit within the width of the layer are wrapped to the next line. If a width is not specified, the layer will grow as much as possible to fit all the items.

```
<layer name="Animate1" width=100>
```

visibility

The `visibility` attribute determines if a layer is visible on the page. A value of `show` displays the layer on the page while a value of `hide` does not display the layer. For nested layers, a setting of `inherit` sets the visibility of the layer according to the visibility of the parent or outer layer.

```
<layer name="Animate1" visibility=show>
```

> **TIP**
>
> Using the **visibility** attribute and JavaScripting, you create simple animation on your web page. Start by creating the consecutive images of your animation and positioning them on the page one on top of the other with the **top** and **left** attributes. Make sure they are in the correct order so the first image is on top and the last on bottom. Then, one by one, you set the visibility attribute to hide and your graphics will become animated.

z-index

The `z-index` attribute allows you to define the order of layers which are overlapped or are stacked on each other. The value is a positive or negative number which determines the positioning in the stack. Layers with higher numbers are displayed on top of layers with lower numbers. Without the `z-index` attribute, layers are positioned in the order they appear in the page with the first layer displayed at the bottom of the stack and the last layer on top.

```
<layer name="Animate1" z-index=1>
```

Layer
Category: JavaScript 1.2

Type	Object				

Browser Support		Navigator 3	Navigator 4	Explorer 3	Explorer 4
	Macintosh	☐	■	☐	☐
	Windows	☐	■	☐	☐

Subset Of Document object

Properties above, background, below, bgcolor, clip, left, name, pagex, pagey, parentlayer, siblingabove, siblingbelow, src, top, visiblity, zindex

Methods moveBy(), moveTo(), moveAbsolute(), resizeBy(), resizeTo(), moveAbove(), moveBelow(), load

Events onBlur, onFocus, onLoad, onMouseout, onmouseover

Syntax document.layerName.property OR document.layers[index].property OR document.layerName.method(parameters) OR document.layer[index].method(parameters)

Layers are a main element of Netscape 4's *Dynamic HTML*. A layer is much like a piece of cellophane placed over the browser window—you can draw any HTML you want on it, see through it, and move it anywhere within the browser window. Furthermore, you can create as many layers as you want, and alter their characteristics (transparency, size, position) on-the-fly using JavaScript.

Initially, a layer is created either using JavaScript Style Sheet Syntax or with the "simpler" <layer> tag.

```
<layer
 id=layerName
 left=horizontal
 top=vertical
 [pagex=horizRelativeToDocWindow]
 [pagey=vertRelativeToDocWindow]
 [src=sourceHTML]
 [z-index | above | below]
 width=layerWidth
 height=layerHeight
 clip=topx,topy,botx,boty
 [visibility]
 [bgcolor=backColor]
 [background=imageURL]
```

```
[onMouseOver="event-handler"]
[onMouseOut="event-handler"]
[onFocus="event-handler"]
[onBlur="event-handler"]
[onLoad="event-handler"]>
```

Figure 1

A page composed of three layers, each of which may contain independent sets of properties.

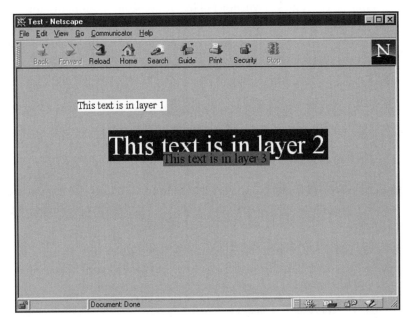

As illustrated in the modern-art-like Figure 1, you can position a layer anywhere on the page. It can have its own background colors, and any HTML elements can be placed within the layer. Once the layer has been created in the HTML, its characteristics are accessible via properties and methods of the JavaScript layer object. Using this object, you can change or modify many of the layer's onscreen attributes on-the-fly, such as visibility, transparency, background color, position, and size.

Layers can quickly become conceptually complex. First, the layer object itself is an element of the layers[] array property of the document object. You can thus refer to a particular layer object by referencing its index in the layers[] array. Layers are indexed in the array according to their creation order in the HTML document. So, the first layer object in a document can be referred to as:

```
document.layers[0]
```

Alternately, if the layer has been given a name via the id attribute of the <layer> tag, you can refer to it by name:

```
document.layerName
```

A layer is treated as a self-contained document. As a result, the `layer` object itself also contains a `document` property which is the `document` object for everything within that layer—which may include subordinate layers. Because layers can be nested, they can grow quickly complex and hard on the brain. Of course, this isn't a comprehensive look at creating and managing layers, per se, but rather a reference source for the `layer` object. For a detailed look at using layers, you may want to read Netscape's "Dynamic HTML in Netscape Communicator" document. As of this writing, it can be found at the URL `http://developer.netscape.com/library/documenta-tion/communicator/dynhtml/index.htm`. Section 2.5 of this document contains extremely detailed information on using JavaScript with layers.

The following section takes a look at each of the `layer` object's properties and methods, and how they reflect and affect the layer.

above **property**

The `above` property is in fact a reference to another `layer` object—the one "above" the current layer in terms of z-order. The z-order is the stacking order that determines whether a layer appears above or behind another layer. Within this stacking order, a layer with a higher z-order integer will appear above a layer with a lower z-order integer (the integers themselves are arbitrary).

Imagine that there are two layers, named *lay1* and *lay2*. The first, *lay1*, has a z-order of 2, while *lay2* has a z-order of 4. Thus, *lay2* is "above" (and will visually appear above) *lay1*. The following code will be a reference to some property of the *lay2* `layer` object:

```
document.lay1.above.property
```

background **property**

The `background` property is an `image` object that contains the background image for the layer. To change the layer's background image, simply assign a new image URL to the `src` property of `background` (because `background` is an `image` object, it has the standard `image` object `src` property).

```
document.layerName.background.src="newimage.jpg"
```

below **property**

The `below` property is in fact a reference to another `layer` object—the one "below" the current layer in terms of z-order. The z-order is the stacking order that determines whether a layer appears above or behind another layer. Within this stacking order, a layer with a lower z-order integer will appear below a layer with a higher z-order integer (the integers themselves are arbitrary).

Imagine that there are two layers, named *lay1* and *lay2*. The first, *lay1*, has a z-order of 2, while *lay2* has a z-order of 1. Thus, *lay1* is "above" (and will visually appear above) *lay2*. The following code will be a reference to some property of the *lay2* `layer` object:

```
document.lay1.below.property
```

bgcolor property

The background color of the layer. Modifying this property results in an immediate onscreen effect, as the background color of any visible portions of the layer change to the newly specified color. Setting the bgcolor property to null will cause the layer's background to be transparent.

```
document.layerName.bgColor="#FAFAFA"
```

> **TIP**
> All color values are specified as a hexadecimal triplet. The triplet indicates the RGB color values in the form of "#RRGGBB," where each color is a hexadecimal value between 00 and FF. Alternatively, you may instead specify a predefined color name; for instance
>
> ```
> document.layerName.bgColor="steelblue"
> ```
>
> You can refer to the color chart in Appendix B for predefined color names and their associated hexadecimal triplet values.

clip properties

The entire layer has a certain width and height, as specified by the width and height attributes of the <layer> tag. However, you can specify that only a portion of the layer should be visible. The clip properties enable you to control the dimensions of the visible portion of the layer.

A common use of clipping is to create a drop-down menu layer. Simply construct a graphic which contains a menu title and several menu items. Initially, the layer is clipped so that its height only reveals the menu title:

```
document.layerName.clip.height=25
```

When the user clicks on the menu title, the clipping height increases to display the rest of the menu.

```
document.layerName.clip.height=100
```

You can use any combination of the below clip properties to immediately alter the clipping size of the layer.

clip.bottom	Bottom edge of clip this many pixels from top edge of layer
clip.height	Height in pixels of whole clip
clip.left	Left edge of clip this many pixels in from left edge of layer
clip.right	Right edge of clip this many pixels from left edge of layer
clip.top	Top edge of clip this many pixels from top edge of layer
clip.width	Width in pixels of whole clip

L

left property

The simple `left` property specifies the left-edge position of the layer with relation to its parent layer, measured in pixels. If the layer is not nested within another layer then its parent layer is the browser window itself.

```
document.layerName.left=10
```

name property

The read-only `name` property merely reflects the name of the layer, as specified by the `id` attribute of the `<layer>` tag.

pageX property

In contrast to the `left` property, the `pageX` property controls the horizontal position of the layer (in pixels) with respect to the whole page, regardless of whether the layer is nested or not. If the layer is not nested within another layer then the `left` and `pageX` properties have the same effect.

```
document.layerName.pageX=15
```

pageY property

In contrast to the `top` property, the `pageY` property controls the vertical position of the layer (in pixels) with respect to the whole page, regardless of whether the layer is nested or not. If the layer is not nested within another layer then the `top` and `pageY` properties have the same effect.

```
document.layerName.pageY=25
```

parentLayer property

The `parentLayer` property is actually a reference to another `layer` object—that which encloses the current layer. In some cases, you may have nested layers, which is when a layer is contained within another layer. Imagine a layer named *layA*, which itself contains two layers, *lay1* and *lay2*. For both *lay1* and *lay2*, *layA* is the parent layer. Thus, both statements below reference the same property of *layA*:

```
document.lay1.parentLayer.property
document.lay2.parentLayer.property
```

Notice, though, that *layA* is not nested within a layer itself. Its parent layer is the `window` object. Therefore, this statement would refer to a property of the `window` object:

```
document.layA.parentLayer.property
```

siblingAbove property

The `siblingAbove` property is in fact a reference to another `layer` object—the one "above" the current layer in terms of z-order which is nested within the same layer. The z-order is the stacking order which determines whether a layer appears above or behind another layer. Within this stacking order, a layer with a higher z-order integer will appear above a layer with a lower z-order integer (the integers themselves are arbitrary).

Imagine that there are two layers, named *lay1* and *lay2*, and both are nested within a parent layer, *layA*. The first, *lay1*, has a z-order of 2, while *lay2* has a z-order of 4. Thus, *lay2* is "above" (and will visually appear above) *lay1*. The following code will be a reference to some property of the *lay2* layer object:

```
document.lay1.siblingAbove.property
```

However, if *lay1* were the highest layer sharing a parent *layA*, the `siblingAbove` property would contain null.

siblingBelow property

The `siblingBelow` property is in fact a reference to another `layer` object—the one "below" the current layer in terms of z-order which is nested within the same layer. The z-order is the stacking order that determines whether a layer appears above or behind another layer. Within this stacking order, a layer with a lower z-order integer will appear below a layer with a higher z-order integer (the integers themselves are arbitrary).

Imagine that there are two layers, named *lay1* and *lay2*, and both are nested within a parent layer, *layA*. The first, *lay1*, has a z-order of 2, while *lay2* has a z-order of 1. Thus, *lay1* is "above" (and will visually appear above) *lay2*. The following code will be a reference to some property of the *lay2* layer object:

```
document.lay1.siblingBelow.property
```

However, if *lay1* were the lowest layer sharing a parent *layA*, the `siblingBelow` property would contain null.

src property

The contents of a layer are defined by standard HTML. Using the `src` property, you can specify which HTML document to display within the layer. You can change the `src` property at any time and the new HTML document will be loaded into the layer. Simply assign a valid file URL to this property.

```
document.layerName.src="http://www.server.com/layer1a.html"
```

top property

The straightforward `top` property specifies the top-edge position of the layer with relation to its parent layer, measured in pixels. If the layer is not nested within another layer then its parent layer is the browser window itself.

```
document.layerName.top=10
```

L

visibility **property**

An entire layer can be hidden or shown using the visibility property. This property may contain one of three possible string values. Assigning any of the below to this property will cause the layer to magically appear or dissappear:

"hide"	layer will disappear from view
"show"	layer will appear into view
"inherit"	layer will appear or disappear in coordination with its parent layer

For instance, to hide *layerName*:

```
document.layerName.visibility="hide"
```

Note that if a layer's parent is the browser window itself then a visibility property of "inherit" will be the same as "show."

zIndex **property**

The z-order is the stacking order that determines whether a layer appears above or behind another layer. Within this stacking order, a layer with a lower z-order integer will appear below a layer with a higher z-order integer (the integers themselves are arbitrary).

The zIndex property contains the layer's z-order integer. By assigning a new integer to a layer object's zIndex property you can make that layer suddenly appear above or below a sibling layer.

Imagine that there are two layers, named *lay1* and *lay2*. The first, *lay1*, has an initial z-order index of 3, while *lay2* has a z-order index of 2. As a result, we can expect that *lay1* will appear above *lay2*, as seen in Figure 2.

Figure 2

Due to z-order indexing, the layer with a higher index appears above the layer with a lower index.

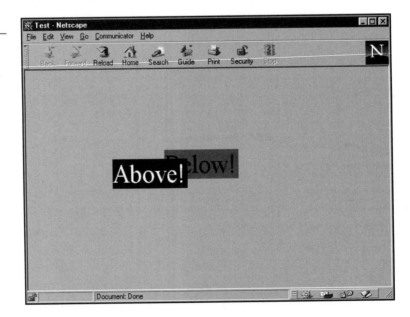

However, simply assign a value higher than 3 to *lay2*'s zIndex property and the tables will be turned.

```
document.lay2.zIndex=4
```

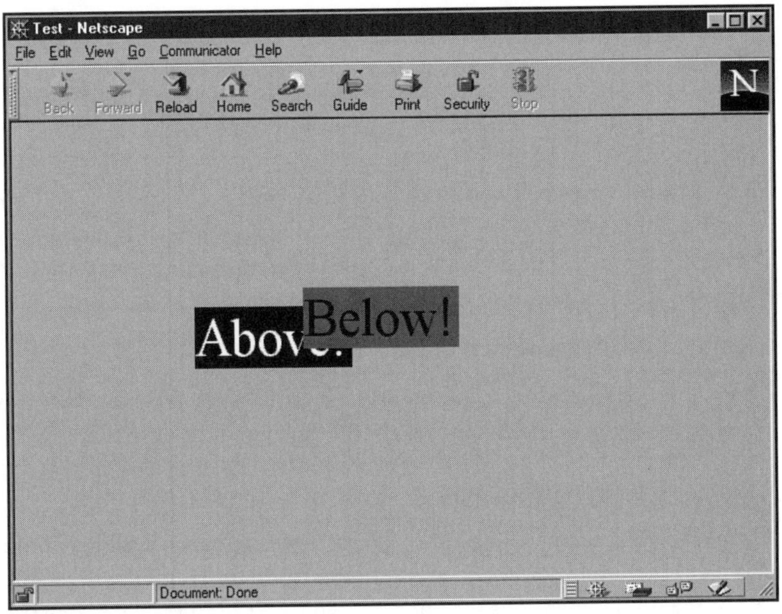

Figure 3

Assigning a higher z-order index to the previous bottom layer brings it to the top.

moveBy() method

A simple shift, the moveBy() method accepts two parameters, *x* and *y*. It shifts the layer by *x* pixels horizontally and *y* pixels vertically.

```
document.layerName.moveBy(10,20)
```

This will move *layerName* 10 pixels to the right and 20 pixels down. You can also use negative values to shift in the reverse direction.

```
document.layerName.moveBy(15,-30)
```

In this case, *layerName* will move 15 pixels to the right and 30 pixels up.

moveTo() method

Whereas the moveBy() method shifted the layer a relative amount, the moveTo() method relocated the layer to the absolute coordinates *x, y* within the parent layer. If the layer is not nested then its parent layer is the browser window.

```
document.layerName.moveTo(20,30)
```

In this example, *layerName* will be moved to the coordinates 20,30 within its parent (be that a parent layer or the browser window).

moveToAbsolute() method

Putting all parenting issues aside, the `moveToAbsolute()` method will relocate the layer to the specified *x, y* coordinates relative to the entire page. Whether or not the layer is nested is irrelevent.

```
document.layerName.moveToAbsolute(0,0)
```

This statement will relocate *layerName* to the upper left corner of the page.

resizeBy() method

The `resizeBy()` method works the same as assigning new clipping coordinates to the `layer` object's `clip` property. By specifying relative *x* and *y* values, this method will modify the visible clip area of the layer. For instance, imagine that *layerName* is currently wholly visible and has a width of 100 and a height of 100.

```
document.layerName.resizeBy(-10,-50)
```

This will reduce the visible clip area of the layer to 90 by 50. Note that this does *not* scale the size of the layer's content—rather, it merely affects how much of the layer is currently visible.

resizeTo() method

The `resizeTo()` method works the same as assigning new clipping coordinates to the `layer` object's `clip.height` and `clip.width` properties. This method will resize the visible clipping area to the pixel dimensions specified by *x* and *y*. For instance, imagine that *layerName* is currently wholly visible and has a width of 100 and a height of 100.

```
document.layerName.resizeTo(90,50)
```

The above will reduce the visible clip area of the layer to 90 by 50. Note that this does *not* scale the size of the layer's content—rather, it merely affects how much of the layer is currently visible.

moveAbove() method

Circumventing direct dealings with the `zIndex` property, you can use the `moveAbove()` method to stack one layer above another. Simply pass this method the reference for the layer you wish to stack above. For instance, consider two layers, *lay1* and *lay2*. Currently, *lay2* is stacked above *lay1*. To reverse that:

```
document.lay1.moveAbove(lay2)
```

moveBelow() method

Like the `moveAbove()` method, you can use the `moveBelow()` method to stack one layer below another without referencing z-order indexes. Simply pass this method the reference for the layer you want to stack below. For instance, consider two layers, *lay1* and *lay2*. Currently, *lay2* is stacked above *lay1*. To reverse that:

```
document.lay2.moveBelow(lay1)
```

load() method

A slight elaboration on the layer object's src property, using the load() method you can simultaneously load new HTML content into a layer and adjust its width. The load() method accepts two parameters: *sourceURL* and *width*. For example, you can load a new HTML document into *layerName*, and specify that *layerName*'s width be changed to 600 pixels:

```
document.layerName.load("http://www.server.com/layer2b.html",600)
```

Event Handlers

Because each layer is considered a self-contained document, the layer object's event handlers behave just as they do in the window object (see window object). If an event occurs where multiple layers are stacked, the topmost layer will handle the event. This rule applies even if the portion of the topmost layer where the event occurred is transparent. Below are brief overviews of each of the layer object's event handlers.

onBlur event handler

Using the Tab key, the user can navigate elements on the page. When a layer which just had focus is tabbed away from, the onBlur event handler is triggered. This lets you know that a user has left a certain layer.

onFocus event handler

Using the Tab key, the user can navigate elements on the page. When the user Tabs onto a layer, it is said to have gained focus. When the layer gains focus, the onFocus event handler is triggered. This lets you know that a user has brought attention to the layer.

onLoad event handler

Each layer contains an HTML document. Once this document has fully loaded into the layer, the onLoad event handler for that layer is triggered. This allows you to know that a layer has been loaded and is "ready to go." Note that the onLoad event handler is triggered whether the layer is visible or hidden.

onMouseOut event handler

If you want to know when the mouse pointer has passed off of a layer, this is the event handler for you. Whenever the mouse leaves a layer's region, an onMouseOut event handler is triggered. Remember that events occur on topmost layers in cases where several layers are stacked.

onMouseOver event handler

If you want to know when the mouse pointer passes over a layer, you'll come to like onMouseOver. Whenever the mouse enters a layer's region, an onMouseOver event handler is triggered. Remember that events occur on topmost layers in cases where several layers are stacked.

L

LBound()
Category: VBScript

Type	Function

Browser Support

	Navigator 3	Navigator 4	Explorer 3	Explorer 4
Macintosh	☐	☐	☐	■
Windows	☐	☐	■	■

Syntax Lbound(arrayName [,dimension])

The LBound() function returns the lowest available index in *arrayName*. In most cases, this function returns the value 0—since that is typically the index of the first element in an array.

```
names=array("harry","bill")
firstidx=lbound(names)
```

Above, firstidx will be assigned the value 0 because that is the index of the first element in the array. If your array contains more than one dimension, you can specify which dimension to report the lbound of using the *dimension* parameter—of course, this will still usually be 0.

The LBound() function, while not incredibly useful in and of itself, has a more utile sibling known as the UBound() function, which can help you to determine the overall size of an array. (See the UBound() function.)

LCase()
Category: VBScript

Type	Function

Browser Support

	Navigator 3	Navigator 4	Explorer 3	Explorer 4
Macintosh	☐	☐	☐	■
Windows	☐	☐	■	■

Syntax LCase(string)

The LCase() function converts all uppercase characters in *string* to lowercase. Any characters that are already lowercase, or non-alphabetical, remain unchanged. If *string* is null, then null is returned.

lcase("CRENSHAW")	returns	"crenshaw"
lcase("honeyDEW")	returns	"honeydew"
lcase("cAnteLOupe!!??")	returns	"canteloupe!!??"

Typically, you would use either the `LCase()` or `UCase()` function (which converts a string to uppercase) to convert user-input data before performing a string comparison. For instance, suppose you need to test whether a user entered the string "yes." However, string comparisons are case-sensitive, and you don't know what sort of capitalization the user typed in his input—thus, you convert his input to a known case before performing the comparison:

```
if lcase(userinput)="yes" then …
```

left

Category: Cascading Style Sheets

Browser Support

	Navigator 3	Navigator 4	Explorer 3	Explorer 4
Macintosh		▆		
Windows		▆		▆

Applies to All elements

Syntax `left : value`

The `left` property defines the position of the left edge of an element on the page. The `left` property accepts any length units (see Appendix D), though pixels are safest to use across browsers and platforms at this time. Percentage values refer to the parent element's width. For elements with absolute positioning, `left` is relative to the upper left corner of the box of the nearest parent element. For relative positioning, `left` is relative to the normally rendered position of the element.

You may also specify the keyword `auto`, which indicates the browser should place the element where it normally would without this property. `Auto` is useful when dealing with inheritance and a parent element which has a previously set value for `left`.

When combined with `top`, and when the `position` property has been set, you can precisely control the layout of objects on your page regardless of the other elements you wish to display. In fact, you can't use `left` unless `position` is also present. See the description of `position` for more information and elaborate examples combining `top` and `left`. Figure 1 shows text displayed to the right and lower using both `left` and `top`.

```
h1 { left: 2in }
```

```
h1 { left: 40% }
```

L

Figure 1

Using left and top to change the position of items on the page.

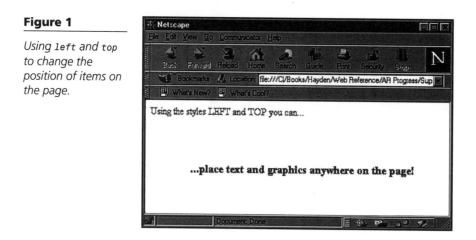

 Explorer 4 associates these percentage values with the size of the browser window. A left value of **50%** means the element will begin halfway across the browser window.

Left()
Category: VBScript

Type	Function

Browser Support

	Navigator 3	Navigator 4	Explorer 3	Explorer 4
Macintosh	☐	☐	☐	■
Windows	☐	☐	■	■

Syntax Left(string, length)

The Left() function returns *length*—the number of characters from the left (e.g. beginning) of *string*. A *length* of 0 will return a zero-length string, while a *length* greater than the string length will return the whole *string*. A *length* less than zero will cause an error.

left("barney",2)	returns	"ba"
left("house warming",0)	returns	""
left("flag waving",30)	returns	"flag waving"
left("doggy",-2)	returns	invalid procedure call error

The Left() function is one of several tools you can use to extract portions of a string—also see the functions Right() and Mid().

Len()
Category: VBScript

Type	Function

Browser Support

	Navigator 3	Navigator 4	Explorer 3	Explorer 4
Macintosh	☐	☐	☐	▉
Windows	☐	☐	▉	▉

Syntax `Len(string)`

The `Len()` function returns the number of characters in *string*. The length of the string includes all spaces, punctuation, newlines, and other control characters.

`len("hello")` returns 5

`len("hi there")` returns 8

`len("")` returns 0

If you pass a value which is numeric, `Len()` returns the number of digits in the number, which is essentially the same as the number of characters in it. There is also an alternate function, `LenB()`, which returns the number of bytes required to represent *string*:

`lenb("hello")` returns 10

`lenb("a")` returns 2

`lenb("")` returns 0

Typically, you use the `Len()` function to determine the character position at the right end of the string, for use with functions such as `InStr()`, `InStrRev()`, and `Mid()`. The rightmost character position in a string is represented by `Len(string)-1`. You may never use the `LenB()` function, as it is of low utility.

L

letter-spacing
Category: Cascading Style Sheets

Browser Support

	Navigator 3	Navigator 4	Explorer 3	Explorer 4
Macintosh	☐	☐	☐	☐
Windows	☐	☐	☐	▉

Applies To	All elements

Syntax `letter-spacing : value`

The letter-spacing property adjusts the space between individual characters. This is also known as *kerning*. Letter-spacing works similarly to word-spacing in that the value is added to the default spacing used by the browser. Likewise, you can specify definitive units for the value as discussed in Appendix D or the word normal to avoid inheriting previous spacing settings.

```
h1 { letter-spacing: 0.1em }
```

```
<h1 style="letter-spacing: 0.2em">
```

Here's an example of letter-spacing at work:

```
<html>
 <style TYPE="text/css">
 <!--
  h1.a { letter-spacing: 10px }
  h1.b { letter-spacing: .3in }
 -->
 </style>
<head>
 <title>Specifying Letter Spacing</title>
</head>
<body>
 <h1>
 Look ma! I can adjust the space between letters!
 </h1>
 <h1 class=a>
 Look ma! I can adjust the space between letters!
 </h1>
 <h1 class=b>
 Look ma! I can adjust the space between letters!
 </h1>
</body>
</html>
```

As Figure 1 shows, the first paragraph is normal text, the second has a letter-spacing of 10 pixels, and the third a spacing of three-tenths of an inch.

Figure 1

Give `letter-spacing` a value and instantly adjust kerning.

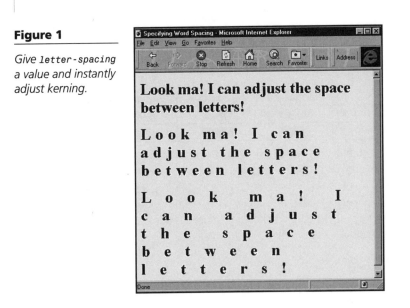

You can also use negative values to achieve overlapping characters, but use this capability wisely. Effective uses of this might be tight kerning for prominent text and artificially created ligatures (since ligatures aren't possible in normal HTML). See both in Figure 2.

L

Figure 2

Negative `letter-spacing` creates the "VoV" effect and the ligature in "fling."

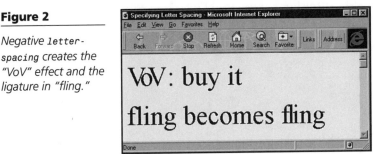

If you justify text with `text-align` (discussed in its own entry), the web browser is usually free to adjust the kerning by itself to make the justification happen. But if you want, you can override this by setting `letter-spacing` to zero:

```
p { letter-spacing: 0 }
```

With that rule set, the browser can achieve justified text by adjusting word spacing, but not by adjusting kerning.

<LI>

Category: HTML

Browser Support

May Contain <A>, <ADDRESS>, <APPLET>, <B>, <BASEFONT>, <BIG>, <BLOCKQUOTE>, <BR>, <CENTER>, <CITE>, <CODE>, <DFN>, <DIR>, <DIV>, <DL>, <EM>, <FONT>, <FORM>, <HR>, <I>, <IMG>, <INPUT>, <KBD>, <MAP>, <MENU>, <OL>, <P>, <PRE>, <SAMP>, <SELECT>, <SMALL>, <STRIKE>, <STRONG>, <SUB>, <SUP>, <TABLE>, <TEXTAREA>, <TT>, <U>, <UL>, <VAR>

May Be Used In <DIR>, <MENU>, <OL>, <UL>

Attributes CLASS, ID, TYPE, VALUE

Syntax <LI>...</LI>

The <LI> tag, used within a <DIR>, <MENU>, <OL>, or <UL> list, denotes a single list item. It signals a visitor's browser to add bullets before and proper spacing between individual list items.

The following example is a plain <DIR> list, but you could substitute <DIR> and </DIR> for <MENU>, <OL>, and/or <UL>, too:

```
<P>Employees<BR>
<DIR><LI>John Smith
<LI>Jane Doe
<LI>Ralph Nesbit
<LI>Kermit the Frog
</DIR>
```

> **NOTE** It is possible to add bullets before something outside a <DIR>, <MENU>, <OL>, or <UL> list by using the <LI> tag—Navigator 3 and Explorer 3 for Mac and for Windows will be cooperative. But most earlier browsers, and other browsers such as Mosaic, will ignore stray <LI> tags and leave out the bullets. So don't count on this kind of HTML syntax as reliable.

CLASS

The CLASS attribute is used to specify the name of a style sheets as it applies to a specific selection on a web page. See the "Cascading Style Sheets Basics" chapter and any individual, related style sheets entries elsewhere in the book for more information.

ID

The ID attribute is used to distinguish individual selections in a web page as pertaining to the use of style sheets. See the "Cascading Style Sheets Basics" chapter and any individual, related style sheets entries elsewhere in the book for more information.

TYPE

The TYPE attribute specifies numbering systems or bullet types in mid-<OL> and <UL> lists.

There are five TYPE values when used in an <OL> list: 1 for Arabic numbers (1, 2, 3, and so on—this is the TYPE default), a for alphanumeric lowercase letters (a, b, c, and so on), A for alphanumeric uppercase letters (A, B, C, and so on), i for lowercase Roman numerals (i, ii, iii, and so on), and I for uppercase Roman numerals (I, II, III, and so on).

There are three TYPE values when used in a <UL> list: circle for open, ring-like bullets, disc for solid, typical bullets, and square for solid, square bullets.

> **NOTE** See the <OL> and <UL> tag entries elsewhere in this book for a longer, more detailed look at how the <LI> tag works within these types of lists.

L

VALUE

The VALUE attribute enables you to resequence or reset the numbering of items in an ordered list.

In the following example, 4 has been specified as the VALUE setting:

```
<DIR><LI VALUE=4>Lions
<LI>Tigers
<LI>Bears
<LI>Oh my!
</DIR>
```

The items in this list, then, would be numbered as 4, 5, 6, and 7. So using the VALUE attribute does not change the overall appearance of a list—it simply enables you to decide where the list numbering begins.

> **NOTE** You can also use the VALUE attribute in combination with the START attribute to arrange list items in a kind of outline format. See the START attribute section of the <OL> tag entry for more information.

`<limittext>`

Category: HTML

Browser Support	WebTV Internet Terminal
Applies To	Text
Attributes	`size, value, width`
Syntax	`<limittext>…</limittext>`

The `<limittext>` tag displays the text associated with the value in a limited area, regardless of the actual size needed for the text. This helps you plan the layout of your page more precisely without leaving extra room for text which may expand or come in larger than you expect. The `value` attribute contains the text to be displayed. The `size` attribute sets the width of the text area in pixels, while the `width` attribute limits the number of characters displayed. Text is scaled with the `size` attribute and or cropped at the character limit if the `width` attribute is used.

```
<limittext value="http://mycompany.com/position.html" size=300>
```

> **NOTE** If you use the `width` and the `size` attribute at the same time, the smaller limit of the two will be used.

size

The `size` attribute defines the width of the area in pixels. You should use this attribute with text where the number of characters remains the same but the size expands from formatting or special characters.

```
<limittext value="http://mycompany.com/intl.html" size=300>
```

value

The `value` attribute defines the url of the text to be displayed within the area.

```
<limittext value="docs/copywrt.html" size=300>
```

width

The `width` attribute limits the number of characters displayed with the `<limittext>` tag. Limiting the characters is helpful when you only need to display the first characters of the text to help the viewer understand your page. For example, you can display the first few words of a more complete text, and then provide a hypertext link for viewers who wish to see the entire content.

```
<limittext value="company/mission.html" width=100>
```

line-height

Category: Cascading Style Sheets

Browser Support		Navigator 3	Navigator 4	Explorer 3	Explorer 4
	Macintosh	☐	■	■	☐
	Windows	☐	■	■	■

Applies To All elements except replaced elements.

Syntax `line-height: value`

The `line-height` property adjusts the distance between the baselines of two adjacent lines of text. The property gives the total height of a line of text, which includes space above and below the line. If you have 12-point text and specify a `line-height` of 16 points, then 4 points are added to the overall height, 2 above the line and 2 below the line.

You can specify `line-height` in one of three ways: number, length, and percentage. When you specify `line-height` by a number, the browser figures out the actual line height by multiplying the font size of the current element by the number you specify. For the purposes of inheritance, when you use a number, child elements will inherit the calculated line height, not the actual `line-height` number.

You can also specify `line-height` using length units, such as `pt` or `em` as discussed in Appendix D. Finally, you can adjust `line-height` through a percentage value. The value you specify is relative to the font size of the element at hand.

```
h1 { line-height: 2 }

<h1 style="line-height: 120%">
```

> **NOTE** Explorer and Navigator both add all the `line-height` spacing *above* the text line, and none after.

> **NOTE** If you ever have a line of text with two different `line-height` values, then the line extends from the top of the highest section to the bottom of the lowest section. Thus, the browser uses the larger of the `line-height` values for determining how it will display the elements.

L

> **TIP** For elements that do not support line-height, such as the `<img>` tag and other tags which are *replaced* when the page is displayed, you can work around this limitation in some browsers by nesting one tag within another as with the following example:
>
> ```
> span { line-height: 200% }
>
> <img src="logo.gif">
> ```

 Actually, Explorer *does* allow you to add `line-height` directly to `<img>` tags. Rules such as this one work fine to space out images vertically:

```
img { line-height: 200% }
```

Here's a more complete example of specifying `line-height` by number. The most interesting aspect of this example is the differences between the way this page is displayed in one browser versus another. See the explanation after this for more information.

```
<html>
 <style type="text/css">
 <!--
  h1 { font-size: 20pt;
       line-height: 1.2 }
  h2 { font-size: 20pt;
       line-height: 2 }
  h3 { font-size: 20pt;
       line-height: 5 }
 -->
 </style>
<head>
 <title>Specifying Leading with Numbers</title>
</head>
<body>
 <h1>Adjusting leading with numbers involves multiplying the number
 by the font size of the element in question.</h1>
 <h2>Adjusting leading with numbers involves multiplying the number
 by the font size of the element in question.</h2>
 <h3>Adjusting leading with numbers involves multiplying the number
 by the font size of the element in question.</h3>
</body>
</html>
```

In this example, the line height calculated by the browser for each of the blocks of text is 24, 40, and 100, respectively (see Figure 1).

Figure 1

Leading defined by number.

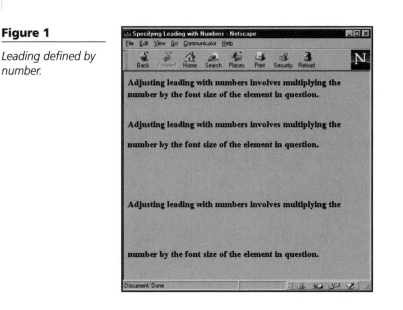

Navigator does this just fine, but Internet Explorer 3 (Mac and Windows) uses absolute `line-height` numbers differently. Check out Figure 2.

Figure 2

The exact same web page viewed in Explorer 3.

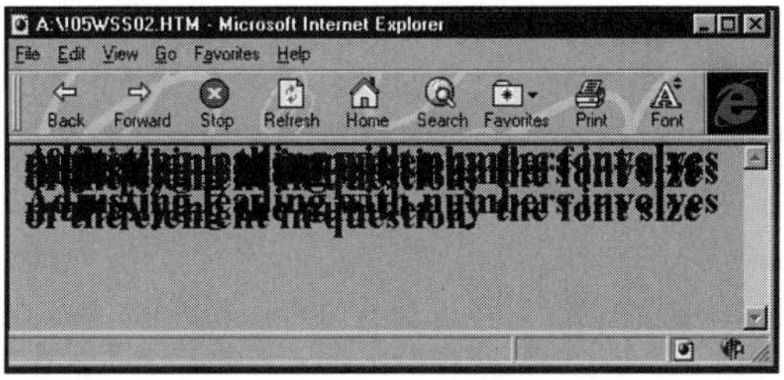

This page is not quite the same (to say the least!). In Explorer 3, `line-height` number matches point-size number in default text display. So, `line-height` for 20-point text is 20 unless set differently (whereas it should be 1 according to the official style sheet rules). If you go too much less than that, text lines start to overlap in Explorer 3, as you can see.

This is not a problem in Explorer 4. Version 4 works correctly, as Navigator does. But the fact that Explorer 3 and Navigator handle `line-height` differently when using absolute values means that you should avoid using numbers for now. Try length or percentage values instead.

lineHeight

Category: JavaScript Style Sheets

Type	Property

Browser Support

	Navigator 3	Navigator 4	Explorer 3	Explorer 4
Macintosh	☐	■	☐	☐
Windows	☐	■	☐	☐

Applies To	Block-level elements
Inherited	Yes
Syntax	lineHeight = "*value*"

lineHeight is used to define the distance between base lines of two adjacent block-level elements. Using this style you can define certain block-level elements to be either closer or further away than normal from adjacent elements. Three types of values can be used for lineHeight; each has a slightly different way in which it is used and how it is inherited.

- ■ "number" is used to specify a multiplier by which the current font size should be increased. (By increasing the font size you will increase the line height) The resulting lineHeight is not inherited by the children; only the multiplier is inherited by the children. lineHeight = 1.2 will increase the lineHeight to 1.2 times the original line height. For more information on units of measurement, see appendix D.

- ■ Using a "length" value, you can specify an exact new value for the line height. lineHeight = "1.2em" This exact value is inherited by all children.

- ■ "percentage" increases the line height to a percentage of the parent elements line height. lineHeight = 1.20 This resulting height is inherited by the children.

The values for lineHeight above all rely on inheritance to pass lineHeight on to child HTML elements. Inheritance means that an element which is considered to be child (for exmaple <p>) of the HTML element that you are working with (for example <body>) will also have the styles that you have defined for the parent HTML element that you are working with.

Defining lineHeight styles for block-level elements allows you to explicitly control the spacing of your document and keep consistency among elements over a document or many documents.

The following example defines a class for the lineHeight. You can use the lineHeight style for only certain paragraphs.

```
<html>
<style TYPE="text/javascript">
tags.p.lineHeight = "1.2em"
classes.pclass.p.lineHeight = "2.00"
</style>
```

```
<body>
<p> Paragraph 1
<p class = "pclass"> Paragraph 2
<p> Paragraph 3
<p> Paragraph 4
</body>
</html>
```

In the previous example only Paragraph 2 will be spaced away from the other paragraphs, as shown in Figure 1.

Figure 1

Taller lineHeight for the second para- graph

The two lines of JSS code in the previous example can be broken down as follows:

- classes and tags are the methods of defining JSSS styles. The classes definition describes the element immediately following it in the dot notation will be a class name. While tags defines that the element immediately following in dot notation will be the element for which the style is being defined.

- pclass is the class name that is being defined. A class name may be any alphanumeric combination.

- p is the HTML element that is being assigned a style in both the classes and tags definitions. This may be any valid HTML element.

- lineHeight is the style property that is being defined for the element.

- "2.0" and "1.2em" are the values of the style properties.

To define a generic `lineHeight` for all `<p>` elements, change the line:

```
classes.pclass.p.lineHeight = "2.00"
```

in the previous text to read:

```
tags.p.lineHeight = "2.00"
```

By doing this, all `<p>`s keep a consistent `lineHeight` style.

Link
Category: JavaScript, JScript, VBScript

		Navigator 3	Navigator 4	Explorer 3	Explorer 4
Type	Object				
Browser Support	Macintosh	■	■	☐	■
	Windows	■	■	■	■
Subset Of	Document object				
Syntax	`document.links[index].property`				

The `link` object provides script access characteristics of the hypertext link, created using the `<a>` tag in HTML. You do not refer to the `link` object by name from within a script; rather, the `link` object is an element within the `links[]` array, which itself is a property of the `document` object (see the `Document` object). For instance, consider the first hyperlink specified in HTML—its `link` object would be referenced from a script as:

```
document.links[0]
```

There are some notable differences between how Netscape Navigator and Internet Explorer handle the `link` object, so it is advised that you read the browser note.

> **NOTE** Within Netscape Navigator or Internet Explorer 4, two qualities of the `link` object should be noted:
>
> 1. Properties of the `link` object *may* be modified. Therefore, you can assign new URL's to a hyperlink. See the `link` object's properties for specific information.
>
> 2. The Document object's `links[]` array can also contain `area` objects, which reflect imagemaps created with the `<area>` tag. Items in this array are indexed according to their order in the HTML. Therefore, if your document contains an `<a>` tag hyperlink, followed by an `<area>` hyperlink, followed by another `<a>` tag hyperlink, the `link` objects would be at index points `links[0]` and `links[2]`, while `links[1]` would contain an `area` object.

Within Internet Explorer 3, *neither* of the above points applies. That is:

1. Properties of the `link` object are *read-only*, and cannot be modified. You cannot assign new URL's to a hyperlink.

2. The `document` object's `links[]` array contains only `link` objects. Internet Explorer 3 does not support the `area` object, and therefore imagemap hyperlinks are ignored in the indexing of the `links[]` array. For this reason, the same HTML document as proposed in point 2 above would contain `link` objects at `links[0]` and `links[1]`.

A `link` object is created using an <a> tag.

```
<a href="locationOrURL"
   [name="anchorName"]
   [target="windowOrFrameName"]
   [onClick="eventHandler"]
   [onMouseOut="eventHandler"]>
   [onMouseOver="eventHandler"]>
   linkTextorImage
</a>
```

hash property

Reflects the anchor portion of an HTTP URL. This includes the hash mark (#) and everything after it. For instance, consider a hyperlink which points to a URL with an anchor named `july`.

```
<a href="http://www.site.com/whatsnew.html#july>What's New Page</a>
```

Assuming that the above is the first hyperlink in the HTML document, then the script statement

```
anchtext = document.links[0].hash
```

Would assign the value "#july" to the variable `anchtext`.

You can also assign a new anchor name to the `hash` property, thereby redirecting the `link` object. In other words, recalling the example above, the script statement

```
document.links[0].hash="august"
```

Would modify the hyperlink to point to

```
http://www.site.com/whatsnew.html#august
```

Modifying the `hash` property is a convenient way to dynamically redirect a hyperlink depending on a certain condition. For instance, you might have a "What's New" page which contains anchors for each month. When the page loads, your script could determine the current date using the `date` object, and modify the `hash` property for the link leading to the "What's New" page. In this way, when the user clicks the "What's New" hyperlink, she'll always be taken to the most current anchor in the page.

Internet Explorer 3 does not support modifying the `hash` property; it is read-only.

hostname property

Reflects the host name or IP address contained in a URL. For instance, consider a hyperlink which points to a URL with the host name `www.site.com`.

```
<a href="http://www.site.com/whatsnew.html>What's New Page</a>
```

Assuming that the above is the first hyperlink in the HTML document, then the script statement

```
hosttext = document.links[0].hostname
```

Would assign the value "www.site.com" to the variable `hosttext`.

You can also assign a new host name to the `hostname` property, thereby redirecting the `link object`. In other words, recalling the example above, the script statement

```
document.links[0].hostname="www.anothersite.com"
```

Would modify the hyperlink to point to

```
http://www.anothersite.com/whatsnew.html#august
```

However, modifying the `hostname` property is not commonly done; in such cases, you'll want to modify the entire URL, via the link object's `href` property.

Internet Explorer 3 does not support modifying the `hostname` property; it is read-only.

host property

Almost exactly the same as the `hostname` property. The only difference is that the `host` property will reflect the server port number if specified in the URL, whereas the `hostname` property will not. Consider the hyperlink

```
<a href="http://www.site.com:6000/whatsnew.html>What's New Page</a>
```

In this URL, server port 6000 is specified. Most URL's do not contain a server port, which cause them to default to 80, the web server standard port. In such a case, the `host` property contains the same value as the `hostname` property.

Assuming that the above is the first hyperlink in the HTML, then

```
hosttext = document.links[0].host
```

Would assign the value "www.site.com:6000" to `hosttext`, whereas

```
hosttext = document.links[0].hostname
```

Would have assigned the value "www.site.com" to hosttext. This is the only difference between the two properties.

> Within Internet Explorer 3 or 4, the host property always contains a port number, even if one was not specified in the URL. Thus, if the location object contained the URL "http://www.site.com", the host property would contain "www.site.com:80". Recall that 80 is the default port when unspecified. Also note that this is the opposite behavior of Netscape, which does not include the port if unspecified in the URL.

> Internet Explorer 3 does not support modifying the host property; it is read-only.

href property

Reflects the entire URL specified in the hyperlink <a> tag. Recall the hyperlink

```
<a href="http://www.site.com/whatsnew.html#july>What's New Page</a>
```

Assuming that this is the first hyperlink in the HTML document, the script statement

```
url = document.links[0].href
```

Would assign the value "http://www.site.com/whatsnew.html#july" to the variable url.

Modifying the href property is the most common way to redirect the destination of a hyperlink. For instance, imagine a page which contains a series of form fields, and a hyperlink containing the text "Click here to advance to the next page."

However, just *which* page is the next page depends on options the user has selected in the various form fields. Therefore, we could write a script function which would test the state of the form fields and, depending upon the results, assign a new URL to the link object.

```
document.links[0].href="newURL"
```

When would this function be executed? Immediately upon the user clicking the hyperlink! This is covered in more detail under the onClick event handler for the link object.

> **NOTE** It's important to understand that assigning a new URL to a link object's href property does *not* immediately load that page. Rather, it merely redirects where the hyperlink *will* lead when and if the user clicks it.

> Internet Explorer 3 does not support modifying the href property; it is read-only.

`pathname` **property**

Reflects the file path portion of a URL. This begins with the first backslash following the host name or port number up until the end of the URL or the presence of a hash mark or question mark.

For instance, consider a hyperlink which points to the following URL:

```
<a href="http://www.site.com/whatsnew.html#july>What's New Page</a>
```

Assuming that the above is the first hyperlink in the HTML document, then the script statement

```
pathtext = document.links[0].pathname
```

Would assign the value "/whatsnew.html" to the variable `pathtext`.

You can also assign a new file path to the `pathname` property, thereby redirecting the `link object`. In other words, recalling the example above, the script statement

```
document.links[0].pathname="/oldwhatnews.html"
```

Would modify the hyperlink to point to

```
http://www.site.com/oldwhatsnew.html#july
```

Notice that the anchor name "july" was not lost from the URL. Assigning a new file path to the `pathname` property only modifies that portion of the URL—the rest of it remains unchanged.

The `pathname` property is rarely modified, however. Generally speaking, when you want to redirect a `link object` you should assign the new URL in its entirety to the `href` property.

> Internet Explorer 3 does not support modifying the `pathname` property; it is read-only.

`port` **property**

Reflects the port number, if specified, for the URL contained in the `link object`. Given the hyperlink

```
<a href="http://www.site.com:4096/whatsnew.html>What's New Page</a>
```

The script statement

```
urlport = document.links[0].port
```

Would assign the value 4096 to the variable `urlport`.

Few URL's specify a port number, however, because most web servers use the default port number 80. If no port number is specified in the URL, the `port` property will be empty (it will *not* contain the value 80).

Although unlikely, you could also assign a new port number to the `port` property, and the URL to which that `link` object points will change accordingly.

```
document.links[0].port=6000
```

Unlike Netscape, when within Internet Explorer 3 and 4 and no port number is specified in the location object, the port property *will* contain the value 80 (the default port for web servers).

Internet Explorer 3 does not support modifying the `port` property; it is read-only.

`protocol` property

Reflects the document delivery protocol for the URL contained in the `link` object, up to and including the colon. Given the hyperlink

```
<a href="http://www.site.com/whatsnew.html>What's New Page</a>
```

The script statement

```
urlprotcol = document.links[0].protocol
```

would assign the value "http:" to the variable `urlprotocol`. Of course, "http:" is the protocol prefix which describes all web pages, so it is the most common protocol to turn up in the `protocol` property. Other, far less common possibilites include

`file`	document is retrieved either from the local computer or remotely through FTP
`ftp`	document is retrieved through FTP
`gopher`	document is retrieved through the old Gopher protocol
`mailto`	hyperlink launches new email message to specified address
`javascript`	hyperlink leads to JavaScript statements

Although rarely modified, you could assign a protocol the `protocol` property, and the URL to which that `link` object points will change accordingly.

```
document.links[0].protocol="ftp:"
```

Internet Explorer 3 does not support modifying the `protocol` property; it is read-only.

search property

Reflects the query string, if specified, for an HTTP URL contained in the `link` object, including the preceding question mark. Given the hyperlink

```
<a href="http://www.site.com/whatsnew.html?m=2&d=10>What's New Page</a>
```

The script statement

```
urlquery = document.links[0].search
```

would assign the value "?m=2&d=10" to the variable `urlport`. The query string is a series of variable and value pairs, which are passed along to a CGI program on the server side for processing. Form data which is submitted via the "get" method are sent using a query string URL.

You could supply a hyperlink with a new query string by assigning it to the `search` property.

```
document.links[0].search = "?m=5&d=14"
```

 Internet Explorer 3 does not support modifying the `search` property; it is read-only.

target property

Reflects the name of the window or frame in which to display the clicked hyperlink, as specified by the `target` attribute of the `<a>` tag. By default, a hyperlink with no set `target` attribute will open into the same window, overwriting the contents of the current page.

However, some pages contain multiple frames. Or, some scripts open new windows on the screen. You can redirect a hyperlink to open into a particular frame or window.

```
document.links[idx].target="frameOrWindowName"
```

Frame names are created within the `<frame>` tag subordinate to the `<frameset>` tag. Window names are created using the `open()` method of the `window object` (see `Window object`).

There is also a set of built-in targets, which you can assign to the `target` property to achieve the following results:

`"_top"`	Open hyperlink into full size of current window
`"_parent"`	Open hyperlink into parent window of current window
`"_self"`	Open hyperlink into same window which hyperlink was clicked
`"_blank"`	Open hyperlink into a new, blank, unnamed window

 Internet Explorer 3 does not support modifying the `target` property; it is read-only.

onClick **event handler**

Located within the <a> tag, this will activate when the user clicks on the hyperlink. Event handler statements will execute before the URL is loaded. For instance, you could call a script function which redirects the link object depending upon certain conditions, when the user clicks the hyperlink.

```
<a href="http://www.site.com/whatsnew.html onClick="return fixlink()">What's New
Page</a>
```

The above HTML sets the onClick event handler to trigger the hypothetical script function fixlink() when the user clicks on the hyperlink. The function fixlink() will execute before the hyperlink is followed—therefore, any modifications made to the link object's properties will affect where the link actually leads when the function has completed execution.

Within Netscape Navigator, if the onClick event handler returns a value of false, the hyperlink will *not* be followed.

onMouseDown **event handler**

Located within the <a> tag, this will activate when the user presses down the mouse button on the link, but before the mouse button is released. This event handler can be used to determine if a user is "holding" the mouse button down over a link, as opposed to clicking (pressing down and releasing).

For instance:

```
<a href="http://www.site.com/dragged.html  onMouseDown="dragfunc();return
true">Drag this link into the dumpster.</a>
```

> **NOTE**   The onMouseDown event handler is only supported beginning with the version 4 releases of Netscape Navigator and Internet Explorer.

onMouseOver **event handler**

Located within the <a> tag, this will activate when the user moves the mouse on to the link, but before it is clicked. Often, this event handler is used to display a description of the hyperlink in the browser's status bar (at the bottom of the browser window border).

For instance:

```
<a href="http://www.site.com/whatsnew.html  onMouseOver="window.status='The
Latest and Greatest News';return  true">What's New Page</a>
```

When the mouse passes over this hyperlink, the browser's status message will display the specified description.

L

Figure 1

Customizing the browser status using the link *object's* onMouseOver *event handler.*

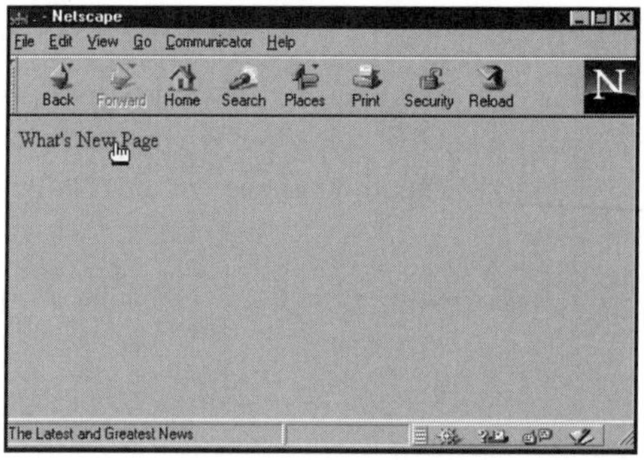

Notice that the onMouseOver event handler returns a value of true—this is necessary for the event handler to function properly.

onMouseOut event handler

Located within the <a> tag, this will activate when the user moves the mouse off the hyperlink. Typically, the onMouseOut event handler will contain statements to disable any functions invoked by the onMouseOver event handler.

In the onMouseOver example earlier, the window status message was modified by the event handler. However, this message remains on the window until the mouse moves over another hyperlink. Clearly, you'd want to remove the status message immediately after the mouse vacated the hyperlink. Simply add an onMouseOut event handler to the <a> tag which assigns an empty string to the window object's status property.

```
<a href="http://www.site.com/whatsnew.html  onMouseOver="window.status='The
Latest and Greatest News';return true"  onMouseOut="window.status='';return
true">What's New Page</a>
```

Figure 2

Using the onMouseOut *event handler, the status message disappears when the mouse moves off the hyperlink.*

Internet Explorer 3 does not support the `onMouseOut` event handler.

onMouseUp event handler

Located within the <a> tag, this will activate when the user releases the mouse button on the link, after having pressed it down. In releasing the mouse button, the user has completed a click—however, the `onMouseUp` event occurs just prior to the `onClick` event. If your `onMouseUp` event handler returns `true`, the `onClick` event will be triggered and/or the link will be followed; if this event handler returns `false`, no `onClick` event will occur and the link will not be followed.

For instance:

```
<a href="http://www.site.com/dragged.html onMouseUp="preclick();return
true">Drag this link into the dumpster.</a>
```

NOTE   The `onMouseUp` event handler is only supported beginning with the version 4 releases of Netscape Navigator and Internet Explorer.

Although Internet Explorer 4 does support the `onMouseUp` event, returning a value of false does not abort the `onClick` event or following the link.

L

<LISTING>

Category: HTML

Browser Support		Navigator 3	Navigator 4	Explorer 3	Explorer 4
	Macintosh	▬	▬	▬	▬
	Windows	▬	▬	▬	▬

May Contain None

May Be Used In <BODY>

Attributes None

Syntax <LISTING>...</LISTING>

The <LISTING> tag is an older HTML tag that renders text in fixed-width type. Theoretically, this enables a full 132 characters to fit on one line.

Only Netscape browsers actually support this part of the tag's features. Internet Explorer will translate <LISTING>-specified text into fixed-width type, but it puts more space between the individual letters so fewer characters can fit on one line. The closing, or </LISTING> tag, is required.

Many HTML authorities do not recommend using the <LISTING> tag to render text in a fixed-width font, nor do they recommend using the equally old <PLAINTEXT> or <XMP> tags, either. Use the <PRE> tag instead to create fixed-width text, and see its entry elsewhere in the book for more information.

`list-style`
Category: Cascading Style Sheets

Browser Support		Navigator 3	Navigator 4	Explorer 3	Explorer 4
	Macintosh	☐	☐	☐	☐
	Windows	☐	☐	☐	☐

Applies To Elements with `display` set to `list-item`

Syntax `<keyword> ¦¦ <position> ¦¦ <url>`

List-style is another shorthand property that enables you to set a number of different properties all at once. In this case, the properties include `list-style-type`, `list-style-image`, and `list-style-position`. See the descriptions for these properties for more information.

```
h1 { list-style: square outside }
```

```
<h1 style="list-style: upper-roman inside">
```

`list-style-image`
Category: Cascading Style Sheets

Browser Support		Navigator 3	Navigator 4	Explorer 3	Explorer 4
	Macintosh	☐	☐	☐	☐
	Windows	☐	☐	☐	☐

Applies To Elements with `display` set to `list-item`

Syntax `list-style-image : url`

The `list-style-image` property allows you to supply a graphic or image for the bullet displayed before items of your list. You supply absolute or relative URL at the `list-style-image` property, and your own custom graphic will serve as the bullet symbol. If this property is set to `none`, or if the browser fails to load the image specified, then the browser will use the value of `list-style-type` instead.

```
h1 { list-style-image: url(../graphics/bullet.gif) }
```

list-style-position

Category: Cascading Style Sheets

Browser Support		Navigator 3	Navigator 4	Explorer 3	Explorer 4
	Macintosh	☐	☐	☐	☐
	Windows	☐	☐	☐	☐

Applies To Elements with `display` set to `list-item`

Syntax `list-style-position : value`

The `list-style-position` property enables you to dictate to the browser how it draws the list item marker, symbol, or graphic with regard to the content of the list. If you set the property to `outside`, the bulleted text appears like we're used to. The bullet (or other symbol) appears "outside" the lines of text as with the item below:

- This is some

  sample text.

If you use the `inside` setting, the text "wraps around" the symbol, more like this:

- This is some
sample text.

- This is more
sample text.

```
h1 { list-style-position: inside }
```

list-style-type

Category: Cascading Style Sheets

Browser Support		Navigator 3	Navigator 4	Explorer 3	Explorer 4
	Macintosh	☐	☐	☐	☐
	Windows	☐	☐	☐	☐

Applies To Elements with `display` set to `list-item`

Syntax `list-style-type : value`

The `list-style-type` property changes the symbol displayed before items in a list. The values you use for the type include `disc`, `circle`, `square`, `decimal`, `lower-roman`, `upper-roman`, `lower-alpha`, `upper-alpha`, and `none`. You can only use this property if you also use the `display` property on the same element, and it is set to `list-item`.

```
h1 { list-style-type: square }
```

L

listStyleType

Category: JavaScript Style Sheets

Type	Property				

Browser Support

	Navigator 3	Navigator 4	Explorer 3	Explorer 4
Macintosh	☐	■	☐	☐
Windows	☐	■	☐	☐

Applies To Elements with display property value of list-item

Inherited Yes

Syntax ListStyleType = "*value*"

Unlike most other JavaScript Style Sheets properties, the listStyleType is fairly restricted in its usage. This property can only be applied against HTML list-items that have a display property. The listStyleType property defines the type of "bullet" for any HTML list item.

However, since this property is an inherited property, it can be defined as a style for non list-type HTML elements and the style will be inherited to any list-type child HTML element. The possible values that can be used for the listStyleType property are the following:

- "disc" changes the list bullets to be solid circles. This is the default value.
- "circle" displays the list bullets as open circles.
- "square" uses solid squares as the list bullets.
- "decimal" displays the list as a normal numbered list. (Using 1., 2., 3., and so on.)
- "upper-roman" displays the bullets as upper-case roman numerals.
- "lower-roman" displays the bullets as lower-case roman numerals.
- "upper-alpha" uses upper case letters as the list bullets. (Using A., B., C., and so on.)
- "lower-alpha" changes the bullet style to lower case letters (a., b., c., and so on).
- "none" causes the browser to choose it's own bullet style, which in the case of Netscape Navigator 4 is the same as circle.

By defining a simple `listStyleType` to be carried through all of your documents, you guarantee consistency as well as good user readability. The user will always know how to look for something in your document. Also, you can define different classes of `listStyleType` and use the styles through your document, as seen in the following code:

```
<HTML>
<HEAD>
<STYLE TYPE="text/JavaScript">
classes.nameclass.UL.listStyleType = "square"
classes.houseclass.UL.listStyleType = "upper-Roman"
</STYLE>
</HEAD>
<BODY>
This is a list of people and the list bullet will be a square.
<UL class="nameclass">
<LI> Kim
<LI> Ken
<LI> Colter
<LI> Colleen
<LI> Chris
<LI> Kristie
</UL>
This is a list of house colors and the list bullet will be
in roman numerals.
<UL class="houseclass">
<LI> Colonial Red
<LI> Forest Green
<LI> Blue
<LI> Stained
</UL>
</BODY>
</HTML>
```

Even in this case we only have two styles to choose from and can use those two styles consistently throughout the document (see Figure 1).

L

Figure 1

Two list style types.

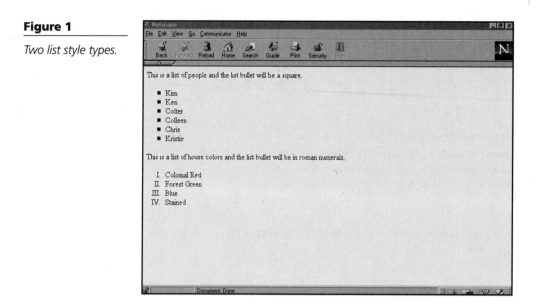

The two JSSS styles that were defined to create Figure 1

```
classes.nameclass.ul.listStyleType = "square"
classes.houseclass.ul.listStyleType = "upper-Roman"
```

can be broken down as follows:

- **classes** one of the methods of defining JSSS styles. The **classes** definition describes the element immediately following it in the dot notation will be a class name.
- **nameclass** and **houseclass** are the class names that are being defined. A class name may be any alphanumeric combination.
- **ul** defines this class to be a class the can be used only in conjunction with `<ul>` elements.
- **listStyleType** is the style property that is being defined for the element.
- **"square"** and **"upper-Roman"** are the values of the style property **listStyleType**.

Location
Category: JavaScript, JScript, and VBScript

| | Type | Object |

Browser Support

	Navigator 3	Navigator 4	Explorer 3	Explorer 4
Macintosh	■	■	□	■
Windows	■	■	▬	■

Subset Of Window object

Properties href, hash, host, hostname, pathname, port, protocol, search

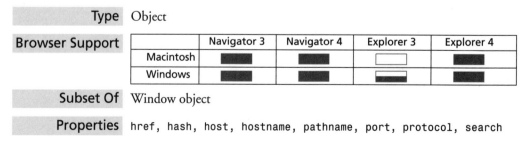

Methods	`reload()`, `replace("url")`
Syntax	`location.property` OR `windowName.frameName.location.property` OR `location.method(parameter)` OR `windowName.frameName.location.method(parameter)`

The `location` object contains the currently loaded URL. Using its properties, you can extract and/or modify various portions of the URL, enabling you to redirect the current window. You can also extract URL information of individual frames in a document by referencing a frame from the frames array; for instance:

`self.frames[1].location`

would reference the `location` object within the second frame of the current window (specified by using the `self` keyword for the *windowName*).

The quick and easy way to open a new page into a window or frame is to assign a new URL to the `location` object

`self.location="http://new.site.com"`

This would immediately load `http://new.site.com` into the current window. Doing so would effectively end the script, since it is lost when the new page is loaded into the same window. This technique is equivalent to assigning a new URL to the `location` object's `href` property.

L

> **NOTE** Remember: anytime you load a new page into the window or frame which contains the current script, that script is lost from memory! Therefore, don't redirect the `location` object of the window or frame containing your script unless you want the script to end.

`href` property

The `href` property reflects the complete current URL for the document currently loaded into the browser window; for example.

`http://www.company.com:8080/products/index.html#stuff?user1`

You can access the URL of the current window using a construction such as

`cururl=self.location.href`

Or, access the URL of the frame named *content* (within the current window) as in

`cururl=self.content.location.href`

The URL in a frame named *content* within a window named *win2* can be found with

`cururl=win2.content.location.href`

Assigning a new URL to the `href` property causes the specified window or frame to immediately load that page:

```
self.location.href="http://new.site.com"
```

You can accomplish the same result as the example above, with fewer keystrokes, by simply assigning the new URL to the location object itself, as described in the introduction to the `location` object.

hash **property**

The `hash` property reflects the anchor portion of a URL. This includes the hash mark (#) and everything after it. For instance, consider the URL

```
http://www.site.com/whatsnew.html#july
```

Assuming that this page is currently loaded into the browser window, then the script statement

```
curhash = self.location.hash
```

would assign the value "#july" to the variable `curhash`.

You can also assign a new anchor name to the `hash` property, thereby redirecting the specified page or frame object. In other words, recalling the example above, the script statement

```
self.location.hash="august"
```

would cause the current page to load the URL

```
http://www.site.com/whatsnew.html#august
```

Typically, you modify the `hash` property when a script in one frame controls the contents of another frame, such as in a classic "table of contents" web site.

```
self.framename.location.hash="newURL"
```

host **property**

The `host` property is almost exactly the same as the `hostname` property. The only difference is that the `host` property will reflect the server port number if specified in the URL, whereas the `hostname` property will not. Consider the hyperlink

```
http://www.site.com:6000/whatsnew.html
```

In this URL, server port 6000 is specified. Most URLs do not contain a server port, which causes the browser to default to port 80—the web server standard port. However, if the server port is not specified, the value of `host` will *not* contain ":80"—it will simply contain the `hostname`. Assuming that the above URL is currently loaded, then

```
curhost = self.location.host
```

would assign the value "`www.site.com:6000`" to `curhost`, whereas

```
curhost = self.location.hostname
```

would assign the value "www.site.com" to curhost. This is the only difference between the two properties host and hostname.

> Within Internet Explorer 3 or 4, the host property always contains a port number, even if one was not specified in the URL. Thus, if the location object contained the URL "http://www.site.com", the host property would contain "www.site.com:80". Recall that 80 is the default port when unspecified. Also note that this is the opposite behavior of Netscape, which does not include the port if unspecified in the URL.

Modifying this property will cause the specified frame or page to immediately re-contact the server and attempt to load the new URL. Commonly, though, you redirect pages by assigning the new URL to the location object itself—see the introduction to the location object.

hostname **property**

The hostname property is almost exactly the same as the host property. The only difference is that the hostname property only reflects the IP name of the host, and not its server port number. Consider the hyperlink

```
http://www.site.com:6000/whatsnew.html
```

In this URL, server port 6000 is specified. Most URLs do not contain a server port, which causes them to default to 80—the web server standard port. Assuming that the above URL is currently loaded, then

```
curhost = self.location.hostname
```

would assign the value "www.site.com" to curhost, omitting the server port number. Needless to say, the absence of a specified port number has no impact on the hostname property.

Modifying this property will cause the specified frame or page to immediately re-contact the server and attempt to load the new URL. Commonly, though, you redirect pages by assigning the new URL to the location object itself—see the introduction to the location object.

pathname **property**

The pathname property reflects the file path portion of a URL. This begins with the first backslash (/) following the host name or port number up until the end of the URL or the presence of a hash mark or question mark.

For instance, consider the following URL:

```
http://www.site.com/whatsnew.html#july
```

Assuming that the above example is currently loaded into the browser window, then the script statement

```
curpath = self.location.pathname
```

would assign the value "/whatsnew.html" to the variable `curpath`. Likewise, you can obtain the path for the URL loaded into a frame or other browser window:

```
curpath = windowname.framename.pathname
```

You can also assign a new file path to the `pathname` property, thereby redirecting the specified window or frame to the new URL.

```
self.frames[1].pathname="/oldwhatnews.html"
```

would load the URL

```
http://www.site.com/oldwhatsnew.html#july
```

into the second frame of the current window. Typically, this modification is used when a script in one frame controls the contents of another frame, such as in a classic "table of contents" web site.

port property

The `port` property reflects the port number, if specified, for the URL loaded into the specified window or frame. Consider the URL

```
http://www.site.com:4096/whatsnew.html
```

In this case, the script statement

```
curport = self.location.port
```

would assign the value 4096 to the variable `curport`.

Few URLs specify a port number, however, because most web servers use the default port number 80. If no port number is specified in the URL, the `port` property will be empty (it will *not* contain the value 80).

Unlike Netscape, when within Internet Explorer 3 and 4 and no port number is specified in the location object, the port property *will* contain the value 80 (the default port for web servers).

Modifying this property will cause the specified frame or page to immediately re-contact the server and attempt to load the new URL. Commonly, though, you redirect pages by assigning the new URL to the `location` object itself—see the introduction to the `location` object.

protocol property

The `protocol` property reflects the document delivery protocol for the URL loaded into the specified window or frame. Consider the URL

```
http://www.site.com/whatsnew.html
```

In this case, the script statement

```
curprotocol = self.location.protocol
```

would assign the value "http:" to the variable `curprotocol`. Of course, "http:" is the protocol prefix that describes all web pages, so it is the most common protocol to turn up in the `protocol` property. Other, far less common possibilities include:

`file`	Document is retrieved either from the local computer or remotely through FTP
`ftp`	Document is retrieved through FTP
`gopher`	Document is retrieved through the old Gopher protocol
`mailto`	Hyperlink launches new email message to specified address
`javascript`	Hyperlink leads to JavaScript statements

Modifying this property will cause the specified frame or page to immediately re-contact the server and attempt to load the new URL. Commonly, though, you redirect pages by assigning the new URL to the `location` object itself—see the introduction to the `location` object.

search **property**

The `search` property reflects the query string, if specified, for the URL. Query strings are data submitted via the "get" method to a web page, as in

```
http://www.altavista.digital.com/cgi-`bin/
query?pg=q&what=web&fmt=.&q=%22barney+beagle%22
```

The previous URL sends a query to Digital's Alta Vista search engine requesting hits for the phrase "barney beagle." For this URL, the script statement

```
curquery = self.location.search
```

would assign the value "?pg=q&what=web&fmt=.&q=%22barney+beagle%22" to the variable `curquery`. The query string is a series of variable and value pairs, each separated by an ampersand (&), which are passed along to a CGI program on the server side for processing.

You could redirect a frame, for instance, to load a page containing a new query by assigning it to that frame's `location` object `search` property.

```
self.frames[1].search = "?new=query"
```

reload() **method**

The `reload()` method forces a reload of the page currently loaded into the specified window or frame. For instance:

```
self.location.reload()
```

reloads the current page.

This reload is slightly different than if you pressed the Reload button in the browser—in this case, form data and global variables are lost and do not survive the reload. Assuming that the user's cache is operating properly, the `reload()` method will *not* retrieve the page from the server *if* the page has not since been modified on the server.

To force a true reload from the server, specify the parameter `true`:

```
self.location.reload(true)
```

Although using the `true` parameter utilizes extra bandwidth, it is sometimes necessary. Some pages include fresh data which is dynamically included from external sources—the server may not report that these pages have "changed," even though their content has. If a true reload is not forced, the user may wind up seeing the older, cached content.

Internet Explorer 3 does not support the `reload()` method.

`replace("url")` method

Use the `replace("url")` method to load a specified page (*"url"*) into a specified window or frame atop the current page's position in the history list. In other words, rather than add a new entry to the history list (the list of URL's visited during the current browsing session—see `history` object), the new page overwrites the current page.

```
self.location.replace("http://www.yahoo.com")
```

This method doesn't affect anything except how the history list is handled. Normally, when a new page is loaded, a new entry is added to the top of the history list—this method simply prevents that and writes the new page's entry in the same history list position as the page it overwrote.

Internet Explorer 3 does not support the `replace()` method.

Log()
Category: VBScript

Type	Function	

Browser Support

	Navigator 3	Navigator 4	Explorer 3	Explorer 4
Macintosh	☐	☐	☐	■
Windows	☐	☐	■	■

Syntax `Log(number)`

The `Log()` function calculates and returns the natural logarithm of a *number*, where *number* is greater than 0. The natural logarithm is the logarithm to the base *e*.

To calculate the logarithm to a different base *n*, divide the Log() function by Log(*n*). For example, to return the base 10 log of a *number,* use the formula:

```
log(number) / log(10)
```

LTrim()
Category: VBScript

		Navigator 3	Navigator 4	Explorer 3	Explorer 4
Type	Function				

Browser Support

	Navigator 3	Navigator 4	Explorer 3	Explorer 4
Macintosh	☐	☐	☐	■
Windows	☐	☐	■	■

Syntax LTrim(string)

The LTrim() function simply removes any leading spaces from the beginning of *string.*

```
ltrim("    hi there!")                 returns  "hi there!"

ltrim("    words of wisdom    ")       returns  "words of wisdom"
```

To strip spaces from the right-hand side of *string,* see the function RTrim(); to strip spaces from both sides of *string,* see Trim().

These functions can be used to remove any extraneous spaces that the user may have typed into input boxes or form fields.

L

```
</STRONG> ■ <TD> </TD> ■ <TH> </TH> ■ <TABLE> </TABLE> ■
<IMG> </IMG> ■ <SCRIPT LANGUAGE = "javascript"> </SCRIPT>
■ <SCRIPT LANGUAGE = "vbscript"> </SCRIPT> ■ <BGSOUND
SRC=gbv.wav LOOP=-1> </BGSOUND> ■ <APPLET CLASS=
"ester's_day" SRC="http://testsite/walla walla washington/"
</APPLET> ■ <FRAME></FRAME>■ <MARQUEE> </MARQUEE> ■   <HTML>
</HTML> ■ <A> </A> ■ <OL> </OL> ■ <UL> </UL> ■ <MENU> </MENU>
■ <STRONG> </STRONG> ■ <TD> </TD> ■ <TH> </TH>
```

<MAP>

Category: HTML

Browser Support

	Navigator 3	Navigator 4	Explorer 3	Explorer 4
Macintosh	■	■	■	■
Windows	■	■	■	■

May Contain <AREA>

May Be Used In <ADDRESS>, <APPLET>, <B>, <BIG>, <BLOCKQUOTE>, <BODY>, <CAPTION>, <CENTER>, <CITE>, <CODE>, <DD>, <DT>, <FONT>, <H1>, <H2>, <H3>, <H4>, <H5>, <H6>, <I>, <KBD>, <LI>, <P>, <SAMP>, <SMALL>, <STRIKE>, <STRONG>, <SUB>, <SUP>, <TD>, <TH>, <TT>, <U>

Attributes NAME

Syntax <MAP>...</MAP>

The <MAP> tag is one of two necessary elements used to create client-side imagemaps. An imagemap is a two-part element on a web page that serves as a navigational tool: a single image or picture file that displays on your web page, and the related, many-sectioned HTML working behind it. Each individual, HTML-specified section of the imagemap links a user to something elsewhere on the web, even though you only use one graphic file for the entire thing.

The <MAP> tag specifies all the instructional imagemap information laid out by the <AREA> tag and its attributes—how many clickable linked areas, or hot spots, are included in the imagemap; what size and shape they are; where each hot spot links the visitor when it is clicked; and more. NAME, the sole <MAP> attribute, assigns a name to this imagemap, which is referenced by the second necessary element—the <IMG> tag. In the case of creating an imagemap, the <IMG> tag specifies the file name of the image displayed on the web page along with certain size and appearance instructions, plus the NAME of the <MAP> tag file.

Here is a simple example of how the <MAP> and <IMG> tags work together to create an imagemap:

```
<IMG SRC="buttonbar.gif" BORDER=0 USEMAP="map1">
<MAP NAME="map1">
<AREA SHAPE="RECT" COORDS="10, 10, 40, 70" HREF="links.html">
<AREA SHAPE="RECT" COORDS="60, 10, 90, 70" HREF="resume.html">
```

```
<AREA SHAPE="RECT" COORDS="110, 10, 140, 70" HREF="gallery.html">
</MAP>
```

Notice that map1 is the same value assigned to both the <IMG> tag USEMAP attribute and the <MAP> tag NAME attribute. This value is the linchpin that holds all this information together to make the imagemap work properly.

The <AREA> tag and its attributes must be placed within the <MAP> tag, so a closing, or </MAP> tag, is needed.

NAME

The NAME attribute of the <MAP> tag is used to assign a name to the <MAP> portion of an imagemap. It is then referenced using the USEMAP attribute within the corresponding <IMG> information to link the two necessary elements together.

In the following example, map1 represents the name of the imagemap:

```
<IMG SRC="buttonbar.gif" BORDER=0 USEMAP="map1">
<MAP NAME="map1">
<AREA SHAPE="RECT" COORDS="10, 10, 40, 70" HREF="links.html">
<AREA SHAPE="RECT" COORDS="60, 10, 90, 70" HREF="resume.html">
<AREA SHAPE="RECT" COORDS="110, 10, 140, 70" HREF="gallery.html">
</MAP>
```

Remember that the NAME-specified information is case-sensitive, so you must type it in correctly when specifying it again in the <IMG> portion using USEMAP, or your imagemap will not work.

---

margin
Category: Cascading Style Sheets

Browser Support		Navigator 3	Navigator 4	Explorer 3	Explorer 4
	Macintosh	☐	■	▬	☐
	Windows	☐	■	▬	■

Applies To All elements

Syntax margin: top_value right_value bottom_value left_value

The margin property is a shorthand property that includes margin-top, margin-bottom, margin-right, and margin-left. You specify the four values of these other properties all at one time in the order top, right, bottom, and finally left. You can likewise set the margins with specific values, percentages, and with the auto keyword. See the descriptions of these other four properties for more information.

```
h1 { margin: 20px 10px 20px 40px }

h1 { margin: 34% 27% }
```

Navigator 4 doesn't support `margin`. You have to use the four individual margin properties instead.

```html
<html>
 <style type="text/css">
 <!--
  body { background: white }
  h3    { margin: 10% 30% 20% 5% }
  -->
 </style>
<head>
 <title>Specifying All Margins</title>
</head>
<body>
 <h3>I'm giddy with the joy that margins bring. Through margin,
 margin-top, margin-right, margin-bottom, and margin-left, I can
 skip merrily along in my Web design, moving text around like I'm
 using a virtual shovel. It is indeed wondrous.</h3>
 <p>Here's a second paragraph.</p>
</body>
</html>
```

In this example, I've specified values for all four margins. According to the official style sheets spec, they should be interpreted by the browser in this order: `margin-top`, `margin-right`, `margin-bottom`, `margin-left`. Internet Explorer is right on the mark: the paragraph is displayed with a top margin of 10%, a right margin of 30%, a bottom margin of 20%, and a left margin of 5% (see Figure 1).

M

Figure 1

Explorer supports percentage values for margin.

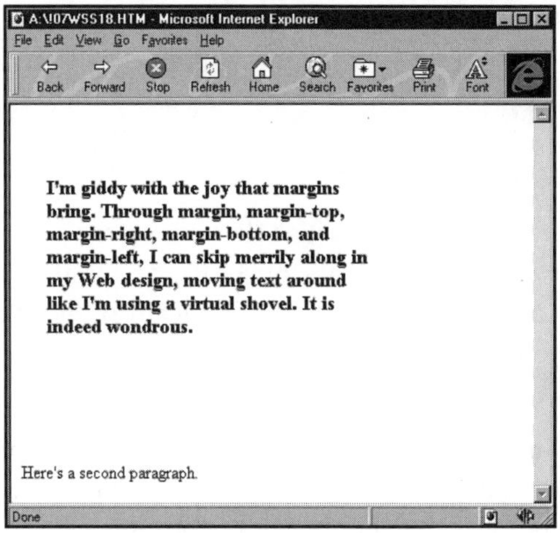

![Screenshot of Microsoft Internet Explorer window titled "A:\07WSS18.HTM - Microsoft Internet Explorer" displaying text: "I'm giddy with the joy that margins bring. Through margin, margin-top, margin-right, margin-bottom, and margin-left, I can skip merrily along in my Web design, moving text around like I'm using a virtual shovel. It is indeed wondrous." followed by "Here's a second paragraph."]

You don't have to provide all four values every time:

- h3 { margin: 20% }

  Listing one value only tells the browser to use that value for every single margin: top, right, bottom, and left.

- h3 { margin: 20% 5% }

  Providing two values tells the browser to take the first value as the top and bottom margins, and the second value as the right and left margins.

- h3 { margin: 20% 5% 12% }

  Use three values, and the first will be the top margin, the second will be the right *and* left margins, and the third will be the bottom margin.

> Percentage values work fine for margin, but in Explorer 3, other values do not. If you list four different pixel values, for instance, Explorer will ignore all but the *first* value. It will then use that first value to specify all the different margins. So, if you have…
>
> h3 { margin: 10px 30px 20px 5px }
>
> …then Explorer will use 10 pixels for *every* margin, even though there are other values specified.

---

margin-bottom
Category: Cascading Style Sheets

Browser Support		Navigator 3	Navigator 4	Explorer 3	Explorer 4
	Macintosh	☐	■	▬	☐
	Windows	☐	■	▬	■

Applies To	All elements

Syntax	margin-bottom: *value*

The margin-bottom property sets the margin below elements on the page. A margin is the space on all four sides of a page between the ends of the physical page and the beginning of the page content or graphics. You can use a specific length value with any of the units discussed in Appendix D. You can also specify a percentage value means that the margin takes its size from the box size of the parent element. 0% means no margin.

Your final choice for margin-bottom is a setting of auto, which means that the browser automatically calculates the element's bottom margin so that the sum of it, the top margin, the top border, the top padding, the element's height, the bottom padding, and the bottom border equals the entire parent element's total box height.

```
h1 { margin-bottom: 20px }
```

```
<h1 style="margin-bottom: auto">
```

Keep in mind that the first beta of Explorer 4 does not support top or bottom margins at all.

Explorer 3 doesn't recognize `margin-bottom` for every single tag. For example, if you give a `margin-bottom` to `<span>` or `<body>`, Explorer ignores it entirely and won't display a bottom margin.

marginBottom
Category: JavaScript Style Sheets

Type	Property

Browser Support		Navigator 3	Navigator 4	Explorer 3	Explorer 4
	Macintosh	☐	▉	☐	☐
	Windows	☐	▉	☐	☐

Applies To	All elements

Inherited	No

Syntax	marginBottom = "value"

marginBottom can be used by itself, or in conjunction with any of the other margin properties (marginTop, marginLeft, marginRight). marginBottom is used to define the margin of an element, where the margin is the distance between the current element and the other elements surrounding it. marginBottom can take two types of values:

- The "length" defines the size of the margin in an absolute font size. The following code segment will make the style for all `<h1>` bottom margins be 1.2 times larger than the font size of the parent element.

  ```
  Tags.h1.marginBottom = "1.2em"
  ```

- "percentage" makes the margin size a percentage of the current element font size. The following code sample makes the same bottom margin style be 150 percent of the current `<h1>` font size.

  ```
  Tags.h1.marginBottom = "1.50"
  ```

By defining the JavaScript Style Sheets property of marginBottom for `<img>` tags, each image will have a larger than normal margin on the bottom.

The following example shows how to align all images along the right-hand border and any text that falls below the image will not crowd the bottom of the image, as can be seen in Figure 1.

```html
<html>
<style TYPE="text/javascript">
with (tags.img) {
align = "right";
marginBottom = "200.00";
}
</style>
<body>
<img SRC=sciex.gif>
<p> After the text stops wrapping around the image to the left
and continues along the bottom of the image, it will leave a margin
on the bottom of 200% the images font size.
<p> After the text stops wrapping around the image to the left
and continues along the bottom of the image, it will leave a margin
on the bottom of 200% the images font size. After the text stops wrappi
ng around the image to the left and continues along the bottom of the image, it
will leave a margin on the bottom of 200% the images font size.

</body>
</html>
```

Figure 1

Image with large bottom margin defined.

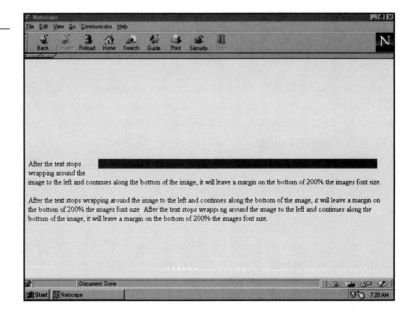

The JSSS code

```
with (tags.img) {
align = "right";
marginBottom = "200.00";
```

that is contained in the HTML used to create Figure 1 can be broken down as follows:

- ■ with {…} do as a JavaScript function used in our example to define multiple style properties for a single HTML element <img> all within a single statement.

- ■ tags is one of the methods of defining JSSS styles. The tags definition describes the element immediately following it if the dot notation will be one of the accepted HTML elements.

- ■ img is the HTML element that is being assigned a style. This may be any valid HTML element.

- ■ marginBottom (and align) are the styles that is being defined for the element. They may be any valid JSSS style.

- ■ "200.00" is the value of the style marginBottom.

Element margins may actually be larger than defined for a particular element style based on the margins, borders, and sizing for styles of other elements. Using the margins property you can be assured that your margin will be at least as large as you have defined it.

M

margin-left
Category: Cascading Style Sheets

Browser Support		Navigator 3	Navigator 4	Explorer 3	Explorer 4
	Macintosh	☐	■	▬	☐
	Windows	☐	■	▬	■

Applies To   All elements

Syntax   margin-right : *value*

Margin-left works just like margin-right (and margin-top and margin-bottom). The property sets the margin to the left of an element. You can use a specific length value with any of the units discussed in Appendix D, or a percentage value that is taken from the box size of the parent element. A setting of auto means that the browser automatically calculates the margin so that the sum of it, the left border, the left padding, the element's width, the right padding, right margin, and the right border equals the entire parent element's total box width.

```
h1 { margin-left: 20px }
```

```
h1 { margin-left: 10% }
```

Although Explorer 4 gives a right margin to an image just fine, it fails to give a left margin to an image.

marginLeft

Category: JavaScript Style Sheets

Type	Property

Browser Support

	Navigator 3	Navigator 4	Explorer 3	Explorer 4
Macintosh	☐	■	☐	☐
Windows	☐	■	☐	☐

Applies To	All elements
Inherited	No
Syntax	marginLeft = "*value*"

marginLeft can be used by itself, or in conjunction with any of the other margin properties (marginTop, marginBottom, marginRight). marginLeft is used to define the left margin of an element, where the margin is the distance between the current element and the other elements surrounding it. marginLeft can take two types of values:

■ The "length" value defines the size of the margin in an absolute font size. The following code segment makes the style for all <h1> left margins be 1.2 times larger than the font size of the parent element.

```
Tags.h1.marginLeft = "1.2em"
```

■ Using the "percentage" will make the margin size a percentage of the current element font size. The following code sample will make the same left margin style be 150 percent of the current <h1> font size.

```
Tags.h1.marginLeft = "1.50"
```

In the following example, by defining the JavaScript Style Sheets property of marginLeft for <img> tags, each image will have a margin on the left-hand side that is four times larger than a default margin.

```
<html>
<style TYPE="text/javascript">
with (tags.img){
align = "right"
marginBottom = "2.00"
marginLeft = "4.00"
}
</style>
<body>
```

```
<img SRC=kim1.gif>
<div> Display text to the left side of the first image
</div>
<img SRC=kim2.gif>
<div> Display more text to the left side of the second image
<p> After the text stops wrapping around the image to the left
and continues along the bottom of the image, it will leave a margin
on the bottom of 200% the images font size.
</div>
</body>
</html>
```

The JSSS code

```
with (tags.img){
align = "right"
marginBottom = "2.00"
marginLeft = "4.00"
```

that is contained in the preceding HTML code can be broken down as follows:

- with {…} do as a JavaScript function used in our example to define multiple style properties for a single HTML element <img> all within a single statement.

- tags is one of the methods of defining JSSS styles. The tags definition describes the element immediately following it if the dot notation will be one of the accepted HTML elements.

- img is the HTML element that is being assigned a style. This may be any valid html element.

- marginLeft (and marginBottom) are the styles that is being defined for the element. They may be any valid JSSS style.

- "4.00" is the value of the style marginLeft.

Element margins may actually be larger than defined for a particular element's style based on the margins, borders, and sizing for styles of other elements. By using the margins property, you can be sure that your margin will be at least as large as you have defined it.

margin-right
Category: Cascading Style Sheets

Browser Support		Navigator 3	Navigator 4	Explorer 3	Explorer 4
	Macintosh	☐	■	■	☐
	Windows	☐	■	■	■

Applies To All elements

Syntax margin-right: *value*

M

margin-right works just like margin-top and margin-bottom, more or less. The property sets the margin to the right of an element. You can use a specific length value with any of the units discussed in Appendix D or a percentage value that is taken from the box size of the parent element. A setting of auto means that the browser automatically calculates the margin so that the sum of it, the left margin, the left border, the left padding, the element's width, the right padding, and the right border equals the entire parent element's total box width.

```
h1 { margin-right: 20px }
```

```
h1 { margin-right: 10% }
```

One thing to note is that you can't use margin-right to add horizontal space between two replaced elements (images, for example). The browsers ignore any attempt to do so. Apparently, the only way to adjust the margin horizontally between two elements (text or replaced elements) is if the two elements are in adjoining table cells.

> **TIP** Restrict margins to block-level elements. Browsers don't handle margin setting of inline elements.

An important thing to note about margin-right (and also margin-left—see the specifics in its own entry) is that horizontal margins are *cumulative*. If you put a 50-pixel right margin on the <body> tag and a 25-pixel margin on <h1>, then all level-one heading text on the page will have a right margin of *75* pixels—the sum of the two applied margins. This is different from normal inheritance; we'd expect the margin on <h1> to be just 25 pixels, but it's not.

This is not the case with margin-top. A margin-top value for <body> will not "trickle down" to other elements on the page. If the same values were applied to margin-top instead of margin-right, then all <h1> text would get just a 25-pixel top margin, not 75 pixels.

marginRight

Category: JavaScript Style Sheets

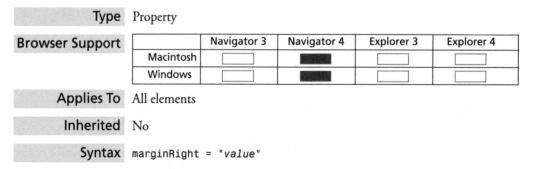

		Navigator 3	Navigator 4	Explorer 3	Explorer 4
Type	Property				
Browser Support					
	Macintosh	☐	■	☐	☐
	Windows	☐	■	☐	☐
Applies To	All elements				
Inherited	No				
Syntax	marginRight = "*value*"				

marginRight can be used by itself, or in conjunction with any of the other margin properties (marginTop, marginLeft, marginBottom). marginRight, like marginLeft and marginTop, is used to define the right margin of an element, where the margin is the distance between the current element and the other elements surrounding it. marginRight can take two types of values:

- "length" defines the size of the margin in an absolute font size. The following code segment will make the style for all <h1> right margins be two times larger than the font size of the parent element.

  ```
  Tags.h1.marginRight= "2.0em"
  ```

- "percentage" makes the margin size a percentage of the current element font size. The following code sample will make the same right margin style be 150 percent of the current <h1> font size.

  ```
  Tags.h1.marginRight= "1.50"
  ```

By defining the JavaScript Style Sheets property of marginRight in conjunction with marginLeft for <p> tags, each paragraph will have a larger than normal margin.

```
<html>
<style TYPE="text/javascript">
with (classes.marginclass.p){
marginRight = "50.00"
marginLeft = "50.00"
}
</style>
<body>
<img src="scisess.gif">
<p> The text in this paragraph does not have increased margin because
it does not have the class of "magrinclass" in it's definition.
<p>
<div class="marginclass"> This text, while it is defined with "marginclass"
do not have large margins because "marginclass" has been defined only to
apply to paragraphs.
<p class="marginclass"> Finally, this text will have the large margins defined
in the style because it a paragraph and has the class in it's definition.
</div>
</body>
</html>
```

Figure 1 shows the display of the previous HTML code segment. If the <p> does not have the class definition included in it's tag then it will not take on the margin style has been defined for use with <p> elements. Also, notice that the margin style is defined for only <p> elements and thus when used for <div> elements that margin style will not be applied.

M

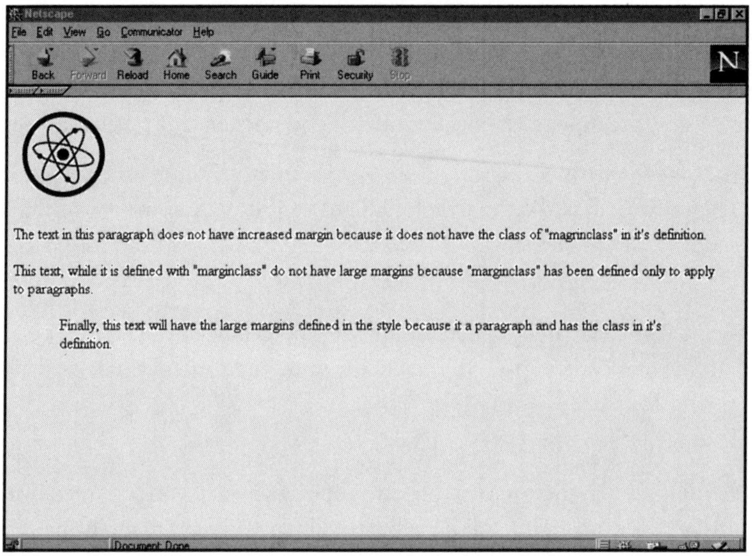

Figure 1

A paragraph with left and right margins defined.

The JSSS code

```
with (classes.marginclass.p){
marginRight = "50.00"
marginLeft = "50.00"
```

that is contained in the HTML used to create Figure 1 is broken down as follows:

- with {...} do as a JavaScript function used in our example to define multiple style properties for a single HTML element <p> all within a single statement.

- classes is one of the methods of defining JSSS styles. The classes definition describes the element immediately following it if the dot notation will be a class name.

- marginclass is the name of class that has been defined for this style. The class name can be any alphanumeric combination.

- p is the html element that is being assigned a style. This may be any valid html element.

- marginRight (and marginLeft) are the styles that is being defined for the element. They may be any valid JSSS style.

- "50.00" is the value of the style marginRight.

Element margins may actually be larger than defined for a particular elements style based on the margins, borders, and sizing for styles of other elements. Using the margins property you can be sure that your margin will be at least as large as you have defined it.

margins()

Category: JavaScript Style Sheets

| | Type | Property |

Type Property

Browser Support

	Navigator 3	Navigator 4	Explorer 3	Explorer 4
Macintosh	☐	■	☐	☐
Windows	☐	■	☐	☐

Applies To All elements

Inherited No

Syntax margins(value1, value2, value3, value4)

The margins() property is a much more consise method for defining the four margin properties (marginLeft, marginRight, marginTop, marginBottom) for an HTML element. The four elements are defined as arguments in the following manner:

```
tags.margins(top,right,bottom,left)
```

margins() is used to define the margins around an element, where the margin is the distance between the current element and the other elements surrounding it. margins() can take two types of values:

- ■ "length" defines the size of the margin in an absolute font size. The following code segment will make the style for all <h1> margins be 2.0 times larger than the font size of the parent element.

    ```
    Tags.h1.margins("2.0em", "2.0em", "2.0em", "2.0em")
    ```

- ■ "percentage" makes the margin size a percentage of the current element font size. The following code sample will make the margin style be 200% of the current <h1> font size.

    ```
    Tags.h1.margins("2.00", "2.00", "2.00", "2.00")
    ```

Using the JavaScript Style Sheets property of margins() allows for all margin properties to be defined in a single statement. The following code:

```
<style TYPE="text/javascript">
with (classes.marginclass.p){
marginRight = "20.00"
marginLeft = "20.00"
marginTop = "70.00"
marginBottom = "20.00"
}
</style>
```

M

was taken from this complete sample code:

```
<html>
<style TYPE="text/javascript">
with (classes.marginclass.p){
marginRight = "20.00"
marginLeft = "20.00"
marginTop = "70.00"
marginBottom = "20.00"
}
</style>
<body>
<img src="scisess.gif">
<p class="marginclass"> This text will have the large margins defined
in the style because it a paragraph and has the class in it's definition.
This text will also be displayed further away from the image
because a large top margin has been defined.
<div class="marginclass"> This text, while it is defined with "marginclass"
do not have large margins because "marginclass" has been defined only to
apply to paragraphs.
<p> This will be a paragraph with no margins
<p class="marginclass"> This text will have the large margins defined
in the style because it a paragraph and has the class in it's definition.
This text will also be displayed further away from the previous element
because a large top margin has been defined.
</div>
</body>
</html>
```

and can be replaced with the following code to obtain the same results, as displayed in Figure 1:

```
<style TYPE="text/javascript">
classes.marginclass.p.margins("70.00", "20.00", "20.00", "20.00")
</style>
```

Figure 1

Image with all margin styles defined using margins()*.*

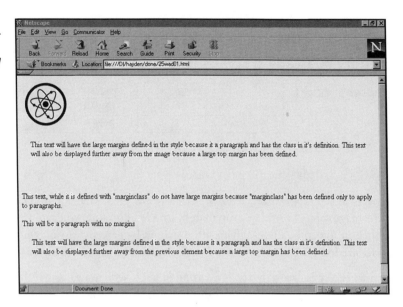

The JSSS code

```
classes.marginclass.p.margins("70.00", "20.00", "20.00", "20.00")
```

that is contained in the HTML used to create Figure 1 is broken down as follows:

M

- classes is one of the methods of defining JSSS styles. The classes definition describes the element immediately following it in the dot notation will be a class name.

- marginclass is the name of class that has been defined for this style. The class name can be any alphanumeric combination.

- p is the HTML element that is being assigned a style. This may be any valid HTML element.

- margins() is the style that is being defined for the element. It may be any valid JSSS style.

- "20.00" and "50.00" are the values of the style margins().

Element margins may actually be larger than defined for a particular elements style based on the margins, borders, and sizing for styles of other elements. Using the margins property you can be assured that your margin will be at least as large as you have defined it.

margin-top

Category: Cascading Style Sheets

Browser Support

	Navigator 3	Navigator 4	Explorer 3	Explorer 4
Macintosh	□	■	▨	□
Windows	□	■	▨	■

Applies To All elements

Syntax `margin-top: value`

The `margin-top` property sets the margin above any given element. You can use any length value or percentage value. In setting a top margin by a length value, you can use any length unit described in Appendix D. Specifying a top margin by percentage value means that the margin takes its size from the box size of the parent element. `0%` means no top margin.

Your final choice for `margin-top` is a setting of `auto`, which means that the browser automatically calculates the element's top margin so that the sum of it, the top border, the top padding, the element's height, the bottom padding, the bottom border, and the bottom margin equals the entire parent element's total box height.

```
h1 { margin-top: 20px }
```

```
h1 { margin-top: 10% }
```

You can apply margins to images as well as to text. The easiest way is to specify a style to the `<img>` tag. But you can also add margin-related tags to another tag, and then have `<img>` inherit those styles.

With Navigator 4 you have to use this inheritance workaround, because this browser ignores any styles the `<img>` tag itself has. You will have to embed the `<img>` tag within another item such as `<span>`.

Explorer 4.0, at least in its first beta version, does not support vertical margins at all (top or bottom)! This should be fixed before the final release.

Let's look at an example:

```
<html>
 <style type="text/css">
 <!--
  span.a { margin-top: 30px;
           font-size: 20pt }
  span.b { margin-top: 1in;
           font-size: 20pt }
```

```
  span.c { font-size: 20pt }
  -->
 </style>
<head>
 <title>Specifying a Top Margin</title>
</head>
<body>
 <img height=10 width=480 SRC="box-sm.gif"><br>
 <span CLASS=c>This is text with a 0 margin.
 <img align=top SRC="box-C.gif"></span>
 <p></p>
 <img height=10 width=480 src="box-sm.gif"><br>
 <span class=a>This is text with a 30-pixel margin.
 <img align=top src="box-C.gif"></span>
 <p></p>
 <img height=10 width=480 src="box-sm.gif"><br>
 <span class=b>This is text with a 1-inch margin.
 <img align=top src="box-C.gif"></span>
</body>
</html>
```

As you can see, both the text lines and the rectangles can be moved down from the base solid line using different values for `margin-top` (see Figure 1).

M

Figure 1

Adjust `margin-top` by a certain length, and you get different top margins. Simple.

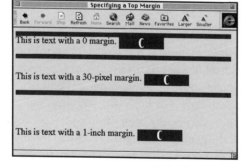

> The Windows 95 version of Explorer 3 is sometimes erratic in how it displays the "ruler units" (inches, centimeters, and so on) for `margin-top`. Often it will add a certain amount of extra space to top margins. With other margins, however, the display seems accurate. The Mac version doesn't have this problem at all.

NOTE   Internet Explorer 3 and Navigator 4 do not support `auto`.

Overlapping text and images is easy by simply giving negative values to `margin-top` as with the following example:

```
<html>
 <style type="text/css">
 <!--
   body { background: gray;
          color: white;
          font-size: 30px }
   h1    { color: black;
          font-family: arial }
   p.a   { margin-top: -33px }
   .b    { margin-top: -33px }
 -->
 </style>
<head>
 <title>Specifying a Negative Top Margin</title>
</head>
<body>
 <img height=50 width=240 src="box-med.gif">
 <p class=a>Negative margins! My stars!</p>
 <p></p>
 <img height=50 width=240 src="box-med.gif">
 <br><span class=b>Negative margins! My stars!</span>
 <p></p>
 <h1>This is unaffected text.</h1>
 <span class=b>Negative margins! My stars!</span>
</body>
</html>
```

Figure 2 shows the results. A negative margin on the white text line brings it right up into the element above it. But even though all of these lines have the same negative margins (–33 pixels), how much they "invade" the element above them depends on the situation. As you can see, there's a <p> between the rectangle and the text in the first example, but only a <br> in the second. So because there would normally be (by browser default) less existing vertical space in the second, the text line overlaps the graphics more than it does in the first.

Figure 2

Negative margin-top values translate into overlapping elements.

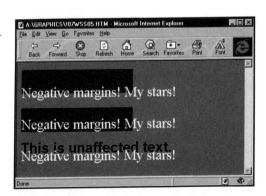

marginTop

Category: JavaScript Style Sheets

Type	Property

Browser Support

	Navigator 3	Navigator 4	Explorer 3	Explorer 4
Macintosh	☐	■	☐	☐
Windows	☐	■	☐	☐

Applies To	All elements
Inherited	No
Syntax	marginTop = "*value*"

marginTop can be used by itself, or in conjunction with any of the other margin properties (marginRight, marginLeft, marginBottom). marginTop, like marginLeft, marginRight, and marginBottom, is used to define the top margin of an element, where the margin is the distance between the current element and the other elements surrounding it. marginTop can take two types of values:

- ■ "length" defines the size of the margin in an absolute font size. The following code segment will make the style for all <h1> top margins be 2.0 times larger than the font size of the parent element.

  ```
  Tags.h1.marginTop = "2.0em"
  ```

- ■ "percentage" makes the margin size a percentage of the current element font size. The following code sample will make the same top margin style be 200 percent of the current <h1> font size.

  ```
  Tags.h1.marginTop = "2.00"
  ```

By defining the JavaScript Style Sheets property of marginTop in conjunction with all the other margin styles for <p> tags, each paragraph will have a wide margin to separate it from other elements.

```
<html>
<style TYPE="text/javascript">
with (classes.marginclass.p){
marginRight = "50.00"
marginLeft = "50.00"
marginTop = "50.00"
}
</style>
<body>
<img src="scisess.gif">
<p class="marginclass"> This text will have the large margins defined
in the style because it a paragraph and has the class in it's definition.
This text will also be displayed further away from the image
because a large top margin has been defined.
```

M

```
<div class="marginclass"> This text, while it is defined with "marginclass"
do not have large margins because "marginclass" has been defined only to
apply to paragraphs.
<p> This will be a paragraph with no margins
<p class="marginclass"> This text will have the large margins defined
in the style because it a paragraph and has the class in it's definition.
This text will also be displayed further away from the previous element
because a large top margin has been defined.
</div>
</body>
</html>
```

Figure 1 shows the display of the previous HTML code segment. If the <p> does not have the class definition included in its tag then it will not take on the margin style has been defined for use with <p> elements. Also, notice that the margin style is defined for only <p> elements and thus when used for <div> elements that margin style will not be applied.

Figure 1

Image with all margin styles defined.

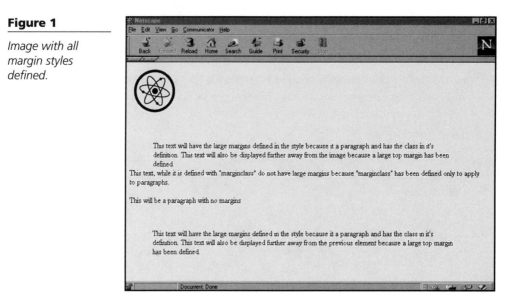

The JSSS code

```
with (classes.marginclass.p){
marginRight = "50.00"
marginLeft = "50.00"
marginTop = "50.00"
```

that is contained in the HTML used to create Figure 1 is broken down as follows:

- with {…} do as a JavaScript function used in our example to define multiple style properties for a single HTML element <p> all within a single statement.

- **classes** is one of the methods of defining JSSS styles. The **classes** definition describes the element immediately following it in the dot notation will be a class name.
- **marginclass** is the name of class that has been defined for this style. The class name can be any alphanumeric combination.
- **p** is the HTML element that is being assigned a style. This may be any valid HTML element.
- **marginTop** (and **marginRight** and **marginLeft**) are the styles that is being defined for the element. They may be any valid JSSS style.
- **"50.00"** is the value of the style **marginTop**.

Element margins may actually be larger than defined for a particular elements style based on the margins, borders, and sizing for styles of other elements. Using the **margins** property you can be assured that your margin will be at least as large as you have defined it.

<MARQUEE>

Category: HTML

Browser Support		Navigator 3	Navigator 4	Explorer 3	Explorer 4
	Macintosh	☐	☐	■	■
	Windows	☐	☐	■	■

May Contain None

May Be Used In `<BLOCKQUOTE>`, `<BODY>`, `<CENTER>`, `<DD>`, `<DIV>`, `<FORM>`, `<LI>`, `<TD>`, `<TH>`

Attributes `ALIGN, BEHAVIOR, BGCOLOR, HEIGHT, HSPACE, LOOP, SCROLLAMOUNT, SCROLLDELAY, VSPACE, WIDTH`

Syntax `<MARQUEE>...</MARQUEE>`

The `<MARQUEE>` tag creates a scrolling text marquee across a particular part of a web page. Its attributes control the action, speed, appearance, and size of the marquee, and a closing, or `</MARQUEE>`, tag is required.

> **NOTE** This tag is not supported by Netscape browsers—any text you specify with `<MARQUEE>` will be displayed as regular non-moving text by Navigator. Because most surfers are using some version of Navigator (at this writing), you should consider this syntactical problem before using `<MARQUEE>` in your page.

This example illustrates the most basic `<MARQUEE>` HTML, minus attribute settings to be established later:

```
<MARQUEE>This is the text that will scroll across the page.</MARQUEE>
```

A marquee with no attributes will automatically scroll in as soon as the text—not the images—is finished loading, with a plain gray background and default font settings, and the marquee text will play continuously.

> **NOTE**   There are other ways to add a marquee to a web page but Java applets or JavaScripts are required. Java applets are not covered in this book, but JavaScripts are—see the "JavaScript Basics" chapter of this book for more information on the available options.

ALIGN

The ALIGN attribute determines the alignment of surrounding text in relation to the marquee. It has six values:

Value	Result
bottom	The surrounding text is aligned with the bottom of the marquee.
center	The surrounding text is aligned with the center of the marquee.
left	The surrounding text is aligned with the left of the marquee. This is the ALIGN attribute default.
middle	The surrounding text is aligned with the middle of the marquee.
right	The surrounding text is aligned with the right of the marquee.
top	The surrounding text is aligned with the center of the marquee.

> **NOTE**   The ALIGN attribute is not supported by Internet Explorer 3 for the Mac or Windows.

BEHAVIOR

The BEHAVIOR attribute determines how the text will behave within the marquee as it passes across the web page. There are three values to choose from:

Value	Result
alternate	The text will bounce back and forth from left to right within the marquee.
scroll	The text will appear from one side, scroll completely across the page, and disappear off the other side before starting again. This is the BEHAVIOR attribute default.
slide	The text will appear from one side, scroll completely across the page, and stop when it arrives at the other side.

The SCROLLDELAY attribute will affect the performance of these values, as it specifies an amount of pause time between marquee runs. If you're going to use both the BEHAVIOR and the SCROLLDELAY attributes together, test your marquee thoroughly.

BGCOLOR

The BGCOLOR attribute establishes a background color for the marquee field with either a color name or a hexadecimal value.

So you can specify the color white by writing either

```
<MARQUEE BGCOLOR="white">This is the text that will scroll across the page.
➡</MARQUEE>
```

or

```
<MARQUEE BGCOLOR="#ffffff">This is the text that will scroll across the page.
➡</MARQUEE>
```

There are 16 colors you can specify in English and dozens of colors you can specify by hexadecimal value. See Appendix B for an in-depth discussion of color choices.

In the following examples, the background color of the entire page has been specified as dark gray and the background color of the marquee has been specified as white—this will enable you to make comparisons even though the figures in this book are black and white only. (The boundaries of the marquee path have been set using the VSPACE, HSPACE, and WIDTH attributes described later in this section.)

Figures 1 and 2 illustrate the effects of the BGCOLOR attribute in Internet Explorer for Mac and Windows.

M

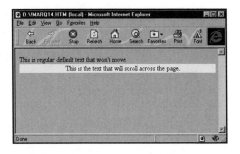

Figure 1

The track of a basic marquee with a white background in Internet Explorer 3 for the Mac.

Figure 2

The track of a basic marquee with a white background in Internet Explorer 3 for Windows.

As you can see, the track of a marquee in Windows is wider than a marquee track with the same left margin, right margin, and width measurements on the Mac. This is a hardware discrepancy—text on a Windows monitor appears taller and with more space between individual characters than on a Mac. There's nothing you can do about this difference in HTML, but you should keep it in mind as you're designing your web page.

DIRECTION

The DIRECTION attribute determines if the marquee will roll in from left to right or right to left. It has two values:

left

The text will scroll from right to left, entering from the right side of the screen and exiting on the left. This is the DIRECTION attribute default.

right

The text will scroll from left to right, entering from the left side of the screen and exiting on the right.

DESIGN NOTE	If you're designing a web page in Arabic, Chinese, or any other language that is read from right to left (the opposite of English and other Western languages, which are read from left to right) your marquees should also roll in from right to left. Otherwise native readers of these languages will be instinctively looking at the wrong side of the browser window when the marquee text begins to scroll across.

HEIGHT

The HEIGHT attribute specifies the height of the marquee either in pixels or as a percentage of the overall screen height.

A pixel-specified setting is established as follows:

<MARQUEE HEIGHT=25>This is the text that will scroll across the page.</MARQUEE>

and a percentage-specified setting is established like this:

<MARQUEE HEIGHT=25%>This is the text that will scroll across the page.</MARQUEE>

Figures 3 and 4 illustrate three marquees apiece—the top with a HEIGHT-specified setting of 25 pixels, the middle at the default width, and the bottom at a HEIGHT-specified setting of 12.5%—in Internet Explorer 3 for the Mac and for Windows. The background color of the marquee tracks have been preserved as white so you can see the contrast in these black and white figures.

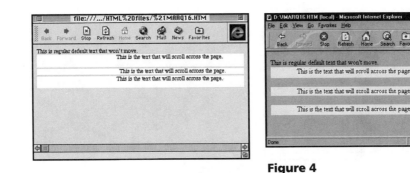

Figure 3

Three example marquee heights in Internet Explorer 3 for the Mac.

Figure 4

Three example marquee heights in Internet Explorer 3 for Windows.

There are a couple things you should note about Figures 3 and 4: first, the text inside the marquee aligns itself along the top of the marquee track, regardless of track width, so you get lots of blank space below the text. Second, which you can see on the screen as well, if you have more than one marquee on a page, they will not move smoothly nor in synch across the screen.

Also, there's an advantage to using a percentage-specified marquee width. The problem with a pixel-specified marquee is directly similar to the problem with a pixel-specified horizontal rule: if a visitor to your web page greatly reduces or enlarges the browser window, a pixel-specified marquee cannot adjust itself and may look strange. A percentage-specified marquee, on the other hand, is already determined by the width and margins of the browser window so if the window is resized the marquee automatically rescales itself.

HSPACE

The HSPACE attribute works in tandem with the VSPACE attribute to specify a buffer zone of blank space around the marquee field. HSPACE establishes the size of the left and right margins while VSPACE establishes the amount of space directly above and below.

In the following example, the HSPACE setting is 30 pixels:

```
<MARQUEE HSPACE=30>This is the text which will scroll across the page.</MARQUEE>
```

Figures 5 and 6 illustrate two different marquees, one with default settings and another with HSPACE- and VSPACE-specified settings of 15 pixels, as displayed by Internet Explorer 3 for the Mac and Windows.

See the VSPACE section later in this entry for the rest of the information you'll need to properly establish blank space around a marquee.

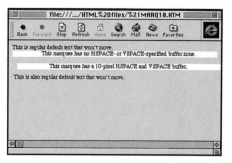

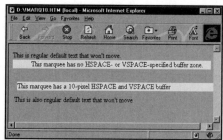

Figure 5

Two example marquees in Internet Explorer 3 for the Mac.

Figure 6

Two example marquees in Internet Explorer 3 for Windows.

LOOP

The LOOP attribute is used to specify the number of times a marquee will scroll after being activated.

In the following example, the LOOP setting of 5 indicates that the marquee text will scroll five times and then stop:

```
<MARQUEE LOOP=5>This is the text that will scroll across the page.</MARQUEE>
```

Setting LOOP to –1 or INFINITE will cause the marquee text to run continuously. (The marquee will also run continuously if you don't use the LOOP attribute at all.)

> **NOTE** If you have questions about the general speed of a marquee, you should perform two tests. Make a test page with three or four marquees of varying text length and launch it in Explorer both on and off the Internet. This will give you a real-time idea of how your marquee will perform, independently of any **LOOP**, **SCROLLAMOUNT**, or **SCROLLDELAY** settings you establish.

SCROLLAMOUNT

The SCROLLAMOUNT attribute specifies an amount of blank space between successive loops of the marquee text. It is directly related to using the LOOP attribute, as a SCROLLAMOUNT setting is only needed if the marquee text will loop more than once.

In the following example, the SCROLLAMOUNT setting of 25 indicates there will be a blank space 25 pixels wide between each loop:

```
<MARQUEE SCROLLAMOUNT=25>This is the text that will scroll across the page.
➡</MARQUEE>
```

The height of this blank space is the same as the height of the marquee field, though field height is not determined or constricted by the height of the marquee text.

SCROLLDELAY

The SCROLLDELAY attribute established the length of time it will take a marquee to complete one loop.

In the following example, the SCROLLDELAY setting is 75 to specify 75 milliseconds, or less than one second (there are 1000 milliseconds in 1 second):

```
<MARQUEE SCROLLDELAY=75>This is the text which will scroll across the page.
➥</MARQUEE>
```

SCROLLDELAY is directly related to the LOOP and SCROLLAMOUNT attribute settings—see these two sections elsewhere in this entry for a complete idea of how you should manage more than one loop of a marquee.

VSPACE

The VSPACE attribute works in tandem with the HSPACE attribute to specify a buffer zone of blank space around the marquee field. VSPACE establishes the amount of space directly above and below the marquee while HSPACE establishes the size of the left and right margins.

In the following example, the VSPACE setting is 30 pixels:

```
<MARQUEE VSPACE=30>This is the text which will scroll across the page.</MARQUEE>
```

Figures 7 and 8 illustrate two different marquees, one with default settings and another with HSPACE- and VSPACE-specified settings of 15 pixels, as displayed by Internet Explorer 3 for the Mac and Windows.

M

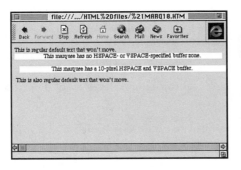

Figure 7

Two example marquees in Internet Explorer 3 for the Mac.

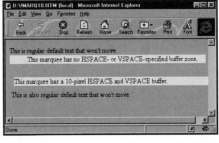

Figure 8

Two example marquees in Internet Explorer 3 for Windows.

See the HSPACE section elsewhere in this entry for the rest of the information you'll need to properly establish blank space around a marquee.

WIDTH

The WIDTH attribute specifies the width of the marquee either in pixels or as a percentage of the overall screen height.

A pixel-specified setting is established as follows:

```
<MARQUEE WIDTH =12>This is the text that will scroll across the page.</MARQUEE>
```

and a percentage-specified setting is established like this:

```
<MARQUEE WIDTH =12%>This is the text that will scroll across the page.</MARQUEE>
```

Figures 9 and 10 illustrate three marquees apiece—the top with a WIDTH-specified setting of 30 pixels, the middle at the default width, and the bottom at a WIDTH-specified setting of 30%—in Internet Explorer 3 for the Mac and Windows. Again, a white background color has been established so you can see the marquee track in these black-and-white figures.

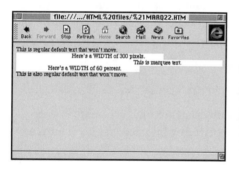

Figure 9

Three example marquee widths in Internet Explorer 3 for the Mac.

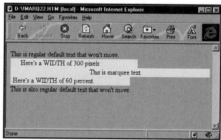

Figure 10

Three example marquee widths in Internet Explorer 3 for Windows.

Without HSPACE and VSPACE settings (or a HEIGHT setting, either) the edges of these three marquees end up blurring to nothing.

There's also problem with a pixel-specified marquee that is directly similar to the problem with a pixel-specified horizontal rule: If a visitor to your web page greatly reduces or enlarges the rowser window, a pixel-specified marquee cannot adjust itself and may look strange. A percentage-specified marquee, on the other hand, is already determined by the width and margins of the browser window so if the window is resized the marquee automatically rescales itself. (For the record, the default marquee will also automatically rescale itself, so don't use the WIDTH attribute unnecessarily.)

Math

Category: JavaScript, JScript

| | **Type** | Object |

	Browser Support		Navigator 3	Navigator 4	Explorer 3	Explorer 4
		Macintosh	■	■	☐	■
		Windows	■	■	■	■

Subset Of Nothing

Properties E, LN2, LN10, LOG2E, LOG10E, PI, SQRT1_2, SQRT2

Methods Abs(), Acos(), Asin(), Atan(), Atan2(), Ceil(), Cos(), Expo(), Floor(), Log(), Max(), Min(), Pow(), Random(), Round(), Sin(), Sqrt(), Tan()

Syntax Math.property OR Math.method(parameters)

The math object is purely a read-only object. All of its properties are mathematical constants, while its methods are various mathematical functions and operations. You use the math object in scripts as your "calculator," when you need to perform arithmetic routines for a particular purpose.

When you need to execute several calculations in a row, you may find it efficient to use the JavaScript with construction:

```
with (Math)
 { a=PI*r*r
   b=abs(100-a)
   c=sqrt(b)
 }
```

In the previous example, the with (Math) construction alleviates the need to specify the Math object preceding each property and method, as in Math.PI, Math.abs(), and Math.sqrt().

Also be sure to capitalize Math as written, because JavaScript is case-sensitive. Similarly, pay special attention to all forms of capitalization illustrated in the following properties and methods—it *is* important.

When approximate values are provided, the "actual" value used within JavaScript usually extends to many more decimal places for full precision. Exact degree of precision may vary from platform to platform.

E property

Euler's constant e, the base of the natural logarithm. The E property always contains this value, which is approximately 2.718.

```
x=Math.E * 100
```

LN2 property

The natural logarithm of 2, which is approximately 0.693.

```
x=Math.LN2
```

LN10 property

The natural logarithm of 10, which is approximately 2.302.

```
x=Math.LN10
```

LOG2E property

The base 2 logarithm of e, which is approximately 1.442.

```
x=Math.LOG2E
```

LOG10E property

The base 10 logarithm of e, which is approximately 0.434.

```
x=Math.LOG10E
```

PI property

The constant pi, which represents the ratio of the circumference of a circle to its diameter. The PI property contains a value of approximately 3.14159.

```
x=Math.PI
```

SQRT1_2 property

The square root of one-half, which is approximately 0.707. But you knew that!

```
x=Math.SQRT1_2
```

SQRT2 property

The square root of 2, which is, you guessed it, approximately 1.414.

```
x=Math.SQRT2
```

abs() method

```
Math.abs(value)
```

Returns the absolute value of *value*. The absolute value of a number is its unsigned magnitude—thus, both statements

```
Math.abs(5) and Math.abs(-5)
```

would return the value 5.

acos() method

`Math.acos(value)`

Returns the arc cosine of *value* in radians. The parameter *value* must contain a value between –1 and 1, otherwise it will return zero or an invalid number ("NaN" in Netscape, "–1.#IND" in Internet Explorer).

asin() method

`Math.asin(value)`

Returns the arc sine of *value* in radians. The parameter *value* must contain a value between –1 and 1, otherwise it will return zero or an invalid number ("NaN" in Netscape, "–1.#IND" in Internet Explorer).

atan() method

`Math.atan(value)`

Returns the arc tangent of *value* in radians.

atan2() method

`Math.atan2(valueX,valueY)`

Returns the counter-clockwise angle (theta) between the positive X axis and the point (*valueX,valueY*), in radians. The *value* parameter in the `atan()` method represents the ratio of *valueX* to *valueY* in the `atan2()` method.

ceil() method

`Math.ceil(value)`

Returns the least integer greater than or equal to *value*. For instance:

`Math.ceil(11.4)`	returns the value 12.
`Math.ceil(-11.4)`	returns the value –11.
`Math.ceil(11)`	returns the value 11.

cos() method

`Math.cos(value)`

Returns the cosine of *value*, where *value* is the size of an angle in radians. The cosine of *value* will fall between –1 and 1.

exp() method

`Math.exp(value)`

Returns e (Euler's constant) raised to the power of *value*.

M

floor() method

`Math.floor(value)`

Returns the greatest integer less than or equal to *value*. For instance:

`Math.floor(25.6)`   returns the value 25.

`Math.floor(-25.6)`   returns the value −26.

`Math.floor(-25)`   returns the value −25.

log() method

`Math.log(value)`

Returns the natural logarithm of *value*, where *value* is a positive number. Passing a *value* of zero or negative may produce unpredictable results, ranging from a value of zero to "infinity."

max() method

`Math.max(value1,value2)`

Returns the greater of *value1* or *value2*. For instance:

`Math.max(5,11)`   returns the value 11.

`Math.max(-11.-5)`   returns the value −5.

min() method

`Math.min(value1,value2)`

Returns the lesser of *value1* or *value2*. For instance:

`Math.min(20,12)`   returns the value 12.

`Math.min(-12,-20)`   returns the value −20.

pow() method

`Math.pow(base,exponent)`

Returns the value of *base* raised to the *exponent* power.

`Math.pow(4,3)` performs the calculation 4^3, returning the value 64.

random() method

`Math.random()`

Returns a random number between 0 and 1, seeded on the current time (technically, a pseudo-random number). Typically, though, you'll want to select a random number between some *lowerbound* and *upperbound*. To do so, use the formula:

`rnumber = Math.random() * (upperbound-lowerbound)+lowerbound`

Or, to generate only random integers between two bounds:

```
rnumber = Math.round(Math.random() * (upperbound-lowerbound))+lowerbound
```

round() method

```
Math.round(value)
```

Returns *value* rounded to the nearest integer. If *value*'s fractional component is .5 or greater, it will be rounded to the next highest integer; if less than .5, it will be rounded down.

```
Math.round(3.532)
```
    returns the value 4.

```
Math.round(3.432)
```
    returns the value 3.

sin() method

```
Math.sin(value)
```

Returns the sine of *value*, where *value* is the size of an angle in radians. The sine of *value* will fall between −1 and 1.

sqrt() method

```
Math.sqrt(value)
```

Returns the square root of *value*, where *value* contains any non-negative number. If *value* does contain a negative number, sqrt() will return unpredictable results, ranging from zero to "NaN" or "−1.#IND".

tan() method

```
Math.tan(value)
```

Returns the tangent of the angle *value*, where *value* is the size of an angle in radians.

<MENU>

Category: HTML

Browser Support		Navigator 3	Navigator 4	Explorer 3	Explorer 4
	Macintosh	■	■	■	■
	Windows	■	■	■	■

May Contain	`<LI>`
May Be Used In	`<BLOCKQUOTE>`, `<BODY>`, `<CENTER>`, `<DD>`, `<DIV>`, `<FORM>`, `<LI>`, `<TD>`, `<TH>`
Attributes	COMPACT
Syntax	`<MENU>...</MENU>`

M

The <MENU> tag is used to create a simple, streamlined list of items. A closing, or </MENU>, tag is required.

The following example is a simple <MENU> list:

```
<MENU>
<LI>Index
<LI>Portfolio
<LI>Site Overview
<LI>About Acme Computing
</MENU>
```

Each item in a <MENU> list should be preceded with an <LI> tag. See the <LI> tag entry for more information on this tag that is used in four kinds of lists.

Figures 1, 2, 3 and 4 illustrate this simple <DL> list in Netscape Navigator 3 and Internet Explorer 3 for both the Mac and Windows.

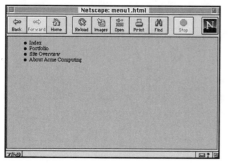

Figure 1

A simple <MENU> list in Netscape Navigator 3 for the Mac.

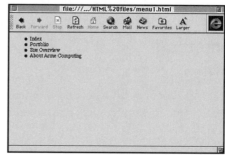

Figure 2

A simple <MENU> list in Internet Explorer 3 for the Mac.

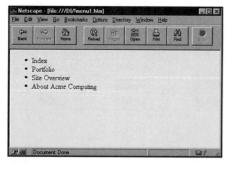

Figure 3

A simple <MENU> list in Netscape Navigator 3 for Windows.

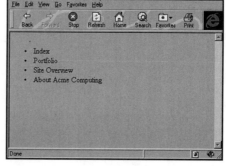

Figure 4

A simple <MENU> list in Internet Explorer 3 for Windows.

COMPACT

The COMPACT attribute is used to tell the browser that items in the list are short, so the list can be tightened accordingly. When this attribute is used within a <DL> list in Netscape Navigator 3, for example, the browser will display two items on one line.

In <MENU> lists, however, neither Navigator nor Internet Explorer 3 will display COMPACT-specified lists any differently than regular <MENU> lists, even when the list items are only one character long. So use of this attribute in these two browsers, on either the Mac or the Windows platforms, seems to serve no purpose at this writing.

<META>

Category: HTML

Browser Support		Navigator 3	Navigator 4	Explorer 3	Explorer 4
	Macintosh	■	■	☐	■
	Windows	■	■	■	■

Applies To Text

May Contain None

May Be Used In None

Attributes CHARSET, CONTENT, NAME, HTTP-EQUIV, URL

Syntax <META>...</META>

The <META> tag is used primarily to give out information about your web page. The following six <META> attributes: CONTENT, NAME, HTTP-EQUIV, REL, REV, and URL work together in different combinations to do different things. CHARSET is the only <META> tag attribute that works alone—it lists a specific character set needed to properly display your web page if it contains special letters or symbols.

The catch is, at this writing, not all clients/servers support the <META> tag. You may find after using the HTML in this section that you can't see or test your web page properly—and even if you can view your page properly, users visiting your page on the web may not. So keep these limitations in mind if you choose to implement the <META> tag. Other special conditions and considerations will be noted as each <META> tag attribute is covered.

CHARSET

The CHARSET attribute is used to specify a special character set needed to properly view your web page. If the CHARSET attribute is written in, and the server can see it, the browser will ask for the character set document along with the web page. This is especially useful for web pages that use non-Western alphabets like Cyrillic, Chinese, or Greek, or if your web page contains mathematical or scientific language.

M

If, for example, cset stands for the special character set needed to read `webpage1.html`, you would write:

```
<META HTTP-EQUIV="character set" CHARSET="cset" URL="webpage1.html">
```

CONTENT

The CONTENT attribute, depending upon other attributes used with it, specifies a description or value. In the following example, the CONTENT attribute is used with the URL attribute to create a meta-refresh or automatic page reloading:

```
<META HTTP-EQUIV=REFRESH CONTENT=3 URL="webpage.html">
```

This HTML enables the browser to automatically reload the web page you specify. The REFRESH instruction activates the process, the 3 value tells your browser to load the page after a three-second pause, and the URL specifies the name of the page to be loaded. Remember that this countdown will begin only after the first web page is finished downloading, so the final effect of a meta-refresh may be affected by connection time and the amount of time it takes to download all the elements of the first web page.

> **NOTE** If you use this combination of <META> tag attributes to create a meta-refresh, do not set the CONTENT value to zero. If you do, users who visit your page will get stuck at your page if they use their browser's Back button—to escape this looping effect, they will have to manually type in a new URL.

NAME

The NAME attribute also specifies a description when used with other <META> tag attributes, but strictly related to your web page's contents. <META> tag instructions are always enclosed within the <HEAD> tag.

Two popular uses of the <META> tag and NAME attribute involve how a web page is displayed by a search engine or index (currently, only Alta Vista and InfoSeek use the <META> tag to do this).

If you include

```
<META NAME="keywords" CONTENT="keyword1, keyword2, keyword3">
```

in your <HEAD> tag information, you're instructing a search engine how to identify the contents of your web page. By including "rollerblading" as a keyword, then, your web page will appear in a keyword search executed by someone entering "rollerblading" in the search window.

> **NOTE** The catch to this keyword-specification trick is that if you include more than seven keywords in the <HEAD> tag of a web page, the search engine will ignore them all.

Similarly, if you include

```
<META NAME="description" CONTENT="This is a web site">
```

in your <HEAD> tag information, too, a search engine that supports the <META> tag will provide the text you specify as the search result page description, rather than the first few lines of your web page.

> **NOTE** There's also a catch to providing your own search result description: you've only got room for about 1,000 characters and not all of them are guaranteed to be used.

HTTP-EQUIV

The HTTP-EQUIV attribute specifies a browser response to instructions given by other <META> attributes used at the same time. For example, if you write the following HTML:

```
<META HTTP-EQUIV="EXPIRES" CONTENT="Mon, 31 Dec 1999, 11:59:59 GMT">
```

in your <HEAD> tag information, this sets an expiration date for your web page. So if your web page is requested from your service provider after the date you establish, the browser executing the request will upload a new copy of your page instead of using a previous copy already stored in its memory cache.

This use of the HTTP-EQUIV attribute and <META> tag can be especially valuable if your web page contains information that's frequently updated—such as sports scores or stock market performance.

URL

The URL attribute, when used in combination with other <META> tag attributes, specifies the location of a web page.

You've already seen an example of how to use this attribute under CONTENT—the sequence of <META> tag attributes and specifications you can write to create a meta-refresh, or automatic loading of another page. However, you can also use similar HTML, including the URL attribute, to create a kind of primitive slide show by specifying several different web pages.

```
<META HTTP-EQUIV=REFRESH CONTENT=5 URL="webpage1.html">
```

```
<META HTTP-EQUIV=REFRESH CONTENT=5 URL="webpage2.html">
```

```
<META HTTP-EQUIV=REFRESH CONTENT=5 URL="webpage3.html">
```

If a browser interprets the <META> tag, it will read these REFRESH instructions in sequence, producing a slow-motion slide show of the three pages you specify. The examples shown here are set up as an entryway sequence—a visitor to this web page would see these first three pages in relatively rapid sequence (five seconds apart) with webpage3.html being the real main page of this entire web site.

M

Mid()
Category: VBScript

| | Type | Function |

Browser Support		Navigator 3	Navigator 4	Explorer 3	Explorer 4
	Macintosh	☐	☐	☐	■
	Windows	☐	☐	■	■

Syntax `Mid(string, start [, length])`

The `Mid()` function extracts a specific subsection from *string*. The function returns *length* characters of *string* beginning at character position *start*. If *length* is omitted or if the number of characters left in the string is less than *length*, all the characters to the end of the string will be returned. A *start* value greater than the string length will return a zero-length string (""). If *string* contains null then a null value is always returned.

`mid("hello there",1,5)`	returns	"hello"
`mid("hello there",4,6)`	returns	"lo the"
`mid("mighty mouse",8)`	returns	"mouse"
`mid("door ajar",15,3)`	returns	""

In certain instances, such as when recovering the value of a cookie, you may find it useful to apply the `Mid()` function. Or, you might want to extract someone's surname from a string containing their full name. Of course, you'll first need to use position-finding functions, such as `InStr()` and `InStrRev()`, to locate the start and end points of the string you want to extract with `Mid()`.

MimeType
Category: JavaScript 1.1

| | Type | Object |

Browser Support		Navigator 3	Navigator 4	Explorer 3	Explorer 4
	Macintosh	■	■	☐	☐
	Windows	■	■	☐	☐

Subset of `Navigator object`

Properties `description, type, suffixes, enabledPlugin`

Syntax `navigator.mimeTypes[index].property` OR
`navigator.plugins[index]mimeTypes[index].property` OR
`navigator.mimeTypes["type/sub-type"].property`

The `mimeType` object contains information about a MIME type configured for the browser. MIME (Multipart Internet Mail Extension) information is sent to the browser by the server whenever a piece of data is downloaded. The MIME type identifies what type of data to expect; each browser is configured to handle particular types of data in specific ways.

For instance, the MIME type:

`text/html`

signifies that the incoming data is a web page because it is of the type "text" and sub-type "html." Another common MIME type is:

`image/jpeg`

which indicates an incoming image in JPEG format. The browser can be configured to handle JPEG images in a particular way, such as calling on an external image viewer.

MIME types are also identified based on the file name's extension; for instance, you could configure the browser such that file names ending in `.jpg` and `.jpeg` are handled as MIME type `image/jpeg` data.

The `navigator` object contains the `mimeTypes array` as a property (see the `navigator` object)—each element in this array is a `mimeType` object reflecting eaching configured MIME type for the user's browser.

Typically, you would use the `mimeType` object to determine whether the user's browser is configured to handle a certain file format.

For instance, suppose a link on your page led to a file in Adobe Acrobat format. When the user clicks the hyperlink to that file, you could first check to see if her browser has been configured to handle such a file type; if not, you could provide information or hyperlinks leading the user to obtain the Adobe Acrobat reader.

Checking for the presence of a particular MIME type is easy, assuming you know the type definition. Suppose that you know the MIME type for Adobe Acrobat format is `application/pdf`. The following `if` statement will follow the true condition if this MIME type has been configured in the user's browser; otherwise, it will follow the false condition.

```
if (navigator.mimeTypes["application/pdf"])
 { true condition statements }
else { false condition statements }
```

 Internet Explorer 3 and 4 do not support the `mimeType` object.

NOTE   For a list of more MIME types, refer to Appendix E.

description property

Some MIME types contain extra descriptive information. The `description` property contains this text. For instance, imagine that the first MIME type configured in the browser is for `image/jpeg`. In that case, the script statement

```
mimetext=navigator.mimeTypes[0].description
```

would assign the text "JPEG Image" to the variable `mimetext`. Not all MIME types contain description text—it depends how they were created in the browser. The `description` property is read-only, and cannot be modified.

Typically, there are few reasons to access this property from a script. If you want to identify the presence of a particular MIME type, it would be more accurate to use the simple test presented at the beginning of this entry.

type property

The `type` property contains the "type" of this MIME type configuration. In plain English, this property contains the official MIME type for this object, such as

```
application/x-pn-realaudio
```

or

```
image/gif
```

or

```
text/plain
```

The `type` property is read-only and cannot be modified via the script.

```
mtype=navigator.mimeTypes[2].type
```

suffixes property

Each MIME type configuration contains a list of related file name extensions, also known as suffixes. For instance, the MIME type `text/html` usually contains the suffixes `html` and `htm`. When the browser downloads a file that contains such a suffix, it looks to its associated MIME type configuration to decide what action to take.

For example, the following code excerpt displays the suffixes associated with the MIME type `image/jpeg`.

```
window.alert(navigator.mimeTypes["image/jpeg"].suffixes)
```

Figure 1

An alert window displaying the contents of the suffixes *property for the* image/jpeg mimeType *object.*

enabledPlugin **property**

In some cases, a MIME type is associated with a plug-in. A plug-in is an external program that is launched to handle a particular type of file; for instance, a RealAudio sound file launches the RealAudio Player, which plays said sound file.

If the mimeType object possesses an associated plug-in, then that plugin object is accessible through the enabledPlugin property. Thus, this property serves two purposes:

1. You can use enabledPlugin to determine whether a user has a plug-in installed for the particular MIME type. If no such plug-in exists, this property contains the value null.

   ```
   if (navigator.mimeType["audio/x-pn-realaudio"].enabledPlugin)
    { statements if plug-in is installed }
   else { statements if plug-in not installed }
   ```

2. You can access properties of the plugin object directly through the enabledPlugin property for a mimeType object. For instance, you can access properties of the plugin object associated with the RealAudio MIME type using the reference

   ```
   navigator.mimeType["audio/x-pn-realaudio"].enabledPlugin.property
   ```

In this way, you do not need to know the element index for the plugin object itself in the plugins array—for details on the properties of the plugin object, see plugin object.

M

Minute()
Category: VBScript

Type	Function			

Browser Support		Navigator 3	Navigator 4	Explorer 3	Explorer 4
	Macintosh	☐	☐	☐	■
	Windows	☐	☐	■	■

Syntax	Minute(*date*)

The Minute() function returns the minute, between 0 and 59, within the specified *date*. The time format within *date* may be in either 24-hour time or AM/PM time.

```
hour("June 11 4:30 PM")          returns          30

hour("05:45:00")                 returns          45

hour("12:00 AM")                 returns          0
```

If the value *date* is null, then a null value is returned. If *date* does not contain a time or minute, then 0 is returned; if *date* contains an invalid time, such as 25:70:00, an error will occur.

Month()

Category: VBScript

Type	Function

Browser Support

	Navigator 3	Navigator 4	Explorer 3	Explorer 4
Macintosh				■
Windows			■	■

Syntax   Month(*date*)

The Month() function returns the month, between 1 and 12, within the specified *date*. The date format within *date* may conform to any of the following examples:

```
month("June 11 4:30 PM")         returns          6
month("4/26/72")                 returns          4
month("15-mar-94")               returns          3
```

If the value *date* is null, then a null value is returned. If *date* contains an invalid date (outside of the valid date range January 1, 100 to December 31, 9999) then an error will occur.

MonthName

Category: VBScript

Type	Function

Browser Support

	Navigator 3	Navigator 4	Explorer 3	Explorer 4
Macintosh				■
Windows			■	■

Syntax   MonthName(*month* [, *abbrev*])

The MonthName() function returns a string containing the name of the specified *month*, where *month* is an integer from 1 to 12. If *abbrev* is omitted or specified as false, the full name of the month will be returned; otherwise, a three-character abbreviation of the month name will be returned.

Typically, you would use the MonthName() function when constructing an output string which should contain a date in the form of "February 12, 1981". Or, you may output a calendar, and use this function to generate the month name for the calendar heading.

monthname(2)	returns	"February"
monthname(2,true)	returns	"Feb"
monthname(14)	returns	invalid procedure call or argument error

MsgBox()
Category: VBScript

Type   Function

Browser Support

	Navigator 3	Navigator 4	Explorer 3	Explorer 4
Macintosh				■
Windows			■	■

Syntax   msgBox(prompt [, buttons][, title][, helpfile, contextID])

The MsgBox() function displays a message in a dialog box. The dialog box can provide several different buttons for the user to click. The function returns a value indicating which button the user selected.

The complex aspect of the MsgBox() function lies with its number of options. Read the following discussions of each parameter carefully—especially the *buttons* parameter, which requires you to consult with several value tables to specify exactly which buttons you want the dialog box to contain.

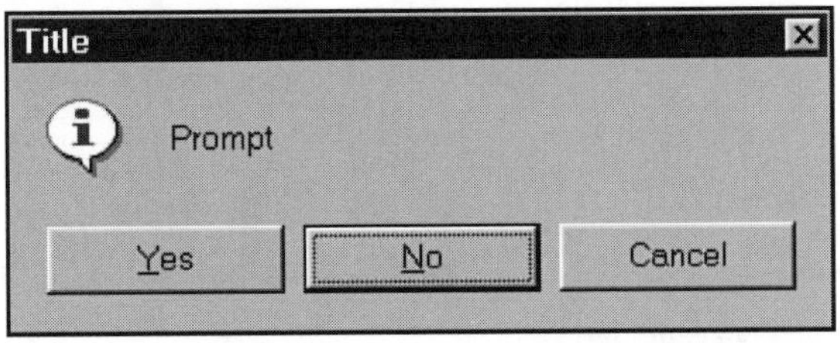

Figure 1

One type of message dialog box, with Yes, No, and Cancel buttons.

The message dialog box illustrated in Figure 1 was created with the statement

```
val=msgbox("Would you like to submit your survey0 information?"&chr(13)&"If you
click NO then your survey will not be submitted.",4+64+256+0,"Survey Finished")
```

Below are explanations of each parameter and how they contribute to the resulting message box:

prompt   A string expression to display in the dialog box. This string may be as long as 1024 characters. Multiple line strings are permitted—use the carriage return (chr(13)) or linefeed (chr(10)) characters or both to separate the lines.

buttons   An integer value that is the sum of the various options you can choose to determine which types of buttons appear in the dialog box. To calculate the correct value for this parameter, you should consult each of the four option tables shown, and add up the values you select from each. For instance, you might select an OK and Cancel button (1), the second button as the default (256), the user can use other applications before dismissing this dialog box (0), and an information icon should appear in the dialog box (64). Add these values together and you have a total of 321, which is what you would specify for the buttons parameter. If this parameter is omitted, it defaults to 0, which provides a dialog box with no icon and only an OK button.

title   A string expression to display in the title bar of the dialog box. If omitted, the application name will be displayed ("Visual Basic").

helpfile   The name of a help file to use to provide context-sensitive help for the dialog box. A Help button will be displayed in the dialog box. If helpfile is provided, contextID must also be provided. You're not likely to use this parameter in web pages.

contextID   The help context number for the appropriate help topic. If *contextID* is provided, *helpfile* must also be provided. You're not likely to use this parameter in web pages.

Button choices for the types of buttons:

0	OK button
1	OK and Cancel buttons
2	Abort, Retry, and Ignore buttons
3	Yes, No, and Cancel buttons
4	Yes and No buttons
5	Retry and Cancel buttons

Button choices for the icon style:

0		No icon
16		Critical Message icon
32		Warning Query icon
48		Warning Message icon
64		Information Message icon

Button choices for the default button:

0	First button is default
256	Second button is default
512	Third button is default, or last button if there are less than three buttons
768	Fourth button is default, or last button if there are less than four buttons

Button choices for the system modality of the message box:

0	The user must attend to the message box before continuing with the application.
4096	The user must attend to the message box before continuing with any application on the system.

Although the parameters may look overwhelming, creating the message box is mostly a matter of choosing items from each preceding table and adding them together to create the *buttons* parameter value. Consider some examples:

Example 1: A critical message dialog box with only an OK button.

```
val=msgbox("You must provide an e-mail address!", 0+16,"Attention!")
```

Example 2: A warning query with a Retry and Cancel button.

```
val=msgbox("You did not enter a name — are you sure you want to remain name-
less?", 5+32,"Nameless?")
```

Example 3: An information query with a Yes, No, and Cancel button. The Cancel button is the default selection.

```
val=msgbox("Is your taxable income over $40K? Choose Cancel if you'd rather not
say.", 3+64+512,"Survey")
```

The MsgBox() function returns an integer based on the type of button pressed:

1	OK
2	Cancel
3	Abort
4	Retry
5	Ignore
6	Yes
7	No

This integer allows your program to know which button the user clicked, and will then take appropriate action.

```
</STRONG> ■ <TD> </TD> ■ <TH> </TH> ■ <TABLE> </TABLE> ■
<IMG> </IMG> ■ <SCRIPT LANGUAGE = "javascript"> </SCRIPT>
■ <SCRIPT LANGUAGE = "vbscript"> </SCRIPT> ■ <BGSOUND
SRC=gbv.wav LOOP=-1> </BGSOUND> ■ <APPLET CLASS=
"ester's_day" SRC="http://testsite/walla walla washington/"
</APPLET> ■ <FRAME></FRAME>■ <MARQUEE> </MARQUEE> ■
<HTML> </HTML> ■ <A> </A> ■ <OL> </OL> ■ <UL> </UL> ■ <MENU>
</MENU> ■ <STRONG> </STRONG> ■ <TD> </TD> ■ <TH> </TH>
```

Navigator

Category: JavaScript, JScript, and VBScript

Type	Object			

Browser Support

	Navigator 3	Navigator 4	Explorer 3	Explorer 4
Macintosh	■	■	☐	■
Windows	■	■	■	■

Properties appCodeName, appName, appVersion, mimeTypes[], plugins[], userAgent, javaEnabled(), taintEnabled()

Syntax navigator.*property* OR navigator.method(parameters)

The navigator object obtains information about the user's browser. This includes internal information such as which version and brand of browser is being used, which MIME types and plug-ins are installed, and whether Java and data tainting are enabled.

Although this object possesses a very "Netscape-centric" name, Microsoft's Internet Explorer supports the navigator object as well (minus a few properties and methods).

Typically, you would use the navigator object's properties and methods to determine whether to proceed with certain script functions or not, depending upon whether the browser supports them.

appCodeName property

The appCodeName property is a read-only string specifying the "code name" of the browser. For instance, the following code

```
code = navigator.appCodeName
```

would assign the following values to the variable code, depending upon which browser the user has:

Browser Used	appCodeName
Navigator 2.0, 3.0, 4.0	"Mozilla"
Internet Explorer 3.0, 4.0	"Mozilla"

Notice that Internet Explorer also returns the `appCodeName` "Mozilla." This is because it tries to pass itself off as Netscape Navigator, on the premise that sites that test for Navigator's presence *should* also work with Internet Explorer. You'll see in the following properties how to truly distinguish between the two browsers.

appName property

The `appName` property is a read-only string specifying the official name of the browser. For instance, the following code

```
browsname = navigator.appName
```

would assign the following values to the variable `browsname`, depending upon which browser the user has:

Browser Used	appName
Navigator 2.0, 3.0, 4.0	"Netscape"
Internet Explorer 3.0, 4.0	"Microsoft Internet Explorer"

One way, then, to determine which browser your visitor is using is a simple `if` statement that tests the `appName` property of the `navigator` object.

JavaScript

```
if (navigator.appName.indexOf("Netscape")>-1)
 {statements if browser is Netscape}
else {statements if browser is not Netscape}
```

VBScript

```
if inStr(navigator.appName,"Internet Explorer")>0 then
 statements if browser is MSIE
else
 statements if browser is not MSIE
end if
```

appVersion property

The `appVersion` property is a read-only string specifying the version of the browser, the operating system version, and whether it is the US or international version. In some cases, such as with Internet Explorer, additional information is included. For instance, the following code

```
browsers = navigator.appVersion
```

might assign the following values to the variable `browsers`, depending upon which browser the user has:

Browser Used	appVersion
Navigator 3.01, Windows 95,	"3.01 (Win95; I) International version"
Internet Explorer 3.01B, Windows 95	"2.0 (compatible; MSIE 3.01; Update B; Windows 95)"
Internet Explorer 4.0	"4.0 (compatible; MSIE 4.0; Windows 95)"

Generally speaking, you'll find the appVersion property most useful when you need to check the browser's version. For instance, you know that the image object is supported in Navigator 3.0 and higher—thus, if the appVersion property reveals that the user's version of Navigator is 2.0, you could avoid calling functions that use the image object during this session. Or, alternatively, display a message alerting the users to the fact that they must use Navigator 3.0 or higher to properly view your page.

You can test the version number for the browser with a statement such as:

```
if (navigator.appVersion.substring(0,1)>2)...
```

In the preceding portion of an if statement, the browser's version is tested against the number 2. Similarly, you can test the browser's version against any number to determine the minimum version of that browser.

mimeTypes[] property

The mimeTypes[] property is an array of MIME types supported by the client's browser. A MIME type, in short, is a definition that pairs a type of file (such as a JPEG image) with a procedure for handling it (such as calling on an external program). Each element in the mimeTypes array is a mimeType object—see mimeType object. The mimeTypes array contains one property of its own: length.

The length property contains the number of elements (that is, mimeType objects) within the mimeTypes[] array.

The construction

```
mimes=navigator.mimeTypes.length
```

would assign the number of MIME types configured for this browser to the variable mimes. This also reflects how many mimeType objects are in the array.

Internet Explorer 3 and 4 do not support the mimeTypes[] property.

plugins[] property

The plugins[] property is an array of plug-ins supported by the client's browser. Plug-ins are typically proprietary files which require a specific third-party program to launch, such as a Macromedia Director file, which must be played with the Shockwave plug-in. Plug-ins are added to a web page using the <embed> tag. Each element in the plugins array is a plugin object—see plugin object. The plugins array contains a property and a method of its own: length and refresh().

The length property contains the number of elements (that is, plugin objects) within the plugins[] array.

The construction

```
plugs=navigator.plugins.length
```

would assign the number of plug-ins configured for this browser to the variable plugs. This also reflects how many plugin objects are in the array.

Using the refresh() method of the plugins[] array, you can update the browser in case the user has installed a new plug-in during this browsing session. This update will make the new plug-ins available, update the plugins[] array, and re-load any open documents which contain plug-ins. Typically, if your page contains a plug-in that the user may need to download, you provide a hyperlink to the installation file, and instructions to the user. Once the user has installed the plug-in, you may provide a button on the web page that the user can click to activate the new plug-in.

```
<input type="button" value="Click to activate new plug-in"
➥onClick="navigator.plugins.refresh()">
```

Internet Explorer 3 does not support the plugins[] property. At the time of this writing, Internet Explorer 4 may support the plugins[] property as a property of the document object rather than the navigator object. Further details are unavailable.

userAgent property

The userAgent property is a read-only string including the appCodeName and appVersion properties. The userAgent property reflects the data sent to the server which identifies the client; it doesn't provide any information not already available through appCodeName and appVersion. For instance, the following code

```
clientinfo = navigator.userAgent
```

would assign the following values to the variable clientinfo, depending upon which browser the user has:

Browser Used	appName
Navigator 3.0, Mac, International version, PowerPC	"Mozilla/3.0 (Macintosh; I; PPC)"
Navigator 3.0, Windows 3.1, International version	"Mozilla/3.0 (Win16; I)"
Navigator 4.0 beta 2, Windows 95, U.S. version	"Mozilla/4.0b2 (Win95; U)"
Internet Explorer 3.0	"Mozilla 2.0 (compatible; MSIE 3.01; Update B; Windows 95)"
Internet Explorer 4.0	"Mozilla/4.0 (compatible; MSIE 4.0; Windows 95)"

javaEnabled() method

The `javaEnabled()` method returns a Boolean value of true or false, indicating if the user has enabled Java support in the browser configuration. Java support, of course, being support for the Java programming language (no true relation to JavaScript) with which web authors can add complex programs to the web page. Some users may disable Java support due to security concerns or performance issues.

```
if (javaEnabled())
{statements if Java is enabled}
else {statements if Java is disabled}
```

For instance, if your page requires Java support to be enabled, you might use an if statement such as the preceding one to test the user's browser, and issue an alert if his Java has been disabled.

 Internet Explorer 3 does not support the `javaEnabled()` method.

taintEnabled() method

The `taintEnabled()` method will return a Boolean value of true or false, indicating whether the user has data tainting enabled. Tainting can prevent certain types of information from being passed to the server by JavaScript, for security and privacy reasons. Tainted data can only be sent to the server if the user has enabled data tainting—see `taint()` function. For instance, you might want to alert the user that your page cannot fully operate with data tainting disabled.

```
if (taintEnabled())
 {statements if tainting is enabled}
else {statements if tainting is disabled, such as alerting the user}
```

 Internet Explorer 3 and 4 do not support the `taintEnabled()` method.

<NEXTID>

Category: HTML

Browser Support	Unreliable
Applies To	None
May Contain	None
May Be Used In	None
Attributes	None
Syntax	<NEXTID>...</NEXTID>

The <NEXTID> tag has been used to provide information about anchor (<A>) elements, but it is no longer widely supported and its use is not recommended.

<NOBR>

Category: HTML

Browser Support

	Navigator 3	Navigator 4	Explorer 3	Explorer 4
Macintosh	☐	☐	■	■
Windows	☐	☐	■	■

Applies To	None
May Contain	None
May Be Used In	<BLOCKQUOTE>, <BODY>, <CENTER>, <DD>, <DIV>, <FORM>, <LI>, <P>, <TD>, <TH>
Attributes	None
Syntax	<NOBR>...</NOBR>

The <NOBR> or "no break" tag is used to enclose text that should not be divided by line breaks. Traditionally <NOBR> has been used to specify strings of programming code or other similar text where a line break or carriage return affects its purpose.

<NOBR> is not supported by Netscape Navigator 3 or Communicator at this writing. The closing, or </NOBR>, tag is needed to reenable the default line breaking capability so it is required.

In the following example, the text that precedes and follows the <NOBR>-specified section would be rendered with line breaks:

```
This line of text would automatically be broken by the browser if it got too
long.
<NOBR>But this line of text would go on right off the edge, as NOBR disables line
breaking.</NOBR>
This text falls outside the closing </NOBR> tag so it can be broken like the top
line.
```

Figures 1, 2, 3, and 4 visually illustrate this example in Internet Explorer 3 for both the Mac and Windows.

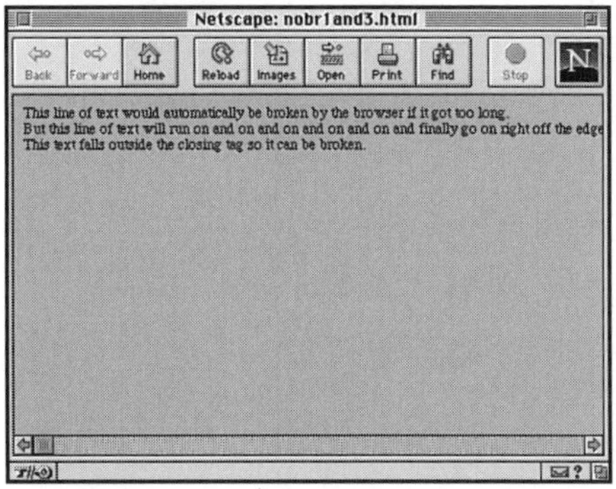

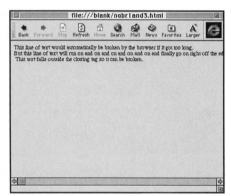

Figure 1

*Comparing broken and unbroken, or
<NOBR>-specified, lines of text in Netscape
Navigator 3 for the Mac.*

Figure 2

*Comparing broken and unbroken, or
<NOBR>-specified, lines of text in Internet
Explorer 3 for the Mac.*

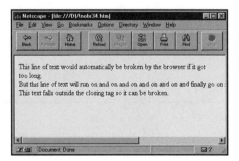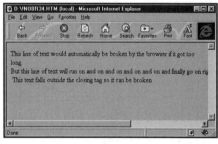

Figure 3

*Comparing broken and unbroken, or
<NOBR>-specified, lines of text in Netscape
Navigator 3 for Windows.*

Figure 4

*Comparing broken and unbroken, or
<NOBR>-specified, lines of text in Internet
Explorer 3 for Windows.*

N

You can insert soft line breaks within a line of \<NOBR\>-specified text, in the rare event that such a thing is needed, by using the \<WBR\> tag. For an example of when this may be necessary and for more information, see the \<WBR\> entry later in the book.

\<NOFRAMES\>

Category: HTML

Browser Support

	Navigator 3	Navigator 4	Explorer 3	Explorer 4
Macintosh	▇	▇	▇	▇
Windows	▇	▇	▇	▇

Applies To None

May Contain None

May Be Used In None

Attributes None

Syntax \<NOFRAMES\>...\</NOFRAMES\>

The \<NOFRAMES\> tag is used specifically within the \<FRAMESET\> tag to create instructions or an alternative web page for visitors using browsers that do not support frames. All page content contained within the \<NOFRAMES\> beginning and closing tags is not displayed by browsers that support frames, so a closing, or \</NOFRAMES\>, tag is required.

In the following example HTML, the \<NOFRAMES\> text points to a second version of the current web page:

```
<FRAMESET>
<NOFRAMES> Click <A HREF=noframes.html>here</A> for a no-frames version of this
➡page.</NOFRAMES>
</FRAMESET>
```

\<NOSCRIPT\>

Category: HTML

Browser Support

	Navigator 3	Navigator 4	Explorer 3	Explorer 4
Macintosh	▇	▇	▇	▇
Windows	▇	▇	▇	▇

Applies To None

May Contain	`<APPLET>`, `<B>`, `<BASEFONT>`, `<BIG>`, ` `, `<CITE>`, `<CODE>`, `<DFN>`, `<EM>`, `<FONT>`, `<I>`, `<IMG>`, `<INPUT>`, `<KBD>`, `<MAP>`, `<SAMP>`, `<SELECT>`, `<SMALL>`, `<STRIKE>`, `<STRONG>`, `<SUB>`, `<SUP>`, `<TEXTAREA>`, `<TT>`, `<U>`, `<VAR>`
May Be Used In	`<BODY>`
Attributes	None
Syntax	`<NOSCRIPT>…</NOSCRIPT>`

The `<NOSCRIPT>` tag is used in tandem with a JavaScript, VBScript, or other script to exclude a portion of a web page you want to remain unaffected by script instructions.

See the "JavaScript Basics" chapter elsewhere in this book for more information on how to use scripts in your web page.

`<NOSMARTQUOTES>`
Category: HTML

Browser Support	WebTV Internet Terminal
Applies To	Text
May Contain	None
May Be Used In	None
Attributes	None
Syntax	`<nosmartquotes>…</nosmartquotes>`

N

The `<nosmartquotes>` tag overrides the WebTV feature that replaces all regular quotes in text with smart quotes and all regular single quotes with single smart quotes. You may want to have regular quotes for special page content such as code examples or excerpts from technical documentation.

```
<nosmartquotes>The "reality" of it all is this. </nosmartquotes>
```

Now
Category: VBScript

| Type | Function |

Browser Support

	Navigator 3	Navigator 4	Explorer 3	Explorer 4
Macintosh	☐	☐	☐	■
Windows	☐	☐	■	■

Syntax Now

The Now function returns the current date and time from the user's machine. The date and time is returned in the format of "mm/dd/yy hh:mm:ss [AM/PM]," or "mm/dd/yyyy hh:mm:ss [AM/PM]" if the year is not in the 1900s. You needn't use parentheses when calling the Now function.

```
dtime=now
```

This function differs from Date in that Date does not return the time, whereas Now returns both the date and time.

</STRONG> ■ <TD> </TD> ■ <TH> </TH> ■ <TABLE> </TABLE>
<IMG> </IMG> ■ <SCRIPT LANGUAGE = "javascript"> </SCRIPT>
■ <SCRIPT LANGUAGE = "vbscript"> </SCRIPT> ■ <BGSOUND
SRC=gbv.wav LOOP=-1> </BGSOUND> ■ <APPLET CLASS=
"ester's_day" SRC="http://testsite/walla walla washington/"
</APPLET> ■ <FRAME></FRAME>■ <MARQUEE> </MARQUEE> ■
<HTML> </HTML>■ <A> </A>■ <OL> </OL>■ <UL> </UL> ■ <MENU>
</MENU> ■ <STRONG> </STRONG> ■ <TD> </TD> ■ <TH> </TH>

O

`<object>`

Category: HTML

Browser Support

	Navigator 3	Navigator 4	Explorer 3	Explorer 4
Macintosh		■		
Windows		■		

Attributes align, border, classid, codebase, codetype, data, declare, height, hspace, id, name, shapes, standby, type, usemap, vspace, width

Applies To Multimedia files, Java applets, embedded objects, component objects

Syntax `<object>…</object>`

The `<object>` tag is a powerful tag aimed at supporting all embedded and referenced objects such as multimedia files, images, and Java applets in a single format and tag. With `<object>`, you have a variety of means to integrate documents and applications on your web pages. For example, you can specify a data file, such as a multimedia presentation, or URL that references the file, along with the type that informs the browser how to handle or display the file.

Object data can be in-line, specified with a collection of named properties, or, as previously stated, defined by a URL. The browser must be able to display the object as defined by the `classid` and/or `data` attributes. These attributes inform the browser what type of object is being loaded and how it should be handled (see below for more information).

Additional properties such as the `type`, `codetype`, and `codebase` help the browser determine how to process the object. If it cannot, you specify an alternate set of actions or HTML data between the `<object>` and `</object>` tags. You use the `<param>` tag to send parameters or data to applications or applets you invoke with the `<object>` tag. The following two examples show how to use the `<object>` tag with, first, a URL to a local Java applet and, second, with an object type and a QuickTime movie.

In the first example, the `<object>` tag is used to execute a Java applet. If the browser does not support Java, a message is displayed to inform the user. The second example shows how to run a QuickTime movie using the `<object>` tag. If the user has not already installed QuickTime, and can therefore not display the movie, a link is provided to download QuickTime.

```
<object classid="java:testapp.class" height=150 width=150>
Your browser does not know how to execute Java applets
</object>
```

```
<object data=testapp.mov type="video/quicktime" width=200 height=200>
Your browser does not support QuickTime movies.
<a href="http://quicktime.apple.com/"> Click to download QuickTime </a>
</object>
```

align

The `align` attribute determines the placement of the object either on the current text line or on a new line relative to the text on that line. The values for `align` are displayed in the following table:

Table 1   Values for align

Value	Alignment
texttop	Top of current font
textmiddle	Middle of current font
textbottom	Bottom of current font
middle	Object middle with baseline
baseline	Object bottom with baseline

```
<object classid="java:testapp.class" align=texttop>
```

border

The `border` attribute determines the width of the border displayed around the object when it is included within a hypertext link. The value can either be fixed units or as a percentage of the display area. A value of 0 indicates no border should be displayed and is the default value.

```
<object classid="java:testapp.class" border=2>
```

classid

The `classid` attribute is a URL that provides the definition of the actual class instantiated when the object is created. The class can be a Java applet, an ActiveX control, or any class that is supported by the object model of the browser. The browser uses the class to determine how to display or handle the object.

The format is *class:url* where *class* defines the object model and the *url* provides the information of the class definition. The following two examples define a Java object class and an ActiveX class, respectively. In the second example, data for the initialization of the object is provided from a location on the web.

```
<object classid="java:clock.start">
<object classid="clsid:663C8FEF-1EF9-11CF-A3DB-080036F12502" data="http://
www.MyCompany.com/USsites/initdata.stm">
```

codebase

The codebase property points to the location of the class implementation in cases where this is needed. For example, the user's browser may not directly support the class but an implementation is available that the browser can use to process and interact with the object. For more common classes such as Java objects, the use of the codebase property is generally not needed. In the following example, the implementation of the class is retrieved from the web.

```
<object classid="java:newclass.start" codebase="http://www.DevOnline.com/Java/
newclass/">
```

codetype

The codetype property further defines the class given with the classid property similar to the way the type property defines the file name or URL of the data property. The value for codetype helps the browser determine if it can process or create the object defined with the classid. If not, the alternate HTML text between the object tags is used instead.

```
<object classid="java:program.start" codetype="application/java-vm">
```

data

The data attribute defines the URL or file name that contains the data of the object. For example, this could be a Gif file or multimedia presentation. You should use the type attribute with the data attribute to help the browser determine what plug-in or application should be used when processing the file. If the browser cannot display or process the file, or if the information supplied with the type property is not valid for the browser, the HTML text between the <object> and </object> tags is processed.

```
<OBJECT data="demo.dcr" type="application/director">
```

declare

The declare property determines if the object is created or instantiated when encountered on the web page. The object is only created when referenced on the page such as with a hypertext link. You might delay the creation of an object if you want to collect data from the user on the page first. For example, with a Java applet, you could then pass the data to the applet using the <param> tag.

height

The height attribute determines the height of the area used by the object on the page. For example, the height and width attributes define the space reserved for the display of a Java applet invoked with the <object> tag. Units for the value can either be a percentage of the display area or actual units, such as inches or pixels.

O

hspace

The hspace attribute defines the space between the left and right side of the object display area and any text that may be on the same line before or after the object. The value is specified in percentage of the viewable area, in this case the distance from the left and right margins, or in absolute units such as pixels or inches.

id

The id attribute defines a document specific identifier for the object. Identifiers can be used in links to other sections on the same page, for example. The value is a text name that must be unique among all the elements on the page.

name

The name property defines a name for the data collected by the object when used in conjunction with forms. If the name property is present and the object is defined within the bounds of a form, the object data is collected and submitted with the rest of the form data. If the declare property is set, however, the object must be referenced or created first before the data will be submitted.

shapes

You use the shapes property to allow the definition of hypertext links within the object display area similar to an image map. If the <object> tag definition contains the shapes property, the browser must examine the contents between the start and end tag to locate any anchors with a shape definition. When the viewer clicks within the defined shape, the link is explored and the coordinates of the click are passed as part of the URL. In the following example, clicking in the page4.htm defined area at the coordinates 25,30 would jump to page4.htm.

```
<object data="arrows.gif" shapes>
<a href=page4.htm shape=rect coords="0,0,50,50">Prev</a>
<a href=page6.htm shape=rect coords="51,0,100,50">Next</a>
</object>
```

standby

The standby property defines text that is displayed while the browser is loading the object data and application. Users see this text until the object can be displayed or executed.

type

The type attribute defines the type of object or media specified with the data attribute of the <object> tag. When processing an object, the browser examines the type to see if the object is supported or can be processed. For example, to play a QuickTime movie, QuickTime must be installed. The browser examines its list of installed applications or plug-ins, and supported file types (image file formats, multimedia files, and so on), to see if the type is supported.

```
<OBJECT data="demo.avi" type="application/avi">
```

usemap

The usemap attribute enables the object to act as a client-side image map in the same fashion as the usemap attribute of the <img> tag. With usemap, you specify the URL of the image map file on the server that should be used when processing clicks on the image of the object.

vspace

The vspace attribute defines the space between the top and bottom of the object display area. The value can be given as units, such as pixels or inches, or as a percentage of the viewable area.

width

The width attribute sets the width of the area used by the object on the page. For example, the height and width attributes define the space reserved for the display of a Java applet invoked with the <object> tag. Units for the actual width can either be a percentage of the display area or actual units such as inches or pixels.

Oct()
Category: VBScript

Type	Function

Browser Support

	Navigator 3	Navigator 4	Explorer 3	Explorer 4
Macintosh				■
Windows			■	■

Syntax   Oct(*number*)

The Oct() function accepts a *number* and returns its octal (base 8) equivalent value. The octal counting system contains eight base values, represented by 0–7. Any numerical value *number* may be passed to Oct(), but fractional values are rounded to the nearest integer before conversion. Passing a null value to the function will return a null value.

oct(5)	returns	5
oct(8)	returns	10
oct(255)	returns	377
oct(0)	returns	0

The octal numbering system is not commonly used—when using a numbering system other than decimal in computer, you'll most likely encounter the hexadecimal system. (See the Hex() function.)

O

<OL>

Category: HTML

		Navigator 3	Navigator 4	Explorer 3	Explorer 4
Browser Support	Macintosh	▬▬▬	▬▬▬	▬▬▬	▬▬▬
	Windows	▬▬▬	▬▬▬	▬▬▬	▬▬▬

Applies To None

May Contain <LI>

May Be Used In <BLOCKQUOTE>, <BODY>, <CENTER>, <DD>, <DIV>, <FORM>, <LI>, <TD>, <TH>

Attributes CLASS, COMPACT, ID, START, TYPE, VALUE

Syntax <OL>...</OL>

The <OL> tag a simple, numbered list of items. A closing, or </OL> tag, is required.

The following example is a simple <OL> list:

```
<OL>
<LI>First item
<LI>Second item
<LI>Third item
</OL>
```

Each item in an <OL> list should be preceded with an <LI> tag. See the <LI> tag entry for more information on this tag, which is used in four kinds of lists.

> **NOTE** If you want to create a bulleted list instead of a numbered list, use the <UL> tag instead. See the <UL> entry for more information.

Figures 1, 2, 3, and 4 illustrate this simple <OL> list in Navigator 3 and Internet Explorer 3 for the Mac and for Windows.

CLASS

The CLASS attribute is used to specify the name of a style sheet as it applies to a specific selection on a web page. See "Cascading Style Sheets Basics" and any individual, related style sheets entries elsewhere in the book for more information.

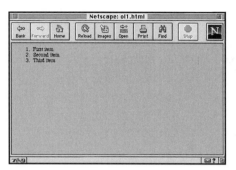

Figure 1

A simple <OL> list in Navigator 3 for the Mac.

Figure 2

A simple <OL> list in Internet Explorer 3 for the Mac.

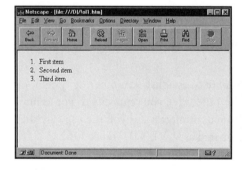

Figure 3

A simple <OL> list in Navigator 3 for Windows.

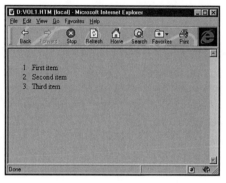

Figure 4

A simple <OL> list in Internet Explorer 3 for Windows.

O

COMPACT

The COMPACT attribute tells the browser that items in the list are short, so the list can be tightened accordingly. When this attribute is used within a <DL> list in Navigator 3, for example, the browser will display two items on one line.

In <OL> lists, however, neither Navigator nor Internet Explorer 3 will display COMPACT-specified lists any differently than regular <OL> lists, even when the list items are only one character long. So use of this attribute in these two browsers, on either the Mac or Windows, seems to serve no purpose at this writing.

ID

The ID attribute is used to distinguish individual selections in a web page as pertaining to the use of style sheets. See "Cascading Style Sheets Basics" and any individual, related style sheets entries elsewhere in the book for more information.

START

The START attribute enables you to resequence or reset the numbering of list items.

In the following example, 3 has been specified as the START value:

```
<OL START=3>
<LI>Me
<LI>You
<LI>A dog named Boo
</OL>
```

The items in this list, then, would be numbered as 3, 4, and 5, respectively. Using the START attribute does not change the general appearance of an <OL> list, just the way that list items are numbered.

Remember that if you have used the TYPE attribute to establish a numbering system, the START attribute will draw its instructions based on the TYPE value you've specified. For example, if you specify I as the TYPE attribute for uppercase Roman numerals and you then specify the START attribute at 5, the items on the list will be numbered as V, VI, VII, and so forth.

See the following TYPE attribute section for more information.

TYPE

The TYPE attribute specifies different kinds of numbering systems.

There are five TYPE values:

1	Arabic numbers (1, 2, 3, and so on) appear sequentially before each item on the list. This is the TYPE attribute's default.
a	Alphanumeric lowercase letters (a, b, c, and so on) appear sequentially before each item on the list.
A	Alphanumeric uppercase letters (A, B, C, and so on) appear sequentially before each item on the list.
i	Lowercase Roman numerals (i, ii, iii, and so on) appear sequentially before each item on the list.
I	Uppercase Roman numerals (I, II, III, and so on) appear sequentially before each item on the list.

In the following example, a TYPE value of a has been specified:

```
<OL TYPE=a>
<LI>Hello.
<LI>Goodbye.
</OL>
```

The two items on this list will subsequently appear numbered with a and b.

Figures 5, 6, 7, and 8 illustrate short <OL> lists with all five numbering TYPE values specified in Navigator 3 and Internet Explorer 3 for the Mac and for Windows.

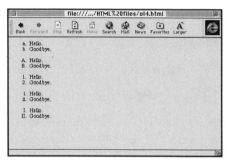

Figure 5

<OL> *lists of all five TYPE settings in Navigator 3 for the Mac.*

Figure 6

<OL> *lists of all five TYPE settings in Internet Explorer 3 for the Mac.*

Figure 7

<OL> *lists of all five TYPE settings in Navigator 3 for Windows.*

Figure 8

<OL> *lists of all five TYPE settings in Internet Explorer 3 for Windows.*

See the <LI> tag entry for more information on the TYPE attribute.

<OPTION>

Category: HTML

Browser Support		Navigator 3	Navigator 4	Explorer 3	Explorer 4
	Macintosh	■	■	■	■
	Windows	■	■	■	■

Applies To None

May Contain None

May Be Used In <SELECT>

Attributes SELECTED, VALUE

Syntax <OPTION>...</OPTION>

The <OPTION> tag is used within the <SELECT> tag to specify individual list items on a form pull-down menu. See the <SELECT> tag entry elsewhere in this book for more information on creating pull-down menus within forms.

The following example HTML demonstrates the proper placement of <OPTION> tag information:

```
<FORM ACTION=http://www.provider.com/cgi-bin/politics METHOD=post>
<P>Political affiliation:<BR>
<SELECT NAME=politics SIZE=3>
<OPTION VALUE=1>Democrat
<OPTION VALUE=2>Republican
<OPTION VALUE=3>Libertarian
<OPTION VALUE=4>Green Party
<OPTION VALUE=5>Communist
<OPTION VALUE=6>Independent
</SELECT>
</FORM>
```

This simple pull-down list will be repeated and shown in figures later on in this entry to demonstrate the function of different <OPTION> attributes.

SELECTED

The SELECTED attribute has a very similar function to the <INPUT> tag's CHECKED attribute: it enables you to preselect one default menu option that will remain selected unless the menu user clicks something else.

The following example HTML shows the same simple list with the first menu item SELECTED:

```
<FORM ACTION=http://www.provider.com/cgi-bin/politics METHOD=post>
<P>Political affiliation:<BR>
<SELECT NAME=politics SIZE=1>
<OPTION VALUE=1 CHECKED>Democrat
<OPTION VALUE=2>Republican
<OPTION VALUE=3>Libertarian
<OPTION VALUE=4>Independent
</SELECT>
</FORM>
```

Figures 1 through 3 illustrate this example HTML in Navigator 3 for Windows and Internet Explorer 3 for the Mac and for Windows. (In Navigator for the Mac, a check mark does not appear next to the menu item specified by the CHECKED attribute.)

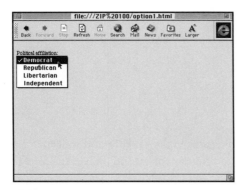

Figure 1

A basic pull-down menu with the first item SELECT-ed in Internet Explorer 3 for the Mac.

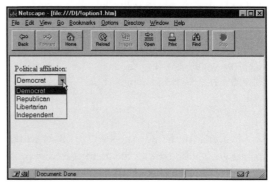

Figure 2

A basic pull-down menu with the first item SELECT-ed in Navigator 3 for Windows.

O

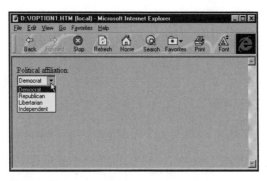

Figure 3

A basic pull-down menu with the first item SELECT-ed in Internet Explorer 3 for Windows.

> **NOTE** To enable the menu user to choose more than one menu option, use the <SELECT> tag's MULTIPLE attribute. See the <SELECT> tag entry elsewhere in the book for more information.

VALUE

The VALUE attribute specifies the hierarchy of menu items by tagging each menu item with an individual identifier.

In the following example HTML, a different VALUE identifier has been given to each item on the menu:

```
<FORM ACTION=http://www.provider.com/cgi-bin/politics METHOD=post>
<P>Political affiliation:<BR>
<SELECT NAME=politics SIZE=1>
<OPTION VALUE=1 CHECKED>Democrat
<OPTION VALUE=2>Republican
<OPTION VALUE=3>Libertarian
<OPTION VALUE=4>Independent
</SELECT>
</FORM>
```

This is similar to the way the NAME attribute works with regards to the <INPUT> and <SELECT> tags, as VALUE also enables the form's gateway program to properly collect and process the form's information.

Option
Category: JavaScript, JScript, and VBScript

Type	Object			

Browser Support		Navigator 3	Navigator 4	Explorer 3	Explorer 4
	Macintosh	■	■	☐	■
	Windows	■	■	■	■

Subset Of	Select object
Properties	defaultSelected, index, selected, text, value
Syntax	document.formName.selectName.options[index].property OR
	document.forms[index].elements[index].options[index].property

The option object provides script access to an item in a selection list, created using the <option> tag within the <select> tag (see Select object). For an entire selection list, each individual option object is stored as an element in the options[] array, which itself is a property of the

`Select` object. By adding or removing `option` objects to the `options[]` array, you can add or remove items from the select field.

> Internet Explorer 3 does not support adding or removing option objects from the `options[]` array; there is no way to modify the item list for a select field.

An option object is created by the `<option>` tag within the `<select>` tag.

`<option value="`*valueToSubmit*`" [selected]> `*textToDisplay*

The `value` attribute specifies a value to send to the server if and when this item is selected *and* the form is submitted to a server. The `selected` attribute specifies whether the item is to be selected by default.

Dynamically Creating and Removing Options

An `option` object can be created and added to a select object's `options[]` array, thereby adding a new item to that select field. To add a new item to *selectName*, use the general construction:

`document.formName.selectName.options[index] = new Option(`*textToDisplay*`, `*value*`,`
defaultSelected`, `*selected*`)`

The parameters `defaultSelected` and `selected` can be either 0 or 1. If you specify 1 for *defaultSelected*, the new item will be selected when the form is reset. If you specify 1 for *selected*, the new item will be selected immediately upon appearing in the select field.

Consider, for example, that you have a select field that contains three items, all of which were specified in the HTML (resulting in Figure 1):

```
<form name=form1>
 <select name="cars" size=6 multiple>
  <option>Toyota</option>
  <option>Honda</option>
  <option>Nissan</option>
 </select>
 <br><input type=text name=newtxt width=10>Enter name of new select item<br>
 <input type=button name=butt1 value="Add new item"
onClick="newitem(this.form.newtxt.value)">
</form>
```

Notice that this form also contains a text field and a button field (which itself contains an `onClick` event handler calling the new item function). Now, you want to code the function that accepts one parameter—the name of a new item—and adds that new item to the above select field.

O

Figure 1

The original select field, with three items, all created within the HTML `<select>` tag.

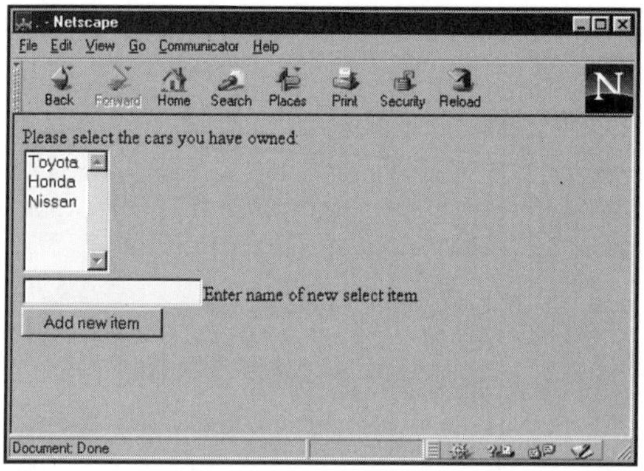

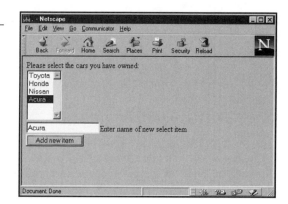

```
function newitem(str)
{
 newidx=document.form1.cars.length;
 document.form1.cars.options[newidx] = new Option(str,str,0,1)
}
```

The first line of this function determines the current number of elements in the `options[]` array. Because index numbering begins at zero, you can add the new `option` object to the array at position `newidx`.

In the second line, you create the new `option` object, which specifies an item whose text is contained in the variable *str*, whose value to submit is also *str*, is not selected by default (0), and is selected upon addition to the list (1).

Now you can type a word into the text field, click the button, and that word is added as an item to the select field, as illustrated handsomely in Figure 2.

Figure 2

The modified select field, with the new item added to the list.

defaultSelected property

Initially, this property reflects the selected attribute of the <option> tag for the particular item. You can modify this property to either true or false, which will cause this item to be selected or unselected by default when and if the form is reset.

```
document.formname.selectname.options[idx].defaultSelected=true
```

> **NOTE**   If the select field is set to accept multiple selections, via the multiple attribute of the <select> tag, resetting the form *will* select any items with true defaultSelected properties, and any currently selected items will remain selected.
>
> If the select field does not accept multiple selections, resetting the form will clear all selections except for the item whose defaultSelected property has most recently been set to true.

 Internet Explorer 3 does not support modification to an option object's defaultSelected property; it is read-only.

index property

The read-only integer that indicates the index of the option object in the options array. The first option object in the array begins at index 0. Therefore, logically,

```
objidx = document.formname.selectname.options[0].index
```

would assign the value 0 to objidx. Of course, this property would become more useful if you did not know for certain which option object in the options array you were currently referencing, such as within a loop situation.

selected property

A Boolean value indicating if the item is currently selected. Contains a value of true if item is selected, otherwise contains false.

```
objsel = document.formname.selectname.options[idx].selected
```

Alternatively, you can assign true or false to the selected property, thereby causing the item to become selected or unselected.

```
document.formname.selectname.options[idx].selected=true
```

Note this works in both Netscape Navigator *and* Internet Explorer!

O

text property

The text that is displayed for the option in the selection list. Originally, this is the text that follows the `<option>` tag. For instance, recall the tag:

`<option>Nissan</option>`

Therefore, assuming we properly reference the option object for this item:

`itemlabel = document.formname.selectname.options[2].text`

would assign the value "Nissan" to `itemlabel`.

Alternatively, you can modify the text that appears for this item in the select field by assigning a new value to the `text` property.

`document.formname.selectname.options[2].text="Integra"`

This would immediately change the item label from "Nissan" to "Integra."

 Internet Explorer 3 does not support assigning a new value to the `text` property; it is read-only.

value property

The text specified by the `value` attribute in the `<option>` tag. This is *not* the text that is displayed by the select list—rather, it is the value that is sent to the server if and when the form is submitted to a server. You can read or modify this property.

```
servval = document.formname.selectname.options[idx].value
document.formname.selectname.options[idx].value="textToSubmit"
```

overflow
Category: Cascading Style Sheets

Browser Support		Navigator 3	Navigator 4	Explorer 3	Explorer 4
	Macintosh	☐	☐	☐	☐
	Windows	☐	☐	☐	☐

Applies To   All elements with `position` of `absolute` or `relative`

Syntax   `overflow: value`

With the `overflow` property, you decide what happens to an element when it exceeds a specified `height` and/or `width` for the element. Set `overflow` to `none`, and the whole of the element will be displayed, even if it goes outside of its declared boundaries. Set this property to `clip`, and the browser will clip off whatever part of the element "goes over the line," so to speak. If line three of a given paragraph goes past the defined height, then that line of text will be cut off and we'll see only the top half or so of the words. Use scroll, and the excess element will be clipped, just as with clip, but this time the browser will display a scrolling mechanism, similar to a frame with scroll bars, to allow the viewer to see the rest of the element. If you have overflow set to none, the browser will do nothing.

```
h1 { overflow: clip }
```

```
h1 { overflow: scroll }
```

O

```
</STRONG> ■ <TD> </TD> ■ <TH> </TH> ■ <TABLE> </TABLE> ■
<IMG> </IMG> ■ <SCRIPT LANGUAGE = "javascript"> </SCRIPT>
■ <SCRIPT LANGUAGE = "vbscript"> </SCRIPT> ■ <BGSOUND
SRC=gbv.wav LOOP=-1> </BGSOUND> ■ <APPLET CLASS=
"ester's_day" SRC="http://testsite/walla walla washington/"
</APPLET> ■ <FRAME></FRAME>■ <MARQUEE> </MARQUEE> ■ <HTML>
</HTML> ■ <A> </A> ■ <OL> </OL> ■ <UL> </UL> ■ <MENU> </MENU>
■ <STRONG> </STRONG> ■ <TD> </TD> ■ <TH> </TH>
```

P

<P>

Category: HTML

Browser Support		Navigator 3	Navigator 4	Explorer 3	Explorer 4
	Macintosh	■■■	■■■	■■■	■■■
	Windows	■■■	■■■	■■■	■■■

May Contain `<A>`, `<APPLET>`, `<B>`, `<BASEFONT>`, `<BIG>`, `<BR>`, `<CITE>`, `<CODE>`, `<DFN>`, `<EM>`, `<FONT>`, `<I>`, `<IMG>`, `<INPUT>`, `<KBD>`, `<MAP>`, `<SAMP>`, `<SELECT>`, `<SMALL>`, `<STRIKE>`, `<STRONG>`, `<SUB>`, `<SUP>`, `<TEXTAREA>`, `<TT>`, `<U>`, `<VAR>`

May Be Used In `<ADDRESS>`, `<BLOCKQUOTE>`, `<BODY>`, `<CENTER>`, `<DD>`, `<DIV>`, `<FORM>`, `<LI>`, `<TD>`, `<TH>`

Attributes `ALIGN, CLASS, ID`

Syntax `<P>…</P>`

The `<P>` tag inserts a paragraph break and specifies a block of text as a paragraph. The closing, or `</P>` tag, is optional.

In the following example, all three paragraphs will display the same way on a web page, even though the closing `</P>` tag is only used in the middle line:

```
<P>This line of text would be one paragraph (it has no closing tag).
<P>This line of text would be another (it does have a closing tag). </P>
<P>This line is another paragraph.
```

Figures 1, 2 and 3 visually illustrate this example in Navigator 3 and Internet Explorer 3 for the Mac and for Windows.

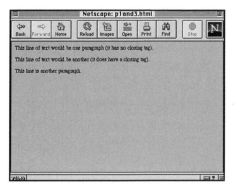

Figure 1

Comparing three paragraphs in Navigator 3 for the Mac.

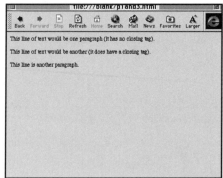

Figure 2

Comparing three paragraphs in Internet Explorer 3 for the Mac.

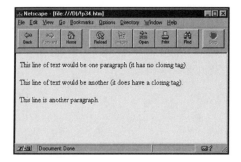

Figure 3

Comparing three paragraphs in Navigator 3 for Windows.

NOTE   Each browser will break and define <P>-specified paragraphs differently. On the average, <P>-specified paragraphs are separated by one to one and a half lines of blank space and are not indented.

The <P> tag should not be used to create blank horizontal space on a web page, because some browsers will add even more white space if more than one <P> tag is present. See the <PRE> and <BR> tag entries elsewhere in the book for more suggestions.

ALIGN

The ALIGN attribute establishes the alignment of a paragraph. It has three values:

center

The paragraph is centered on the web page with ragged right and left edges.

`left`

The paragraph sits flush against the left side of the web page with a ragged right edge. This is the `ALIGN` attribute default.

`right`

The paragraph sits flush against the right side of the web page with a ragged left edge. This value is not supported by Internet Explorer.

Figures 5 and 6 illustrate all three alignment options in Navigator and Internet Explorer for the Mac.

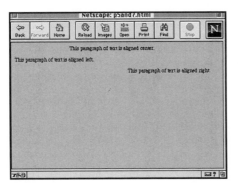

Figure 5

Comparing three paragraph alignments in Navigator 3 for the Mac.

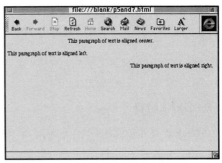

Figure 6

Comparing three paragraph alignments in Internet Explorer 3 for the Mac.

Figures 7 and 8 illustrate all three alignment options in Navigator and Internet Explorer for Windows.

Figure 7

Comparing three paragraph alignments in Navigator 3 for Windows.

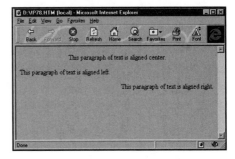

Figure 8

Comparing three paragraph alignments in Internet Explorer 3 for Windows.

Some browsers other than Navigator and Internet Explorer will not apply an `ALIGN` center or an `ALIGN` right setting if the paragraph is not closed with a `</P>` tag.

Also, if a <P>-specified paragraph with an ALIGN-specified alignment setting is enclosed within a <DIV> tag, the <DIV> tag's alignment will override the <P> tag's—even if an alignment setting is not specified and is left by default.

CLASS

The CLASS attribute is used to specify the name of a style sheets as it applies to a specific selection on a web page. See the "Cascading Style Sheets Basics" chapter and any individual, related style sheets entries elsewhere in the book for more information.

ID

The ID attribute is used to distinguish individual selections in a web page as pertaining to the use of style sheets. See the "Cascading Style Sheets Basics" chapter and any individual, related style sheets entries elsewhere in the book for more information.

padding

Category: Cascading Style Sheets

Browser Support		Navigator 3	Navigator 4	Explorer 3	Explorer 4
	Macintosh				
	Windows				

Applies To Block and replaced elements

Syntax `padding: top_value left_value bottom_value right_value`

The padding property enables you to set the top, left, bottom, and right padding values with a single statement. Padding is the space between the border and margin of an element, and the actual element. You can use padding to change the layout of your page or make elements stand alone by themselves. See the section on "Positioning and Layout" in "Cascading Style Sheets Basics" for more information. As with the other padding properties, you may specify either a length in units or a percentage of the block of the element. See the descriptions for margin-top, margin-left, margin-bottom, and margin-right for more information on the individual settings.

```
h1 { padding: 20px 10px 20px 40px }
```

```
<h1 style="padding: 1.2in">
```

Navigator 4 doesn't support this particular **padding**. You have to use the four individual padding properties instead.

padding-bottom
Category: Cascading Style Sheets

Browser Support		Navigator 3	Navigator 4	Explorer 3	Explorer 4
	Macintosh		■		
	Windows		■		

Applies To   Block and replaced elements

Syntax   `padding-bottom: value`

The `padding-bottom` property sets the padding below any given block-level element or replaced element such as the `<img>` tag. The padding is the space between the actual element and any bottom border. You can use any length value or percentage value for padding properties. By default, `padding-bottom` is set to `0`, or no extra bottom padding. Negative values are not supported. For more information on padding and layout, see the section "Positioning and Layout" in "Cascading Style Sheets Basics" earlier in this book.

```
h1 { padding-bottom: 20px }
```

```
<h1 style="padding-bottom: 1.2in">
```

 Explorer 3 and 4 do not support *any* kind of padding. No top, bottom, right, or left.

paddingBottom
Category: JavaScript Style Sheets

Type   Property

Browser Support		Navigator 3	Navigator 4	Explorer 3	Explorer 4
	Macintosh		■		
	Windows		■		

Applies To   All elements

Inherited   No

Syntax   `paddingBottom = "value"`

`paddingBottom` is one of the five padding styles that can be defined for all elements. `paddingBottom` can be used by itself, in conjunction with any of the other padding properties (`paddingTop`, `paddingLeft`, `paddingRight`), or can be defined using the `paddings()` property.

`paddingBottom` is used to define the padding, or space that is left between the border of an element and its content. `paddingBottom` has two possible values:

- "length" defines the size of the padded space in an absolute font size. Using "2.0em" sets a space of 2.0 times larger than the font size of the parent element.

- "percentage" makes the padding space size a percentage of the current element's font size. "1.50" sets the space for 150 percent of the current font size.

> **NOTE** Padding values cannot be negative.

The following code sample shows how to define a style for the body element where the space between the content of the body and the bottom border of the body is 400 percent larger than the size of the parent font. This will cause a large gap between the last element in the body and the end of the body. The JSSS paddingBottom property enables you to define padding space, through code, based on the various document properties. See paddings() for a detailed example.

The following code segment shows the definition of a paddingBottom property:

```
<style TYPE="text/javascript">
tags.body.paddingBottom = "4.00"
</style>
```

The JSSS code can be broken down as follows:

- tags defines that the element immediately following in dot notation will be the element for which the style is being defined.

- body is the html element that is being assigned a style in the tags definitions. This may be any valid HTML element.

- paddingBottom is the style property that is being defined for the element.

- "4.00" is the value of the paddingBottom property.

The initial value for paddingBottom is 0, so there will be no extra space in an element if the style is not used. Element padding can be more consisly defined using the paddings() property.

padding-left

Category: Cascading Style Sheets

Browser Support		Navigator 3	Navigator 4	Explorer 3	Explorer 4
	Macintosh	☐	■	☐	☐
	Windows	☐	■	☐	☐

Applies To	Block and replaced elements
Syntax	padding-left: *value*

The padding-left property sets the padding to the left of an element. The padding is the space between the actual element and any left border such as the edge of the page. You can use any length value or percentage value for padding properties. By default, padding-left is set to 0, or no extra bottom padding. You can't adjust the horizontal padding between two adjacent elements (unless they're in different table cells). Negative values are not supported. For more information on padding and layout, see the section "Positioning and Layout" in "Cascading Style Sheets Basics" earlier in this book.

```
h1 { padding-left: 20px }
```

```
<h1 style="padding-left: 1.2in">
```

Explorer 3 and 4 do not support *any* kind of padding. No top, bottom, right, or left.

N

Navigator 4 overprints text if you ever give padding to inline tags. It also doesn't allow padding to be applied to images.

paddingLeft

Category: JavaScript Style Sheets

Type	Property				
Browser Support		Navigator 3	Navigator 4	Explorer 3	Explorer 4
	Macintosh	☐	■	☐	☐
	Windows	☐	■	☐	☐
Applies To	All elements				
Inherited	No				
Syntax	paddingLeft = "*value*"				

paddingLeft is one of the five padding styles that can be defined for all elements. paddingLeft can be used by itself, in conjunction with any of the other padding properties (paddingTop, paddingBottom, paddingRight), or defined in the paddings() property.

paddingLeft is used to define the padding, or space that is left between the border of an element and its content. paddingLeft has two values:

- ■ "length" defines the size of the padded space in an absolute font size. Using "2.0em" will set a space of 2.0 times larger than the font size of the parent element.

- ■ "percentage" makes the padding space size a percentage of the current element's font size. "1.50" sets the space for 150 percent of the current font size.

NOTE   Padding values cannot be negative.

The following code sample shows how to define a style for the body element where the space between the content of the body and the bottom border of the body is 400 percent larger than the size of the parent font, and the space on the left is 200 percent larger. Using the JavaScript Style Sheets padding style enables you to progamatically define padding space based on the various document properties. See `paddings()` for a detailed example.

```
<style TYPE="text/javascript">
tags.body.paddingBottom = "4.00"
tags.body.paddingLeft = "2.00"
</style>
```

The JSSS code can be broken down as follows:

- `tags` defines that the element immediately following in dot notation will be the element for which the style is being defined.

- `body` is the html element that is being assigned a style in the `tags` definitions. This may be any valid html element.

- `paddingLeft` (and `paddingBottom`) are the style properties that are being defined for the element.

- `"2.00"` (and `"4.00"`) are the values of the `paddingLeft` (and `paddingBottom`) properties.

The initial value for `paddingLeft` is 0, so there is no extra space in an element if the style is not used. Element padding can be more consisly defined using the `paddings()` property.

padding-right

Category: Cascading Style Sheets

Browser Support		Navigator 3	Navigator 4	Explorer 3	Explorer 4
	Macintosh	☐	■	☐	☐
	Windows	☐	■	☐	☐

Applies To Block and replaced elements

Syntax `padding-right: value`

The `padding-right` property sets the padding to the right of an element. The padding is the space between the actual element and any right border. You can use any length value or percentage value for padding properties. By default, `padding-right` is set to `0`, or no extra bottom padding. You can't adjust the horizontal padding between two adjacent elements (unless they're in different table cells). Negative values are not supported. For more information on padding and layout, see the section "Positioning and Layout" in "Cascading Style Sheets Basics" earlier in this book.

```
h1 { padding-right: 20px }
```

```
<h1 style="padding-right: 1.2in">
```

Explorer 3 and 4 do not support *any* kind of padding. No top, bottom, right, or left.

Navigator 4 overprints text if you ever give padding to inline tags and it doesn't allow padding to be applied to images.

---

paddingRight
Category: JavaScript Style Sheets

| Type | Property |

Browser Support		Navigator 3	Navigator 4	Explorer 3	Explorer 4
	Macintosh		■		
	Windows		■		

| Applies To | All elements |

| Inherited | No |

| Syntax | paddingRight = "*value*" |

paddingRight is one of the five padding styles that can be defined for all elements. paddingRight can be used by itself, or in conjunction with any of the other padding properties (paddingTop, paddingBottom, paddingLeft). (Or its definition can be encompassed in a paddings() property definition.)

paddingRight is used to define the padding, or space that is left between the border of an element and its content. paddingRight has two values:

- "length" defines the size of the padded space in an absolute font size. Using "2.0em" will set a space of 2.0 times larger than the font size of the parent element.
- "percentage" makes the padding space size a percentage of the current element's font size. "1.50" sets the space for 150 percent of the current font size.

> **NOTE** Padding values cannot be negative.

The following code sample shows how to define a style for the body element where the space between the content of the body and the bottom border of the body is 400 percent larger than the size of the parent font, and the space on the right is 200% larger. Using the JavaScript Style Sheets padding style enables you to progamatically define padding space based on the various document properties. See paddings() for a detailed example.

```
<style TYPE="text/javascript">
tags.body.paddingBottom = "4.00"
tags.body.paddingRight = "2.00"
</style>
```

The JSSS code can be broken down as follows:

- **tags** defines that the element immediately following in dot notation will be the element for which the style is being defined.

- **body** is the html element that is being assigned a style in the **tags** definitions. This may be any valid HTML element.

- **paddingRight** (and **paddingBottom**) are the style properties that are being defined for the element.

- **"2.00"** (and **"4.00"**) are the values of the **paddingRight** (and **paddingBottom**) properties.

The initial value for **paddingRight** is 0, so there is no extra space in an element if the style is not used. Element padding can be more consisly defined using the **paddings()** property.

paddings()

Category: JavaScript Style Sheets

	Type	Property

Browser Support		Navigator 3	Navigator 4	Explorer 3	Explorer 4
	Macintosh		■		
	Windows		■		

	Applies To	All elements
	Inherited	No
	Syntax	paddings(value1, value2, value3, value4)

paddings() is one of the five padding styles that can be defined for all elements. **paddings()** is used to define the padding, or space that is left between the border of an element and its content. Using **paddings()** replaces the need to define a style for each of the four specific padding elements—paddingLeft, paddingBottom, paddingRight, paddingTop.

The syntax for the **paddings()** property is:

```
tags.paddings(top,right,bottom,left)
```

Each of the four arguments for the **paddings()** property can be one of two values:

- **"length"** defines the size of the padded space in an absolute font size. Using "2.0em" will set a space of 2.0 times larger than the font size of the parent element.

- **"percentage"** makes the padding space size a percentage of the current element's font size. "1.50" sets the space for 150 percent of the current font size.

> **NOTE** Padding values cannot be negative.

The following code sample shows how to define a style for the body element where the space between the content of the body and all borders of the body are at least 200 percent larger than the size of the parent font(and the top is 400 percent larger):

```
<style TYPE="text/javascript">
tags.body.paddings("4.00", "2.00", "2.00", "2.00")
</style>
```

This style definition is the same as defining each property seperately as shown in the following example:

```
<style TYPE="text/javascript">
tags.body.paddingBottom = "2.00"
tags.body.paddingLeft = "2.00"
tags.body.paddingRight = "2.00"
tags.body.paddingTop = "4.00"
</style>
```

Using the JavaScript Style Sheets `padding` style enables you to define padding space based on the various document properties. Note that the `paddingTop` is much larger (an extra 200 percent larger) than the other padding styles. This means that the content at the top of the body will always be spaced further away from the border than any of the other three borders.

```
<html>
<head>
<style TYPE="text/javascript">
tags.body.paddings("200.00", "100.00", "100.00", "100.00")
</style>
<img src="sciex.gif">
</head>
<body>
<p>Without paddings the text is displayed to the extreme
left and top of the document. And seems to close to the image
to make the page easily readable.
<p>
<p> With the paddings() in the body of the document, the text
is moved in from the left and top of the body thus making the
image less crowded
</body>
</html>
```

Figure 1 shows the result when the `<style>` for paddings is not included in the previous code segment and Figure 2 shows the result when the `paddings()` style is implemented.

P

Figure 1

*Document with no
padding in body.*

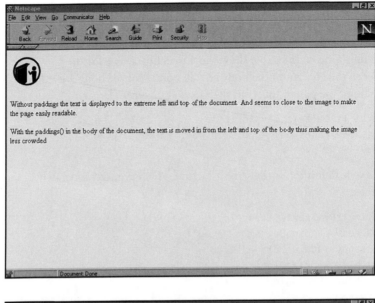

Figure 2

*Body of document is
padded.*

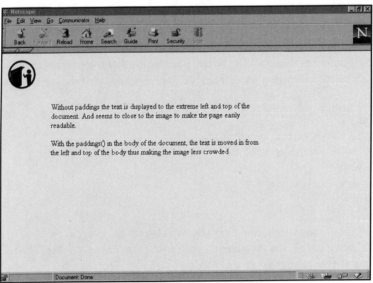

The difference between the top padding in Figures 1 and 2 is very minor, because the percentage increase isn't a large amount, but the padding on the top is indeed slightly bigger than the padding on the other three sides.

The JSSS code

```
tags.body.paddings("200.00", "100.00", "100.00", "100.00")
```

that is contained in the HTML used to create Figure 2 is broken down as follows:

- `tags` is one of the methods of defining JSSS styles. The `tags` definition describes the element immediately following it in the dot notation a valid HTML element.
- `body` is the html element that is being assigned a style. This may be any valid html element.
- `paddings()` is the style that is being defined for the element. It may be any valid JSSS style.
- `"200.00"` and `"100.00"` are the values of the style `paddings()`.

The initial value for all padding styles is 0, so there is no extra space in an element if the style is not used.

padding-top
Category: Cascading Style Sheets

Browser Support		Navigator 3	Navigator 4	Explorer 3	Explorer 4
	Macintosh		■		
	Windows		■		

Applies To Block and replaced elements

Syntax `padding-top: value`

The `padding-top` property sets the padding above any given block-level element or replaced element such as the `<img>` tag. The padding is the space between the actual element and any top border. You can use any length value or percentage value for padding properties. By default, `padding-top` is set to `0`, or no extra top padding. Negative values are not supported. For more information on padding and layout, see the section "Positioning and Layout" in "Cascading Style Sheets Basics" earlier in this book.

```
h1 { padding-top: 20px }

<h1 style="padding-top: 1.2in">
```

 Explorer 3 and 4 do not support *any* kind of padding. No top, bottom, right, or left.

P

paddingTop

Category: JavaScript Style Sheets

Type	Property

Browser Support

	Navigator 3	Navigator 4	Explorer 3	Explorer 4
Macintosh	☐	■	☐	☐
Windows	☐	■	☐	☐

Applies To	All elements
Inherited	No
Syntax	paddingTop = "*value*"

paddingTop is one of the five padding styles that can be defined for all elements. paddingTop can be used by itself, or in conjunction with any of the other padding properties (paddingLeft, paddingBottom, paddingRight).

paddingTop is used to define the padding, or space that is left between the border of an element and its content. paddingTop has two values:

- "length" defines the size of the padded space in an absolute font size. Using "2.0em" will set a space of 2.0 times larger than the font size of the parent element.
- "percentage" makes the padding space size a percentage of the current element's font size. "1.50" sets the space for 150 percent of the current font size.

> **NOTE** Padding values cannot be negative.

The following code sample shows how to define a style for the body element where the space between the content of the body and all borders of the body are 200 percent larger than the size of the parent font. Using the JavaScript Style Sheets padding style enalbes you to progamatically define padding space based on the various document properties. Note that the paddingTop is much larger (an extra 200 percent) than the other padding styles. This means that the content at the top of the body will always be spaced further away from the border than on any of the other three borders.

```
<style TYPE="text/javascript">
tags.body.paddingBottom = "2.00"
tags.body.paddingLeft = "2.00"
tags.body.paddingRight = "2.00"
tags.body.paddingTop = "4.00"
</style>
```

The JSSS code is broken down as follows:

- tags defines that the element immediately following in dot notation will be the element for which the style is being defined.
- body is the html element that is being assigned a style in the tags definitions. This may be any valid HTML element.
- paddingTop (and paddingBottom, paddingLeft, and paddingRight) are the style properties that are being defined for the element.
- "4.00" (and "2.00") are the values of the paddingTop (and paddingBottom, paddingLeft, and paddingRight) properties.

The initial value for paddingTop is 0, so there is no extra space in an element if the style is not used. Element padding can be more consisly defined using the paddings() property. See paddings() for a detailed example.

parseFloat()

Category: JavaScript, JScript

| **Type** | Function |

Browser Support

	Navigator 3	Navigator 4	Explorer 3	Explorer 4
Macintosh	■	■	☐	■
Windows	■	■	■	■

Syntax   parseFloat(*string*)

The purpose of parseFloat() is to convert a given *string* into a floating point number (that is, a number with decimal places). Legal characters that may appear within *string* include:

- a sign, + or – as the first character
- a numeral, 0 through 9
- one decimal point
- an exponent, e or E

Examples best illustrate the parseFloat() function:

parseFloat("510.33")	returns	510.33
parseFloat("-23.173")	returns	–23.173
parseFloat("12")	returns	12
parseFloat("3e+2")	returns	300
parseFloat("3E-2")	returns	0.03
parseFloat("34feet4")	returns	34

P

Parsing of *string* stops at the first instance of an illegal character, as illustrated in the last example. If an illegal character is the first character in the string, parseFloat() returns "NaN" ("Not a Number"), which represents a failure to return a valid number. You check for "NaN" using the isNaN() function (see isNaN() function).

parseInt()
Category: JavaScript, JScript

	Type	Function

Browser Support

	Navigator 3	Navigator 4	Explorer 3	Explorer 4
Macintosh	■	■	☐	■
Windows	■	■	■	■

Syntax parseInt(string[,radix])

The purpose of the parseInt() function is relatively straightforward: convert the given *string* into an integer in base *radix* units.

The common numbering system familiar to most of us is base 10. Based on that radix, consider the following examples:

parseInt("3",10)	returns	3
parseInt("200.7323",10)	returns	200
parseInt("42*3+hiya",10)	returns	42

Notice that when a radix is specified, as it is in this example, the string is parsed only until it reaches a non-numeric characters. In the third example parsing stops after "42".

Another common numbering system in computing is hexadecimal, or base 16. In this system there are 16 basic units, numbered 0 through F. Thus:

parseInt("F",16)	returns	15
parseInt("AA",16)	returns	170

If you omit the *radix* parameter, base 10 will be assumed, unless you precede the string value with "0x" to indicate base 16 or "0" to indicate base 8 (octal). For instance:

parseInt("0xAA")	returns	170 (base 16 was indicated)
parseInt("017")	returns	15 (base 8 was indicated)
parseInt("420")	returns	420 (base 10 was implied)

The previous results hold even if the *radix* is specified, because the "0x" and "0" prependages override any base specified by *radix*.

If you pass a *string* that cannot be evaluated, such as one that begins with a non-numeric characters, or a character invalid for the base, "NaN" ("Not a Number") will be returned. You test for the return of "NaN" using the `isNaN()` function (see `isNan() function`).

The following examples would all return "NaN" because they cannot produce a valid number:

`parseInt("Joey")`	because	begins with non-numeric character
`parseInt("0xGA")`	because	first character "G" is invalid base 16
`parseInt("21101",2)`	because	first character "2" is invalid base 2

Although these examples may seem complicated, you'll most commonly use `parseInt()` to convert a string into a base 10 number for some calculation.

Password
Category: JavaScript, JScript, VBScript

Type	Object	

Browser Support

	Navigator 3	Navigator 4	Explorer 3	Explorer 4
Macintosh	■	■	☐	■
Windows	■	■	■	■

Subset Of Form object

Properties `defaultValue, form, name, type, value`

Methods `blur(), focus(), select()`

Event Handlers `onBlur, onFocus`

Syntax
```
document.formName.passwordName.property OR
document.forms[index].elements[index].property OR
document.formName.passwordName.method(parameters) OR
document.forms[index].elements[index].method(parameters)
```

The password form field is a variation on the `text` form field. However, data entered into the password form field is not displayed onscreen; rather, asterisks are shown as placeholders. Although often used to accept private information from a user, such as a password, keep in mind that this form field only obscures the true data from sight in the browser window—it does not encrypt the data sent to the server. The `password` object provides script access to this form field, allowing the programmer to modify or view the password element's contents. A password element is created using the `<input>` tag.

```
<input
   type="password"
   name="passwordName"
```

```
[value="initialValue"]
size=lengthOfBox
[onBlur="eventHandler"]
[onFocus="eventHandler"]
```

Figure 1

A standard password
object.

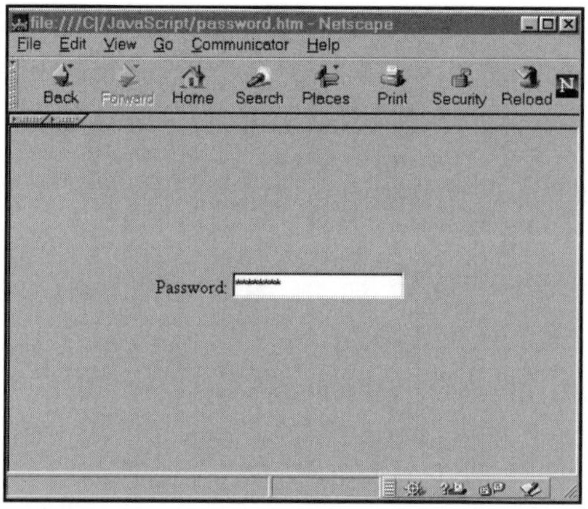

defaultValue property

The initial text displayed (in asterisks) in the password field, specified by the `value` attribute in the `<input>` tag. This property is read-only.

```
startval = document.formname.passwordname.defaultValue
```

form property

The read-only reference to the `form` object that contains the `password` object. This is a useful way to refer to another object in the same form. For instance, imagine a scenario where you want to reference a `text` object, named *text1*, which resides within the same form as the `password` object *password1*. This can be used to code in shorthand, or eliminate the need to explicitly reference the full path to every element within a single form, as in the code excerpts:

JavaScript

```
path=document.forms[0].password1
value1=path.value
value2=path.form.text1.value
```

VBScript

```
set path=document.forms(0).password1
value1=path.value
value2=path.form.text1.value
```

name **property**

The read-only name of the `password` object, specified by the `name` attribute in the `<input>` tag.

```
objname = document.formname.passwordname.name
objval = document.formname.objname.defaultValue
```

type **property**

The input type specified by the `type` attribute in the `<input>` tag. Of course, this always contains the value "password" when referencing a password element.

```
objtype = document.formname.passwordname.type
```

> Internet Explorer 3 does not support the **type** property.

value **property**

The `value` property contains the text recorded into the password field. This can be changed by the user modifying the text in the password field, or internally via a script assignment. The initial value of the password field is specified by the `value` attribute in the `<input>` tag, and stored in the `defaultValue` property. Because the text that appears in the password is obscured, and usually used for private data, it's uncommon to need to modify this property from within a script.

WARNING   Under certain circumstances, you can read the contents of the value property, but remember that this private data is *not* encrypted. Therefore, if you send it to a server for processing without using some form of encryption, the private data could be intercepted and utilized by someone on the network.

```
passval = document.formname.passwordname.value
```

Within Netscape 3.0 and higher, user-input password field data cannot be properly "seen" with JavaScript unless data-tainting is enabled. This is a security feature, explained briefly in the entry for the JavaScript `taint()` function.

blur( ) **method**

This method simulates the user losing focus from the password field. Therefore, if the user currently has focus on the password field, somehow triggering the following code would remove the focus:

```
document.formname.passwordname.blur()
```

P

focus() method

This method simulates the user gaining focus on the password field. You could use this method to call a user's attention to the password field.

```
document.formname.textname.focus()
```

Be careful when and if you use the focus() method on a password field that also contains an onFocus() event handler. In some scenarios within Netscape, this may result in an infinite loop wherein the onFocus event handler is repeated seemingly indefinitely. If your page is not operating as intended, this may be a cause to investigate.

select() method

This method selects the group of asterisks in password field. This is a good way to draw the user's attention to the password field for modification, as seen in Figure 2.

```
document.formname.passwordname.select()
```

Figure 2

Text in the password field selected, either by the user or the select() method.

Enter your password:

onBlur event handler

Located within the <input> tag, this activates when the user loses focus (that is, clicks or tabs elsewhere in the browser) from the password field.

```
<input type="password" name=passwordname value="initialtext"
➥onBlur="eventHandler">
```

onFocus event handler

Located within the <input> tag, this activates when the user clicks or tabs onto the password field, unless the field already had focus.

```
<input type="password" name=passwordname value="initialtext"
➥onFocus="eventHandler">
```

<PLAINTEXT>

Category: HTML

Browser Support		Navigator 3	Navigator 4	Explorer 3	Explorer 4
	Macintosh	■■	■■	■■	■■
	Windows	■■	■■	■■	■■

Applies To None

May Contain None

May Be Used In None

Attributes None

Syntax `<PLAINTEXT>...</PLAINTEXT>`

The `<PLAINTEXT>` tag renders formatted text, typically in fixed-width type with white space and an ending line break. Both Navigator and Internet Explorer support it (although HTML 3.2 specifications only list Netscape support), but each browser translates this tag in a different way. For this reason, many HTML authorities recommend using the `<PRE>` tag in its place to accomplish the same results. See the `<PRE>` tag entry elsewhere in the book for more information.

Here's the problem: in Navigator, the closing, or `</PLAINTEXT>` tag, is not required:

`This text is normal plain text <PLAINTEXT> but this is PLAINTEXT-type text.`

However, Internet Explorer does require a `</PLAINTEXT>` closing tag:

`This text is normal plain text <PLAINTEXT> but this is PLAINTEXT-type text.`
`➥</PLAINTEXT>`

Here's the catch: if you include the `</PLAINTEXT>` tag, Navigator will write it out on your web page like regular text. But if you leave the `</PLAINTEXT>` closing tag off, Explorer won't apply the `<PLAINTEXT>` tag at all. So you cannot cover all your bases.

P

Plugin

Category: JavaScript 1.1

Type Object

Browser Support		Navigator 3	Navigator 4	Explorer 3	Explorer 4
	Macintosh	■■	■■	☐	☐
	Windows	■■	■■	☐	☐

Subset Of Navigator object

Properties description, name, filename, length

Syntax navigator.plugins[*index*].*property* OR
navigator.plugins["*pluginName*"].*property* OR
navigator.mimeTypes[*index*].enabledPlugin.*property*

Plug-ins are external programs that the browser launches when a file of an associated MIME type is downloaded. Each plugin object allows read-only script access to configuration characteristics for each plug-in; plugin objects are elements of the plugins array, which itself is a property of the navigator object. (See the navigator object). Common plug-ins include the RealAudio Player, QuickTime, and Macromedia Shockwave. Plug-ins are placed in a web page via the <embed> tag.

Using this tag, a particular file is "embedded" into the web page. Upon loading the page, the browser encounters this embedded file, and attempts to launch whichever plug-in is associated with that type of file. So, you might embed a QuickTime movie into your page. When a visitor loads this page, his browser will determine if a plug-in has been installed to handle a QuickTime movie. If yes, the QuickTime plug-in will be launched and the movie played. If no, a pop-up dialog box will alert the user that this plug-in is unknown to the browser.

Generally, you would access a plugin object to determine whether a user has a particular plug-in installed. If your page requires a certain plug-in, you could alert the user to the problem. If you know the official name of the plug-in, testing for it is straightfoward:

```
if (navigator.plugins["pluginName"])
{ statements if plug-in is installed }
else { statements if plug-in not installed }
```

However, if you're interested in determining whether a *particular* plug-in is installed for a *particular* MIME type, you'd find it easier to use the enabledPlugin property of the mimeType object. (See the MimeType object.)

Plugin objects can be referenced either directly through the plugins array, or through the enabledPlugin property of the mimeType object (see MimeType object).

Additionally, each plugin object is also an array, containing one mimeType object element for each MIME type associated with that plug-in. Thus, a plug-in that has three associated MIME types would be reflected as a plugin object array containing three elements, each of which is a mimeType object.

For instance, the following code excerpt would display the MIME type definition for the first MIME type associated with the second plug-in:

```
window.alert(navigator.plugins[1][0].type)
```

Internet Explorer 3 does not support the `plugin` object. At the time of this writing, Internet Explorer 4 appears to support a `plugins[]` array under the `document` object. However, additional details are unavailable.

NOTE For a listing of some frequently used MIME types, check out Appendix E.

`description` property

Some plug-ins, when installed, contain additional description text for humans' benefit. The following script statement writes the description text for the first installed plug-in:

```
document.write(navigator.plugins[0].description)
```

`name` property

Each plug-in possesses a name, by which it can be identified. You can also use this name in place of the index number in the `plugins` array to refer to a particular `plugin` object.

```
plgname=navigator.plugins[0].name
document.write(navigator.plugins[plgname].description)
```

In the preceding script excerpt, the first plug-in's name is assigned to the variable `plgname`. In the second statement, `plgname` is used in a `plugin` object reference, outputting its `description`. For instance, if `navigator.plugins[0]` references the QuickTime `plugin` object, the `name` property will contain the string "QuickTime Plug-In."

`filename` property

The `filename` property contains the filesystem path to where the plug-in resides on the user's computer. For instance, the following script statement outputs the file path for the LiveAudio plug-in:

```
document.write(navigator.plugins["LiveAudio"].filename)
```

Output to the page is the text:

```
C:\INTERNET\NETSCAPE\PROGRAM\plugins\NPAUDIO.DLL
```

Of course, the file path varies from system to system, and between different operating systems.

`length` property

As explained earlier, each `plugin` object is also an array containing elements for each `mimeType` object associated with it. The `length` property reflects the number of `mimeType` object elements in the array, and thus, the number of MIME types that the specific plug-in recognizes. Do not confuse this property with the length property of the `plugins` array, which reflects the number of plug-ins installed. (See the `navigator` object.)

P

For instance, the script statement

```
xmimes=navigator.plugins["LiveAudio"].length
```

would assign the number of MIME types associated with the LiveAudio plug-in to the variable `xmimes`.

position

Category: Cascading Style Sheets

Browser Support		Navigator 3	Navigator 4	Explorer 3	Explorer 4
	Macintosh	☐	■	☐	☐
	Windows	☐	■	☐	■

Applies To All elements

Syntax position: *value*

`position` is the property that opens new doors for controlled page layout. When combined with the `top` and `left` properties discussed in this book, you can more accurately define where any element (text or replaced element) appears onscreen. This property also establishes an exact coordinate system on the page for placing child elements relative to the parent. The three values you can specify for `position` are:

- `absolute` positioning enables you to precisely position elements totally independently of any other elements around them.

- `relative` positioning involves specifying the position of elements relative to their natural position in the document's flow.

- `static` turns off positioning and returns the layout to what HTML normally does without style sheets. A static element cannot be positioned, nor does it define a coordinate system by which some other child element could be positioned.

```
h1 { position: relative }
```

```
<h1 style="position: absolute">
```

When you position an element with `absolute`, you give it a specific rectangular area that will contain the contents of the element. This new rectangle can be controlled independently of any other element on the page with the `top` and `left` properties as with the following example:

```
<html>
 <style type="text/css">
 <!--
  body { background: white }
  div  { position: absolute;
        left: 40px;
```

```
             top: 70px }
    P     { position: absolute;
             left: 200px;
             top: 100px }
  -->
  </style>
<head>
  <title>Absolute Positioning</title>
</head>
<body>
  Here is some body text that appears after BODY but before
  any other HTML tags. Standard stuff.
  <div>Now I've started a division, and the text you see
  here is within DIV. It gets positioned independently,
  based on the coordinate system defined by BODY.
  <p>And here is P text within the DIV. It's positioned
  independently based on DIV's coordinate system.</p>
  </div>
</body>
</html>
```

The result is shown in Figure 1. Figure 2 illustrates the various coordinate systems at work. The `<div>` text is positioned absolutely and the browser creates a new coordinate system based on its parent element, `<body>`. The `<div>` text (the "box" around `<div>`, actually) begins at a point that is 40 pixels from the left edge of `<body>`'s normal display area, and 70 pixels down from the top. Similarly, when the browser sees that `<p>` is a child of `<div>`, it creates yet another coordinate system for `<p>` that is based on the starting point of `<div>` text (the upper-left corner of the box that surrounds the `<div>` element). So, from that point, it goes across 200 pixels and down 100 pixels, and then begins to display `<p>` text.

P

Figure 1

Absolute positioning means you can control layout according to coordinate systems.

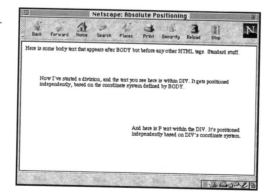

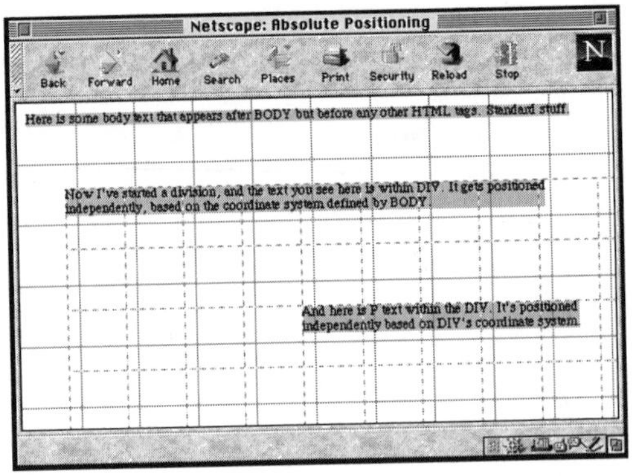

Figure 2

Here is the position-ing going on behind the scenes. You can see the boxes for each element, and the two coordinate systems (solid lines for <body>'s, dashed lines for <div>'s).

For some reason, Explorer 4 positions the <div> text correctly, but *not* the <p> text. The <p> text appears to be absolutely positioned, but not according to the units specified.

Absolute positioning can also be used on replaced elements such as images, as with the following example:

```html
<html>
 <style type="text/css">
 <!--
  body { background: black;
         color: white }
   .a  { position: absolute;
         left: 300px;
         top: 0px }
   P   { position: absolute;
         left: -40px;
         top: 80px }
 -->
 </style>
<head>
 <title>Absolute Positioning</title>
</head>
<body>
 <h2>Muir Woods: Your Path to Peace</h2>
 <span class=a><img src="woods.jpg">
 <p>Stepping into Muir Woods is like stepping into the
 quietest part of your soul. The wind in the trees slows
 the racing mind...</p>
```

```
  </span>
 </body>
 </html>
```

Figure 4 shows the magic happening. The image is positioned 300 pixels from the left edge of
<body> (which is also the edge of the browser window). Because the top value is set to 0 pixels,
it's brought right up to the top edge of the window (definitely something difficult to do in
standard HTML!). Then, the line of <p> text is positioned based on the coordinate system the
image creates: 80 pixels down from the top of the image, and –40 pixels to the right (that is, 40
pixels to the left) of the image's left edge.

When layering occurs while you're using position, the child elements always appear on top of
their parents. That's why the text is displayed on top of the image in Figure 3.

Figure 3

*Absolute positioning
with images and
negative values can
create interesting
results.*

 In the current beta, Explorer 4 does not seem to absolutely position images.
Hopefully this will be fixed as well.

When you position an element with relative, it's placed relative to its parent element, more or
less like current HTML. But even though the element does retain its natural formatting on the
page, it can receive some of the special abilities that absolute offers. For example, you can
position child elements relative to it, and you can also use it to layer with other elements as with
this example:

```
<html>
 <style type="text/css">
 <!--
  body { background: white }
  i    { position: relative;
         left: 10px;
         top: 50px }
```

P

```
-->
</style>
<head>
 <title>Relative Positioning</title>
</head>
<body>
 <h4>Here's some normal body text.
 <i>When you position an element with relative, it's placed relative to its
parent element, more or less like we're used to in HTML. But even though the
element does retain its natural formatting on the page, it can receive some of
the special abilities that absolute offers.
 </i></h4>
</body>
</html>
```

In this example, the browser is told to position the italicized text relative to the regular text. Specifically, the instructions are to begin displaying the italicized text 10 pixels across and 50 pixels down from *where it would otherwise be displayed* by default (see Figure 4). There is a coordinate system at work here, but the coordinates begin *not* at the beginning of an element, but at the "end." So, after the period after "text," the browser goes down 50 pixels and across 10 before displaying the other text.

Figure 4

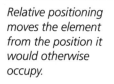

Relative positioning moves the element from the position it would otherwise occupy.

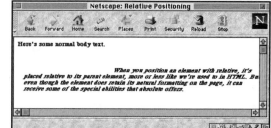

Notice how the other lines in the italicized section continue to wrap (more or less) like the first, using its left margin. That's because the text continues to be formatted like its parent. That's the difference between `relative` and `absolute`.

 The first beta of Explorer 4 does not support `relative` positioning at all.

<PRE>

Category: HTML

	Navigator 3	Navigator 4	Explorer 3	Explorer 4
Browser Support Macintosh	▬	▬	▬	▬
Windows	▬	▬	▬	▬

May Contain <A>, <APPLET>, <B>, <BASEFONT>, <BR>, <CITE>, <CODE>, <DFN>, <EM>, <I>, <INPUT>, <KBD>, <MAP>, <SAMP>, <SELECT>, <STRIKE>, <STRONG>, <TEXTAREA>, <TT>, <U>, <VAR>

May Be Used In <BLOCKQUOTE>, <BODY>, <CENTER>, <DD>, <DIV>, <FORM>, <LI> <TD>, <TH>

Attributes WIDTH

Syntax <PRE>...</PRE>

The <PRE> tag specifies a block of preformatted text to be inserted in a web page exactly as you type it in. A closing, or </PRE>, tag, is required.

The following example is part of *Romeo and Juliet*, the Shakespearean drama, and requires certain precise spacing to be transcribed in Elizabethan style:

```
<PRE>          When he shall die,
Take him and cut him out in little stars.
    And he will make the face of heaven so fine,
That all the world will be in love with night,
    And pay no worship to the garish sun.</PRE>
```

When this HTML is translated by a browser, the exact spacing and line breaks will be preserved as typed in above, until the closing </PRE> tag reimposes the web page's default or customized settings.

The spacing in the previous examples shown was established with the space bar, not the Tab key. Using the Tab key will not guarantee precise or accurate results, as different browsers translate the width of a Tab space differently.

Believe it or not, the same amount of space was created on each line in each passage, first using the space bar and then using the Tab key, in the HTML for each of these pages. Both the top and bottom passages should look exactly the same, but in all four instances, the browser software has interpreted a Tab key space very differently, sometimes even varying Tab key space from line to line. This is why you want to measure <PRE> space using the space bar—if you use the Tab key instead, you are far less likely to get acceptable results.

P

> **NOTE**   If you are using the <PRE> tag to show example strings of HTML code or some other programming language where <, >, and & are actual characters, you cannot simply cut and paste such strings in between <PRE> and </PRE>. Browsers interpret the <, >, and & characters as instructions, not letters or symbols, so you must replace them with their correct character entities. See Appendix A for more information on character mapping and alternative alphabets.

WIDTH

The WIDTH attribute is an optional instruction sometimes used to specify the width of the <PRE>-specified text block.

Specifying a width in this manner enables the browsers to choose an appropriate font and font size, but at this writing, WIDTH is not widely supported. It does not work, for example, in Navigator 3 or Internet Explorer 3 for the Mac.

In the following example, a text area width of 40, roughly half the default space, is suggested:

```
<PRE WIDTH="40"> When he shall die,
Take him and cut him out in little stars.
     And he will make the face of heaven so fine,
That all the world will be in love with night,
     And pay no worship to the garish sun.</PRE>
```

In the following test figures—Figures 1 and 2—compare the default, nonspecified width of the top quotation (usually about 80 characters) to the second quote where the width is specified, as in the preceding example, at 40.

Figure 1

Different WIDTH settings in Navigator 3 for the Mac.

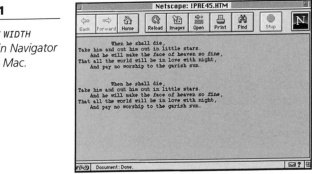

Figure 2

Different WIDTH settings in Internet Explorer 3 for the Mac.

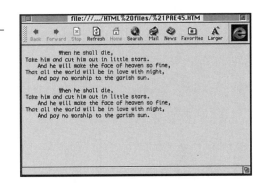

> **NOTE**
> Remember that Windows monitors display text differently than Mac monitors—on PCs, individual letters are wider and taller; there's more space between them; and blank spaces like line breaks and margins are also more generous. This difference will also affect the way attributes such as WIDTH are interpreted.

Many web page authors also use the <PRE> tag to insert blank space—just blank space, space bar spaces, and carriage returns—no text. This is not the use for which this tag was intended, and it doesn't work with precision, either. As already mentioned (several times) units of space are translated differently from browser to browser and platform to platform, from the tiny pixel measurement to the larger line and character width.

If this discrepancy will not affect the design of your page, or if you're only looking for an approximate amount of blank horizontal space, then you might be satisfied with the <PRE> tag.

> **DESIGN NOTE**
> If you've experimented with the <PRE> tag and don't care for the results, there's a relatively new trick called the "Single Pixel GIF" that you might investigate. This method of inserting horizontal and vertical space involves creating an "image" that's one pixel by one pixel in a program like Photoshop, which you then save as a GIF file and insert in your web page with the <IMG> tag. Because you use this GIF file as an image, its size remains constant regardless of the platform or browser a visitor to your page is using.
>
> There's more to it than that, however—if you want to learn all the ins and outs of the Single Pixel GIF, consult David Siegel's *Killer Web Sites* tutorial pages located on the web at:
>
> `http://www.killersites.com`

P

<IMG> </IMG> ■ <SCRIPT LANGUAGE = "javascript"> </SCRIPT>
■ <SCRIPT LANGUAGE = "vbscript"> </SCRIPT> ■ <BGSOUND
SRC=gbv.wav LOOP=-1> </BGSOUND> ■ <APPLET CLASS=
"ester's_day" SRC="http://testsite/walla walla washington/"
</APPLET> ■ <FRAME></FRAME>■ <MARQUEE> </MARQUEE> ■
<HTML> </HTML> ■ <A> </A> ■ <OL> </OL> ■ <UL> </UL> ■ <MENU>
</MENU> ■ <STRONG> </STRONG> ■ <TD> </TD> ■ <TH> </TH>

Radio

Category: JavaScript, JScript, VBScript

Type	Object

Browser Support

	Navigator 3	Navigator 4	Explorer 3	Explorer 4
Macintosh	■	■	☐	■
Windows	■	■	■	■

Subset Of Form object

Properties checked, defaultChecked, form, name, type, length, value

Methods Blur(), Focus(), Click()

Event Handlers onBlur, onFocus, onClick

Syntax
```
document.formName.radioName[index].property OR
document.forms[index].elements[index].property OR
document.formName.radioName[index].method(parameters) OR
document.forms[index].elements[index].method(parameters)
```

The radio object is an on/off form field element. Checking the radio button will result in a "on" (true) setting, whereas an unchecked radio button will have a "off" (false) setting. What separates radio buttons from checkboxes is that radio buttons are typically used in mutually exclusive groupings. That is, a group wherein only one choice from a set of choices can be selected. Consider, for instance, querying the user's gender, which can be *either* male or female, but never both nor neither. In this case, you might have two radio buttons, one labeled "Male" and the other labelled "Female". When the user selects one of the button, the other is automatically deselected, as seen in Figure 1.

Radio buttons are grouped together by giving them the same name, as specified by the name attribute. Within a script, an individual `radio` object refers to an individual radio button. A radio object is referenced via an indexed array within the radio button group name. For instance:

```
document.formName.radioName[0].property
```

references the `radio` object corresponding to the first radio button in the group of radio buttons named *radioName*.

A radio object is created using the `<input>` tag. The default value of the radio button object will be unchecked unless the `checked` attribute is supplied.

```
<input
    type="radio"
    name="radioGroupName"
    value="valueToSubmit"
    [checked]
    [onBlur="eventHandler"]
    [onClick="eventHandler"]
    [onFocus="eventHandler"]>
    RadioButtonText
```

checked **property**

A Boolean value indicating the status of the radio button. The value will be true for a checked radio button and false for an unchecked radio button.

```
radioval = document.formname.radiogroup[0].checked
```

In the preceding statement, `radioval` will be assigned the `checked` status of the first radio button within the group named `radiogroup`.

Alternatively, you may set this property to true or false with script code, and the appearance of the radio button will change accordingly.

```
document.formname.radiogroup[1].checked=true
```

When one radio button's checked property is set to true, the rest in that group will be set to false.

Recall this entry's opening image (Figure 1), which contained a group of two radio buttons representing gender choices. Imagine that this grouping was created with the following HTML:

```
<form name=firstform>
<h3>Please select your gender:<br></h3>
<input type=radio name=gender checked>Male<br>
<input type=radio name=gender>Female<br>
</form>
```

You can see that the `name` for this radio button group is `gender`. Thus, you could programmatically set the second radio button—Female—to true:

```
document.firstform.gender[1].checked=true
```

As a consequence, the result would be as seen in Figure 2.

Figure 2

Assigning a value of true to the `checked` *property of the second* `radio` *object in this group.*

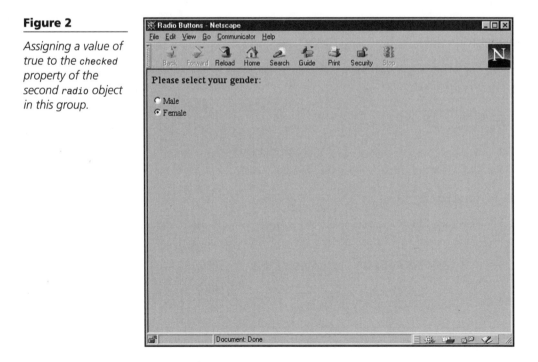

R

defaultChecked **property**

A Boolean value true or false indicating the default value of the radio button, indicated by whether the `checked` attribute was supplied or not in the `<input>` tag.

```
defval = document.formname.radiogroup[0].defaultChecked
```

 Internet Explorer 3.0 does not support the `defaultChecked` property for the `radio` object.

form **property**

The read-only reference to the `form` object that contains the radio `object`. This is a useful way to refer to another object in the same form. For instance, imagine a scenario where you want to reference a `text` object, named *text1*, which resides within the same form as the `radio` object *radiogroup[1]*. This can be used to code in shorthand, or eliminate the need to explicitly reference the full path to every element within a single form, as in the code excerpts:

JavaScript

```
path=document.forms[0].radiogroup[1]
value1=path.value
value2=path.form.text1.value
```

VBScript

```
set path=document.forms(0).radiogroup(1)
value1=path.value
value2=path.form.text1.value
```

name **property**

The name of the group within which the `radio` object resides, specified by the `name` attribute in the `<input>` tag.

```
objname = document.formname.radiogroup[0].name
objval = document.formname.objname.value
```

type **property**

The input type specified by the `type` attribute in the `<input>` tag. Of course, this always contains the value "radio" when referencing a radio button element.

```
objtype = document.formname.radiogroup[0].type
```

 Internet Explorer 3 does not support the `type` property.

length property

This read-only property contains the number of radio buttons in the group specified by the name attribute of the radio button's <input> tag. For instance, for a group of three radio buttons:

```
<input type="radio" name="car">Toyota
<input type="radio" name="car">Honda
<input type="radio" name="car">Nissan
```

The script excerpt:

```
howmany = document.formname.car.length
```

Would assign a value of 3 to howmany, because there are three radio buttons in the group.

value property

The data (string or numeric) specified by the value attribute in the <input> tag. This is *not* the text that is displayed by the radio button. Rather, it is the data that is sent to the server, when the form is submitted, when this radio button is checked on.

```
radioval = document.formname.radiogroup[2].value
```

Within Netscape Navigator and Internet Explorer 4, if the value attribute was not specified in the HTML, this property defaults to the string "on."

Within Internet Explorer 3, if the value attribute was not specified in the HTML, this property contains an empty value.

blur() method

This method simulates the user losing focus from the radio button. Therefore, if the user currently has focus on the radio button, somehow triggering the following code would remove the focus:

```
document.formname.radiogroup[index].blur()
```

 Internet Explorer 3.0 does not support the blur() method for the radio object.

focus() method

The focus() method simulates the user gaining focus on the radio button. You could use this method to call a user's attention to a particular radio button.

```
document.formname.radiogroup[index].focus()
```

> **WARNING** Be careful when and if you use the `focus()` method on a radio button that also contains an `onFocus()` event handler. In some scenarios within Netscape, this may result in an infinite loop wherein the `onFocus` event handler is repeated seemingly indefinitely. If your page is not operating as intended, this may be a cause to investigate.

click() method

This method simulates the user clicking on the radio button. Essentially, this has the same effect as assigning a true value to a `radio` object's `checked` property: the clicked button will become checked onscreen, and its `checked` property will contain true; all other `radio` object checked properties within the group will be set to false.

```
document.formname.radiogroup[index].click()
```

Within Netscape Navigator and Internet Explorer 4, the `click()` method also triggers any `onClick` event handler defined for the particular radio button.

Within Internet Explorer 3, the `click()` method does not trigger an `onClick` event handler, although it does set the `radio` object's `checked` property to true and update the radio buttons onscreen.

onBlur event handler

Located within the `<input>` tag, this will activate when the user loses focus (that is, clicks or tabs elsewhere in the browser) from the radio button element.

```
<input type="radio" name=radiogroup onBlur="eventHandler">
```

 Internet Explorer 3.0 does not support the `onBlur` event handler for the radio object.

onFocus event handler

Located within the `<input>` tag, this will activate when the user brings focus to the radio button element. When the user is using a mouse, the only way to bring focus to the button is to click on it—therefore, the `onClick` event handler is more commonly used. The user can also bring focus to the button using the Tab key, however, which consecutively brings focus to each element on the page. In this case, the `onFocus` event handler could be triggered without also triggering an `onClick` event.

```
<input type="radio" name=radiogroup onFocus="eventHandler">
```

 Internet Explorer 3.0 does not support the `onFocus` event handler for the radio object.

onClick **event handler**

Located within the <input> tag, this will activate when the user clicks on and releases from the radio button. Typically, the onClick event handler is used for the radio object when you want to trigger an action immediately conditional upon the state of a particular radio button. For instance, imagine that you have three radio buttons, each representing a different background color for the current page. You would use an onClick event handler for each radio button to trigger a change in the page's background color.

```
<input type="radio" name="bgcolor" checked onClick="document.bgColor='red'">Red
<input type="radio" name="bgcolor" onClick="document.bgColor='green'">Green
<input type="radio" name="bgcolor" onClick="document.bgColor='white'">White
```

Replace()

Category: VBScript

		Navigator 3	Navigator 4	Explorer 3	Explorer 4
Type	Function				
Browser Support	Macintosh				■
	Windows			■	■

Syntax   `replace(string, find, replacewith[, start][, count])`

The Replace() function performs a "search-and-replace" on *string*. Within *string*, the function will replace *count* instances of the string *find* with the string *replacewith*, and return the resulting string. The search-and-replace begins at the beginning of *string*, unless you specify an alternate *start* position. The original *string* is not modified itself.

Assuming the variable str contains "my name is not your name":

`replace(str,"name","nom")`   returns   "my nom is not your nom"

`replace(str,"name","nom",1,1)` returns   "my nom is not your name"

`replace(str,"name","nom",9)`   returns   "is not your nom"

`replace(str,"","nom")`   returns   "my name is not your name"

`replace(str,"name","")`   returns   "my is not your"

If you pass a null *string* to the function, an error will occur. The Replace() function is well suited to construction form-letter style strings, in which you substitute one word repeatedly in several places.

R

Reset

Category: JavaScript, JScript, VBScript

Type Object

Browser Support

	Navigator 3	Navigator 4	Explorer 3	Explorer 4
Macintosh	■	■	□	■
Windows	■	■	■	■

Subset Of `Form` object

Properties `form, name, type, value`

Methods `blur(), focus(), click()`

Events `onBlur, onFocus, onClick, onMouseDown, onMouseUp`

Syntax `document.formName.resetName.property` OR
`document.forms[index].elements[index].property` OR
`document.formName.resetName.method(parameters)` OR
`document.forms[index].elements[index].method(parameters)`

A reset button form field is typically used in tandem with the submit button. When the reset button is clicked, it resets all the elements within the form to their default values. The `reset` object, much like the `submit` and `button` objects, provides script access to the reset button's characteristics. A reset form field is created using the `<input>` tag.

```
<input
   type="reset"
   name="buttonName"
   value="buttonCaption"
   [onBlur="eventHandler"]
   [onClick="evnetHandler"]
   [onFocus="eventHandler"]>
```

`form` property

The read-only reference to the `form` object that contains the `reset` object. This is a useful way to refer to another object in the same form. For instance, imagine a scenario where you want to reference a `text` object, named *text1*, which resides within the same form as the `reset` object *reset1*. This can be used to code in shorthand, or eliminate the need to explicitly reference the full path to every element within a single form, as in the code excerpts:

JavaScript

```
path=document.forms[0].reset1
value1=path.value
value2=path.form.text1.value
```

VBScript

```
set path=document.forms(0).reset1
value1=path.value
value2=path.form.text1.value
```

name property

The read-only name of the reset object, specified by the name attribute in the <input> tag.

```
objname = document.formname.resetname.name
objval = document.formname.objname.value
```

type property

The input type specified by the type attribute in the <input> tag. Of course, this always contains the value "reset" when referencing a reset element.

```
objtype = document.formname.resetname.type
```

 Internet Explorer 3 does not support the type property.

value property

The read-only text displayed on the reset button, specified by the value attribute in the <input> tag. You *cannot* modify the text on the face of the reset button using the value property—it *is* read-only.

```
caption = document.formname.resetname.value
```

Typically, the reset button contains a caption that indicates that it *is* a reset button, such as "Reset Form" or "Clear Form".

R

TIP In the case of a reset button which has no value attribute specified in HTML, it's value property will contain the string "Reset" (which will also appear on the face of the submit button onscreen).

blur() method

This method simulates the user losing focus from the reset button. Therefore, if the user currently has focus on the reset button, somehow triggering the following code would remove the focus:

```
document.formname.resetname.blur()
```

Internet Explorer 3.0 does not support the `blur()` method for the `reset` object.

focus() method

 This method simulates the user gaining focus on the reset button. When the reset button element has focus, a thin dotted line appears around its perimeter.

You could use this method to cajole the user into paying attention to the reset button:

```
document.formname.resetname.focus()
```

WARNING Be careful when and if you use the `focus()` method on a reset button that also contains an `onFocus()` event handler. In some scenarios within Netscape, this may result in an infinite loop wherein the `onFocus` event handler is repeated seemingly indefinitely. If your page is not operating as intended, this may be a cause to investigate.

 Internet Explorer 3.0 does not support the `focus()` method for the `reset` object.

click() method

This method simulates the user pressing the left (or only) mouse button atop the reset button element.

```
document.formname.resetname.click()
```

In the case of Netscape Navigator and Internet Explorer 4, the `click()` method will generate an `onReset` event for the form, triggering any `onReset` event-handler defined in the `<form>` tag. Whether or not an `onReset` event handler is defined, the form data will then be reset, just as if the user had clicked the reset button.

Within Internet Explorer 3.0, the `click()` method *does not* generate an `onReset` event, but it *does* reset the form data.

onBlur event handler

Located within the `<input>` tag, this will activate when the user loses focus (that is, clicks or tabs elsewhere in the browser) from the reset button.

```
<input type="reset" name=resetname value="captiontext" onBlur="eventHandler">
```

Internet Explorer 3.0 does not support the `onBlur` event handler for the `reset` object.

onFocus **event handler**

Located within the `<input>` tag, this will activate when the user brings focus to the reset button. When using a mouse, the only way to bring focus to the reset button is to click on it—which, in turn, would generate an onClick event followed by an onReset event. However, the user can also bring focus to the button using the Tab key, which consecutively brings focus to each element on the page. In this case, the `onFocus` event handler could be triggered without also triggering an `onClick` or `onSubmit` event.

```
<input type="reset" name=resetname value="captiontext"  onFocus="eventHandler">
```

 Internet Explorer 3.0 does not support the `onFocus` event handler for the `reset` object.

onClick **event handler**

Located within the `<input>` tag, this activates when the user clicks on and releases from the reset button. Of course, clicking a reset button generates an onReset event, which is an event handler of the form object. Thus, if you'd like any script to intervene before the form data is reset, you should do so using the onReset event rather than the onClick event.

Nonetheless, if you *can* think of a reason to use the onClick event for the reset object:

```
<input type="reset" name=resetname value="captiontext"
onClick="eventHandler">
```

onMouseDown **event handler**

Located within the `<a>` tag, this will activate when the user presses down the mouse button on the reset button, but before the mouse button is released. This event handler can be used to determine if a user is "holding" the mouse button down over the button, as opposed to clicking (pressing down and releasing).

For instance:

```
<input type="reset" name=resetname value="captiontext"
onMouseDown="eventHandler">
```

NOTE   The onMouseDown event handler is only supported beginning with the version 4 releases of Netscape Navigator and Internet Explorer.

R

onMouseUp **event handler**

Located within the <a> tag, this will activate when the user releases the mouse button on the reset button, after having pressed it down. In releasing the mouse button, the user has completed a click—however, the onMouseUp event occurs just prior to the onClick event. If your onMouseUp event handler returns true, the onClick event will be triggered and/or the form will be reset; if this event handler returns false, no onClick event will occur and the form will not be reset.

For instance:

```
<input type="reset" name=resetname value="captiontext"
onMouseDown="eventHandler">
```

> **NOTE** The onMouseUp event handler is only supported beginning with the version 4 releases of Netscape Navigator and Internet Explorer.

Right()

Category: VBScript

	Type	Function

Browser Support

	Navigator 3	Navigator 4	Explorer 3	Explorer 4
Macintosh				■
Windows			■	■

Syntax Right(string, length)

The Right() function returns *length*—the number of characters from the right end of *string*. A *length* of 0 will return a zero-length string, whereas a *length* greater than the string length will return the whole *string*. A *length* less than zero will cause an error.

right("barney",2)	returns	"ey"
right("house warming",0)	returns	""
right("flag waving",30)	returns	"flag waving"
right("doggy",-2)	returns	invalid procedure call error

The Right() function is one of several tools you can use to extract portions of a string—also see the functions Left() and Mid().

Rnd ( )

Category: VBScript

Type	Function

Browser Support

	Navigator 3	Navigator 4	Explorer 3	Explorer 4
Macintosh	☐	☐	☐	■
Windows	☐	☐	■	■

Syntax `Rnd[(number)]`

The `Rnd()` function generates and returns a random number. Before using the `rnd()` function, you should execute the `randomize` statement, which sets a seed for the pseudo-random number generator (as seen in the example at the end of this entry).

The type of random number generated depends on the *number* parameter. An integer less than 0 will produce the same number every time, using the *number* as the seed—this may be useful for debugging. A positive *number*, or omitting the parameter, will generate the next number in the pseudo-random sequence. A *number* of 0 returns the most recently generated number.

The numbers returned by the `rnd()` function are floating-point numbers ranging from 0 to 1. To create random integers within any range (between *lowerbound* and *upperbound*) you can use the following formula:

```
Int((upperbound - lowerbound + 1) * Rnd + lowerbound)
```

The following VBScript function accepts two integers' parameters, a lower- and upperbound, and returns a random number between those bounds:

```
function randnum(lb,ub)
 randomize
 randnum=int((ub-lb+1)*Rnd+lb)
 end function
```

For instance, we could call the above function procedure in an assignment statement:

```
number = randnum(50,100)
```

Based upon our `randnum()` function, the preceding code would assign a random integer between 50 and 100 to the variable `number`.

R

RTrim( )

Category: VBScript

Type Function

Browser Support

	Navigator 3	Navigator 4	Explorer 3	Explorer 4
Macintosh	☐	☐	☐	■
Windows	☐	☐	■	■

Syntax RTrim(*string*)

The RTrim( ) function simply removes any trailing spaces from the end of *string*.

rtrim("hi there! ")	returns	"hi there!"
rtrim(" words of wisdom ")	returns	" words of wisdom"

To strip spaces from the left-hand side of *string*, see the function LTrim( ); to strip spaces from both sides of *string*, see Trim( ).

These functions can be used to remove any extraneous spaces that the user may have typed. If the input *string* contains a null value, RTrim( ) will return null.

<IMG> </IMG> ■ <SCRIPT LANGUAGE = "javascript"> </SCRIPT>
■ <SCRIPT LANGUAGE = "vbscript"> </SCRIPT> ■ <BGSOUND
SRC=gbv.wav LOOP=-1> </BGSOUND> ■ <APPLET CLASS=
"ester's_day" SRC="http://testsite/walla walla washington/"
</APPLET> ■ <FRAME></FRAME>■ <MARQUEE> </MARQUEE> ■   <HTML>
</HTML> ■ <A> </A>■ <OL> </OL> ■ <UL> </UL> ■ <MENU> </MENU>
■ <STRONG> </STRONG> ■ <TD> </TD> ■ <TH> </TH>

S

<S>

Category: HTML

Browser Support		Navigator 3	Navigator 4	Explorer 3	Explorer 4
	Macintosh	■■	■■	■■	■■
	Windows	■■	■■	■■	■■

Applies To None

May Contain <APPLET>, <B>, <BASEFONT>, <BIG>, <BR>, <CITE>, <CODE>, <DFN>, <EM>, <FONT>, <I>, <IMG>, <INPUT>, <KBD>, <MAP>, <SAMP>, <SELECT>, <SMALL>, <STRIKE>, <STRONG>, <SUB>, <SUP>, <TEXTAREA>, <TT>, <U>, <VAR>

May Be Used In <ADDRESS>, <APPLET>, <B>, <BIG>, <BLOCKQUOTE>, <BODY>, <CAPTION>, <CENTER>, <CITE>, <CODE>, <DD>, <DT>, <FONT>, <H1>, <H2>, <H3>, <H4>, <H5>, <H6>, <I>, <KBD>, <LI>, <P>, <SAMP>, <SMALL>, <STRIKE>, <STRONG>, <SUB>, <SUP>, <TD>, <TH>, <TT>, <U>

Attributes None

Syntax <S>...</S>

The <S> tag is used to strike out a specified amount of text (display it with a horizontal line drawn through it, as if it were crossed out). Everything written between the beginning and closing, or </S> tag, is stricken out.

For example:

<S>This text has been stricken out using the S tag.</S>

This text is normal default text.

Figure 1 displays this HTML in Netscape Navigator 3 for the Mac.

Figure 1

Strikeout text as defined by the <S> tag, compared with plain default text on the second line.

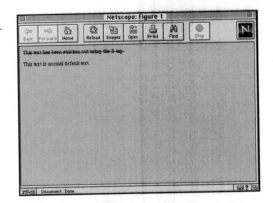

> **NOTE**
> The <STRIKE> tag serves exactly the same purpose as the <S> tag in both Navigator and Internet Explorer (all versions tested) and on both Mac and Windows platforms. However, the <S> tag is older and more widely supported, whereas the <STRIKE> tag is relatively new, so you may want to use <S> for greater reliability.

<SAMP>

Category: HTML

Browser Support

	Navigator 3	Navigator 4	Explorer 3	Explorer 4
Macintosh			■	■
Windows			■	■

Applies To None

May Contain <APPLET>, <B>, <BASEFONT>, <BIG>, <BR>, <CITE>, <CODE>, <DFN>, <EM>, <FONT>, <I>, <IMG>, <INPUT>, <KBD>, <MAP>, <SELECT>, <SMALL>, <STRIKE>, <STRONG>, <SUB>, <SUP>, <TEXTAREA>, <TT>, <U>, <VAR>

May Be Used In <ADDRESS>, <APPLET>, <B>, <BIG>, <BLOCKQUOTE>, <BODY>, <CAPTION>, <CENTER>, <CITE>, <CODE>, <DD>, <DT>, <FONT>, <H1>, <H2>, <H3>, <H4>, <H5>, <H6>, <I>, <KBD>, <LI>, <P>, <SAMP>, <SMALL>, <STRIKE>, <STRONG>, <SUB>, <SUP>, <TD>, <TH>, <TT>, <U>

Attributes None

Syntax <SAMP>...</SAMP>

The <SAMP> tag is an older, Explorer-only tag used in a tutorial or other instructional exercise to specify a bit of text to be typed in exactly as shown. Everything written between the beginning and closing, or </SAMP>, tags will be displayed in a monotype font as shown in the example:

```
<SAMP>This text is displayed in monospace by using the SAMP tag.</SAMP>
This text is plain default text.
```

Figure 1 displays this HTML in Navigator 3 for the Mac.

Figure 1

Text written in monospace by using the <SAMP> tag, compared to plain default text.

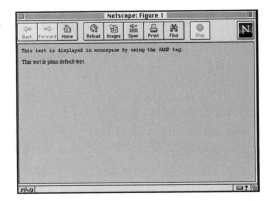

There's no functional difference between text displayed in a monospace font using the <SAMP> tag versus using the <CODE> tag or the <KBD> tag, as shown in Figure 2. Use any of these tags for monospaced plain text as you prefer.

Figure 2

The <SAMP> tag versus the <CODE> tag and/or the <KBD> tag—there's no difference.

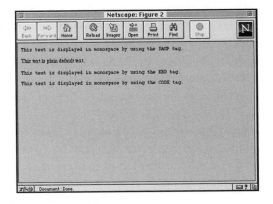

S

However, there is a difference between the way Navigator displays <KBD>-specified text versus Internet Explorer. Figure 3 displays the same HTML as shown in Figure 2—the <SAMP>-specified text is properly monospaced, but the <KBD>-specified text is monospaced and bolded, too.

Figure 3

The <KBD>, <CODE>, and <SAMP> tags— Internet Explorer bolds and monospaces <KBD>- specified text.

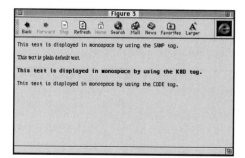

Screen

Category: JavaScript 1.2

Type	Object

Browser Support

	Navigator 3	Navigator 4	Explorer 3	Explorer 4
Macintosh	☐	■	☐	☐
Windows	☐	■	☐	☐

Subset Of	Nothing

Properties	availHeight, availWidth, colorDepth, height, pixelDepth, width

Syntax	screen.property

The simple but useful screen object provides information about the user's screen resolution and color capacity. Clearly, the properties of this object are useful in calculating custom creations, such as opening a window on the user's screen. For instance, you might test whether a user's horizontal resolution is at least 800 pixels wide—if so, you can open a new window that is 800 pixels wide; if not, you may open a window that is 640 pixels wide.

availHeight property

This property contains the height of the user's screen resolution, measured in pixels, not counting permanent visual obstacles that are part of the operating system. In other words, consider the Windows 95 taskbar. When sitting at the bottom of the screen, for example, it blocks anything that might appear in that space. The availHeight property reflects the amount of "visible" screen space, by subtracting such operating system obstacles from the total available screen height.

```
aheight=screen.availHeight
```

availWidth property

The availWidth property contains the width of the user's screen resolution, measured in pixels, not counting permanent visual obstacles that are part of the operating system. In other words, consider the Windows 95 taskbar. When sitting, at the bottom of the screen, for example, it does not block any width of the viewable screen area. However, some users move the taskbar to the left or right side of their desktop. The `availWidth` property reflects the amount of "visible" screen space, by subtracting such operating system obstacles from the total available screen width.

```
awidth=screen.availWidth
```

`colorDepth` property

This property is supposed to reflect the number of possible colors the user's screen can display. As of this writing, in our extensive laboratory testing, the `colorDepth` property seems to return the same value as the `pixelDepth` property—see the `pixelDepth` property.

`height` property

Simply, the height of the user's screen, measured in pixels. Common, standard screen heights are 480, 600, and 768.

```
vres=screen.height
```

`pixelDepth` property

Using the `pixelDepth` property, you can determine whether the user has a high-color or low-color display. This may reflect which images you choose to load into a page, or perhaps a warning message that your site requires a certain color capacity to truly appreciate. This property returns a pixel depth value, which is correlated with a color capacity as shown below:

Pixel depth	Color capacity
24	16.8 million colors
25	65,000 colors
26	256 colors
27	16 colors

If your site has a lot of graphics, users will probably need pixel depths of at least 16 to fully "get the picture." Because some users may have high color capacity but have not configured their operating system to use it, you may test the `pixelDepth` property and offer a warning or explanation to users who may need to configure their system for higher color capacity.

`width` property

Simply, the width of the user's screen, measured in pixels. Common, standard screen widths are 640, 800, and 1024.

```
hres=screen.width
```

S

<SCRIPT>

Category: HTML

Browser Support		Navigator 3	Navigator 4	Explorer 3	Explorer 4
	Macintosh	▇	▇	▇	▇
	Windows	▇	▇	▇	▇

Applies To None

May Contain Scripts in plain text only

May Be Used In <HEAD>

Attributes None

Syntax <SCRIPT>…</SCRIPT>

The <SCRIPT> tag is used to specify a JavaScript, VBScript, or other "scripts" included on a web page. A closing, or </SCRIPT>, tag is required.

See the "JavaScript Basics" chapter elsewhere in this book for more information on how to use scripts in your web page.

Second()

Category: VBScript

Type Function

Browser Support		Navigator 3	Navigator 4	Explorer 3	Explorer 4
	Macintosh	☐	☐	☐	▇
	Windows	☐	☐	▇	▇

Syntax Second(date)

The Second() function returns the second, between 0 and 59, within the specified *date*. The time format within *date* may be in either 24-hour time or AM/PM time.

second("June 11 4:30:21 PM")	returns	21
second("05:45:06")	returns	6
second("12:00 AM")	returns	0

If the value *date* is null, then a null value is returned. If *date* does not contain a time or second value, then 0 is returned; if *date* contains an invalid time, such as 12:20:82, an error will occur.

<SELECT>

Category: HTML

Browser Support		Navigator 3	Navigator 4	Explorer 3	Explorer 4
	Macintosh	▬	▬	▬	▬
	Windows	▬	▬	▬	▬

Applies To None

May Contain <OPTION>

May Be Used In <A>, <ADDRESS>, <APPLET>, <B>, <BIG>, <BLOCKQUOTE>, <CAPTION>—but only if these elements are enclosed by the <FORM> tag, <CENTER>, <CITE>, <CODE>, <DD>, <DFN>, <DIV>, <DT>, <EM>, <FONT>, <FORM>, <H1>, <H2>, <H3>, <H4>, <H5>, <H6>, <I>, <KBD>, <LI>, <P>, <PRE>, <SAMP>, <SMALL>, <STRIKE>, <STRONG>, <SUB>, <SUP>, <TD>, <TH>, <TT>, <U>, <VAR>

Attributes MULTIPLE, NAME, SIZE

Syntax <SELECT>…</SELECT>

The <SELECT> tag specifies a pull-down menu and its associated text box within a form. It also encloses the <OPTION> tag, which is used to specify individual menu items (see the <OPTION> and <FORM> tag entries elsewhere in this book for more information) so the closing, or </SELECT> tag, is required.

The HTML for a basic <SELECT> pull-down menu as it appears enclosed within the <FORM> tag looks like:

```
<FORM ACTION=http://www.provider.com/cgi-bin/tvquiz METHOD=post>
<P>Who's your favorite classic TV family?<BR>
<SELECT NAME=tvfamilies SIZE=1>
<OPTION VALUE=1>The Bradys
<OPTION VALUE=1>The Keatons
<OPTION VALUE=1>The Cunninghams
</SELECT>
</FORM>
```

Figures 1 through 4 illustrate this basic pull-down menu in Navigator 3 and Internet Explorer 3 for the Mac and for Windows.

S

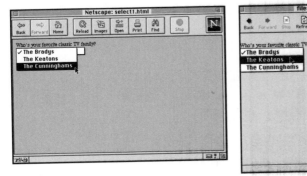

Figure 1

A basic <SELECT> pull-down menu in Navigator 3 for the Mac.

Figure 2

A basic <SELECT> pull-down menu in Internet Explorer 3 for the Mac.

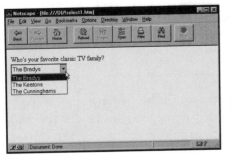

Figure 3

A basic <SELECT> pull-down menu in Navigator 3 for Windows.

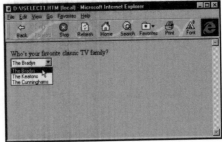

Figure 4

A basic <SELECT> pull-down menu in Internet Explorer 3 for Windows.

MULTIPLE

The MULTIPLE attribute enables the user of a pull-down menu to select more than one menu item.

In the following HTML, MULTIPLE is correctly written into the basic pull-down menu shown in Figures 1 through 4:

```
<FORM ACTION=http://www.provider.com/cgi-bin/tvquiz METHOD=post>
<P>Choose your favorite classic TV family (you can vote more than once):
```

```
<SELECT NAME=tvfamilies SIZE=1 MULTIPLE>
<OPTION VALUE=1>The Bradys
<OPTION VALUE=2>The Keatons
<OPTION VALUE=3>The Cunninghams
</SELECT>
</FORM>
```

It's good netiquette to include some sort of indication that form users can choose more than one menu option, which is why the new paragraph of text was added just above the pull-down menu in the preceding example. Using MULTIPLE doesn't affect the appearance of a web page, just its functionality.

NAME

The NAME attribute specifies the description of the text control that corresponds to the gateway program that processes any information submitted via the form. Without the NAME attribute and the identifier it specifies, the gateway program will not work properly and the form user will not get a response. This is the reason why you cannot choose a form control's NAME value randomly; it must correspond to the part of the form's CGI script or other gateway program that processes the control's information.

Take another look at the example HTML and related Figures 1 through 4 in the opening section of this entry to see how the NAME attribute should be written.

SIZE

The SIZE attribute specifies how many menu options will be shown on the web page, and therefore, whether or not the pull-down menu will scroll.

In the following example HTML, the SIZE value is specified at 1:

```
<FORM ACTION=http://www.provider.com/cgi-bin/tvquiz METHOD=post>
<P>Choose your favorite TV dog:<BR>
<SELECT NAME=tvdogs SIZE=1>
<OPTION VALUE=1>Lassie
<OPTION VALUE=2>Rin Tin Tin
<OPTION VALUE=3>Eddie
<OPTION VALUE=4>Murray
<OPTION VALUE=5>Scooby Doo
</SELECT>
</FORM>
```

If the SIZE value were specified instead as 3, for example, the first three items on the menu would appear on the web page along with a slider bar that the form user would click-and-drag to choose her favorite TV dog.

Figures 5 through 8 display a pull-down menu that scrolls in Navigator 3 and Internet Explorer 3 for the Mac and for Windows.

S

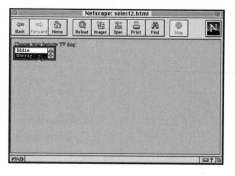

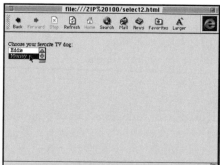

Figure 5

A scrolling pull-down menu in Navigator 3 for the Mac.

Figure 6

A scrolling pull-down menu in Internet Explorer 3 for the Mac.

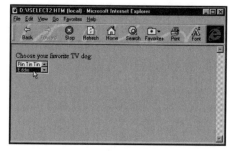

Figure 7

A scrolling pull-down menu in Navigator 3 for Windows.

Figure 8

A scrolling pull-down menu in Internet Explorer 3 for Windows.

Select

Category: JavaScript, JScript, VBScript

	Type	Object

Type Object

Browser Support

	Navigator 3	Navigator 4	Explorer 3	Explorer 4
Macintosh	■	■	☐	■
Windows	■	■	■	■

Subset Of Form object

Properties `form, length, name, options[], selectIndex, type`

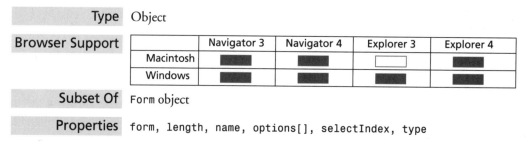

Methods	blur(), focus()
Event Handler	onBlur, onFocus, onChange
Syntax	document.formName.selectName.property OR
	document.forms[index].elements[index].property OR
	document.formName.selectName.method(parameters) OR
	document.forms[index].elements[index].method(parameters)

The select form field allows the user to choose one or more items from a list of choices. It differs from the radio button because the choices need not be mutually exclusive; for example, the user could possibly select three choices out of five. The select object provides script access to view or modify characteristics of the select form field element. A select field is created using the <select> tag with subordinate <option> tag specifying the various choices in the list.

```
<select
    name="selectName"
    [size="optionsVisible"]
    [multiple]
    [onBlur="eventHandler"]
    [onChange="eventHandler"]
    [onFocus="eventHandler"]>
    <option value="valueToSubmit" [selected]> textToDisplay
    [… <option value="valueToSubmit" [selected]>Ø textToDisplay]
</select>
```

A select list can be displayed in two different forms, as a drop-down list or in a box with scroll bars. Omitting the size attribute or setting it to 1 *and* omitting the multiple attribute will display a drop-down list. Setting the size attribute to an integer greater than 1 will display the list as a box with scrollbars and a height of *integer* lines. Specifying the multiple attribute enables the user to select multiple items from the list, by holding down a key while clicking on the desired option (the exact key varies from platform to platform—for Windows, you use the Control key).

The <option> tag defines each item in the list. For information on the scripting abilities specific to the option elements, see the Option object.

S

Figure 1

A select object as a pop-up list and scrolling list box.

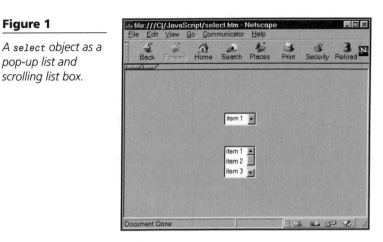

Internet Explorer 3 does not support dynamic modification of the selection field. Any following examples that add, remove, or otherwise modify items in the selection field (other than those created in HTML with the `<option>` tag) do not apply to Internet Explorer 3.

`form` property

The read-only reference to the `form` object which contains the `select` object. This is a useful way to refer to another object in the same form. For instance, imagine a scenario in which you want to reference a `text` object, named *text1*, which resides within the same form as the `select` object *select1*. This can be used to code in shorthand, or eliminate the need to explicitly reference the full path to every element within a single form, as in the following code excerpts:

JavaScript

```
path=document.forms[0].select1
value1=path.value
value2=path.form.text1.value
```

VBScript

```
set path=document.forms(0).select1
value1=path.value
value2=path.form.text1.value
```

`length` property

An integer reflecting the current number of items in the select field. For instance, for a select field which contains three `<option>` tags,

```
items = document.formname.selectname.length
```

Would assign the value 3 to items; assuming, of course, that we've not added or removed any of the items from the select object.

The length property also refers to the number elements in the options[] array. Adding new elements to the options[] array will dynamically modify the size of the selection list—for specifics, see the Option object.

name **property**

The read-only name of the selection form field, specified by the name attribute in the <input> tag.

```
objname = document.formname.selectname.name
objval = document.formname.objname.length
```

options[] **property**

In fact, options[] is an array of objects, each of which reflects one item in the list, originally created with the <option> tag. Each object in the options[] array can be modified or removed, and new items can be added to the select field by adding new option objects to the options[] array. For specific usage information on the options array and option objects, see the Option object.

selectedIndex **property**

An integer that indicates the index of the item selected in the select object. For instance, if you have a select field with three items, and the first item is currently selected, then

```
item = document.formname.selectname.selectedIndex
```

would assign the value 0 to item. If no items are selected, then selectedIndex will reflect the value 1.

When the multiple attribute of the <select> tag is specified in the HTML, the user can select multiple items from the list. However, the selectedIndex property will *only* return the index of the first item selected! To determine which items are selected in the case of multiple-selection, you will have to script a loop that individually tests the state of each option object in the options array. The following example functions accept one parameter—the select object—and pops up a window showing the indexes for each item selected in that select field, as seen in Figure 2.

You would modify and call this function, either in an event handler or from some other portion of script, as

```
selected(document.formname.selectname)
```

JavaScript

```
function selected(selobj)
{
tmpstr="";
```

```
  for (var j = 0; j < selobj.length; j++)
   { if (selobj.options[j].selected)
    { tmpstr=tmpstr+" "+j }}
window.alert("Selected items: "+tmpstr)
}
```

VBScript

```
function selected(selobj)
 tmpstr=""
 for j=0 to selobj.length -1
  if selobj.options(j).selected then tmpstr=tmpstr&" "&j
 next
 window.alert("Selected items: "&tmpstr)
end function
```

> **NOTE**   In the VBScript example of `selected()`, note that we use a function delcaration rather than a sub declaration, although no value is returned. While the procedure could just as well be defined as a sub, if you modify this procedure for use in a real program, it will probably need to return a value indicating which options have been selected—therefore, it will need to be a function. For a refresher on VBScript sub and function procedures, see the "VBScript Basics" chapter at the beginning of this book.

Figure 2

An example
function, which
returns the index
numbers for each
item selected in the
select field.

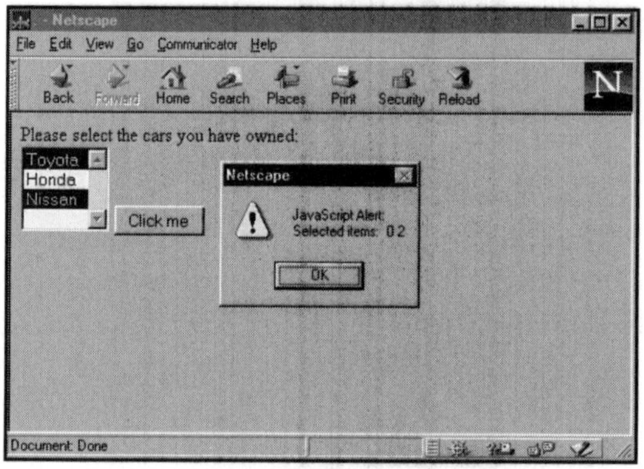

type property

Reflects either "select-one" or "select-multiple" depending on whether the `multiple` attribute is specified in the `<select>` tag.

```
seltype = document.formname.selectname.type
```

Internet Explorer 3 does not support the **type** property.

blur() method

This method simulates the user losing focus from the select field. Therefore, if the user currently has focus on the select field, somehow triggering the following code would remove the focus:

```
document.formname.selectname.blur()
```

focus() method

This method simulates the user gaining focus on the select field. You could use this method to cajole a user's attention (and, possibly, keystrokes) toward the select field.

```
document.formname.selectname.focus()
```

WARNING   Be careful when and if you use the **focus()** method on a select field that also contains an **onFocus()** event handler. In some scenarios within Netscape, this may result in an infinite loop wherein the **onFocus** event handler is repeated seemingly indefinitely. If your page is not operating as intended, this may be a cause to investigate.

onBlur event handler

Located within the <select> tag, this will activate when the user loses focus (that is, clicks or tabs elsewhere in the browser) from the select field.

```
<select name=selectname size=5 onBlur="eventHandler">
```

onFocus event handler

Located within the <select> tag, this will activate when the user brings focus to the select element.

```
<select name=selectname size=5 onFocus="eventHandler">
```

onChange event handler

Located within the <select> tag, this will activate when the user makes a change to the select field. This is the most often used event handler for a select field—use it to trigger a function that updates some other portion of the page that is dependent upon the currently selected item in the select field.

For instance, imagine that we have a second select field on the page, whose items depend on which item is selected in the first select field. We could code a function which modifies the options in the second select field (see the Option object), and launch this function with an onChange event handler in the first select field.

```
<select name=select1 size=5 onChange="changeSelect2()">
```

S

Sgn()
Category: VBScript

Type	Function			

Browser Support

	Navigator 3	Navigator 4	Explorer 3	Explorer 4
Macintosh	☐	☐	☐	■
Windows	☐	☐	■	■

Syntax   `Sgn(number)`

The `Sgn()` function determines the sign of *number*. The function will return 1 if *number* is positive, 0 if *number* is 0, and –1 if *number* is negative. Any non-numerical *number* will cause an error.

`sgn(3)`   returns   1

`sgn(0)`   returns   0

`sgn(-9)`   returns   –1

In spirit, the `Sgn()` function is the companion to the `Abs()` function—`Abs()` returns only the magnitude of a number, while `Sgn()` returns only the sign.

<SHADOW>
Category: HTML

Browser Support	WebTV Internet Terminal
Applies To	Text
May Contain	None
May Be Used In	None
Attributes	None
Syntax	`<SHADOW>...</SHADOW>`

The `<SHADOW>` tag adds a thin shadow to text on your page. Shadows help to add depth to your text and create a page that is visually appealing. The shadow is displayed down and to the right of the text enclosed within the `<SHADOW>` tags.

`<H6> News of the <shadow>Weird</shadow></h6>`

Sin()

Category: VBScript

| Type | Function |

Browser Support

	Navigator 3	Navigator 4	Explorer 3	Explorer 4
Macintosh				■
Windows			■	■

| Syntax | Sin(*number*) |

The sin() function calculates and returns the sine of *number*, which is an angle expressed in radians. The sine of *number* represents the ratio between two sides of a right triangle: length of the side opposite the angle divided by the length of the hypotenuse. The ratio returned can range from –1 to 1.

> **NOTE** VBScript does not provide an asin() function. Use the following formula to calculate the inverse sine:
>
> atn(x / sqr(-1 * x * x + 1))

<SMALL>

Category: HTML

Browser Support

	Navigator 3	Navigator 4	Explorer 3	Explorer 4
Macintosh	■	■	■	■
Windows	■	■	■	■

| Applies To | None |

May Contain <APPLET>, <B>, <BASEFONT>, <BIG>, <BR>, <CITE>, <CODE>, <DFN>, <EM>, <FONT>, <I>, <IMG>, <INPUT>, <KBD>, <MAP>, <SAMP>, <SELECT>, <SMALL>, <STRIKE>, <STRONG>, <SUB>, <SUP>, <TEXTAREA>, <TT>, <U>, <VAR>

May Be Used In <ADDRESS>, <APPLET>, <B>, <BIG>, <BLOCKQUOTE>, <BODY>, <CAPTION>, <CENTER>, <CITE>, <CODE>, <DD>, <DT>, <FONT>, <H1>, <H2>, <H3>, <H4>, <H5>, <H6>, <I>, <KBD>, <LI>, <P>, <SAMP>, <SMALL>, <STRIKE>, <STRONG>, <SUB>, <SUP>, <TD>, <TH>, <TT>, <U>

| Attributes | None |

| Syntax | <SMALL>...</SMALL> |

S

The <SMALL> tag decreases the point size of plain text by one size to 10. Everything written between the required start and closing, or </SMALL>, tag will be displayed on a web page one point size smaller, as shown in the example:

`<SMALL>This text is smaller than default text.</SMALL>`

So just as the <BIG> tag increases font size, the <SMALL> tag is used to decrease the point size of a specified block of text by one screen font size increment. In other words, text displayed on a web page is sized in 8-, 10-, 12-, 14-, 18-, and 24-point increments, so that if the rest of the text on a web page is 12-point, any text specified as <SMALL> will be 10-point instead.

Figure 1 displays three text sizes—from top to bottom: text defined by the <BIG> tag, default text, and text defined by the <SMALL> tag.

Figure 1

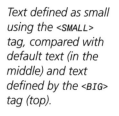

Text defined as small using the <SMALL> tag, compared with default text (in the middle) and text defined by the <BIG> tag (top).

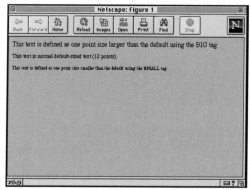

<SOUND>

Category: HTML

Browser Support	None (Mosaic)
Applies To	None
May Contain	None
May Be Used In	None
Attributes	AUTOSTART, HEIGHT, SRC, WIDTH
Syntax	<SOUND>...</SOUND>

The <SOUND> tag was created for use with the Mosaic browser—when a web page loads up, so does the sound file, providing a sort of short soundtrack.

At this writing, however, the <SOUND> tag is not supported by any version of Navigator or Internet Explorer. It may eventually become supported in future updated versions, but for now its use in Navigator and Internet Explorer is not reliable.

Space()

Category: VBScript

Type	Function

Browser Support		Navigator 3	Navigator 4	Explorer 3	Explorer 4
	Macintosh	☐	☐	☐	■
	Windows	☐	☐	■	■

Syntax	Space(*number*)

The Space() function simply returns a string containing *number* spaces. A non-numeric or negative *number* will cause an error. To create a string full of other characters use the String() function.

```
space(5)          returns          "     "
```

```
space(0)          returns          ""
```

Split()

Category: VBScript

Type	Function

Browser Support		Navigator 3	Navigator 4	Explorer 3	Explorer 4
	Macintosh	☐	☐	☐	■
	Windows	☐	☐	■	■

Syntax	Split(string[, delimiter][, count])

The Split() function accepts a single *string*, which it then breaks into substrings at each *delimiter* for *count* instances. The function returns an array, each of whose elements contain a substring produced by the split. If no *delimiter* is specified, then the space character is used as the delimiter.

```
letters = split("a b c d")
```

The above example returns an array to letters, whose elements contain:

```
letters(0) "a"
```

```
letters(1) "b"
```

```
letters(2) "c"
```

```
letters(3) "d"
```

S

Whereas the following example would split the string at the letter "c":

```
letters = split("a b c d","c")
```

Resulting in the array:

```
letters(0)       "a b "
```

```
letters(1)       " d"
```

Lastly, you can specify a *count* parameter to limit the number of splits that occur:

```
letters=split("a:b:c:d:e",":",3)
```

Resulting in the array:

```
letters(0)       "a"
```

```
letters(1)       "b"
```

```
letters(2)       "c:d:e"
```

StrComp()
Category: VBScript

	Type	Function

Browser Support		Navigator 3	Navigator 4	Explorer 3	Explorer 4
	Macintosh				███
	Windows			███	███

Syntax StrComp(string1, string2 [, compare])

The StrComp() function compares two strings, *string1* and *string2*, and returns a value indicating the result of the comparison. Omitting the *compare* parameter is the same as setting it to 0, which performs a binary-based (case-sensitive) comparison, whereas setting *compare* to 1 performs a text-based (case-insensitive) comparison.

After comparing the two strings, StrComp() returns –1 if *string1* is less than *string2*; 0 if the two strings are equivalent, and 1 if *string1* is greater than *string2*.

Of course, when comparing alphabetical strings, you're interested in whether they are equal (0) or not equal (–1 or 1), rather than which is "greater" than the other.

When comparing strings which contain numeric values, it is useful to consider which string is greater than the other.

strcomp("hello","Hello")	returns	1 (not equal, case-sensitive)
strcomp("hello","Hello",1)	returns	0 (equal, case-insensitive)

strcomp("12","40")   returns -1 (*string1<string2*)

strcomp("24","8")   returns 1 (*string1>string2*)

If *string1* or *string2* is null, then null is returned. You typically don't *need* to use the StrComp() function, but it can serve to compact longer constructions of if statements.

<STRIKE>

Category: HTML

Browser Support		Navigator 3	Navigator 4	Explorer 3	Explorer 4
	Macintosh	▬	▬	▬	▬
	Windows	▬	▬	▬	▬

Applies To None

May Contain `<APPLET>`, `<B>`, `<BASEFONT>`, `<BIG>`, `<BR>`, `<CITE>`, `<CODE>`, `<DFN>`, `<EM>`, `<FONT>`, `<I>`, `<IMG>`, `<INPUT>`, `<KBD>`, `<MAP>`, `<SAMP>`, `<SELECT>`, `<SMALL>`, `<STRIKE>`, `<STRONG>`, `<SUB>`, `<SUP>`, `<TEXTAREA>`, `<TT>`, `<U>`, `<VAR>`

May Be Used In `<ADDRESS>`, `<APPLET>`, `<B>`, `<BIG>`, `<BLOCKQUOTE>`, `<BODY>`, `<CAPTION>`, `<CENTER>`, `<CITE>`, `<CODE>`, `<DD>`, `<DT>`, `<FONT>`, `<H1>`, `<H2>`, `<H3>`, `<H4>`, `<H5>`, `<H6>`, `<I>`, `<KBD>`, `<LI>`, `<P>`, `<SAMP>`, `<SMALL>`, `<STRIKE>`, `<STRONG>`, `<SUB>`, `<SUP>`, `<TD>`, `<TH>`, `<TT>`, `<U>`

Attributes None

Syntax `<STRIKE>…</STRIKE>`

The `<STRIKE>` tag is used to strike out a specified amount of text (display it with a horizontal line drawn through it, as if it were crossed out). Everything written between the beginning and closing, or `</STRIKE>` tag, is stricken out as shown in the example:

`<STRIKE>This text has been stricken out using the STRIKE tag.</STRIKE>`

`<STRIKE>` is a relatively new tag to the HTML syntax so support for it is not universal at this writing. The `<S>` tag serves exactly the same purpose as the `<STRIKE>` tag in both Navigator and Internet Explorer (all versions tested) and on both the Mac and Windows. Use the `<S>` tag instead if you want greater guarantee—see the `<S>` tag entry elsewhere in the book for more information.

Figure 1 displays this HTML in Navigator 3 for the Mac.

S

Figure 1

Strikeout text as defined by the <STRIKE> tag, compared with plain default text on the second line.

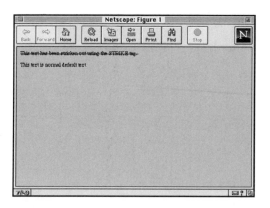

String

Category: JavaScript, JScript

| Type | Object |

Browser Support		Navigator 3	Navigator 4	Explorer 3	Explorer 4
	Macintosh	■■■	■■■	☐	■■■
	Windows	■■■	■■■	■■■	■■■

Properties `length`

Methods `anchor()`, `big()`, `blink()`, `bold()`, `charat()`, `fixed()`, `fontColor()`, `fontSize()`, `indexOf()`, `italics()`, `lastIndexOf()`, `link()`, `small()`, `split()`, `strike()`, `sub()`, `subString()`, `sup()`, `toLowerCase()`, `toUpperCase()`

Syntax `stringName.property` OR `stringName.method(parameters)`

The `string` object is used to manipulate strings, in many cases, to parse them for segments of data. Additionally, the `string` object possesses many methods which return a string marked up with HTML tags which, if and when output, will render a particular style. At its most basic, a string is a grouping of any characters. We always represent string values enclosed within double or single quotation marks, to differentiate them from numeric values or variable names. Thus, any of the following are perfectly valid strings: "a", "13", 'hi there!?', and 'WHOA nellie'.

You may use the properties and methods of the `string` object on any type of string data value, such as string literals, string variables, or string properties of other objects. For instance, all of the following examples are valid uses of the `string` object's methods:

```
"Don't Panic!".substring(7,11)
myPhrase.substring(7,11)
document.form1.textbox.value.substring(7,11)
```

Note that none of the `string` object's methods directly alters the original string itself—string manipulations are returned by the method. Of course, to alter the original string, simply assign the method to that string.

```
stringName = stringName.method(parameters)
```

Typically, there are two main reasons for manipulating strings and thus using the property and methods described below:

- Parsing for information—often, you'll want to extract a segment of data from a string. For instance, in retrieving a cookie value, you'd need to extract the portion of the string following the cookie name up until the delimiting semicolon. In other cases, you may simply need to determine whether a certain "phrase" resides within a string—for example, checking the property `navigator.appName` for the phrase "Netscape."

- Preparing a string for output—several of the methods below can "prep" a string, from converting its characters to upper- or lowercase, to embedding it between HTML tags, for possible future output. Typically "future output" refers to using the `write()` or `writeln()` methods of the `document` object to output a string to a browser window (see the `document` object). When outputting strings to a window, they are rendered in HTML. Therefore, if you will want the string "Welcome" to be output in the HTML bold style, you would need to output the string "`<b>Welcome</b>`". Many of the `string` object's "prep" methods can return a string encoded with HTML tags which will render to a particular style.

Imagine, for instance, that the variable `username` currently contained the string value, "Frank Fountain". You want to output this name to the browser window named `invoice`, in the HTML italic style. Simply call on the `string` object's `italics()` method:

```
invoice.document.writeln(username.italics())
```

> **TIP** Because the `string` object's methods return `string` objects, you can "append" `string` methods in sequence as a form of shorthand. For instance, the two statements
>
> ```
>         stringName.big()
>         stringName.italics()
> ```
>
> could also be written as:
>
> ```
>         stringName.big().italics()
> ```
>
> The methods will be executed in order from left to right; thus, the `big()` method will operate on *stringName* first and then `italics()` will operate on *stringName*.`big()`. You can string together any number of string methods in this manner.

S

`length` property

The `length` property simply contains the number of characters in the string. To quote the now no-longer–defunct Depeche Mode, "Everything counts"—spaces, punctuation, newline characters, and any other control characters are all included in the `length` count. Each of the following examples evaluates to the value 7:

```
"?seven?".length
"one two".length
"one\ntwo".length
```

> **NOTE** Note in the third example of the `length` property above that "\n" is a newline character, and thus counts as one character.

`anchor()` method

```
stringName.anchor("anchorName")
```

The `anchor()` method returns *stringName* enclosed within anchor (<a>) tags. The *anchorName* string is assigned to the name of the anchor via the `name` attribute.

```
"What's New".anchor("jan")
```

returns the string:

```
<A NAME="jan">What's New</A>
```

`big()` method

```
stringName.big()
```

The `big()` method returns *stringName* enclosed within <big> tags, which increase the font size by one step.

```
"Welcome to 1997!".big()
```

returns the string:

```
<BIG>Welcome to 1997!</BIG>
```

`blink()` method

```
stringName.blink()
```

The `blink()` method returns *stringName* enclosed within the much reviled <blink> tags, which cause text to blink on the web page—to many people's great annoyance.

```
"Wilkommen".blink()
```

returns the string:

```
<BLINK>Wilkommen</BLINK>
```

bold() method

`stringName.bold()`

The `bold()` method returns *stringName* enclosed within `<b>` tags, which render the text in boldface on the page.

`"Ouch!".bold()`

returns the string:

`<B>Ouch!</B>`

charAt() method

`stringName.charAt(index)`

The `charAt()` method returns the single character at the *index* position in the string. The first (leftmost) character in the string is considered position 0. Requesting an index outside the length of the string will return an empty string ("").

`"Long John Silver".charAt(5)`

would return the value `"J"`.

The `charAt()` method can be useful when you only need to know one character in a string. For example, imagine a form field where a user had to type a reply "yes" or "no." However, you don't know whether the user typed "yes" or "y" or "yessirree" or "ya." Well, it doesn't necessarily matter, because you need only verify the first character of the response—if it's a "y" then you consider it to be a "yes."

```
if (document.formName.textName.value.charAt(0)=="y")
{ statements in case of "yes" }
else { statements otherwise }
```

Of course, the flaw in the above code is that you can't be sure the user keyed in lowercase. For the solution to that, see the `toLowerCase()` and `toUpperCase()` methods of this `string` object.

fixed() method

`stringName.fixed()`

The `fixed()` method returns *stringName* enclosed within `<tt>` tags, which render text in fixed-width type on the page.

`"Memo".fixed()`

returns the string:

`<TT>Memo</TT>`

S

fontcolor() method

`stringName.fontcolor(colorValue)`

The `fontcolor()` method returns *stringName* enclosed within `<font>` tags, with the `color` attribute set to *colorValue*. The *colorValue* may be a predefined color name or an RGB hexadecimal triplet (see Appendix B).

`"YellowText".fontcolor("yellow")`

returns the string:

`<FONT COLOR="yellow">YellowText</FONT>`

fontsize() method

`stringName.fontsize(sizeValue)`

The `fontsize()` method returns *stringName* enclosed within `<font>` tags, with the `size` attribute set to *sizeValue*. The *sizeValue* may be a positive or negative integer, reflecting how many size steps to increase or decrease from default font size.

`"Some Tiny Text".fontsize(-3)`

returns the string:

`<FONT SIZE="-3">Some Tiny Text</FONT>`

indexOf() method

`stringName.indexOf(searchString, [startIndex])`

The `indexOf()` method returns an integer indicating at what index *searchString* is contained within *stringName*. The optional parameter *startIndex* tells the method where within *stringName* to start the search.

The `indexOf()` method will search from that point until the end of the string, finding the first instance of *searchString*. The value returned indicates the index at which the first character of *searchString* occurs within *stringName*. Without a specified *startIndex* parameter, the search begins at index 0. If the search fails to find a match, the method returns a value of −1.

This method is a useful way to determine whether a string exists at all within another string. For instance, to determine whether the string "Netscape" appears within the contents of `navigator.appName` (see `navigator` object):

`navigator.appName.indexOf("Netscape")`

In the following example, `indexOf()` returns a value of 11:

`"Little Boy Blue Big Blue".indexOf("Blue")`

Whereas the next example returns −1:

`"Oy Vey".indexOf("cow")`

italics() method

stringName.italics()

The italics() method returns *stringName* enclosed within <i> tags, which render the text italicized on the page.

"Noto Bene:".italics()

returns the string:

<I>Noto Bene:</I>

lastIndexOf() method

stringName.lastIndexOf(searchString, [startIndex])

Very similar to the indexOf() method, lastIndexOf() returns an integer indicating at what index *searchString* is contained within *stringName*. However, this method searches from right to left within *stringName*, thereby finding the match nearest the end of the string.

The optional parameter *startIndex* tells the method where within *stringName* to start the search—lastIndexOf() will then search from right to left starting at *startIndex*..

The value returned indicates the index at which the first character of *searchString* occurs within *stringName*. Without a specified *startIndex* parameter, the search begins at index *stringName*.length–1. If the search fails to find a match, the method returns a value of –1.

In the following example, lastIndexOf() returns a value of 20:

"Little Boy Blue Big Blue".lastIndexOf("Blue")

Whereas the next example returns –1:

"Apple Brown Betty".lastIndexOf("Marsha")

link() method

stringName.link(URL)

The link() method returns *stringName* enclosed within <a> tags, with the href attribute set to *URL*, creating a hyperlink on the page.

"Amazing Home Page".link("http://chebucto.ns.ca/~af227")

returns the string:

<A HREF="http://chebucto.ns.ca/~af227">Amazing Home Page</A>

small() method

stringName.small()

The small() method returns *stringName* enclosed within <small> tags, which decrease the font size by one step.

S

```
"Bye Bye".small()
```

returns the string:

```
<SMALL>Bye Bye</SMALL>
```

split() method

```
stringName.split(separatorCharacter)
```

The split() method breaks *stringName* into smaller strings, splitting at each occurrence of *separatorCharacter*. The resulting strings are returned as elements in an array. Consider the following statement:

```
newstr = "Monday,Tuesday,Wednesday".split(",")
```

The above example will split the specified string at each comma, and return the three resulting strings in an array assigned to newstr.

newstr[0] will contain "Monday"

newstr[1] will contain "Tuesday"

newstr[2] will contain "Wednesday"

Notice that the *separatorCharacter* is not included in any of the resultant strings. Your separator character can actually be longer than one character—if you had called split("Tuesday"), then the resulting two strings would have been "Monday," and ",Wednesday."

If you do not specify a *separatorCharacter*, the entire *stringName* will be returned as the first element in the array:

```
newstr = "Monday,Tuesday,Wednesday".split("")
```

newstr[0] will contain "Monday,Tuesday,Wednesday".

> To use the split() method in Internet Explorer 3, you must have installed the JScript Version 2 update available from Microsoft.

strike() method

```
stringName.strike()
```

The strike() method returns *stringName* enclosed within <strike> tags, which render text in strikethrough appearance on the page.

```
"Censored".strike()
```

returns the string:

```
<STRIKE>Censored</STRIKE>
```

sub() method

```
stringName.sub()
```

The sub() method returns *stringName* enclosed within <sub> tags, which render text in subscript on the page.

```
"H"+"2".sub()+"O"
```

returns the string:

```
H<SUB>2</SUB>O
```

substring() method

```
stringName.substring(indexA, indexB)
```

Like a pair of scissors, the substring() method extracts and returns a section of the string starting at *indexA* up to *the character before indexB*. Thus, the statement

```
"Hello Dolly".substring(0,4)
```

would return "Hell." The order of indexes is not important—

```
"Hello Dolly".substring(4,0)
```

also returns "Hell."

If *indexA* is equal to *indexB* then an empty string ("") is returned.

Often, you'll use the substring() method as the final step in a series when trying to extract data from a string. Typically, you use position finding methods, such as indexOf(), to locate a string segment within a larger string, and after you've determined the start- and endpoints of the segment, substring() finishes the job.

sup() method

```
stringName.sup()
```

The sup() method returns *stringName* enclosed within <sup> tags, which render text in superscript on the page.

```
"E=MC"+"2".sup()
```

returns the string:

```
E=MC<SUP>2</SUP>
```

toLowerCase() method

```
stringName.toLowerCase()
```

The toLowerCase() method returns *stringName* entirely in lowercase characters. Of course, this only affects alphabetical characters, and not numbers or symbols contained within the string.

S

```
"I want YOU!".toLowerCase()
```

returns the string:

```
i want you!
```

You may find this method useful when processing user-input data, so that you need not worry about whether the user entered text in lower- or uppercase:

```
if (document.formName.textName.value.charAt(0).toLowerCase()=="y")
{ statements in case of "yes" }
else { statements otherwise }
```

toUpperCase() method

```
stringName.toUpperCase()
```

The toUpperCase() method returns *stringName* entirely in uppercase characters. Of course, this only affects alphabetical characters, and not numbers or symbols contained within the string.

```
"poems by ee cummings".toUpperCase()
```

returns the string:

```
POEMS BY EE CUMMINGS
```

You may find this method useful when comparing two strings whose cases are unknown—perhaps they are user-input. Simply convert the strings toUpperCase() before the comparison.

```
if (question1.toUpperCase() == answer1.toUpperCase()) {…}
```

String()
Category: VBScript

	Type	Function

Browser Support		Navigator 3	Navigator 4	Explorer 3	Explorer 4
	Macintosh				■
	Windows			■	■

Syntax `String(number, character)`

The String() function creates and returns a string containing *number* instances of the specified *character*. You can specify *character* either as an ASCII character code or as a single-character string. If *character* is null, then the function returns null.

`string(5,"a")`	returns	"aaaaa"
`string(10,68)`	returns	"DDDDDDDDDD"
`string(3,"hello")`	returns	"hhh"

```
string(0,34)          returns          " "

string(-1,"r")        returns          invalid procedure call error
```

The String() function is a quick and easy way to create long strings of a single character—for instance, a line of 72 dash marks that act as a visual separator:

```
string(72,"-")
```

<STRONG>

Category: HTML

Browser Support		Navigator 3	Navigator 4	Explorer 3	Explorer 4
	Macintosh	▬	▬	▬	▬
	Windows	▬	▬	▬	▬

Applies To Nothing

May Contain <APPLET>, <B>, <BASEFONT>, <BIG>, <BR>, <CITE>, <CODE>, <DFN>, <EM>, <FONT>, <I>, <IMG>, <INPUT>, <KBD>, <MAP>, <SAMP>, <SELECT>, <SMALL>, <STRIKE>, <SUB>, <SUP>, <TEXTAREA>, <TT>, <U>, <VAR>

May Be Used In <ADDRESS>, <APPLET>, <B>, <BIG>, <BLOCKQUOTE>, <CAPTION>, <CENTER>, <CITE>, <CODE>, <DD>, <DT>, <FONT>, <H1>, <H2>, <H3>, <H4>, <H5>, <H6>, <I>, <KBD>, <LI>, <P>, <SAMP>, <SMALL>, <STRIKE>, <SUB>, <SUP>, <TD>, <TH>, <TT>, <U>

Attributes None

Syntax <STRONG>...</STRONG>

The <STRONG> tag emphasizes a specified amount of text by displaying it in boldface. Everything between the beginning and closing, or </STRONG> tag, will be bolded as shown in the example:

```
<STRONG>This text has been emphasized using the STRONG tag.</STRONG>
```

Figure 1 compares <STRONG>-specified text with plain default text in Navigator 3 for the Mac.

S

Figure 1

Emphasized text as defined by the <STRONG> tag, compared with plain default text on the second line.

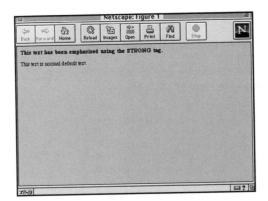

You can achieve the same results in both Navigator and Internet Explorer, on both platforms, by using the <B> or boldface tag instead of <STRONG>. See Figure 2 to compare the similarities between these tags.

Figure 2

The first and third lines look the same, although the top is specified with the <STRONG> tag and the third with the <B> tag, compared with plain default text on the second line.

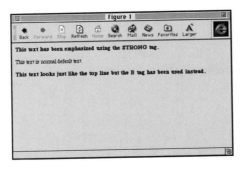

StrReverse()

Category: VBScript

Type	Function	

Browser Support

	Navigator 3	Navigator 4	Explorer 3	Explorer 4
Macintosh				▬
Windows			▬	▬

Syntax StrReverse(*string*)

The very simple StrReverse() function returns *string* with its characters in the reverse order. It does not directly modify *string* itself. If *string* is zero-length (""), then a zero-length string is returned; if *string* is null, then null is returned.

```
strreverse("Palindrome?")        returns        "?emordnilaP"

strreverse("Otto")               returns        "ottO"

strreverse("123")                returns        "321"
```

\<style\>

Category: HTML

Browser Support		Navigator 3	Navigator 4	Explorer 3	Explorer 4
	Macintosh	☐	■	■	☐
	Windows	☐	■	■	■

Applies To Cascading Style Sheets

Attributes None

Syntax `<style>…</style>`

You use the `<style>` tag to embed style sheets directly on your HTML page. The styles defined within the `<style>` and `</style>` tags effect the elements on the given page only and not the other pages on your site. See "Cascading Style Sheets Basics" for more information on defining and linking in styles. You must specify a value of "text/css" for the `type` attribute for the styles to be used.

```
<style type="text/css">
<!--
h1 { color: blue }
h2 { color: green }
-->
</style>
```

TIP You should make sure to hide style sheet tags from older browsers. Some browsers don't support style sheets. These browsers will ignore the `<STYLE>` tags, but not the rules themselves, because they're not surrounded by brackets. To avoid this problem, put your style definitions within *comments* as shown in the previous code, beginning with `<!--` and ending with `-->`. Browsers that support style sheets will pay attention to the style rules, while older browsers will ignore this "commented out" code.

S

> **NOTE**   Styles can be added to individual tags using `style` as an attribute. You specify the styles within quotes as with the following example:
>
> `<h4 style="color:green"> Famous Quotes </h4>`
>
> The styles only affect a specific tag regardless of whether the exact same tag—in this example, `<h4>`—is used to modified other elements later in the page.

<SUB>

Category: HTML

Browser Support		Navigator 3	Navigator 4	Explorer 3	Explorer 4
	Macintosh	■■■■	■■■■	■■■■	■■■■
	Windows	■■■■	■■■■	■■■■	■■■■

Applies To   Text

May Contain   `<APPLET>`, `<B>`, `<BASEFONT>`, `<BIG>`, `<BR>`, `<CITE>`, `<CODE>`, `<DFN>`, `<EM>`, `<FONT>`, `<I>`, `<IMG>`, `<INPUT>`, `<KBD>`, `<MAP>`, `<SAMP>`, `<SELECT>`, `<SMALL>`, `<STRIKE>`, `<STRONG>`, `<SUP>`, `<TEXTAREA>`, `<TT>`, `<U>`, `<VAR>`

May Be Used In   `<ADDRESS>`, `<APPLET>`, `<B>`, `<BIG>`, `<BLOCKQUOTE>`, `<CAPTION>`, `<CENTER>`, `<CITE>`, `<CODE>`, `<DD>`, `<DT>`, `<FONT>`, `<H1>`, `<H2>`, `<H3>`, `<H4>`, `<H5>`, `<H6>`, `<I>`, `<KBD>`, `<LI>`, `<P>`, `<SAMP>`, `<SMALL>`, `<STRIKE>`, `<STRONG>`, `<SUP>`, `<TD>`, `<TH>`, `<TT>`, `<U>`

Attributes   None

Syntax   `<SUB>...</SUB>`

The `<SUB>` tag displays a specified amount of text in subscript—text that has been reduced by one point size and dropped just below the normal line of text. Everything written between the beginning and closing, or `</SUB>` tag, will be subscripted. Subscript generally is used to properly write out chemical compounds or similar scientific data as shown in the example:

```
This text is normal default-type text but
<SUB>this text has been written as subscript using the SUB tag.</SUB>
```

Figure 1 displays this HTML in Navigator 3 for the Mac.

Figure 1

Subscript text as defined by the <SUB> tag, compared with plain default text.

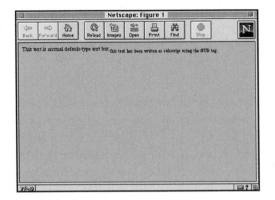

Submit

Category: JavaScript, JScript, VBScript

Type	Object		

Browser Support

	Navigator 3	Navigator 4	Explorer 3	Explorer 4
Macintosh	■	■	☐	■
Windows	■	■	■	■

Subset Of	Form object
Properties	form, name, type, value
Methods	blur(), focus(), click()
Events	onBlur, onFocus, onClick, onMouseDown, onMouseUp
Syntax	document.formName.submitName.property OR
	document.forms[index].elements[index].property OR
	document.formName.submitName.method(parameters) OR
	document.forms[index].elements[index].method(parameters)

The submit form field looks like a standard button. However, when the submit button is clicked, it submits the data within the form fields to the URL specified by the <form> tag's action attribute. Typically, the form data is sent to a CGI program on the web server (CGI programs are often UNIX scripts which are programmed to process the form data in some manner). Nearly exactly like the button object, the submit object allows script access to the submit form field element. The submit element is created using the <input> tag.

```
<input
   type="submit"
   name="buttonName"
   value="buttonCaption"
```

S

```
[onBlur="eventHandler"]
[onClick="eventHandler"]
[onFocus="eventHandler"]>
```

form property

The read-only reference to the form object that contains the submit object. This is a useful way to refer to another object in the same form. For instance, imagine a scenario where you want to reference a text object, named *text1*, which resides within the same form as the currently interesting submit object, *submit1*. This can be used to code in shorthand, or eliminate the need to explicitly reference the full path to every element within a single form, as in the code excerpts:

JavaScript

```
path=document.forms[0].submit1
value1=path.value
value2=path.form.text1.value
```

VBScript

```
set path=document.forms(0).submit1
value1=path.value
value2=path.form.text1.value
```

name property

The read-only name of the submit object, specified by the name attribute in the <input> tag.

```
objname = document.formname.submitname.name
objval = document.formname.objname.value
```

type property

The input type specified by the type attribute in the <input> tag. Of course, this always contains the value "submit" when referencing a submit element.

```
objtype = document.formname.submitname.type
```

 Internet Explorer 3 does not support the type property.

value property

The read-only text displayed on the submit button, specified by the value attribute in the <input> tag. You *cannot* modify the text on the face of the submit button using the value property—it *is* read-only.

```
caption = document.formname.submitname.value
```

Typically, the submit button contains a caption, which indicates that it *is* a submit button, such as "Submit" or "Submit Form."

> **TIP** In the case of a submit button appearing in Netscape Navigator or Internet Explorer 4 which has no `value` attribute specified in HTML, it's `value` property will contain the string "Submit Query" (which will also appear on the face of the submit button onscreen).
>
> Within Internet Explorer 3, the `value` property of a submit button which has no specified `value` attribute will contain the string "Submit" (which will appear on the face of the submit button onscreen).

`blur()` method

This method simulates the user losing focus from the submit button. Therefore, if the user currently has focus on the submit button, somehow triggering the following code would remove the focus:

```
document.formname.submitname.blur()
```

 Internet Explorer 3.0 does not support the `blur()` method for the `submit` object.

`focus()` method

 This method simulates the user gaining focus on the submit button. When the submit button element has focus, a thin dotted line appears around its perimeter.

You could use this method to call a user's attention to the submit button.

```
document.formname.submitname.focus()
```

> **WARNING** Be careful when and if you use the `focus()` method on a submit button that also contains an `onFocus()` event handler. In some scenarios within Netscape, this may result in an infinite loop wherein the `onFocus` event handler is repeated seemingly indefinitely. If your page is not operating as intended, this may be a cause to investigate.

S

 Internet Explorer 3.0 does not support the `focus()` method for the `submit` object.

`click()` method

This method simulates the user pressing the left (or only) mouse button atop the submit button element.

```
document.formname.submitname.click()
```

In the case of Netscape Navigator and Internet Explorer 4, the `click()` method will generate an `onSubmit` event for the form, and, unless the `onSubmit` event handler returns a value of false, submission of the form as specifed by the `<form>` tag's `action` attribute will proceed.

Within Internet Explorer 3.0, the `click()` method *does not* generate an `onSubmit` event, but it *does* proceed with submission of the form.

onBlur **event handler**

Located within the `<input>` tag, this will activate when the user loses focus (that is, clicks or tabs elsewhere in the browser) from the submit button.

`<input type="submit" name=submitname value="captiontext" onBlur="eventHandler">`

 Internet Explorer 3.0 does not support the `onBlur` event handler for the `submit` object.

onFocus **event handler**

Located within the `<input>` tag, this activates when the user brings focus to the submit button. When using a mouse, the only way to bring focus to the submit button is to click on it—which generates, in turn, an `onClick` event followed by an `onSubmit` event.

However, the user can also bring focus to the button using the tab key, which consecutively brings focus to each element on the page. In this case, the `onFocus` event handler could be triggered without also triggering an `onClick` or `onSubmit` event.

`<input type="submit" name=submitname value="captiontext" onFocus="eventHandler">`

 Internet Explorer 3.0 does not support the `onFocus` event handler for the `submit` object.

onClick **event handler**

Located within the `<input>` tag, this activates when the user clicks on and releases from the submit button. Of course, clicking a submit button generates an `onSubmit` event, which is an event handler of the `form` object. Thus, if you'd like to process or verify the form data before it is submitted to a server, you should do so using the `onSubmit` event rather than the `onClick` event.

Nonetheless, if you *can* think of a reason to use the `onClick` event for the `submit` object:

`<input type="submit" name=submitname value="captiontext" onClick="eventHandler">`

onMouseDown event handler

Located within the <a> tag, this will activate when the user presses down the mouse button on the submit button, but before the mouse button is released. This event handler can be used to determine whether a user is "holding" the mouse button down over the button, as opposed to clicking (pressing down and releasing).

For instance:

```
<input type="submit" name=submitname value="captiontext"
onMouseDown="eventHandler">
```

> **NOTE** The onMouseDown event handler is only supported beginning with the version 4 releases of Netscape Navigator and Internet Explorer.

onMouseUp event handler

Located within the <a> tag, this will activate when the user releases the mouse button on the submit button, after having pressed it down. In releasing the mouse button, the user has completed a click—however, the onMouseUp event occurs just prior to the onClick event. If your onMouseUp event handler returns true, the onClick event will be triggered and/or the form will be submitted; if this event handler returns false, no onClick event will occur and the form will not be submitted.

For instance:

```
<input type="submit" name=submitname value="captiontext"
onMouseUp="eventHandler">
```

> **NOTE** The onMouseUp event handler is only supported beginning with the version 4 releases of Netscape Navigator and Internet Explorer.

<SUP>

Category: HTML

Browser Support

	Navigator 3	Navigator 4	Explorer 3	Explorer 4
Macintosh	■	■	■	■
Windows	■	■	■	■

Applies To None

S

May Contain	\<APPLET\>, \<B\>, \<BASEFONT\>, \<BIG\>, \<BR\>, \<CITE\>, \<CODE\>, \<DFN\>, \<EM\>, \<FONT\>, \<I\>, \<IMG\>, \<INPUT\>, \<KBD\>, \<MAP\>, \<SAMP\>, \<SELECT\>, \<SMALL\>, \<STRIKE\>, \<STRONG\>, \<SUB\>, \<TEXTAREA\>, \<TT\>, \<U\>, \<VAR\>
May Be Used In	\<ADDRESS\>, \<APPLET\>, \<B\>, \<BIG\>, \<BLOCKQUOTE\>, \<CAPTION\>, \<CENTER\>, \<CITE\>, \<CODE\>, \<DD\>, \<DT\>, \<FONT\>, \<H1\>, \<H2\>, \<H3\>, \<H4\>, \<H5\>, \<H6\>, \<I\>, \<KBD\>, \<LI\>, \<P\>, \<SAMP\>, \<SMALL\>, \<STRIKE\>, \<STRONG\>, \<SUB\>, \<TD\>, \<TH\>, \<TT\>, \<U\>
Attributes	None
Syntax	\<SUP\>...\</SUP\>

The \<SUP\> tag displays a specified amount of text in superscript—text that has been reduced by one point size and elevated just above the normal line of text. Everything written between the beginning and closing, or \</SUP\> tag, will be superscripted. Superscript generally is used to properly display and number a footnote as shown in the example:

```
<P>This text is normal default-type text but
<SUP>this text has been written as superscript using the SUP tag.</SUP>
```

Figure 1 displays this HTML in Navigator 3 for the Mac.

Figure 1

Superscript text as defined by the \<SUP\> tag, compared with plain default text.

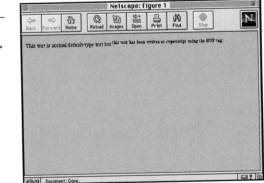

```
</STRONG> ■ <TD> </TD> ■ <TH> </TH> ■ <TABLE> </TABLE> ■
<IMG> </IMG> ■ <SCRIPT LANGUAGE = "javascript"> </SCRIPT>
■ <SCRIPT LANGUAGE = "vbscript"> </SCRIPT> ■ <BGSOUND
SRC=gbv.wav LOOP=-1> </BGSOUND> ■ <APPLET CLASS=
"ester's_day" SRC="http://testsite/walla walla washington/"
</APPLET> ■ <FRAME></FRAME>■ <MARQUEE> </MARQUEE> ■   <HTML>
</HTML> ■ <A> </A>■ <OL> </OL>■ <UL> </UL> ■ <MENU> </MENU>
■ <STRONG> </STRONG> ■ <TD> </TD> ■ <TH> </TH>
```

T

\<TABLE\>

Category: HTML

Browser Support

	Navigator 3	Navigator 4	Explorer 3	Explorer 4
Macintosh	■	■	■	■
Windows	■	■	■	■

May Contain \<CAPTION\> (once), \<TR\>

May Be Used In \<BLOCKQUOTE\>, \<BODY\>, \<CENTER\>, \<DD\>, \<DIV\>, \<FORM\>, \<LI\>, \<TD\>, \<TH\>

Attributes ALIGN, BACKGROUND, BORDER, BORDERCOLOR, BORDERCOLORDARK, BORDERCOLORLIGHT, CELLPADDING, CELLSPACING, CLASS, CLEAR, FRAME, HEIGHT, ID, NOWRAP, RULES, VALIGN, WIDTH

Syntax \<TABLE\>...\</TABLE\>

The \<TABLE\> tag is the most important tag used to create tables—bordered graphs on a web page consisting of rows and columns of cells. A closing, or \</TABLE\>, tag is required.

Tables were previously used to display numbers and numerical data, like spreadsheets, but now they are being widely used to arrange everything from images to inline video because of the control and precision that \<TABLE\> tags can provide.

The following example is the HTML for a very basic, four-cell table:

```
<TABLE>
<TR>
<TD>Cell No. 1</TD><TD>Cell No. 2</TD>
</TR>
<TR>
<TD>Cell No. 3</TD><TD>Cell No. 4</TD>
</TR>
</TABLE>
```

As you can see, the \<TABLE\> tag encompasses all the other table elements: the border or lines, the cells, the columns, and the spaces between. If the \<TABLE\> tag were missing, a browser could not correctly interpret this information as a table. (The \<TR\> and \<TD\> tags are explained more thoroughly in their own entries found elsewhere in the book.)

Figures 1, 2, 3, and 4 illustrate two plain tables—one with a plain border and one without a border—in Navigator 3 and Internet Explorer 3 for the Macintosh and for Windows.

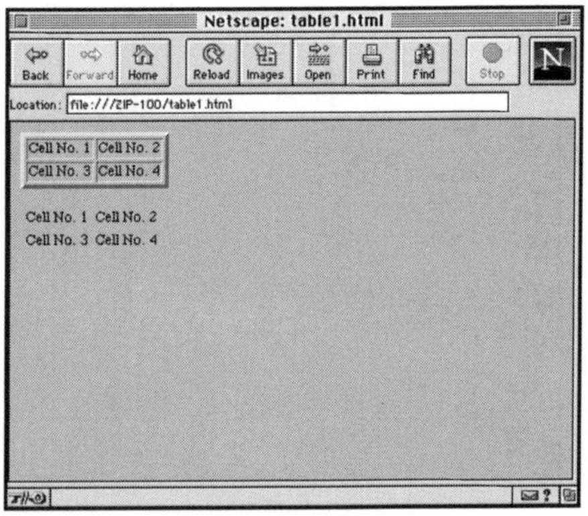

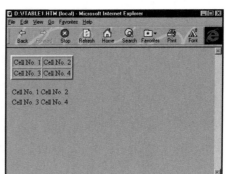

Figure 1

Basic four-cell tables in Navigator 3 for the Macintosh.

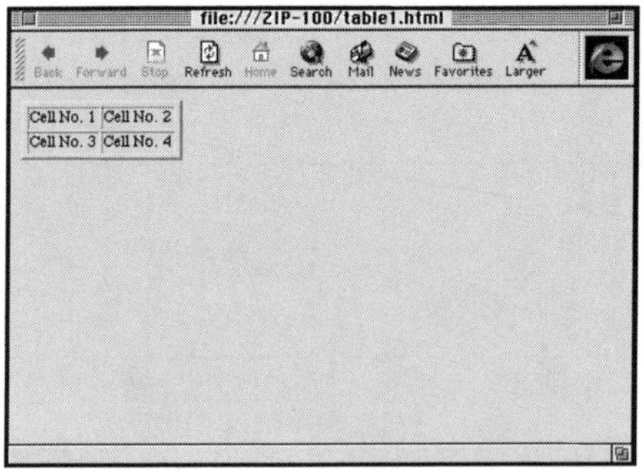

Figure 2

Basic four-cell tables in Internet Explorer 3 for the Macintosh.

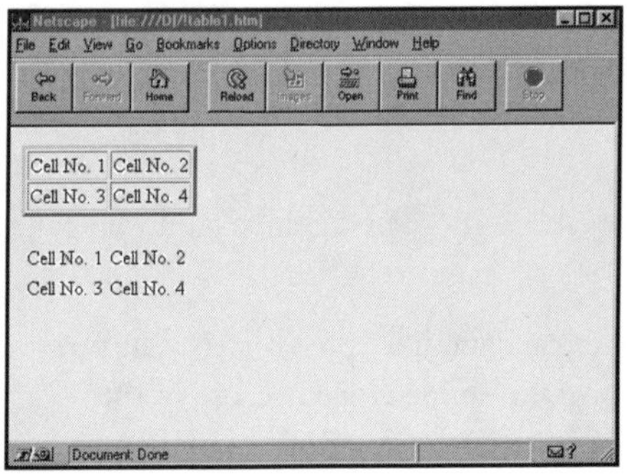

Figure 3

Basic four-cell tables in Navigator 3 for Windows.

Figure 4

Basic four-cell tables in Internet Explorer 3 for Windows.

There are more complicated types of tables, such as tables that use headers, column-spanning elements, and row-spanning elements, which will be covered elsewhere in the <TD> and <TH> tag entries, respectively.

ALIGN

The ALIGN attribute is supposed to specify table alignment in Internet Explorer only, yet at this writing neither Internet Explorer 3 for the Macintosh nor version 3 for Windows will properly support it.

There are six ALIGN values listed in several Internet Explorer HTML references:

bleedleft

The table will bleed into the left-hand margin.

bleedright

The table will bleed into the right-hand margin.

center

The table will appear centered on the page.

justify

The table will appear justified to both the left and right margins.

left

The table will float along the left side of the browser window. This is the ALIGN default.

right

The table will float along the right side of the browser window. If the table area is smaller than the browser window, any text that follows the table will wrap along the left side.

In the following example, the ALIGN value has been specified as right:

```
<TABLE ALIGN=right>
<TR>
<TD>Cell No. 1</TD><TD>Cell No. 2</TD>
</TR>
<TR>
<TD>Cell No. 3</TD><TD>Cell No. 4</TD>
</TR>
</TABLE>
```

It is possible that this attribute and its values will be supported by forthcoming versions of Explorer (version 4) and Navigator (Netscape Communicator). At this writing, however, using the ALIGN attribute in either browser is not recommended.

BACKGROUND

The BACKGROUND attribute is an Internet Explorer–only feature that tiles a background pattern behind every table cell, similar to the way the <BODY> tag's BACKGROUND attribute tiles a pattern behind the text on an entire web page.

In the following example, pattern.gif represents the file name of the background pattern:

```
<TABLE BACKGROUND=pattern.gif>
<TR>
<TD>Cell No. 1</TD><TD>Cell No. 2</TD>
</TR>
<TR>
```

T

```
<TD>Cell No. 3</TD><TD>Cell No. 4</TD>
</TR>
</TABLE>
```

The background pattern can be in any file format supported by Internet Explorer.

Figure 5 illustrates a BACKGROUND-specified pattern tiled behind a four-cell table in Internet Explorer 3 for Windows. (This attribute is not supported by Explorer 3 for the Macintosh.)

Figure 5

A four-cell table with a BACKGROUND-specified pattern in Internet Explorer 3 for Windows.

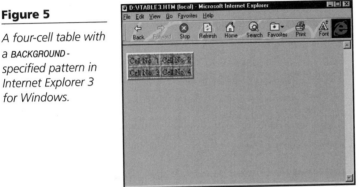

> **DESIGN NOTE** If you want to tile a background pattern behind a table, keep these considerations in mind: first, visitors need to read the text or see the images you're putting in your tables so choose something that's not too busy, and second, use the background color or pattern behind your entire page as a guideline so you don't choose a table pattern that clashes. Also remember that support for this attribute is extremely limited at this time, so don't rely on it.

BGCOLOR

The BGCOLOR attribute specifies a custom background color for table cells, using a color name or a hexadecimal color value. (See Appendix B for a chart of all the colors you can specify by name and all the colors you can specify by hex value.)

In the following example, white is used by its hex value:

```
<TABLE BORDER BGCOLOR=#ffffff>
<TR>
<TD>Cell No. 1</TD><TD>Cell No. 2</TD>
</TR>
<TR>
<TD>Cell No. 3</TD><TD>Cell No. 4</TD>
</TR>
</TABLE>
```

White is one of 16 colors you can also specify by name if you prefer—for more information on color choices and color issues, see Appendix B.

Figures 6, 7, 8, and 9 illustrate this example HTML in Navigator 3 and Internet Explorer 3 for the Macintosh and for Windows. White is used as the background color so the effect of using BACKGROUND will be visible in these black-and-white figures.

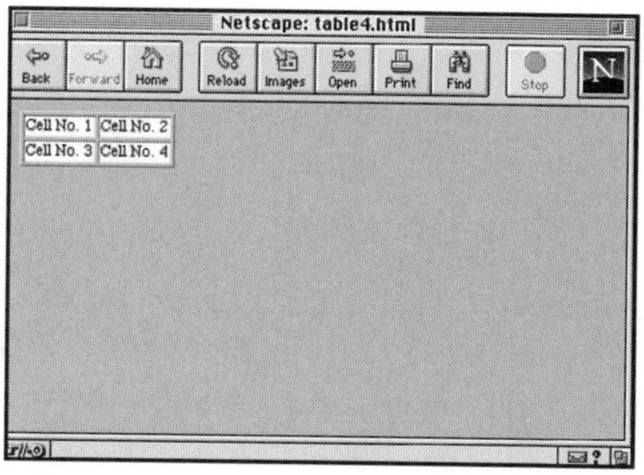

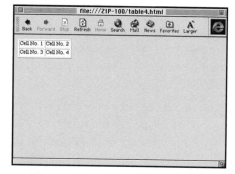

Figure 6

A four-cell table with a white background in Navigator 3 for the Macintosh.

Figure 7

A four-cell table with a white background in Internet Explorer 3 for the Macintosh.

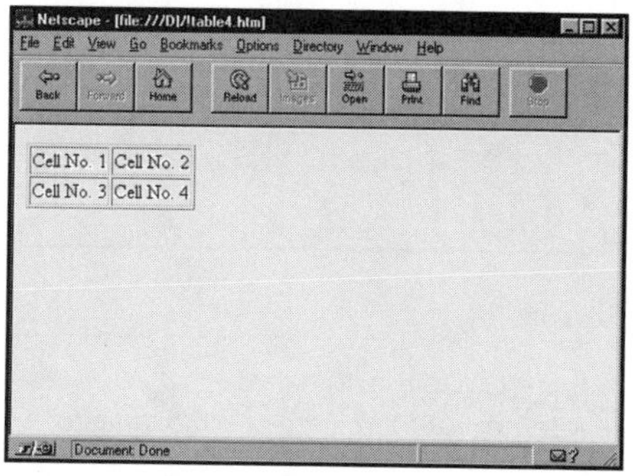

Figure 8

A four-cell table with a white background in Navigator 3 for Windows.

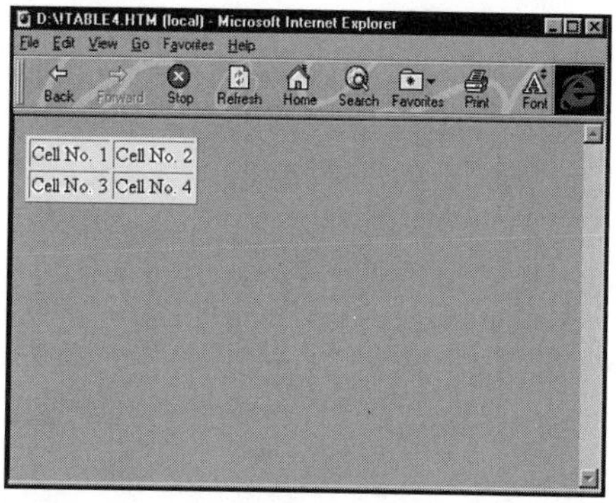

Figure 9

A four-cell table with a white background in Internet Explorer 3 for Windows.

T

DESIGN NOTE The suggestions mentioned elsewhere in this book about choosing a background pattern still remain in effect—your page is there to be read, not to blind or hypnotize, and your overall background color or pattern must be taken into consideration.

BORDER

The BORDER attribute specifies the presence and the width of a border around each cell and column in a table.

In the following example, the BORDER width has been specified as 10:

```
<TABLE BORDER=10>
<TR>
<TD>Cell No. 1</TD><TD>Cell No. 2</TD>
</TR>
<TR>
<TD>Cell No. 3</TD><TD>Cell No. 4</TD>
</TR>
</TABLE>
```

The resulting border will be ten pixels wide. Figures 10, 11, 12, and 13 illustrate a 10-pixel border in Navigator 3 and Internet Explorer 3 for the Macintosh and for Windows. Compare this width to the default BORDER width as shown in Figures 1 through 4.

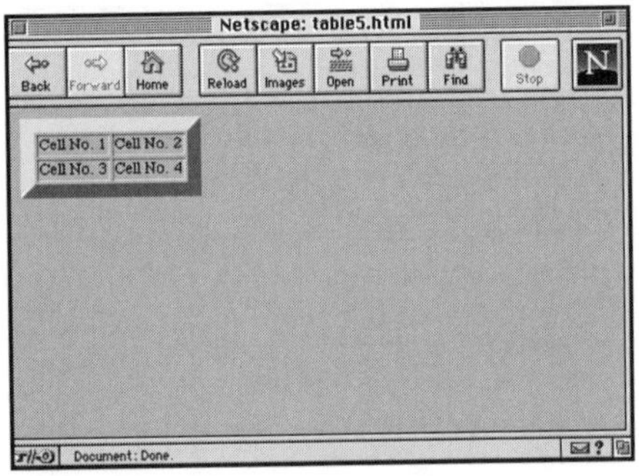

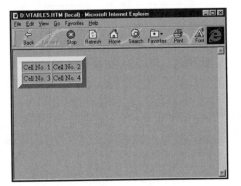

Figure 10

A four-cell table with a BORDER of 10 pixels in Navigator 3 for the Macintosh.

Figure 11

A four-cell table with a BORDER of 10 pixels in Internet Explorer 3 for the Macintosh.

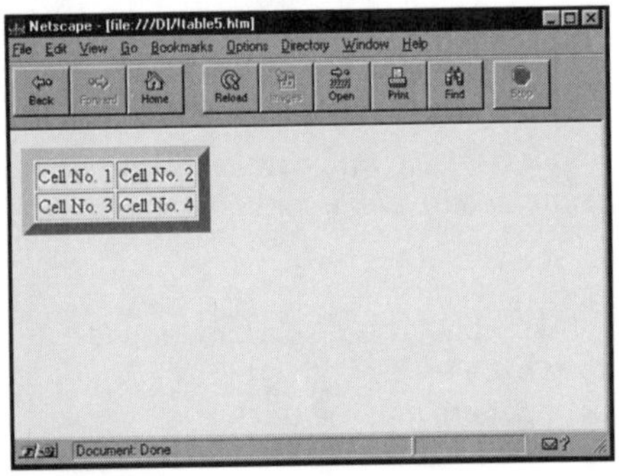

Figure 12

A four-cell table with a BORDER of 10 pixels in Navigator 3 for Windows.

Figure 13

A four-cell table with a BORDER of 10 pixels in Internet Explorer 3 for Windows.

The BORDER tag also works in tandem with three Internet Explorer—only <TABLE> tag attributes—BORDERCOLOR, BORDERCOLORLIGHT, and BORDERCOLORDARK—to create color customized solid and 3-D table borders.

It also works with the Internet Explorer—only FRAME and RULES attributes to customize border displays. See these subsequent sections later on in this entry for more information.

BORDERCOLOR

The BORDERCOLOR attribute is an Internet Explorer—only attribute that specifies a solid custom border color.

There is no equivalent attribute for Navigator, so no matter what color you specify using BORDERCOLOR, visitors to your site using Navigator will see all tables bordered in black.

BORDERCOLOR color values are specified either by name or by hexadecimal value. (See Appendix B for a chart of all the colors you can specify by name and all the colors you can specify by hex value.)

In the following example, magenta is specified by hex value:

```
<TABLE BORDER BORDERCOLOR=#ff00ff>
<TR>
<TD>Cell No. 1</TD><TD>Cell No. 2</TD>
</TR>
<TR>
<TD>Cell No. 3</TD><TD>Cell No. 4</TD>
</TR>
</TABLE>
```

Magenta is another color you can specify by name if you like—for the complete list of such colors and more information about other color issues, see Appendix B.

You must use the BORDER attribute with BGCOLOR or your borders will appear in default black. See the BORDER attribute section earlier in this entry for more information.

Figures 14 and 15 illustrate this example HTML in Internet Explorer 3 for the Macintosh and for Windows. White is used as the border color so the effect of using BACKGROUND will be visible in these black-and-white figures.

T

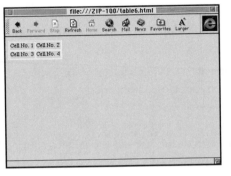

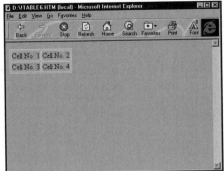

Figure 14

A four-cell table with white borders in Internet Explorer 3 for the Macintosh.

Figure 15

A four-cell table with white borders in Internet Explorer 3 for Windows.

DESIGN NOTE Do NOT choose border colors that a) won't show up against your table or page background color (as in white borders on a yellow background), b) match your customized link colors (or visitors will click your tables thinking they're links), and c) clash with any other customized colors on your page.

BORDERCOLORDARK

The BORDERCOLORDARK attribute is an Internet Explorer–only attribute that specifies the darker of two border colors that overlap to create a 3-D effect.

There is no equivalent attribute for Navigator, so no matter what color you specify using BORDERCOLORDARK, all visitors to your web site using Navigator will view your table borders as solid black.

BORDERCOLORDARK color values are specified either by name or by hexadecimal value. (See Appendix B for a chart of all the colors you can specify by name and all the colors you can specify by hex value.)

In the following example, blue is specified in both instances as the BORDERCOLORDARK value by hex value:

```
<TABLE BORDER BORDERCOLORLIGHT=#00ffff BORDERCOLORDARK=#0000ff>
<TR>
<TD>Cell No. 1</TD><TD>Cell No. 2</TD>
</TR>
<TR>
<TD>Cell No. 3</TD><TD>Cell No. 4</TD>
</TR>
</TABLE>
```

Blue can also be specified by name—for more information on doing this, and for more information on other color issues, see Appendix B.

You must use both the BORDER and the BORDERCOLORLIGHT attributes and appropriate values along with a BORDERCOLORDARK value to make this color 3-D effect work. If you leave out one or both of these other attributes, your borders will remain plain gray and white.

Figures 16 and 17 illustrate this example HTML in Internet Explorer 3 for the Macintosh and for Windows. White is used as the BORDERCOLORLIGHT value and medium gray as the BORDERCOLORDARK value so the effect of using these attributes will be visible in these black-and-white figures.

Figure 16

A four-cell table with a white and gray 3-D border in Internet Explorer 3 for the Macintosh.

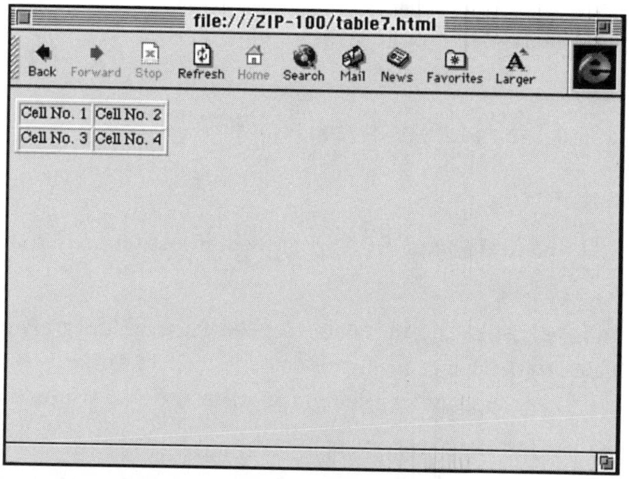

Figure 17

A four-cell table with a white and gray 3-D border in Internet Explorer 3 for Windows.

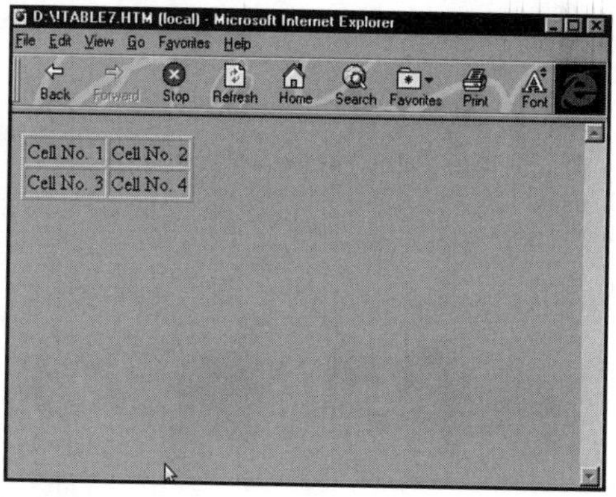

BORDERCOLORLIGHT

The BORDERCOLORLIGHT attribute is an Internet Explorer–only attribute that specifies the lighter of two border colors that overlap to create a 3-D effect.

There is no equivalent attribute for Navigator, so no matter what color you specify using BORDERCOLORLIGHT, all visitors to your web site using Navigator will view your table borders as solid black.

BORDERCOLORLIGHT color values are specified either by name or by hexadecimal value. (See Appendix B for a chart of all the colors you can specify by name and all the colors you can specify by hex value.)

In the following example, cyan is specified in both instances as the BORDERCOLORLIGHT value by hex value:

```
<TABLE BORDER BORDERCOLORLIGHT=#00ffff BORDERCOLORDARK=#0000ff>
<TR>
<TD>Cell No. 1</TD><TD>Cell No. 2</TD>
</TR>
<TR>
<TD>Cell No. 3</TD><TD>Cell No. 4</TD>
</TR>
</TABLE>
```

Cyan can be used by name if you prefer—for more information on this and other color issues, see Appendix B.

You must use both the BORDER and the BORDERCOLORDARK attributes and appropriate values along with a BORDERCOLORLIGHT value to make this color 3-D effect work. If you leave out one or both of these other attributes, your borders will remain plain gray and white.

Figures 18 and 19 illustrate this example HTML in Internet Explorer 3 for the Macintosh and for Windows. White is used as the BORDERCOLORLIGHT value and medium gray as the BORDERCOLORDARK value so the effect of using these attributes will be visible in these black-and-white figures.

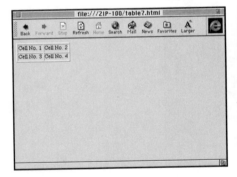

Figure 18

A four-cell table with a white and gray 3-D border in Internet Explorer 3 for the Macintosh.

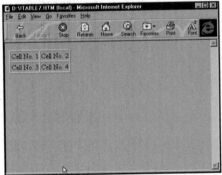

Figure 19

A four-cell table with a white and gray 3-D border in Internet Explorer 3 for Windows.

CELLPADDING

The CELLPADDING attribute determines the amount of blank space between a table cell border and the cell's contents (text, images, and so on).

In the following example, the CELLPADDING value has been established at 3:

```
<TABLE BORDER CELLPADDING=3 CELLSPACING=3>
<TR>
<TD>Cell No. 1</TD><TD>Cell No. 2</TD>
</TR>
<TR>
<TD>Cell No. 3</TD><TD>Cell No. 4</TD>
</TR>
</TABLE>
```

The default CELLPADDING value is 1. If you want no "elbow room" between the border and cell contents—if you're using an image within a cell, for example—you would set the CELLPADDING value at 0.

Using a CELLSPACING value whenever you establish CELLPADDING is not required, but it will produce better spacing proportions. In the example HTML above, the CELLSPACING value is also set at 3 so all the relative spacings within the table will be equal. This is a good rule of thumb, or else visitors to your page may think there's a problem with your HTML. See the CELLSPACING attribute section of this entry for more information.

Figures 20, 21, 22, and 23 display a table with the three-pixel CELLPADDING and CELLSPACING settings in place in Navigator 3 and Internet Explorer 3 for the Macintosh and for Windows.

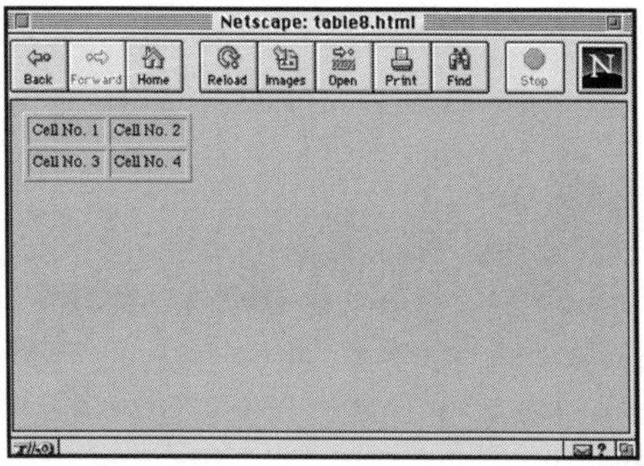

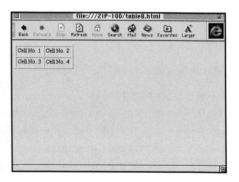

Figure 20

A four-cell table with three-pixel CELL-PADDING in Navigator 3 for the Macintosh.

Figure 21

A four-cell table with three-pixel CELL-PADDING in Internet Explorer 3 for the Macintosh.

T

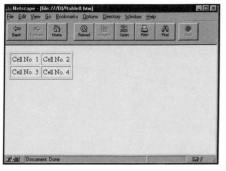

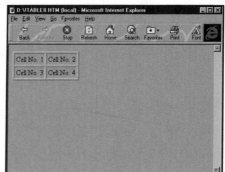

Figure 22

A four-cell table with a three-pixel CELL-PADDING in Navigator 3 for Windows.

Figure 23

A four-cell table with three-pixel CELL-PADDING in Internet Explorer 3 for Windows.

CELLSPACING

The CELLSPACING attribute determines the amount of blank space between two individual table cells.

In the following example, the CELLSPACING value has been established at 3:

```
<TABLE BORDER CELLPADDING=3 CELLSPACING=3>
<TR>
<TD>Cell No. 1</TD><TD>Cell No. 2</TD>
</TR>
<TR>
<TD>Cell No. 3</TD><TD>Cell No. 4</TD>
</TR>
</TABLE>
```

The default CELLSPACING value is 2.

Using a CELLSPACING value whenever you establish CELLPADDING is not required, but it will produce better spacing proportions. In the example HTML above, the CELLPADDING value is also set at 3 so all the relative spacings within the table will be equal. This is a good rule of thumb, or else visitors to your page may think there's a problem with your HTML. See the CELLPADDING attribute section of this entry for more information.

Figures 24, 25, 26, and 27 display a table with the three-pixel CELLSPACING and CELLPADDING settings in place in Navigator 3 and Internet Explorer 3 for the Macintosh and for Windows.

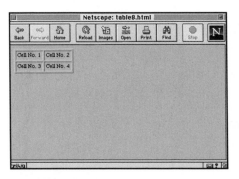

Figure 24

A four-cell table with three-pixel CELL-SPACING in Navigator 3 for the Macintosh.

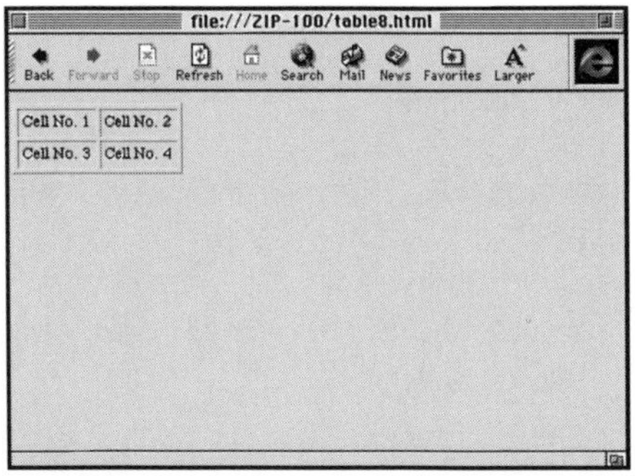

Figure 25

A four-cell table with three-pixel CELL-SPACING in Internet Explorer 3 for the Macintosh.

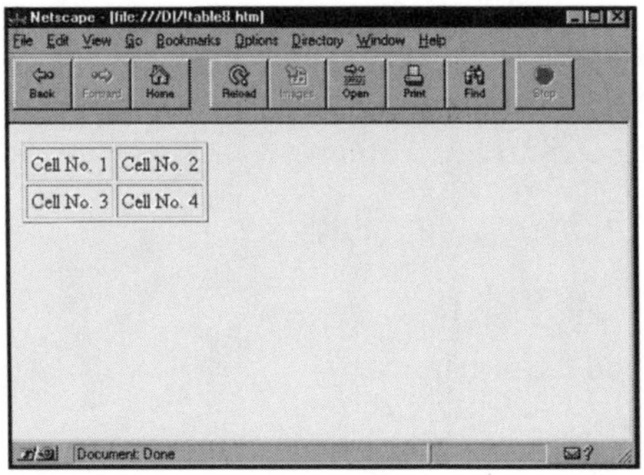

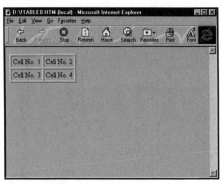

Figure 26

A four-cell table with a three-pixel CELL-SPACING in Navigator 3 for Windows.

Figure 27

A four-cell table with three-pixel CELL-SPACING in Internet Explorer 3 for Windows.

CLASS

The CLASS attribute is used to specify the name of a style sheet as it applies to a specific selection on a web page. See the "Cascading Style Sheets Basics" chapter and any individual, related style sheets entries elsewhere in the book for more information.

COLS

The COLS attribute specifies the number of columns present in a table.

It does not affect or alter the appearance of a table, but it may help a browser interpret long or complex tables more quickly so that your web page, in turn, will also load up more quickly.

In the following example, the number of columns has been specified as 2:

```
<TABLE COLS=2>
<TR>
<TD>Cell No. 1</TD><TD>Cell No. 2</TD>
</TR>
<TR>
<TD>Cell No. 3</TD><TD>Cell No. 4</TD>
</TR>
</TABLE>
```

Do not confuse the COL attribute with column tags, such as <COLSPAN>, <COLGROUP>, or the very similarly named <COL> tag. See these other tag entries elsewhere in the book for more information about formatting table columns.

CLEAR

The CLEAR attribute reportedly specifies the alignment of any text following a table in Navigator and Internet Explorer. However, at this writing CLEAR is not supported by any version of Netscape Navigator/Communicator or Microsoft Internet Explorer.

However, various HTML references report it as having four values:

all

The text appears justified with both the left and right margins.

left

The text appears on the first available line aligned left.

no

The text appears on the first available line with no alignment. This is the CLEAR attribute default.

right

The text appears on the first available line aligned right.

In the following example, the CLEAR attribute value has been established as left:

```
<TABLE BORDER CLEAR=left>
<TR>
<TD>Cell No. 1</TD><TD>Cell No. 2</TD>
</TR>
<TR>
<TD>Cell No. 3</TD><TD>Cell No. 4</TD>
</TR>
</TABLE>
This text will wrap as specified by the CLEAR value.
```

It is possible that this attribute and values will be supported in updated versions of Netscape Communicator and Explorer 4, but at this writing, CLEAR is not a reliable <TABLE> attribute.

FRAME

FRAME is an Internet Explorer–only attribute that disables the display of certain *borders*—or exterior table lines.

It must be used with the BORDER attribute as in the following example:

```
<TABLE BORDER FRAME=void>
<TR>
<TD>Cell No. 1</TD><TD>Cell No. 2</TD>
</TR>
<TR>
<TD>Cell No. 3</TD><TD>Cell No. 4</TD>
</TR>
</TABLE>
```

If the BORDER attribute is not present, the browser will ignore any FRAME value you specify and display all the table borders.

The FRAME attribute has nine values:

above

Only the outside edge border along the top of the table will be displayed.

below

Only the outside edge border along the bottom of the table will be displayed.

border

All outside borders will be displayed. This is the FRAME attribute default.

box

Only the outside top, bottom, left, and right borders will be displayed, enclosing the table in a box.

hsides

Only the borders along the horizontal edges of the table will be displayed (the top and bottom).

lhs

Only the border on the left edge of the table will be displayed.

rhs

Only the border on the right edge of the table will be displayed.

void

No borders will be displayed.

vsides

Only the borders along the vertical edges of the table will be displayed (the left and right).

T

Figures 28 and 29 display all nine FRAME values in Internet Explorer 3 for the Macintosh. Figures 30 and 31 display these values in Internet Explorer 3 for Windows.

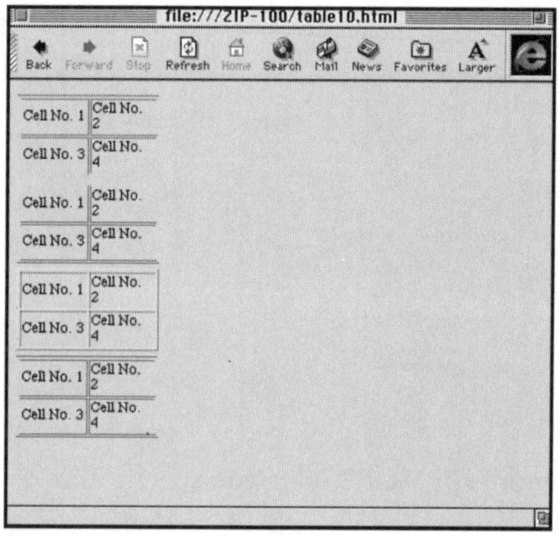

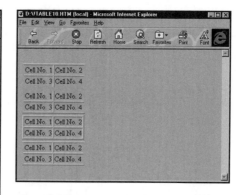

Figure 28

FRAME `above, below, border, box,` and `hsides` in Internet Explorer 3 for the Macintosh.

Figure 29

FRAME `lhs, rhs, void,` and `vsides` in Internet Explorer 3 for the Macintosh.

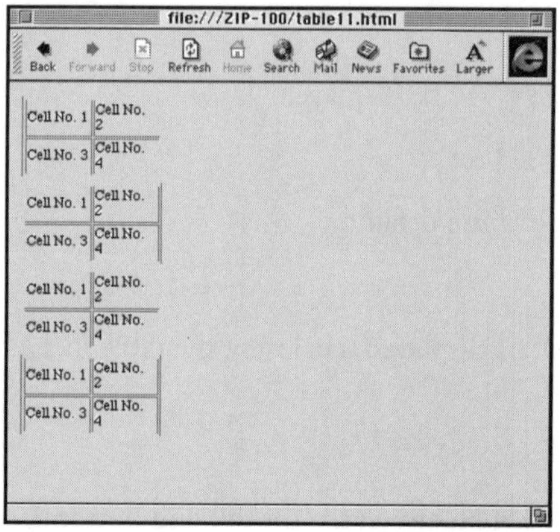

Figure 30

FRAME `above, below, border, box,` and `hsides` in Internet Explorer 3 for Windows.

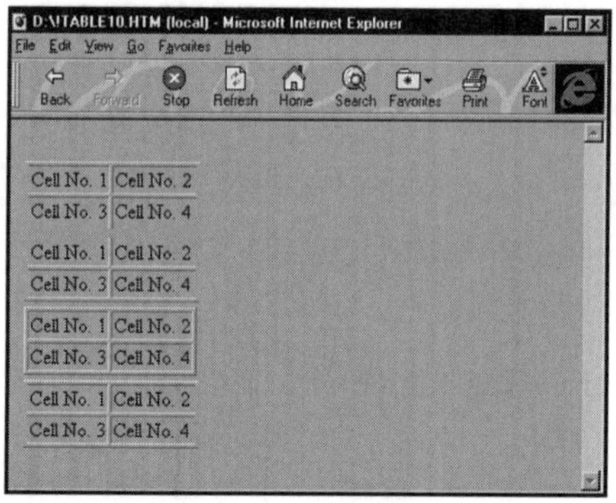

Figure 31

FRAME `lhs, rhs, void,` and `vsides` in Internet Explorer 3 for Windows.

> **NOTE**   If you want to disable or turn off the display of the internal table lines, use the RULES attribute—although it is also, like FRAME, supported by Internet Explorer only. See the RULES section of this entry for more information.

HEIGHT

The HEIGHT attribute specifies an exact table height, in either pixels or as a percentage of the browser window.

It should be accompanied by a WIDTH attribute setting—see the WIDTH attribute section of this entry for more information.

In the following example, HEIGHT is specified as 200 pixels:

```
<TABLE BORDER HEIGHT=200 WIDTH=300>
<TR>
<TD>Cell No. 1</TD><TD>Cell No. 2</TD>
</TR>
<TR>
<TD>Cell No. 3</TD><TD>Cell No. 4</TD>
</TR>
</TABLE>
<TABLE BORDER HEIGHT=15% WIDTH=15%>
<TR>
<TD>Cell No. 1</TD><TD>Cell No. 2</TD>
</TR>
<TR>
<TD>Cell No. 3</TD><TD>Cell No. 4</TD>
</TR>
</TABLE>
```

Figures 32, 33, 34, and 35 display this example HTML in Navigator 3 and Internet Explorer 3 for the Macintosh and for Windows.

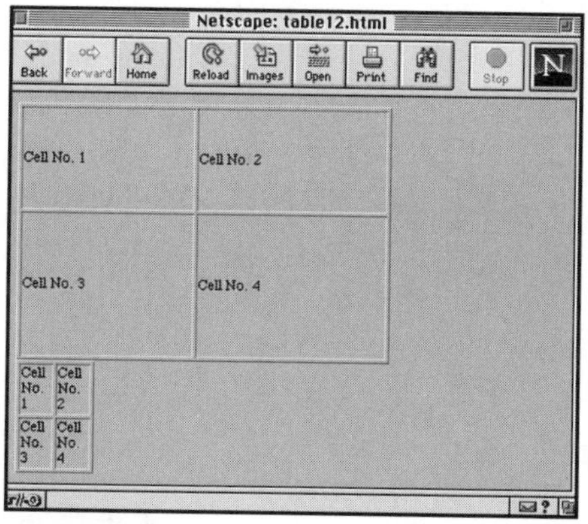

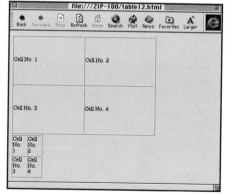

Figure 32

Customizing a table using HEIGHT and WIDTH in Navigator 3 for the Macintosh.

Figure 33

Customizing a table using HEIGHT and WIDTH in Internet Explorer 3 for the Macintosh.

T

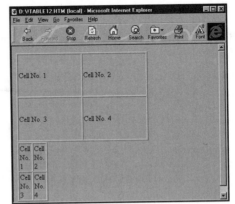

Figure 34

Customizing a table using HEIGHT and WIDTH in Navigator 3 for Windows.

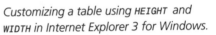

Figure 35

Customizing a table using HEIGHT and WIDTH in Internet Explorer 3 for Windows.

ID

The ID attribute is used to distinguish individual selections in a web page as pertaining to the use of style sheets. See the "Cascading Style Sheets Basics" chapter and any individual, related style sheets entries elsewhere in the book for more information.

NOWRAP

The NOWRAP attribute supposedly prevents rows from wrapping if a table extends into the right margin. Ordinarily, Navigator and Internet Explorer will automatically wrap table information down to the next line, as they do with plain text.

In the following example, the NOWRAP attribute is placed properly within the opening <TABLE> tag with no values:

```
<TABLE BORDER NOWRAP>
<TR>
<TD>Cell No. 1</TD><TD>Cell No. 2</TD>
</TR>
<TR>
<TD>Cell No. 3</TD><TD>Cell No. 4</TD>
</TR>
</TABLE>
```

It is possible that this attribute will be supported by forthcoming versions of Navigator (Netscape Communicator) and Explorer (version 4), but at this writing, using NOWRAP is not recommended.

RULES

RULES is an Internet Explorer–only attribute that disables the display of certain *rules*—or interior table borders.

It must be used with the BORDER attribute and with <THEAD>-, <TBODY>-, and <TFOOT>-specified table sections—these three table section tags are also only supported by Internet Explorer.

In the following example, everything the RULES attribute needs to work with is in place:

```
<TABLE BORDER RULES=none>
<THEAD>
<TR>
<TD>Cell No. 1</TD><TD>Cell No. 2</TD>
</TR>
<TBODY>
<TR>
<TD>Cell No. 3</TD><TD>Cell No. 4</TD>
</TR>
<TFOOT>
<TR>
<TD>Cell No. 3</TD><TD>Cell No. 4</TD>
</TR>
</TABLE>
```

If the BORDER attribute and <THEAD>, <TBODY>, and <TFOOT> attributes are not present, the browser will ignore any RULES value you specify and display all the interior table borders.

The RULES attribute has six values:

```
all
```

All the internal rules are displayed. This value is not supported by Internet Explorer 3 for the Macintosh.

```
basic
```

Only the rules between the <THEAD>, <TBODY>, and <TFOOT> text are displayed. This value is not supported by Internet Explorer 3 for the Macintosh.

```
cols
```

Only the rules between the columns are displayed.

```
groups
```

Only the horizontal rules between table groups are displayed. (These groups are specified by the <COLGROUP>, <THEAD>, <TBODY>, and <TFOOT> tags—the <COLGROUP> tag is additionally required to make this value work properly.) This value is not supported by Internet Explorer 3 for the Macintosh.

```
none
```

No internal rules are displayed.

```
rows
```

Only the rules between the rows are displayed.

T

Figures 36 and 37 display six tables each, illustrating the six and three RULES attributes as marked in Internet Explorer 3 for the Macintosh and for Windows.

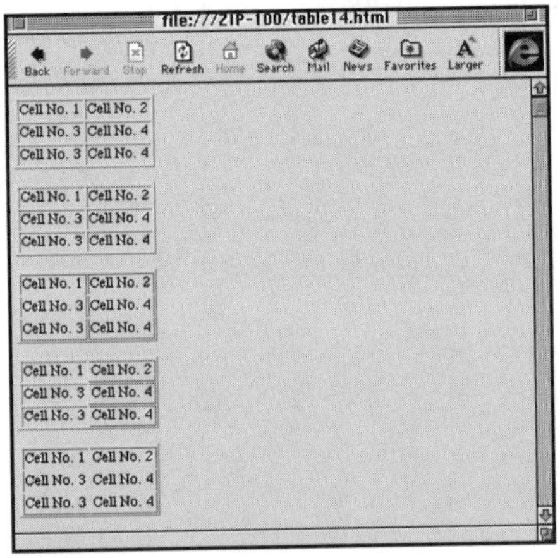

Figure 36

The three RULES values in Internet Explorer 3 for the Macintosh.

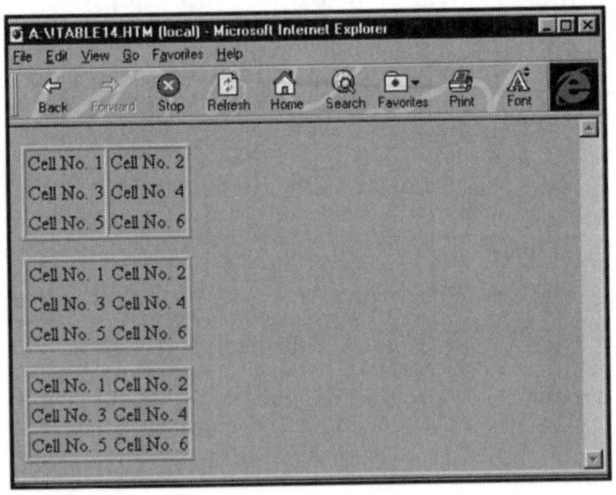

Figure 37

The six RULES values in Internet Explorer 3 for Windows.

> **NOTE** If you want to disable or turn off the display of the external table lines, use the FRAME attribute—although it is also, like RULES, supported by Internet Explorer only. See the FRAME section of this entry for more information.

VALIGN

The VALIGN attribute is supposedly an Internet Explorer–only feature that specifies the vertical alignment of table cell contents.

Various Explorer HTML sources say VALIGN has two values:

`left`

The contents of all the table cells is aligned with the left side of the column.

`right`

The contents of all the table cells is aligned with the right side of the column.

The HTML for this VALIGN attribute would look like this:

```
<TABLE VALIGN=right>
<TR>
```

```
<TD>Cell No. 1</TD><TD>Cell No. 2</TD>
</TR>
<TR>
<TD>Cell No. 3</TD><TD>Cell No. 4</TD>
</TR>
</TABLE>
```

It is possible that this attribute and its values will be supported in updated versions of Netscape Communicator and Explorer 4, but at this writing, VALIGN does not provide reliable performance.

WIDTH

The WIDTH attribute specifies an exact table height in either pixels or as a percentage of the browser window.

It should be accompanied by a HEIGHT attribute setting—see the HEIGHT attribute section of this entry for more information.

In the following example, WIDTH is specified as 200 pixels:

```
<TABLE BORDER HEIGHT=200 WIDTH=300>
<TR>
<TD>Cell No. 1</TD><TD>Cell No. 2</TD>
</TR>
<TR>
<TD>Cell No. 3</TD><TD>Cell No. 4</TD>
</TR>
</TABLE>
<TABLE BORDER HEIGHT=15% WIDTH=15%>
<TR>
<TD>Cell No. 1</TD><TD>Cell No. 2</TD>
</TR>
<TR>
<TD>Cell No. 3</TD><TD>Cell No. 4</TD>
</TR>
</TABLE>
```

Figures 38, 39, 40, and 41 display this example HTML in Navigator 3 and Internet Explorer 3 for the Macintosh and for Windows.

T

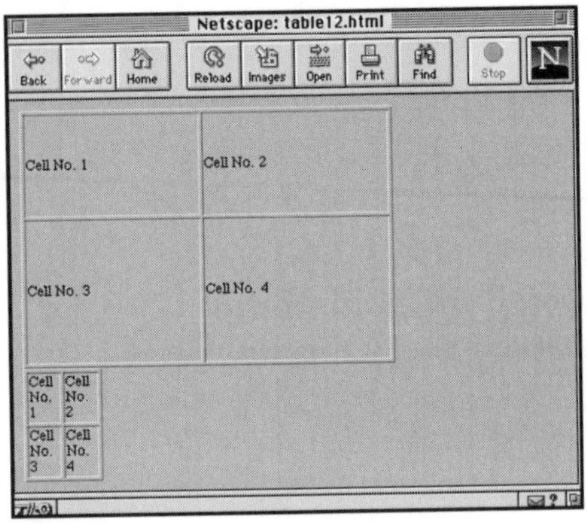

Figure 38

Customizing a table using HEIGHT and WIDTH in Navigator 3 for the Macintosh.

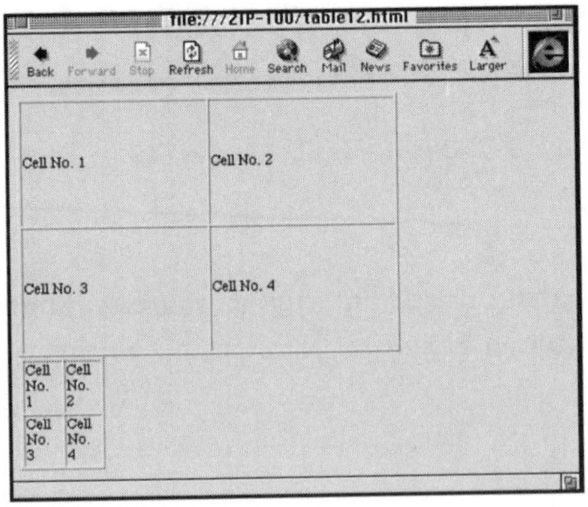

Figure 39

Customizing a table using HEIGHT and WIDTH in Internet Explorer 3 for the Macintosh.

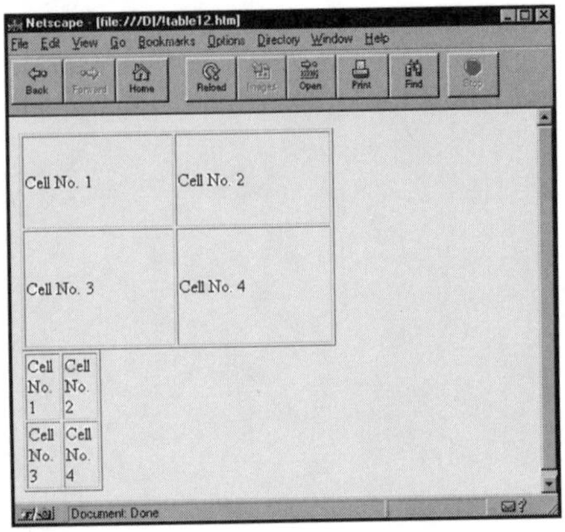

Figure 40

Customizing a table using HEIGHT and WIDTH in Navigator 3 for Windows.

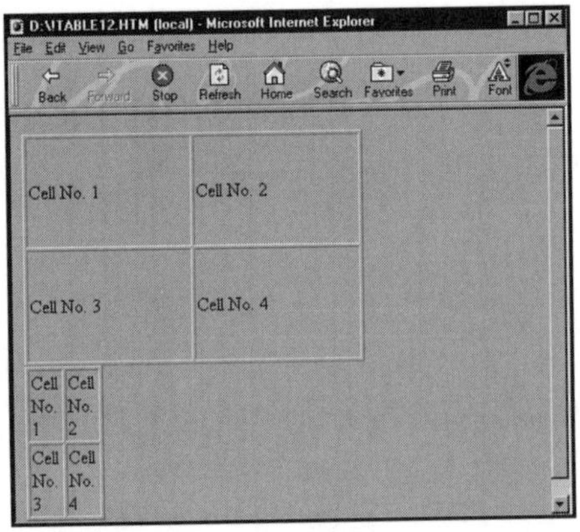

Figure 41

Customizing a table using HEIGHT and WIDTH in Internet Explorer 3 for Windows.

tags

Category: JavaScript Style Sheets

	Navigator 3	Navigator 4	Explorer 3	Explorer 4
Type	Selector			

Browser Support

	Navigator 3	Navigator 4	Explorer 3	Explorer 4
Macintosh	☐	■	☐	☐
Windows	☐	■	☐	☐

Applies To	All elements
Inherited	Yes
Syntax	`tags.element.proprety = "value"`

The `tags` property is a JavaScript object property that is one of three properties (the others are `classes` and `ids`) that can be used to define styles in JavaScript Style Sheets.

The `tags` property is defined using dot notation and takes as its first modifier any valid HTML element. For example, `tags.body.` or `tags.h1.` are both valid tags.element combinations.

The property modifier of this object can be any valid JavaScript Style Sheets property, which are listed in the alphabetical listing in this book under the category: JavaScript Style Sheets, type: property.

> **NOTE** The `tags` property actually applies to the document object of the current document, but is assumed when `tags` are defined. Therefore,
>
> `tags.body.color = "red"`
>
> and
>
> `document.tags.body.color = "red"`
>
> will have the same meaning.

The `tags` property must always be used with the `<style></style>` elements; thus defining it as a property used only for JavaScript Style Sheets.

By defining your styles using the `tags` property, you will need to make no other reference to the style in the document itself. Each usage of the HTML element in the document will take on the defined style.

In the following simple example, `<h2>` headers are underlined. No other reference to the style declaration is made outside of the style definition, but remember that this style will apply to all `<h2>` elements.

```
<html>
<head>
<style type="text/javascript">
tags.h2.textDecoration ="underline";
</style>
</head>
<body>
<h1> This header will not be underlined.</h1>
<h1> Note that the style has only been applied to the h2 header</h1>
<h2> This header will be underlined.</h2>
</body>
</html>
```

T

The results of this code are shown in Figure 1.

Figure 1

*Underlined <h2>
elements.*

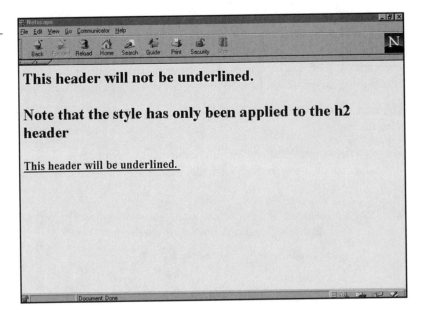

In the preceding example the important JSSS code is in the single line of code

```
tags.h2.textDecoration ="underline";
```

where

- **tags** denotes that this style is applicable to an HTML element. This notation tells JSSS that the property immediately following in the dot notation will be a valid HTML element.
- **<h2>** is the HTML element that the style will be applied to. This can be any valid HTML element.
- **textDecoration** is the style that will be applied to the <h2> element. Any valid JSSS style property can be used here.
- **"underline"** is the value of the style that will be applied. Each style property has its own set of defined values.

It is also worthy to note that some styles can be inherited to child elements, so when using the high-level **tags** property remember that this style may not be for just <h2> but also for all child elements.

`taint()`

Category: JavaScript 1.1

Type	Function

Browser Support		Navigator 3	Navigator 4	Explorer 3	Explorer 4
	Macintosh	■	■	☐	■
	Windows	▭	■	☐	▭

Syntax	`taintedVar = taint(value)`

Data tainting is a security feature that prevents or allows scripts to pass data across the network or to access data from another server in an open frame or browser window.

When a piece of data is said to be *tainted*, it is then subject to tainting restrictions—if the user has enabled tainting.

When tainting is enabled, your script *can* access tainted data, but it is subject to the following restriction:

When your script tries to send tainted data, or any data derived thereof, across the network such as via a form or submission, a dialog box appears allowing the user to accept or cancel the action.

If the user has not enabled data tainting, then your script cannot access tainted data at all.

> **NOTE** The `taint()` function only works in Windows 95 in Netscape Navigator 3 and Internet Explorer 4.

What is Tainted Data?

Data that has been tainted is "marked," as in "marked bills" that track the flow of counterfeit money. You can taint the value of a variable, property, function, or object. Alternatively, you can taint the entire window containing the script. Some data is tainted by default in JavaScript—see the following note for details.

To manually taint any piece of data you wish, use the `taint()` function. This function returns a tainted copy of the value of the specified variable, property, function, or object:

```
tstatus = taint(window.status)
```

The variable `tstatus` is now a tainted variable that contains the value of `window.status`. If the user has enabled data tainting and refuses the dialog box that requests such permission, you might not be able to pass `tstatus` across the network. Additionally, scripts in other browser windows or frames that originate from a different server will not be able to access `tstatus` without the user's permission (or at all, if data tainting is not enabled by the user).

T

Importantly, any data *derived* from tstatus will likewise be tainted: any data returned from a function that uses tstatus, any substrings of tstatus, and so forth. If tstatus is evaluated in a scripted if, while, or for statement, then that script also becomes tainted.

Alternatively, you can taint the entire window containing the script (and thus every value within it) using the simple statement:

taint()

Any value that you have tainted can later be untainted. (See the Untaint() function.)

NOTE By default, the most vulnerable data is automatically tainted in JavaScript, so you don't need to use the taint() function for these values. For each object listed you can see which of its properties are tainted by default.

Object	Tainted properties
document object	cookie, domain, forms, lastModified, links, referrer, title, URL
form object	action
button object	name, value
checkbox object	checked, defaultChecked, name, value
fileUpload object	name, value
hidden object	name, value
password object	defaultValue, name, value
radio object	checked, defaultChecked, name, value
reset object	name, value
submit object	name, value
text object	defaultValue, name, value
textarea object	defaultValue, name, value
history object	current, next, previous
select object	defaultSelected, selected, text, value
link object	hash, host, hostname, href, pathname, port, protocol, search
location object	hash, host, hostname, href, pathname, port, protocol, search
window object	defaultStatus, status

How Does the User Enable Data Tainting?

By default, data tainting is *not* enabled. This means that you *cannot* access data from another server that is in a frame or browser window. To allow such access, and therefore render the taint() and untaint() functions useful, the user must manually enable data tainting. This is done by setting the environment variable NS_ENABLE_TAINT to any value. The exact procedure varies from platform to platform as described.

Windows

In your autoexec.bat file you must add the line:

```
set NS_ENABLE_TAINT=1
```

Make sure to include the underscores between MS, ENABLE, and TAINT=1!

Macintosh

Edit the resource with type "Envi" and number 128 in the Netscape application by removing the two ASCII slashes "//" before the NS_ENABLE_TAINT text at the end of the resource.

Unix

At the shell prompt, or in your .cshrc file, execute the command:

```
setenv NS_ENABLE_TAINT 1
```

Make sure to include the underscores between ME, ENABLE, and TAINT!

Tan( )
Category: VBScript

| | Type | Function |

Browser Support

	Navigator 3	Navigator 4	Explorer 3	Explorer 4
Macintosh				▮
Windows			▬	▬

Syntax Tan(number)

The Tan() function calculates and returns the tangent of an angle measured in radians, specified by *number*. The tangent of *number* represents the ratio between two sides of a right triangle: the length of the side opposite the angle divided by the length of the side adjacent to the angle. The Atn() function can be used to calculate the inverse tangent. (See the Atn() function.)

The Tan() function only works on Windows 95 machines in Internet Explorer.

<TBODY>

Category: HTML

Browser Support		Navigator 3	Navigator 4	Explorer 3	Explorer 4
	Macintosh	☐	☐	■	■
	Windows	☐	☐	■	■

May Contain   <APPLET>, <B>, <BASEFONT>, <BIG>, <BR>, <CITE>, <CODE>, <DFN>, <EM>, <FONT>, <I>, <IMG>, <INPUT>, <KBD>, <MAP>, <SAMP>, <SELECT>, <SMALL>, <STRIKE>, <STRONG>, <SUB>, <SUP>, <TEXTAREA>, <TT>, <U>, <VAR>

May Be Used In   <TABLE>

Attributes   CLASS, ID

Syntax   <TBODY>...</TBODY>

The <TBODY> tag designates particular groups of table rows so that the RULES attribute knows where to draw interior horizontal lines.

It is an Internet Explorer–specific tag used in tandem with the <TFOOT> and <THEAD> tags when the RULES attribute has been specified in the <TABLE> tag. The closing, or </TBODY>, tag is optional (you can leave it out and your web page will still work), but it is used in this entry to better distinguish <TBODY>-specified sections.

In the following example, the <TBODY> tag groups the two middle rows together for the sake of the RULES attribute:

```
<TABLE BORDER RULES=basic>
<THEAD>This is a table header.</THEAD>
<TR>
<TD>Cell No. 1</TD><TD>Cell No. 2</TD>
</TR>
<TBODY>
<TR>
<TD>Cell No. 3</TD><TD>Cell No. 4</TD>
</TR>
<TR>
<TD>Cell No. 5</TD><TD>Cell No. 6</TD>
</TR>
</TBODY>
<TR>
<TD>Cell No. 7</TD><TD>Cell No. 8</TD>
</TR>
<TFOOT>This is the table footer.</TFOOT>
</TABLE>
```

The RULES attribute value of basic will only apply to the middle two rows (cells 3 to 6). See the RULES attribute section of the <TABLE> tag entry for a list of all RULES values.

Figures 1 and 2 illustrate this example HTML in Internet Explorer 3 for the Macintosh and for Windows.

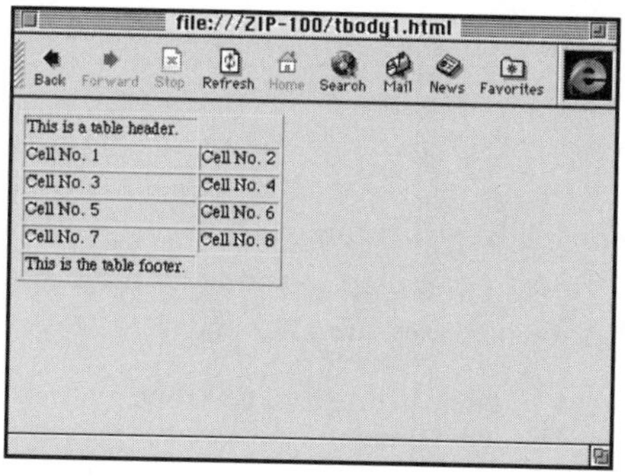

Figure 1

Using the <TBODY> tag to apply the RULES attribute in Internet Explorer 3 for the Macintosh.

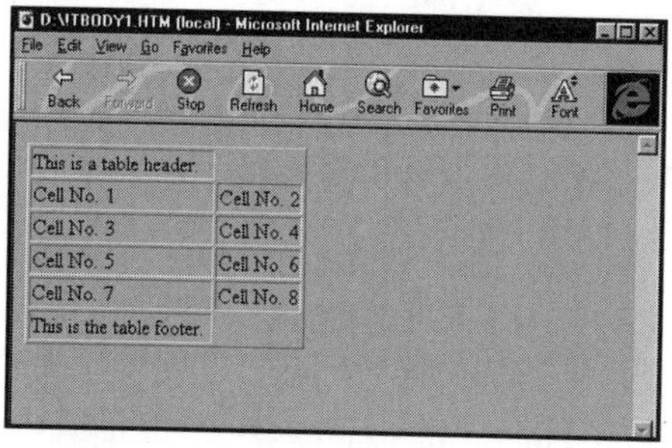

Figure 2

Using the <TBODY> tag to apply the RULES attribute in Internet Explorer 3 for Windows.

CLASS

The CLASS attribute is used to specify the name of a style sheet as it applies to a specific selection on a web page. See the "Cascading Style Sheet Basics" chapter and any individual, related style sheets entries elsewhere in the book for more information.

ID

The ID attribute is used to distinguish individual selections in a web page as pertaining to the use of style sheets. See the "Cascading Style Sheets Basics" chapter and any individual, related style sheets entries elsewhere in the book for more information.

<TD>

Category: HTML

Browser Support

	Navigator 3	Navigator 4	Explorer 3	Explorer 4
Macintosh	▪	▪	▪	▪
Windows	▪	▪	▪	▪

May Contain <A>, <ADDRESS>, <APPLET>, <B>, <BASEFONT>, <BIG>, <BLOCKQUOTE>, <BR>, <CENTER>, <CITE>, <CODE>, <DFN>, <DIR>, <DIV>, <DL>, <EM>, <FONT>, <FORM>, <H1>, <H2>, <H3>, <H4>, <H5>, <H6>, <HR>, <I>, <IMG>, <INPUT>, <KBD>, <MAP>, <MENU>,

T

```
<OL>, <P>, <PRE>, <SAMP>, <SELECT>, <SMALL>, <STRIKE>,
<STRONG>, <SUB>, <SUP>, <TABLE>, <TEXTAREA>, <TT>, <U>, <UL>,
<VAR>
```

May Be Used In   <TR>

Attributes   ALIGN, BACKGROUND, BGCOLOR, BORDERCOLOR, BORDERCOLORDARK,
BORDERCOLORLIGHT, CLASS, CLSPAN, ID, NOWRAP, ROWSPAN, VALIGN,
WIDTH

Syntax   <TD>...</TD>

The <TD> tag specifies each individual *cell*—small boxes containing text or images that sit side by side in a table. It is one of three fundamental <TABLE> tags used to construct the basic framework of a table (the others, covered elsewhere in their own entries, are <TR> and <TABLE>).

In the following example, <TD> is used with <TR> to enclose one two-cell row:

```
<TR>
<TD>Cell No. 1</TD><TD>Cell No. 2</TD>
</TR>
```

and there are two rows with two cells each in this complete, simple example table:

```
<TABLE BORDER>
<TR>
<TD>Cell No. 1</TD><TD>Cell No. 2</TD>
</TR>
<TR>
<TD>Cell No. 3</TD><TD>Cell No. 4</TD>
</TR>
</TABLE>
```

Figures 1 and 2 illustrate this simple table in Navigator 3 and Internet Explorer 3 for Windows.

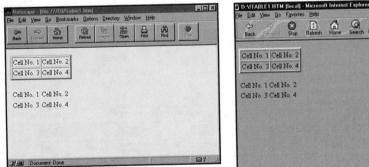
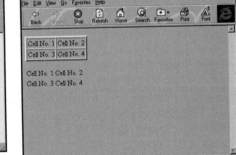

Figure 1

Basic four-cell tables in Navigator 3 for Windows.

Figure 2

Basic four-cell tables in Internet Explorer 3 for Windows.

ALIGN

The ALIGN attribute establishes the horizontal alignment of text in an individual cell. (To set vertical alignment, see the VALIGN tag later in this entry.)

It has four values:

center

The cell text is centered. This is the ALIGN attribute default.

justify

The cell text is justified to both left and right margins.

left

The cell text is left-aligned with the left margin. This is the ALIGN attribute default in Navigator for the Mac.

right

The cell text is right-aligned with the right margin.

In the following example, the ALIGN setting has been established in the first row of cells, with the first cell as right and the second as left:

```
<TABLE>
<TH>Header No. 1</TH><TH>Header No. 2</TH>
<TR>
<TD ALIGN=right>Cell No. 1</TD><TD ALIGN=center>Cell No. 2</TD>
</TR>
<TR>
<TD>Cell No. 3</TD><TD>Cell No. 4</TD>
</TR>
</TABLE>
```

Figures 3, 4, 5, and 6 contain sample tables demonstrating each of the supported ALIGN values in Navigator 3 and Internet Explorer 3 for the Mac and for Windows.

T

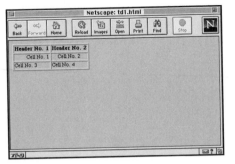

Figure 3

ALIGN values in Navigator 3 for the Mac.

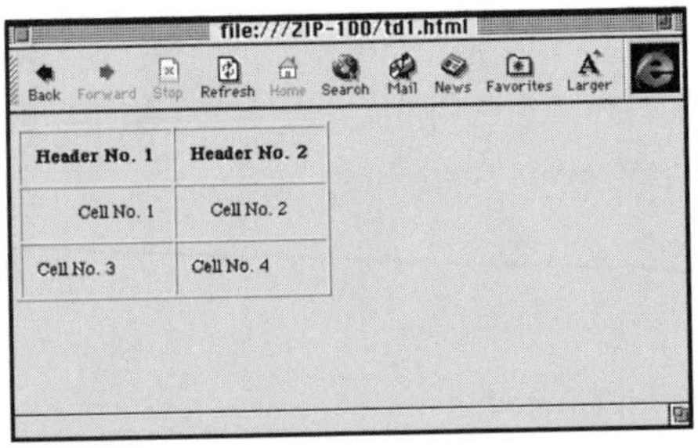

Figure 4

ALIGN values in Internet Explorer 3 for the Mac.

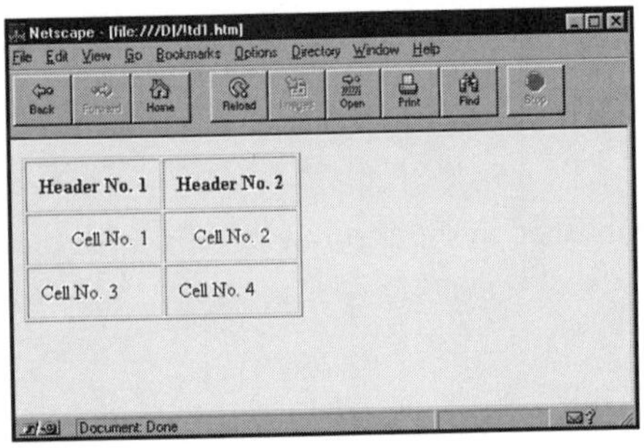

Figure 5

ALIGN values in Navigator 3 for Windows.

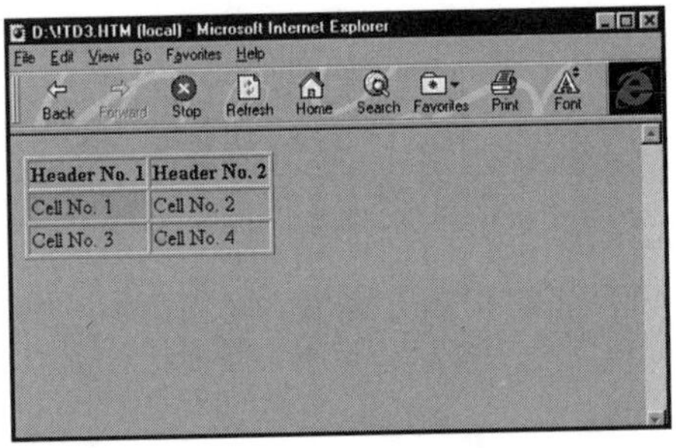

Figure 6

ALIGN values in Internet Explorer 3 for Windows.

DESIGN NOTE   If you establish either (or both) an `ALIGN` or `VALIGN` value to a "cell," these settings will override any `ALIGN` or `VALIGN` settings established for the entire "row."

BACKGROUND

The BACKGROUND attribute is an Internet Explorer–only feature that tiles a background pattern behind an individual, specified table cell, similar to the way the `<BODY>` tag's BACKGROUND attribute tiles a pattern behind the text on an entire web page.

In the following example, `pattern.gif` represents the file name of the background pattern:

```
<TABLE BORDER>
<TR>
<TD BACKGROUND=pattern.gif>Cell No. 1</TD><TD>Cell No. 2</TD>
</TR>
```

```
<TR>
<TD>Cell No. 3</TD><TD>Cell No. 4</TD>
</TR>
</TABLE>
```

The first cell in the first row (cell 1) will appear with a background pattern, while the other three will remain default gray.

The background pattern can be in any file format supported by Internet Explorer.

Figures 7 and 8 illustrate a BACKGROUND-specified pattern tiled behind a four-cell table in Internet Explorer 3 for the Mac and for Windows.

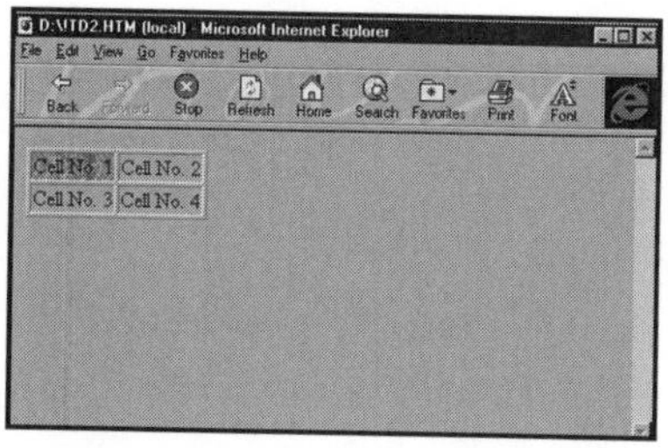

Figure 7

A four-cell table with one BACK-GROUND-specified cell in Internet Explorer 3 for the Mac.

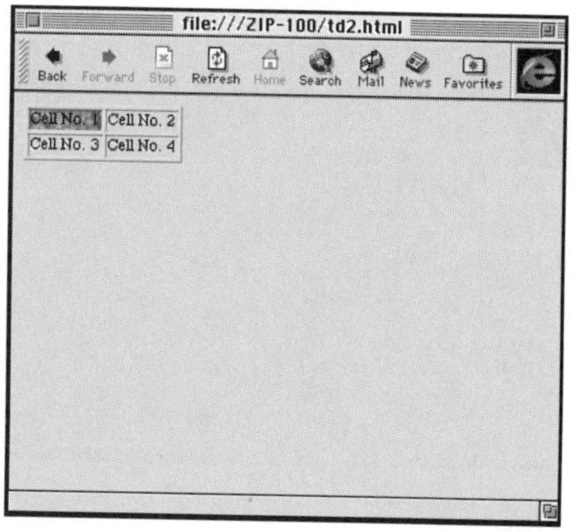

Figure 8

A four-cell table with one BACKGROUND-specified cell in Internet Explorer 3 for Windows.

DESIGN NOTE

If you want to tile a background pattern behind a table cell, keep these considerations in mind: first, visitors need to read the text or see the images you're putting in your tables so choose something that's not too busy, and second, use the background color or pattern behind your entire page as a guideline so you don't choose a table pattern that clashes.

T

BGCOLOR

The BGCOLOR attribute is an Internet Explorer–only feature that specifies a custom background color for an individual cell, either with a color name or a hexadecimal value. (See Appendix B for a chart of all the colors you can specify by name and all the colors you can specify by hex value.)

In the following example, cyan (or aqua blue) is specified as the first cell's background color:

```
<TABLE>
<TH>Header No. 1</TH><TH ALIGN=left>Header No. 2</TH><TR>
```

```
<TD BGCOLOR=cyan>Cell No. 1</TD><TD>Cell No. 2</TD>
</TR>
<TR>
<TD>Cell No. 3</TD><TD>Cell No. 4</TD>
</TR>
</TABLE>
```

You could also substitute cyan's hexadecimal value for the color name and achieve the same effect.

Figures 9 and 10 illustrate this example HTML in Internet Explorer 3 for the Mac and for Windows. The first row's background color is specified as cyan (which will appear as a lighter gray in these black-and-white figures), while the second row will remain default gray.

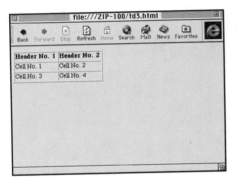

Figure 9

BGCOLOR *background cell colors in Internet Explorer 3 for the Mac.*

Figure 10

BGCOLOR *background cell colors in Internet Explorer 3 for Windows.*

BORDERCOLOR

The BORDERCOLOR attribute is an Internet Explorer–only attribute that specifies a solid custom border color around an individual table cell. There is no equivalent attribute for Navigator, so no matter what color you specify using BORDERCOLOR, visitors to your site using Navigator will see all table cells bordered in default gray.

BORDERCOLOR color values are specified either by name or by hexadecimal value. (See Appendix B for a chart of all the colors you can specify by name and all the colors you can specify by hex value.)

In the following example, aqua is specified in the first cell in the first row and black in the second cell in the first row:

```
<TABLE>
<TH>Header No. 1</TH><TH>Header No. 2</TH><TR>
<TR>
<TD BORDERCOLOR=aqua>Cell No. 1</TD><TD BORDERCOLOR=black>Cell No. 2</TD>
```

```
</TR>
<TR>
<TD>Cell No. 3</TD><TD>Cell No. 4</TD>
</TR>
</TABLE>
```

Again, you could also substitute the appropriate hexadecimal values for the color names and achieve the same effect.

Figures 11 and 12 illustrate this example HTML in Internet Explorer 3 for the Mac and for Windows. The first cell's border color will appear as a lighter gray, although the second will, for once, appear black as specified.

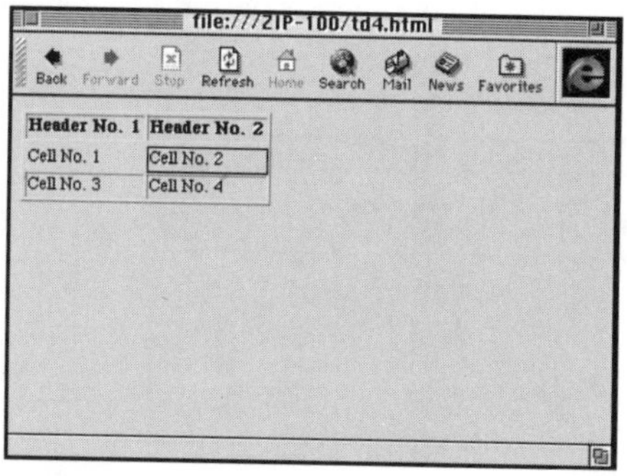

Figure 11

BORDERCOLOR cell colors in Internet Explorer 3 for the Mac.

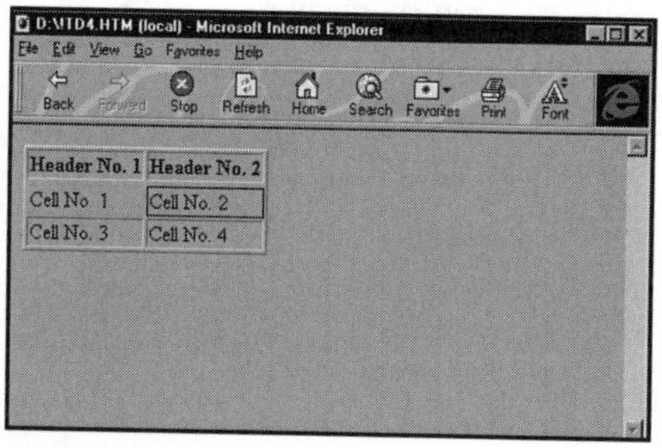

Figure 12

BORDERCOLOR cell colors in Internet Explorer 3 for Windows.

DESIGN NOTE	Do NOT choose cell border colors that a) won't show up against your table or page background color (as in white borders on a yellow background), b) match your customized link colors (or visitors will click your headers thinking they're links), and c) clash with any other customized colors on your page.

BORDERCOLORDARK

The BORDERCOLORDARK attribute is an Internet Explorer–only attribute that specifies the darker of two cell border colors that overlap to create a 3-D effect. (If you've already read the <TABLE> and <TR> tag entries, you know they also have a similar BORDERCOLORDARK, which works pretty much the same way.)

There is no equivalent attribute for Navigator, so no matter what color you specify using BORDERCOLORDARK, visitors to your site using Navigator will see all cell borders in default gray.

BORDERCOLORDARK color values are specified either by name or by hexadecimal value. (See Appendix B for a chart of all the colors you can specify by name and all the colors you can specify by hex value.)

T

In the following examples, `black` is specified as the BORDERCOLORDARK value in cell 1:

```
<TABLE>
<TH>Header No. 1</TH><TH ALIGN=left>Header No. 2</TH>
<TR>
<TD BORDERCOLORDARK=black BORDERCOLORLIGHT=white>Cell No. 1</TD><TD>Cell No. 2</
TD>
</TR>
<TR>
<TD>Cell No. 3</TD><TD>Cell No. 4</TD>
</TR>
</TABLE>
```

In both examples, the borders of the other three cells have been left as default gray for comparison. Figure 13 illustrates this example HTML in Internet Explorer 3 for the Mac.

Figure 13

BORDERCOLORLIGHT and BORDERCOLOR-DARK cell colors in Internet Explorer 3 for the Mac.

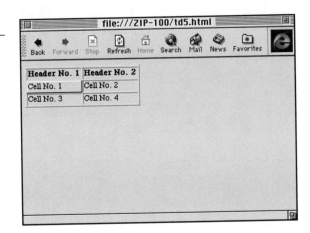

BORDERCOLORLIGHT

The BORDERCOLORLIGHT attribute is an Internet Explorer–only attribute that specifies the darker of two row cell colors that overlap to create a 3-D effect. (If you've already read the \<TABLE> and \<TR> tag entries, you know they also have a similar BORDERCOLORLIGHT, which works pretty much the same way.)

There is no equivalent attribute for Navigator, so no matter what color you specify using BORDERCOLORLIGHT, visitors to your site using Navigator will see all cell borders in default gray.

BORDERCOLORLIGHT color values are specified either by name or by hexadecimal value. (See Appendix B for a chart of all the colors you can specify by name and all the colors you can specify by hex value.)

In the following examples, `black` is specified as the BORDERCOLORLIGHT value of cell 1:

```
<TABLE>
<TH>Header No. 1</TH><TH ALIGN=left>Header No. 2</TH>
```

```
<TR>
<TD BORDERCOLORDARK=black BORDERCOLORLIGHT=white>Cell No. 1</TD><TD>Cell No. 2
➥</TD>
</TR>
<TR>
<TD>Cell No. 3</TD><TD>Cell No. 4</TD>
</TR>
</TABLE>
```

The borders of the other cells have been left as default gray for comparison.

Figure 14 illustrates this example HTML in Internet Explorer 3 for the Mac.

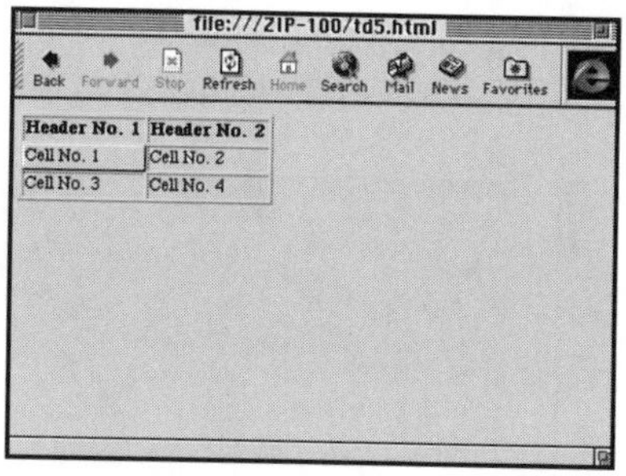

Figure 14

BORDERCOLORLIGHT and BORDERCOLORDARK cell colors in Internet Explorer 3 for the Mac.

CLASS

The CLASS attribute is used to specify the name of a style sheet as it applies to a specific selection on a web page. See the "Cascading Style Sheet Basics" chapter and any individual, related style sheets entries elsewhere in the book for more information.

COLSPAN

The COLSPAN attribute specifies more than one column to be spanned by the same cell.

In the following example three-column table, COLSPAN has been assigned a value of 2 to stretch the first cell across the first and second columns in one long double-width cell:

```
<TABLE BORDER>
<TH>Header No. 1</TH><TH>Header No. 2</TH><TH>Header No. 3</TH>
<TR>
<TD COLSPAN=2>Cell No. 1</TD><TD>Cell No. 2</TD>
</TR>
<TR>
<TD>Cell No. 3</TD><TD>Cell No. 4</TD><TD>Cell No. 5</TD>
</TR>
</TABLE>
```

Figures 14, 15, 16, and 17 illustrate this sample table in Navigator 3 and Internet Explorer 3 for the Mac and for Windows.

T

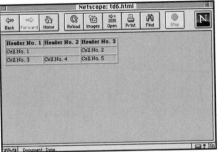

Figure 15

A COLSPAN double-width cell in Navigator 3 for the Mac.

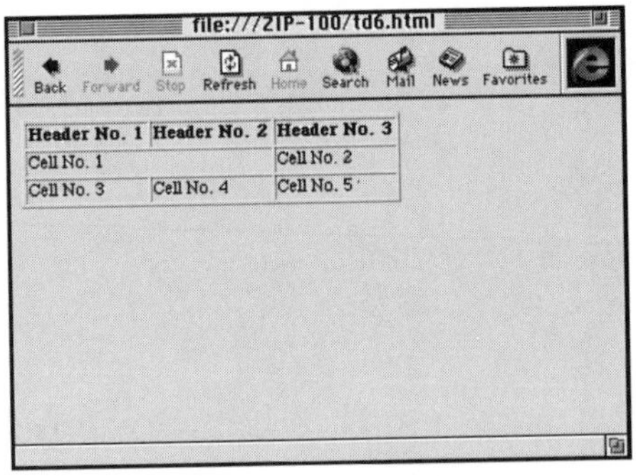

Figure 16

A COLSPAN double-width cell in Internet Explorer 3 for the Mac.

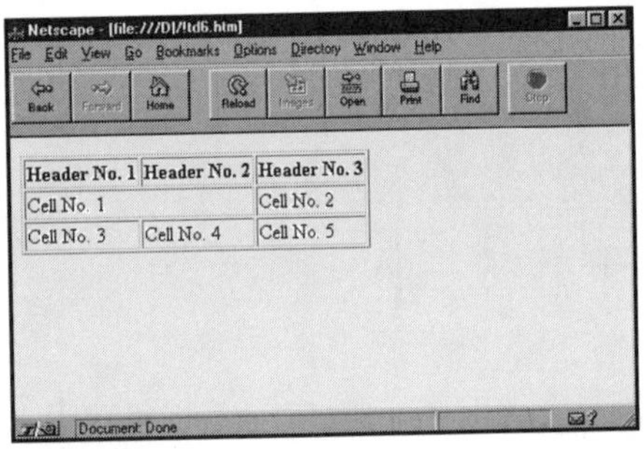

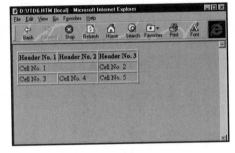

Figure 17

A COLSPAN double-width cell in Navigator 3 for Windows.

Figure 18

A COLSPAN double-width cell in Internet Explorer 3 for Windows.

ID

The ID attribute is used to distinguish individual selections in a web page as pertaining to the use of style sheets. See the "Cascading Style Sheets Basics" chapter and any individual, related style sheets entries elsewhere in the book for more information.

NOWRAP

The NOWRAP attribute is an Internet Explorer–specific feature that prevents cell text from wrapping down to a second line. Ordinarily, both Navigator and Internet Explorer will automatically wrap cell text down to the next line if it's too long for the margins. Using <NOWRAP> prevents this from happening.

In the following example, the NOWRAP attribute is placed properly within the appropriate <TD> tag with no values:

```
<TABLE>
<TH>Header No. 1</TH><TH>Header No. 2</TH>
<TR>
<TD>Cell No. 1</TD><TD NOWRAP>Cell No. 2</TD>
</TR>
<TR>
<TD>Cell No. 3</TD><TD>Cell No. 4</TD>
</TR>
</TABLE>
```

Obviously in this example table, there isn't enough text in cell 2 to merit using the NOWRAP attribute, but in Figures 19 and 20, the first cell has been extended out and should run right off the page.

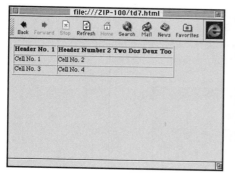

Figure 19

Using NOWRAP in Internet Explorer 3 for the Mac.

Figure 20

Using NOWRAP in Internet Explorer 3 for Windows.

ROWSPAN

The ROWSPAN attribute is similar to the COLSPAN attribute in that it specifies a cell as more than one row wide (as opposed to more than one column wide).

In the following example three-column table, ROWSPAN has been assigned a value of 2 to stretch the first two cells across the second and third rows in one long double-width cell:

```
<TABLE BORDER>
<TH>Header No. 1</TH><TH>Header No. 2</TH><TH>Header No. 3</TH>
<TR>
<TD ROWSPAN=2>Cell No. 1</TD><TD>Cell No. 2</TD><TD>Cell No. 3</TD>
</TR>
<TR>
<TD>Cell No. 4</TD><TD>Cell No. 5</TD>
</TR>
</TABLE>
```

T

Figures 21, 22, and 23 illustrate this sample table in Navigator 3 for the Macintosh and Internet Explorer 3 for the Mac and for Windows.

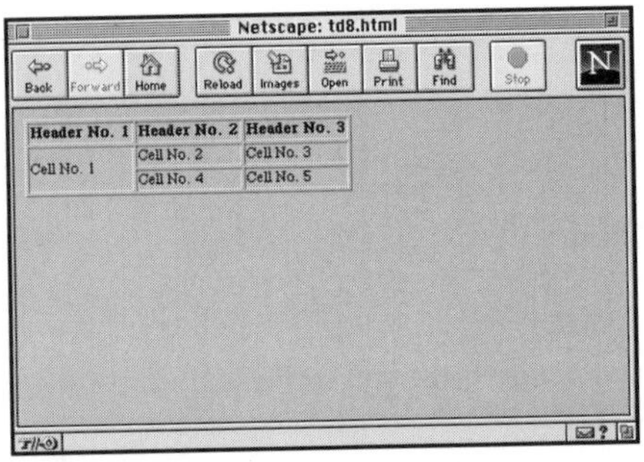

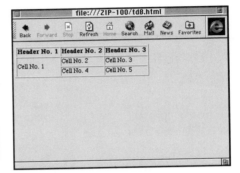

Figure 21

A ROWSPAN double-width cell in Navigator 3 for the Mac.

Figure 22

A ROWSPAN double-width cell in Internet Explorer 3 for the Mac

Figure 23

A ROWSPAN double-width cell in Internet Explorer 3 for Windows.

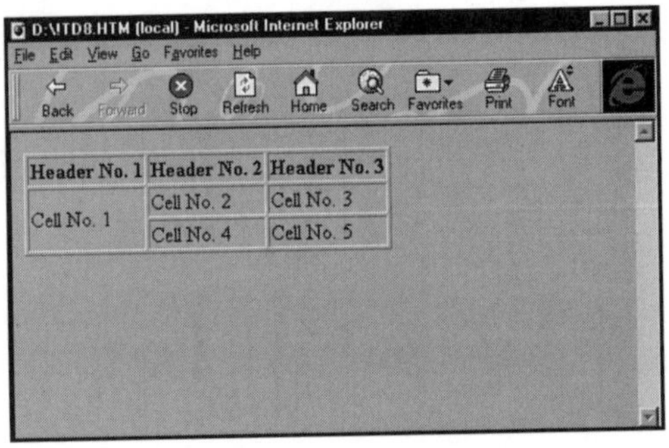

VALIGN

The VALIGN attribute controls the vertical alignment of cell text. It has four values:

baseline

The cell text is aligned on a shared, common baseline.

bottom

The cell text is aligned with the bottom of each cell.

middle

The cell text is aligned with the middle of each cell. This is the VALIGN attribute default.

top

The cell text is aligned with the top of each cell.

In the following example, the VALIGN setting has been established in cell 1 as middle and then in cell 2 as bottom:

```
<TABLE>
<TH>Header No. 1</TH><TH>Header No. 2</TH>
<TR>
<TD VALIGN=middle>Cell No. 1</TD><TD VALIGN=bottom>Cell No. 2</TD>
</TR>
<TR>
<TD>Cell No. 3</TD><TD>Cell No. 4</TD>
</TR>
</TABLE>
```

> **NOTE** To establish horizontal alignment, use the ALIGN attribute. It's covered in its own section earlier in this entry.

WIDTH

The WIDTH attribute specifies the width of the table header in columns.

In the following example HTML, WIDTH has been established as 2:

```
<TABLE BORDER>
<TH>Header No. 1</TH><TH WIDTH=2>Header No. 2</TH>
<TR>
<TD>Cell No. 1</TD><TD>Cell No. 2</TD><TD>Cell No. 3</TD>
</TR>
<TR>
<TD>Cell No. 4</TD><TD>Cell No. 5</TD><TD>Cell No. 6</TD>
</TR>
</TABLE>
```

The second header will then span the width of the second and third columns in a double-wide, single cell.

Text

Category: JavaScript, JScript, VBScript

Type	Object

Browser Support

	Navigator 3	Navigator 4	Explorer 3	Explorer 4
Macintosh	■	■	☐	■
Windows	▭	■	▬	▬

Subset Of	Form object

T

Properties	defaultValue, form, name, type, value
Methods	blur(), focus(), select()
Event Handlers	onblur, onfocus, onchange, onselect
Syntax	document.formName.textName.property OR document.forms[index].elements[index].property OR document.formName.textName.method(parameters) OR document.forms[index].elements[index].method(parameters)

The text object provides a way for the script to access and/or modify the contents of a single-line text form field element. Multi-line text elements are a separate input type and accessed through the textarea object. By accessing the text object's value property, you can "see" the data currently input into the text element. For instance, you might use this technique to help validate a form entry (for example, checking a ZIP code format) before the form data is actually submitted to a server-side processor. Conversely, you can also modify the text object's value property to change the data appearing in the text element. This practice is often used as a way of displaying messages to the user, as a sort of "message box."

The text object references the text form field element HTML:

```
<input
    type="text"
    name="textName"
    value="initialValue"
    size=lengthOfBox
    maxlength=maxCharsAllowed
    [onBlur="eventHandler"]
    [onChange="eventHandler"]
    [onFocus="eventHandler"]
    [onSelect="eventHandler"]>
```

NOTE The Text object only works in Windows 95 in Netscape Navigator 3 and Internet Explorer 3 and 4.

defaultValue **property**

The initial text displayed in the text form field, specified by the value attribute in the <input> tag. This property is read-only.

```
startval = document.formname.textname.defaultValue
```

form **property**

The read-only reference to the form object that contains the text object. This is a useful way to refer to another object in the same form. For instance, imagine a scenario where you want to reference another text object, named *text2*, which resides within the same form as the text object *text1*. This can be used to code in shorthand, or eliminate the need to explicitly reference the full path to every element within a single form, as in the code excerpts:

JavaScript:

```
path=document.forms[0].text1
value1=path.value
value2=path.form.text2.value
```

VBScript:

```
set path=document.forms(0).text1
value1=path.value
value2=path.form.text2.value
```

name **property**

The read-only name of the text object, specified by the name attribute in the <input> tag.

```
objname = document.formname.textname.name
objval = document.formname.objname.value
```

type **property**

The input type specified by the type attribute in the <input> tag. Of course, this read-only property always contains the value "text" when referencing a text element.

```
objtype = document.formname.textname.type
```

 Internet Explorer 3 does not support the **type** property.

value **property**

This represents text displayed in the text form field element. The contents of the value property will change when the user modifies the data in the text element. For instance, we could validate the user's input against specified criteria:

JavaScript:

```
if (document.forms[0].text1.value>18)
 { true condition statements }
else { false condition statements }
```

VBScript:

```
if document.forms(0).text1.value>18 then
 true condition statements
else
 false condition statements
end if
```

Alternatively, you can change the text displayed in the form field by assigning a new value to this property. Taking another example, this time using code compatible with either scripting language:

```
document.formName.text1.value="That option is not valid"
```

blur() method

This method simulates the user losing focus from the text form field. Therefore, if the user currently has focus on the text element, somehow triggering the following code would remove the focus:

```
document.formname.textname.blur()
```

focus() method

This method simulates the user gaining focus on the text form field. You could use this method to call a user's attention to a particular text field.

```
document.formname.textname.focus()
```

> **WARNING** Be careful when and if you use the focus() method on a text element that also contains an onFocus() event handler. In some scenarios within Netscape, this may result in an infinite loop wherein the onFocus event handler is repeated seemingly indefinitely. If your page is not operating as intended, this may be a cause to investigate.

select() method

The select() method selects the text in the text form field, as if the user had clicked and dragged his mouse over the text himself. This is a good way to draw the user's attention to a specific text object for modification, such as to indicate that the data in a text field needs to be changed (perhaps the original data failed to pass a validation test). Modifying the earlier validation example:

JavaScript:

```
if (document.forms[0].text1.value>18)
 { true condition statements }
else { window.alert ("You must enter a number greater than 18");
       document.forms[0].text1.select()}
```

VBScript:

```
if document.forms(0).text1.value>18 then
 true condition statements
else
 window.alert ("You must enter a number greater than 18")
 document.forms(0).text1.select()
end if
```

In either scripting language, the above code will—if the user's form field input fails to meet the "greater than 18" validation test—pop up a message window using the alert() method of the window object, and then automatically select the data in the text element so that the user can modify it.

> **TIP** To help the user quickly modify the selected text, call the focus() method immediately before or after select().

onBlur event handler

Located within the <input> tag, this event will occur when the user loses focus (that is, clicks or tabs elsewhere in the browser) from the text form field.

```
<input type="text" name=textname value="initialtext"  onBlur="eventHandler">
```

onFocus event handler

Located within the <input> tag, this activates when the user clicks or tabs onto the text field, unless the text field already had focus. For instance, you might use this event handler to pop up a window of instructions when the user brings focus to a field that requires explanation.

```
<input type="text" name=textname value="initialtext"  onFocus="window.alert('To
use this field…')">
```

onChange event handler

Located within the <input> tag, this activates when the user makes a change to the text field and clicks or tabs away. Commonly, you would use this event handler to launch a validation function. This way, the user's input will be validated immediately after the user has completed modifying the form field. Consider pairing the form field HTML with a validation script function, as illustrated.

JavaScript:

```
<input type="text" name="text1" width=5 onBlur="validate(this.form,18)">
function validate(theform,minlimit)
{ if (theform.text1.value<minlimit)
   { window.alert ("You must enter a number greater than "+minlimit);
     theform.text1.focus(); theform.text1.select()}
}
```

VBScript:

```
<form name=form1>
<input type="text" name="text1" width=5 onBlur="validate
document.form1,18">
function validate(theform,minlimit)
 if int(theform.text1.value)<int(minlimit) then
```

T

```
window.alert("You must enter a number greater than "&minlimit)
theform.text1.focus():theform.text1.select()
end if
end function
```

> **NOTE** In the JavaScript version of the event handler in this `<input>` tag, the object *this.form* is passed to the `validate()` function. Doing so passes the current form object to the function. VBScript does not support the *this* object, and so in the VBScript code we must pass the current form object to the `validate()` function by explicitly referencing it, as in `document.form1`.

onSelect event handler

Located within the `<input>` tag, this will activate when the user selects some or all of the text in the text form field. You might, for instance, want to prevent the user from modifying the text in a particular text element—when she tries to select the existing text, you could pop up an appropriate message and then restore the text field to its original message.

```
<input type="text" name=textname value="initialtext"  onSelect="window.alert('You
may not change this field…');document.forms[0].textname.value='initialtext'">
```

---

text-decoration
Category: Cascading Style Sheets

Browser Support

	Navigator 3	Navigator 4	Explorer 3	Explorer 4
Macintosh	☐	▬	▬	☐
Windows	☐	▬	▬	▬

Applies To All elements

Syntax `text-decoration: value`

Similar to `text-transform`, `text-decoration` enables you to create interesting effects with your text. Values for this property include:

- ▪ `underline` imparts an underline to the text
- ▪ `overline` adds a line above the text
- ▪ `line-through` gives a strike-through appearance
- ▪ `blink` is all too familiar
- ▪ `none` neutralizes any inherited settings and brings things back to normal

```
h1 { text-decoration: underline }
```

```
h1 { text-decoration: line-through }
```

Explorer 3 doesn't support `overline` and `blink`. Explorer 4 does support `overline`, but not `blink`.

 Everything works in Navigator except `overline`, which causes underlining instead of overlining.

A great use of `text-decoration` is to remove the underlines that browsers give to linked text. The "Cascading Style Sheets Basics" chapter explains how to use the pseudo-classes `A:link`, `A:visited`, and `A:active` to modify the attributes of Hypertext links on your pages. See this section for more information.

`A:link, A:visited, A:active { text-decoration: none }`

The `text-decoration` property is not inherited, but you should make sure elements match their parent(s). If all `<h1>` text is underlined, then all `<b>` text within that level-one heading should be underlined too.

---

text-indent

Category: Cascading Style Sheets

Browser Support		Navigator 3	Navigator 4	Explorer 3	Explorer 4
	Macintosh	☐	■	■	☐
	Windows	☐	■	■	■

Applies To Block level elements

Syntax `text-indent: number`

The `text-indent` defines the amount of indentation of the first formatted line of a block element including `<p>`, `<h1>`-`<h6>`, `<blockquote>`, and `<ul>`. You can specify an indentation of any of length and in any of the units discussed in Appendix D. You can also specify a percentage value that is a percentage of width of the block. In the second example following, the first line of `<h1>` text would be indented 10% of the width that `<h1>` would otherwise have that isn't necessarily the entire browser window. Figure 1 shows the text of a story on a web page where the first line of each paragraph is indented to help the viewer see the paragraphs on the page.

T

Figure 1

Paragraph indents help your viewers see where each paragraph or block begins.

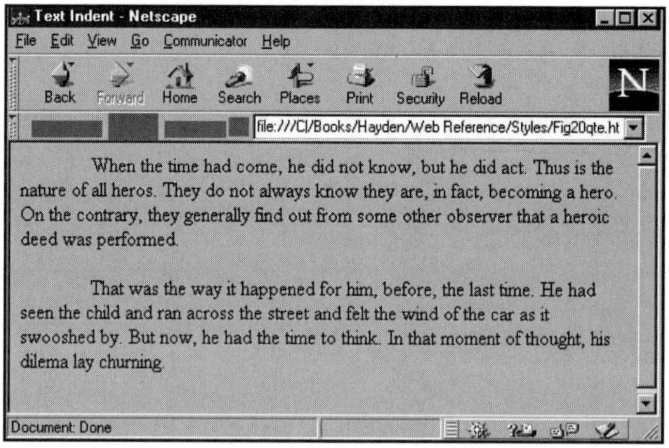

```
h1 { text-indent: 2em }

<h1 style="text-indent: 10%">
```

> **NOTE** Indents are not used in the middle of an element that is broken by another element. So if a <br> is inserted within a <p></p>, the next line will not be indented.

If you want a so-called "hanging indent," you can set text-indent to a negative value as with the HTML text below (see Figure 2):

```
<html>
 <style type="text/css">
 <!--
  h1          { text-indent: -.4in }
  blockquote { text-indent: -5% }
 -->
 </style>
<head>
 <title>Specifying Negative Indents</title>
</head>
<body>
 <h1>
 Behold the wonders of text-indent, which can be specified with a
 negative value so the result is a cool hanging indent. Style sheets
 are wondrous, are they not? I bow before them and give thanks.
 </h1>
 <blockquote>
```

```
Yes, they certainly are, even for us lowly blockquote tags, which
can also enjoy the treats that style sheets have to offer. The makers
of HTML would be proud to see their language grow thusly.
</blockquote>
</body>
</html>
```

Figure 2

Negative text-indent gives you a hanging indent.

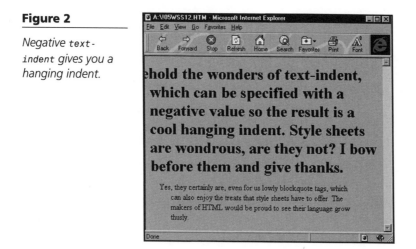

Of course, the big danger with using hanging indents is that words can get cut off, as you can see in the figure.

Navigator ignores hanging indents if any words will get cut off, but otherwise it supports them.

text-transform

Category: Cascading Style Sheets

Browser Support

	Navigator 3	Navigator 4	Explorer 3	Explorer 4
Macintosh		▬		
Windows		▬		▬

Applies To All elements

Syntax `text-transform: value`

The `text-transform` property enables you to display text in interesting and specific styles. The values you specify include:

- `capitalize` if you want the first character in every word capitalized, but the rest of the characters left alone
- `uppercase` if you want every single character capitalized
- `lowercase` if you want none of the characters capitalized
- `none` if you want to negate any inherited value that might impact capitalization

```
h1 { text-transform: uppercase }
```

 Explorer 3 doesn't support any of `text-transform`.

The following example displays non-transformed lines along with a transformed line (see Figure 1). Note that <SPAN> automatically negates the rule and tells the browser to go back to the initial text display.

```
<html>
 <style type="text/css">
 <!--
  body  { font-size: 20pt }
  SPAN  { text-transform: none }
  p.cap { text-transform: capitalize }
  p.up  { text-transform: uppercase }
  p.low { text-transform: lowercase }
 -->
 </style>
<head>
 <title>Specifying Uppercase and Lowercase</title>
</head>
<body>
 <p>Here I am, Great Text to be played with.
 </p>
 <p class=cap>Here I am, Great Text to be played with.<br>
 <span>Here I am, Great Text to be played with.</span>
 </p>
 <p class=up>Here I am, Great Text to be played with.<br>
 <span>Here I am, Great Text to be played with.</span>
 </p>
 <p class=low>Here I am, Great Text to be played with.<br>
 <span>Here I am, Great Text to be played with.</span>
 </p>
</body>
</html>
```

Figure 1

Examples of playing with case via text-transform.

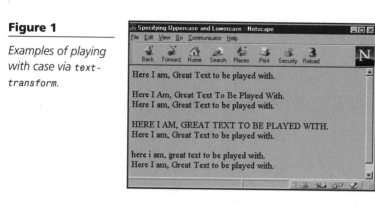

text-align

Category: Cascading Style Sheets

Browser Support

	Navigator 3	Navigator 4	Explorer 3	Explorer 4
Macintosh			▬	
Windows		▬	▬	▬

Applies To Block-level and replaced elements

Syntax text-align: *value*

The text-align property is used to align a block of text or fully justify the text. This property works only on block-level elements—that is, elements that on their own define a new paragraph, such as `<p>`, `<h1>`-`<h6>`, `<blockquote>`, and `<ul>`. It also works for aligning "replaced elements" such as images and applets. The value for text-align can be left, right, center, or justify. The default value is left. Figure 1 shows a `<blockquote>` right-aligned. Note that text is aligned relative to the edges of the element, not necessarily to the edge of the browser window.

Figure 1

Right-aligned text.

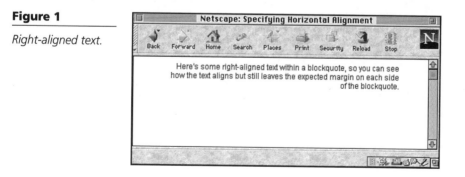

T

```
h1 { text-align: center }
```

```
<h1 style="text-align: right">
```

 Explorer 3 and 4 don't support `justify`. They display justified text as left-aligned.

 Explorer 3 doesn't always restrict alignment to the edge of the element. Right-aligned blockquote text, for example, gets aligned all the way to the edge of the browser window.

textAlign

Category: JavaScript Style Sheets

Type	Property

Browser Support		Navigator 3	Navigator 4	Explorer 3	Explorer 4
	Macintosh	☐	■	☐	☐
	Windows	☐	■	☐	☐

Applies To	Block-level elements

Inherited	Yes

Syntax	textAlign = "*value*"

The `textAlign` property enables you to specify the alignment style for the text within the HTML element itself. "Within the element" means any text that lies between the start and end tags (`<h1>...</h1>`) of an HTML element. There are currently three universally supported values and one value dependent on the browser.

- ■ `"left"` aligns text to the left within the element.
- ■ `"right"` aligns text to the right within the element.
- ■ `"center"` aligns text in the center of the element.
- ■ `"justify"` gives varied results based on the browser's interpretation of justify.

Even though the results of `justify` are browser dependent, you can be guaranteed of the current results because Netscape 4 is the only browser that will support JavaScript Style Sheets.

NOTE Although Navigator 4 is the only browser supporting JavaScript Style Sheets at this time, caution should be taken when using `"justify"` with `textAlign` in style sheets as the results may vary in browsers, and browser verisons.

The values for textAlign will all change the alignment style of the text within the allowed width element and not the alignment relative to the canvas. If a particular element also has a paddings() or margins() style, then the text will align relative to those already applied margins and not take into account the entire document width.

The following example defines a JSSS property class for aligning text.

```html
<html>
<head>
<style type="text/javascript">
classes.alignclass.p.textAlign = "center"
</style>
</head>
<body>
<p class="alignclass"> This paragraph will be aligned in the center
<p> This paragraph will not be aligned in the center
</body>
</html>
```

Figure 1 shows the results of the following code sample. The paragraph has a border and is aligned within the center of the <p> element itself.

Figure 1

Paragraph aligned in the center using textAlign.

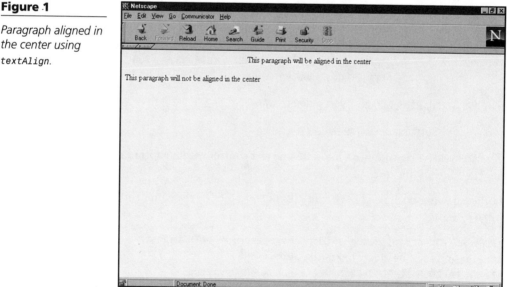

The previous simple example of HTML code includes a single line of JSSS code

```
classes.alignclass.p.textAlign = "center"
```

that can be broken down to:

- classes one of the methods of defining JSSS styles. The classes definition specifies the element immediately following it in the dot notation, which will be a class name.
- alignclass is the class name that is being defined. A class name may be any alphanumeric combination.
- p defines this class to be available for use only with <p> HTML elements.
- textAlign is the style property that is being defined for the element.
- "center" is the value that is assigned to the style property.

<TEXTAREA>

Category: HTML

Browser Support		Navigator 3	Navigator 4	Explorer 3	Explorer 4
	Macintosh	■	■	■	■
	Windows	■	■	■	■

May Contain Plain text only

May Be Used In <A>, <ADDRESS>, <APPLET>, <B>, <BIG>, <BLOCKQUOTE>, <CAPTION>—but only within the <FORM> tag, <CENTER>, <CITE>, <CODE>, <DD>, <DFN>, <DIV>, <DT>, <EM>, <FONT>, <FORM>, <H1>, <H2>, <H3>, <H4>, <H5>, <H6>, <I>, <KBD>, <LI>, <P>, <PRE>, <SAMP>, <SMALL>, <STRIKE>, <STRONG>, <SUB>, <SUP>, <TD>, <TH>, <TT>, <U>, <VAR>

Attributes COLS, NAME, ROWS, WRAP

Syntax <TEXTAREA>...</TEXTAREA>

The <TEXTAREA> tag specifies a multiple-line text control within a form in which the form user may type in and edit text.

In the following example HTML, the <TEXTAREA> specifies the comment area on a feedback web page:

```
<FORM ACTION=http://www.provider.com/cgiscript METHOD=post>
<P>Please leave us your comments below:<BR>
<TEXTAREA COLS=30 ROWS=50 NAME=feedback WRAP=virtual>
</FORM>
```

COLS

The COLS attribute specifies the number of vertical columns to be displayed as a measurement of the width of a text control. Each individual measurement is the width of a character, so a COLS value of 40, for example, would equal the total width of 40 characters on the web page.

COLS is used in tandem with the ROWS attribute (which measures the height of the text control also in single-character widths) to create a complete control measurement, as in the following example HTML:

```
<FORM ACTION=http://www.provider.com/cgiscript METHOD=post>
<P>Please leave us your comments below:<BR>
<TEXTAREA COLS=30 ROWS=50 NAME=feedback WRAP=virtual>
</FORM>
```

Figures 1 and 2 illustrate this example HTML in Internet Explorer 3 for the Macintosh and Windows.

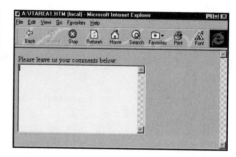

Figure 1

A basic text control measured in COLS and ROWS in Internet Explorer 3 for the Macintosh.

Figure 2

A basic text control measured in COLS and ROWS in Internet Explorer 3 for Windows.

See the ROWS section of this entry for more information.

NAME

The NAME attribute specifies the description of the text control that corresponds to the gateway program that processes any information submitted via the form. Without the NAME attribute and the identifier it specifies, the gateway program will not work properly and the form user will not get a response. This is the reason why you cannot choose a form control's NAME value randomly; it must correspond to the part of the form's CGI script or other gateway program that processes the control's information.

In the following example HTML, NAME has been specified with a logical identifier, feedback, because you're asking for comments:

```
<FORM ACTION=http://www.provider.com/cgiscript METHOD=post>
<P>Please leave us your comments below:<BR>
<TEXTAREA COLS=30 ROWS=50 NAME=feedback WRAP=virtual>
</FORM>
```

T

See the example HTML and corresponding figures in the previous section of this entry for another example of how the NAME attribute is written properly.

ROWS

The ROWS attribute specifies the number of horizontal columns to be displayed as a measurement of the width of a text control. Each individual measurement is the height of a character, so a ROWS value of 20, for example, would equal the total height of 20 characters on the web page.

ROWS is used in tandem with the COLS attribute (which measures the width of the text control also in single-character increments) to create a complete control measurement, as in the following example HTML:

```
<FORM ACTION=http://www.provider.com/cgiscript METHOD=post>
<P>Please leave us your comments below:<BR>
<TEXTAREA COLS=30 ROWS=50 NAME=feedback WRAP=virtual>
</FORM>
```

Figures 3 and 4 illustrate this example HTML in Internet Explorer 3 for the Macintosh and for Windows.

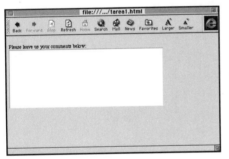

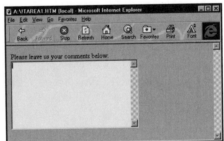

Figure 3

A basic text control measured in COLS and ROWS in Internet Explorer 3 for the Macintosh.

Figure 4

A basic text control measured in COLS and ROWS in Internet Explorer 3 for Windows.

See the COLS section of this entry for more information.

WRAP

The WRAP attribute determines whether or not the text being typed into the <TEXTAREA> control will wrap down or continue on the same line. Its presence or absence does not affect how the CGI script would receive the information, but not using WRAP makes it difficult for the form user to read what has been typed.

In the following example HTML, WRAP has been placed properly inside the <TEXTAREA> tag:

```
<FORM ACTION=http://www.provider.com/cgiscript METHOD=post>
<P>Please leave us your comments below:<BR>
<TEXTAREA COLS=30 ROWS=50 NAME=feedback WRAP=virtual>
</FORM>
```

In Figures 5 and 6, the first of the two text controls is specified with WRAP and the next is not.

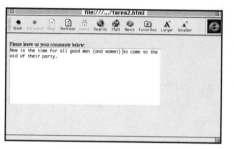

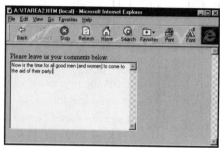

Figure 5

To WRAP or not to WRAP in Internet Explorer 3 for the Macintosh.

Figure 6

To WRAP or not to WRAP in Internet Explorer 3 for Windows.

textDecoration

Category: JavaScript Style Sheets

	Type	Property

Browser Support

	Navigator 3	Navigator 4	Explorer 3	Explorer 4
Macintosh		▓		
Windows		▓		

Applies To All elements

Inherited No

Syntax textDecoration = "value"

textDecoration is a rather elaborate term for a process that is used frequently in text documents. textDecoration is nothing more than the capability to underline, overline, or put a line through text. Okay, so maybe there is a little more to it than that. You can also make the text blink. The five acceptable values for textDecoration are:

- ▓ "none" will do just as its name implies—it will give the HTML element no decoration. This would most commonly be used to negate a previously implemented style.

- ▓ "underline" draws a line underneath the text of the element.

- ■ "overline" draws a line above the text of the element.
- ■ "line-through" puts a line through, otherwise known as a strike-through, the element. It is drawn through the center of the text.
- ■ The "blink" value causes an obvious reaction: The text of the object will blink.

It is important to remember when using textDecoration that it will only have effect on the text of an element. The property may be used with non-textual elements, such as <em>, but there will be no change to the display of the element.

Although this property is not inherited to the children, for consistency, the children should use the same decoration as their parents. This will have to be done explicitly by the programmer for each child element.

The capability to decorate text inside of JavaScript code gives you the option to define styles that will be applied in certain instances. For example, you may need to have certain text elements underlined only if the browser is Netscape Navigator.

```
<html>
<head>
<style type="text/javascript">
if (navigator.appName == "Netscape") {
tags.h3.textDecoration = "underline"
}
</style>
</head>
<body>
<h1> document heading one
<h2> document heading two
<p> This paragraph will not be affected.
<h3> document heading three

<p> this paragraph will be affected, because it inherits the property.
</body>
</html>
```

The JSSS code contained within the function call in the previous example can be broken down as follows:

- ■ tags is one of the methods of defining JSSS styles. The tags definition describes the element immediately following it in the dot notation will be one of the accepted HTML elements.
- ■ h3 is the HTML element that is being assigned a style. This may be any valid HTML element.
- ■ textDecoration is the style that is being defined for the element. This may be any valid JSSS style.
- ■ "underline" is the value of the style textDecoration. This value means that the HTML element defined with this style will be underlined.

In Figure 1, you can see the results of the previous code sample if the browser is Navigator. Obviously at this printing JSSS is supported by Navigator only, but in the future when other browsers support JSSS this example would be extremely useful.

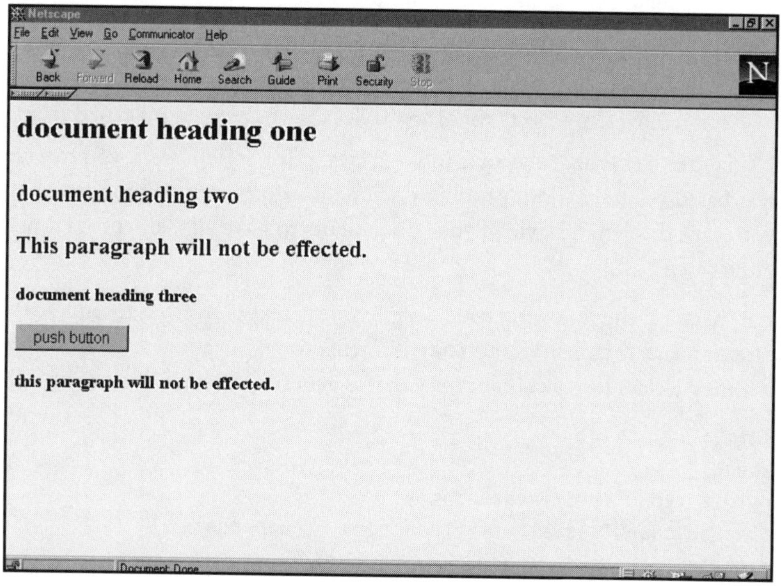

Figure 1

Document result if browser is Navigator.

Figure 1

Document result if browser is Navigator.

The concept of `textDecoration` seems to suggest the need for color as well as formatting styles, but colors are handled seperately using the `color` property.

textTransform

Category: JavaScript Style Sheets

Type	Property	

Browser Support

	Navigator 3	Navigator 4	Explorer 3	Explorer 4
Macintosh	☐	■	☐	☐
Windows	☐	■	☐	☐

Applies To All elements

Inherited Yes

Syntax `textTransform = "value"`

When applied to text objects, the `textTransform` property will convert, based on the value, the case of the text. Text can be changed to uppercase, lowercase, or first letters capitals with the available JSSS property values.

T

- ■ "capitalize" formats the first letter of each word in the text to first letter uppercase. This will not format the first letter of sentence, but the first letter of each word. For example, "the big brown dog" will be converted to "The Big Brown Dog."

- ■ "uppercase" formats the entire text in uppercase letters.

- ■ "lowercase" formats the text into lowercase letters.

- ■ "none" removes any case changes on the text from previous textTransform styles, as well as removes any textTransform styles that have been inherited from parent elements.

Using the textTransform style in your JavaScript Style Sheets, you can change the casing of your text based on usage input or other document information. This kind of style is also useful when you want the generic style of your documents to have all elements of a particular type using the same case.

For instance, the following code sample shows text converted to uppercase to match the corporate standard for all <h1> and <h2> elements to be in captial letters. You can accomplish this by defining a class for textTransform that is generic across all documents.

```
<html>
<head>
<style type="text/javascript">
classes.caseClass.all.textTransform = "uppercase"
</style>
</head>
<body>
<h1 class="caseClass"> Heading type 1 in upper case.
</h1>
<h2 class="caseClass"> Heading type 2 also in upper case
</h2>
<p> Regular body text not transformed to upper case
</body>
</html>
```

Figure 1 shows the results of this code.

Figure 1

Text converted to uppercase.

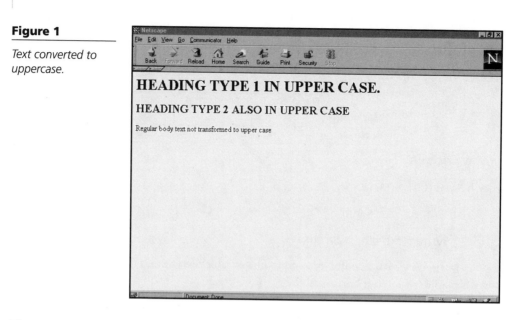

The important line of code in the example shown is

```
classes.caseClass.all.textTransform = "uppercase"
```

This code can be broken down to:

- `classes` is one of the methods of defining JSSS styles. The `classes` definition specifies the element immediately following it in the dot notation, which will be a class name.
- `caseclass` is the class name for the style property. This may be any alphanumeric combination.
- `all` defines this class to be available for use with all HTML elements.
- `textTransform` is the style that is being defined for the element. This may be any valid JSSS style.
- `"uppercase"` is the value of the style `textTransform`. This value means that the HTML element defined with this class will be changed to uppercase.

A more generic method would be to define the style in an external JavaScript Style Sheet, and that style could then be used by multiple documents.

T

<TFOOT>

Category: HTML

Browser Support		Navigator 3	Navigator 4	Explorer 3	Explorer 4
	Macintosh			■■■	■■■
	Windows			■■■	■■■

May Contain None

May Be Used In <TABLE>

Attributes CLASS, ID

Syntax <TFOOT>...</TFOOT>

The <TFOOT> tag designates a footer, or bottom line of table text, so that the RULES attribute knows where to draw interior horizontal lines.

It is an Internet Explorer-specific tag used in tandem with <TBODY> and <THEAD> when the RULES attribute has been specified in the <TABLE> tag. The closing, or </TFOOT>, tag is optional (you can leave it out and your web page will still work), but it is used in this entry to better distinguish <TFOOT>-specified sections.

In the following example, the <TFOOT> tag groups the two middle rows together for the sake of the RULES attribute:

```
<TABLE BORDER RULES=cols>
<THEAD>This is a table header.</THEAD>
<TR>
<TD>Cell No. 1</TD><TD>Cell No. 2</TD>
</TR>
<TBODY>
<TR>
<TD>Cell No. 3</TD><TD>Cell No. 4</TD>
</TR>
<TR>
<TD>Cell No. 5</TD><TD>Cell No. 6</TD>
</TR></TBODY>
<TFOOT>This is the table footer.</TFOOT>
<TR>
<TD>Cell No. 7</TD><TD>Cell No. 8</TD>
</TR>
</TABLE>
```

The RULES attribute value of cols will only apply to the middle two rows (cells 3 to 6). See the RULES attribute section of the <TABLE> tag entry for a list of all RULES values.

Figures 1 and 2 illustrate this example HTML Internet Explorer 3 for the Macintosh and for Windows.

Figure 1

Using the <TBODY> and <TFOOT> tags to apply the RULES attribute in Internet Explorer 3 for the Macintosh.

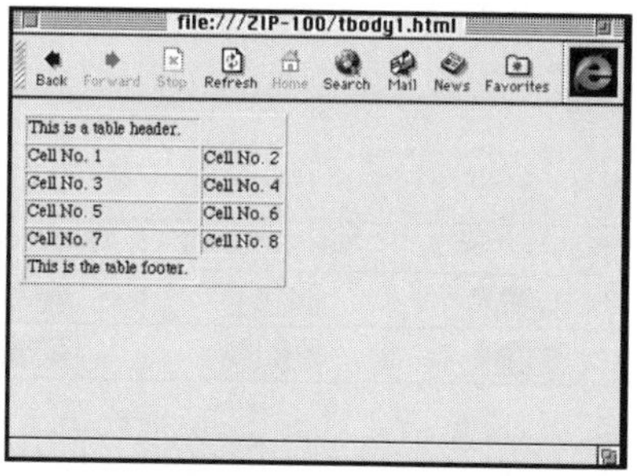

Figure 2

Using the <TBODY> and <TFOOT> tags to apply the RULES attribute in Internet Explorer 3 for Windows.

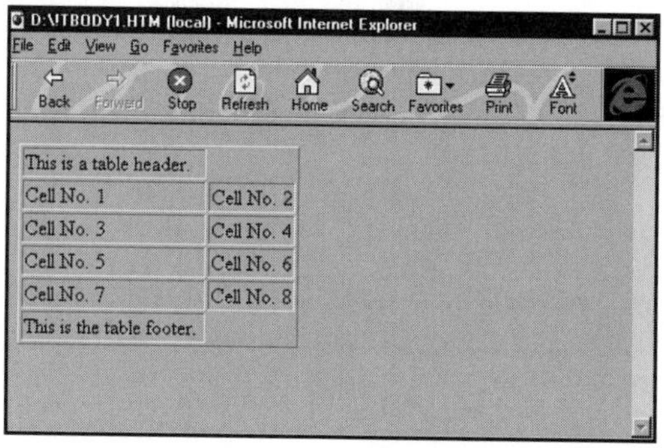

CLASS

The CLASS attribute is used to specify the name of a style sheet as it applies to a specific selection on a web page. See the "Cascading Style Sheets Basics" chapter and any individual, related style sheets entries elsewhere in the book for more information.

ID

The ID attribute is used to distinguish individual selections in a web page as pertaining to the use of style sheets. See the "Cascading Style Sheets Basics" chapter and any individual, related style sheets entries elsewhere in the book for more information.

T

<TH>

Category: HTML

	Navigator 3	Navigator 4	Explorer 3	Explorer 4
Browser Support				
Macintosh	■	■	■	■
Windows	■	■	■	■

May Contain <A>, <ADDRESS>, <APPLET>, <B>, <BASEFONT>, <BIG>, <BLOCKQUOTE>, <BR>, <CENTER>, <CITE>, <CODE>, <DFN>, <DIR>, <DIV>, <DL>, <EM>, <FONT>, <FORM>, <H1>, <H2>, <H3>, <H4>, <H5>, <H6>, <HR>, <I>, <IMG>, <INPUT>, <KBD>, <MAP>, <MENU>, <OL>, <P>, <PRE>, <SAMP>, <SELECT>, <SMALL>, <STRIKE>, <STRONG>, <SUB>, <SUP>, <TABLE>, <TEXTAREA>, <TT>, <U>, <UL>, <VAR>

May Be Used In <TR>

Attributes ALIGN, BGCOLOR, BORDERCOLOR, BORDERCOLORDARK, BORDERCOLORLIGHT, CLASS, COLSPAN, ID, NOWRAP, ROWSPAN, VALIGN, WIDTH

Syntax <TH>...</TH>

The <TH> tag specifies a *header*, or description, of a column within a table. The closing, or </TH>, tag is optional—some HTML authorities recommend it and others don't, but it won't adversely affect your web page if you leave it out. It has, however, been used in this entry to better distinguish heading text.

In the following example, the <TH> tag adds headers to both a row and a column within a simple four-cell, two-row table:

```
<TABLE BORDER>
<TH>Header No. 1</TH><TH>Header No. 2</TH>
<TR>
<TD>Cell No. 1</TD><TD>Cell No. 2</TD>
</TR>
<TR>
<TD>Cell No. 3</TD><TD>Cell No. 4</TD>
</TR>
</TABLE>
```

Figures 1, 2, 3, and 4 illustrate this simple table with headers in Navigator 3 and Internet Explorer 3 for the Macintosh and for Windows.

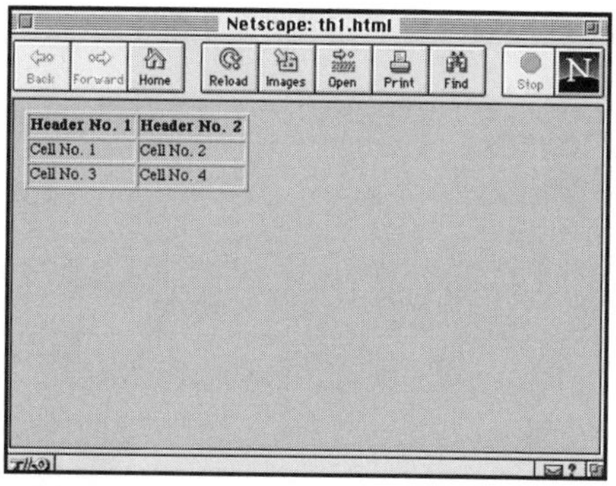

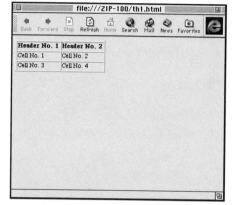

Figure 1

Basic table with headers in Navigator 3 for the Macintosh.

Figure 2

Basic table with headers in Internet Explorer 3 for the Macintosh.

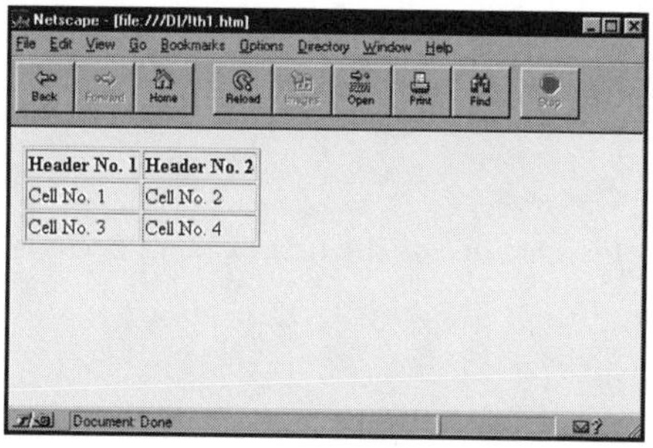

Figure 3

Basic table with headers in Navigator 3 for Windows.

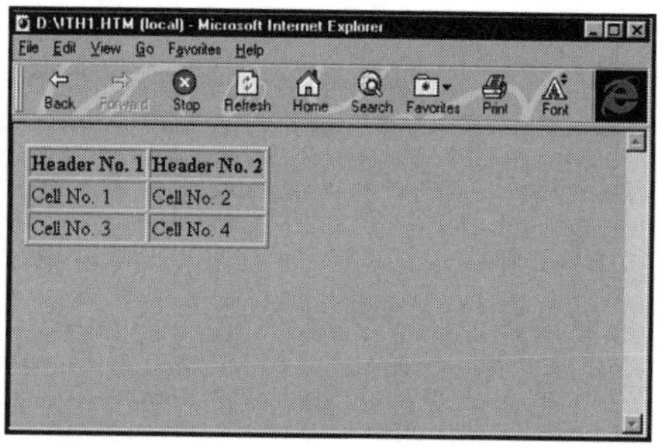

Figure 4

Basic table with headers in Internet Explorer 3 for Windows.

ALIGN

The ALIGN attribute establishes the horizontal alignment of header text. It has four values:

center

The header text is centered. This is the ALIGN attribute default.

justify

The header text is justified to both left and right margins.

left

The header text is left-aligned with the left margin.

right

The header text is right-aligned with the right margin.

T

In the following example, the ALIGN setting has been established first as right and then as left:

```
<TABLE>
<TH ALIGN=right>Header No. 1</TH><TH ALIGN=left>Header No. 2</TH>
<TR >
<TD>Cell No. 1</TD><TD>Cell No. 2</TD>
</TR>
<TR ALIGN=left>
<TD>Cell No. 3</TD><TD>Cell No. 4</TD>
</TR>
</TABLE>
```

> **NOTE**   To establish vertical alignment, use the VALIGN attribute. It's covered in its own section later on in this entry.

BGCOLOR

The BGCOLOR attribute is an Internet Explorer–only feature that specifies a custom background color for an individual header, either with a color name or a hexadecimal value. (See Appendix B for a chart of all the colors you can specify by name and all the colors you can specify by hex value.)

In the following examples, cyan (or aqua blue) is specified as the first header's background color in both instances, first by name:

```
<TABLE>
<TH BGCOLOR=cyan>Header No. 1</TH><TH ALIGN=left>Header No. 2</TH><TR>
<TD>Cell No. 1</TD><TD>Cell No. 2</TD>
</TR>
<TR ALIGN=left>
<TD>Cell No. 3</TD><TD>Cell No. 4</TD>
</TR>
</TABLE>
```

and then by hex value:

```
<TABLE>
<TH BGCOLOR=#00ffff>Header No. 1</TH><TH ALIGN=left>Header No. 2</TH><TR>
<TR>
<TD>Cell No. 1</TD><TD>Cell No. 2</TD>
</TR>
<TR ALIGN=left>
<TD>Cell No. 3</TD><TD>Cell No. 4</TD>
</TR>
</TABLE>
```

Figures 5 and 6 illustrate this example HTML in Internet Explorer 3 for the Macintosh and for Windows. The first row's background color is specified as cyan (which will appear as a lighter gray in these black-and-white figures), while the second row will remain default gray.

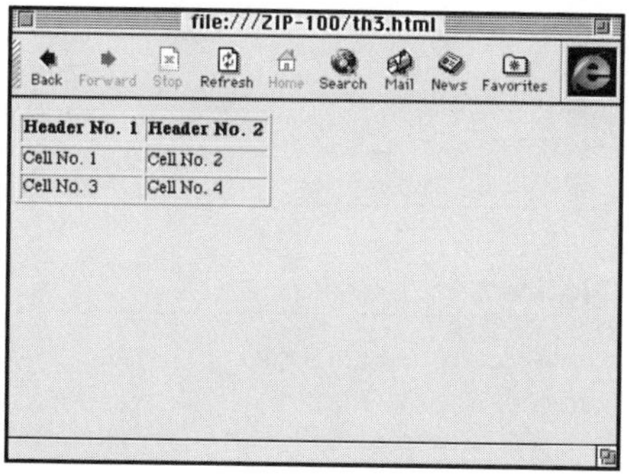

Figure 5

BGCOLOR *background colors in Internet Explorer 3 for the Macintosh.*

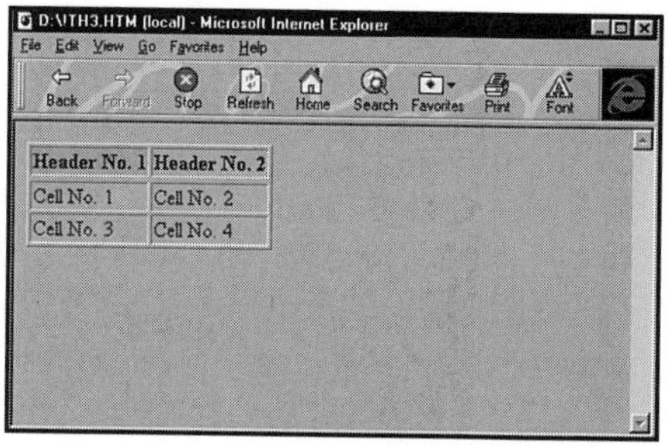

Figure 6

BGCOLOR *background colors in Internet Explorer 3 for Windows.*

BORDERCOLOR

The BORDERCOLOR attribute is an Internet Explorer–only attribute that specifies a solid custom border color around a table header. There is no equivalent attribute for Navigator, so no matter what color you specify using BORDERCOLOR, visitors to your site using Navigator will see all table headers bordered in default gray.

BORDERCOLOR color values are specified either by name or by hexadecimal value. (See Appendix B for a chart of all the colors you can specify by name and all the colors you can specify by hex value.)

In the following examples, aqua is specified in the first row and black in the second.

```
<TABLE>
<TH BORDERCOLOR=aqua>Header No. 1</TH><TH BORDERCOLOR=black>Header No. 2</TH><TR>
<TR>
<TD>Cell No. 1</TD><TD>Cell No. 2</TD>
</TR>
<TR>
<TD>Cell No. 3</TD><TD>Cell No. 4</TD>
</TR>
</TABLE>
```

These colors may also be identified by hexadecimal value instead—see Appendix B on color and hexadecimal value for more information.

Figures 7 and 8 illustrate this example HTML in Internet Explorer 3 for the Macintosh and for Windows. The first header's border color will appear as a lighter gray, although the second will, for once, appear black as specified.

T

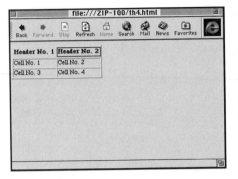

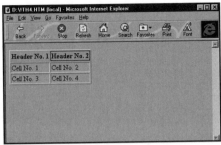

Figure 8

BORDERCOLOR header colors in Internet Explorer 3 for Windows.

Figure 7

BORDERCOLOR header colors in Internet Explorer 3 for the Macintosh.

DESIGN NOTE	Do NOT choose header border colors that a) won't show up against your table or page background color (as in white borders on a yellow background), b) match your customized link colors (or visitors will click your headers thinking they're links), and c) clash with any other customized colors on your page.

BORDERCOLORDARK

The BORDERCOLORDARK attribute is an Internet Explorer–only attribute that specifies the darker of two row header colors that overlap to create a 3-D effect. (If you've already read the <TABLE> and <TR> tag entries, you know they also have a similar BORDERCOLORDARK, which works pretty much the same way.)

There is no equivalent attribute for Navigator, so no matter what color you specify using BORDERCOLORDARK, visitors to your site using Navigator will see all header borders in default gray.

BORDERCOLORDARK color values are specified either by name or by hexadecimal value. (See Appendix B for a chart of all the colors you can specify by name and all the colors you can specify by hex value.)

In the following examples, black is specified as the BORDERCOLORDARK value by hex value:

```
<TABLE>
<TH BORDERCOLORDARK=#ffffff BORDERCOLORLIGHT=#000000>Header No. 1</TH><TH
➥ALIGN=left>Header No. 2</TH>
<TR>
<TD>Cell No. 1</TD><TD>Cell No. 2</TD>
</TR>
<TR>
<TD>Cell No. 3</TD><TD>Cell No. 4</TD>
</TR>
</TABLE>
```

In both examples, the borders of the second header in the table have been left as default gray for comparison. You can also specify certain colors (16 with complete cross-platform certainty) by name rather than by hex value. See Appendix B for more information on color and color choices.

Figures 9 and 10 illustrate this example HTML in Internet Explorer 3 for the Macintosh and for Windows.

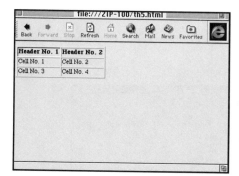

Figure 9

BORDERCOLORLIGHT and BORDERCOLOR-DARK header colors in Internet Explorer 3 for the Macintosh.

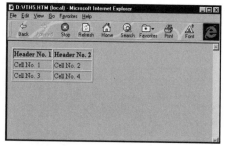

Figure 10

BORDERCOLORLIGHT and BORDERCOLOR-DARK header colors in Internet Explorer 3 for Windows.

BORDERCOLORLIGHT

The BORDERCOLORLIGHT attribute is an Internet Explorer–only attribute that specifies the darker of two row header colors that overlap to create a 3-D effect. (If you've already read the <TABLE> and <TR> tag entries, you know they also have a similar BORDERCOLORLIGHT that works pretty much the same way.)

There is no equivalent attribute for Navigator, so no matter what color you specify using BORDERCOLORLIGHT, visitors to your site using Navigator will see all header borders in default gray.

BORDERCOLORLIGHT color values are specified either by name or by hexadecimal value. (See Appendix B for a chart of all the colors you can specify by name and all the colors you can specify by hex value.)

In the following examples, black is specified as the BORDERCOLORLIGHT value by hex value:

```
<TABLE>
<TH BORDERCOLORDARK=#ffffff BORDERCOLORLIGHT=#000000>Header No. 1</TH><TH
➥ALIGN=left>Header No. 2</TH>
<TR>
<TD>Cell No. 1</TD><TD>Cell No. 2</TD>
</TR>
```

T

```
<TR>
<TD>Cell No. 3</TD><TD>Cell No. 4</TD>
</TR>
</TABLE>
```

In both examples, the borders of the second header in the table have been left as default gray for comparison. Again, you can specify some colors by name if you prefer—see Appendix B for more detailed information on color and color choices.

Figures 11 and 12 illustrate this example HTML in Internet Explorer 3 for the Macintosh and for Windows.

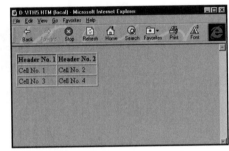

Figure 11

BORDERCOLORLIGHT and *BORDERCOLOR-DARK* header colors in Internet Explorer 3 for the Macintosh.

Figure 12

BORDERCOLORLIGHT and *BORDERCOLOR-DARK* header colors in Internet Explorer 3 for Windows.

CLASS

The CLASS attribute is used to specify the name of a style sheet as it applies to a specific selection on a web page. See the "Cascading Style Sheets Basics" chapter and any individual, related style sheets entries elsewhere in the book for more information.

COLSPAN

The COLSPAN attribute specifies more than one column to be spanned by the same header.

In the following example three-column table, COLSPAN has been assigned a value of 2 to stretch the second header across the second and third columns in one long double-width cell:

```
<TABLE BORDER>
<TH>Header No. 1</TH><TH COLSPAN=2>Header No. 2</TH>
<TR>
<TD>Cell No. 1</TD><TD>Cell No. 2</TD><TD>Cell No. 3</TD>
</TR>
```

```
<TR>
<TD>Cell No. 4</TD><TD>Cell No. 5</TD><TD>Cell No. 6</TD>
</TR>
</TABLE>
```

Figures 13, 14, 15, and 16 illustrate this sample table in Navigator 3 and Internet Explorer 3 for the Macintosh and for Windows.

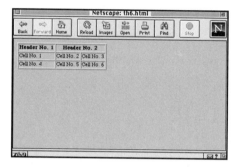

Figure 13

A COLSPAN double-width header in Navigator 3 for the Macintosh.

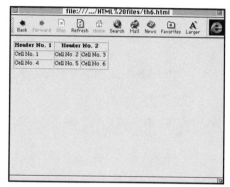

Figure 14

A COLSPAN double-width header in Internet Explorer 3 for the Macintosh.

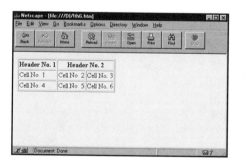

Figure 15

A COLSPAN double-width header in Navigator 3 for Windows.

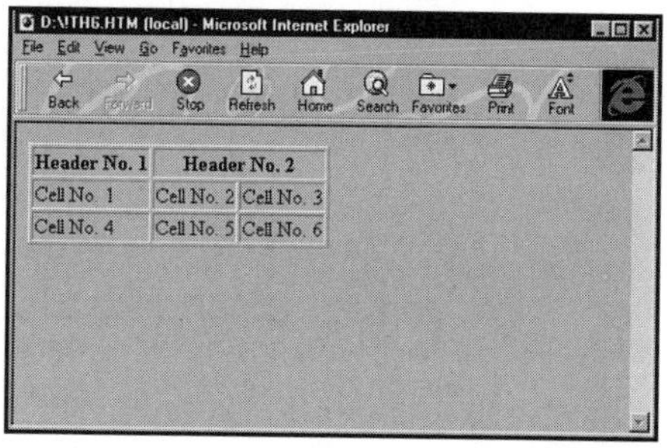

Figure 16

A COLSPAN double-width header in Internet Explorer 3 for Windows.

ID

The ID attribute is used to distinguish individual selections in a web page as pertaining to the use of style sheets. See the "Cascading Style Sheets Basics" chapter and any individual, related style sheets entries elsewhere in the book for more information.

NOWRAP

The NOWRAP attribute is an Internet Explorer–specific feature that prevents header text from wrapping down to a second line. Ordinarily, both Navigator and Internet Explorer will automatically wrap a header down to the next line if it's too long for the margins.

In the following example, the NOWRAP attribute is placed properly within the appropriate <TH> tag with no values:

```
<TABLE>
<TH>Header No. 1</TH><TH NOWRAP>Header No. 2</TH>
<TR>
<TD>Cell No. 1</TD><TD>Cell No. 2</TD>
</TR>
<TR>
<TD>Cell No. 3</TD><TD>Cell No. 4</TD>
</TR>
</TABLE>
```

Obviously in this example table, there isn't enough text in the second header to merit using the NOWRAP attribute, but in Figures 17 and 18, the first header has been extended out and should run right off the page.

Figure 17

Using NOWRAP in Internet Explorer 3 for the Macintosh.

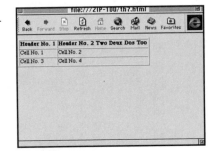

Figure 18

Using NOWRAP in Internet Explorer 3 for Windows.

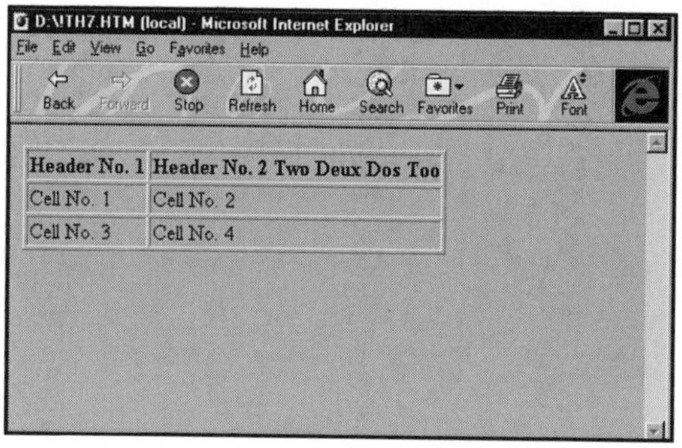

ROWSPAN

The ROWSPAN attribute is similar to the COLSPAN attribute in that it specifies a header as more than one row wide (as opposed to more than one column wide).

In the following example three-column table, ROWSPAN has been assigned a value of 2 to stretch the second header across the second and third rows in one long double-width cell:

```
<TABLE BORDER>
<TH>Header No. 1</TH><TH ROWSPAN=2>Header No. 2</TH>
<TR>
<TD>Cell No. 1</TD><TD>Cell No. 2</TD><TD>Cell No. 3</TD>
</TR>
<TR>
<TD>Cell No. 4</TD><TD>Cell No. 5</TD><TD>Cell No. 6</TD>
</TR>
</TABLE>
```

Figures 19, 20, 21, and 22 illustrate this sample table in Navigator 3 and Internet Explorer 3 for the Macintosh and for Windows.

T

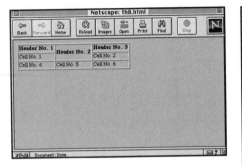

Figure 19

A ROWSPAN *double-width header in Navigator 3 for the Macintosh.*

Figure 20

A ROWSPAN *double-width header in Internet Explorer 3 for the Macintosh.*

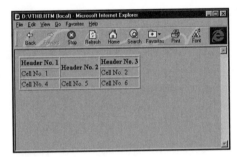

Figure 21

A ROWSPAN *double-width header in Navigator 3 for Windows.*

Figure 22

A ROWSPAN *double-width header in Internet Explorer 3 for Windows.*

VALIGN

The VALIGN attribute controls the vertical alignment of header text. It has four values:

baseline

The header text is aligned on a shared, common baseline.

bottom

The header text is aligned with the bottom of each cell.

middle

The header text is aligned with the middle of each cell.

top

The header text is aligned with the top of each cell. This is the VALIGN attribute default.

In the following example, the VALIGN setting has been established first as middle and then as bottom:

```
<TABLE>
<TH VALIGN=middle>Header No. 1</TH><TH VALIGN=bottom>Header No. 2</TH>
<TR>
<TD>Cell No. 1</TD><TD>Cell No. 2</TD>
</TR>
<TR>
<TD>Cell No. 3</TD><TD>Cell No. 4</TD>
</TR>
</TABLE>
```

NOTE To establish horizontal alignment, use the ALIGN attribute. It's covered in its own section earlier in this entry.

WIDTH

The WIDTH attribute specifies the width of the table header in columns.

In the following HTML example, WIDTH has been established as 2:

```
<TABLE BORDER>
<TH>Header No. 1</TH><TH WIDTH=2>Header No. 2</TH>
<TR>
<TD>Cell No. 1</TD><TD>Cell No. 2</TD><TD>Cell No. 3</TD>
</TR>
<TR>
<TD>Cell No. 4</TD><TD>Cell No. 5</TD><TD>Cell No. 6</TD>
</TR>
</TABLE>
```

The second header will then span the width of the second and third columns in a double-wide, single cell.

<THEAD>

Category: HTML

Browser Support

	Navigator 3	Navigator 4	Explorer 3	Explorer 4
Macintosh			▬	▬
Windows			▬	▬

May Contain <A>, <ADDRESS>, <APPLET>, <B>, <BASEFONT>, <BIG>, <BR>, <CITE>, <CODE>, <DFN>, <EM>, <FONT>, <H1>, <H2>, <H3>, <H4>, <H5>, <H6>, <I>, <IMG>, <INPUT>, <KBD>, <MAP>, <SAMP>, <SELECT>, <SMALL>, <STRIKE>, <STRONG>, <SUB>, <SUP>, <TEXTAREA>, <TT>, <U>, <VAR>

T

May Be Used In	<TABLE>
Attributes	ALIGN, CLASS, ID, VALIGN
Syntax	<THEAD>...</THEAD>

The <THEAD> tag defines a table header exactly as the <TH> tag.

It is an Internet Explorer–specific tag used in tandem with the <TFOOT> and <TBODY> tags when the RULES attribute has been specified in the <TABLE> tag. The closing, or </THEAD>, tag is optional (you can leave it out and your web page will still work), but it is used in this entry to better distinguish <THEAD>-specified sections.

In the following example, the <THEAD> tag specifies the header text:

```
<TABLE BORDER RULES=cols>
<THEAD>This is a table header.</THEAD>
<TBODY>
<TR>
<TD>Cell No. 1</TD><TD>Cell No. 2</TD>
</TR>
<TR>
<TD>Cell No. 3</TD><TD>Cell No. 4</TD>
</TR>
<TR>
<TD>Cell No. 5</TD><TD>Cell No. 6</TD>
</TR>
</TBODY>
<TR>
<TD>Cell No. 7</TD><TD>Cell No. 8</TD>
</TR>
<TFOOT>This is the table footer.</TFOOT>
</TABLE>
```

See the RULES attribute section of the <TABLE> tag entry for a list of all RULES values.

ALIGN

The ALIGN attribute specifies the horizontal alignment of the table header. It has four values:

center

The table header will be centered. This is the ALIGN attribute default.

justify

The table header will be justified between the left and right margins.

left

The table header will be left-aligned.

right

The table header will be right-aligned.

In the following example, ALIGN has been established as left:

```
<TABLE BORDER RULES=cols>
<THEAD ALIGN=left>This is a table header.</THEAD>
<TBODY>
<TR>
<TD>Cell No. 1</TD><TD>Cell No. 2</TD>
</TR>
<TR>
<TD>Cell No. 3</TD><TD>Cell No. 4</TD>
</TR>
<TR>
<TD>Cell No. 5</TD><TD>Cell No. 6</TD>
</TR>
</TBODY>
<TR>
<TD>Cell No. 7</TD><TD>Cell No. 8</TD>
</TR>
<TFOOT>This is the table footer.</TFOOT>
</TABLE>
```

Figures 1 and 2 illustrate this example HTML in Internet Explorer 3 for the Macintosh and for Windows.

Figure 1

Using the <THEAD> tag ALIGN attribute in Internet Explorer 3 for the Macintosh.

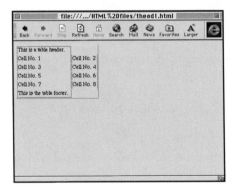

T

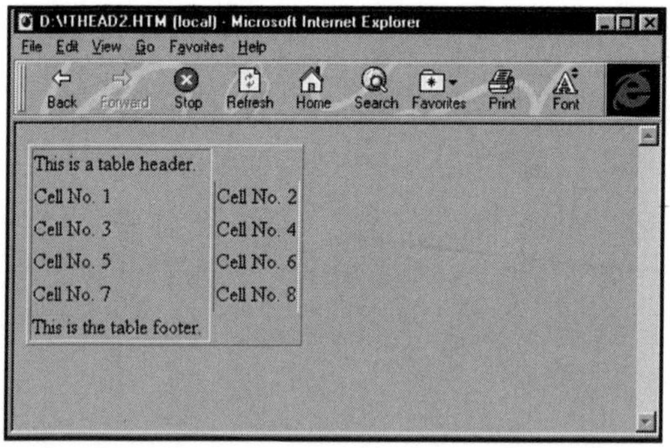

Figure 2

*Using the <THEAD>
tag ALIGN attribute
in Internet Explorer 3
for Windows.*

> **NOTE**   The VALIGN attribute establishes vertical alignment of the header text. See its
> section later on in this entry.

CLASS

The CLASS attribute is used to specify the name of a style sheet as it applies to a specific selection on a web page. See the "Cascading Style Sheets Basics" chapter and any individual, related style sheets entries elsewhere in the book for more information.

ID

The ID attribute is used to distinguish individual selections in a web page as pertaining to the use of style sheets. See the "Cascading Style Sheets Basics" chapter and any individual, related style sheets entries elsewhere in the book for more information.

VALIGN

The VALIGN attribute specifies the vertical alignment of the header text. It has three values:

`bottom`

The table header will be aligned with the bottom of the header cell.

`middle`

The table header will be aligned with the middle of the header cell. This is the VALIGN attribute default.

`top`

The table header will be aligned with the top of the header cell.

In the following example, VALIGN has been established as bottom:

```
<TABLE BORDER RULES=cols>
<THEAD VALIGN=bottom>This is a table header.</THEAD>
<TBODY>
<TR>
<TD>Cell No. 1</TD><TD>Cell No. 2</TD>
</TR>
<TR>
<TD>Cell No. 3</TD><TD>Cell No. 4</TD>
</TR>
<TR>
<TD>Cell No. 5</TD><TD>Cell No. 6</TD>
</TR>
</TBODY>
<TR>
<TD>Cell No. 7</TD><TD>Cell No. 8</TD>
</TR>
<TFOOT>This is the table footer.</TFOOT>
</TABLE>
```

> **NOTE**   The ALIGN attribute establishes horizontal alignment of the header text. See its section earlier in this entry.

Time

Category: VBScript

Type   Function

Browser Support

	Navigator 3	Navigator 4	Explorer 3	Explorer 4
Macintosh				■
Windows			■	■

Syntax   Time

The Time function returns the current time from the user's machine. The time is returned in the format "hh:mm:ss [AM/PM]."

time returns   5:10:16 PM

TimeSerial()

Category: VBScript

Type	Function

Browser Support

	Navigator 3	Navigator 4	Explorer 3	Explorer 4
Macintosh				▓▓▓
Windows			▓▓▓	▓▓▓

Syntax `TimeSerial(hour, minute, second)`

The `TimeSerial()` function returns the time value specified by the numeric *hour, minute,* and *second* parameters. While *hour* must be a number between 0 and 23, *minute* and *second* may be any number—if they fall outside the range of 0 to 59 then the entire time will update accordingly. The resulting time is returned in the format "hh:mm:ss [AM/PM]."

`timeserial(5,30,10)`   returns 5:30:10 AM

`timeserial(17,70,25)`   returns 6:10:25 PM

`timeserial(14,59,62)`   returns 3:00:02 PM

You can use the `TimeSerial()` function to quickly add or subtract time. For instance, the below example adds 5 minutes and 30 seconds to the time 2:15 PM:

`timeserial(14,15+5,0+30)`   returns 2:20:30 PM

TimeValue()

Category: VBScript

Type	Function

Browser Support

	Navigator 3	Navigator 4	Explorer 3	Explorer 4
Macintosh				▓▓▓
Windows			▓▓▓	▓▓▓

Syntax `TimeValue(time)`

The `TimeValue()` function accepts a string expression containing a valid *time*, and returns a variant subtype of date with the time information. You may include date information in *time*, but the function will only return the time—if only the date is specified, the function will return the time in the format of "12:00:00 AM." Although date information is not returned, an invalid date will produce an error. A null *time* will, as usual, return null.

You may specify *time* in either 24-hour or AM/PM format:

`timevalue("12:05PM")`	returns	12:05:00 PM
`timevalue("18:30:45")`	returns	6:30:45 PM
`timevalue("Jan 11 1998 05:20")`	returns	5:20:00 AM
`timevalue("Mar 45 1945 12:30")`	returns	`invalid procedure call error`

\<TITLE\>

Category: HTML

Browser Support		Navigator 3	Navigator 4	Explorer 3	Explorer 4
	Macintosh	■	■	■	■
	Windows	■	■	■	■

May Contain   Plain text only

May Be Used In   \<HEAD\>

Syntax   \<TITLE\>...\</TITLE\>

The \<TITLE\> tag specifies the title of a web page. It must be enclosed within the \<HEAD\> tag as follows:

```
<HEAD>
<TITLE>A Look at Domestic Short Hair Cats></TITLE>
</HEAD>
```

> **NOTE**   Choose your \<TITLE\> tag text very carefully, as it will appear out of context separately from the contents of your web page. Using a specific word is a good choice because it describes the structure of the web site, some of the content, and the general site design theme.

top

Category: Cascading Style Sheets

Browser Support		Navigator 3	Navigator 4	Explorer 3	Explorer 4
	Macintosh	☐	■	☐	☐
	Windows	☐	■	☐	■

Applies To   All elements

Syntax   top: *value*

The top property sets the position of the top of an element on the page. You may specify units as discussed in Appendix D or a percentage that refers to the parent element's width. For elements with absolute positioning, top is relative to the upper-left corner of the box of the nearest parent element. For relative positioning, top is relative to the normal position of the element.

You may also specify the keyword auto that indicates the browser should place the element where it normally would without this property. Auto is useful when dealing with inheritance and a parent element has a previously set value for left.

When combined with left, and when the position property has been set, you can precisely control the layout of objects on your page regardless of the other elements you wish to display. In fact, you can't use top unless position is also present. See the description of position for more information and elaborate examples combining top and left.

```
h1 { top: 2in }
```

```
<h1 style="top: 40%">
```

Figure 1

Using left and top to change the position of items on the page.

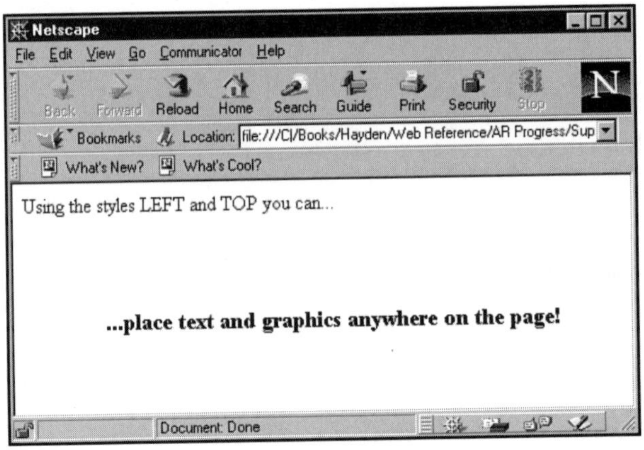

<TR>

Category: HTML

Browser Support

	Navigator 3	Navigator 4	Explorer 3	Explorer 4
Macintosh	▬	▬	▬	▬
Windows	▬	▬	▬	▬

May Contain   <TD>, <TH>

May Be Used In <TABLE>

Attributes ALIGN, BGCOLOR, BORDERCOLOR, BORDERCOLORDARK,
BORDERCOLORLIGHT, CLASS, ID, NOWRAP, VALIGN

The <TR> tag specifies each single row of table *cells*—each horizontal line of individual boxes containing text or images that sit side by side.

<TR> is one of three fundamental <TABLE> tags used to construct the basic framework of a table (the others, covered elsewhere in their own entries, are <TD> and <TABLE>).

In the following example, <TR> is used with <TD> to enclose one two-cell row:

```
<TR>
<TD>Cell No. 1</TD><TD>Cell No. 2</TD>
</TR>
```

and there are two rows with two cells each in this complete, simple example table:

```
<TABLE>
<TR>
<TD>Cell No. 1</TD><TD>Cell No. 2</TD>
</TR>
<TR>
<TD>Cell No. 3</TD><TD>Cell No. 4</TD>
</TR>
</TABLE>
```

Figure 1 1illustrates this simple table in Navigator 3 for the Macintosh.

Figure 1

Basic four-cell tables in Navigator 3 for the Macintosh.

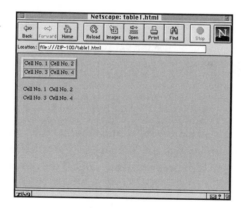

T

ALIGN

The ALIGN attribute controls the horizontal alignment of text within the cells in a single row. It has four values:

center

The text in the row cells is centered. This is the ALIGN attribute default.

justify

The text in the row cells is justified to both left and right margins. This value is not supported by Navigator.

left

The text in the row cells is left-aligned with the left margin.

right

The text in the row cells is right-aligned with the right margin.

In the following example, the ALIGN setting has been established first as right and then as left:

```
<TABLE>
<TR ALIGN=right>
<TD>Cell No. 1</TD><TD>Cell No. 2</TD>
</TR>
<TR ALIGN=left>
<TD>Cell No. 3</TD><TD>Cell No. 4</TD>
</TR>
</TABLE>
```

> **NOTE** To establish vertical alignment, use the VALIGN attribute. It's covered in its own section later on in this entry.

BGCOLOR

The BGCOLOR attribute is an Internet Explorer–only feature that specifies a custom background color to all the cells in a <TR> row, either with a color name or a hexadecimal value. (See Appendix B for a chart of all the colors you can specify by name and all the colors you can specify by hex value.)

In the following examples, cyan (or aqua blue) is specified as the first row's background color by hex value:

```
<TABLE>
<TR BGCOLOR=#00ffff>
<TD>Cell No. 1</TD><TD>Cell No. 2</TD>
</TR>
```

```
<TR ALIGN=left>
<TD>Cell No. 3</TD><TD>Cell No. 4</TD>
</TR>
</TABLE>
```

You can also specify cyan (and 15 other colors) by name if you prefer—for more information on color and color choices, see Appendix B.

BORDERCOLOR

The BORDERCOLOR attribute is an Internet Explorer–only attribute that specifies a solid custom border color around a table row.

There is no equivalent attribute for Navigator, so no matter what color you specify using BORDERCOLOR, visitors to your site using Navigator will see all table rows bordered in default gray.

BORDERCOLOR color values are specified either by name or by hexadecimal value. (See Appendix B for a chart of all the colors you can specify by name and all the colors you can specify by hex value.)

In the following example, aqua is specified in the first row and black in the second by hex value:

```
<TABLE>
<TR BGCOLOR=#00ffff>
<TD>Cell No. 1</TD><TD>Cell No. 2</TD>
</TR>
<TR BORDERCOLOR=#000000>
<TD>Cell No. 3</TD><TD>Cell No. 4</TD>
</TR>
</TABLE>
```

You can also specify aqua and black by name if you prefer—for more information on color and color choices, see Appendix B.

DESIGN NOTE
Do NOT choose row border colors that a) won't show up against your table or page background color (as in white borders on a yellow background), b) match your customized link colors (or visitors will click your tables thinking they're links), and c) clash with any other customized colors on your page.

T

BORDERCOLORDARK

The BORDERCOLORDARK attribute is an Internet Explorer–only attribute that specifies the darker of two row border colors that overlap to create a 3-D effect. (If you've already read the <TABLE> tag entry, you know it also has a similar BORDERCOLORDARK, which works pretty much the same way.)

There is no equivalent attribute for Navigator, so no matter what color you specify using BORDERCOLORDARK, all visitors to your site using Navigator will view your row borders as default gray.

BORDERCOLORDARK color values are specified either by name or by hexadecimal value. (See Appendix B for a chart of all the colors you can specify by name and all the colors you can specify by hex value.)

In the following examples, black is specified in both instances as the BORDERCOLORDARK value by hex value:

```
<TABLE>
<TR BORDERCOLORLIGHT=#ffffff BORDERCOLORDARK=#000000 >
<TD>Cell No. 1</TD><TD>Cell No. 2</TD>
</TR>
<TR>
<TD>Cell No. 3</TD><TD>Cell No. 4</TD>
</TR>
</TABLE>
```

In both examples, the borders of the second row in the table have been left as default gray for comparison. You can specify black and a few other colors by name if you prefer—see Appendix B for more information on color selection and choices.

BORDERCOLORLIGHT

The BORDERCOLORLIGHT attribute is an Internet Explorer–only attribute that specifies the darker of two row border colors that overlap to create a 3-D effect. (If you've already read the <TABLE> tag entry, you know it also has a similar BORDERCOLORLIGHT, which works pretty much the same way.)

There is no equivalent attribute for Navigator, so no matter what color you specify using BORDERCOLORLIGHT, all visitors to your site using Navigator will view your row borders as default gray.

BORDERCOLORLIGHT color values are specified either by name or by hexadecimal value. (See Appendix B for a chart of all the colors you can specify by name and all the colors you can specify by hex value.)

In the following example, white is specified as the BORDERCOLORLIGHT value by hex value:

```
<TABLE>
<TR BORDERCOLORLIGHT=#ffffff BORDERCOLORDARK=#000000 >
<TD>Cell No. 1</TD><TD>Cell No. 2</TD>
</TR>
<TR>
<TD>Cell No. 3</TD><TD>Cell No. 4</TD>
</TR>
</TABLE>
```

CLASS

The CLASS attribute is used to specify the name of a style sheet as it applies to a specific selection on a web page. See the "Cascading Style Sheets Basics" chapter and any individual, related style sheets entries elsewhere in the book for more information.

ID

The ID attribute is used to distinguish individual selections in a web page as pertaining to the use of style sheets. See the "Cascading Style Sheets Basics" chapter and any individual, related style sheets entries elsewhere in the book for more information.

NOWRAP

The NOWRAP attribute is an Internet Explorer–specific feature that prevents individual rows from wrapping if they extend past other rows into the right margin. Ordinarily, both Navigator and Internet Explorer will automatically wrap table information down to the next line, as they do with plain text.

In the following example, the NOWRAP attribute is placed properly within the appropriate <TR> tag with no values:

```
<TABLE>
<TR NOWRAP>
<TD>Cell No. 1</TD><TD>Cell No. 2</TD>
</TR>
<TR>
<TD>Cell No. 3</TD><TD>Cell No. 4</TD>
</TR>
</TABLE>
```

VALIGN

The VALIGN attribute controls the vertical alignment of text within the cells in a single row. It has four values:

`baseline`

The text in the row cells is aligned on a shared, common baseline.

`bottom`

The text in the row cells is aligned with the bottom of each cell.

`middle`

The text in the row cells is aligned with the middle of each cell. This is the VALIGN attribute default.

T

top

The text in the row cells is aligned with the top of each cell.

In the following example, the VALIGN setting has been established first as top and then as bottom:

```
<TABLE>
<TR VALIGN=top>
<TD>Cell No. 1</TD><TD>Cell No. 2</TD>
</TR>
<TR VALIGN=bottom>
<TD>Cell No. 3</TD><TD>Cell No. 4</TD>
</TR>
</TABLE>
```

> **NOTE** To establish horizontal alignment, use the ALIGN attribute. It's covered in its own section earlier in this entry.

Trim()

Category: VBScript

Type Function

Browser Support

	Navigator 3	Navigator 4	Explorer 3	Explorer 4
Macintosh				■
Windows			■	■

Syntax Trim(string)

The Trim() function removes any leading and trailing spaces from *string*. This function is often used on user input data to ensure that it has a consistent format. Trim() is the equivalent of combining both LTrim() and RTrim() (which remove leading or trailing spaces, respectively).

trim(" hi there! ")	returns	"hi there!"
trim("joe q. public ")	returns	"joe q. public"
trim(" ouch.")	returns	"ouch."

<TT>

Category: HTML

Browser Support

	Navigator 3	Navigator 4	Explorer 3	Explorer 4
Macintosh	■	■	■	■
Windows	■	■	■	■

May Contain	<APPLET>, <B>, <BASEFONT>, <BIG>, , <CITE>, <CODE>, <DFN>, <EM>, <FONT>, <I>, <IMG>, <INPUT>, <KBD>, <MAP>, <SAMP>, <SELECT>, <SMALL>, <STRIKE>, <STRONG>, <SUB>, <SUP>, <TEXTAREA>, <TT>, <U>, <VAR>
May Be Used In	<ADDRESS>, <APPLET>, <B>, <BIG>, <BLOCKQUOTE>, <CAPTION>, <CENTER>, <CITE>, <CODE>, <DD>, <DT>, <FONT>, <H1>, <H2>, <H3>, <H4>, <H5>, <H6>, <I>, <KBD>, <LI>, <P>, <SAMP>, <SMALL>, <STRIKE>, <STRONG>, <SUB>, <SUP>, <TD>, <TH>, <TT>, <U>
Attributes	None
Syntax	<TT>...</TT>

The <TT> tag displays a specified amount of text as teletype—text that has been rendered in fixed-width type as if it were produced by a typewriter. Everything written between the beginning and closing, or </TT>, tag will be displayed as teletype as shown in the example:

```
<TT>This text has been displayed as teletype using the TT tag.</TT>
```

Figures 1 and 2 display this HTML in Navigator 3 and Internet Explorer 3 for the Macintosh.

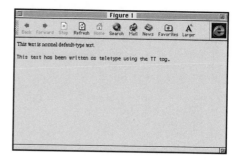

Figure 1

Teletype rendered using the <TT> tag compared with plain default text in Navigator 3 for the Macintosh.

Figure 2

Teletype rendered using the <TT> tag compared with plain default text in Internet Explorer 3 for the Macintosh.

T

The appearance of teletype text on a web page is also determined by browser font defaults—compare Figures 1 and 2, both of which display the same HTML page, as an example of this discrepancy.

<IMG> </IMG> ■ <SCRIPT LANGUAGE = "javascript"> </SCRIPT>
■ <SCRIPT LANGUAGE = "vbscript"> </SCRIPT> ■ <BGSOUND
SRC=gbv.wav LOOP=-1> </BGSOUND> ■ <APPLET CLASS=
"ester's_day" SRC="http://testsite/walla walla washington/"
</APPLET> ■ <FRAME></FRAME>■ <MARQUEE> </MARQUEE> ■
<HTML> </HTML> ■ <A> </A> ■ <OL> </OL> ■ <UL> </UL> ■ <MENU>
</MENU> ■ <STRONG> </STRONG> ■ <TD> </TD> ■ <TH> </TH>

U

<U>

Category: HTML

Browser Support		Navigator 3	Navigator 4	Explorer 3	Explorer 4
	Macintosh	■	■	■	■
	Windows	■	■	■	■

May Contain <APPLET>, <B>, <BASEFONT>, <BIG>, <BR>, <CITE>, <CODE>, <DFN>, <EM>, <FONT>, <I>, <IMG>, <INPUT>, <KBD>, <MAP>, <SAMP>, <SELECT>, <SMALL>, <STRIKE>, <STRONG>, <SUB>, <SUP>, <TEXTAREA>, <TT>, <VAR>

May Be Used In <ADDRESS>, <APPLET>, <B>, <BIG>, <BLOCKQUOTE>, <BODY>, <CAPTION>, <CENTER>, <CITE>, <CODE>, <DD>, <DT>, <FONT>, <H1>, <H2>, <H3>, <H4>, <H5>, <H6>, <I>, <KBD>, <LI>, <P>, <SAMP>, <SMALL>, <STRIKE>, <STRONG>, <SUB>, <SUP>, <TD>, <TH>, <TT>, <VAR>

Attributes None

Syntax <U>...</U>

The <U> tag underlines a specified amount of text. Everything written between the beginning and closing, or </U>, tags will be underlined as shown in the example:

```
<P>This text is normal default-type text.<BR>
<U>This text has been underlined using the U tag.</U>
```

Figure 1 displays this HTML in Navigator 3 for the Macintosh.

Figure 1

Text that has been underlined by using the <u> tag compared with plain default text.

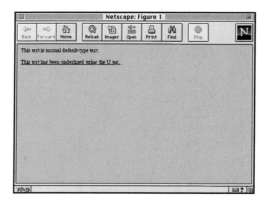

Figure 2 illustrates the problem with using the <U> tag in a web page. It has become standard procedure to display text links as underlined bits of text (although you can turn the underlining off in some browsers via Preferences menus). So most experienced visitors to your web page will react to an unlinked, but underlined, bit of text as some sort of <A> tag or LINK attribute mistake.

In other words, don't underline plain text on your page. Use italics (the <I> tag) or place emphasis by increasing the font size (the <BIG> tag) instead.

Figure 2

In the context of an ordinary web page—that is, a page with text links—underlined plain text looks like some kind of mistake.

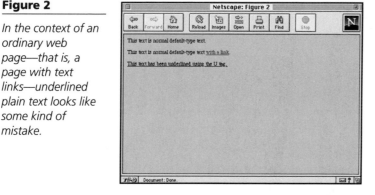

UBound()

Category: VBScript

Type	Function			

Browser Support

	Navigator 3	Navigator 4	Explorer 3	Explorer 4
Macintosh				▅
Windows			▅	▅

Syntax   Ubound(*arrayName* [,*dimension*])

The `UBound()` function returns the highest available index in *arrayName*. This enables you to determine the size of the array, such as how many elements it contains. Because the first element in an array is typically at index 0, the total number of elements in the array is `ubound(`*arrayName*`)+1`.

```
names=array("harry","bill")
lastidx=ubound(names)
```

In the preceding example, `lastidx` will be assigned the value 1 because this array contains two elements, the second being at index 1. This also means that the array contains `ubound()+1` elements in total, or 2. You can use this value to construct a loop if you need to perform some operation on each element in an array.

```
for j=0 to ubound(names)
 some code using names(j)
 next
```

If your array contains more than one dimension, you can specify which dimension to report the ubound to by using the *dimension* parameter. Consider the three-dimensional array autos:

```
dim autos(20,5,2)
```

For the each dimension in the array autos:

`ubound(autos,1)`	returns	19
`ubound(autos,2)`	returns	4
`ubound(autos,3)`	returns	1

UCase( )

Category: VBScript

Type	Function

Browser Support

	Navigator 3	Navigator 4	Explorer 3	Explorer 4
Macintosh				▓
Windows			▓	▓

Syntax `UCase(`*string*`)`

The `UCase()` function converts all lowercase characters in *string* to uppercase. Any characters that are already uppercase, or non-alphabetical, remain unchanged. If *string* is null, then null is returned.

`ucase("crenshaw")`	returns	"CRENSHAW"
`ucase("HONEYdew")`	returns	"HONEYDEW"
`ucase("cAnteLOupe!!??")`	returns	"CANTELOUPE!!??"

U

Typically, you would use either the `LCase()` or `UCase()` function to convert user-input data before performing a string comparison. For instance, suppose you need to test whether a user entered the string "yes." However, string comparisons are case-sensitive, and you don't know what sort of capitalization the user typed in his input—thus, you convert his input to a known case before performing the comparison:

```
if ucase(userinput)="YES" then…
```

<UL>

Category: HTML

Browser Support

	Navigator 3	Navigator 4	Explorer 3	Explorer 4
Macintosh	███	███	███	███
Windows	███	███	███	███

May Contain `<LI>`

May Be Used In `<BLOCKQUOTE>`, `<BODY>`, `<CENTER>`, `<DD>`, `<DIV>`, `<FORM>`, `<LI>`, `<TD>`, `<TH>`

Attributes `CLASS, COMPACT, ID, TYPE`

Syntax `<UL>…</UL>`

The `<UL>` tag creates a simple, bulleted list of items. A closing, or `</UL>` tag, is required

The following example is a simple `<UL>` list:

```
<UL>
<LI>This item
<LI>That item
<LI>Another item
</UL>
```

Each item in a `<UL>` list should be preceded with an `<LI>` tag. See the `<LI>` tag entry for more information on this tag, which is used in four kinds of lists.

> **NOTE** If you want to create a numbered list instead of an unnumbered list, use the `<OL>` tag. See the `<OL>` entry elsewhere in this book for more information.

Figures 1, 2, 3, and 4 illustrate this simple `<UL>` list in Navigator 3 and Internet Explorer 3 for the Macintosh and for Windows.

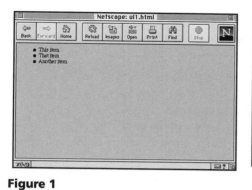

Figure 1

A simple <UL> list in Navigator 3 for the Macintosh.

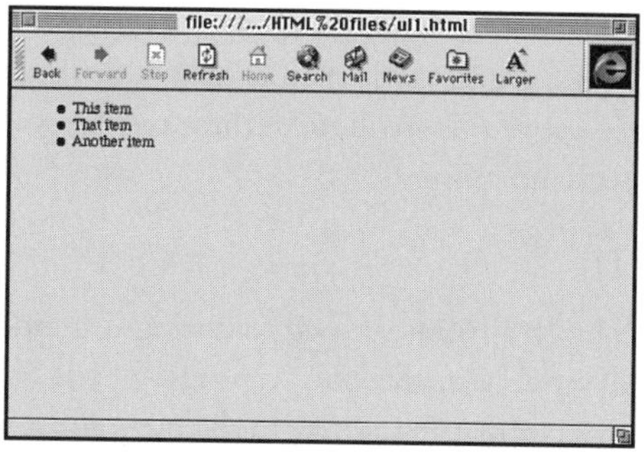

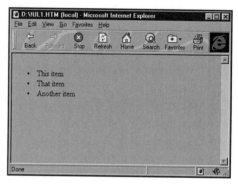

Figure 2

A simple <UL> list in Internet Explorer 3 for the Macintosh.

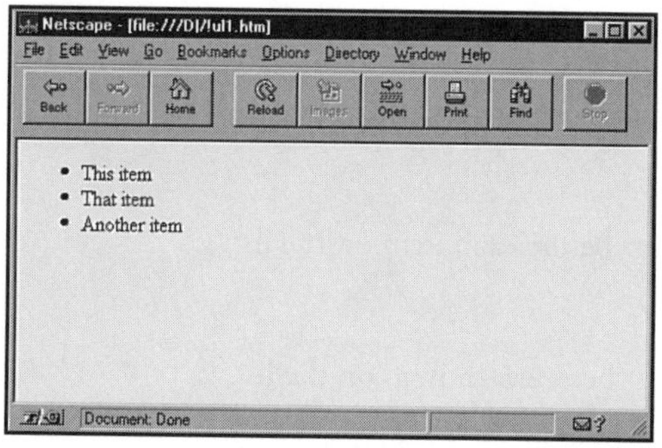

Figure 3

A simple <UL> list in Navigator 3 for Windows.

Figure 4

A simple <UL> list in Internet Explorer 3 for Windows.

CLASS

The CLASS attribute is used to specify the name of a style sheets as it applies to a specific selection on a web page. See the "Cascading Style Sheets Basics" chapter and any individual, related style sheets entries elsewhere in the book for more information.

COMPACT

The COMPACT attribute tells the browser that items in the list are short, so the list can be tightened accordingly. When this attribute is used within a <DL> list in Navigator 3, for example, the browser will display two items on one line.

U

In <UL> lists, however, neither Navigator 3 nor Internet Explorer 3 will display COMPACT-specified lists any differently than regular <UL> lists, even when the list items are only one character long. So use of this attribute in these two browsers, on either the Macintosh or Windows, seems to serve no purpose.

ID

The ID attribute is used to distinguish individual selections in a web page as pertaining to the use of style sheets. See the "Cascading Style Sheets Basics" chapter and any individual, related style sheets entries elsewhere in the book for more information.

TYPE

The TYPE attribute specifies different kinds of bullets.

There are three TYPE values:

circle

This value causes an open, ring-like bullet to appear before each item on the list.

disc

This value causes a solid, typical bullet to appear before each item on the list.

square

This value causes a solid, square bullet to appear before each item on the list.

In the following example, square bullets are specified using the square value:

```
<UL TYPE=square>
<LI>Tom
<IL>Dick
<LI>Harry
</UL>
```

Figures 5, 6, and 7 illustrate short <UL> lists with all three bullet type values specified in Navigator 3 for Macintosh and Windows and Internet Explorer 3 for Macintosh.

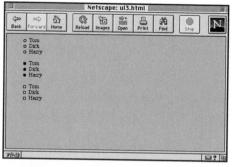

Figure 5

<UL> lists of all three *TYPE* settings in Navigator 3 for the Macintosh.

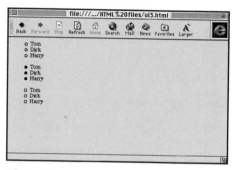

Figure 6

<UL> lists of all three *TYPE* settings in Internet Explorer 3 for the Macintosh.

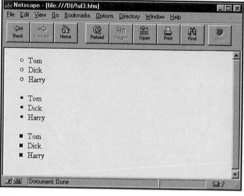

Figure 7

<UL> lists of all three *TYPE* settings in Navigator 3 for Windows.

See the <LI> tag entry for more information on the TYPE attribute.

---

unescape()

Category: JavaScript, JScript

Type	Function

Browser Support

	Navigator 3	Navigator 4	Explorer 3	Explorer 4
Macintosh	■	■	☐	■
Windows	■	■	■	■

Syntax unescape(*string*)

U

The unescape( ) function returns a *string* decoded from the Latin ISO-1 character set into the local character set, including spaces, punctuation, and other special characters that were represented as escape codes.

For instance:

`unescape("Hey%20buddy")`   returns the string "Hey buddy"

In the preceding example, the escape code %20 represents a space.

As described in the entry for escape( ), you would use the unescape( ) function to read data that needed to be encoded before passing across the network. Use unescape( ) to restore spaces, punctuation, and other special characters to the string.

For instance, when you retrieve a cookie, its value was probably escaped to encode spaces and punctuation (as explained in the entry for the Escape( ) function). Therefore, you need to unescape( ) the cookie value upon retrieving it:

`cookval=unescape(document.cookie.substring(6,11))`

untaint()
Category: JavaScript 1.1

	Type	Function

Browser Support

	Navigator 3	Navigator 4	Explorer 3	Explorer 4
Macintosh	■	■	☐	☐
Windows	■	■	☐	☐

Syntax untaint(*value*)

To properly use the untaint( ) function you **must** read the entry for taint( )—see the taint( ) function.

You can use untaint( ) to create an "unmarked" copy of the value of a variable, property, function, or object. Typically, you would use this function to "undo" a taint( ) that you have previously created.

For instance, suppose you create a tainted copy of the value of the window object's status property:

`tstatus = taint(window.status)`

You may later want to undo this taint, so that the value can be passed across the network or accessed by another script without tainting restrictions:

`tstatus = untaint(window.status)`

If you don't specify a parameter, you can use untaint( ) to remove tainting from the entire script:

`untaint()`

TIP   The entry for `taint()` contains a list of all JavaScript properties that are tainted by default. You *can* use the `untaint()` function to create untainted copies of these values.

U

</STRONG> ■ <TD> </TD> ■ <TH> </TH> ■ <TABLE> </TABLE> ■
<IMG> </IMG> ■ <SCRIPT LANGUAGE = "javascript"> </SCRIPT>
■ <SCRIPT LANGUAGE = "vbscript"> </SCRIPT> ■ <BGSOUND
SRC=gbv.wav LOOP=-1> </BGSOUND> ■ <APPLET CLASS=
"ester's_day" SRC="http://testsite/walla walla washington/"
</APPLET> ■ <FRAME></FRAME>■ <MARQUEE> </MARQUEE> ■
<HTML> </HTML> ■ <A> </A> ■ <OL> </OL> ■ <UL> </UL> ■ <MENU>
</MENU> ■ <STRONG> </STRONG> ■ <TD> </TD> ■ <TH> </TH>

V

<VAR>

Category: HTML

	Navigator 3	Navigator 4	Explorer 3	Explorer 4
Macintosh	▬	▬	▬	▬
Windows	▬	▬	▬	▬

Browser Support

May Contain   <APPLET>, <B>, <BASEFONT>, <BIG>, <BR>, <CITE>, <CODE>, <DFN>, <EM>, <FONT>, <I>, <IMG>, <INPUT>, <KBD>, <MAP>, <SAMP>, <SELECT>, <SMALL>, <STRIKE>, <STRONG>, <SUB>, <SUP>, <TEXTAREA>, <TT>, <U>, <VAR>

May Be Used In   <ADDRESS>, <APPLET>, <B>, <BIG>, <BLOCKQUOTE>, <CAPTION>, <CENTER>, <CITE>, <CODE>, <DD>, <DT>, <FONT>, <H1>, <H2>, <H3>, <H4>, <H5>, <H6>, <I>, <KBD>, <LI>, <P>, <SAMP>, <SMALL>, <STRIKE>, <STRONG>, <SUB>, <SUP>, <TD>, <TH>, <TT>, <U>

Attributes   None

Syntax   <VAR>...</VAR>

The <VAR> tag is an older tag that specifies a bit of text as a programming variable. Everything written between the beginning and closing, or </VAR>, tags will be displayed in italics as shown in the example:

```
<VAR> This text is displayed in italics by using the VAR tag. </VAR>.
This text is plain default text.
```

Figure 1 displays this HTML in Navigator 3 for the Macintosh.

Figure 1

Text written in italics by using the <VAR> tag compared to plain default text.

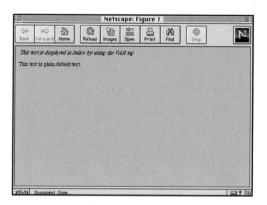

There's no functional difference between italicized text created using the <VAR> tag versus using the <I> tag, <CITE> tag, or the <EM> tag, as shown in Figure 2. Use any of these tags for italicizing text as you prefer.

Figure 2

The <VAR> tag versus the <I> tag, <CITE> tag, and/or the <EM> tag—there's no difference.

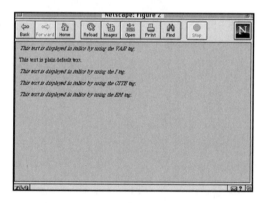

vertical-align

Category: Cascading Style Sheets

Browser Support

	Navigator 3	Navigator 4	Explorer 3	Explorer 4
Macintosh				
Windows				▬▬▬▬▬

Applies To   Inline and replaced elements

Syntax   vertical-align: *value*

This property enables you to control the vertical alignment of inline text as well as images. Some of these values correspond to what the HTML attribute `align` accomplishes. The alignment can be set according to some other elements on the page, such as the parent of the current item, or a percentage of the line height. Most of the keyword values you can use are relative to the parent of the element in question. These are:

- `baseline` ensures that the baseline of the element is aligned with the baseline of the parent.
- `sub` puts the element in subscript.
- `super` puts the element in superscript.
- `text-top` aligns the top of the element with the top of the font of the parent element.
- `middle` places the vertical midpoint of the element aligned with the baseline of the parent plus half the x-height (x-height refers to the height of the lowercase letters of a font). `middle` is often used for aligning images.
- `text-bottom` aligns the bottom of the element with the bottom of the font of the parent element.

Two other keyword values are relative not to the parent, but instead to the formatted line that the element is part of. These are:

- `top` aligns the top of the element with the tallest element on the line.
- `bottom` aligns the bottom of the element with the lowest element on the line.

Finally, you can also use percentage values to specify `vertical-align`. Percentage values refer to the `line-height` of the element itself. A positive value raises the alignment while a negative value lowers the baseline appropriately. A value of –100% actually places the baseline of the element exactly the same place as the baseline of the text line underneath.

```
h1 { vertical-align: top }

<h1 style="vertical-align: 40%">
```

V

Explorer 4 only recognizes the sub and super values of vertical-align (see Figure 1).

Figure 1

Vertically aligned text with the super keyword is good for footnotes.

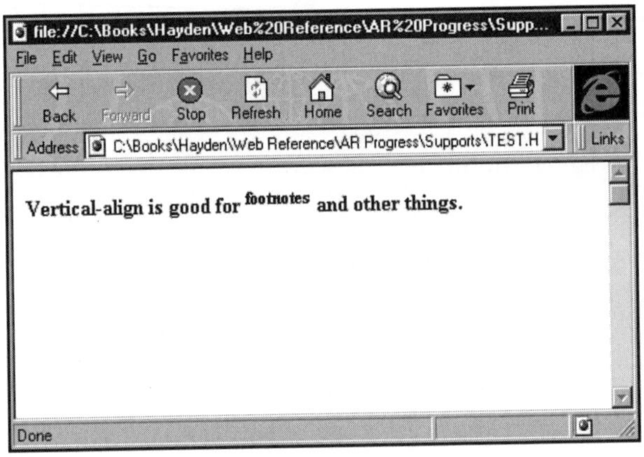

> Vertical-align is good for ᶠᵒᵒᵗⁿᵒᵗᵉˢ and other things.

verticalAlign

Category: JavaScript Style Sheets

Type	Property

Browser Support

	Navigator 3	Navigator 4	Explorer 3	Explorer 4
Macintosh		■		
Windows		■		

Applies To	All elements
Inherited	Yes
Syntax	verticalAlign = "*value*"

The verticalAlign property can be used as a style for all elements, and it is used to define the vertical positioning of the element in the document. There are three types of positioning that can be used:

- Vertical position relative to the parent element (type 1).
- Vertical position relative to the formatted line that the element is on (type 2).
- Vertical positioning of the element in relation to itself (type 3).

The three types of positioning refer to three different uses for the verticalAlign property. An HTML element can be vertically aligned three different ways. The first six values in the following list are used for type 1 positioning, the next two values (top and bottom) for type 2, and the last value (percentage) for type 3.

Type 1:

- baseline aligns the baseline of the element with the baseline of the parent element.
- sub displays the element in subscript.
- super displays the element in superscript.
- middle is typically used for images, and will align the vertical midpoint of the image with the baseline of the parent plus one half of the parent's x-height. x-height is the height of the character X.
- text-top aligns the top of the element with the top of the parent element.
- text-bottom aligns the bottom of the element with the bottom of the parent element.

Type 2:

- top aligns the element with the top of tallest element on the same formatted line.
- bottom aligns the element with the bottom of the lowest element on the formatted line.

Type 3:

- percentage is applied against the line height of the current element and does not relate itself to any other elements. verticalAlign = +25 will move the element a quarter of the way up the current line height.

WARNING Use caution when using **top** and **bottom** elements because it is easy to find yourself in the condition in which unsolvable element dependencies will get you into an unending loop.

Using the verticalAlign value of "middle", we can define a style to be used for <img> elements that will cause the text immediately following the image to always be displayed in the middle of the image.

```
<html>
<style TYPE="text/javascript">
tags.img.verticalAlign = "middle"
</style>
<body>
<img src="school.gif">
Text that would display after the image is vertically
aligned in the middle of the image.
</body>
</html>
```

V

The JSSS in this code segment can be broken down as follows:

- ▪ `tags` is one of the methods of defining JSSS styles. The `tags` definition denotes that the element immediately following it in the dot notation will be one of the accepted HTML elements.
- ▪ `img` is the HTML element that is being assigned a style. This may be any valid HTML element.
- ▪ `verticalAlign` is the style that is being defined for the `<img>` element. This may be any valid JSSS style.
- ▪ `"middle"` is the value of the style `verticalAlign`. This value means that the HTML element defined with this style will be aligned in the middle of the parent HTML element.

Figure 1 shows the document that would be generated from the previous code segment if the JSSS style defintion for `verticalAlign` were removed.

Figure 1

With no verticalAlign style.

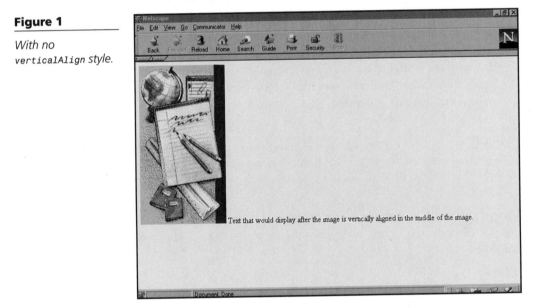

Figure 2 shows what the document will look like after the style has been applied.

Figure 2

With verticalAlign style.

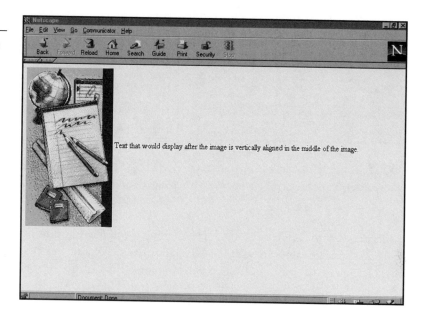

The most important use of this style is the use defined previously. The other uses, in which the verticalAlign is used on a formatted line or with the single element are less useful in style sheets and can get you into infinite loops of display styles if caution is not taken during style definition.

Remember that previously defined style sheets that are linked to documents can have their styles overridden by styles within the document. Overriding a previous style may cause problems such as the loop discussed earlier.

visibility

Category: Cascading Style Sheets

Browser Support

	Navigator 3	Navigator 4	Explorer 3	Explorer 4
Macintosh	▢	▢	▢	▢
Windows	▢	▢	▢	▉

Applies To All elements

Syntax visibility: *value*

V

The visibility property enables you to decide the initial display state of an element and whether or not it is displayed on the page. This affects the appearance of a page, but it doesn't affect the layout. The element is still there, you just can't see it (see Figures 1 and 2).

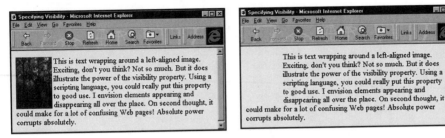

Figure 1

Now you see it. Text wrapping around an image.

Figure 2

Now you don't. The image is set to hidden, *but the text still wraps around it.*

By default, visibility is set to inherit, meaning it will inherit its display state from its parent. The other possible values are visible, which displays the object, and hidden, which makes it invisible. Here is the way the elements will look for either visible or inherit:

```
h1 { visibility: visible }
h1 { visibility: inherit }
```

When combined with scripting, setting or changing the visibility of an object can create some interesting results and simple, but clever, animation.

</STRONG> ■ <TD> </TD> ■ <TH> </TH> ■ <TABLE> </TABLE> ■
<IMG> </IMG> ■ <SCRIPT LANGUAGE = "javascript"> </SCRIPT>
■ <SCRIPT LANGUAGE = "vbscript"> </SCRIPT> ■ <BGSOUND
SRC=gbv.wav LOOP=-1> </BGSOUND> ■ <APPLET CLASS=
"ester's_day" SRC="http://testsite/walla walla washington/"
</APPLET> ■ <FRAME></FRAME>■ <MARQUEE> </MARQUEE> ■ <HTML>
</HTML> ■ <A> </A>■ <OL> </OL>■ <UL> </UL> ■ <MENU> </MENU>
■ <STRONG> </STRONG> ■ <TD> </TD> ■ <TH> </TH>

W

<WBR>

Category: HTML

Browser Support		Navigator 3	Navigator 4	Explorer 3	Explorer 4
	Macintosh	■	■	■	■
	Windows	■	■	■	■

May Contain <APPLET>, <B>, <BASEFONT>, <BIG>, <BR>, <CITE>, <CODE>, <DFN>, <EM>, <FONT>, <I>, <IMG>, <INPUT>, <KBD>, <MAP>, <SAMP>, <SELECT>, <SMALL>, <STRIKE>, <STRONG>, <SUB>, <SUP>, <TEXTAREA>, <TT>, <U>, <VAR>

May Be Used In <ADDRESS>, <APPLET>, <B>, <BIG>, <BLOCKQUOTE>, <CAPTION>, <CENTER>, <CITE>, <CODE>, <DD>, <DT>, <FONT>, <H1>, <H2>, <H3>, <H4>, <H5>, <H6>, <I>, <KBD>, <LI>, <P>, <SAMP>, <SMALL>, <STRIKE>, <STRONG>, <SUB>, <SUP>, <TD>, <TH>, <TT>, <U>

Attributes None

Syntax <WBR>...</WBR>

The <WBR> tag inserts a soft line break in the very rare event that one is needed within a line of text specified by the <NOBR> tag.

In the following example, the first line of text will not break, no matter what a visitor does to his browser window:

```
<NOBR>No matter how much the browser window is narrowed, this line of text won't
➥break, nope, no sir, never.
<WBR>This line of text, however, will, absolutely, positively, every time, yes
➥sir, always.</NOBR>
```

The second sentence follows the <WBR> tag but falls within the <NOBR> and </NOBR> tags, so the browser window will insert a line break, if necessary, at the place where <WBR> is written in.

Figures 1, 2, 3, and 4 illustrate this comparison in Navigator 3 and Internet Explorer 3 for the Macintosh and for Windows.

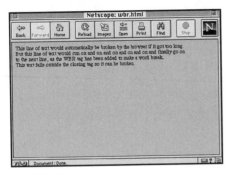

Figure 1

<NOBR> versus <WBR> in Navigator 3 for the Macintosh.

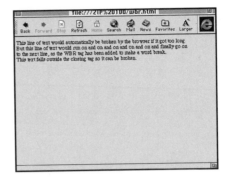

Figure 2

<NOBR> versus <WBR> in Internet Explorer 3 for the Macintosh.

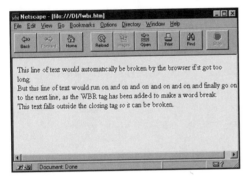

Figure 3

<NOBR> versus <WBR> in Navigator 3 for Windows.

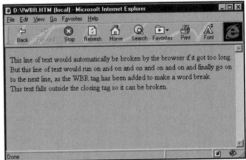

Figure 4

<NOBR> versus <WBR> in Internet Explorer 3 for Windows.

Weekday()

Category: VBScript

Type	Function			

Browser Support		Navigator 3	Navigator 4	Explorer 3	Explorer 4
	Macintosh	☐	☐	☐	▬
	Windows	☐	☐	▬	▬

Syntax Weekday(date, [firstDay])

The Weekday() function accepts a *date* and returns an integer representing the day of the week. Sunday is considered the first day of the week, unless you specify an alternate first day via the *firstDay* parameter, from 1 (Sunday) to 7 (Saturday).

The function returns a value from 1 (Sunday) to 7 (Saturday), unless *date* is null or invalid, in which case null is returned or an error occurs. However, if you've specified an alternate *firstDay*, then the value that the function returns is shifted.

```
weekday("may 25 1997")        returns  1 (Sunday)
```

```
weekday("may 25 1997",7)      returns  2 (Sunday, because Saturday (day 7) was specified as being day 1)
```

```
weekday("may 25 1997",2)      returns  7 (Sunday, because Monday (day 2) was specified as being day 1)
```

To avoid confusion, you can also use the following constants in place of the numbers 1 to 7 to represent each day: vbSunday, vbMonday, vbTuesday, vbWednesday, vbThursday, vbFriday, vbSaturday.

```
weekday("may 25, 1997",vbSaturday)     returns  2
```

WeekDayName( )

Category: VBScript

Type	Function				

Browser Support		Navigator 3	Navigator 4	Explorer 3	Explorer 4
	Macintosh	☐	☐	☐	■
	Windows	☐	☐	■	■

Syntax WeekDayName(*weekday*, [*abbrev*], [*firstDay*])

The WeekDayName( ) function accepts a number from 1 to 7 representing a *weekday* and returns the name of that day.

If you omit *abbrev* or specify false, then the full day name is returned; if specified as true, a three-letter abbreviation is returned.

Sunday is considered the first day of the week, unless you specify an alternate first day via the *firstDay* parameter, from 1 (Sunday) to 7 (Saturday).

```
WeekDayName(1)          returns    "Sunday"
```

```
WeekDayName(1,true)     returns    "Sun"
```

```
WeekDayName(2,false,3)  returns    "Wednesday" (because Tuesday (day 3) was specified as being day 1)
```

To avoid confusion, you can also use the following constants in place of the numbers 1 to 7 to represent each day: vbSunday, vbMonday, vbTuesday, vbWednesday, vbThursday, vbFriday, vbSaturday.

```
WeekDayName(2,false,vbTuesday)     returns        "Wednesday"
```

W

white-space
Category: Cascading Style Sheets

Browser Support

	Navigator 3	Navigator 4	Explorer 3	Explorer 4
Macintosh	☐	▉	☐	☐
Windows	☐	▉	☐	☐

Applies To Block level elements

Syntax `white-space: value`

With the `white-space` property, you can finally instruct the browser on exactly what it should do when it comes across whitespace within an element. Whitespace includes spaces in between words, tabs, and even the returns at the end of a line. If you set this property to `normal`, the default value, the whitespace will collapse as it normally does with current HTML. That is, when browsers come upon a number of spaces in traditional `<p>` HTML text, they collapse that whitespace to a single space. If you set it to `pre`, all extra spaces will be respected as if you had used the `<pre>` tag. Using `nowrap` tells the browser *not* to wrap to a new line unless it comes across a `<br>` tag.

`h1 { white-space: pre }`

 Netscape Navigator supports `pre`, but not `nowrap`.

whiteSpace
Category: JavaScript Style Sheets

Type Property

Browser Support

	Navigator 3	Navigator 4	Explorer 3	Explorer 4
Macintosh	☐	▉	☐	☐
Windows	☐	▉	☐	☐

Applies To Block-level elements

Inherited Yes

Syntax `whiteSpace = "value"`

The `whiteSpace` property is used to define how `whiteSpace` in an element will be handled. Whitespace is the blank space the can appear between words on a text line. This blank space may appear at the beginning or end of line as well as between words in the middle of a line, and may be purposefully used to make text appear set off from other text on the same line. `whiteSpace` only has two possible values that can be used when defining it in your JavaScript Style Sheets.

- ■ `"normal"` treats whitespace with the default HTML method. The whitespace is collapsed with in the element.

- ■ `"pre"` causes whitespace to be treated in the same manner as whitespace in the <pre> tag. All whitespace is displayed exactly as defined.

Defining a JavaScript Style Sheets class that can be used for any block-level element using the "all" notation gives you the capability to apply the class to each HTML element individually. In the following basic code sample, if the `squeezedocument` variable is set to "No" then all elements with the class of `whiteclass` will be displayed as inputted.

```
<html>
<style TYPE="text/javascript">

var squeezedocument
squeezedocument = "Yes"

if (squeezedocument == "No"){
classes.whiteclass.all.whiteSpace = "pre";
}
if (squeezedocument == "Yes"){
classes.whiteclass.all.whiteSpace = "normal";
}
</style>
<body>
<p class="whiteclass"> This paragraph will
squeeze                    together
when squeezedocument is on.
<div class="whiteclass"> This division will
also               squeeze when
squeezedocument is on.</div>
<p> This paragraph will ALWAYS                squeeze
together because it does
not use the class=whiteclass
</body>
</html>
```

The single line of code in the `if` statement in the preceeding example can be broken down as follows:

- ■ `classes` one of the methods of defining JSSS styles. The `classes` definition describes the element immediately following it if the dot notation will be a class name.

W

- `whiteclass` is the class name that is being defined. A class name may be any alphanumeric combination.

- `all` defines this class to be a class the can be used with all HTML elements.

- `whiteSpace` is the style property that is being defined for the element.

- `"normal"` and `"pre"` are the values of the style properties.

The results of the preceding code sample are displayed in Figure 1. Notice that the first <p> and the <div> will be displayed as they are entered when `squeezedocument` is off.

Figure 1

Squeezedocument is off, text displays as entered.

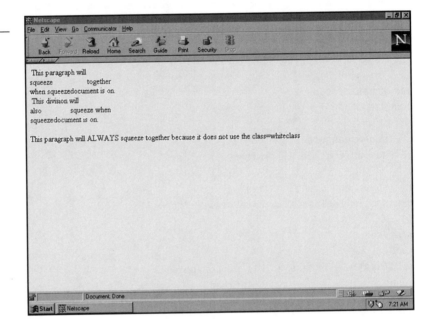

In Figure 2, whitespace will be removed when `squeezedocument` is on because the property value is changed to `"normal"`.

Figure 2

Squeezedocument is on, text displays squeeze together.

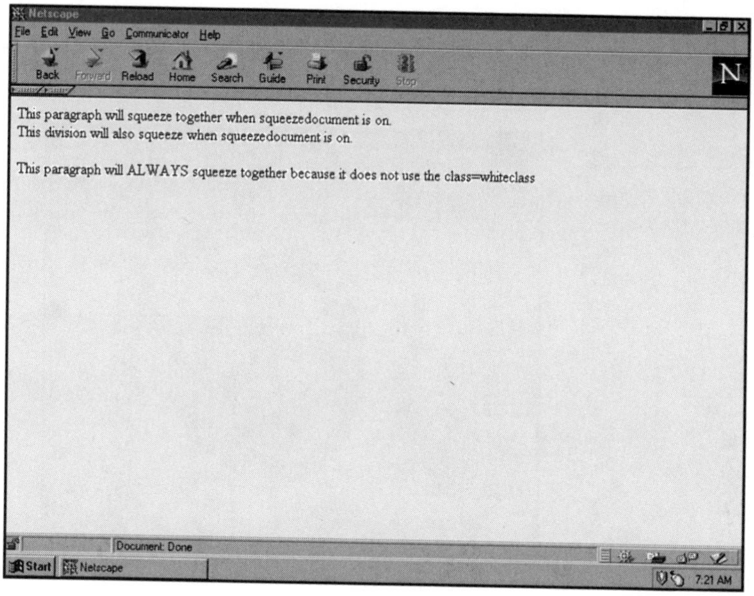

Note in both figures that the second <p> will take on the default whitespace behavior because it has no class definition.

width

Category: Cascading Style Sheets

Browser Support

	Navigator 3	Navigator 4	Explorer 3	Explorer 4
Macintosh		▬		
Windows		▬		

Applies To All elements

Syntax width: *value*

With the width property, you can pre-set the width for tags or elements on your page in units or percentages. The width property works much in the same way as the HTML width property for tags. The units may be any of those discussed in Appendix D. With the width and height properties, you can force text or an image to a certain dimension. You may also use the auto keyword that reverts the width of the element to the width it would normally have on the page. auto is especially useful for inherited attributes.

```
h1 { width: 200px }

<h1 style="width: 150%">
```

W

Explorer 4 supports `width` for replaced elements, though not for text (see Figure 1).

Figure 1

The original image, followed by images with greater width.

The first image on the left shows the original image size. The second is set to 100 pixels wide. The third is set to 50%. Percentage values are relative to the size of the browser window. Thus, the image is half as wide as the entire window.

In an ideal browser, when you set `width` on an image, that image is stretched to fit the declared space. It stretches out of proportion, so the height of the image will not change.

 Explorer 4, however, will always increase an image's size proportionally if only the `width` or the `height` is set.

If you set the `height` property, however, to `auto` (see the description of `height`), then the height will indeed change proportionally to the change in width. Theoretically, all of this also works on block-level text elements.

width

Category: JavaScript Style Sheets

Type	Property				
Browser Support		Navigator 3	Navigator 4	Explorer 3	Explorer 4
	Macintosh	☐	■	☐	☐
	Windows	☐	■	☐	☐
Applies To	Block-level elements and replace elements				
Inherited	No				
Syntax	Width = "*value*"				

The `width` style is most useful for sizing the width of image in the document. Although this style can be applied to all block-level elements, it is meant for the purpose of changing the width of `<img>`. Only two types of values are allowed for `width`:

- ▪ `"length"` is the numeric value for the exact width of the element.
- ▪ `"auto"` is the default style. `"auto"` is best used when the `height` of the element has been assigned a `length` and the element should be auto-sized (scaled) to the correct height.

`width` and `height` are compatible properties and you should use caution when setting both property styles. Explicitly setting both properties may produce an HTML element that is no longer displayed to scale. By specifying the `width` property and leaving the `height` as `"auto"` you are more likely to get a reasonably scaled element.

The following example shows two class defintions for scaling and `<img>` element. Notice that for the `bclass`, both the `height` and `width` have be explicitly set.

```
<html>
<style TYPE="text/javascript">
classes.hclass.img.width = "10"
with (classes.bclass.img) {
width = "1000"
height = "10"
}
</style>
<body>
<img class="hclass" src="school.gif">
<img class="bclass" src="school.gif">
</body>
</html>
```

Using the preceding sample you let the first `<img>` auto scale the `height` after defining `width`, whereas in the second image, you have set both properties.

W

> **WARNING** The `width` property does not function as defined in Netscape Navigator 4.0.

The second image is completely out of scale and does not display well because both the `height` and `width` were defined explicitly.

The important JSSS code that was used to define the document in the previous code sample is:

```
classes.hclass.img.width = "10"
with (classes.bclass.img) {
width = "1000"
height = "10"
}
```

The code can be broken down as follows:

- `with {…} do` is a JavaScript function used in our example to define multiple style properties for a single HTML element `<img>` class all within a single statement.
- `classes` is one of the methods of defining JSSS styles. The `classes` definition describes the element immediately following it if the dot notation will be a class name.
- `hclass` and `bclass` are the class names that are being defined. A class name may be any alphanumeric combination.
- `img` is the html element that is being assigned a style in both of the classes. This may be any valid html element.
- `height` and `width` are the style properties that are being defined for the element.
- `"10"` and `"1000"` are the values of the style properties.

This JSSS defintion uses two different methods to define JSSS class style properties. One is a single, complete line defintion and the other uses a `with {…} do` grouping to define multiple styles.

window

Category: JavaScript, JScript, VBScript

Type	Object			
Browser Support		Navigator 3	Navigator 4	Explorer 3	Explorer 4

	Navigator 3	Navigator 4	Explorer 3	Explorer 4
Macintosh	■	■	☐	■
Windows	■	■	■	■

Properties closed, defaultStatus, document, frames, history, innerHeight, innerWidth, location, name, opener, outerHeight, outerWidth, pageXOffset, pageYOffset, parent, self, status, top, window

Methods	`alert()`, `blur()`, `clearTimeout()`, `close()`, `confirm()`, `find()`, `focus()`, `home()`, `moveBy()`, `moveTo()`, `open()`, `prompt()`, `resizeBy()`, `resizeTo()`, `scroll()`, `scrollBy()`, `scrollTo()`, `setTimeout()`, `stop()`
Event Handlers	`onBlur`, `onError`, `onFocus`, `onLoad`, `onUnload`
Subset Of	Nothing—window is the top-level object
Syntax	`[windowName.]`*`property`* OR `[windowName.]method(`*`parameters`*`)`

The `window` object encompasses all other objects. It is King of the Hill. The `window` object gives you direct access to features such as the browser's status bar, dialog boxes, and the ability to create and destroy additional windows.

For scripting purposes, all of the `window` object properties and methods also apply to the `frame` object, which is itself a `window` object. (See `frame` object.)

There are several occasions where you'll want to use the `window` object—opening and closing new windows, of course, but also when using a script in one window to influence the content in another. In other scenarios, you may use the `window` object to access the browser's status bar as a way to communicate messages to the user. Important notices can be made to pop up in an alert box, which the user must acknowledge.

As the topmost object, the `window` object is quite flexible and powerful. Of course, because all other objects reside below the `window` object, you're technically *always* using the `window` object, even without specifying it!

> **NOTE** For all properties and methods of the `window` object, you need only specify the `windowName` portion of the syntax when referring to a window other than that within which the script resides.

> **NOTE** Because the window object is the top-level object, it does not need to be explicitly named when referring to the current window. For example, you may refer to the `window.alert()` method simply as `alert()`. However, the properties of `parent`, `self`, `top`, and `window` refer to specific windows and cannot be preceded by a reference to the current window. That is, do not refer `window.self.status`, but refer to it as `self.status`. The only time you must refer to the window object is opening or closing a window with the `window.open()` and `window.close()` methods, or when referencing a window other than the one in which your script resides.

W

The window object only works on Windows 95 machines in Internet Explorer 3 and 4.

closed property

The closed property is a read-only Boolean value that indicates if a window is closed. When a window, which you have previously opened, is closed, the window object that represents it will still exist, and its closed property will be set to true. Otherwise, if the window remains open, the closed property will be set to false.

You can use this to test if the user has closed a window that your script has created. Because you cannot modify any properties of a closed window, you should use a test such as the one below to be sure the target window is still open.

```
if (windowName.closed)
 { void(0) }
else { statements if window is open }
```

In the preceding example, nothing will occur if the window has been closed; otherwise, *statements if window is open* will execute.

 Internet Explorer 3 does not support the closed property.

defaultStatus property

The defaultStatus property is a string that represents the message that is displayed on the browser's status bar when the mouse is not over any link or image map. When the mouse does move over a link, its URL is normally displayed in the status bar, although you can show alternative messages using the onMouseOver and onMouseOut events of the link object. (See the link object.)

By default, the defaultStatus property is empty, and no message is displayed in the status bar until the mouse moves over a hyperlink. At any time, you can assign a string to this property, which will then be displayed in the status bar.

```
defaultStatus="Please select a link on the page"
```

To change the defaultStatus of a window other than that in which the script resides:

```
windowName.defaultStatus="Please select a link on the page"
```

document property

The document property is an object with which you can access characteristics of the HTML document that resides within the window, such as its color properties, or output new HTML content to the page—see the document object.

```
windowName.document.property
```

or

```
windowName.document.method()
```

> **NOTE** Remember that you don't need to specify windowName unless you intend to reference a window other than the one containing the script.

frames property

The frames property is an array of all the frames within the specified window. Each element in the frames[] array is reference to a frame object—see the frame object.

```
windowName.frames[index].property
```

or

```
windowName.frames[index].method()
```

> **NOTE** Remember that you don't need to specify *windowName* unless you intend to reference a window other than the one containing the script.

history property

The history property references the history object, which possesses a list of URLs recently visited by the user. You can use this object, for instance, to simulate clicking the browser's Back and Forward buttons in either a window or frame—see the history object.

innerHeight property

The innerHeight property reflects the height, measured in pixels, of the content area of the brower window (that is, where the web page is displayed). You can assign a new value to this property to instantly make the content area shorter or taller.

```
windowName.innerHeight=450
```

W

> The innerHeight property is new to JavaScript 1.2, and therefore only supported in Netscape Navigator 4.

innerWidth **property**

The innerWidth property reflects the horizontal width, measured in pixels, of the content area of the brower window (that is, where the web page is displayed). You can assign a new value to this property to instantly make the content area thinner or wider.

```
windowName.innerWidth=500
```

 The innerWidth property is new to JavaScript 1.2, and therefore only supported in Netscape Navigator 4.

location **property**

The location property references the location object, which contains information about the URL of the specified window. You can use this object to access or, more commonly, modify the window's URL, thereby redirecting it to a new page—see the location object.

name **property**

This can be confusing: a window may actually have two different "names":

1. The name property contains the name of the window as specified in the *winName* parameter of the open() method. This name is typically used in the target attribute of the <a> and <form> tags.

2. When referencing a window in a script statement, you use *windowName*, which is the variable name the window is assigned to, as specified in the *windowName*=open() construction. (See the open() method.) This is *not* related to the name property.

Consider the following call to the open() method (see the open() method entry for a full explanation):

```
window1=open("","New Window","toolbar=yes,location=no,directories=no,
status=yes,menubar=yes,scrollbars=yes,resizable=no,width=640,height=400")
```

In this example, the name property for this newly created window object would contain the value "New Window", because that is the specified *winName* parameter in the open() call. Distinctly, the variable window1 contains this window object. Later, you would use this variable name when calling a property or method of this window; for example, window1.close().

The name property is read-only; it's not often used, although you may use it when constructing HTML strings to output to a window (see the document object), within which you require specified target attributes of <a> or <form> tags:

```
windowName1.document.write("<a href='http://www.yahoo.com'
➥target="+windowName2.name+">The Yahoo Catalog")
```

The preceding snippet of code would create an HTML hyperlink within the window *windowName1*, which, when clicked, opens http://www.yahoo.com in the window *windowName2*.

opener property

For a window object that was spawned by another window object (that is, was created using the open() method), the opener property references the originating window object. To clarify: imagine that *windowName1* spawned *windowName2*. A script within *windowName2* could reference

windowName2.opener.*property*

or

self.opener.*property*

Either of which would be the equivalent of *windowName1*. Thus, a script within *windowName2* could execute the statement

self.opener.close()

which would close *windowName1*. Using the opener property, you can access any of the properties or methods of the window object that spawned the current window.

Internet Explorer 3 does not support the **opener** property.

outerHeight property

The outerHeight property reflects the height, measured in pixels, of the entire browser window. You can assign a new value to this property to instantly make the browser shorter or taller.

windowName.outerHeight=600

The **outerHeight** property is new to JavaScript 1.2, and therefore only supported in Netscape Navigator 4.

outerWidth property

The innerWidth property reflects the horizontal width, measured in pixels, of the entire brower window. You can assign a new value to this property to instantly make the browser thinner or wider.

windowName.outerWidth=800

W

The **outerWidth** property is new to JavaScript 1.2, and therefore only supported in Netscape Navigator 4.

pageXOffset property

Technically speaking, the read-only `pageXOffset` property reflects how many horizontal pixels the viewed page is offset from the left edge of the content area. Put more plainly: when a web page is wider than the width of the browser window, the user can scroll the page sideways using the horizontal scrollbar. This property returns how many pixels sideways (relative to the left edge, which equals 0) the user has scrolled the page.

```
pixelsfromleft=windowName.pageXOffset
```

Typically, you would use the `pageXOffset` property to determine the current position of the page when calling the `scrollTo()` or `scrollBy()` methods of the `window` object.

 The `pageXOffset` property is new to JavaScript 1.2, and therefore only supported in Netscape Navigator 4.

pageYOffset property

Technically speaking, the read-only `pageYOffset` property reflects how many horizontal pixels the viewed page is offset from the top edge of the content area. Put more plainly: when a web page is longer than the height of the browser window, the user can scroll the page up and down using the vertical scrollbar. This property returns how many pixels down (relative to the top edge, which equals 0) the user has scrolled the page.

```
pixelsfromtop=windowName.pageYOffset
```

Typically, you would use the `pageYOffset` property to determine the current position of the page when calling the `scrollTo()` or `scrollBy()` methods of the `window` object.

 The `pageYOffset` property is new to JavaScript 1.2, and therefore only supported in Netscape Navigator 4.

parent property

Within a frame, the `parent` property refers to the window within which the entire frameset resides. The `parent` property applies to frames—for a detailed explanation, see the `parent` property in the `frame` object.

self property

The `self` property refers to the current window. It is generally not required, but can help make script code more readable and less ambiguous. The following statements are equivalent:

```
status="message"
```

and

```
self.status="message"
```

Imagine, for instance, that you named a `form` object "status." In your script code, you may find it unclear whether an occurrence of "status" refers to the `form` object or the `window` object's `status` property—using the `self.status` construction for the `window` object helps keep matters clear.

`status` property

Assigning a string to the `status` property will display that string on the status bar of the browser window. Typically, the status bar displays the loading status of a document or the URL of a hyperlink or image map. Setting the status property will override any of these typical messages.

```
self.status="new message"
```

or

```
windowName.status="new message"
```

Frequently, this property is used within the `onMouseOver` and `onMouseOut` event handlers of hyperlinks—see the `link` object for specific script examples.

`top` property

The `top` property refers to the window within which any framesets, including nested framesets, reside. For instance, for a window that contains two frames, a script in either frame can make the statment:

```
top.status="new message"
```

The preceding code will modify the status message in the browser window, because `top` refers to the topmost `window` object in which the frame resides. Importantly, even child frames within a frame can use the same `top` property to refer to the topmost window. Imagine two frames, *frame1* and *frame2*. Within *frame2* there are three child frames: *frameA, frameB,* and *frameC.* A script within *frameC* could access a property of *frame1* as simply as

```
top.frame1.property
```

or

```
top.frames[0].property
```

`window` property

The `window` property refers the current window or frame. It is equivalent to the `self` property, although it is recommended to use the `self` property in most cases due to its lack of ambiguity. However, you may prefer to use the `window` property if you find code more readable that way.

```
window.status="new message"
window.close()
```

W

alert() method

Supplied with a string, the alert method will display that string in a dialog box with an OK button. The button must be pressed by the user to dismiss the dialog box. No further browser activity can occur until the alert dialog box has been dismissed. Because the user must interrupt his actions to deal with the alert box, it should be used sparingly, lest visitors grow quickly annoyed with your page.

```
alert(stringMessage)
```

An alert box such as the one shown in Figure 1 could be used as an onClick event handler for a "Help" button, for instance:

```
alert("Instructions: the object of this game is to maneuver each of the numbered
➡tiles until they are in ascending order from 1 to 20. Click on a tile adjacent
➡to the blank space to slide it over. Good luck!")
```

Figure 1

An alert dialog box that provides instructions to a hypothetical (yet fun) game.

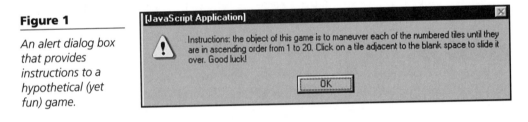

> **TIP** Remember that the alert() method produces a dialog box with only an OK button—if you need to create a dialog box with both an OK and Cancel button, use the confirm() method.

blur() method

The blur() method removes focus from the specified window, thereby pushing it behind any other open windows.

```
self.blur()
```

will hide the current browser window behind other windows.

```
windowName2.blur()
```

will cause the window referenced by *windowName2* to be hidden behind any other open windows. Although there may be occasions where you may want to bring the user's attention to a window via the focus() method, it's rarer still to usefully exploit the blur() method.

Internet Explorer 3 does not support the `blur()` method.

`clearTimeout()` method

Given a *timeOutID,* which was returned from a `setTimeout()` method, the `clearTimeout()` method will prevent the *expression* in the `setTimeout()` method from executing. Typically, you would use the `clearTimeout()` method to exit from a recursive loop, or, with respect to the "Hangman" example described in the `setTimeout()` method, to abort an impending call of a particular function. In short, use this method to cancel a previously set `setTimeout()` method (see the `setTimeout()` method).

```
clearTimeout(timeOutID)
```

`close()` method

The `close()` method closes the specified window, with some exceptions (see warning).

```
windowName.close()
```

will close *windowName,* although the variable *windowName* will remain pointing to the now-closed `window` object (see also the `closed` property). If no *windowName* is specified, the current window will attempt to close.

WARNING Within Netscape Navigator 3 or Internet Explorer 3, the statement

```
self.close()
```

will close the current window, even if the current window is the original browser window. This essentially shuts down the browser, forcing the user to re-launch it. Some unscrupulous types have created web pages that contain this code, shutting down the user's browser upon visiting the malicious page.

Both Netscape Navigator 4 and Internet Explorer 4 introduce a new security restriction to prevent this problem: the `close()` method will only automatically close windows spawned by the script itself. If the script attempts to close any other window, such as the original browser window, a confirm dialog box appears that enables the user to prevent the window from closing.

`confirm()` method

This method will display *stringMessage* (typically a question to the user) in a dialog box with both an OK and a Cancel button. The method returns a value of true or false depending upon whether the user selected OK or Cancel, respectively.

```
confirm(stringMessage)
```

To create the confirmation dialog box seen in Figure 2, you could call the `confirm()` method as the condition of an `if` statement.

W

JavaScript

```
if (confirm("Are you sure you want to quit this page?")) { self.close() }
```

VBScript

```
if confirm("Are you sure you want to quit this page?") then self.close()
end if
```

Figure 2

A confirm dialog box.

You could, for instance, attach a `confirm()` method to an `onSubmit` event handler for a form:

```
<form name=form1 method=get action="processor.cgi" onSubmit="return confirm('Do
you really want to submit this form data?')">
```

Remember that the form data will only be submitted if the `onSubmit` event handler returns a value of true. Thus, if the `confirm()` method returns true, that is passed onto the event handler and the form data is submitted; otherwise, submission is cancelled.

`find()` method

Using the `find()` method, you can search for a text string within the loaded document. This is equivalent to the user selecting the Find in Page item under the Edit menu in Navigator 4. To use the `find()` method, refer to the template:

```
windowName.find(["string"][,true|false][,true|false])
```

As shown in the template, the `find()` method takes three parameters, each of which are optional. The first parameter, *string*, represents the text string to search for in the document. If you omit this parameter, the Find in Page dialog box will pop up for the user, just as if he had selected this menu item from the Edit menu.

The second parameter, if specified as true, will perform a case-sensitive search (meaning that uppercase letters are considered different from lowercase letters). If specified as false or omitted, a case-insensitive search will be performed.

Last, if you specify the third parameter as true, the search will operate backward in the page, proceeding from the current cursor position to the top of the document. If specified as false or omitted, the search will proceed forward, from the current cursor position to the bottom of the document.

> **NOTE** You must specify both the case-sensitivity and search direction parameters if you want to specify either of them.

The find() method is new to JavaScript 1.2, and therefore only supported in Netscape Navigator 4.

focus() method

The focus() method brings focus to the specified window, causing it to appear in front of any other windows.

windowName.focus()

This is a useful way to bring attention to small sub-windows that may get hidden behind the main large browser window.

Internet Explorer 3 does not support the focus() method.

home() method

Quite simply, calling the home() method directs the browser window to the user's "home page," as configured by the user in his preferences settings. This is equivalent to the user clicking the Home icon on the navigational toolbar.

windowName.home()

The home() method is new to JavaScript 1.2, and therefore only supported in Netscape Navigator 4.

moveBy() method

Using the moveBy() method, you can relocate the entire browser window on the user's screen. Simply specify the number of pixels to move in both the horizontal and vertical directions:

windowName.moveBy(horiz,vert)

You can pass positive (right and down) or negative (left and up) integers, as in the following examples:

W

`moveBy(5,100)`	Moves browser 5 pixels right, 100 pixels down
`moveBy(-20,-5)`	Moves browser 20 pixels left, 5 pixels up
`moveBy(30,-75)`	Moves browser 30 pixels right, 75 pixels up

 The `moveBy()` method is new to JavaScript 1.2, and therefore only supported in Netscape Navigator 4.

moveTo() method

Using the `moveTo()` method, you can relocate the entire browser window on the user's screen. Simply specify the horizontal and vertical coordinates, in pixels, to where on the screen the window should relocate.

`windowName.moveTo(x,y)`

The x coordinate represents the position of the left edge of the browser window, while the y coordinate represents the top edge. To move the browser to the upper-left corner of the screen, for instance, call the method:

`moveTo(0,0)`

 The `moveTo()` method is new to JavaScript 1.2, and therefore only supported in Netscape Navigator 4.

open() method

The `open()` method creates an additional browser window, assigned to the variable *windowName*. Should the creation be unsuccessful, a value of null will be assigned to *windowName*.

`windowName=open(URL, winName, ["windowFeatures"])`

The *URL* parameter specifies which URL to load into the new window. If you'd like the new window to start out empty, simply pass a null string ("") for this parameter.

The *winName* parameter names the window for `target` attributes of the `<a>` and `<form>` tags. This *winName* is also reflected in the `name` property of the `window` object.

The *windowFeatures* parameter takes the form of a comma-delimited list of the following options:

Option	Displays
`toolbar[=yes¦no]¦[=1¦0]`	Navigational button bar
`location[=yes¦no]¦[=1¦0]`	Field displaying the current URL
`directories[=yes¦no]¦[=1¦0]`	Sirectory buttons
`status[=yes¦no]¦[=1¦0]`	Status bar on the bottom of the window
`menubar[=yes¦no]¦[=1¦0]`	Displays menu bar
`scrollbars[=yes¦no]¦[=1¦0]`	Scrollbars if document is to large for the window
`resizable[=yes¦no]¦[=1¦0]`	Allows window resizing
`width=pixels`	Size of window width in pixels
`height=pixels`	Size of window height in pixels

For instance, to assign to the variable *window_new* a new blank window, named *NewWin*, which contains a navigational toolbar, a status bar, a menu bar, and scrollbars, but does not contain the location field or directory buttons, is not resizable, and has the dimensions 640 by 400:

```
window_new=open("","NewWin","toolbar=yes,location=no,directories=no,
status=yes,menubar=yes,scrollbars=yes,resizable=no,width=640,height=400")
```

Figure 3

A brand new baby window, courtesy of the open() method.

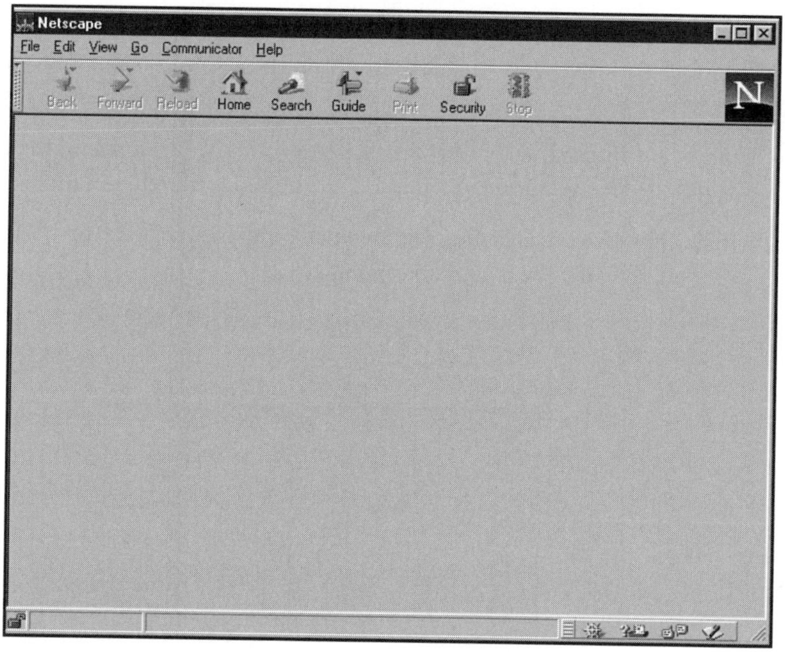

W

> **NOTE**   Internet Explorer 3 supports an additional two features in the *windowFeatures* parameter:
>
> > `top=pixels`   number of pixels from top of screen to position new window
> >
> > `left=pixels`   number of pixels from left edge of screen to position new window

> **NOTE**   The *menubar* and *resizable* options will not effect Mac browser versions. The menu bar is not part of the browser window on the Macintosh, and Mac windows are always resizable.

If the *windowFeatures* parameter is omitted, the new window will have the same format as the browser default style set by the user's specifications.

prompt() method

The `prompt()` method displays a dialog box with *stringMessage*, a data input field, an OK and a Cancel button. Initially, the data input field will contain *stringDefaultAnswer*.

```
prompt(stringMessage, stringDefaultAnswer)
```

If *stringDefaultAnswer* is not provided in the `prompt()` method, the default answer will be the string `<undefined>`. If you want the input field to default to blank, pass the *stringDefaultAnswer* parameter as a null string ("").

The `prompt()` method will return the string value in the input field if the OK button was pressed. If the Cancel button was pressed, the method will return a null value.

The following example asks the user how many toppings he'd like on his pizza—if the variable `tops` is null, then the user chose no toppings.

```
tops=prompt("How many toppings would you like on your pizza? (click Cancel for no toppings)",2)
```

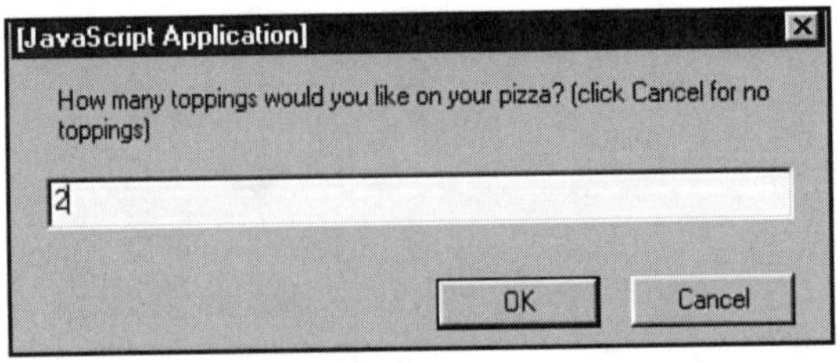

Figure 4

A prompt dialog box. I recommend pepperoni and mushrooms.

resizeBy() method

Using the resizeBy() method, you can modify the size of the entire browser window on the user's screen. Relative to the lower-right corner of the window, specify the number of pixels to resize by in both the horizontal and vertical directions:

windowName.resizeBy(*horiz,vert*)

You can pass positive (right and down) or negative (left and up) integers, as in the following examples:

resizeBy(5,10)   Stretches the lower-right corner 5 pixels right, 10 pixels down

moveBy(-20,-5)   Stretches the lower-right corner 20 pixels left, 5 pixels up

moveBy(30,-5)   Stretches the lower-right corner 30 pixels right, 5 pixels up

 The resizeBy() method is new to JavaScript 1.2, and therefore only supported in Netscape Navigator 4.

resizeTo() method

Using the resizeTo() method, you can modify the size of the entire browser window on the user's screen. Simply specify the width and height, in pixels, to resize the browser to these new dimensions.

windowName.resizeTo(*width,height*)

For example, to resize the browser window to the dimensions 640 by 400 pixels, call the method:

resizeTo(640,400)

NOTE   Calling the resizeTo() method is equivalent to assigning new values to the outerHeight and outerWidth properties.

 The resizeTo() method is new to JavaScript 1.2, and therefore only supported in Netscape Navigator 4.

scroll() method

The scroll() method scrolls the document such that the coordinates specified will be in the upper left corner of the browser window. However, because exact pixel placement of HTML elements varies between platforms and screen resolutions, this method may not produce the exact results desired.

W

```
scroll(horizontalCoord, verticalCoord)
```

The coordinates 0,0 always refer to the top of a page—to scroll the current window to the top of the page:

```
self.scroll(0,0)
```

Or you can scroll a specified window:

```
windowName.scroll(0,0)
```

 Internet Explorer 3 does not support the `scroll()` method. At the time of this writing, it is unclear whether Internet Explorer 4 supports the `scroll()` method.

scrollBy() method

Using the `scrollBy()` method, you can scroll the page within the browser window. Simply specify the number of pixels to scroll in both the horizontal and vertical directions:

```
windowName.scrollBy(horiz,vert)
```

You can pass positive (right and down) or negative (left and up) integers, as in the following examples:

`scrollBy(5,100)`	Scrolls page 5 pixels right, 100 pixels down
`scrollBy(-20,-5)`	Scrolls page 20 pixels left, 5 pixels up
`scrollBy(30,-75)`	Scrolls page 30 pixels right, 75 pixels up

 The `scrollBy()` method is new to JavaScript 1.2, and therefore only supported in Netscape Navigator 4.

scrollTo() method

Using the `scrollTo()` method, you can scroll the page within the browser window to a specified coordinate appears in the upper-left corner of the window. Simply specify the pixel coordinates for a location on the page, and the page will be scrolled so that the specified location will appear in the upper-left corner of the window.

```
windowName.scrollTo(x,y)
```

For example, to scroll the page such that the portion of the page 100 pixels down and 50 pixels right appears in the upper-left corner of the browser, call the method:

```
scrollTo(100,50)
```

The `scrollTo()` method is new to JavaScript 1.2, and therefore only supported in Netscape Navigator 4.

setTimeout() method

A potentially confusing but useful method, `setTimeout()` evaluates the supplied *expression* after an interval of *msec* milliseconds. The method will assign an ID number to a variable (`clearID`), which can later be used with the `clearTimeout()` method to cancel the `setTimeout()` method before *msec* has elapsed.

```
clearID=setTimeout("expression", msec)
```

This method has been used very creatively by programmers for a variety of purposes, some rather complex. Consider first a straightfoward example: your page and script provide some sort of timed game, such as "Hangman." The player has 10 seconds to guess the word after choosing a letter. After the player has chosen a letter, you might execute a statement such as

```
clearID=setTimeout(loser(),10000)
```

The preceding example would, after a delay of 10 seconds (10,000 milliseconds), call the hypothetical function `loser()`, which would break the news that the player has lost. If the user guesses an answer before 10 seconds have elapsed, you can use the variable `clearID` with the `clearTimeout()` method to cancel the impending `loser()` function call.

Some increasingly complex examples of using the `setTimeout()` method include:

- A web page–based real-time clock. The script retrieves the current time from the `date` object, and displays it in a text form field via the `text` object. Using a recursive `setTimeout()` method, the clock update function is called every second, which re-sets the `setTimeout()` method to trigger again one second later, and so on.

- A scrolling "ticker tape" status bar message. Given a message string, you first pad it with a large number of leading spaces. Next, setup a recursive loop that first assigns an increasingly smaller portion of the message string (chopping out the leading spaces using the `string` object's `substr()` method) to the `window` object's `status` property; then use a `setTimeout()` method to delay one second before calling the same function again, chopping out more spaces from the message and re-setting the delay. Ultimately, the effect will be a new message appearing every second in the status bar, which has one less leading space each time—a scrolling ticker tape!

stop() method

As if the user has clicked the Stop button in the browser, calling the `stop()` method immediately aborts any page activity, such as downloading from the server, or sending information to the server.

```
windowName.stop()
```

W

The `stop()` method is new to JavaScript 1.2, and therefore only supported in Netscape Navigator 4.

onBlur **event handler**

The `onBlur` event handler is triggered when the user loses focus from a window or frame. The `onBlur` event handler for a window is placed in the `<body>` tag of the HTML document that is loaded into that window.

```
<body background="#FFFFFF" onBlur="eventHandler">
```

However, HTML documents that contain a frameset do not possess a `<body>` tag—in this case, the event handler is placed in the `<frameset>` tag.

```
<frameset rows="20%,80%" onBlur="eventHandler">
```

In either case, the `onBlur` event handler is triggered when focus is lost from the *window*. To set an `onBlur` event for a *frame*, you must manually assign an event handler to the `onblur` property of the `frame` object—see the `frame` object for full details.

 TIP If a frame that possesses an `onBlur` event handler contains an HTML document which itself possesses an `onBlur` event handler in its `<body>` tag, the event handler for the frame takes precedence and is triggered when focus is lost.

 Internet Explorer 3 does not support the `onBlur` event handler.

onError **event handler**

The `onError` event handler is not set in a tag, but treated as a property: *window.onerror.*

This event handler will activate if an error occurs from JavaScript, but not if a browser error occurs (such as "404 Not Found"). Setting the event handler to *null* will suppress all error messages caused by your script.

```
window.onerror=null
```

Setting the event handler to the name of a function will execute that function. Three parameters will be passed to that function: an error message, the URL of the document causing the error, and the line number in which the error occurred.

```
window.onerror=errfunc(msg,docurl,line)
```

If your error handling function returns a value of true, the standard JavaScript error dialog box will be suppressed. This enables your script to track or "notice" any errors it has caused without having them pop up dialog boxes that interrupt the page.

Internet Explorer 3 and 4 do not support the `onError` event handler.

onFocus event handler

The `onFocus` event handler is triggered when the user brings focus to a window or frame. The `onFocus` event handler for a window is placed in the `<body>` tag of the HTML document that is loaded into that window.

```
<body background="#FFFFFF" onFocus="eventHandler">
```

However, HTML documents that contain a frameset do not possess a `<body>` tag—in this case, the event handler is placed in the `<frameset>` tag.

```
<frameset rows="20%,80%" onFocus="eventHandler">
```

In either case, the `onFocus` event handler is triggered when focus is gained from the *window*. To set an `onFocus` event for a *frame*, you must manually assign an event handler to the `onfocus` property of the `frame` object—see the `frame` object for full details.

A focus event is not triggered when the window or frame initially appears—it must first lose focus and then gain it again before the `onFocus` event occurs.

TIP   If a frame that possesses an **onFocus** event handler contains an HTML document which itself possesses an **onFocus** event handler in its **<body>** tag, the event handler for the frame takes precedence and is triggered when focus is gained.

WARNING   Use caution when including an **alert()** method in an **onFocus** event handler! When the user dismisses the alert dialog box, focus is regained on the window, triggering the **onFocus** event handler again, possibly causing the **alert()** method to be called again. In short, this can result in an infinite loop from which there may be no escape.

Internet Explorer 3 does not support the `onFocus` event handler.

onLoad event handler

An `onLoad` event is triggered when a document is fully loaded into a window or frame. The event is placed within the `<body>` or `<frameset>` tag:

```
<body background="#FFFFFF" onLoad="eventHandler">
<frameset rows="20%,80%" onLoad="eventHandler">
```

W

In the case of a frameset, the onLoad event handler is triggered *only* after all frames have been fully loaded. An onLoad event handler that resides within the <body> tag of a document loaded into a frame will trigger before the onLoad event for the entire frameset.

Typically, you use the onLoad event handler to display an opening message to the user or to call functions that initialize the state of variables that will later be used in other functions.

onUnload event handler

An onUnload event is triggered when a document is exited—that is, a new document is loaded into the current window by any means. Immediately prior to displaying the new document, the onUnload event handler is executed. The event is placed within the <body> or <frameset> tag:

```
<body background="#FFFFFF" onUnload="eventHandler">
<frameset rows="20%,80%" onUnload="eventHandler">
```

In the case of a frameset, an onUnload event handler that resides within the <body> tag of a document loaded into a frame will trigger before the onUnload event for the entire frameset.

Typically, you use the onUnload event handler to display a goodbye message to the user or to call functions that cleanup any remnants of the script, such as closing down open windows that were spawned.

---

word-spacing

Category: Cascading Style Sheets

Browser Support		Navigator 3	Navigator 4	Explorer 3	Explorer 4
	Macintosh				
	Windows				

Applies To All elements

Syntax word-spacing: *value*

The word-spacing property controls the horizontal space between words. The value you use will be *added* to the default space that occurs between words. It won't simply replace the default. You can use a unit length for the spacing or the reserved word normal. See Appendix D for an explanation of units. A value of normal will guarantee that the default word spacing is used instead of any inherited value. In the first following example, the space between each word would be 0.3 ems more than what the browser would normally display.

```
h1 { word-spacing: 0.3em }

<h1 style="word-spacing: 0.5em">
```

NOTE   As of this writing, neither browser supports the word-spacing property.

</STRONG> ■ <TD> </TD> ■ <TH> </TH> ■ <TABLE> </TABLE> ■
<IMG> </IMG> ■ <SCRIPT LANGUAGE = "javascript"> </SCRIPT>
■ <SCRIPT LANGUAGE = "vbscript"> </SCRIPT> ■ <BGSOUND
SRC=gbv.wav LOOP=-1> </BGSOUND> ■ <APPLET CLASS=
"ester's_day" SRC="http://testsite/walla walla washington/"
</APPLET> ■ <FRAME></FRAME>■ <MARQUEE> </MARQUEE> ■ <HTML>
</HTML>■ <A> </A>■ <OL> </OL>■ <UL> </UL> ■ <MENU> </
MENU> ■ <STRONG> </STRONG> ■ <TD> </TD> ■ <TH> </TH>

<XMP>

Category: HTML

		Navigator 3	Navigator 4	Explorer 3	Explorer 4
Browser Support	Macintosh	■	■	■	■
	Windows	■	■	■	■

May Contain <APPLET>, <B>, <BASEFONT>, <BIG>, <BR>, <CITE>, <CODE>, <DFN>, <EM>, <FONT>, <I>, <IMG>, <INPUT>, <KBD>, <MAP>, <SAMP>, <SELECT>, <SMALL>, <STRIKE>, <STRONG>, <SUB>, <SUP>, <TEXTAREA>, <TT>, <U>, <VAR>

May Be Used In <ADDRESS>, <APPLET>, <B>, <BIG>, <BLOCKQUOTE>, <CAPTION>, <CENTER>, <CITE>, <CODE>, <DD>, <DT>, <FONT>, <H1>, <H2>, <H3>, <H4>, <H5>, <H6>, <I>, <KBD>, <LI>, <P>, <SAMP>, <SMALL>, <STRIKE>, <STRONG>, <SUB>, <SUP>, <TD>, <TH>, <TT>, <U>

Attributes None

Syntax <XMP>...</XMP>

The <XMP> tag renders all the text enclosed between the beginning and closing, or </XMP>, tags in fixed-width type. Like <LISTING> and <PLAINTEXT>, this is an older HTML tag that predates the better choice for fixed-width type: the <PRE> tag.

If you want to render a block of text in fixed-width type, use the <PRE> tag instead, and see its entry elsewhere in the book for more information.

<IMG> </IMG> ■ <SCRIPT LANGUAGE = "javascript"> </SCRIPT> ■ <SCRIPT LANGUAGE = "vbscript"> </SCRIPT> ■ <BGSOUND SRC=gbv.wav LOOP=-1> </BGSOUND> ■ <APPLET CLASS= "ester's_day" SRC="http://testsite/walla walla washington/" </APPLET> ■ <FRAME></FRAME>■ <MARQUEE> </MARQUEE> ■ <HTML> </HTML> ■ <A> </A> ■ <OL> </OL> ■ <UL> </UL> ■ <MENU> </MENU> ■ <STRONG> </STRONG> ■ <TD> </TD> ■ <TH> </TH>

Y

Year()

Category: VBScript

Type Function

Browser Support

	Navigator 3	Navigator 4	Explorer 3	Explorer 4
Macintosh	□	□	□	■
Windows	□	□	■	■

Syntax `Year(date)`

The `Year()` function accepts a valid *date* string and returns the four-digit year. If date is null, then null is returned. An invalid date causes an error.

`year("sept 8 2067")`	returns	2067
`year("10/10/47")`	returns	1947
`year("81,2,1")`	returns	1981

Z

z-index

Category: Cascading Style Sheets

Browser Support		Navigator 3	Navigator 4	Explorer 3	Explorer 4
	Macintosh		▬		
	Windows		▬		

Applies To All elements with `position` of `absolute` or `relative`

Syntax `z-index: value`

The `z-index` property determines the order, or stacking, of elements that overlap, or are layered, on their page. With the `left`, `top`, and `position` properties, you can place elements anywhere you want on a page. This means that items can be made to overlap, or even stack directly on top of each other. Each item on the page can have a `z-index` value, a positive or negative integer, which determines what is on top of what. Elements with higher values are on top of ones with lower values. For nested elements, ones with negative `z-index`s are actually displayed below the parent element. Otherwise, children are displayed on top of the parent (and at the same `z-index` as well). `z-index` works only with elements that have a `position` property.

```
h1 { z-index: 2 }
```

```
h1 { z-index: auto }
```

The following is an example of `z-index`. A large image is positioned right up to the edge of the browser window with two smaller children images. These two "sibling" elements would normally be layered in the order they appear in the HTML: the face image first, the woods photo second and therefore on top. With `z-index` in play, however, that order is reversed. The face gets a higher `z-index` than the woods image, and so the face appears on top as displayed in Figure 1).

```
<html>
 <style type="text/css">
 <!--
  body { background: white }
  .a   { position: absolute;
         left: 0px;
         top: 0px }
  .b   { position: absolute;
         left: 150px;
```

```
           top: 110px;
           z-index: 2 }
    b      { position: absolute;
           left: 100px;
           top: 70px;
           z-index: 1 }
-->
</style>
<head>
<title>Specifying Layering Order</title>
</head>
<body>
<div class=a>
<img src="../graphics/world.jpg">
<span class=b><img src="../graphics/face2.gif"></span>
<b><img src="../graphics/woods.jpg"></b>
</div>
</body>
</html>
```

Figure 1

Among sibling elements, higher `z-index` values get you on top.

 Navigator 4 works fine with positive integer values, but not negative. There's no way to layer a child element so it's displayed below its parent.

```
<IMG> </IMG> ■ <SCRIPT LANGUAGE = "javascript"> </SCRIPT>
■ <SCRIPT LANGUAGE = "vbscript"> </SCRIPT> ■ <BGSOUND
SRC=gbv.wav LOOP=-1> </BGSOUND> ■ <APPLET CLASS=
"ester's_day" SRC="http://testsite/walla_walla_washington/"
</APPLET> ■ <FRAME></FRAME>■ <MARQUE
<HTML> </HTML> ■ <A> </A> ■ <OL> </OL> ■ <UL> </UL> ■ <MENU>
</MENU> ■ <STRONG> </STRONG> ■ <TD> </TD> ■ <TH> </TH>
```

Appendix A

Special Characters and Entities

The following table contains the characters in the ISO-Latin-1 character set. Use these values if you want to insert the special characters listed into your HTML code.

Character	Numeric Entity	Character Entity	Description
	&#00;–&#08		Unused
				Horizontal Tab

	
		Line Feed

	&#11;–&#31		Unused
	 		Space
!	!		Exclaimation mark
"	"	"	Quotation Mark
#	#		Number sign
$	$		Dollar sign
%	%		Percentage sign
&	&	&	Ampersand
'	'		Apostrophe
(	(		Left parenthesis
)	)		Right paranthesis
*	*		Asterisk
+	+		Plus sign
,	,		Comma
-	-		Hyphen
.	.		Period
/	/		Solidus (slash)
0–9	0–9		Digits 0–9
:	:		Colon
;	;		Semi-colon

Character	Numeric Entity	Character Entity	Description
<	`&#60;`	`&lt;`	Less than
=	`&#61;`		Equal sign
>	`&#62;`	`&gt;`	Greater than
?	`&#63;`		Question mark
@	`&#64;`		Commerical "at"
A–Z	`&#65;–&#90;`		Letters A–Z
[	`&#91;`		Left square bracket
\	`&#92;`		Reverse Solidus (backslash)
]	`&#93;`		Right square bracket
^	`&#94;`		Caret
_	`&#95;`		Horizontal bar
`	`&#96;`		Grave accent
a–z	`&#97;–&#122;`		Letters a–z
{	`&#123;`		Left curly bracket
|	`&#124;`		Vertical bar
}	`&#125;`		Right curly bracket
~	`&#126;`		Tilde
	`&#127;– `		Unused
¡	`&#161;`	`&iexcl;`	Inverted Exclaimation
¢	`&#162;`	`&cent;`	Cent sign
£	`&#163;`	`&pound;`	Pound sterling
¤	`&#164;`	`&curren;`	General currency sign
¥	`&#165;`	`&yen;`	Yen sign
¦	`&#166;`	`&brvbar; or brkbar;`	Broken vertical bar
§	`&#167;`	`&sect;`	Section sign
¨	`&#168;`	`&uml;`	Umlaut
©	`&#169;`	`&copy;`	Copyright
ª	`&#170;`	`&ordf;`	Feminine ordinal
«	`&#171;`	`&laquo;`	Left angle quote

Character	Numeric Entity	Character Entity	Description
¬	&#172;	&not;	Not sign
–	&#173;	&shy;	Soft hyphen
®	&#174;	&reg;	Registered trademark
‾	&#175;	&hibar;	Macron accent
°	&#176;	&deg;	Degree sign
±	&#177;	&plusmn;	Plus or minus sign
²	&#178;	&sup2;	Superscript two
³	&#179;	&sup3;	Superscript three
´	&#180;	&acute;	Acute accent
µ	&#181;	&micro;	Micro sign
¶	&#182;	&para;	Paragraph sign
·	&#183;	&middot;	Middle dot
¸	&#184;	&cedil;	Cedilla
¹	&#185;	&sup1;	Superscript one
º	&#186;	&ordm;	Masculine ordinal
›	&#187;	&raquo;	Right angle quote
¼	&#188;	&frac14;	Fraction, one-fourth
½	&#189;	&frac12;	Fraction, one-half
¾	&#190;	&frac34;	Fraction, three-fourths
¿	&#191;	&iquest;	Inverted question mark
À	&#192;	&Agrave;	Capital A, grave accent
Á	&#193;	&Aacute;	Capital A, acute accent
Â	&#194;	&Acirc;	Capital A, circumflex accent
Ã	&#195;	&Atilde;	Capital A, tilde
Ä	&#196;	&Auml;	Capital A, umlaut
Å	&#197;	&Aring;	Capital A, ring
Æ	&#198;	&Aelig;	Capital AE dipthong
Ç	&#199;	&Ccedil;	Capital C, cedilla

Character	Numeric Entity	Character Entity	Description
È	È	È	Capital E, grave accent
É	É	É	Capital E, acute accent
Ê	Ê	ˆ	Capital E, circumflex accent
Ë	Ë	Ë	Capital E, umlaut
Ì	Ì	Ì	Capital I, grave accent
Í	Í	Í	Capital I, acute accent
û	Î	Î	Capital I, cimcumflex accent
Ï	Ï	Ï	Capital I, umlaut
Ð	Ð	Ð	Capital ETH, Icelandic
Ñ	Ñ	Ñ	Capital N, cedilla
Ò	Ò	Ò	Capital O, grave accent
Ó	Ó	Ó	Capital O, acute accent
Ô	Ô	Ô	Capital O, circum flex accent
Õ	Õ	Õ	Capital O, tilde
Ö	Ö	Ö	Capital O, umlaut
×	×	&times	Multiplication sign
Ø	Ø	Ø	Capital O, slash
Ù	Ù	Ù	Capital U, grave accent
Ú	Ú	Ú	Capital U, acute accent
Û	Û	Î	Capital U, circumflex
Ü	Ü	Ü	Capital U, umlaut
Ý	Ý	Ý	Capital Y, acute accent

Character	Numeric Entity	Character Entity	Description
þ	&#222;	&THORN;	Capital Thorn, Icelandic
ß	&#223;	&szlig;	German sz
à	&#224;	&agrave;	Small a, grave accent
á	&#225;	&aacute;	Small a, acute accent
â	&#226;	&acirc;	Small a, circumflex accent
ã	&#227;	&atilde;	Small a, tilde
ä	&#228;	&aauml;	Small a, umlaut
å	&#229;	&aring;	Small a, ring
æ	&#230;	&aelig;	Small ae, dipthong
ç	&#231;	&ccedil;	Small c, tilde
è	&#232;	&egrave;	Small e, grave accent
é	&#233;	&eacute;	Small e, acute accent
ê	&#234;	&ecirc;	Small e, circumflex accent
ë	&#235;	&euml;	Small e, umlaut
ì	&#236;	&igrave;	Small i, grave accent
í	&#237;	&iacute;	Small i, acute accent
î	&#238;	&icirc;	Small i, circumflex accent
ï	&#239;	&iuml;	Small i, umlaut
ð	&#240;	&eth;	Small eth, Icelandic
ñ	&#241;	&ntilde;	Small n, tilde
ò	&#242;	&ograve;	Small o, grave accent
ó	&#243;	&oacute;	Small o, acute accent

Character	Numeric Entity	Character Entity	Description
ô	&#244;	&ocirc;	Small o, circumflex accent
õ	&#245;	&otilde;	Small o, tilde
ö	&#246;	&ouml;	Small o, umlaut
÷	&#247;	&divide	Division sign
ø	&#248;	&oslash;	Small o, slash
ù	&#249;	&ugrave;	Small u, grave accent
ú	&#250;	&uacute;	Small u, acute accent
û	&#251;	&ucirc;	Small u, circumflex
ü	&#252;	&uuml;	Small u, umlaut
ý	&#253;	&yacute;	Small y, acute
þ	&#254;	&thorn;	Small thorn, Icelandic
ÿ	&#255;	&yuml;	Small y, umlaut

<IMG> </IMG> ■ <SCRIPT LANGUAGE = "javascript"> </SCRIPT>
■ <SCRIPT LANGUAGE = "vbscript"> </SCRIPT> ■ <BGSOUND
SRC=gbv.wav LOOP=-1> </BGSOUND> ■ <APPLET CLASS=
"ester's_day" SRC="http://testsite/w
</APPLET> ■ <FRAME></FRAME>■ <MARQU
<HTML> </HTML> ■ <A> </A> ■ <OL> </OL> ■ <UL> </UL> ■ <MENU>
</MENU> ■ <STRONG> </STRONG> ■ <TD> </TD> ■ <TH> </TH>

Appendix

B

Colors by Name and HEX Value

Table B.1 contains a list of all the color names recognized by Netscape Navigator 2.0 and also includes their corresponding HEX Triplet values. To see all these colors correctly, you must have a 256-color or better video card and the appropriate video drivers installed. Also, depending on the operating system and computer platform you are running, some colors may not appear exactly as you expect them to.

Table B.1   Color Values and HEX Triplet Equivalents

Color Name	HEX Triplet
ALICEBLUE	#A0CE00
ANTIQUEWHITE	#FAEBD7
AQUA	#00FFFF
AQUAMARINE	#7FFFD4
AZURE	#F0FFFF
BEIGE	#F5F5DC
BISQUE	#FFE4C4
BLACK	#000000
BLANCHEDALMOND	#FFEBCD
BLUE	#0000FF
BLUEVIOLET	#8A2BE2
BROWN	#A52A2A
BURLYWOOD	#DEB887
CADETBLUE	#5F9EA0
CHARTREUSE	#7FFF00
CHOCOLATE	#D2691E
CORAL	#FF7F50
CORNFLOWERBLUE	#6495ED

continues

Table B.1   continued

Color Name	HEX Triplet
CORNSILK	#FFF8DC
CRIMSON	#DC143C
CYAN	#00FFFF
DARKBLUE	#00008B
DARKCYAN	#008B8B
DARKGOLDENROD	#B8860B
DARKGRAY	#A9A9A9
DARKGREEN	#006400
DARKKHAKI	#BDB76B
DARKMAGENTA	#8B008B
DARKOLIVEGREEN	#556B2F
DARKORANGE	#FF8C00
DARKORCHID	#9932CC
DARKRED	#8B0000
DARKSALMON	#E9967A
DARKSEAGREEN	#8FBC8F
DARKSLATEBLUE	#483D8B
DARKSLATEGRAY	#2F4F4F
DARKTURQUOISE	#00CED1
DARKVIOLET	#9400D3
DEEPPINK	#FF1493
DEEPSKYBLUE	#00BFFF
DIMGRAY	#696969
DODGERBLUE	#1E90FF
FIREBRICK	#B22222
FLORALWHITE	#FFFAF0
FORESTGREEN	#228B22
FUCHSIA	#FF00FF
GAINSBORO	#DCDCDC
GHOSTWHITE	#F8F8FF
GOLD	#FFD700
GOLDENROD	#DAA520
GRAY	#808080

Color Name	HEX Triplet
GREEN	#008000
GREENYELLOW	#ADFF2F
HONEYDEW	#F0FFF0
HOTPINK	#FF69B4
INDIANRED	#CD5C5C
INDIGO	#4B0082
IVORY	#FFFFF0
KHAKI	#F0E68C
LAVENDER	#E6E6FA
LAVENDERBLUSH	#FFF0F5
LEMONCHIFFON	#FFFACD
LIGHTBLUE	#ADD8E6
LIGHTCORAL	#F08080
LIGHTCYAN	#E0FFFF
LIGHTGOLDENRODYELLOW	#FAFAD2
LIGHTGREEN	#90EE90
LIGHTGRAY	#D3D3D3
LIGHTPINK	#FFB6C1
LIGHTSALMON	#FFA07A
LIGHTSEAGREEN	#20B2AA
LIGHTSKYBLUE	#87CEFA
LIGHTSLATEGRAY	#778899
LIGHTSTEELBLUE	#B0C4DE
LIGHTYELLOW	#FFFFE0
LIME	#00FF00
LIMEGREEN	#32CD32
LINEN	#FAF0E6
MAGENTA	#FF00FF
MAROON	#800000
MEDIUMAQUAMARINE	#66CDAA
MEDIUMBLUE	#0000CD
MEDIUMORCHID	#BA55D3

continues

Table B.1 continued

Color Name	HEX Triplet
MEDIUMPURPLE	#9370DB
MEDIUMSEAGREEN	#3CB371
MEDIUMSLATEBLUE	#7B68EE
MEDIUMSPRINGGREEN	#00FA9A
MEDIUMTURQUOISE	#48D1CC
MEDIUMVIOLETRED	#C71585
MIDNIGHTBLUE	#191970
MINTCREAM	#F5FFFA
MISTYROSE	#FFE4E1
NAVAJOWHITE	#FFDEAD
NAVY	#000080
OLDLACE	#FDF5E6
OLIVE	#808000
OLIVEDRAB	#6B8E23
ORANGE	#FFA500
ORANGERED	#FF4500
ORCHID	#DA70D6
PALEGOLDENROD	#EEE8AA
PALEGREEN	#98FB98
PALETURQUOISE	#AFEEEE
PALEVIOLETRED	#DB7093
PAPAYAWHIP	#FFEFD5
PEACHPUFF	#FFDAB9
PERU	#CD853F
PINK	#FFC0CB
PLUM	#DDA0DD
POWDERBLUE	#B0E0E6
PURPLE	#800080
RED	#FF0000
ROSYBROWN	#BC8F8F
ROYALBLUE	#4169E1
SADDLEBROWN	#8B4513

Color Name	HEX Triplet
SALMON	#FA8072
SANDYBROWN	#F4A460
SEAGREEN	#2E8B57
SEASHELL	#FFF5EE
SIENNA	#A0522D
SILVER	#C0C0C0
SKYBLUE	#87CEEB
SLATEBLUE	#6A5ACD
SLATEGRAY	#708090
SNOW	#FFFAFA
SPRINGGREEN	#00FF7F
STEELBLUE	#4682B4
TAN	#D2B48C
TEAL	#008080
THISTLE	#D8BFD8
TOMATO	#FF6347
TURQUOISE	#40E0D0
VIOLET	#EE82EE
WHEAT	#F5DEB3
WHITE	#FFFFFF
WHITESMOKE	#F5F5F5
YELLOW	#FFFF00
YELLOWGREEN	#9ACD32

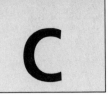

```
</STRONG> ■ <TD> </TD> ■ <TH> </TH> ■ <TABLE> </TABLE> ■
<IMG> </IMG> ■ <SCRIPT LANGUAGE = "javascript"> </SCRIPT>
■ <SCRIPT LANGUAGE = "vbscript"> </SCRIPT> ■ <BGSOUND
SRC=gbv.wav LOOP=-1> </BGSOUND> ■ <APPLET CLASS=
"ester's_day" SRC="http://testsite/wa
</APPLET> ■ <FRAME></FRAME>■ <MARQUE
</HTML> ■ <A> </A> ■ <OL> </OL> ■ <UL> </UL> ■ <MENU> </MENU>
■ <STRONG> </STRONG> ■ <TD> </TD> ■ <TH> </TH>
```

Appendix | **C**

Font Faces

There is no sure-fire way to guarantee that visitors will have on their systems the font face you specify. You can of course specify that rare but cool font anyway and hope that visitors have it and can view it. Or you can play it safe and use a font that you're pretty sure all visitors will have.

This appendix was written just for this purpose—to give you both the "sure bet" fonts and the "best guess" fonts.

"Sure Bet" Fonts

There are some fonts that come with every computer. Unfortunately, those fonts aren't the same for Mac as they are for Windows.

The fonts that currently ship with new Mac systems include the following:

- Chicago
- Courier
- Geneva
- Helvetica
- Monaco
- New York
- Palatino
- Symbol
- Times
- Zapf Dingbats

If your audience uses only Macs, then using any of these fonts is a safe bet.

The fonts that ship with Windows 95, Windows 3.1x, and Windows NT include the following:

- Arial
- Comic Sans
- Courier New
- Modern
- MS Sans Serif
- Symbol
- Times New Roman
- WingDings

> **NOTE** For some reason, Netscape Navigator doesn't display Comic Sans, MS Sans Serif, or WingDings, regardless of how they're spelled. And it likes Courier, but not Courier New. (Internet Explorer displays all of these just fine.)

> **NOTE** There are a lot of font faces that Netscape Navigator *should* display, but does not (especially on the Mac). Test often, and try not to get too discouraged.

What do all these systems have in common? What are the fonts that you can always use on any page and never have to worry? The master list:

- Arial and Helvetica (they look alike; make sure to name both for each use)
- Courier
- Symbol
- Times

> **NOTE** Fortunately, Courier and Times work across platforms even though the names vary slightly. If you use Times as the value of the style sheet property `font-family`, for instance, the Windows browser recognizes it as Times New Roman. But to be safe among the many browsers out there, you might still want to refer to both Times and Times New Roman, and do the same for Courier and Courier New.

There are three fonts to choose from for text (I'm not including the Symbol font). Not exactly a lot of flexibility. This is why Microsoft, Adobe, and others are racing to develop new type standards such as OpenType that will enable web designers to transfer actual *font information* right along with web pages, so visitors can see fonts even if they don't have them installed on their systems.

In the meantime, we have to abandon "sure bet" fonts much of the time and make some guesses.

"Best Guess" Fonts

Okay, here is where you have to be willing to take some risks. If visitors don't have the font you specify, what will they see? Well, there's no good answer other than your own diligence in testing the different fonts on various browsers and platforms. And remember, make sure you test and test and test before going to sleep at night, because you can never be too safe. This section attempts to help you in your quest.

Internet Explorer Fonts

If your audience is Internet Explorer, your options expand a bit. Internet Explorer 3 for Windows 95 ships with these fonts included:

- Arial Black
- Comic Sans MS
- Impact
- Verdana

The final version of Internet Explorer 4 will ship with these fonts as well, if not more.

Meanwhile, the full version of Internet Explorer 3 for Mac ships with these fonts:

- Arial
- Arial Black
- Comic Sans MS
- Courier New
- Georgia
- Impact
- Times New Roman
- Trebuchet
- Verdana
- WingDings

So if your audience is definitely using Internet Explorer, you can add most of these font faces to your "sure bet" column.

Netscape's Dynamic Fonts

Netscape-licensed technology from Bitstream, Inc., has another way to try to get around the problem of limited font choices. Built into Netscape Navigator 4 is the capability of displaying fonts even if those fonts *aren't* on the user's system. This technology, called TrueDoc, maintains the look and feel of any font across all platforms, including onscreen display and printing. It even anti-aliases the font, so there are no ugly jaggies.

Basically, here's how it works: You specify any font you want in your HTML document. When a visitor comes to your page, the browser checks your system for the font. If it's there, great. If not, TrueDoc's font processors will closely approximate the font for temporary use. That is, the visitor will see the font onscreen and be able to print it, but will be unable to keep the font for other uses. When the page is gone, so is the font.

Of course, keep in mind that this dynamic font technology gives you font freedom only if your audience is entirely using Navigator. (Unfortunately, as of this writing, this dynamic font technology is not yet part of the Netscape Navigator 4 beta. But Netscape promises it will be part of the final version.)

OpenType

This is a good time to mention OpenType, which is a font initiative somewhat like TrueDoc. OpenType is currently being co-developed by Microsoft and Adobe. The very fact that these two companies are teaming up for something means that OpenType stands a good chance at becoming a standard.

OpenType is a new font format, a superset of existing TrueType and Type 1 fonts, which will allow for fast downloading of font information over the web. It will enable web designers to embed specific fonts into a web page, so that even visitors without those fonts installed will be able to view them temporarily. These high-quality onscreen fonts and font technology will be cross-platform and (many of us pray) cross-browser as well.

Details on OpenType are still sketchy at this point. Neither browser supports OpenType in their 4 versions. But it's definitely something to watch for in the future!

Microsoft Office Fonts

Everyone's got Microsoft Office, right? Or at least Microsoft Word? Well, no, but a lot of people do. And that might be reason enough to use the following fonts, which ship with various versions of Office (97, 95, NT, 4.3, and 4.2):

Font	97	95	NT	4.3 (Win)	4.2 (Mac)
Algerian	✓	✓	✓	✓	
Arial Black	✓	✓	✓	✓	
Arial MT					✓
Arial Narrow	✓	✓	✓	✓	✓
Arial Rounded Bold	✓	✓	✓	✓	✓
Bauhaus 93					✓
Book Antiqua	✓	✓	✓	✓	✓
Bookman Old Style	✓	✓	✓	✓	✓
Braggadocio	✓	✓	✓	✓	✓
Brittanic Bold	✓	✓	✓	✓	✓

Font	97	95	NT	4.3 (Win)	4.2 (Mac)
Brush Script MT	✓	✓	✓	✓	✓
Century Gothic	✓	✓	✓	✓	✓
Century Schoolbook	✓	✓	✓	✓	
Colonna MT	✓	✓	✓	✓	✓
Courier					✓
Desdemona	✓	✓	✓	✓	✓
Footlight MT Light	✓	✓	✓	✓	✓
Garamond	✓	✓	✓	✓	
Greek Symbols	✓	✓	✓	✓	
Haettenschweiler	✓	✓	✓	✓	
Iconic Symbols ext	✓	✓	✓	✓	
Impact	✓	✓	✓	✓	✓
Kino MT	✓	✓	✓	✓	✓
Math ext	✓	✓	✓	✓	
Matura MT Script Capitals	✓	✓	✓	✓	✓
Mistral	✓				
Monotype Corsiva	✓				
Monotype Sorts	✓				
MS LineDraw	✓	✓	✓	✓	
Multinational ext	✓	✓	✓	✓	
Playbill	✓	✓	✓	✓	✓
Stencil					✓
Times New Roman PS MT					✓
Typographic	✓	✓	✓	✓	
Vivaldi					✓
Wide Latin	✓	✓	✓	✓	✓
WingDings					✓

Obviously, the fonts that cross all versions of Office are even better guesses of fonts to use on your web pages. Watch for varying spellings, however!

Free Downloadable Fonts

Another thing we're seeing to increase font choice is the giveaway of fonts. There are many sites that provide free downloadable fonts, and *way* too many fonts to list here. One concern is that many of these free fonts are variations of other, more standard font families. Names vary wildly, so be careful.

Microsoft is pushing hard to make a core set of TrueType fonts freely available at its Typography site (`http://www.microsoft.com/truetype/`). These are solid fonts and are worth adding to your list of options.

The free fonts from Microsoft, which are available for both Mac *and* Windows, include:

- Arial
- Arial Black
- Comic Sans
- Courier New
- Georgia
- Impact
- Times New Roman
- Trebuchet
- Verdana

Yes, some of these already come installed with Windows or Microsoft Office. But these web versions, Microsoft tells us, contain more characters that future versions of Internet Explorer can take advantage of.

NOTE Verdana is fast becoming a font of choice for many web designers. It was designed specifically for the screen, and so is very readable, even at small sizes. A lot of sites are using it already.

Other Guesses

After the fonts previously listed, I'm afraid you're on your own. If you've got a good feeling that some other particular font is popular and that many people have it, feel free to take your chance with it.

Here are few other fonts that I personally think might be ubiquitous enough across platforms to use. Happy hunting, and may the fonts be with you.

- Bauhaus 93
- Book Antiqua
- Bookman Old Style
- Brittanic Bold

- Brush Script
- Century Gothic
- Century Schoolbook
- Colonna MT
- Franklin Gothic
- Garamond
- Gill Sans
- Goudy
- Kino
- Stencil

</STRONG> ■ <TD> </TD> ■ <TH> </TH> ■ <TABLE> </TABLE> ■
<IMG> </IMG> ■ <SCRIPT LANGUAGE = "javascript"> </SCRIPT>
■ <SCRIPT LANGUAGE = "vbscript"> </SCRIPT> ■ <BGSOUND
SRC=gbv.wav LOOP=-1> </BGSOUND> ■ <APPLET CLASS=
"ester's_day" SRC="http://testsite/w
</APPLET> ■ <FRAME></FRAME>■ <MARQU
<HTML> </HTML> ■ <A> </A> ■ <OL> </OL> ■ <UL> </UL> ■ <MENU>
</MENU> ■ <STRONG> </STRONG> ■ <TD> </TD> ■ <TH> </TH>

Appendix D

Style Sheets Units

Throughout the book you've seen style sheet rules that use a variety of units for their values: pixels, ems, percentages, and so on. This appendix explains what each unit represents and what values are allowed for each unit. It also reveals which ones actually work or don't work in the various browsers. Coverage includes units for:

- Absolute dimensions
- Relative dimensions
- Percentages

Absolute Dimensions

Absolute dimensions are the units of measurement we're most used to in the physical world: inches, centimeters, points, picas, and so on. Here are the available units and how they look, in this case, within style sheet rules:

- Inches: H1 { margin: 1.5in }
- Centimeters: H1 { line-height: 4cm }
- Millimeters: H1 { word-spacing: 4mm }
- Points: H1 { font-size: 14pt }
- Picas: H1 { font-size: 1pc }

> **NOTE** Netscape Navigator is apparently dead set against any kind of absolutes on the Internet because Netscape Navigator 4 supports none of these values. That's right, no inches, no centimeters, no millimeters, no points, no picas. No luck.
>
> If you use one of these units, Netscape Navigator ignores the unit and treats the number as if you mean pixels. Try to indent 1 inch, and Netscape Navigator translates that into 1 pixel. Try to indent 30 millimeters, and Netscape Navigator indents 30 pixels. If you try to define a text size of 1 inch, Navigator displays the text 1 pixel tall.
>
> Internet Explorer does it right. It supports all of these units. In beta 3, Internet Explorer supports all of these units except pica.

Here are some helpful translation formulas (numbers are approximate):

- 1 in = 2.54 cm = 25.4 mm = 72 points = 6 picas
- 1 cm = .39 in = 10 mm = 28.1 points = 2.34 picas
- 1 mm = .039 in = .1 cm = 2.81 points = .234 picas
- 1 point = .0139 in = .0353 cm = .353 mm = .0833 picas
- 1 pica = .167 in = .424 cm = 4.24 mm = 12 points

Unfortunately, such absolute precision is just about impossible, because an inch or centimeter in the digital world is fairly meaningless. There's a good chance that what takes up an inch on my screen doesn't take up exactly an inch on yours—especially across platforms.

> **NOTE** Heck, inches aren't even honored in real space anymore. Have you measured your monitor lately? That monitor that was advertised as 15-inches in diagonal screen size is probably not.

Keep in mind that you can also specify these values as *negative* units. That is, the following rule would specify a negative margin:

```
<C1>H1 { margin: -1.5in }
```

Not all browsers support negative values, so use them at your own risk. Browsers that don't support negative values will find the nearest value they do support (probably 0). You can also put a plus sign (+) in front of values, but because the plus is already assumed, you aren't required to do so.

If the browser simply can't display something at a specified absolute value, then it will approximate to come as close as it can.

Relative Dimensions

Relative lengths can be flexible and powerful within style sheets. They specify a dimension that's relative to the dimension of another property. The relative dimension units available under style sheets include:

- Em: `H1 { margin: 1.5em }`

  An em is a unit of distance equal to the point size of a font. In 14-point type, an em is 14 points wide. An em is relative to font size.

- X-height: `H1 { margin: 1ex }`

  X-height refers to the height of the lowercase letters (not including ascenders or descenders, such as "h" or "p" have) of a font. X-height is relative to font size.

- Pixels: `H1 { font-size: 12px }`

  A pixel is the smallest discrete unit of a display screen or printed page. It is relative to the resolution of the "canvas."

> **NOTE** Internet Explorer 3 and 4 for Windows 95 do not support em or ex values. (If you use em or ex, Internet Explorer 3 assumes you mean pixels instead.)
>
> The Mac version does support both em and ex; both versions support px values.
>
> Netscape Navigator supports pixels (px). But it appears to only sometimes support em and ex. (In my tests, Netscape Navigator recognized em and ex when used for text-indent but not when used for font-size.)

> **TIP** The bottom line? Although no unit can be guaranteed to work in all situations across all browsers and platforms, the pixel comes the closest at this time.

We're used to measuring by pixels, of course, and we rely on them for more consistent and predictable measurement for onscreen display, because most monitors are 72 ppi (pixels per inch). But I've also seen 96 ppi monitors. And if you were to print the web page to a 300 dpi laser printer, all hell would break loose. It doesn't, fortunately, because good web browsers rescale pixel values when they print (Explorer 3 for Windows, however, doesn't do this). Otherwise everything would be very tiny on paper. But remember that pixels are always measured relative to the size of the canvas (most often a monitor in our case, but TV set-top boxes and web phones are on the way, so look out!). The style sheets specification recommends a "reference pixel" that is the "visual angle of one pixel on a device with a pixel density of 90 dpi and a distance from the reader of an arm's length."

Style sheets that use relative units will more easily scale from one medium to another, so keep this in mind as you design. Style rules that use ems for unique letterspacing, for example, will remain more true to original intent than rules that use centimeters for letterspacing. When you print the document, ems will scale from a computer monitor to a printer; centimeters (and other absolute measurements) might not.

As with absolute units, relative units can occur in negative values. Simply append a minus sign (–). The plus sign (+) is the default. Browsers that don't support negative values will find the nearest value that they do support.

Also, if browsers can't support the specified value, they will approximate to do the best they can. For all style sheet properties, any further computations or inheritance should be based on this approximated value, not the original one.

One important thing to note about how relative units are inherited in style sheets: Child elements inherit the *computed* value, not the relative value.

```
<HTML>
<STYLE TYPE="text/css">
<!--
P { font-size: 14pt;
text-indent: 2em }    /* i.e., 28pt */
B { font-size: 18pt }
-->
</STYLE>
<HEAD>
<TITLE>Inheritance and Relative Units</TITLE>
</HEAD>
<BODY>
<P>This is normal text indented 28 points.</P>
<P><B>What am I? Also indented 28 points, even though my size
is different.</B></P>
</BODY>
</HTML>
```

The text-indent value of anything within <B> displays at 28 points, not 36 points. The indent as originally calculated for <P> "trickles down" to all the child elements, and isn't recalculated when the browser hits <B>.

Percentages

Percentage values are straightforward: They always represent a value relative to a length unit. To specify a percentage value, just include a number (with or without a decimal point) that is immediately followed by %:

```
H1 { line-height: 140% }
```

You can use percentage values only with certain properties, and each of these properties also defines what length unit is referred to by the percentage.

In all style sheet properties, child elements inherit the result, not the percentage value.

```
<HTML>
<STYLE TYPE="text/css">
<!--
P { font-size: 14pt;
line-height: 200% }    /* i.e., 28pt */
B { font-size: 24pt }
-->
</STYLE>
<HEAD>
<TITLE>Inheritance and Percentage Units</TITLE>
</HEAD>
<BODY>
<P>This is normal text with a line-height of 28 points. I'll
add more text here so you can see it wrap and get a feel for
the leading.</P>
<P><B>What am I? Also with a line-height of 28 points, even
though my text size is different. And here's more text so you
can see it wrap.</B></P>
</BODY>
</HTML>
```

Percentage units like that for line-height are calculated once for the entire document, not multiple times for different selectors.

```
</STRONG> ■ <TD> </TD> ■ <TH> </TH> ■ <TABLE> </TABLE> ■
<IMG> </IMG> ■ <SCRIPT LANGUAGE = "javascript"> </SCRIPT>
■ <SCRIPT LANGUAGE = "vbscript"> </SCRIPT> ■ <BGSOUND
SRC=gbv.wav LOOP=.1> </BGSOUND> ■ <APPLET CLASS=
"ester's_day" SRC="http://testsite/wa    wa    washington">
</APPLET> ■ <FRAME></FRAME> ■ <MARQUE
<HTML> </HTML> ■ <A> </A> ■ <OL> </OL> ■ <UL> </UL> ■ <MENU>
</MENU> ■ <STRONG> </STRONG> ■ <TD> </TD> ■ <TH> </TH>
```

Appendix E

MIME Types

Table E.1 lists the file extensions and MIME Content-types supported by many popular web servers. If your server does not list an extension for a particular content-type or if the type you want to use is not listed at all, you will have to add support for that type to your server configuration.

Table E.1   MIME Types and HTTPD Support

MIME Type	What It Is (If Noted)	File Extensions
application/acad	AutoCAD Drawing files	dwg, DWG
application/arj		arj
application/clariscad	ClarisCAD files	CCAD
application/drafting	MATRA Prelude drafting	DRW
application/dxf	DXF (AutoCAD)	dxf, DXF
application/excel	Microsoft Excel	xl
application/i-deas	SDRC I-DEAS files	unv, UNV
application/iges	IGES graphics format	igs, iges, IGS, IGES
application/mac-binhex40	Macintosh BinHex format	hqx
application/msword	Microsoft Word	word, w6w, doc
application/mswrite	Microsoft Write	wri
application/octet-stream	Uninterpreted binary	bin
application/oda		oda
application/pdf	PDF (Adobe Acrobat)	pdf
application/postscript	PostScript	ai, PS, ps, eps
application/pro_eng	PTC Pro/ENGINEER	prt, PRT, part
application/rtf	Rich Text Format	rtf
application/set	SET (French CAD standard)	set, SET

continues

Table E.1   continued

MIME Type	What It Is (If Noted)	File Extensions
application/sla	Stereolithography	stl, STL
application/solids	MATRA Prelude Solids	SOL
application/STEP	ISO-10303 STEP data files	stp, STP, step, STEP
application/vda	VDA-FS Surface data	vda, VDA
application/x-director	Macromedia Director	dir, dcr, dxr
application/x-mif	FrameMaker MIF Format	mif
application/x-csh	C-shell script	csh
application/x-dvi	TeX dvi	dvi
application/x-gzip	GNU Zip	gz, gzip
application/x-hdf	NCSA HDF Data File	hdf
application/x-latex	LaTeX source	latex
application/x-netcdf	Unidata netCDF	nc, cdf
application/x-sh	Bourne shell script	sh
application/x-stuffit	StiffIt Archive	sit
application/x-tcl	TCL script	tcl
application/x-tex	TeX source	tex
application/x-texinfo	Texinfo (emacs)	texinfo, texi
application/x-troff	troff	t, tr, roff
application/x-troff-man	troff with MAN macros	man
application/x-troff-me	troff with ME macros	me
application/x-troff-ms	troff with MS macros	ms
application/x-wais-source	WAIS source	src
application/x-bcpio	Old binary CPIO	bcpio
application/x-cpio	POSIX CPIO	cpio
application/x-gtar	GNU tar	gtar
application/x-shar	Shell archive	shar
application/x-sv4cpio	SVR4 CPIO	sv4cpio
application/x-sv4crc	SVR4 CPIO with CRC	sv4crc
application/x-tar	4.3BSD tar format	tar
application/x-ustar	POSIX tar format	ustar

MIME Type	What It Is (If Noted)	File Extensions
application/x-winhelp	Windows Help	hlp
application/zip	ZIP archive	zip
audio/basic	Basic audio (usually μ-law)	au, snd
audio/x-aiff	AIFF audio	aif, aiff, aifc
audio/x-pn-realaudio	RealAudio	ra, ram
audio/x-pn-realaudio-plugin	RealAudio (plug-in)	rpm
audio/x-wav	Windows WAVE audio	wav
image/gif	GIF image	gif
image/ief	Image Exchange Format	ief
image/jpeg	JPEG image	jpg, JPG, JPE, jpe, JPEG, jpeg
image/pict	Macintosh PICT	pict
image/tiff	TIFF image	tiff, tif
image/x-cmu-raster	CMU raster	ras
image/x-portable-anymap	PBM Anymap format	pnm
image/x-portable-bitmap	PBM Bitmap format	pbm
image/x-portable-graymap	PBM Graymap format	pgm
image/x-portable-pixmap	PBM Pixmap format	ppm
image/x-rgb	RGB Image	rgb
image/x-xbitmap	X Bitmap	xbm
image/x-xpixmap	X Pixmap	xpm
image/x-xwindowdump	X Windows dump (xwd) format	xwd
multipart/x-zip	PKZIP Archive	zip
multipart/x-gzip	GNU ZIP Archive	gzip
text/html	HTML	html, htm
text/plain	Plain text	txt, g, h, C, cc, hh, m, f90
text/richtext	MIME Richtext	rtx
text/tab-separated-values	Text with tab separated values	tsv
text/x-setext	Struct enhanced text	etx

continues

Table E.1   continued

MIME Type	What It Is (If Noted)	File Extensions
video/mpeg	MPEG video	mpeg, mpg, MPG, MPE, mpe, MPEG, mpeg
video/quicktime	QuickTime Video	qt, mov
video/msvideo	Microsoft Windows Video	avi
video/x-sgi-movie	SGI movieplayer format	movie
x-world/x-vrml	VRML Worlds	wrl

```
</STRONG> ■ <TD> </TD> ■ <TH> </TH> ■ <TABLE> </TABLE> ■
<IMG> </IMG> ■ <SCRIPT LANGUAGE = "javascript"> </SCRIPT>
■ <SCRIPT LANGUAGE = "vbscript"> </SCRIPT> ■ <BGSOUND
SRC=gbv.wav LOOP=-1> </BGSOUND> ■ <APPLET CLASS=
"ester's_day" SRC="http://testsite/walla walla washington/"
</APPLET> <FRAME></FRAME>■ <MARQU
<HTML> </HTML> ■ <A> </A> ■ <OL> </OL>■ <UL> </UL> ■ <MENU>
</MENU> ■ <STRONG> </STRONG> ■ <TD> </TD> ■ <TH> </TH>
```

Appendix | F

Online Resources

In addition to the entries in this book, we would like to direct you to the following URLs to supplement your reading.

Dynamic HTML

By the time this book goes to press, some of the material on Dynamic HTML may be out of date. If you are planning to use Dynamic HTML in your web pages, make sure to be aware of changes that take place in both Netscape's and Mircosoft's vision of the extended technology. These web sites are a good place to start that search.

Netscape

http://developer.netscape.com/library/documentation/communicator/comdocs.html

http://home.netscape.com/eng/beta_central/

http://home.netscape.com/comprod/products/communicator/layers/canvas_syntax.html

Microsoft

http://www.microsoft.com/workshop/prog/aplatfrm/dynthml-f.htm

http://www.microsoft.com/ie/ie40/authors

http://www.microsoft.com/workshop/prog/ie4

JavaScript, JScript, and VBScript

JavaScript 1.1 Reference Online

http://home.netscape.com/eng/mozilla/3.0/handbook/javascript/index.html

JavaScript 1.1 Reference—Downloadable Archive

http://developer.netscape.com/library/documentation/jshtm.zip

JavaScript 1.2 Additions

http://developer.netscape.com/library/documentation/communicator/jsguide/js1_2.htm

VBScript Main Page

`http://www.microsoft.com/vbscript/`

VBScript Documentation Online and/or Downloadable

`http://www.microsoft.com/vbscript/us/techinfo/vbsdocs.htm`

JScript Main Page

`http://www.microsoft.com/jscript/`

JScript Documentation Online and/or Downloadable

`http://www.microsoft.com/JScript/us/techinfo/jsdocs.htm`

Microsoft Scripting Object Model (applies to JScript and VBScript)

`http://www.microsoft.com/workshop/prog/sdk/docs/scriptom/`

HTML

The premier HTML online reference for all HTML-related information

`http://www.htmlhelp.com`

A well-recommended introduction to HTML, with examples…

`http://www.cwru.edu/help/introHTML/toc.html`

…and its successor, for intermediate HTML

`http://www.cwru.edu/help/interHTML/toc.html`

Design Issues and General Reference

The World Wide Web Consortium home page

`http://www.w3.org`

The place to keep an eye on browser support for HTML

`http://www.browserwatch.com`

The HTML Writer's Guild home page

`http://www.hwg.org`

David Siegel's site on HTML and page design

`http://www.killersites.com`

The HTML discussion newsgroup

`comp.infosystems.www.authoring.html`

```
</STRONG> ■ <TD> </TD> ■ <TH> </TH> ■ <TABLE> </TABLE> ■
<IMG> </IMG> ■ <SCRIPT LANGUAGE = "javascript"> </SCRIPT>
■ <SCRIPT LANGUAGE = "vbscript"> </SCRIPT> ■ <BGSOUND
SRC=gbv.wav LOOP=-1> </BGSOUND> ■ <APPLET CLASS=
"ester's_day" SRC="http://testsite/walla walla washington/"
</APPLET> ■ <FRAME></FRAME>■ <MARQUEE> </MARQUEE
</HTML> ■ <A> </A>■ <OL> </OL>■ <UL> </UL>■
■ <STRONG> </STRONG> ■ <TD> </TD> ■ <TH> </TH>
```

Index